DICTIONARY OF PRINTING AND PUBLISHING

second edition

Titles in the series

Dictionary of Accounting	0-948549-27-0
Dictionary of Agriculture, 2nd ed	0-948549-78-5
Dictionary of American Bus.	0-948549-11-4
Dictionary of Automobile Engineering	0-948549-66-1
Dictionary of Banking & Finance	0-948549-12-2
Dictionary of Business, 2nd ed	0-948549-51-3
Dictionary of Computing, 2nd edition	0-948549-44-0
Dictionary of Ecology & Environment, 3rd ed	0-948549-74-2
Dictionary of Government & Politics, 2nd ed	0-948549-89-0
Dictionary of Hotels, Tourism, Catering	0-948549-40-8
Dictionary of Human Resources & Personnel, 2nd ed	0-948549-79-3
Dictionary of Information Technology, 2nd ed	0-948549-88-2
Dictionary of Law, 2nd ed	0-948549-33-5
Dictionary of Library & Information Management	0-948549-68-8
Dictionary of Marketing, 2nd ed	0-948549-73-4
Dictionary of Medicine, 2nd ed	0-948549-36-X
Dictionary of Printing & Publishing, 2nd ed	0-948549-99-8
Dictionary of Science & Technology	0-948549-67-X

For a complete catalogue with full details of all our dictionaries, please write to:

Peter Collin Publishing
1 Cambridge Road
Middx. TW11 8DT

or visit our web site: http://www.pcp.co.uk

DICTIONARY OF **PRINTING AND PUBLISHING**

second edition

P.H. Collin

PETER COLLIN PUBLISHING

First published in Great Britain 1989
Second edition 1997

Published by Peter Collin Publishing Ltd
1 Cambridge Road, Teddington, Middlesex, TW11 8DT

British Library Cataloguing in Publication Data
A catalogue record for this book is available from the British Library

ISBN 0-948549-99-8

Text set by PCP
Printed and bound in Finland by WSOY
Cover design by Gary Weston

PREFACE TO THE FIRST EDITION

The aim of this dictionary is to provide the user with a comprehensive vocabulary of terms and expressions used in printing, publishing and other allied trades. The vocabulary ranges from that used in metal setting to desk-top publishing, from bookselling to copy-editing.

The main words are explained in simple English, with many examples of usage. Encyclopaedic notes expand on the definitions and give further useful information about the person, device or process being defined.

The Supplement at the back of the book gives charts and documents which will be of use to people in all areas of printing and publishing.

We are particularly grateful to many people who have read the text and made suggestions for its improvement: in particular John Holmes, Stephen Curtis, and Dr A.K. Maitra of the London College of Printing.

PREFACE TO THE SECOND EDITION

Many new technologies have entered the printing world since the first edition of this dictionary, and the text has now been completely revised and expanded. We are particularly grateful again to John Holmes for making many useful comments and suggestions. Liz Greasby gave invaluable help in preparing the text for printing.

Aa

a circle *US* **a ring** *noun* 'a' with a small circle over it (å) used in Scandinavian languages

A format paperback *noun* paperback with the format 178 x 111mm

A series *or* **A sizes (A1, A2, A3, A4, A5)** *noun* ISO recommended international standard sizes of paper (also used for sizes of computer screen); ***you must photocopy the spreadsheet on A3 paper; we must order some more A4 headed notepaper; a standard 300 d.p.i. black and white A4 monitor;*** *see also* B SERIES, C SERIES ⇨APPENDIX

> COMMENT: A sizes of paper are based on the largest size (A0), which is 1189 x 841mm; folded once, this gives A1 (841 x 594mm), which if folded once gives A2 (594 x 420mm), and so on. See the table in the Appendix for the list of paper sizes

AAs = AUTHOR'S ALTERATIONS

ABA = AMERICAN BOOKSELLERS ASSOCIATION (NOTE: the bookfair sponsored by the ABA, and formerly also called 'the ABA' has changed its name to BookExpo America)

abbreviate *verb* to make something shorter; ***the words 'out of stock' are usually abbreviated to 'O/S';*** **abbreviated text** = text which is shorter than the original

abbreviation *noun* something which is shorter than the original, especially single letters used to represent words; ***the abbreviation 'O/S' stands for 'out of stock' and 'O/P' stands for 'out of print';*** **list of abbreviations** = note in a reference book which lists the abbreviations used and what they stand for (usually printed at the beginning of the text, after the prelims, or, in some reference works such as dictionaries, on the endpapers)

abrasion resistance *noun* ability of a surface (such as a printing plate) to resist rubbing without showing scratches or other signs of wear

abridge *verb* to make a shorter version of a book; ***an abridged version of 'War and Peace'; the abridged version will sell in the educational market***

abridgement *noun* shortened version of a book

absorb *verb* **(a)** to take up liquid; ***glossy paper does not absorb ink very well*** **(b)** to take in a small item so as to form part of a larger one; **overheads have absorbed all our profits** = all our profits have gone in paying overhead expenses

absorbency *noun* ability to absorb moisture; ***the paper has a high absorbency level;*** **absorbency test** = test carried out in a laboratory to test how absorbent a sample of paper is

absorbent *adjective* which takes up moisture; ***highly absorbent paper***

absorption *noun* **(a)** taking up moisture; ***the absorption of ink by the paper*** **(b)** **absorption costing** = costing method, which takes into account the time taken, the overhead costs (including machining costs) for each part of a job, rather than dealing with the job on a single-cost basis

> COMMENT: paper is a relatively absorbent substrate because there are

> pores in between the fibres and mineral particles. Liquids such as oil or water can be absorbed through these pores. Water absorbency and oil absorbency are quite different properties, and as most printing inks are oil-based, the printer is more concerned with the oil absorbency of paper than its water absorbency. Oil absorbency can be measured using the PIRA Surface Oil Absorbency Tester (SOAT), the K & N method or the IGT method

abstract 1 *noun* **(a)** short summary of what is said in a learned article; ***English abstracts of the articles are printed at the back of the journal*** **(b)** short form of a report *or* document; ***to make an abstract of the company accounts*** **2** *verb* to make a short summary of what is said in an article; **abstracting and indexing (A & I)** = making summaries and indexes for articles and books

a/c *or* **acc** = ACCOUNT

academic *adjective* concerned with or aimed at the university and polytechnic market; ***an academic publisher; they publish three academic journals; he has made his career in academic publishing***

accelerator *noun* chemical such as borax, used to make photographic film develop more rapidly

accent *noun* small sign placed on, above or below a printed or written character to show that it is pronounced in a different way; **acute accent** = accent above a character, which slopes upwards to the right; **circumflex accent** = accent above a character, shaped like an upside down 'v'; **grave accent** = accent above a character, which slopes upwards to the left; *see also* CEDILLA, TILDE, UMLAUT ⇨APPENDIX

accented *adjective* (letter) with an accent on it

accept *verb* to agree to something which is being offered; ***he accepted the estimate for printing; she has accepted our terms; he will not accept the job unless we increase the salary;*** **to accept a book for publication** = to agree to publish a book; **to accept delivery of a shipment** = to take goods into the warehouse officially when they are delivered

acceptable *adjective* which can be accepted; ***his manuscript is not acceptable as it stands, and will need rewriting; the terms of the contract are not acceptable to the agent***

acceptance *noun* taking *or* agreeing to something; ***acceptance of a book for publication; on his acceptance of the terms, we will send him a contract; the first part of the advance will be paid on acceptance;*** **acceptance of an offer** = agreeing to an offer; **to give an offer a conditional acceptance** = to accept provided that certain things happen *or* that certain terms apply; **we have his letter of acceptance** = we have received a letter from him accepting the offer; **acceptance sampling** = testing a small part of a batch to see if the whole batch is good enough

access 1 *noun* ability to reach data stored in a computer; **random access** = calling up data in a computer immediately in any order; **sequential access** *or* **serial access** = calling up data stored in a computer by reading through the data in order; **access time** = time needed for the file to become available on the screen *or* time taken by a computer to find data stored in it **2** *verb* to call up (data) which is stored in a computer; ***she accessed the address file on the computer;*** **to access a computer file** = to call up and start examining a computer file

accessions *noun* new books which are added to a library; **accession number** = serial number used in a library indexing system (numbered to show when the book was acquired)

accordion fold *or* **concertina fold** *or* **fanfold** *noun* (i) method of folding a printed sheet in parallel folds, with one fold in one direction, and the next in the other, so that it will unfold sideways; (ii) method of folding continuous paper, one page in one direction, the next page in the opposite direction, allowing the paper to be fed into a printer continuously with no action on the part of the user; **accordion insert** = insert in a magazine which is folded in this way

account 1 *noun* **(a)** record of money paid *or* owed; ***please send me your account or a detailed or an itemized account;*** **representative's expense account** = money which a company allows a representative to spend on travelling and entertaining clients in connection with his business; ***he charged his hotel bill to his expense account*** **(b)** customer who does a large amount of business with a firm and has an account; ***he is one of our largest accounts; our salesmen call on their best accounts twice a month;*** **account executive** = employee who looks after certain customers *or* who is the link between certain customers and his company **(c) the accounts of a business** *or* **a company's accounts** = detailed record of a company's financial affairs; **to keep the accounts** = to write each sum of money in the account book; **annual accounts** = accounts prepared at the end of a financial year; **management accounts** = financial information (sales, expenditure, credit, and profitability) prepared so as to assist a manager in taking decisions; **profit and loss account** = accounts for a company with expenditure and income balanced to show a final profit or loss; **accounts department** = department in a company which deals with money paid, received, borrowed or owed; **accounts manager** = manager of an accounts department; **accounts payable** = money owed by a company; **accounts receivable** = money owed to a company **(d) sum paid on account** = sum paid in advance *or* as a first payment **2** *verb* **to account for** = to explain and record a money deal; ***the editor was asked to account for a loss or a discrepancy in his budget; the reps have to account for all their expenses to the sales manager***

accountant *noun* person who keeps a company's accounts *or* person who advises a company on its finances *or* person who examines accounts for individuals and prepares tax returns; ***the chief accountant of a manufacturing group; most authors send all their income tax queries to an accountant;*** **management accountant** = accountant who prepares financial information for managers so that they can take decisions

account book *noun* ledger in which accounts are kept; **account-book binding** = binding style which is used for books which are to be written in, and therefore must lie flat when open (also called 'stationery binding')

accounting *noun* work of recording money paid, received, borrowed or owed; **accounting period** = period usually covered by a firm's accounts; **cost accounting** = preparing special accounts of manufacturing and sales costs; **current cost accounting** = method of accounting which notes the cost of replacing assets at current prices, rather than valuing assets at their original cost

accredited *adjective* (agent) who is appointed by a company to act on its behalf

acct = ACCOUNT

acetate *noun* sheet of transparent film used for marking the designer's instructions, for placing CRC, for making overlays or for laminating a glossy book cover; proofs can also be taken from acetates; ***the colour separations are on acetate***

achromatic *adjective* without any colour; **achromatic colour** = (grey) colour within the range between black and white displayed by a graphics adapter; **achromatic separations** = colour separations on a scanner by using the very minimum of primary colours and adding black

acid *noun* chemical compound containing hydrogen, which reacts with an alkali to form a salt and water, and turns litmus paper red; acids are used to etch printing plates; **acid-free paper** = paper which has had certain acid chemicals removed; if they are left in, the paper will become yellow and brittle with age; acid-free paper is used to wrap and preserve documents and other works of art which might be affected by the acid in normal wrapping paper; **acid process** = process of making chemical paper pulp using acid

acknowledge *verb* to tell a sender that a letter *or* package *or* shipment has arrived; ***he has still not acknowledged my letter of the 24th; we acknowledge receipt of your order of June 14th***

acknowledgement *noun* **(a)** act of acknowledging; ***she sent an acknowledgement of receipt; they sent a letter of acknowledgement*** **(b)** **acknowledgements** = text printed at the beginning of a book, where the author *or* publisher thanks people who have helped in its preparation

> COMMENT: the acknowledgements may also include references to institutions which have given permission to quote copyright material or to use copyright photographs. The acknowledgements are usually placed after the verso of the title page and before the preface; if short, they can be listed at the end of the preface itself

acoustic *adjective* referring to sound; **acoustic hood** = soundproof hood placed over a printer to reduce the noise

acoustic coupler *noun* device that connects to a telephone handset, converting binary computer data into sound signals to allow data to be transmitted down a telephone line

> COMMENT: the acoustic coupler also converts sound signals back to digital signals when receiving messages; it is basically the same as a modem but uses a handset on which a loudspeaker is placed to send the signals rather than direct connection to the phone line. It is portable, and clips over both ends of a normal telephone handset; it can be used even in a public phone booth

acquire *verb* to buy; ***to acquire the paperback rights to a new novel;*** US **acquiring editor** = ACQUISITIONS EDITOR

acquisition *noun* book *or* rights bought; act of getting *or* buying something; **new acquisitions** = new books which have been acquired by a library; **acquisitions editor** *or* US **acquiring editor** = editor who is responsible for building a list by acquiring titles from packagers *or* from other publishers; **data acquisition** *or* **acquisition of data** = obtaining and classifying data

Acrobat™ *noun* file format (developed by Adobe Systems) that describes a graphics, text and indexing system that allows the same screen image or page layout file to be displayed on different hardware; for example, an Acrobat file can be viewed on a Macintosh and a PC or from Internet browsers such as NetScape

acronym *noun* abbreviation, usually formed from the initial letters of a group of words, which make up a word which can be pronounced; ***the acronym RAM means Random Access Memory***

ACs = AUTHOR'S CORRECTIONS

actual 1 *adjective* real *or* correct; ***what is the actual cost of one unit? the specimen page is actual size; the pictures reproduced are half the actual size*** **2** *noun* **actuals** = real figures

acute *adjective* **(a)** very sharp *or* clear (image) **(b)** **acute accent** = small sign (é) placed above a vowel to show that it is pronounced in a special way or to indicate stress

ad *noun informal* = ADVERTISEMENT ***we put an ad in the paper; she answered an ad in the paper; he found his job through an ad in the paper;*** **coupon ad** = advertisement with a form attached, which is to be cut out and returned to the advertiser with your name and address for further information; **display ad** = DISPLAY ADVERTISEMENT

adapt *verb* to change a work so that it fits a different medium *or* market; ***the novel has been adapted for television; he wants to adapt the textbook for the American market***

adaptation *noun* work which has been adapted; ***he paid $50,000 for the screen adaptation; his adaptation of the novel was turned down by the editorial board***

adapter *or* **adaptor** *noun* **(a)** person who has done an adaptation; ***he was the adapter of the novel for the TV series*** **(b)** device that allows two *or* more incompatible devices to be connected together; **graphics adapter** = electronic device (normally on an expansion card) in a computer that converts software commands into electrical signals that display graphics on a connected monitor

add *verb* **(a)** to put figures together to make a total; ***to add home and export sales*** **(b)** to put things together to make a large group; ***we are adding to the sales force; they have added two new lists to their range of homecare titles***

added entry *noun* secondary file entry in a library catalogue

addendum *noun* text which is added (such as late copy, which reaches the publisher after the main text has been printed and is added as a supplement); ***he attached an addendum to the contract; the encyclopaedia appeared with twenty pages of addenda;*** (NOTE: plural is **addenda)**

addition *noun* **(a)** thing *or* person added; ***we are exhibiting several additions to our reference list; the marketing director is the latest addition to the board*** **(b)** text which is added at proof stage; ***author's additions and corrections are charged extra;*** **in addition to** = added to *or* as well as; ***there is a twelve-page supplement in addition to the new colour pictures***

additional *adjective* extra *or* which is added; ***there is no room for any additional text matter; the agent has proposed additional clauses to the contract; you pay extra for additional material***

additive *adjective* produced by adding; **additive colour mixing** = mixing different colours to give the final colour that is wanted; **additive colours** *or* **additive primary colours** *or* **additive primaries** = primary colours (red, blue and green pigments) which when added together form white light, and are used to make all other colours

address 1 *noun* **(a)** details of number, street and town where an office is or a person lives; ***my business address and phone number are printed on the card;*** **accommodation address** = address used for receiving messages but which is not the real address of the company; **cable address** = short address for sending cables; **forwarding address** = address to which a person's mail can be sent on; **home address** = address of a house or flat where someone lives; ***please send the documents to my home address;*** **address list** = list of addresses; ***we are continually updating our address list of clients in Europe*** **(b)** point in a computer file where a certain piece of information has been stored, and the code which allows the user to access it **2** *verb* **(a)** to write the details of an address on an envelope, etc.; ***to address a letter*** *or* ***a parcel; please address your enquiries to the manager; a letter addressed to the author, care of his publisher; an incorrectly addressed package*** **(b)** to speak; ***to address a meeting***

addressee *noun* person to whom a letter *or* package is addressed

addressing machine *noun* machine which puts addresses on envelopes automatically

adhere *verb* to stick to something

adhesion *noun* ability to stick

adhesive 1 *noun* glue, substance which sticks; ***the company has developed a range of adhesives for perfect binding; the books are bound using special adhesive for tropical climates;*** **hot melt adhesive** = binding glue which is heated before being used; **spray adhesive** = glue in an aerosol can, which is used for pasting up artwork and allows the designer to reposition the artwork if necessary **2** *adjective* which sticks; ***the posters are stuck to the back of the stand with adhesive tape; the display boards have adhesive backing;*** **adhesive binding** *or* **perfect binding** = binding where the folds of the signatures are trimmed, and not sewn, the cover being glued to the cut pages (the pages are cut roughly so as to help the glue adhere properly); **adhesive lettering** = letters with an adhesive backing, used to make display paste-ups

adjust *verb* **(a)** to change something to fit new conditions; ***to adjust prices to take account of inflation; prices are adjusted for inflation; the text will be adjusted at page make-up stage; the pages have been adjusted to allow for the extra material which the author has sent in*** **(b)** *(in word-processing)* feature which automatically changes the right-hand margin when new text is inserted

adjustment *noun* act of adjusting; slight change; ***to make an adjustment to the page layout; some adjustment of prices is needed to take account of rising paper costs***

adman *noun informal* man who works in advertising; ***the admen are using balloons as promotional material***

admin *noun (informal)* **(a)** work of administration, especially paperwork; ***all this admin work takes a lot of my time; there is too much admin in this job; the admin people have sent the report back*** **(b)** administration staff; ***admin say they need the report immediately***

administer *verb* to organize *or* to manage; *US* **administered price** = price fixed by a manufacturer which cannot be varied by a retailer

administration *noun* organization *or* control *or* management of a company; **the expenses of the administration** *or* **administration expenses** = costs of management, not including production, marketing or distribution costs

administrative *adjective* referring to administration

Adobe™ *noun* software company that developed products including Acrobat, ATM, and PostScript

Adobe Illustrator™ vector image and editing software; a drawing program

Adobe Photoshop™ raster image creation, editing and format translation software; a paint program

Adobe Type Manager™ *or* **ATM** software technology for describing scalable fonts - most commonly used with Apple System 7 and Microsoft Windows to provide fonts that can be scaled to almost any point size, and printed on almost any printer; *see also* OUTLINE FONT *compare with* BIT-MAPPED FONT

adopt *verb* **(a)** to agree to (something) *or* to accept (something); ***to adopt a resolution; the proposals were adopted unanimously*** **(b)** to put a textbook on an official list of books to be used in state schools; ***the English course has been adopted by the State of Texas***

adoption *noun* agreement that a textbook shall be used in state schools; ***the company is hoping for an adoption in Texas***

ADS = ADVERTISEMENT DELIVERY SYSTEM digital file format used in the transmission of mono and colour images

adult *noun* person who is older than a child *or* over 18 years of age; ***adult paperback market; they have started a new list of adult nonfiction titles;*** **adult education** = education of older people; ***the course book is aimed at adult education classes;*** **adult literacy programme** = programme to teach adults to read and write

advance 1 *noun* **(a)** (i) money paid as a loan or as a part of a payment to be made later; (ii) money paid by a publisher to an author before a book is published which will be covered by future royalties; ***to pay an author an advance of £1,000 against a royalty of 10 per cent; the paperback houses pay advances of over $50,000 to established authors*** **(b)** **advance copies** *or* **advances** *or* **advance sheets** = copies of a book (or of printed sheets) sent by the printer direct to the publisher's office, before the bulk stock is sent to the warehouse; ***the marketing department needs twenty advance copies for the exhibition; don't forget to send advance jackets to the reps*** **(c)** **in advance** = early *or* before something happens; ***freight payable in***

advance; price fixed in advance **(d)** early; ***advance booking of advertising space; we have recorded over 10,000 advance orders for the title;*** **advance feed** = the first part of a paper tape, with sprocket holes which carry the tape into the machine; **advance selling** *or* **pre-publication selling** = selling of a book by a bookseller before the official publication date set by the publisher **2** *verb* **(a)** to lend; ***the bank advanced him £100,000 against the security of his house*** **(b)** to make something happen earlier; ***the publication date has been advanced to May 10th; the meeting with the German distributors has been advanced from 11.00 to 09.30***

adverse *adjective* bad *or* not helpful; ***adverse publicity about the author did not help the sales of the book;*** **adverse trading conditions** = bad conditions for trade

advert *noun GB informal* = ADVERTISEMENT

advertise *verb* to announce that something is for sale *or* that a job is vacant *or* that a service is offered; ***to advertise a vacancy in the production department; to advertise for a secretary; the author has phoned to ask what we are doing to advertise his new title***

advertisement *noun* **(a)** notice which shows that something is for sale *or* that a service is offered *or* that someone wants something *or* that a job is vacant, etc.; ***to put an advertisement in the paper; to answer an advertisement in the paper;*** **classified advertisements** = advertisements listed in a newspaper under special headings (such as 'property for sale' or 'jobs wanted'); **display advertisement** = advertisement which is well designed to attract attention; **advertisement manager** = manager in charge of the advertisement section of a newspaper; **advertisement page** = page facing the title page of a book, which may have a list of other works in the same series or by the same author **(b) advertisement delivery system (ADS)** = digital file format used in the transmission of mono and colour images

advertiser *noun* person *or* company which advertises; ***the advertisers will complain if circulation drops***

advertising *noun* business of announcing that something is for sale *or* of trying to persuade customers to buy a product or service; ***she works in advertising; he has a job with an advertising agency;*** **advertising agency** = company which plans, designs and manages advertising for other companies; **advertising copy** = text written for an advertisement; **advertising manager** = manager in charge of advertising a company's products; **advertising rates** = amount of money charged for advertising space in a newspaper *or* advertising time on TV; **advertising space** = space in a newspaper set aside for advertisements; **to take advertising space in a paper** = to book space for an advertisement in a newspaper

advertorial *noun* text in a magazine, which is not written by the editorial staff but by an advertiser

advice *noun* **(a) advice note** = written notice to a customer giving details of goods ordered and shipped but not yet delivered; **as per advice** = according to what is written on the advice note **(b)** opinion as to what action to take; **to take legal advice** = to ask a lawyer to say what should be done; ***the advice of the libel lawyer was to go ahead and publish; we sent the documents to the police on the advice of the accountant*** *or* ***we took the accountant's advice and sent the documents to the police***

advise *verb* **(a)** to tell someone about something; ***we are advised that the shipment will arrive next week; he was advised that some of the material in the book could be libellous*** **(b)** to suggest to someone what should be done; ***the accountant advised us to send the documents to the police***

advise against *verb* to suggest that something should not be done; ***the lawyers advised against publishing the MP's memoirs***

adviser *or* **advisor** *noun* person who suggests what should be done; ***he is***

consulting the company's legal adviser; **financial adviser** = person *or* company which gives advice on financial problems for a fee

advisory *adjective* as an adviser; ***he is acting in an advisory capacity;*** **an advisory board** = a group of advisers

afterword *noun* short text placed at the end of a book (sometimes used for a note about the author, especially if the author has died since the first printing of the book)

against *preposition* as part of; ***to pay an advance against royalty; can I have an advance against next month's salary?;*** *see also* GRAIN

agate *noun* former type size equal to five and a half points (still used in the USA); *US* **agate line** = (i) line on a rule, measured in agates; (ii) depth of an advertising column in a newspaper, equal to about one thirteenth of a column inch

agency *noun* **(a)** job of representing another company in an area; office which represents; ***they signed an agency agreement*** *or* ***an agency contract;*** **sole agency** = agreement to be the only person *or* company allowed to represent a company *or* to sell a product in a certain area **(b)** office *or* business which arranges things for other companies; **advertising agency** = office which plans *or* designs and manages advertising for companies; **employment agency** = office which finds jobs for staff; **literary agency** = office which represents authors in their negotiations with publishers, and finds publishers for new works by authors, for a commission (usually a percentage of the authors' royalties); **news agency** = office which distributes news to newspapers and television stations

agent *noun* **(a)** person who represents a company *or* another person in an area (such as an agent representing a publishing company); **sole agent** = person who has the sole agency for a company in an area; **agent's commission** = money (usually a percentage of sales) paid to an agent **(b)** person in charge of an agency; **authors' agent** = LITERARY AGENT **commission agent** = agent who is paid by commission, not by fee; **forwarding agent** = person *or* company which arranges shipping and customs documents; **literary agent** = person who acts on behalf of an author, negotiates with publishers and receives a percentage of the author's fees or royalties; **paper agent** = person who represents paper suppliers and receives a percentage of any sale which he makes for them

AGM = ANNUAL GENERAL MEETING

agree *verb* **(a)** to decide on *or* to approve; ***we have agreed the budgets for next year; terms of the contract are still to be agreed*** **(b)** to say yes *or* to accept; ***it has been agreed that the contract will run for 25 years; after some discussion he agreed to our offer; the bank will never agree to lend the company £250,000; we all agreed on the publishing programme*** **(c) to agree to do something** = to say that you will do something; ***she agreed to be chairman; will the finance director agree to pay the costs?***

agreement *noun* contract between two parties which explains how they will act; ***written agreement; unwritten*** *or* ***verbal agreement; to draw up*** *or* ***to draft an agreement; to break an agreement; to sign an agreement; to witness an agreement; an agreement has been reached*** *or* ***concluded*** *or* ***come to; to reach an agreement*** *or* ***to come to an agreement on prices*** *or* ***salaries; an international agreement on trade; ;collective wage agreement; an agency agreement; a marketing agreement*** **blanket agreement** = agreement which covers many different items; **exclusive agreement** = agreement where a company is appointed sole agent for a product in a market; **publisher's agreement** = contract between a publisher and the copyright holder *or* author *or* agent *or* another publisher, which lays down the terms under which the publisher will publish the book for the copyright holder

agree with *verb* **(a)** to say that your opinions are the same as someone else's; ***I agree with the chairman about the need to boost sales*** **(b)** to be the same as; ***the auditors' figures do not agree with those***

produced by the the accounts department; the figures for sales by title do not agree with reps' sales by area

A & I = ABSTRACTING AND INDEXING making summaries and indexes for articles and books

air *noun* **(a)** white space on a printed page; ***we need to give the text some more air*** **(b)** method of travelling *or* sending goods using aircraft; ***to send a letter*** *or* ***a shipment by air;*** **air carrier** = company which sends cargo *or* passengers by air; **air forwarding** = arranging for goods to be shipped by air; **air letter** = special sheet of thin blue paper which when folded can be sent by air mail without an envelope **(c) air-dried paper** = good quality paper made and dried slowly in air, instead of being passed over heated rollers; **paper which is air dry** = paper which is as dry as the air around it (taken to be paper with 10% moisture content)

airbrush 1 *noun* machine which uses compressed air to spray ink or paint; ***he uses an airbrush to create soft background effects*** **2** *verb* to paint using an airbrush; **to airbrush out** = to remove (a detail) using an airbrush; ***we got the art department to airbrush out some of the lines on the author's photograph***

air cargo *noun* goods sent by air

air freight *noun* method of shipping goods in an aircraft; ***to send a shipment by air freight; air freight charges*** *or* ***rates***

airfreight *verb* to send goods by air; ***to airfreight a consignment to Mexico; we airfreighted the shipment because our agent ran out of stock***

airmail 1 *noun* way of sending letters *or* parcels by air; ***to send the proofs by airmail;*** **airmail envelope** = very light envelope for sending airmail letters; **airmail paper** = very thin light writing paper; **airmail sticker** = blue sticker with the words 'by air mail' which can be stuck to an envelope or packet to show it is being sent by air **2** *verb* to send letters *or* parcels by air; ***to airmail a document to New York***

airtight *adjective* which does not allow air to get in; ***the goods are packed in airtight containers***

ALA = AMERICAN LIBRARY ASSOCIATION

Albion press *noun* make of solid old hand press, made of cast iron, still used for printing lithographs and other fine art printing work

album *noun* large book of pictures; large book with blank pages in which you can fix pictures; ***reps carry photographs of the jackets of new titles in a loose-leaf album;*** **album paper** = thick antique paper, used for making the pages of photograph albums

align *verb* **(a)** to make sure that the characters to be printed are spaced and lined up correctly (either horizontally or vertically, although strictly speaking, alignment refers to horizontal positioning and ranging refers to vertical positioning); ***some of the characters are not aligned properly;*** *compare* RANGE **(b)** to put on the same line as something else; ***align the bottom of the text with the bottom of the illustration; make sure the paper is correctly aligned in the printer;*** **aligning numerals** = LINING FIGURES

aligner *noun* device used to make sure that the paper in a typewriter is straight

aligning edge *noun* edge of a optical character recognition system used to position a document

alignment *noun* correct spacing and levelling of printed characters; **in alignment** = correctly aligned; **out of alignment** = not aligned correctly; **base alignment** = making sure that the bottom lines of several columns are level; **vertical alignment** = spacing of matter so that items are correctly placed above each other on the page

all-in *adjective* including everything; **all-in price** *or* **rate** = price which covers all items in a purchase (goods, delivery, tax, insurance); **all in hand** = setting job which is with the compositors; **all up** = setting job where the compositors have finished setting the copy

alpha *noun* first letter of the Greek alphabet; **alpha pulp** = wood pulp with almost all the cellulose removed

alphabet *noun* the letters used to make words; ***we have fonts for the Roman and Greek alphabets, but not the Russian;*** **alphabet length** = space (measured in points) taken by the 26 lower case letters of the alphabet in a particular typeface (used in character samples and cast-offs); **Cyrillic alphabet** = the Russian alphabet, also used in some other Slavonic languages such as Ukrainian and Bulgarian; **Greek alphabet** = the alphabet used in Greek, with 28 letters; **Latin alphabet** = (i) alphabet used for Latin, with 21 characters (no j, u, w, y or z); (ii) modern European alphabet with 26 letters, used in most European languages

alphabetic character set *noun* characters (capitals and small letters) that make up the alphabet; **alphabetic shift** = shift key which activates the letter on an alphanumeric pad

alphabetical *adjective* in the same order as the letters of the alphabet (A,B,C,D, etc.); ***the authors' names are given in alphabetical order;*** **alphabetical index** = index where the items are listed in the order of the letters of the alphabet; **alphabetical order** = arrangement of records (such as files, index cards) in the order of the letters of the alphabet (A,B,C,D, etc.)

alphabetically *adverb* in alphabetical order; ***the files are arranged alphabetically under the customer's name***

alphabetize *verb* to put into alphabetical order; ***enter the bibliographical information and alphabetize it***

alphameric = ALPHANUMERIC

alphamosaic *adjective* (character set) used in teletext to provide alphanumeric and graphics characters

alphanumeric *adjective* **alphanumeric characters** *or* **alphanumerics** *or* **alphanumeric set** = letters and Arabic numerals (and other signs such as punctuation marks); **alphanumeric data** = data shown by the letters of the alphabet and the Arabic numerals; **alphanumeric display** = display device able to show characters as well as numbers; **alphanumeric keyboard** = keyboard containing character keys as well as numerical keys

alphaphotographic *adjective* which represents pictures using predefined characters, for teletext services

alphasort *verb* to sort data into alphabetical order

alter *verb* to change; ***to alter the terms of a contract; the author wants to alter his preface***

alteration *noun* change which is made; ***he made some alterations to the print specifications; the agreement was signed without any alterations; the proofs were passed for press with no alterations;*** **author's alterations (AAs)** = changes made by the author to the proofs, which are usually charged to the author by the publishers (and often are deducted from royalties)

> COMMENT: an alteration is a change made by the author or publisher to a proof, where there is no error on the part of the printer. Changes to correct errors made by the printer are called 'corrections'

amend *verb* to change and make more correct *or* acceptable; ***please amend your copy of the contract accordingly; the title has been amended to avoid possible legal action***

amendment *noun* change to a document; ***to propose an amendment to the agreement; his agent wants to make amendments to the draft contract***

American *adjective* referring to the United States of America; ***she is asking for American paperback rights; the American edition is not for sale in Europe;*** **American Booksellers' Association (ABA)** = organization representing American booksellers; it sponsors an annual convention at which publishing companies have stands showing their new titles; **American Library Association (ALA)** = organization representing American libraries and librarians; it holds an annual convention at which academic and reference publishers have stands showing their new titles; **American Publishers Association (APA)** = organization which represents American publishers; **American Standard Code for Information Interchange (ASCII)** = coding system for computerizing printed characters; **American groove** *see* GROOVE

americanization *noun* changing the spelling and style of a book written in English from British to American; (NOTE: the reverse process is **briticization**)

americanize *verb* to change the spelling and style of a book written in English from British to American

> COMMENT: American rights are the permission given by a publisher from outside the USA to an American publisher to publish an American edition of a work; this usually includes the right to publish the book in Canada. In the case of works first published in Great Britain, the rights will cover the americanization of the spelling and syntax. It is sometimes not easy for a British publisher to limit the market for an American edition to the USA alone, nor to prevent the edition from being sold in markets outside the UK where American publishing companies have a strong marketing presence, such as Australia. See also BRITISH TRADITIONAL MARKET

ampersand *noun* printing sign (&) which means 'and'

analog computer *noun* computer that processes data in analog form (that is, data which is represented by a continuously varying signal - as opposed to digital data)

analyse *or* **analyze** *verb* to examine in detail; ***to analyse a statement of account; to analyse the market potential***

analysis *noun* detailed examination and report; ***job analysis; market analysis; sales analysis; to carry out an analysis of the market potential; to write an analysis of the sales position;*** **cost analysis** = examination in advance of the costs of a new product; **systems analysis** = using a computer to suggest how a company can work more efficiently by analysing the way in which it works at present; (NOTE: plural is **analyses**)

analyst *noun* person who analyses; ***market analyst; systems analyst***

ancestral file *noun* system of backing up computer files (son to father to grandfather file), where the son is the current working file

angle *noun* **(a)** corner where two sides join; **angle bars** = turner bars, metal rods on a rotary press which turn the web of paper so that it is running in a different direction; **angle brackets** = signs (< and >) used in mathematical setting; **angle cutter** = machine for cutting paper from a reel **(b) screen angle** = angle at which a screen is set before the photograph is taken (different angles are used for the four process colours so as to avoid a moiré effect); the normal angles are black: 45°; magenta: 75°; yellow: 90°; cyan: 105°; *see also* DUPLEX HALFTONE

aniline dyes *noun* synthetic dyes made from a benzene base; **aniline foil** = foil used in blocking covers, which contains aniline dyes; **aniline ink** = type of quick-drying ink

anilo roller *noun* roller used in flexography to apply aniline ink

animal sized paper *or* **animal tub-sized (ATS) paper** *noun* paper which has been treated by passing it through a bath of gelatine

annexe *US* **annex 1** *noun* (i) document added *or* attached to a contract; (ii); *US* supplement to a specialized book **2** *verb* to attach (a document)

annotate *verb* to make notes; **annotated bibliography** = bibliography with notes;

annotated text = text with notes written by an editor

annotations *noun* **(a)** captions to illustrations **(b)** notes made to a text

announce *verb* to tell something to the public; ***the publishing house has announced its titles for the Spring list; the results of the literary prize will be announced next week***

announcement *noun* telling something to the public; ***the company delayed the announcement of its spring publishing programme***

annual 1 *adjective* which happens each year; ***annual catalogue; an annual price increase; she has six weeks' annual leave;*** **annual report** = report of a company's financial situation at the end of a year, sent to all the shareholders; **on an annual basis** = each year; ***the figures are revised on an annual basis*** **2** *noun* **children's annual** = book published each year, usually at Christmas, with stories, games, articles, etc., intended for children; often based on a popular TV series or cartoon character

annual general meeting (AGM) *noun* meeting of all the shareholders, when the company's financial situation is discussed with the directors

annually *adverb* each year; ***our prices are raised annually on March 1st***

anodized plate *noun* plate used in offset printing, which is specially coated to prevent wear

anon *abbreviation for* ANONYMOUS (NOTE: used in bibliographies, catalogues, etc., when referring to an author whose name is not known)

anonymous *adjective* author whose name is not known; ***a book by an anonymous author has been entered for the literary prize and everyone is trying to guess who wrote it***

answer *noun* reply *or* letter written following an order; publisher's answers are usually computerized, and take the form of recognized abbreviations, such as RP/ND or OP

antedate *verb* to put an earlier date on a document; ***the invoice was antedated to January 1st***

anthology *noun* book containing poems *or* stories by different authors *or* by the same author, which have been selected by an editor; ***a poetry anthology; 'The London Anthology of 19th Century Verse';*** **anthology piece** = poem *or* passage which appears frequently in anthologies

anthologize *verb* to put into an anthology

anti- *prefix* against

anti-aliasing *adjective (in graphics)* reducing the effects of jagged edges in graphics by using shades of grey to blend in along edges

anti-dumping *adjective* which protects a country against dumping; ***anti-dumping legislation***

anti-halation backing *noun* backing to a film which prevents halation (the halo effect caused by reflection from the emulsion)

antimony *noun* metal which forms part of the alloy used in metal type

> COMMENT: the other metals in the alloy are lead and tin. Antimony is added to make the alloy harder, and better able to make very thin lines

Antiqua *noun* German name for roman typeface

antiquarian *noun* very large size of handmade paper; **antiquarian bookseller** = bookseller who specializes in expensive old books

antique *adjective* very old; **antique face** = one of a range of old-style typefaces; **antique finish** = paper with a rough surface which is bulky but light in weight; **featherweight antique** = light very thick paper, formerly used for children's books and annuals

anti-setoff *adjective* which prevents the ink of one page staining the facing page; **anti-setoff paper** = thin sheet of transparent paper put between the pages of an expensive illustrated book; **anti-setoff spray** = fine powder used on a press to prevent set-off between sheets

APA = AMERICAN PUBLISHERS ASSOCIATION

apostrophe *noun* printing character (') which shows that another character has been left out, also used (in 's) to indicate possession

apparent density *noun* weight of a certain volume of paper, calculated by dividing the basic weight by the thickness

appeal 1 *noun* attractiveness; ***science fiction novels show no sign of losing their appeal; the illustrations have a lot to do with the book's continuing appeal;*** **customer appeal** = being attractive to customers; **sales appeal** = quality which makes customers want to buy **2** *verb* to attract; ***these titles should appeal to the under-25 market; the idea of working in Australia for six months appealed to her***

appear *verb* **(a)** to be published; ***the book is advertised to appear in the spring; the second volume will appear shortly*** **(b)** to seem; ***the company appeared to be doing well; the managing director appears to be in control***

appearing size *noun* size of a printed character on the page (not the same as body size); (NOTE: the maximum appearing size of a face is the distance between the ascender and descender lines. The body size is indicated by points, and the appearing size may be several points smaller)

appendix *noun* section at the back of a book, containing additional information; ***there is an appendix giving the names of all the presidents of the USA; see appendix B for paper sizes; for further details see the appendices; a complete list is printed in the appendix;*** (NOTE: plural is **appendices**)

> COMMENT: appendices are always printed at the back of a book, always starting on a right-hand page; they must be laid out in a way which shows clearly that they are not part of the main text

Apple Mac *or* **Apple Macintosh** ™ **computer** *noun* range of personal computer developed by Apple Inc. that has a graphical user interface and uses the 68000 family of processors

applet *noun* utility application program

approve *verb* **(a) to approve of** = to think something is good; ***the chairman approves of the new company letter heading; no one approves of the book jacket*** **(b)** to agree to something officially; ***to approve the terms of a contract; the proposal was approved by the board***

approval *noun* **(a)** agreement; ***all jackets must be submitted to the author's agent for approval*** **(b) approval copy** = inspection copy, book sent to a teacher, which may be kept without payment if a class set of the book is ordered for the students; **on approval** = sale where the buyer only pays for goods if they are satisfactory; ***they let us have the photocopier on approval for two weeks***

apron *noun* **(a)** *(in papermaking)* strip of rubber at the end of the flow box to close the gap beneath the wire mesh **(b)** *US* extra wide margin on a page which has a fold-out

APR Plate = ASAHI PHOTOPOLYMER RESIN printing plate made from photopolymer resin, used in flexography and rotary letterpress

aquatint *noun* (i) printing process using a copper plate, which is etched to produce halftones; (ii) print made in this way

AR = ASPECT RATIO

Arabic *adjective* coming from Arabia *or* from the Arabs; **Arabic numerals** *or* **numbers** *or* **figures** = normal numbers (such as 1, 2, 3, etc.) as opposed to Roman numerals (I, II, III, IV, etc.); ***the page***

numbers are written in Arabic figures; *see also* LINING, NON-LINING FIGURES

archetype *noun* document *or* book that illustrates the styles of a particular time and subject

architecture *noun* layout and interconnection of a computer's internal hardware and the logical relationships between CPU, memory and I/O devices

archive 1 *noun* **(a) archives** = documents relating to an organization, person or company, kept for many years; ***the company's archives contain documents referring to the founders of the company in the 18th century*** **(b)** storage of computer data over a long period; **archive file** = file containing data which is out of date, but which is kept for future reference **2** *verb* to put data in storage; **archived copy** = copy kept in storage

archival paper *noun* special acid-free paper used for important documents such as wills, which may have to be kept for a very long time

archivist *noun* librarian with special training in dealing with archives

area *noun* **(a)** measurement of the space taken up by something (calculated by multiplying the length by the width); ***the area of this office is 3,400 square feet; we are looking for a shop with a sales area of about 100 square metres;*** **area composition** = composition of pages so that as many elements as possible are in place to reduce or eliminate page make-up; **area fill** = graphics instruction to fill an area of the screen *or* an enclosed pattern with a colour *or* pattern; **area graph** = line graph in which the area below the line is filled with a pattern or colour; **area layout** = layout of the printing area of a page, made up during area make-up; **type area** = amount of room on a page taken up by the type; ***the type area is 150mm by 98mm on a trim size of 172 by 124*** **(b)** part of a country, a division for commercial purposes; ***his sales area is the North-West; he finds it difficult to cover all his area in a week***

area code *noun* special telephone number which is given to a particular area; ***the area code for London is 01***

area manager *noun* manager who is responsible for a part of the country

arrow *noun* printing sign ➡ which points in a certain direction

arrowhead *noun* printed sign ▶ which is usually used to show a cross-reference

art *noun* **(a)** painting *or* drawing *or* music *or* sculpture, etc.; **art board** = shiny woodfree coated card used for colour covers; **art book** = book with illustrations, dealing with a painter *or* sculptor *or* style of design, etc.; **art department** = section of a publishing company which deals with illustrations *or* book jackets; **art editor** = (i) person who is in charge of illustrations and book jackets; (ii) person who edits a list of art books; **art paper** = shiny paper, coated on one or both sides with china clay and size, used for illustrations, especially halftones; **art publisher** = publisher who specializes in art books **(b)** *US* = ARTWORK

article *noun* **(a)** section of a legal agreement; ***see article 8 of the contract;*** **articles of association** *or* *US* **articles of incorporation** = document which regulates the way in which a company's affairs are managed; **articles of partnership** = document which sets up the legal conditions of a partnership; ***this procedure is not allowed under the articles of association of the company*** **(b)** section of a long publication; ***he wrote an article on Chinese music for a Sunday newspaper;*** **review article** = very long review of a book, in which the reviewer discusses the subject of the book rather than the book itself; **dictionary article** *or* **encyclopaedia article** = small section of a dictionary *or* encyclopaedia, dealing with a single word

artwork (a/w) *noun* drawings *or* designs *or* photographs, etc. used in printing (the term is used to describe any camera-ready copy); ***the artwork has to be delivered by August 17th, so that we can do the colour separations***

Asahi photopolymer resin *see* APR

ascender *noun* part of a lower case letter (such as 'd' or 'b') which rises above the x-height of the row of type; **ascender line** = line marking the top of the ascenders in a row of type (slightly higher than the cap line); *compare* DESCENDER

ascending letters *noun* letters which have ascenders (such as 'b', 'd', 'l', etc.)

ASCII = AMERICAN STANDARD CODE FOR INFORMATION INTERCHANGE code which represents alphanumeric characters in binary code ⇨ APPENDIX; **ASCII character** = character which is in the ASCII list of codes; **ASCII file** = stored file containing only ASCII coded character data; ***make an ASCII file of the document for clients who use different word-processing software;*** **ASCII keyboard** = keyboard which gives all the ASCII characters

aspect ratio (AR) *noun* ratio of the width to the height of an illustration, used especially in computer graphics (such as 5:3, where the width is 5cm and the height 3cm)

ASPIC = AUTHOR'S STANDARD PRE-PRESS INTERFACING CODE codes adopted by the BPIF as standard for marking up text

assemble *verb* to put together the various parts which make up a product; ***pop-up books are assembled in South America; the type and illustrations are assembled to make up the page***

assembly *noun* putting together the various parts of an item; ***they put in an estimate for the assembly of the learning kits; the editor wants to check the page assembly of the film positives***

assign *verb* **(a)** to give legally; ***to assign a right to someone; the authors have assigned their copyright to the church*** **(b)** to give someone a job of work; ***he was assigned the job of checking the index***

assignee *noun* person who receives something which has been assigned

assignment *noun* **(a)** legal transfer of a property *or* of a right; ***assignment of a copyright; to sign a deed of assignment*** **(b)** particular job of work; ***my assignment as commissioning editor is to build a list of gardening books***

assignor *noun* person who assigns a right to someone

> COMMENT: if an author assigns the copyright in his work to someone else, usually for a fee, this means that he no longer has any interest in the work. In some cases (such as where the book sells badly) this is a better deal for the author than a normal publishing agreement, where the author licenses a publisher to publish his work against payment of a royalty. The outright purchase of a copyright was common until the 20th century, and is still practised by some publishers

assist *verb* to help; ***can you assist the stock controller in counting the stock? he assists me with the publicity***

assistant *noun* person who helps; a clerical employee; **editorial assistant** = person who helps an editor; **personal assistant** = secretary who also helps a manager in various ways; **assistant editor** *or* **assistant manager** = deputy who can replace an editor *or* manager when he or she is away

associate 1 *adjective* linked; **associate director** = director who attends board meetings, but has not been elected by the shareholders **2** *noun* person who works in the same business as someone; ***she is a business associate of mine***

association *noun* **(a)** group of people *or* of companies with the same interest; ***a book trade association; a printers' association*** **(b)** **articles of association** = document which sets up a company and says what work it will do **(c)** **association copy** = copy of a book which has a connection with the author (such as a copy given by the author to a friend *or* the author's own copy with his notes in it)

assortment *noun* mixed lot of bargain books, with books on various subjects often all sold at the same price

asterisk *noun* printing sign (*) used to refer to something (often used to indicate a reference or a footnote)

asterisked *adjective* with an asterisk attached; ***the asterisked titles are also available in hardback***

as to press *noun* proofs of a colour magazine showing the correct position of the colour work

asymmetric typography *noun* typographic style which achieves strength and liveliness by ranging left or right and avoiding centred lines

asymmetry *noun* lack of symmetry *or* lack of balance between two parts

asynchronous *adjective* referring to data which are sent as soon as they are ready, rather than at fixed intervals; **asynchronous transfer mode (ATM)** = broadband switching technology for transferring large volumes of digital data

ATC = AUTHORIZATION TO COPY

> COMMENT: some software companies have introduced ATC schemes which allow users of certain software to make duplicates of the companies' programs for a fee

atlas *noun* book of maps of the world *or* of a country; **ornithological atlas** = atlas showing maps of where certain birds breed; **pocket atlas** = small atlas which can fit in the pocket; **road atlas** = book showing clearly the roads in a country, so that drivers can find their way

ATM = ASYNCHRONOUS TRANSFER MODE

ATS = ANIMAL TUB-SIZED paper which has been dipped in size

attribute *noun (in printers, display)* a single bit that defines whether the font has a particular characteristic, for example, whether it is displayed in normal, bold or underlined; **screen attributes** = variables defining the shape, size and colour of text *or* graphics displayed; ***pressing Ctrl and B keys at the same time will set the bold attribute for this paragraph of text***

auction 1 *noun* **(a) book auction** = sale of secondhand or rare books, where buyers bid for the books, the person making the highest bid buying the book; **book auction house** = company which specializes in the sale of old books by auction **(b)** selling of rights in a book where publishers offer bids, and the book is sold to the person who makes the highest offer; ***the rights manager has announced that there will be an auction for the film rights;*** **paperback auction** = auction where the paperback rights in a book are for sale to the highest bidder; **to put something up for auction** = to offer an item for sale at an auction; ***his agent has decided to put my next novel up for auction*** **2** *verb* to sell at an auction; ***the paperback rights were auctioned for $500,000; the copy of the Gutenberg Bible was auctioned for more than $10 million***

audio-typing *noun* typing to dictation from a recording

audio-typist *noun* typist who types to dictation from a recording on a dictating machine

audio-visual (AV) *adjective* (educational material) which involves both tapes *or* cassettes to listen to, and slides *or* films to watch; **audio-visual aids** = equipment used in teaching, which includes both sound and pictures

audit 1 *noun* examination of the books and accounts of a company; ***to carry out the annual audit*** **2** *verb* to examine the books and accounts of a company; ***to audit the accounts; the books have not yet been audited***

auditing *noun* action of examining the books and accounts

auditor *noun* person who audits; ***the AGM appoints the company's auditors***

Augustijn *noun* 12 point type unit used in the Netherlands, corresponding to the UK pica em

authentic *adjective* true *or* real; ***the book contains authentic documents written by the murderer; she says it is Shakespeare's signature, but I doubt whether it is authentic***

authenticate *verb* to say that something is true

authenticity *noun* being real; ***the author has tried to get authenticity in his descriptions of American political meetings***

author 1 *noun* person who writes a book *or* article; ***he is the author of a book on bee-keeping; who is the author of this biography? she is a best-selling children's author;*** **author's agent** = person who represents an author and takes a percentage of his or her royalty; **author's corrections (ACs)** *or* US **author's alterations (AAs)** = changes to proofs which are made by an author, and which are charged to him if they are excessive; **author's contract** = contract between a publisher and an author (as opposed to an editor); **author's copies** = free copies of a book given to the author under the terms of his contract with the publisher (normally, an author is given six free copies, but may receive fewer if the book is a very expensive one); **author's discount** = discount allowed to an author who wants to buy copies of his or her own works (or sometimes to buy copies of other books published by his publisher); **author promotion tour** = tour made by an author to promote his or her book (appearing on local radio programmes, signing copies in bookshops, etc.); **author's proofs** = proofs checked by the printer's reader and sent to the author for him to read and correct; **author questionnaire** = form sent to the author of a book, asking for details of his or her life, and also for ideas on the best markets for the book (the answers are used by the publisher's publicity department); **author's standard pre-press interfacing code (ASPIC)** = codes adopted by the BPIF as standard for marking up text **2** *verb* **(a)** to be the author of something; ***the book is authored by a college professor*** **(b)** to create a multimedia presentation or application by combining text, video, sound and images using a programming language or special multimedia authoring system; **authoring** = creating a multimedia application by combining sound, video and images, usually using a script or authoring language

authorship *noun* being the author of something; ***she is credited with the authorship of several of the poems; they are trying to discover the authorship of the book about the President;*** **joint authorship** = situation where several authors have written a book together and share the rights in it

authority *noun* power to do something; ***he has no authority to act on our behalf***

authorization *noun* permission *or* power to do something; ***do you have authorization for this expenditure? the bookshop cannot return copies without the publisher's authorization;*** **authorization to copy** *see* ATC

authorize *verb* **(a)** to give permission for something to be done; ***to authorize payment of £10,000*** **(b)** to give someone the authority to do something; ***to authorize someone to act on the company's behalf***

authorized *adjective* permitted; **authorized biography** = biography which has been written with the permission of the subject (or, if the subject is dead, with the permission of the relatives or the estate); (NOTE: the opposite is an **unauthorized biography**)

auto- *prefix* done automatically; **auto-indexing** = automatic indexing using a computer program; **auto-indent** = instruction for the automatic indenting of a text by a typesetter

autobiography *noun* story of the author's own life; **ghosted autobiography** = autobiography written by a ghost writer but said to be by the subject

autoflow *noun (in DTP or wordprocessor)* text that automatically flows around a graphic image or from one page to the next

autograph 1 *noun* handwritten work by the author in person; ***an autograph manuscript of the famous novel*** **2** *verb (of an author)* to sign a copy of the book; ***he gave an autographed copy of his novel to the library;*** **autographing session** = type of publicity party where the author signs copies of his or her book in a bookshop for people who have bought them

automatic *adjective* which works *or* takes place without any person making it happen; **automatic carriage return** = system where the cursor automatically returns to the beginning of a new line when it reaches the end of the previous one; **automatic data processing** = data processing done by a computer; **automatic dictionary** = dictionary of words in a spelling check program; **automatic font downloading** = process in which special font information is sent to a printer by the application; **automatic heading** = making of headings automatically by the computer page make-up program; **automatic hyphenation and justification** = process where a typesetting machine hyphenates words at the ends of lines and justifies the lines automatically; **automatic page make-up** = process where the typesetting machine makes the text into pages automatically; **automatic reel change** = flying paster, device on a rotary printing press which changes the reel of paper automatically when one reel comes to an end; **automatic sewer** = automatic sewing machine

automatically *adverb* working without a person giving instructions; ***address labels are printed automatically at the same time as the invoices; the typesetting machine justifies lines automatically***

autopaster *noun* flying paster, device on a rotary printing press which changes the reel of paper automatically when one reel comes to an end

autoplate *noun* machine which makes curved printing plates

autopositive *noun* positive photographic image made without a negative stage

AV = AUDIO-VISUAL

availability *noun* being easily obtainable; **offer subject to availability** = the offer is valid only if the goods are available

available *adjective* which can be obtained *or* bought; **the title is no longer available** = the book is out of print; **not yet available** = report on an invoice that a book is not ready immediately (because it has not yet been published or is reprinting)

a/w = ARTWORK

award 1 *noun* **(a)** prize; ***the novel was chosen for the annual award;*** **award-winning** = which has won a prize; ***an award-winning TV play; an award-winning science fiction author*** **(b)** decision by a court which settles a dispute; ***an award by an industrial tribunal; the arbitrator's award was set aside on appeal*** **2** *verb* **(a)** to give a prize; ***the novel was awarded first prize*** **(b)** to decide the amount of money to be given to someone; ***to award someone a salary increase; the judge awarded costs to the defendant;*** **to award a contract to someone** = to decide that someone will have the contract to do work

axe *US* **ax 1** *noun* **the project got the axe** = the project was stopped **2** *verb* to cut *or* to stop; ***to axe the publicity budget; several jobs are to be axed in the printing industry***

axis *noun* (i) line around which something turns; (ii) reference line which is the basis for coordinates on a graph; **horizontal axis** *or* **vertical axis** = reference lines used for horizontal and vertical coordinates on a graph; (NOTE: plural is **axes**)

azerty keyboard *noun* keyboard where the keys are arranged with the first line beginning AZERTY (used mainly in Europe); *see also* QWERTY

azure *noun* light blue; **azure laid** = blue writing paper, with laid lines; **azure wove** = blue writing paper without laid lines

Bb

B = BINDING

B & W = BLACK AND WHITE

B format paperback *noun* paperback with the format 198 x 129mm

B series *or* **B sizes** *noun* ISO recommended paper sizes for posters and other large printed items, the basic size being 1414 x 1000mm; *see also* A SERIES, C SERIES ⇨APPENDIX

BA = BOOKSELLERS ASSOCIATION

back 1 *noun* **(a)** opposite side to the front; ***conditions of sale are printed on the back of the invoice; the printer's colophon should be placed on the back of the leaflet; we normally put the bibliographic material on the back of the title page;*** **back to back** = printing on the back of a printed sheet **(b)** the last pages of a book *or* magazine; ***the supplements are at the back of the book;*** **back of book** = the last pages of a magazine containing advertisements **(c)** opposite cover of a book to the front; ***the ISBN and bar code should be printed at the lower right hand corner of the back; the cover has a four colour photograph on the front, but the back is blank apart from the ISBN*** **(d)** spine of a book, the part of the cover of a book which covers the inside of the pages; ***the book needs to be rebound because the back has broken;*** **rounded back** = style of binding where the spine which is made slightly round; **square back** = style of binding where the spine is flat **(e) back of a page** = gutter, the part of a page nearest to the spine **2** *adjective* **(a)** referring to the back of a book; **back board** = the board which forms the back of a book; **back cover** = the cover at the back of a book *or* magazine (which can have publicity matter or details of the author); **back flap** *or* **back jacket flap** = flap of a book jacket which is folded inside the back cover **(b)** referring to the spine of a book; **back lining** = piece of thin cloth or paper glued to the sewn spine of a book before the cover is attached; **back margin** = margin on a printed page which is near the spine of the book **(c)** referring to the past; **back copy** = copy of an old issue of a newspaper *or* magazine; **back number** = copy of an old issue of a journal *or* periodical; **back orders** = orders received in the past and not fulfilled (usually because the item is out of stock); ***after the strike it took the factory six weeks to clear all the accumulated back orders*** **3** *verb* to put a back *or* spine on a book; ***the book is cloth bound, backed in leather***

backbone *noun* **(a)** *US* spine of a book **(b)** high-speed, high-capacity connection path that links smaller sub-networks

backdate *verb* to put an earlier date on a cheque *or* an invoice; ***backdate your invoice to April 1st; the pay increase is backdated to January 1st***

backer *noun* card at the back of a dump bin, which draws attention to the books in the bin

background *noun* **(a)** (i) part of an illustration which is behind the main items, furthest from the viewer; (ii) a flat colour on which a design is placed; ***the cover design is of black letters on a yellow background; the background on the halftones should be made lighter;*** **background art** = artwork (such as a pattern) which forms the background of a design; **background colour** = colour of a computer screen display (characters and graphics are displayed in a different foreground colour); *compare* FOREGROUND **background printing** =

printing from a computer while it is processing another task **(b)** past work *or* experience; ***the author's background as a financial correspondent; the company is looking for someone with a background of success in building a children's list; she has a publishing background; what is his background*** *or* ***do you know anything about his background?***

backing *noun* **(a)** action of putting the backstrip on a book; **backing boards** = heavy boards between which the folded signatures of a book are held while being prepared for having the cover attached; **backing machine** = machine which backs books **(b)** material used to back a book; ***we use a cloth backing for the library editions*** **(c)** layer of paper *or* film on the back of a sheet of stickers *or* transfer letters, which can be peeled off

backing up *noun* **(a)** printing on the back of a printed sheet **(b)** building up a plate to the right height

backlist *noun* books which have been published some time ago and which are still available; ***the company relies heavily on its medical backlist for cash flow; backlist titles are still selling strongly to libraries;*** *see also* FRONTLIST

backlog *noun* work (such as orders *or* letters) which has piled up waiting to be done; ***the warehouse is trying to cope with a backlog of orders; my secretary can't cope with the backlog of paperwork***

back matter *noun* end matter, printed pages at the back of a book (including notes, supplements, etc.)

back number *noun* old copy of a journal *or* periodical

backplaning *noun* removing a thin layer from the back of a stereo *or* plate, to make it the right height

backslant *noun* typeface which slopes towards the left (as opposed to italic, which slopes to the right)

backspace *noun* movement of a cursor *or* printhead back by one character; **backspace character** = code that causes a backspace action in a display device; **backspace key** = key which moves the cursor back one space

backstrip *noun* long piece of paper or linen glued down the spine of a book after the pages have been sewn and rounded, but before the case is put on

back up *verb* **(a)** to make a copy of a computer file; ***the company accounts were backed up on disk as a protection against fire damage; the program enables users to back up hard disk files*** **(b)** to print on the back of a sheet (done in such a way that the lines of type on both sides are in the same position on the pages, which avoids showthrough and improves legibility)

backup *noun* **(a)** printing on the back of a printed sheet **(b)** action *or* help after something has happened; ***we offer a free backup service to users of our system; after sending the publicity material, we send a backup letter two weeks later;*** **backup ad** = advertisement printed in a magazine in which the advertiser has put an insert; **backup machine** = second machine used in case of emergencies **(c) backup** *or* **backup file** *or* **backup copy** = copy of a computer file *or* set of data kept for security purposes in case the original is lost, damaged or altered; **backup procedure** = method of making backup copies of files

backwater *noun* water removed from the pulp during the first stages of papermaking

bad *adjective* **bad break** = (i) wrong hyphenation; (ii) awkward break of a word at the end of a line of text (as when a hyphen occurs at the end of a page); (iii) awkward placing of text in page make-up (as when a hyphenated word ends a page, or when a single word ends a paragraph at the top of a page, or a section heading is the last line on a page); **bad copy** = manuscript which is difficult to read; illegible *or* badly edited manuscript which the typesetter will not accept; **bad buy** = thing bought which was not worth the money paid for it; **bad debt** =

debt which will not be paid; ***the company has written off £30,000 in bad debts;*** **bad sheets** = sheets which have been badly printed

.BAK suffix to a filename, indicating the previous version of a file

baked *adjective* type which has become stuck together; **baked images** = printing plate which has been heated to make the etched surface harder

balance 1 *noun* **(a)** pleasing layout of a page, where text and illustrations and captions, etc., all are in proportion to each other **(b)** amount in an account which makes the total debits and credits equal; **credit balance** = balance in an account showing that more money has been received than is owed; **debit balance** = balance in an account showing that more money is owed than has been received; **balance in hand** = cash held to pay small debts; **balance brought forward** *or* **balance carried forward** = amount entered in an account at the end of a period to balance the expenditure and income which is then taken forward to start the new period **(c)** (i) rest of an amount of money owed; (ii) rest of a quantity of material bought; ***you can pay £100 deposit and the balance within 60 days; half the sheets are to be bound immediately, and the balance is to be shipped to our warehouse*** **2** *verb* **(a)** to calculate the amount needed to make the two sides of an account equal; ***I have finished balancing the accounts for March;*** **the February accounts do not balance** = the two sides are not equal **(b)** to make the two sides of a design equal; to make sure the colours in four-colour work are of equal strength; ***the two columns do not balance; you can use a halftone illustration to balance the block of text on the facing page***

balloon *noun* circle containing the words 'spoken' by a character in a cartoon; **balloon former** = former on a web machine which takes the folded sheets of a newspaper as they are printed

ban 1 *noun* order which forbids someone from doing something; ***a government ban on the import of subversive literature; a ban on the export of computer software;*** **overtime ban** = order by a trade union which forbids overtime work by its members **2** *verb* to forbid something *or* to make something illegal; ***the government has banned the publication of the book***

band *noun* **(a)** strip of paper which is put round a book; ***the book has a band marked 'Winner of the 1997 Booker Prize'*** **(b)** (i) strip of cloth which goes across the back of the book, to which the signatures are sewn, the edges of the band being glued to the cover boards; (ii) raised strip on the back of a leather-bound book covering the strings **(c)** strong plastic tape put round bundles of newspapers *or* magazines to pack them; **band strapper** = machine for bundling newspapers *or* magazines and attaching them with a plastic band

banda *noun* trade name for a type of duplicator, where the image is drawn on a sheet of special paper which is then attached to a rotating drum, which prints on sheets as they pass under it

bandwidth *noun* **(a)** measure of the amount of data that can be transmitted along a cable *or* channel *or* other medium; ***telephone bandwidth is 3100 Hz; this fibre-optic cable has a greater bandwidth than the old copper cable and so it can carry data at higher speeds*** **(b)** measure of the range of frequencies that a monitor or CRT will accept and display; high resolution monitors display more pixels per area so need high speed data input and so a higher bandwidth

bank *noun* **(a)** business which holds money for its clients, which lends money at interest, and trades generally in money; **bank account** = account which a customer has with a bank, where the customer can deposit and withdraw money; **bank balance** = state of a bank account at any particular time; **bank charges** = charges which a bank makes for carrying out work for a customer; **bank draft** = order by one bank telling another bank (usually in another country) to pay money to someone; **bank loan** *or* **bank advance** = loan from a bank **(b) data bank** = store of information in a computer **(c)** thin writing or typing paper (less than 60gsm) used for air mail letters, flimsies, etc. **(d)** wooden table on which the printed signatures are placed before going for gathering

banker *noun* person who runs a bank; **bankers envelope** = rectangular envelope with the flap along the top

banner *noun* heading *or* title extending across the width of a page; **banner headlines** = large headlines on a newspaper running across the width of the page

bar *noun* **(a)** thing which stops you doing something; ***government legislation is a bar to foreign trade*** **(b)** thick line; ***the page is divided in two by a horizontal bar***

bar chart *or* **bar graph** *noun* chart where values *or* quantities are shown as thick columns of different heights

bar code *US* **bar graphics** *noun* system of lines printed on a product which when read by a computer give a reference number or price; **bar code reader** = optical device that reads data from a bar code

COMMENT: bar codes are found on most goods and their packages; the width and position of the stripes is sensed by a light pen or optical wand and provides information about the goods, such as price, stock quantity, etc. The main type of bar code used in Europe is the European Article Number (EAN) or the Universal Product Code (UPC). Bar codes are used on the backs of books, giving their ISBN number, and so helping the computerized stock control in bookshops

bargain books *noun* books which are sold at a cheaper price (as remainders, special offers, etc.)

barge *noun* case with small compartments for type, used when making corrections

baronial envelope *noun* *US* square pocket envelope

baryta paper *noun* coated matt paper used for high quality repro or proofs from which typematter or photographs can be made

base *noun* **(a)** lowest or first position; **base alignment** = aligning characters of different fonts to the base line; *see also* DATABASE **(b)** flat surface which supports something, such as the flat plate supporting film or the bottom plate used in letterpress printing **(c)** background colour; ***the title is reversed out of a dark blue base;*** **base artwork** = artwork to which further illustrations have to be added **(d) base material** = material which is to be coated; **base paper** = thick paper used to make coated paper

base line *noun* **(a)** bottom reference line used when typesetting to make sure characters are correctly located (the line of the bottoms of characters, such as 'a' or 'x', which have no descenders, or the bottoms of capitals) **(b)** *US* last line on a typeset page

basic 1 *adjective* **(a)** normal; **basic discount** = normal discount without extra percentages; ***our basic discount is 20%, but we offer 5% extra for rapid settlement;*** **basic sizes** = (i) normal paper sizes which a printer carries; (ii) *US* size of paper for calculating the basis weight; **basic weight** = weight of printing paper per 500 sheets **(b)** simple *or* from which everything starts; ***he has a basic knowledge of typography*** **2** *noun* **(a) basics** = simple and important facts; ***he has studied the basics of page make-up;*** **to get back to basics** = to consider the basic facts again **(b)** *US* first edition of a text which has been revised

BASIC *noun* = BEGINNER'S ALL-PURPOSE SYMBOLIC INSTRUCTION CODE simple language for computer programming

basis *noun* **(a)** point *or* number from which calculations are made **(b)** general terms of agreement; ***work will be invoiced on a cost-plus basis;*** **on a short-term** *or* **long-term basis** = for a short *or* long period; ***he has been appointed on a short-term basis; we have three people working on a freelance basis;*** (NOTE: the plural is **bases**)

basis weight *noun* **(a)** weight of paper in grams per square metre (gsm) **(b)** *US* basic weight, the weight of 500 sheets of paper (i.e. a ream) of a standard 25 x 38 inch size, measured in pounds

> COMMENT: in the USA basis weight can also be given for 1,000 sheets, in which case it is followed by the letter 'M': so 120M is the same as 60 pounds basis weight per 500 sheets

Baskerville *noun* typeface designed by John Baskerville (1706-1775), very popular in the 18th and 19th centuries and still widely used

bastard *adjective* **bastard font** = (i) font which combines features of two or more styles of type; (ii) type which is set on a larger body than the point size (such as 8 on 9 point), giving the same effect as leading; **bastard progressives** = progressive colour proofs showing different combinations of colours, but not necessarily in order of printing; **bastard size** = odd non-standard size of paper; **bastard title** = HALF-TITLE

.BAT suffix to a filename, showing that the text is a batch file

batch 1 *noun* **(a)** group of items which are made at one time; ***this batch of books has been wrongly collated*** **(b)** group of documents which are processed at the same time; ***a batch of invoices; today's batch of orders; we deal with the orders in batches of fifty;*** **batch file** = file into which data is collected before being processed; **batch processing** = system of data processing where information is collected into batches before being processed by the computer in one machine run; *compare* INTERACTIVE PROCESSING **2** *verb* to put items together in groups; ***to batch invoices** or **cheques***

batch number *noun* number attached to a batch; ***when making a complaint always quote the batch number on the advice note***

bath *noun* large open container for liquids, such as one for developing photographs; **fixing bath** = bath in which developed negatives are fixed

batter *verb* to hit and harm; *US* **battered books** = books which have been damaged in a bookshop and are sold cheaply; **battered type** = old metal type which has become damaged through use

baud *or* **baud rate** *noun* measure of the number of signals transmitted per second

> COMMENT: baud rate is often considered as the same as bits-per-second, but in fact it depends on the protocol used and the error checking (300 baud is roughly equivalent to 30 characters per second using standard error checking)

BDG = BINDING **BDG/ND** = BINDING NO DATE

> COMMENT: BDG is used by publishers as a report on invoices to bookshops, indicating that a book is unavailable because it is being bound

bds = BOARDS

bear *verb* **(a)** to have (a name); to have something written on it; ***the cheque bears the signature of the company secretary; envelope which bears a London postmark; binding which bears the signature of a famous binder*** **(b)** to pay costs; ***the costs of the exhibition will be borne by the company; the company bore the legal costs of both parties***

bearer *noun* wooden *or* metal bar placed beside metal type to prevent the press from pressing down too hard

bear off *verb US* to adjust the spaces between letters or words to make a line justify

beard *noun* **(a)** bevel and shoulder, the space from the edge of the face of a metal character to the edge of the body of the type **(b)** dirty mark on a typeset character

beat *verb* to hit hard

beater *or* **beating engine** *or* **beating machine** *noun (in papermaking)* container with a heavy roll with steel knives attached, which turns against a bedplate, which also has knives fixed on it, and chops up the pulp as it passes through

COMMENT: wood pulp is beaten to make it finer and more suitable for papermaking; it also makes it less opaque. If it is beaten for a long time, it produces semi-transparent paper such as tracing paper. During beating, china clay or other loadings can be added to make the paper more opaque

bed *noun* flat surface on which the metal type in its chase is placed, or on which flat printing plates are placed; **to put a paper to bed** = to finalize the last corrections on a newspaper before printing starts; *see also* FLATBED

bedplate *noun* **(a)** bottom plate on which type is placed **(b)** plate with metal knives against which the beater roll turns

Bekk instrument *noun* air-leak tester for measuring the smoothness of paper

belly *noun* **(a)** **belly band** = paper band put round the middle of the book **(b)** front of a piece of type with a nick or notch in it (so that the compositor can tell by feel which is the front of the piece)

below *preposition* lower down than *or* less than; ***the captions should be placed below the illustrations;*** **see below** = note meaning that the reader has to look further on in the text to find a reference

belt press *noun* letterpress machine which has plastic printing plates attached to an endless belt; *see also* CAMERON PRESS

Ben Day *or* **Benday tints** *noun* transparent sheets with dots, shading or stippled design, used to give an impression of tone on the printed page, invented by Benjamin Day (1838-1916)

bending rollers *noun* rollers which turn a web of paper in a different direction

Berne Convention *noun* international agreement on copyright, signed in Berne in 1886

COMMENT: under the Berne Convention , any book which is copyrighted in a country which has signed the convention is automatically copyrighted in the other countries. Some countries (notably the USA) did not sign the Convention, and the UCC (Universal Copyright Convention) was signed in Geneva in 1952, under the auspices of the United Nations, to try to bring together all countries under a uniform copyright agreement

bestseller *noun* (i) book which sells very well; (ii) author whose books sell very well; **bestseller list** = list of books which are selling very well in bookshops

best-selling *adjective* which sells very well; ***the best-selling novelist, Mr Archer***

beta ray gauge *noun* device for measuring the weight of paper by using radio isotopes

beta test *noun* second stage of tests performed on new software just before it is due to be released

bevel *noun* sloping edge, especially (i) the sloping edge of a piece of type, between the face and the shoulder; (ii) the sloping edge of a stereotype, which is attached by clamps to the base

bevelled *adjective* with a sloping edge; **bevelled boards** = cover boards, with bevelled edges, sometimes used on large books

Bézier curve *noun* geometric curve; the overall shape is defined by two midpoints, called control handles

COMMENT: Bézier curves are a feature of many high-end design software packages; they allow a designer to create smooth curves by defining a number of points. The PostScript page description language uses Bézier curves to define the shapes of characters during printing

bf = BOLDFACE

Bible paper *noun* extremely thin good quality opaque paper (about 30gsm), which is nevertheless quite strong, used for printing books with a large number of pages, such as Bibles, where the length of the text would make the book very thick if ordinary paper were used

biblio *noun (informal)* reverse of title page, the page which gives bibliographical details about the book (such as the address of the publisher, the copyright line, the ISBN number, the date of publication, the Cataloguing in Publication notice)

bibliographer *noun* person who writes a bibliography

bibliographic *or* **bibliographical** *adjective* referring to details of a book *or* author; ***the obituary of the author ended with bibliographical details of his published works; the catalogue gives a full bibliographical description for each book;*** **bibliographical information** = information about a book (name of author, number of pages, ISBN, etc.) which is used for library cataloguing

> COMMENT: references in a bibliography usually include: name of author or editor; title of book (in upper and lower case italic); title of chapter or article (in roman in double quotes); volume number; name of publisher and town of publication; date of publication

bibliography *noun* **(a)** science of classifying books and authors; printed list of books and authors; **British National Bibliography (BNB)** = classified list of books and authors published in the UK **(b)** details of a single book *or* an author's works, including number of pages, format, number of illustrations, etc.; ***the bibliography is printed on the reverse of the title page; the catalogue gives a full bibliography for each title*** **(c) subject bibliography** = list of documents, articles and books which are relevant to a certain subject, with details of author, publisher, date of publication, etc.; ***the book has a bibliography at the end of each chapter***

bibliophile *noun* person who likes books, especially old or beautiful books, and collects them; ***the book has been published as a limited edition for bibliophiles***

bid 1 *noun* offer to pay a certain price, made at an auction; **opening bid** = first offer; **closing bid** = last bid *or* the bid which is successful **2** *verb* to make an offer at an auction

bidder *noun* person who makes a bid at an auction

bidding *noun* making of offers at an auction; ***the bidding for paperback rights started at $1m***

bidirectional *adjective* (operation *or* process) that can work forwards or backwards; **bidirectional printer** = printer which is able to print characters from left to right and from right to left as the head moves forwards and backwards across the paper

bilingual *adjective* in two languages; **bilingual dictionary** = dictionary which gives translations from one language into another; **bilingual text** = text which is given in two languages (usually with the texts on facing pages)

bill 1 *noun* **(a)** written list of charges to be paid; ***does the bill include VAT? the bill is made out to Smith Ltd; the printer has sent in his bill*** **(b)** written paper promising to pay money; **bill of exchange** = document which tells a bank to pay a person (usually used in payments in foreign currency) **(c) bill of lading** = list of goods being shipped, which the transporter gives to the person sending the goods to show that the goods have been loaded **(d)** poster, piece of advertising material which is stuck on a wall **(e)** set of various quantities of pieces of type in a font **2** *verb* to present a bill to someone so that it can be paid; ***the printer billed us for the author's corrections***

billing *noun* writing of invoices or bills

bimetallic plate *or* **bimetal plate** *noun* printing plate made of two metals, with the printing surface and characters of one metal (such as copper) on a chromium or steel base

bin *noun* (i) large container; (ii) separate section of shelves in a warehouse; ***the bulk stock is kept in the bins at the back of the warehouse;*** **bin stock** = stock held in a section of a warehouse where it can be reached easily (this is the current stock, as opposed to the bulk stock which is held separately until needed); **dump bin** = display container like a large round box, filled with books for sale

binary system *noun* number system based on two digits only (computers work on the binary digits 1 and 0)

bind *verb* to tie *or* to attach the pages of a book and put a cover on it; ***the book is bound in simili leather; the sheets have been delivered to the binder, and binding should start within two days***

binder *noun* **(a)** company which binds books; **the binder's** = the factory which binds books; ***the sheets were delivered to the binder's last week; how soon can you get the jackets to the binder's?;*** **binder's brass** *or* US **binder's die** = brass stamp with a design which is stamped on the cover of a book **(b)** stiff cardboard cover for papers; cover for a loose-leaf book; decorated cover into which sections of a partwork are fitted as they are bought; **ring binder** = cover with rings in it which fit into special holes made in sheets of paper

binder's board *noun* **(a)** stiff board binding, formerly used by publishers to cover books which were then rebound in leather by the owner **(b)** US **binder's boards** = stiff board case covered with cloth **(c)** board (such as millboard) used for binding

bindery *noun* factory *or* workshop which binds books

binding 1 *noun* **(a)** action of attaching pages together and putting a cover on a book; ***we have asked for estimates for binding 2,000 copies in hardback, and 10,000 in paperback; we are returning the copies because of faulty binding;*** **binding board** = BINDER'S BOARD **binding cloth** = cloth used to cover the case in case binding; **binding offset** = extra wide margin on the inside of a printed page (left margin on a right hand page, right margin on a left hand page) to prevent text being hidden during binding **(b)** material which binds a book; cover of a book; ***the binding has come apart; we have produced the series in a uniform binding;*** *see also* BURST BINDING, CASE BINDING, HARDBOUND, MECHANICAL BINDING, NOTCHED BINDING, PERFECT BINDING, SEWN BINDING, SOFT BINDING, SPIRAL BINDING, THREAD SEALING **2** *adjective* which legally forces someone to do something; ***a binding contract; this document is not legally binding;*** **the agreement is binding on all parties** = all parties signing it must do what is agreed

biographer *noun* person who writes the story of someone's life

biographical *adjective* referring to the story of someone's life; ***the biographical details of the author are given on the front flyleaf***

biography book which describes the story of a person's life; ***we are publishing a biography of Winston Churchill;*** **authorized biography** = biography which is written with the permission of the subject (or if the subject is dead, with the permission of the relatives or estate); **unauthorized biography** = biography written without the permission of the subject or relatives of the subject, and which may be more critical than an authorized biography, and therefore more liable to prosecution

bit *noun* binary digit *or* the smallest unit of data which a computer system can handle; **bit image** = collection of bits that represent the pixels that make up an image on screen or on a printer; **bit plane** = memory which stores the bits that make up a picture; **bits per inch (bpi)** = number of bits that can be recorded per inch of recording medium; **bits per pixel (BPP)** = number of bits assigned to store the colour of each pixel; one bit provides black or white, four bits gives 16 colour combinations, eight bits gives 256 colour combinations; **bits per second (bps)** = number of binary digits transmitted every second

bite *noun* the effect of acid eating into metal when making blocks or engraving plates

bit map *or* **bitmp** *noun* **(a)** image whose individual pixels can be controlled by changing the value of its stored bit (one is on, zero is off; in colour displays, more than one bit is used to provide control for the three colours - Red, Green, Blue); ***in Windows, every icon picture is stored as a small bitmap image*** **(b)** binary representation in which each bit or set of bits corresponds to some object (image, font, etc.) or condition **(c)** file format for storing images in which data in the file represents the value of each pixel; **bit-mapped font** = font whose characters are made up of patterns of pixels; ***bit-mapped fonts are quick and easy for a computer or printer to use;*** *see also* ADOBE TYPE MANAGER *compare with* VECTOR FONT **bit-mapped graphics** = image whose individual pixels can be controlled by changing the value of its stored bit (one is on, zero is off; in colour displays, more than one bit is used to provide control for the three colours - Red, Green, Blue)

black 1 *adjective & noun* **black and white (b & w)** = printing using black and tints of black only; **black box** = device used for converting protocols from one computer system to another, such as for converting data from a micro to a phototypesetter; **black liquor** = liquid left after dissolving fibres; **black patch** = black or red film used to make windows on film **2** *noun* spot on a printed sheet, caused when part of the leading is too high and touches the paper

blackening *noun* defect in papermaking, when the surface of the paper becomes spotted, caused when the paper is too damp when being calendered

black letter *noun* old type character based on medieval handwriting (black letter faces include Old English, Gothic, etc.); black letter was the first typeface to be developed by Gutenberg in the 15th century, and was still used in Germany until quite recently. It is commonly used in Europe for mastheads of newspapers; *see also* FRAKTUR, GOTHIC, TEXTURA (NOTE: US English calls this face text)

black printer *or* **black plate** *noun* the plate which prints in black, usually with the text of a colour book, and which is changed if the text is changed (as when the book is printed in another language)

black step *noun* method of ensuring that no signature is out of order or missing when the signatures are gathered together, by printing black marks on the folds of the signature; **black step marks** = marks (like thick black lines) printed on the fold of each signature, which move down from the top in each successive signature

blad *noun* dummy copy of a book to show what the binding and part of the text will be like; ***the reps are showing blads to all the leading bookshop buyers***

blade coating *noun* type of coating where the coating liquid is applied to the paper and then spread evenly using a blade

blag *verb informal* to obtain something by asking for a sample for review *or* testing; ***when you visit the show, can you blag me a pocket calculator?***

blank 1 *adjective* with nothing printed *or* written on it; ***there are four blank pages at the back of the book; the first seven pages are prelims, then we have a blank page and start the text on the next left-hand page; leave two blank lines before starting the next paragraph;*** **a blank cheque** = a cheque with no amount of money or name written on it, but signed by the drawer **2** *noun* **(a)** white page with nothing printed on it; ***leave two blanks before the index*** **(b)** space on a form which has to be completed; ***fill in the blanks and return the form to your local office*** **(c)** thick white paper used for posters **3** *verb* to make a white space (by painting with white ink); ***the art department will blank out the extra lines on the line drawing***

blanket *noun* **(a)** **blanket agreement** = agreement which covers many items **(b)** rubber sheet which goes round the offset cylinder in an offset press and accepts the image to be printed on the paper; **blanket contamination** = spotting caused by dirt on the blanket; **blanket cylinder** *or* **offset cylinder** *or* **transfer cylinder** = cylinder in an offset press which accepts the image onto the blanket; **blanket-to-blanket printing** = offset printing where both sides of the paper are printed at the same time, using two blanket cylinders and two blankets

COMMENT: the blanket is a layer of different tissues, covered with a fine rubber surface. It must be cleaned carefully before each printing run

bleach *verb* to make white; **bleached paper** = paper which has been treated with chemicals to make it white

bleaching *noun* process of making paper white, by passing the pulp through a series of bleaching towers, where a solution of chlorine is added

bleed 1 *noun* **(a)** (i) page design where the illustrations run off the edge of the trimmed page; (ii) illustration which runs off the edge of the paper; ***the double-page spreads are all bleeds*** **(b)** overtrimmed margins when binding, cutting off the edge of the type **(c)** ink which changes colour, often by chemical reaction when laminating **2** *verb* **to bleed off** = to run the illustrations to the edge of the trimmed page; ***all the illustrations bleed off*** *or* ***are to be bled off; the bled-off plates are all in one section;***

COMMENT: bleeding has the advantage of increasing the size of illustrations on the paper, but has the disadvantage of needing larger printing sheets in a sheet-fed press, to allow for the extra trim. Normally 3mm of print beyond the trimmed edge should be allowed to make sure the bleed is correct

blind *adjective* without ink or gold leaf; **blind blocking** *or* **blind stamping** *or* **blind embossing** = stamping a design on the cover material without using any ink or gold leaf; **blind finishing** = BLIND BLOCKING **blind folio** page number which is not printed; **blind P** = printed symbol ¶ which is used to mark the beginning of a paragraph; **blind page** = page (such as a half-title) with no printed folio number, although the page is included in the total pagination of the book; **blind tooling** = blind blocking with hot stamps to give a dark impression on the surface of a leather binding

blinding *or* **blinding in** *noun* blind blocking

blister *noun* bubble which forms on the surface of paper as it dries

blister pack *noun* type of packing where the item for sale is covered with a stiff plastic bubble sealed to a card backing

block 1 *noun* **(a)** piece of metal with a design in relief on the surface, used for printing an illustration by letterpress; **block pull** = proof taken directly from a block; **halftone block** = illustration on a copper block where the image has been broken up by a screen so that it is made up of a series of dots of different sizes; **line block** = illustration on a metal block (usually zinc) where the design is shown by raised lines; **four-colour blocks** = blocks for printing in four colours; (NOTE: in US English this is **cut**) **(b)** stamp used to press a design on a cover (with or without metal foil or ink) **(c)** **block capitals** *or* **block letters** = capital letters (such as A, B, C) **(d)** wide printed bar; **block diagram** = graphical representation of a system *or* program operation; **block letter** = thick heavy sans serif letter cut in wood **2** *verb* **(a)** to stamp a design on the cover of a book; **a gold-blocked cover** = cover with a design *or* title stamped on it in gold leaf **(b)** **to block in** = to sketch roughly the main items of a design

blocking *noun* stamping a design on the cover of a book, using gold leaf, foil or ink; **blocking die** = brass for stamping the cover of a book; **blocking foil** = film with a layer of gold or other metal, used to stamp designs on a cover; **blocking machine** *or* **blocking press**

= machine which automatically stamps the covers of a run of books with a design and glues the metal foil to it

blockmaker *noun* person *or* company who makes the blocks for printing illustrations

blockmaking *noun* the process of making printing blocks

block out *verb* to cover up a section of type *or* part of an illustration; ***the art department will block out the two extra lines***

blotting paper *noun* absorbent paper, which is not sized or coated in any way, used to soak up excess ink

blow up *verb* to make larger; ***the photographs will be blown up to six times their size to make the cover artwork***

blow-up *noun* enlarged photograph or other artwork

blue 1 *adjective* **blue key** = proofs taken from films contacted on a coated paper (usually blue, but can also be brown or black); **blue line key** = paper with a key for the page layout drawn in blue, on which camera-ready copy or artwork is positioned (the blue lines disappear when photographed) **2** *noun US* blueprint, proof taken from a film contacted on coated paper; *see also* DIAZO, OZALID, VANDYKE (NOTE: GB English is usually **ozalid**)

blue pencil 1 *noun* pencil used to mark corrections **2** *verb* to censor by crossing out offensive material

blueprint *noun* **(a)** proof in the form of a positive photographic print taken from film (same as an ozalid); **blueprint paper** = special coated paper, used to make blueprints **(b)** copy of an original set of specifications *or* design in graphical form, made on special paper

blur *noun* image where the edges *or* colours are not clear

blurb *noun* piece of advertising, especially a description of a book written by the publisher, and used in advertisements or printed on the jacket of the book; ***the blurb is very misleading; it says in the blurb that the author is a former member of the police force***

blurbwriter *noun* person (usually a member of an advertising department) who writes blurbs for books

blurred *adjective* not clear; ***we can't use this blurred photograph on the book jacket; the author's colour photographs are too blurred to use in the text***

BNB = BRITISH NATIONAL BIBLIOGRAPHY

B/ND = BINDING/NO DATE

board *noun* **(a)** (i) thick stiff paper (usually over 220gsm) used for the covers of paperbacks; (ii) stiff board used for making cased books; ***the binding material is 240gsm board; please quote for binding in 240gsm board*** **(b) boards (front board and back board)** = the front and back covers of a book; **a series of titles in paper boards** = a series of books in thick paper covers; **board papers** = the endpapers, which are glued to the cover boards; **binder's boards** = (i) stiff board binding, formerly used by publishers to cover books which were then rebound in leather by the owner; (ii) board (such as millboard) used for binding; **cloth boards** = cover made of stiff board covered with cloth **(c)** group of people who advise *or* decide; **advisory board** = group of advisors; **editorial board** = group of editors (such as the group which decides on editorial policy for a learned journal, a publishing company, or a large reference book project); **board of directors** = group of directors elected by the shareholders to run a company; **board meeting** = meeting of the directors of a company **(d) on board** = on a ship *or* plane *or* train; **free on board (f.o.b.)** = price includes all the seller's costs until the goods are on the ship for transportation

> COMMENT: board is a stiff paper product used for binding books; heavy board is also used for making rigid boxes and cartons. Boards used in bookbinding can be divided into two groups: **(a)** boards, usually

180-280gsm, which are used for paperbacks (*see also* ART BOARD, IVORY BOARD PULP BOARD) **(b)** boards used for the front and back covers of cased books, usually covered with paper or a binding material such as cloth or leather (*see also* CHIPBOARD, GREY BOARD, MILLBOARD, PASTEBOARD, STRAWBOARD)

Bodoni *noun* typeface designed by Giambattista Bodoni (1740-1813), with very thick stems and very thin serifs, giving a rigid appearance

body *noun* **(a)** heavy *or* solid part of something; **body paper** *or* **body stock** = thick paper used to make coated paper **(b)** main section of text in a document, either the main part of the text on a page (excluding the headings) or the main part of the text of a book (excluding the prelims and back matter); ***the body of the text is set in Times Roman;*** **body size** = length of a section of text from top to bottom in points; **body matter** = main section of text (excluding prelims, supplements, etc.); *US* **body type** = font used for the main part of the text, as opposed to the style of type used for headings, notes, etc. **(c)** thickness and darkness of ink **(d)** (i) measurement from the top to bottom of a piece of type, measured in points; (ii) stem, the main part of a piece of metal type; **body size** = size of the metal body of a piece of type, measured from the top of the ascenders to the bottom of the descenders; **body width** = size of the metal body of a piece of type, measured across

COMMENT: both body size and body width are measured in points. The typeface may not be the same size as its body. If an 8pt face is cast on a 10pt body, this will have the effect of giving extra leading between the lines: this would be called '8 on 10 point' or 8/10

'Boekblad' Dutch magazine dealing with publishing matters

bold *adjective & noun* dark font with thicker lines than roman; ***for the heading we use Univers 9pt bold;*** **bold-condensed** = bold faced type which is narrower than normal

boldface *or* **bold-faced type (bf)** *noun* version of a typeface which is thick and appears dark on the page

COMMENT: to show that a piece of text has to be set in boldface, a sub-editor will underline it with a wavy line

bolle-a *noun* 'a' with a small circle over it (å) used in Scandinavian languages

bolts *noun* folded edges of the pages of a book which has been gathered and sewn, but not trimmed; if a book is bound in this state it is said to be 'uncut', that is, the pages are still folded at the head and foredge

bond *noun* **bond paper** = good quality thin rag paper (more than 50gsm), used for letter paper; **bond ink** = ink which dries by gelation

book *noun* **(a)** set of printed sheets of paper attached together in a cover; **book publisher** = company which publishes books, as opposed to newspapers *or* lithographic prints, etc.; **book block** = book which has been printed, folded, gathered and sewn ready for binding; **book case** = stiff card cover of a cased book; **book cloth** = covering material for cased books, especially library editions; **book cover** *or* **book jacket** *or* **book wrapper** = paper cover which is put on a book to protect it *or* to make it attractive; **book designer** = person who designs books; **book inks** = printing inks used for printing books; **book paper** = special paper used for printing books (as opposed to newsprint or cover paper); **book proofs** = page proofs of a book which are bound up in a paper cover, often used as advance proofs; **book review** = comments written about a book, published in a newspaper *or* magazine; **book reviews page** = special page of a newspaper, which gives reviews of recent books, and usually carries advertisements from publishers; **book token** = coupon which is given to someone as a present, and which can be exchanged for a book; **the book trade** = the business of making *or* selling books **(b) a company's books** = the financial records of a company;

account book = book which records sales and purchases; **cash book** = record of money received or spent; **order book** = record of orders; **the company has a full order book** = it has sufficient orders to keep the workforce occupied; **book value** = value of an asset as recorded in the company's books **(c) bank book** = book which shows money which you have deposited or withdrawn from a bank account; **cheque book** = book of new cheques; **phone book** *or* **telephone book** = book which lists names of people or companies with their addresses and telephone numbers

bookbinder *noun* person *or* company which binds books

bookbinding *noun* the art of binding books

bookbuyer *noun* (i) person who buys books; (ii) person who buys books wholesale for a large bookshop

bookcase *noun* special piece of furniture with shelves (and usually doors), for keeping books

book club *noun* club whose members have the right to buy books at specially low prices; ***the book club rights have been sold for £10,000;*** **book club edition** = edition of a book specially printed for a book club

COMMENT: book clubs do not always charge their members a subscription, though members usually have to guarantee that they will purchase a certain number of books from the club each year. For the publisher, the sale of a title to a book club is a useful (and sometimes crucial) increase to the printrun, as it is assumed that most book club members would not purchase the book through a bookshop if it were not offered to them by the club. The publisher usually sells the book to a club at a discount off the normal published price and the club sells it to its members at a similar discount. If the publisher sells the book at 75% off the retail price, the club will resell it at 25% below the retail price. So a book retailing at £16, will be sold by the publisher to the club at £4 and the club will sell it to the members at £12. Some discounts are higher than this, and are similar to remainder prices

BookExpo America *noun* bookfair held in Chicago in May/June, formerly called the 'ABA'

book fair *noun* meeting where many publishers come together to show their books to buyers or to foreign publishers

COMMENT: the major international fairs are held all year round. The most important are the London Book Fair (April); the Bologna Book Fair (April/May); the Paris Salon du Livre (May); the BookExpo America (May/June); the Moscow Book Fair (September); the Frankfurt Book Fair (October). There are many other book fairs in various countries; and many specialized fairs as well. Book fairs have existed as meetings for trade since books were invented: the Frankfurt Book Fair existed even in the later Middle Ages. Originally they were places where merchants could buy and sell manuscripts; they have always had an international element, and even the earliest book fairs were patronised by dealers from various countries in Europe. Book fairs can now be divided into two main categories: (a) rights fairs (like the Frankfurt Book Fair, or the London Book Fair), where publishers sell rights in books to publishers from other countries, and also meet agents and representatives; and (b) selling fairs (such as the Geneva Book Fair) where books can be sold to the visitors from the stands. The main book fairs are listed in the APPENDIX

booklet *noun* small book with a paper cover

bookmark *noun* piece of paper *or* ribbon used to put in between the pages of a book to keep one's place

bookmobile *noun* travelling library

bookplate *noun* special printed label stuck into the inside of a book to show who owns it (sometimes designed and printed specially for a person, but otherwise bought from a stationer's)

book post *noun* specially cheap postage rates for sending books

bookseller *noun* person who sells books; **'The Bookseller'** = British weekly magazine dealing with publishing and bookselling matters; **the Booksellers Association (BA)** = organization representing the interests of British booksellers

bookselling *noun* the business of selling books

bookshop *noun* shop which sells books

bookstall *noun* small open bookshop (as in a railway station)

bookstore *noun US* shop which sells books

bookwork *noun* **(a)** printing and binding of books (including the choice of paper, the layout of the page, the binding style, etc.) **(b)** keeping of financial records

boost 1 *noun* something that helps, increases or improves; ***this court case will give sales a boost; winning a prize is a tremendous boost to the author*** **2** *verb* to make something increase; to give something publicity; ***we expect our publicity campaign to boost sales by 25%; the author's signing sessions should boost the book***

boot up *verb* to load the operating system *or* programs automatically into a computer

bootstrap *noun* set of instructions which are executed by a computer before a program is loaded, usually to load the operating system after the computer has been switched on

booth *noun US* section of a commercial fair where a company exhibits its products or services; (NOTE: the GB English for this is **stand**)

borax *noun* chemical substance used to develop photographic film quickly

border *noun* (i) area around printed *or* displayed text; blank space round the edge of printed matter; (ii) decoration which goes round the edge of a printed text (it can be a decorated pattern, or simply a straight rule); **ruled border** = frame to a page made up of a straight line round the edge

borrow *verb* **(a)** to take something (such as money *or* a library book) from someone for a time, returning it at the end of the period; ***she borrowed a book on computer typesetting*** **(b)** to take material from someone; ***the idea for the series was borrowed from an American publisher; they are complaining that our author borrowed half his text from one of their publications***

borrower *noun* person who borrows; ***borrowers from the library are allowed to keep books for two weeks***

borrowings *noun* books borrowed from a library

'Börsenblatt' German weekly magazine dealing with publishing matters

bottleneck *noun* situation in which one section of an operation cannot cope with the amount of work it has to do, and business activity is slowed down as a result; ***a bottleneck in the production department; there are serious bottlenecks in editorial***

bottom *noun* lowest part *or* point; ***the folios are centred at the bottom of each page;*** **bottom space** = blank lines at the bottom of a page of printed text

bottom out *verb US* to arrange the typeset text so that there are no widows or orphans

bound *adjective* (i) (book) covered with a binding; (ii) traditionally, a book where the cover boards have been attached to the book block before being covered in the inside with the endpapers and on the outside with leather, cloth or paper; **clothbound** = covered with a cloth binding; *see also* CASEBOUND, HARDBOUND, LEATHERBOUND

bounding box *noun* rectangle that determines the size, position, and shape of a graphic image or video clip; in graphics applications there is normally a tool that allows you to select an area of an image to operate on: this area is shown as a dashed or flashing bounding box and can be stretched by moving the mouse

bourgeois *noun* type size now no longer used, equivalent to 9pt

bow *verb (of pages)* to curl *or* not to lie flat

> COMMENT: the pages of a book will bow if the book is printed with the grain of the paper running across the page, as opposed to down the page from top to bottom

bowdlerize *verb* to remove 'indecent' words from a text

bowl *noun* line forming the rounded part of a letter (such as the round part of a 'b' or 'p' or 'c'); the space inside the bowl is the 'counter'

box *noun* **(a)** cardboard *or* wood *or* plastic container; ***the books were sent in strong cardboard boxes;*** **box board** = the board used for making cardboard boxes; **box file** = file (for papers) made like a box **(b) box number** = reference number used as a reply address (either in a post office or addressed to a magazine) used to avoid giving the advertiser's actual address; ***please reply to Box No. 209; our address is: P.O. Box 74209, Edinburgh*** **(c)** straight rule running round a section of text or an illustration; ***the sections in boxes give hints on legal problems***

boxed *adjective* put in a box *or* sold in a box; **boxed set** = set of books sold together in a box

box in *verb* to surround a section of text with a rule

bpi = BITS PER INCH

BPIF = BRITISH PRINTING INDUSTRIES FEDERATION organization representing the interests of British printing companies

BPOP = BULK-PACKED ON PALLETS

BPS *or* **bps** = BITS PER SECOND rate at which information is sent equal to the number of bits transmitted or received per second

brace *noun* printing sign { } like a decorative bracket, which shows that items on different lines should be linked together; ***put braces round the pairs of figures in column two***

bracket 1 *noun* printing sign [ ] or ( ) to show that a piece of text is separated from the rest; ***the items in brackets are not obligatory; the brackets in the phonetics show sounds which are not always pronounced; the four words underlined should be put in brackets;*** **round brackets** *or* **parentheses** = printing symbol ( ) which encloses words or characters and separates them from the rest of the text; **square brackets** = printing symbol [ ] used to enclose certain types of text (used in particular to enclose phonetics in dictionaries, or the dates of Acts of Parliament in legal texts); (NOTE: among printers the word **brackets** is used to refer to **square brackets** only, as distinct from **parentheses**) **2** *verb* **to bracket together** = to print brackets round several items to show that they are treated in the same way and separated from the rest of the text

bracketed *adjective* (serif) which is joined to the main part of a letter with a curved line

Braille *noun* system of printing for blind people where characters are shown as series of raised dots on the surface of the page which can be read by passing the fingers over them; ***the book has been published in Braille; the library has ordered a copy of the Braille edition***

brake *noun* device which regulates the tension of paper as it runs through a machine

brass *noun* **(a)** alloy made of copper and zinc; **brass rule** = rule made of brass, used for long lines or borders in letterpress **(b) binder's brass** = brass stamp with a design which is stamped on the cover of a book;

(NOTE: in US English this is **binder's die**) **front cover brass** = brass with the words to be used on a front cover; **spine brass** = stamp with the words to be used on a spine; *see also* CHEMAC

brayer *noun* roller for putting ink on a plate by hand, when taking proofs

breach *noun* failure to carry out the terms of an agreement; **breach of contract** = failing to do something which is in a contract; **the company is in breach of contract** = it has failed to carry out the duties of the contract

break 1 *noun* **(a)** point at which a word is split at the end of a line; ***we must check the page proofs for incorrect line breaks** or **for bad breaks;*** **break line** = the last line (usually a short line) at the end of a paragraph **(b)** point at which something *or* someone stops working; ***she typed for two hours without a break; the print run was held up by several paper breaks** or **several breaks in the paper*** **2** *verb* **(a)** to come to pieces *or* to tear; ***the paper broke twice during the print run*** **(b)** to split a word at the end of a line; ***can we break 'revolution' after the 'u'?*** **(c)** *US* to separate colours **(d)** to fail to carry out the duties of a contract; ***the company has broken the contract** or **the agreement;*** **to break an engagement to do something** = not to do what has been agreed **(e)** to cancel (a contract); ***the company is hoping to be able to break the contract without paying any compensation***

break down *verb* **(a)** to stop working because of mechanical failure; ***the collating machine has broken down; what do you do when your photocopier breaks down?*** **(b)** to show all the items in a total list of costs *or* expenditure; ***we broke the expenditure down into fixed and variable costs; can you break down this invoice into paper, print and binding?***

breakdown *noun* **(a)** stopping work because of mechanical failure; ***we cannot continue with the printrun because of a breakdown in the paper feed*** **(b)** showing details item by item; ***give me a breakdown of production costs***

breaker *noun* vat in which paper pulp is broken and washed before being bleached

break even *verb* to balance costs and receipts, but not make a profit; ***last year the company only just broke even; we broke even in our first two months of trading; the novel will break even at 4,562 copies***

breakeven point *noun* point at which sales cover costs, but do not show a profit; ***the breakeven point for this title is 4,562 copies***

break off *noun* editor's instruction to a typesetter showing that text has to start a new line

break up *verb* to take a forme of type apart when it is no longer needed and distribute the pieces of type

breve *noun* symbol ˘ used above a vowel to show that it is pronounced short

> COMMENT: the breve is used particularly in printing Latin poetry

brevier *noun* old type size equivalent to 8 point

bright *adjective* clear and light; ***the jacket must be brighter, with more red and yellow; we need a bright design for the title page***

brighten *verb* to make brighter; ***can you brighten up this cover design?***

brilliant *noun* old type size equivalent to 4 point

bring down *verb* **(a)** to put something lower down; ***can you bring down the illustration to the bottom of the page?*** **(b)** to make smaller; ***if we brought the point size down to 7 point, what effect would this have on the extent? by bringing the captions down to 4 point, we risk making them illegible***

bring forward *verb* to make earlier; ***the publicity department wants us to bring forward the publication date; the date of the***

next meeting has been brought forward to March

bring out *verb* to publish a new book; ***we hope to bring out the series in time for Christmas; they brought out a book on British football***

brisk *adjective* selling actively; ***sales are brisk; the demand for gardening books is particularly brisk at this time of year***

Bristol (board) *noun* fine white card, made of several sheets stuck together, used especially for printing visiting cards and business cards

briticization *noun* changing style and spelling from American to British English

briticize *verb* to change the spelling and style of a book written in English from American to British

British *adjective* referring to Great Britain; **British traditional market** = the Commonwealth, seen as the normal exclusive market for a British edition

> COMMENT: publishing contracts between British and American companies formerly allotted the British traditional market to the British publisher, leaving the USA itself (and usually Canada) to the American publisher. This arrangement is now not so common, and territories like Australia are becoming 'open' or indeed are the subject of special territorial licences. See also EUROPEAN MARKET

British National Bibliography (BNB) classified list of books and authors published in the UK

British Printing Industries Federation (BPIF) organization representing the interests of British printing companies

British Standards Institution (BSI) British national body which sets and monitors standards

broadcast 1 *noun* radio programme; ***the author has made a broadcast on the BBC World Service;*** **schools broadcasts** = radio programmes for schools **2** *verb* to make a radio programme; ***the dramatization of the novel was broadcast last night;*** **broadcasting rights** = the right to perform a play *or* to read sections of a book, etc. on radio

broad fold *noun* way of folding sheets of printed paper to form a book, so that the grain of the paper runs from top to bottom of a page, parallel to the spine of the book

broadsheet *noun* **(a)** uncut sheet of paper, paper which has printing on one side only and is not folded (such as an advertising poster) **(b)** large format newspaper with paper about A2 size

broadside *noun* **(a)** (i) uncut sheet of paper; (ii) paper which has printing on one side only and is not folded (such as an advertising poster) **(b)** *US* publicity leaflet **(c)** *US* landscape page, page which is printed sideways, reading from bottom to top, used for tables and charts

brochure *noun* booklet, often printed for publicity purpose

> COMMENT: a brochure usually has only a few pages (typically 8 or 16) and is not sewn, but can be saddle-stitched. It usually has a self-cover

broke *noun* odd bits of paper collected during the papermaking process and reused

broken *adjective* in pieces; **broken letter** = metal letter which has been broken; **broken line** = line made of a series of dashes; **broken ream** = paper left from a ream which has not been used up on the previous job

bromide *or* **bromide print** *noun* **(a)** photographic print from a typeset film *or* positive photographic print from a negative *or* the finished print from a phototypesetting machine printed on shiny photographic paper; ***in 24 hours we had bromides ready to film; the typesetter has sent us the bromides for checking; can you supply a bromide of the corrections to pages 124 and 125?*** **(b)** **bromide (paper)** = photosensitive paper used to make bromide prints

bronzing *noun* sprinkling metal dust on freshly printed or varnished sheets to give a metallic effect

brown print *or* **brownline** *noun* *see* VANDYKE

browse *verb* to view data in a database or online system; **browsing** = moving through text or a multimedia application in no particular order, controlled by the user

browser *noun* software utility or front-end that allows a user to easily access and search through text or a database; ***a browser can decode the HTML tags that are used to format pages on the Internet and can display images and text***

brush coating *noun* process of coating paper by painting it with brushes in a brush-coating machine

BSI = BRITISH STANDARDS INSTITUTION

bubble *noun* round shape containing the 'spoken' words in a cartoon; **bubble pack** = BLISTER PACK

Buchmesse German book fair, such as the Frankfurt Book Fair

buckle *verb (of film)* to swell because of heat; **buckle folding** = method of folding paper where the sheet is made to buckle by pulling it through rollers against a metal plate

buckling *noun* distortion and bending of a film due to heat *or* dryness

buckram *noun* thick closely-woven stiff cotton cloth used as a covering material over boards in library bindings

budget 1 *noun* (i) plan of expected spending and income (usually for one year); (ii) total amount of money allowed to be spent on a specific item; ***the publicity department has been asked to draw up an advertising budget for the book; the budget for the entire project is only £100,000; we have agreed the budgets for next year;*** **advertising budget** = money planned for spending on advertising; **cash budget** = plan of cash income and expenditure; **overhead budget** = plan of probable overhead costs; **production budget** = plan of expected expenditure on production; **publicity budget** = money allowed for expected expenditure on publicity; **sales budget** = plan of probable sales **2** *verb* to plan probable income and expenditure; ***we are budgeting for £10,000 of sales next year***

buff *adjective* pale brown colour (as of manilla envelopes)

buffer *noun* temporary storage area for data, such as one for data being sent from a computer to a printer

bug *noun informal* error in a computer program which makes it run incorrectly

build *verb* to make something by putting pieces together; to make a list by publishing a series of titles; ***the new editor has a lot of list-building experience***

build into *verb* to add something to something which is being set up; ***you must build all the forecasts into the budget;*** **we have built 10% for contingencies into our cost forecast** = we have added 10% to our basic forecast to allow for items which may appear suddenly

build up *verb* **(a)** to create something by adding pieces together; ***he bought several small lists and gradually built up a publishing company*** **(b)** to expand something gradually; ***to build up a profitable business; to build up a team of salesmen***

bulk 1 *noun* **(a)** thickness of a book (excluding the covers); ***the title needs more bulk to carry a higher price; you need to know the bulk of the book before you can design the jacket*** **(b)** thickness of paper (not necessarily related to its weight); ***we will still use an 80gsm paper, but we need one with more bulk;*** *US* **bulk factor** = way of measuring paper bulk, the number of pages of a certain type of paper which make one inch in height (usually expressed as p.p.i. (pages per inch); *see* VOLUME FACTOR **(c)** large *or* main quantity of goods; ***the bulk of the***

printrun will be delivered next week; **in bulk** = in large quantities; **bulk buying** *or* **bulk purchase** = buying large quantities of goods at a lower price; **bulk order** = order for a large quantity of material; **bulk stock** = large quantity of stock of a book, held in a separate part of the warehouse from the bin stock; **bulk wrapping** = wrapping several copies of a magazine *or* small book for dispatch **2** *verb* **to bulk up** = to use bulky paper to make a book appear thicker; ***the book is only 96 pages but we bulked it up so that we can price it at £9.95***

bulking *noun* general thickness of a book; **bulking dummy** = dummy book, made with the correct paper and binding, to test its weight and overall appearance; *US* **bulking index** = measurement of paper bulk, calculated by dividing the thickness (in p.p.i.) by the basis weight; **bulking number** = measurement of the number of sheets per inch (i.e. half the p.p.i.); **bulking paper** = specially thick paper which is used to make a book thicker

bulk-packed *adjective* not in parcels; **bulk-packed on pallets (BPOP)** = packed loose on pallets but shrink-wrapped for security; ***paper is often bulk-packed on pallets as distinct from ream-wrapped;*** *compare* REAM-WRAPPED

bulky *adjective* thick (paper); ***we used especially bulky paper for the children's books***

> COMMENT: in Europe, paper bulk is measured either in microns (the thickness of one leaf) or by giving a volume factor which gives the bulk in millimetres of 200 pages of 100gsm. In the USA, bulk is measured by the number of pages per inch of thickness (p.p.i.). Hardwood pulp produces paper which is bulkier than softwood. Bulky mechanicals are used particularly for paperbacks. Light bulky paper (such as antique featherweight) is used for children's books

bullet *noun* **(a)** solid area of typeset tone **(b)** large black dot ● used to indicate an important section of text

bump colour *noun* special colour added to a four-colour separation to enhance tonal range

bundling *noun* **(a)** tying items up into bundles for transport (such as packs of newspapers or magazines) **(b)** stacking printed and folded sections for storage until required (the sections are piled with the foredge alternately the the right and left side of the stack, so that the pile stays flat) **(c)** *US* pressing sewn signatures, so that they lie flat

bureau *noun* office which specializes in a certain process; **computer bureau** = office which offers to do work on its computers for companies which do not own their own computers; **information bureau** = office which gives information; **word-processing bureau** = office which specializes in word-processing; ***we farm out the office typing to a local bureau;*** (NOTE: the plural is **bureaux**)

burin *noun* tool like a needle used to engrave on copper plates

burn *noun* the length of exposure of a metal plate

burnishing *noun* **(a)** *(in engraving)* making gold or silver stamping more sharp by running the paper through the press a second time, with copper foil covering the die **(b)** *(in bookbinding)* polishing the gold or silver leaf on edges of books to give it a brighter appearance

burst *verb* **burst binding** = type of perfect binding where the collated pages are slashed in the spines before the glue and covers are put on; **burst test** = test of the strength of paper; **burst tester** = device for testing the strength of paper

burster *noun* machine which cuts continuous stationery into separate sheets

bus *noun* **(a)** communication link consisting of a set of leads *or* wires which connects different parts of a computer hardware system, and over which data is transmitted and received by various circuits in the system

(b) central source of information which supplies several devices

buy *verb* to get something by paying money; ***he bought 10 tonnes of paper; the company has been bought by its leading supplier; to buy wholesale and sell retail; to buy for cash;*** **to buy forward** = to buy foreign currency before you need it, in order to be sure of the exchange rate

buy around *verb* to buy stock of books in contravention of exclusive market arrangements; ***some Australian bookstores may try to buy around to get books more cheaply than from the exclusive distributors***

buyer *noun* **(a)** person who buys; **a buyers' market** = market where products are sold cheaply because there are few buyers **(b)** person who buys a certain type of goods from a wholesaler, which are then stocked by a large store; **children's book buyer** *or* **fiction buyer** = person in a bookshop who is in charge of buying stocks of children's books *or* of fiction; **print buyer** = person in the production department of a publishing company whose job is to place orders with printers **(c)** publisher who buys the reprint rights in a book from the original publisher (especially the right to reprint the book in another country)

buy in *verb* to buy a book ready made and publish it, rather than editing it from the manuscript; ***we rely on bought-in titles to build up the list***

buying *noun* getting something for money; **buying around** = buying stock of a book more cheaply in contravention of exclusive market arrangements; **bulk buying** = getting large quantities of goods at low prices; **forward buying** *or* **buying forward** = buying paper *or* currency for delivery at a later date; **print buying** = placing orders for printing and binding; **buying department** = department in a company which buys raw materials or goods for use in the company

by-line *noun* line at the beginning or end of an article, giving the name of the journalist who wrote it

byte *noun* storage unit in a computer, equal to one character, a group of (usually eight) bits *or* binary digits which a computer operates on as a single unit; ***one byte can hold numbers between zero and 255***

Cc

© copyright symbol

> COMMENT: the symbol adopted by the Universal Copyright Convention in Geneva in 1952. Publications bearing the symbol are automatically covered by the convention. The copyright line in a book should give the © followed by the name of the copyright holder and the date

c & lc = CAPS AND LOWER CASE

c & sc = CAPS AND SMALL CAPS

C format paperback *noun* paperback with the format 234 x 156mm

C series *or* **C sizes** *noun* ISO standard sizes of paper for envelopes (corresponding to the A series for sheets of paper, an A4 sheet fits into a C4 envelope); *see also* A SERIES, B SERIES ⇨APPENDIX

cabinet *noun* piece of furniture for storing records or for display; **display cabinet** = piece of furniture with a glass top or glass doors for showing goods for sale (used particularly in antiquarian bookshops)

cache memory *noun* section of high-speed memory which stores data that the computer can access quickly

CAD = COMPUTER-AIDED DESIGN the use of a computer and graphics terminal to help a designer in his work; **CAD/CAM** = COMPUTER-AIDED DESIGN/ COMPUTER-AIDED MANUFACTURE interaction between computers used for designing products and those used for manufacturing them

caesura *noun* break (in a line of poetry)

caked *adjective* type which has become stuck together

calculate *verb* **(a)** to find the answer to a problem using numbers; ***the estimator calculated the extent of the novel*** **(b)** to estimate; ***I calculate that we have two months' stock left of this title and should consider putting a reprint in hand***

calculation *noun* answer to a problem in mathematics; **rough calculation** = approximate answer; ***I made some rough calculations on the back of an envelope; according to my calculations, we have two months' stock left***

calculator *noun* electronic machine which works out the answers to problems in mathematics; ***my pocket calculator needs a new battery; he worked out the discount on his calculator***

calendar *noun* book *or* set of sheets of paper showing the days and months in a year, often attached to pictures; ***for the New Year the garage sent me a calendar with photographs of old cars;*** **calendar month** = a whole month as on a calendar, from the 1st to the 30th or 31st; **calendar year** = year from the 1st January to 31st December

calender 1 *noun* series of pairs of rollers through which paper is passed to give it a smooth finish **2** *verb* to pass paper through rollers so that it has a shiny finish; ***the book is printed on calendered paper;*** **calender stack** = set of rollers for calendering paper

calendering *noun* rolling paper to give it a smooth finish; *see also* SUPERCALENDERING

calf *noun* soft leather used for binding books; **half-calf** = binding where the spine and corners of the book are bound in leather, and the rest in paper or cloth; **calf cloth** = imitation leather made of woven material

California job case *noun* case for metal type, where the upper and lower case characters are on the same level, now rarely used

caliper *noun* **(a)** type of measuring instrument which calculates the thickness of paper **(b)** thickness of paper

> COMMENT: in the UK, paper was formerly measured in mils (1 mil = one thousandth of an inch), but it is now measured in microns (1 micron = one thousandth of a millimetre). Mils are still used in the USA

call 1 *noun* **(a)** conversation on the telephone; **local call** = call to a number on the same exchange; **trunk call** *or* **long-distance call** = call to a number in a different zone *or* area; **overseas call** *or* **international call** = call to another country; **person-to-person call** = call where you ask the operator to connect you with a named person; **transferred charge call** *or* US **collect call** = call where the person receiving the call agrees to pay for it **(b)** visit; ***the reps make six calls a day;*** **cold call** = sales visit where the salesman has no appointment and the client is not an established customer; **call rate** = number of calls (per day or per week) made by a salesman **2** *verb* **to call on someone** = to visit on business; ***our salesmen call on their best accounts twice a month***

calligraphy *noun* art of drawing letters by hand in a beautiful way

calligrapher *noun* person who specializes in drawing letters

calligraphic pen *noun* pen with a special nib, used for fine drawing of letters

camera *noun* machine which takes photographs, especially in printing, a machine which takes photographs of the made-up pages of a book; **camera-ready copy (CRC** *or* **crc)** *or* **camera-ready paste-up (CRPU)** = final text, illustrations, headings, folios, etc., pasted up ready to be filmed

Cameron press *noun* type of rotary letterpress printing machine, in which plastic plates are attached to an endless belt, as opposed to cylinders; the books are printed, gathered and bound in one single operation

campaign *noun* planned method of working; **sales campaign** = planned work to achieve higher sales; **publicity campaign** *or* **advertising campaign** = planned period when publicity takes place; ***they are working on a campaign to launch a new series of gardening books***

cancel 1 *noun* set of printed pages (or a single leaf) which take the place of other pages in a printed book; ***we printed a four-page cancel for the prelims of the book club edition;*** **cancel pages** *or* **cancels** = pages which are used to replace other printed pages which have errors on them *or* to give an alternative text (as for the prelim section for a special edition; ***the publisher is late in supplying copy for the cancel pages*** **2** *verb* **(a)** to remove a defective page *or* section from a book and put another in its place **(b)** to stop something which has been agreed *or* planned; ***to cancel an appointment*** *or* ***a meeting; to cancel a contract; the bookshop has cancelled the thousand copy subscription order***

cancellation *noun* stopping something which has been agreed *or* planned *or* instructed; **cancellation clause** = clause in a contract which states the terms on which the contract may be cancelled

cap = CAPITAL (LETTER) **cap height** = height of a capital letter from the base line to the top; **cap line** = line marking the top of a series of capital letters

caps *noun* capital letters; ***the heading is printed in caps throughout; put the chapter title in caps and lower case;*** **caps & lc** *or* **caps and lower case** = style of setting where the first letters of the main words are in capitals, and the rest of the words in lower case; **caps**

& sc *or* **caps and small caps** *or* **caps and smalls** = capitals and small capitals, style of setting where the first letter of each word is a capital, and all the other letters are small capitals; **caps lock** = key on a keyboard *or* typewriter that allows all characters to be entered as capitals

capacity *noun* **(a)** amount which can be produced *or* amount of work which can be done; ***we have some spare typesetting capacity; the factory is buying extra presses to increase production capacity;*** **to work at full capacity** = to do as much work as possible; **to use up spare** *or* **excess capacity** = to make use of time *or* space which is not fully used **(b)** amount of space; **storage capacity** = space available for storage; **warehouse capacity** = space available in a warehouse **(c)** amount of storage space available in a computer system *or* on a disk; **storage capacity** = space available for storage; ***total storage capacity is now 3Mb***

capital *noun* **(a)** **capital letters** *or* **block capitals** *or* **caps** = letters written as A, B, C, D, etc., and not a, b, c, d; ***the title is in 12-point capitals reversed out of a dark blue background; does the word 'French' always take a capital in English?;*** **small capitals** *or* **small caps** = capital letters which are smaller than full size **(b)** money, property and assets used in a business; ***company with £10,000 capital*** *or* ***with a capital of £10,000;*** **capital assets** = property *or* machines, etc. which a company owns and uses; **capital equipment** = equipment which a factory or office uses to work; **capital expenditure** *or* **investment** *or* **outlay** = money spent on fixed assets (property, machines, furniture); **fixed capital** = capital in the form of buildings and machinery; **risk capital** *or* **venture capital** = capital for investment which may easily be lost in risky projects; **share capital** = value of the assets of a company held as shares, less its debts; **working capital** = capital in cash and stocks needed for a company to be able to work

capitalize *verb* **(a)** to write a word in capital letters; ***the name of the company is always capitalized in notices to shareholders*** **(b)** to supply money to a working company; **company capitalized at £10,000** = company with a working capital of £10,000

capitalize on *verb* to make a profit from; ***they capitalized on the popularity of the author's TV show***

capitalization *noun* **(a)** putting a word into capital letters **(b)** **market capitalization** = value of a company calculated by multiplying the price of its shares on the stock exchange by the number of shares issued; ***company with a £1m capitalization***

caption 1 *noun* **(a)** legend, the title to an illustration which is printed near to it; note *or* explanation under or next to a picture *or* diagram; ***set the captions in 8 point roman; the captions should fall under each illustration*** **(b)** heading printed above an illustration **2** *verb* to print a caption

captive market *noun* market where one supplier has a monopoly and the buyer has no choice over the product which he must purchase

capture 1 *noun* **data capture** = action of taking data into a computer system (either by keyboarding *or* by scanning, etc.) **2** *verb* to take data into a computer system; ***the software allows captured images to be edited; scanners usually capture images at a resolution of 300 dots per inch (dpi)***

car stock *noun* stock of books which a rep carries in the back of his car, so that he can supply bookshops quickly

carbon *noun* **(a)** carbon paper; ***you forgot to put a carbon in the typewriter*** **(b)** carbon copy; ***make a top copy and two carbons***

carbon black *noun* very black pigment used in making printing ink

carbon copy *noun* copy made with carbon paper; ***give me the original, and file the carbon copy***

carbonless *adjective* which makes a copy without using carbon paper; ***our reps use carbonless order pads;*** **carbonless paper** = paper that transfers writing without carbon paper; *see also* NCR

carbon paper *noun* thin paper with a coating of black substance on one side, used to make copies in a typewriter *or* printer; ***you put the carbon paper in the wrong way round***

carbon process *or* **wet carbon process** *noun* colour correction process used in gravure, involving three-colour carbon tissues

carbon ribbon *noun* thin plastic ribbon, coated with black ink, used in printers and typewriters

carbon set *noun* forms with carbon paper attached

carbon tissue *noun* **(a)** thin paper with a coating of carbon powder **(b)** sheet of light-sensitive material used in photogravure

Carbro process *noun* colour correction process used in gravure printing, where each process colour is carried on gelatine, to allow the colour to be checked

card *noun* **(a)** stiff paper; ***we have printed the instructions on thick white card; the printer will supply the 100gsm card*** **(b)** small piece of stiff paper *or* plastic; **business card** = card showing a businessman's name and the address of the company he works for; **credit card** = plastic card which allows you to borrow money or to buy goods without paying for them immediately; ***the bookshop has reported increased credit card sales;*** **filing card** = card with information written on it, used to classify information in correct order; **index card** = card used to make a card index; **punched card** = card with holes punched in it which a computer can read; **card chase** = small chase for type *or* plates to print business cards and other small items of stationery; **card punch** = machine with a keyboard which punches holes in cards

cardboard *noun* thick stiff paper used for making boxes; **cardboard box** = box made of cardboard; **cardboard tube** = tube made of cardboard, used for sending posters, covers, etc., rolled up

card index *noun* series of cards with information written on them, kept in special order so that the information can be found easily; **card-index file** = information kept on filing cards

card-index *verb* to put information onto a card index

card-indexing *noun* putting information onto a card index; ***no one can understand her card-indexing system***

carding *noun* putting strips of card or thin leading between type to give extra space or to make a page longer

caret (sign) *noun* written sign used by proofreaders to indicate that a piece of text is missing and that something has to be inserted in the text; the sign is written in the margin of the proof, next to the additional text, and a line is inserted at the place in the proofed text where the addition is to be made

caricature 1 *noun* funny drawing which exaggerates a person's appearance **2** *verb* to draw a caricature of someone

carnet *noun* international document which allows dutiable goods to cross several European countries by road without paying duty until the goods reach their final destination

carriage *noun* **(a)** transporting goods from one place to another; cost of transport of goods; ***to pay for carriage; to allow 10% for carriage; carriage is 15% of the total cost;*** **carriage free** = deal where the customer does not pay for the shipping; **carriage paid** = deal where the seller has paid for the shipping; **carriage forward** = deal where the customer will pay for the shipping when the goods arrive **(b)** mechanical section of a typewriter *or* printer that correctly feeds *or* spaces *or* moves paper that is being printed; **carriage control** = codes that control the movements of a printer carriage; **carriage return (CR)** = signal *or* key which moves the cursor *or* print head to the beginning of the next line of print *or* display; **carriage return/line feed (CR/LF)** = key that moves the cursor *or* print head to the beginning of the next line and moves the paper *or* text up by one line **(c)** section of a printing press which holds and moves the forme

carrier *noun* **(a)** company which transports goods; ***we only use reputable carriers;*** **air carrier** = company which sends cargo *or* passengers by air **(b)** substance that holds the ink for photocopying *or* printing processes **(c)** device that holds a section of microfilm **(d)** continuous high frequency waveform that can be modulated by a signal

carry *verb* **(a)** to take from one place to another; ***the van was carrying a delivery of new stock when it caught fire; all our reps carry car stock at Christmas*** **(b)** to move text from one place to another; ***the compositor was instructed to carry three lines over to the next page*** **(c)** to keep in stock; ***the bookshop carries the full range of our paperbacks; we do not carry specialist titles***

cartography *noun* drawing of maps

cartographer *noun* person who draws maps

cartographical *adjective* referring to maps

carton *noun* **(a)** thick cardboard; ***a folder made of carton*** **(b)** box made of cardboard

cartoon *noun* funny drawing; **cartoon character** = character who appears in cartoons (such as Asterix or Donald Duck); ***a cartoon book*** *or* ***a book of cartoons; the gardening title is illustrated by cartoons***

cartoonist *noun* person who draws cartoons

cartouche *noun* decorative box which frames a text (sometimes used for titles)

cartridge *noun* **(a)** removable device made of a closed box, containing a disk *or* tape *or* program *or* data; **cartridge fonts** = hardware which can be attached to a printer, providing a choice of typefaces, but still limited to the typefaces and styles included in the cartridge; **cartridge ribbon** = printer ribbon in a closed cartridge **(b) cartridge paper** = good quality paper for drawing *or* printing; **offset cartridge** = paper of inferior quality to ordinary cartridge, made on a twin-wire machine and so smooth on both sides, used in offset printing

> COMMENT: cartridge paper is so called because it was originally used for making cartridges for bullets. It is made from chemical pulp, sized, and is very white

case 1 *noun* **(a)** stiff cardboard cover glued onto a book (formed of two pieces of cardboard and the spine); ***the library edition has a case and jacket; have you remembered to order the blocking for the spine of the case?*** **(b)** cardboard or wooden box for packing and carrying goods; **a packing case** = large wooden box for carrying items which can be easily broken **(c) display case** = table or counter with a glass top, used for displaying items for sale **(d)** box in which metal type is kept, divided into sections for the various pieces of type; **upper case** = capital letters; **lower case** = ordinary small letters; **upper and lower case** = style of printing where the first letter of each word is a capital, and all the others are small; ***he corrected the word 'coMputer', replacing the upper case M with a lower case letter;*** **case change** = key used to change from upper to lower case on a word-processor **2** *verb* **(a)** to bind a book in a stiff cardboard cover; **cased book** = book which is bound in a hard cover **(b)** to pack in a case

case binding *noun* **(a)** stiff cardboard cover; ***the trade edition has a case binding*** **(b)** action of binding a book in a hard cardboard cover

casebound *adjective* (book) which is bound in a hard cover; (NOTE: the opposite is **limp**)

case-making machine *noun* machine for cutting the cardboard which forms the cover of a book

casing *or* **casing in** *noun* action of putting a hard cover on a book, attaching it by glueing it to the endpapers and the hinge flaps; **casing-in machine** = machine which attaches cases to book blocks

casein glue *noun* glue used in bookbinding and in making coated papers, which is almost acid-free (it has a pH value of 10)

Caslon *noun* typeface designed by William Caslon (1692-1766), the first major English typefounder

cassette *noun* small plastic box with a magnetic tape on which words or information can be recorded; ***copy the information from the computer onto a cassette***

cassie *noun* dirty or torn paper in a ream (the first and last sheets in the pile)

cast *verb* to make a piece of type out of hot metal

caster *or* **casting machine** *noun* machine that produces metal type, such as the Monotype or Linotype machines

casting box *noun* special box in which metal printing plates (stereos) are cast

cast-coated paper *noun* shiny coated paper, which has been dried under pressure from hot rollers

cast off 1 *noun* calculation of the extent of a book, that is the number of pages required to print a text in a certain typeface and point size, done by counting the characters, including the punctuation marks and spaces **2** *verb* to calculate the amount of space needed to print a text in a certain font

casting off *or* **casting up** *noun* calculating the amount of space required to print text in a certain font, and thus the number of pages in the finished book

cast up *noun* calculation of the amount of setting needed for a book (including spaces and headings) which leads to an estimate of typesetting costs

catalogue *US* **catalog 1** *noun* list of items for sale, usually with prices; ***the publisher's autumn catalogue; they sent us a catalogue of their new range of shelving;*** **mail order catalogue** = catalogue from which a customer orders items to be sent by mail; **catalogue price** = price as marked in a catalogue **2** *verb* to put an item into a catalogue

cataloguer *noun* person who catalogues books in a library

Cataloguing in Publication (CIP) *US* **Cataloging in Publication** *noun* system whereby new books are catalogued before publication by the British Library or by the Library of Congress based on details about each book supplied by the publisher; the cataloguing information is then sent by the Library to the publisher, who then prints it in the book, usually on the verso of the title page

catchline *noun* headline which is written at the top of a page of manuscript or printed at the top of proofs, and discarded when the proofs are made up into pages

catch mounts *noun* special mounts which allow a page to be removed from the imposed forme and another page put in its place

catch stitch = KETTLESTITCH

catch up *noun* situation where the non-image areas of a lithographic print take in ink; (NOTE: also called **scumming**)

catchword *noun* word which is highlighted in some way, such as the first and last words on a dictionary page which are repeated in the headline, or a word at the bottom of a page which links to the text on the next page

category *noun* type *or* sort of item; ***the book does not fall into any of the normal categories***

cater for *verb* to deal with *or* to provide for; ***the bookshop caters mainly for polytechnic students***

cathode ray tube (CRT) *noun* output device used in a VDU or phototypesetter for displaying text or figures or graphics

COMMENT: a CRT consists of a vacuum tube, one end of which is flat and coated with phosphor; the other end contains an electron beam source. Characters becomes visible when the electron beam makes the phosphor coating glow

caveat *noun* warning; **to enter a caveat** = to warn legally that you have an interest in a case, and that no steps can be taken without your permission

caveat emptor = LET THE BUYER BEWARE phrase meaning that the buyer is himself responsible for checking that what he buys is in good order

cc = COPIES (NOTE: **cc** is put on a letter to show who has received a copy of it)

CCD = CHARGE-COUPLED DEVICE electronic device that has an array of tiny elements whose electrical charge changes with light; each element represents a pixel and its state can be examined to record the light intensity at that point; used in some scanners and video cameras

CCITT = COMITE CONSULTATIF INTERNATIONAL TELEPHONIQUE ET TELEGRAPHIQUE international committee that defines communications protocols and standards

CCTV = CLOSED CIRCUIT TELEVISION

CD-I = COMPACT DISC-INTERACTIVE hardware and software standards that combine sound, data, video and text onto a compact disc and allow a user to interact with the software stored on a CD-ROM; the standard defines encoding, compression and display functions

CD-ROM *or* **CD** = COMPACT DISC-READ ONLY MEMORY small plastic disc that is used as a high-capacity ROM device, with data stored in binary form which is read by a laser; **CD-ROM drive** = disc drive that allows a computer to read data stored on a CD-ROM; the player spins the disc and uses a laser beam to read etched patterns on the surface of the CD-ROM that represent data bits; **CD-ROM player** = disc drive that allows a computer to read data stored on a CD-ROM; the player uses a laser beam to read etched patterns on the surface of the CD-ROM that represent data bits

CD-WO = COMPACT DISC WRITE ONCE CD-ROM disc and drive technology that allows a user to write data to the disc once only and is useful for storing archived documents or for testing a CD-ROM before it is duplicated

cede *verb* to give up (a right); ***the author has ceded the film rights to a well-known charity;*** *see also* CESSION

cedilla *noun* accent used with the letter c (ç) in some languages to show a change in pronunciation; ***in 'plus ça change' the first 'c' is written with a cedilla***

cell *noun* indentation which holds ink on a gravure cylinder

cello foils *noun* vinyl foils, thin material for blocking on plastic book covers

cellophane *noun* trade mark for a transparent film; ***the books are packed in cellophane wrapping***

cellulose *noun* chemical substance, a compound of carbon, hydrogen and oxygen; **cellulose acetate** = sheet of transparent film used for making overlays; ***the colour separations are on acetate;*** **cellulose film** = transparent film made from cellulose

COMMENT: cellulose forms the fibres in plants, and so becomes the fibre which constitutes paper. Cellulose fibres have the following properties: they are inert, that is, they do not react easily with other chemical substances; they absorb water and so can be made into the liquid pulp which when dried forms paper; they are colourless, transparent and very strong

censor 1 *verb* to remove sections of books *or* articles in newspapers *or* to ban the sale of a book *or* newspaper because it offends official views **2** *noun* person who censors; ***all imported magazines are examined by the official censor***

censorship *noun* action to ban books *or* newspapers or remove parts of them; ***all imported newspapers are subject to strict censorship; the writers' union has set up a committee to monitor censorship***

centimetre *US* **centimeter** *noun* measurement of length (one hundredth of a metre); ***the paper is fifteen centimetres wide;*** (NOTE: **centimetre** is usually written cm after figures: 260cm)

central *adjective* organized around one main point; **central office** = main office which controls all smaller offices; **central processing unit (CPU)** = the circuits which form the main part of a computer; **central purchasing** = purchasing organized by a central office for all branches of a company

centralization *noun* organization of everything from a central point

centralize *verb* to organize from a central point; ***all purchasing has been centralized in our main office; the group benefits from a highly centralized organizational structure***

centre *US* **center 1** *noun* **(a)** point in the middle of an area; ***the illustration should be in the centre of the page; the folio numbers should be in the bottom centre;*** **centre heading** = heading at the middle of the top of a page; **centre holes** = location holes along the centre of punched tape; **centre margin ring** = metal ring round the edge of the cylinder holding printing plates; **centre notes** = notes printed in the centre of a page between two columns of type; **centre spread** = double page spread which is in the middle of a signature; **centre sprocket feed** = central paper tape sprocket holes that line up with coding hole positions **(b)** group of items in an account; **cost centre** = person or group whose costs can be itemized; **profit centre** = person or department which is considered separately for the purposes of calculating a profit **2** *verb* (i) to put in the middle; (ii) to arrange a piece of text so that the middle of the text is in the middle of the line on the page; ***the text is centred, but the headings should be ranged left;*** (NOTE: the opposite is asymmetric) **centred dot** *or US* **centered dot** = dot which is raised above the base line to the middle of the x-height, used in some countries as a decimal point, as an indication of a new paragraph or section, and also in the USA as a way of indicating syllables in headwords in a dictionary

centering *noun* action of putting text in the centre of the piece of paper; ***centering of headings is easily done, using this function key***

centrefold *noun* double page in the middle of a newspaper *or* magazine; ***we have placed an ad on the centrefold of the next issue***

centrifugal pulp cleaner *noun* type of spinning drum which separates dirt from wood pulp as it is prepared for papermaking

Century *noun* American typeface designed for the 'Century' magazine in 1895 by Theodore Lowe de Vinne (1828-1914), now mainly used (especially for reference books) in a form called 'Century Schoolbook'

CEO = CHIEF EXECUTIVE OFFICER

cerfs *or* **kerfs** *noun* grooves cut into the backs of signatures, into which the thread fits

certificate *noun* official document which shows that something is true; **clearance certificate** = document showing that goods have been passed by customs; **certificate of approval** = document showing that an item has been officially approved; **certificate of deposit** = (i) document from a central library which shows that a book has been officially and legally deposited; (ii) document from a bank showing that money has been deposited; **certificate of origin** = document showing where goods were made

cession *noun* giving up of a right to someone; *see also* CEDE

cessionary *noun* person to whom a right has been transferred

cf *abbreviation* (= CONFER) used to refer to a footnote or to another part of the text

CGA = COLOUR GRAPHICS ADAPTER video display standard developed by IBM that provided low-resolution text and graphics (now superseded by EGA and VGA); the CGA standard could display images at a resolution of 320x200 pixels

chad *noun* little round pieces of paper which are removed when holes are punched in tape

chain *noun* **(a)** series of stores belonging to the same company; ***a chain of newsagents*** *or* ***a newsagents chain; the chairman of a large paperback chain; he runs a chain of specialist shops*** **(b) chain lines** *or* *US* **chain marks** = faint lines which run across laid paper, made by the wire mesh in the papermaking machine; **chain printer** = printer whose characters are located on a continuous belt

chain store *noun* one store in a chain

chalking *noun* **(a)** printing fault where the ink dries and flakes off instead of being incorporated into the paper **(b)** dusting leaves with powdered chalk before applying glue to gild the edges (it prevents the leaves sticking together)

chancery *noun* type of italic, such as Bembo; **Chancery script** = 15th century Italian writing style, used for official documents, from which italic type was derived

change 1 *noun* making something different; ***the author has made extensive changes to the text which will affect the page layout*** **2** *verb* **(a)** to make something different; ***adding an extra page of prelims will change the whole page make-up; we have decided to change the text typeface from Times Roman to Baskerville*** **(b) to change hands** = to be sold to a new owner; ***the bookshop changed hands for £100,000***

channel *noun* route by which information *or* instructions are passed from one place *or* person to another; **to go through the official channels** = to deal with government officials (especially when making a request); **distribution channels** *or* **channels of distribution** = ways of sending goods from the manufacturer for sale by retailers

chapbook *noun* cheap little book in paper covers, sold by street traders in the 17th to 19th centuries

chapel *noun* union branch in the printing and publishing industries; ***the factory has closed because of a mandatory chapel meeting*** *or* ***a mandatory meeting of the union chapel;*** (NOTE: the chairman of a union branch in the printing and publishing industries is known as the **Father of the Chapel** or the **Mother of the Chapel**)

chapter *noun* main section of a book, usually taking up several pages; ***the chapter on race relations should come before the one on government legislation; the footnotes can be placed at the end of each chapter; each chapter should start on a right hand page;*** **chapter drop** = number of blank lines *or* millimetres between the top of the type area and a chapter title; **chapter heading** *or* **chapter head** *or* **chapter title** = title and number of a chapter which is printed in larger letters at the beginning of the chapter; ***chapter headings are in 15 point Univers, and are dropped 20mm;*** **chapter opening** = beginning of a chapter, usually marked with a chapter title and a suitable chapter drop

character *noun* **(a)** letter *or* number *or* sign used in typesetting, such as a letter of the alphabet, a number or a punctuation mark; ***the column allows for a width of about 25 characters;*** **character assembly** = method of designing characters in pixels on a computer screen; **character block** = the pattern of dots that will make up a character on a screen *or* printer; **character byte** = byte of data containing the character code and any error check bits; **character count** = (i) counting the number of characters in a line to work out the approximate total number of characters in a manuscript; (ii) automatic count of the number of characters and spaces which have been keyed into a computer *or* typeset by a typesetter; **character generation** = formation of characters either by computer or from film; **character key** = word processor control used to process text one character at a time; **character printer** = device that prints characters one at a time (a typewriter is a character printer); **character reader** = OPTICAL CHARACTER READER **character recognition** = system that reads written *or* printed characters into a computer by recognizing their shapes; *see also* OCR **character rounding** = making a displayed character more pleasant to look at (within the limits of pixel size); **character set** = (i) list of all the characters that can be displayed; (ii) series of characters in a font; **character skew** = angle of a character in comparison to its correct position; **characters per inch (cpi)** = number of printed characters which fit within the space of one inch on a line, used as a guide to the total extent of a book; **characters per line (cpl)** = numbers of characters estimated in each line, used as a guide to the total extent of a book; **characters per second (cps)** = number of characters which are transmitted *or* printed per second; **optical character recognition (OCR)** = being able to recognize a character and store it in a computer memory **(b)** person *or* animal who appears in a book

COMMENT: characters are important properties in themselves, and can be merchandised in many ways. Publishers who represent the original copyright holders in characters, can license the production of dolls, calendars, playing cards, soap, cups, etc., in the form of the characters. Vice versa, a film or TV company which holds the copyright in a screen character, may license a publisher to publish books about the character

charge 1 *noun* money which must be paid *or* price of a service; ***to make no charge for delivery; to make a small charge for rental;*** **handling charge** = money to be paid for packing *or* invoicing *or* dealing with goods which are being shipped; **inclusive charge** = charge which includes all items; **free of charge** = free *or* with no payment to be made **2** *verb* to ask someone to pay for services; **to charge the packing to the customer** *or* **to charge the customer with the packing** = to make the customer pay for packing; **he charges £10 an hour** = he asks to be paid £10 for an hour's work

charge-coupled device *see* CCD

chart *noun* **(a)** diagram showing information as a series of lines *or* blocks, etc.; **bar chart** = diagram where quantities and values are shown as thick columns of different heights *or* lengths; **flow chart** = diagram showing the arrangement of various work processes in a series; **organization chart** = diagram showing how a company *or* an office is organized; **pie chart** = diagram where information is shown as a circle cut up into sections of different sizes; **sales chart** = diagram showing how sales vary from month to month **(b)** map of the sea

charter *noun* **(a)** hiring transport for a special purpose; **charter flight** = flight in an aircraft which has been hired for that purpose; **charter plane** = plane which has been chartered **(b) charter bookseller** = bookseller who stocks a wide range of titles and who has special terms from publishers

chase 1 *noun* metal frame in which metal type and blocks are placed and held ready to print by letterpress **2** *verb* **(a)** to try to speed up work by asking how it is progressing; ***we are trying to chase up the accounts department for the cheque; we will chase your order with the production department*** **(b)** to gild the edges of a book

chaser *noun* **(a) progress chaser** = person whose job is to check that work is being carried out on schedule *or* that orders are fulfilled on time **(b)** letter to remind someone of something (especially to remind a customer that an invoice has not been paid)

CHC = CYCLOHEXYLAMINE CARBONATE **CHC paper** = paper impregnated with CHC, used to deacidify the pages of old books

cheap edition *noun* special edition of a book which is sold at a lower price than the normal edition (and is usually printed on cheap paper, or bound in a cheap binding)

check 1 *noun* **(a) check digit** = a digit added at the end of a string of digits, to check if they are all accurate (the last digit in an ISBN number is a check digit); **check sample** = sample to be used to see if a consignment is acceptable **(b)** investigation *or* examination; ***the editorial department has carried out a check to see if the MS was returned to the author; the admin people have authorized a routine check of the fire equipment*** **(c)** *US* = CHEQUE **(d)** *US* mark on paper to show that something is correct (used by a proofreader in the margin, to show that the text should not be changed); (NOTE: GB English is **tick**) **2** *verb* **(a)** to examine *or* to investigate; ***to check that an invoice is correct; to check and sign for goods;*** **he checked the computer printout against the author's copy** = he examined the printout and the copy to see if there were any mistakes **(b)** *US* to mark with a sign to show that something is correct

checklist *noun* list of items which have to be done *or* examined

chemac *noun* binder's die used for blocking book covers (cheaper and made of softer metal than a brass, so not used for long runs)

chemical *adjective* **chemical ghosting** = faint images which appear on printed sheets, as an effect of the chemicals in the ink; **chemical paper** = paper made from chemical pulp; **chemical (wood) pulp** = wood pulp which has been made by treating small chips of wood with chemicals such as caustic soda to make them soft and clean and to remove the natural acids (as opposed to mechanical paper, where the pulp is simply ground up by machines); **part-chemical paper** = paper which uses a proportion of chemical pulp and a proportion of mechanical pulp

chemically pure paper *noun* paper which is acid-free, used to repair or protect old books or maps

cheque *US* **check** *noun* note to a bank asking for money to be paid from an account to the account of the person whose name is written on the note; **cheque account** = bank account which allows the customer to write cheques; **cheque paper** = special paper for printing cheques, sensitized to prevent fraud; **crossed cheque** = cheque with two lines across it showing that it can only be deposited at a bank and not exchanged for cash; **open** *or* **uncrossed cheque** = cheque which can be cashed anywhere; **blank cheque** = cheque with the amount of money and the payee left blank, but signed by the drawer

cheque book *noun* booklet with new cheques

Chicago Manual of Style *see* MANUAL

china clay *noun* kaolin, fine white clay used for loading and coating paper

chinagraph pencil *noun* pencil used for making clear marks on film or negative ozalids

chip *noun* **(a)** very small piece of wood, used to be ground into pulp for papermaking **(b)** device made of a piece of crystal etched with transistors, resistors, etc., which performs a function in a computer

chipboard *noun* cheap rough board used for making boxes and binding cases

chlorine number *noun* the amount of chlorine which is absorbed by a sample of pulp, used to calculate the amount required to add to produce a white paper

choice *noun* **(a)** thing which is chosen; ***you must give the customer time to make his choice;*** **book club choice** = book which has been chosen by a book club as a special offer for its members; ***his novel is the Book Club Choice for November*** **(b)** range of items to choose from; ***we have only a limited choice of suppliers;*** **the shop carries a good choice of paper** = the shop carries many types of paper to choose from

choose *verb* to decide to do a particular thing *or* to buy a particular item (as opposed to something else); ***there were several good candidates to choose from; they chose the only woman applicant as sales director; the book club has chosen his novel as their***

Christmas special; you must give the customers plenty of time to choose

Christmas *noun* 25th December, the major festival in most Christian countries; **Christmas card** = greetings card which is sent at Christmas; **Christmas gift book** = special book which is given as a present at Christmas; **Christmas list** = list of books specially produced for sale at Christmas

chromo paper *noun* expensive paper, heavily coated on one side, used for block proofing or printing

chromolithography *noun* colour printing by lithography (a technique developed in the 19th century), each colour requiring a separately drawn plate

chronological order *noun* arrangement of records (files, invoices, etc.) in order of their dates

chumship *noun (in Scotland)* group of compositors working together on the same job

cicero *noun* a point size, more or less the equivalent of a pica, used in Europe, but not in Britain or the USA (the cicero is 4.511mm or 12 Didot points); *compare* DIDOT

c.i.f. = COST, INSURANCE AND FREIGHT ***the books can be supplied at £1.30 ex works from Singapore or £1.45 c.i.f. London***

CIP = CATALOGUING IN PUBLICATION

circular 1 *adjective* **circular letter** = letter sent to many people; **circular letter of credit** = letter of credit sent to all branches of the bank which issues it **2** *noun* leaflet *or* letter sent to many people; ***they sent out a circular offering a 10% discount***

circularize *verb* to send a circular to; ***the committee has agreed to circularize the members; they circularized all their customers with a new list of prices***

circulate *verb* to send information to; ***they circulated a new list of prices to all their customers***

circulating *adjective* which is moving about freely; **circulating library** *or* **subscription library** = library run on a commercial basis, where the members pay to borrow books

circulation *noun* **(a)** movement; ***the company is trying to improve the circulation of information between departments*** **(b)** *(of newspapers)* number of copies sold; *(of library books)* number of times a book has been borrowed; ***the audited circulation of the newspaper is 60,000; the new editor hopes to improve the circulation;*** **a circulation battle** = competition between two papers to try to sell more copies in the same market

circumflex *noun* printed accent (like a small 'v' printed upside down) placed above a vowel, which may change the pronunciation *or* distinguish the letter from others (used over vowels: â, ê, î, etc.)

cite *verb* to mention as an example; ***the author has cited several well-known doctors who support his theory; she cited the latest sales figures to back up her point***

citation *noun* **(a)** mentioning as an example **(b)** *US* quotation from a text

clamp *noun* device which holds something tightly; **clamp allowance** = part of the paper which is held by clamp bars and is not used for printing; **clamp bar** = metal bar which holds the paper in the press as it is being printed

class *noun* category *or* group into which things are classified according to quality or price; **first-class** = top quality *or* most expensive; **first-class mail** = more expensive mail service, designed to be faster; **second-class mail** = (i) *GB* less expensive, slower mail service; (ii) *US* postal service for newspapers and other printed matter

classic *noun* famous work of literature; ***'the Lord of the Flies' has become a modern***

classic; they have published a series of nineteenth-century classics

classify *verb* to put into classes *or* categories; **classified advertisements** = advertisements listed in a newspaper under special headings (such as 'property for sale' or 'jobs wanted'), but without illustrations; **classified catalogue** = catalogue where the items are arranged in different categories; **classified directory** = book which lists businesses grouped under various headings (such as computer shops *or* newsagents); **classified index** = index where the items are arranged under different headings

classification *noun* way of putting into classes; **classification system** = way of arranging books into various categories

clause *noun* section of a contract; *there are ten clauses in the contract; according to clause six, payments will not be due until next year;* **exclusion clause** = clause in an insurance policy *or* warranty which says which items are not covered by the policy; **penalty clause** = clause which lists the penalties which will be incurred if the contract is not fulfilled; **termination clause** = clause which explains how and when a contract can be terminated

clean *adjective* without any mistakes; *the estimate for typesetting assumes the publisher will submit clean copy;* **clean copy** = manuscript *or* text for typesetting which has no alterations and is easy to read; **clean proof** = proof which does not need any corrections; **clean tape** = computer tape with data which has been corrected

clear 1 *adjective* **(a)** easily understood; *he made it clear that he wanted the manager to resign; you will have to make it clear to the staff that productivity is falling* **(b) clear profit** = profit after all expenses have been paid; *we made $6,000 clear profit on the sale* **(c)** free *or* total period of time; **three clear days** = three whole working days; *allow three clear days for the cheque to be paid into the bank* **2** *verb* **(a)** to sell cheaply in order to get rid of stock; *'last year's diaries to clear'* **(b) to clear goods through customs** = to have all documentation passed by customs so that goods can leave the country **(c)** to remove data from memory or off a computer screen

clearance *noun* **customs clearance** = passing goods through customs so that they can enter or leave the country; **to effect customs clearance** = to clear goods through customs; **clearance certificate** = certificate showing that goods have been passed by the customs

clearing *noun* **(a) clearing of goods through customs** = passing of goods through customs **(b) clearing house** = central office where information from various sources is pooled; central office where orders from many sources are consolidated; **Booksellers Clearing House** = system used in the UK for payments of publishers' accounts by booksellers: each bookseller adds together the total of the accounts due to all publishers, and sends them with one cheque to the clearing house, which then consolidates the payments from all the booksellers and settles each publisher's account separately **(c)** removing of formes after a book is printed, by distributing the type, and preparing the formes for another job

clerical *adjective* (work) done in an office *or* done by a clerk; **clerical error** = mistake made in an office; **clerical staff** = staff of an office; **clerical work** = paperwork done in an office; **clerical worker** = person who works in an office

cliché *noun* French word for a printing block

clicker *noun* old term for a foreman compositor

client *noun (in a network)* a workstation *or* PC *or* terminal connected to a network that can send instructions to a server and display results

clip-art *noun* set of pre-drawn images or drawings that a user can incorporate into a presentation or graphic; *we have used some clip-art to enhance our presentation*

clipboard *noun* part of the screen in DTP page assembly used for storing text and diagrams ready to assemble

clipping *noun* reference to a client *or* company *or* author in a newspaper *or* magazine which is cut out of the paper and filed for reference; **clipping agency** *or* **service** = office which cuts out references to a client from newspapers and sends them to him for a fee

clock *noun* circuit that generates pulses used to synchronize equipment; ***the central processing unit normally carries out one instruction every clock pulse, so the faster the clock the more instructions it carries out;*** **clock pulse** = regular pulse used for timing *or* synchronizing purposes; **clock rate** *or* **speed** = number of pulses that a clock generates every second

close *verb* to end **(a)** to stop doing business for the day; ***the office closes at 5.30; we close early on Saturdays*** **(b) to close the accounts** = to come to the end of an accounting period and make up the profit and loss account **(c) to close an account** = (i) to stop supplying a customer on credit; (ii) to take all the money out of a bank account and stop the account **(d) to close inverted commas** = to indicate the end of a quotation

closed *adjective* **(a)** shut *or* not open *or* not doing business; ***the office is closed on Mondays; all the banks are closed on the National Day*** **(b)** restricted; **closed circuit television (CCTV)** = television which operates over a restricted area only (such as a conference hall, a shopping centre, etc.); **closed shop** = system where a company agrees to employ only union members in certain jobs; **closed market** = market where a supplier deals only with one agent *or* distributor and does not supply any others direct; ***they signed a closed market agreement with an Egyptian company*** **(c) closed signature** = signature where the bolts (the folded edges) have not been cut

closeup *noun* photography taken a very short distance away from the subject; ***we need a closeup of the murder victim to put on the front cover***

close up *verb* to reduce the space between characters or lines; ***if the text is closed up a little we will save a page***

cloth *noun* material used to cover a hardbound book; ***the book is bound in green cloth*** *or* ***is in a green cloth binding;*** **cloth joint** = strip of linen pasted along the fold of the endpaper to strengthen the joint; **cloth-lined paper** = paper with cloth pasted on the back, used for folding maps

clothbound *adjective* (book) which is cased and bound in cloth or in imitation cloth

club line *noun* first line of a paragraph which appears at the bottom of a page; (NOTE: compare **widow**)

clumps *noun* metal spacers or leads, cast on thicker bodies, used to space out type matter

cm = CENTIMETRE

CMYK = CYAN-MAGENTA-YELLOW-KEY (BLACK) *(in graphics or DTP)* method of describing a colour by the percentage content of its four component colours

c/o = CARE OF

Co. = COMPANY ***J. Smith & Co. Ltd***

co- *prefix* working *or* acting together; *see also* CO-EDITION, COPRODUCTION, COPUBLISH

coauthor 1 *noun* person who writes a book together with another author **2** *verb* to write a book with another author; ***she coauthored the book on Churchill***

coarse *adjective* rough (surface); (screen) with wide spaces between the lines; (NOTE: the opposite is **fine**)

> COMMENT: a coarse screen is used when printing halftones on coarse paper, as in newspapers; it can be up to about 80 lines per inch

coat *verb* to cover with a layer (of clay, paint or varnish); **coated paper** = art paper or shiny paper, coated on one or both sides with a mixture of china clay and size, used for illustrations, especially halftones; **coated one side (C1S)** = coated paper with the coating on one side only, suitable for posters or covers; **coated two sides (C2S)** = coated paper with the coating on both sides; (NOTE: US English is also **enamel paper**) *see also* DULL-COATED, MACHINE-COATED

coating *noun* **(a)** action of covering paper with a mixture of clay and size; *see also* BRUSH COATING **(b) coating (slip)** = material used to cover paper to make it smooth; **coating binder** = the substance in coating slip which makes it adhere to the surface of the paper; **coating machine** = machine which applies the coating to paper

co-axial cable *or* **co-ax** *noun* transmission line made up of two conductors, one inside the other, to cancel out interfering radiation

Cobb sizing test *noun* test to measure the rate of absorption of water by paper

COMMENT: the Cobb test is used to measure absorption by the surface only (as opposed to the penetration of water right through paper or board)

COBOL = COMMON BUSINESS-ORIENTED LANGUAGE a computer programming language

cockle 1 *noun* bump *or* wrinkle on the edge of a sheet of paper (caused by damp) **2** *verb* to bulge and wrinkle; ***the paper has cockled and will have to be dried***

cockroach *noun* text which has been set in lower case only

cock-up *noun* **(a)** superior letter (as in N) **(b)** initial capital which is larger than the rest of the line

COD *or* **c.o.d.** = CASH ON DELIVERY

code *noun* system of signs *or* numbers *or* letters which mean something; **area code** = numbers which indicate an area for telephoning; **bar code** = system of lines printed on a product which can be read by a computer to give a reference number or price; **international dialling code** = numbers used for dialling to another country; **machine-readable codes** = sets of signs or letters (such as bar codes *or* post codes) which can be read by computers; **post code** *or* *US* **zip code** = letters and numbers used to indicate a town or street in an address on an envelope; **stock code** = numbers and letters which refer to an item of stock

co-edit *verb* to edit a book with another person

co-edition *noun* publication of a book by two publishing companies in different countries; the first company has originated the work, and then sells sheets to the second publisher (or licenses the second publisher to reprint the book locally); ***we have sold co-editions of our book on garden flowers to publishers in France and Greece***

co-editor *noun* person who has edited a book with another person

COMMENT: note the difference in meaning between 'co-edit' and 'co-edition'

coffee table book *noun* large well-illustrated book which can be left on a table for visitors to look at (it may be too heavy to read comfortably without being rested on a table, and in any case probably has little text matter)

cold *adjective* **(a)** not hot; **cold composition** *or* **cold metal setting** *or* **cold type** = using hand set type, typewritten material, or other material made by a machine which prints by striking the paper, as a basis for printing (as opposed to hot metal setting); **cold melt** = glue used for binding which does not need to be heated; **cold-pressed paper** = NOT **cold set ink** = ink which sets on the paper without being dried under heat **(b)** without being prepared; **cold call** = sales call where the salesman has no appointment and the client is not an established customer; **cold start** = (i) starting a new business *or* opening a new shop where there was none before; (ii) starting up a computer for the first time, or for the first time after a period when it has not been used

collaborate *verb* to work together; ***she collaborated with a French film star on a book on the cinema***

collaboration *noun* working together; ***their collaboration on the project was very profitable***

collaborator *noun* person who works with another person

collage *noun* illustration made by sticking together various pieces of photographs, line drawings, etc.

collate *verb* **(a)** to check that the various parts of a book (text pages *or* colour illustrations *or* insert maps) are gathered in the correct order before the book is bound; (NOTE: US English is **conflate**) **(b)** to check one text against another to make sure that it is all there

collating *noun* action of checking the gathered sections of a book *or* of checking a text; **collating machine** = machine which collates signatures of a book *or* pages of a document in correct order ready for binding; **collating marks** = marks printed on the spine of a signature so that the binder can see if they have been collated in correct order; **collating sequence** = order in which signatures are stacked for printing

collation *noun* action of checking that the sections of a book have been gathered in the correct order

collator *noun* machine which takes sheets *or* printed signatures and puts them in order for stapling *or* binding; **collator marks** = COLLATING MARKS

collect 1 *verb* **(a)** to bring things together to form a group; ***he collects books about trains; she collects old newspapers; his short stories have been published in a collected edition;*** **the collected works of Shakespeare** = all the works of Shakespeare published together in one book; **collecting cylinder** = cylinder which collects the printed sheets from a web press before they are folded **(b)** to take things away from a place; ***we have to collect the stock from the warehouse; can you collect my letters from the typing pool?*** **2** *adverb & adjective* US (phone call) where the person receiving the call agrees to pay for it; ***to make a collect call; he called his office collect***

collection *noun* **(a)** bringing things together; texts brought together in a book; ***he has a fine collection of eighteenth century colour-plate books; she has edited a collection of 20th century poetry*** **(b)** action of bringing together the printed sheets from a rotary press **(c)** fetching of goods; ***the stock is in the warehouse awaiting collection;*** **collection charges** *or* **collection rates** = charge for collecting something; **to hand something in for collection** = to leave something for someone to come and take away

collective 1 *adjective* working together; **collective authorship** = situation where a group of people have written a work together; **free collective bargaining** = negotiations about wage increases and working conditions between management and trade unions; **they signed a collective wage agreement** = an agreement was signed between management and the trade union about wages **2** *noun* group of people who work together, and share the profits of their business equally

collector *noun* person who collects; ***he is a collector of books on bees***

college *noun* place where people can study after they have left full-time school; **business college** *or* **commercial college** = college which teaches general business methods; **secretarial college** = college which teaches shorthand, typing and word-processing; **college bookstore** = special bookshop attached to a college, where the students can buy books; **College electro** = special type of electro (developed at the London College of Printing)

collotype *noun* rare printing process, where illustrations are printed from a glass surface coated with hardened gelatine (used especially for art books and reproductions of paintings)

> COMMENT: collotype printing follows the same principle as lithography. The image on the surface of the gelatine attracts greasy ink, while the blank parts are damp and repel the ink. The result is a continuous tone, hence its suitability for reproducing original paintings

colon *noun* printing sign (:)

colophon *noun* **(a)** design *or* symbol *or* company name, used on a printed item to show the names of the publisher and the printer; ***their colophon is a boat with sails*** **(b)** details of the printer, and the place of printing, given on the last page of a book (common outside the UK) **(c)** *(in medieval manuscripts and incunabula)* text at the end of the work giving the name of the writer *or* copyist

> COMMENT: usually the publisher's colophon will appear on the title page and spine of a book, and on all publicity matter; a printer's colophon is likely to appear on private press books and other art books, and is often printed on the last page of the book

colour *US* **color** *noun* **colour bar** = strip of bars of colour in the margin of a four-colour proof, used to check that the tones of the colours are correct and to allow the density of the colour reproduction to be checked; **colour chart** = chart showing different colours available for printing; **colour comp print** = print taken from a colour transparency; **colour correction** = correcting faulty colours manually, by changes to the colour separations; **colour depth** = number of bits used to describe the colour of a pixel; for example, if four bits are used to describe each pixel, it can support 16 different colours and has a depth of 4-bits; **colour-fast red** = red colour which is not affected by light or chemicals; **colour film** = film for printing in colour; **colour filter** = sheet of coloured glass or plastic placed in front of a camera, which cuts off some colours and lets others pass, used in making colour separations; **colour guide** = (i) the designer's instruction for colour, written on his artwork; (ii); = PROGRESSIVE PROOFS **colour masking** = correcting faults in colour printing by masking the separations; **colour matching** = preparing colours according to specifications on a standard system of swatches (as in the Pantone system); **colour negative** *or* **positive** = negative *or* positive film for printing in colour; **colour palette** = range of colours which can be used (on a printer or display); **colour plate** = plate printed in colour; **colour-plate book** = book with colour plates (the term usually refers to an antiquarian book); **colour primaries** = the three primary colours (red, green and blue) which make white light, or the three process colours (cyan, magenta and yellow) used in colour printing; **colour printer** = printer that can produce hard copy in colour; includes colour ink-jet, colour dot-matrix and thermal-transfer printers; **colour proof** = proof in colour; ***the printer has submitted colour proofs of the jacket;*** **colour register** = correctly positioning each colour on the previous one, so that the final result is perfect; **colour separation** = process by which colours are separated into their primary colours; **colour swatch** = sample of colour given by an artist for the printer to match; **colour transparency (C/T)** = small photograph on positive colour film which can be used to print from **(b)** lightness or darkness of a certain typeface, when compared to other faces

colour coding *noun* system of coding a MS or a proof using different colours to indicate different changes

> COMMENT: a MS may be marked up in colour by the sub-editor, with, for example, chapter headings indicated in green, paragraph headings in purple, etc., making sure always that an explanation of the colours and the typography required is given on the first pages of the MS for the compositor to follow. For corrections to proofs, normal colour coding is that the printer marks his corrections in green; any corrections noticed by the publisher or author which

they believe to be mistakes made by the printer are marked in red; all other changes are shown in blue or black

coloured *adjective* in colour; **coloured edges** *or* **coloured top** = edges *or* top of the pages of a book block which have been dyed with colour

colouring book *noun* children's book of black and white drawings, which the child can colour in paint

colour separation *noun* **(a)** separating the various colours from a design into the process colours (magenta, cyan, yellow and black) to make a series of four films for printing **(b)** film for a single colour

COMMENT: the colours are separated by electronic scanning or by photographing the original using filters to isolate each colour in turn. Each colour is then printed as a separate proof for checking purposes: this is a colour separation negative

column *noun* **(a)** section of printed words in a book *or* newspaper *or* magazine, printed as a vertical part of the page and not running across the whole page width (very wide columns are difficult to read, as the eye has difficulty in following the characters along the line; 20 or 22 pica ems is usually taken to be the maximum legible column width); ***the dictionary is set in two columns per page; can we get three columns per page for the index? magazines can have up to eight columns per page;*** **single column** = printed in one column; **double column** = printed in two columns; **column balancing** = automatic adjustment of columns on a page, so that they are the same length; **column break** = bad break which occurs in a column; **columns across** = printing a newspaper with the columns running across the cylinder; **columns around** = printing a newspaper with the columns running round the plate cylinder; **column-centimetre** *or* **column-inch** = depth in centimetres or inches of a space in a newspaper column, used for calculating charges for advertising; **column rule** = rule running down the page of a newspaper from top to bottom, separating the columns **(b)** regular article which a journalist writes in a newspaper *or* magazine; ***he writes a weekly gardening column for the local paper; she has a syndicated health and beauty column in six national newspapers*** **(c)** series of characters *or* numbers, one under the other; ***to add up a column of figures; put the total at the bottom of the column;*** **credit column** = right-hand side in accounts showing money received; **debit column** = left-hand side in accounts showing money paid or owed; **80-column printer** = printer which has a maximum line width of 80 characters

columnar *adjective* in columns; **columnar graph** = graph on which values are shown as vertical *or* horizontal bars; **columnar working** = showing information in columns

columnist *noun* journalist who writes a regular column in a paper

comb binding *noun* type of mechanical binding, where loose pages are attached by the teeth of a plastic comb, which are then rolled round to form a spine

combine *verb* to put two or more things together; **combined halftone and line** = using both halftones and line artwork in the same design

combination *noun* **combination line and halftone** *or* **combination plate** = plate which uses both line artwork or text and photographs in the same design

coming-and-going *noun* fore-and-aft *or* two-up, method of printing two copies of a book at the same time, with the pages joined head to head

Comité Consultatif International Téléphonique et Télégraphique (CCITT) international committee that defines communications protocols and standards

comma *noun* printed *or* written sign (,) which indicates a small break in the sense of a sentence; **inverted commas** = printing signs (“ ”, ‘ ’) which are put round words which are being quoted, or round titles; **single inverted commas** *or* **double inverted commas** = signs (‘ ’) or (“ ”); **open** *or* **close inverted commas** = to start *or* stop inverted commas round a quotation

command *noun* instruction to a computer

commentary *noun* text which comments on another text; ***a series of commentaries on the books of the Bible; he has written a commentary on Shakespeare's 'Hamlet'***

commerce *noun* business *or* buying and selling of goods and services; **Chamber of Commerce** = group of local businessmen who meet to discuss problems which they have in common and to promote business in their town

commercial 1 *adjective* referring to business; **commercial a** = printing sign (@) which means ‘at’; **commercial artist** = artist who designs advertisements *or* posters, etc., for payment; **commercial college** = college which teaches business studies; **commercial course** = course where business skills are studied; **commercial law** = laws regarding business; **commercial printer** = printing company which prints for business clients other than publishers; **commercial traveller** = salesman who travels round an area visiting customers on behalf of his company; **sample only - of no commercial value** = not worth anything if sold **2** *noun* advertisement on television

commission 1 *noun* **(a)** money paid to a salesman *or* an agent, usually a percentage of the sales made; ***she gets 10% commission on everything she sells;*** **he charges 10% commission** = he asks for 10% of sales as his payment; **commission agent** = agent who is paid a percentage of sales; **commission rep** *or* **commission salesman** = representative who is not paid a salary, but receives a commission on sales; **commission sale** *or* **sale on commission** = sale where the salesman is paid a commission **(b)** special job given to a person *or* company to do; ***he has an interesting commission - to write a history of museums*** **(c)** group of people officially appointed to examine some problem; ***the government has appointed a commission of inquiry to look into the problems of small exporters; he is the chairman of the government commission on export subsidies*** **2** *verb* to order someone to do some work; ***he was commissioned to design a new logo;*** **to commission a book** = to ask an author to write a book; ***she has commissioned a series of books on world history; they never publish works submitted on spec, and commission everything in their list;*** **commissioning editor** = editor whose job is to think of an idea for a book and ask an author to write it

commit *verb* **to be committed to do something** = to be legally obliged to do something; ***the contract commits the publisher to publish the book***

commitment *noun* being obliged to do something

comp (a) = COMPOSITOR **(b)** = COMPREHENSIVE LAYOUT **(c) comp list** = list of people who receive complimentary copies

compact disc interactive (CD-I) hardware and software standards that combine sound, data, video and text onto a compact disc and allow a user to interact with the software stored on a CD-ROM; the standard defines encoding, compression and display functions

compact disc ROM *or* **CD-ROM** small plastic disc that is used as a high capacity ROM device, data is stored in binary form as holes etched on the surface which are then read by a laser

compact disc write once (CD-WO) CD-ROM disc and drive technology that allows a user to write data to the disc once only and is useful for storing archived documents or for testing a CD-ROM before it is duplicated

companionship *noun* group of compositors working together on the same job

compatible *adjective* (two hardware *or* software devices) that function correctly together

compatibility *noun (of two devices or programs)* ability to function together

> COMMENT: by conforming to the standards of another manufacturer or organization, compatibility of hardware and software allows programs and devices to be interchanged without modification; text, for example, can be written on one machine using a word-processing package and edited on another machine using a page make-up package

compensating guard *see* GUARD

compensating roller *noun* jockey roller, a roller in a web-fed press, which compensates for the uneven tension in the reel of paper

compete *verb* **to compete with someone** *or* **with a company** = to try to do better than another person *or* another company; ***we have to compete with cheap printing in the Far East; they were competing unsuccessfully with local companies on their home territory;*** **the two companies are competing for a market share** = each company is trying to win a larger part of the market

competing *adjective* which competes; **competing firms** = firms which compete with each other; **competing titles** = (i) books published by different companies which have similar subjects and titles and are sold in the same markets at similar prices; (ii) books on the same subject written by the same author for different publishers in the same market (a contract will usually forbid the selling of competing works)

competition *noun* **(a)** trying to do better than another supplier; **free competition** = being free to compete without government interference; **keen competition** = strong competition; ***we are facing keen competition from European manufacturers*** **(b) the competition** = companies which are trying to compete with your product

compile *verb* to put together (a list); ***she has compiled a dictionary of common names; he is compiling a list of databases***

compilation *noun* putting things together in a list

compiler *noun* **(a)** person who compiles a dictionary, an anthology, a puzzle book, etc. **(b)** computer program that converts an encoded program into machine code

complementary *adjective* (two things) that complete each other *or* go well together; **complementary colours** = two colours that when optically combined produce white

complete 1 *adjective* **(a)** whole *or* with nothing missing; ***the complete plays of Shakespeare; the order is complete and ready for dispatch; the order should be accepted only if it is complete; the signatures are all complete and ready for binding*** **(b)** finished; ***the spelling check is complete*** **2** *verb* to finish; ***the factory completed the order in two weeks; how long will it take you to complete the job? when you have completed the keyboarding, pass the text through the spelling checker***

completely *adverb* all *or* totally; ***the cargo was completely ruined by water; the warehouse was completely destroyed by fire***

completion *noun* act of finishing something; **completion date** = date when something will be finished; ***completion date for dispatch of bound copies is November 15th***

complimentary *adjective* free *or* given as a present; ***the author got three complimentary copies of his book; he asked for a complimentary copy to be sent to his father***

compliments slip *noun* piece of paper with the name of the company printed on it, sent with a book *or* document *or* gifts, etc. instead of a letter

compose *verb* to put text into type ready for printing, using any method, such as hot metal setting, photocomposition, etc.; ***to compose a book in Times roman;***

composing frame = a compositor's storage unit, with cases for different types; **composing machine** = machine which sets type automatically in hot metal, from instructions given on a paper tape, punched by the compositor using a keyboard similar to a typewriter keyboard; **composing room** = section of a printer's works *or* of a newspaper, where the text is typeset and made up into pages; **composing stick** = narrow metal holder in which the compositor places the pieces of type as he sets each line

composite *adjective* **composite artwork** = artwork which includes various elements (such as text, halftones, sketch maps, etc.); **composite block** = printing block with halftones and line blocks or parts of different blocks

composition *noun* creating typeset text, either using metal type *or* by keyboarding on a computer typesetter; ***the composition has been done by Smith Ltd; composition costs are cheaper in Spain;*** **composition costs** = cost of typesetting a book; **composition size** = printing type size which can be set by machine (up to 14 point), as opposed to display sizes; *see also* PHOTOCOMPOSITION

compositor *noun* **(a)** person who sets up the required type prior to printing, either by hand (using metal type) or by keyboarding; (NOTE: US English is **typographer)** **electronic compositor** = computer that allows a user to arrange text easily on screen before it is electronically typeset **(b)** *US* person who makes corrections to metal type or who sets technical material

comprehensive (layout) *noun US* finished artwork *or* graphics *or* photographs *or* illustrations, used as part of a printed output; (NOTE: GB English is **visual)**

compression *noun* varying the gain of a device depending on input level to maintain an output signal within certain limits; **compression ratio** = ratio of the size of an original, uncompressed file to the final, compressed file that has been more efficiently encoded; **data compression** = means of reducing the size of blocks of data by removing spaces, empty sections and unused material

comptometer *noun* machine which counts automatically

compulsory *adjective* which is forced *or* ordered; **compulsory liquidation** = liquidation which is ordered by a court

CompuServe ™ one of the largest US-based online information services; the service provides company databases, support for software and hardware together with weather, travel and hotel booking

computer *noun* electronic machine which calculates, stores information and processes it automatically; **computer-assisted composition** = composition using digitally recorded text, which generates characters and automatically inserts spaces, as well as hyphenating, justifying and paginating; **computer-assisted design (CAD)** = design which is done with a computer; **computer bureau** = office which offers to do work on its computers for companies which do not have their own computers; **computer department** = department in a company which manages the company's computers; **computer error** = mistake made by a computer; **computer file** = section of information on a computer (such as the payroll, list of addresses, customer accounts); **computer graphics** = information represented graphically on a computer display and then printed out for use as an illustration in a book *or* magazine; **computer language** = system of signs, letters and words used to instruct a computer; **computer listing** = printout of a list of items taken from data stored in a computer; **computer manager** = person in charge of a computer department; **computer program** = instructions to a computer, telling it to do a particular piece of work; **computer programmer** = person who writes computer programs; **computer services** = work using a computer, done by a computer bureau; **computer time** = time when a computer is being used (paid for at an hourly rate); **computer typesetting** = typesetting which is done automatically by a computer, using instructions keyed on disk or tape; **business computer** = powerful small computer which is programmed for special business uses; **personal computer** *or* **home computer** = small computer which can be used in the home

> COMMENT: computers are now used in all stages of book and magazine production. The original text is keyboarded (often by an author or journalist); a sub-editor may code it for typesetting, and it is passed either on disk or via a modem to a typesetting computer. The typesetting computer has been programmed to recognize certain codes and output text in certain typefaces, point sizes, formats, etc., according to the codes inserted by the editors or compositors. Finally, the printing process itself is computerized, with inbuilt computers in the printing and binding machines programmed to accept printing instructions

computerize *verb* to change from a manual system to one using computers; ***our typesetting*** *or* ***our stock control has been completely computerized***

computerized *adjective* worked by computers; ***the book was set using computerized typesetting; a computerized invoicing system***

computer-readable *adjective* which can be read and understood by a computer; ***computer-readable codes***

computer to plate (CTP) *noun* system by which the publisher supplies the printer with text on disk, usually in PostScript format, and the printer outputs it direct to plate, without going through the CRC and film stages

concertina fold *or* **accordion fold** *noun* **(a)** method of folding advertising pages, where each parallel fold in a sheet goes in the opposite direction to the previous one **(b)** method of parallel folding of continuous paper, one sheet in one direction, the next sheet in the opposite direction, allowing the paper to be fed into a printer continuously with no action on the part of the user

conciliation *noun* bringing together the parties in a dispute so that the dispute can be settled

conclude *verb* to complete successfully; ***we have concluded a distribution agreement with a German distributor***

concordance *noun* index *or* reference book, which lists words used in a large work in alphabetical order; **a concordance to the Bible** *or* **a Shakespeare Concordance** = reference book listing the main words used in the Bible or in Shakespeare's works, giving references to where they occur in the original text

condense *verb* to make shorter; to make text take up less space; ***the book is a condensed version of the novel; the printer was asked to condense the text to 96 pages***

condensed *adjective & noun* typeface with narrower characters than normal, taking less room on the line (as opposed to extended typeface); ***the headwords are set in bold Univers condensed***

condition 1 *noun* **(a)** term of a contract *or* duties which have to be carried out as part of a contract *or* something which has to be agreed before a contract becomes valid; **conditions of employment** *or* **conditions of service** = terms of a contract of employment; **conditions of sale** = agreed ways in which a sale takes place (such as discounts *or* credit terms); **on condition that** = provided that; ***they were granted the lease on condition that they paid the legal costs*** **(b)** general state; ***the union has complained of the bad working conditions in the design department; the books were returned in good condition; what condition was the consignment of books in when it was opened? adverse trading conditions have reduced profits this year*** **2** *verb* to prepare paper for printing by exposing it to the temperature and humidity levels in the pressroom; **mill conditioned paper** = paper which has been prepared in the mill for normal humidity levels

conditional *adjective* provided that certain things take place; **to give a conditional acceptance** = to accept, provided that certain things happen *or* certain terms apply; **the offer is conditional on the board's acceptance** = the offer is firm, provided the board accepts; **he made a conditional offer** = he offered to buy, provided that certain terms applied

conduct *verb* to carry on; ***they had to conduct the conversation in Russian; the chairman conducted the negotiations very efficiently***

confectioners *see* CTN

confidence *noun* **(a)** being able to trust *or* feeling certain about; ***the sales teams do not have much confidence in their manager; his confidence that the book would sell well was justified; the board has total confidence in the managing director*** **(b) in confidence** = in secret; ***I will show you the report in confidence***

confident *adjective* certain *or* sure; ***I am confident the turnover will increase rapidly; are you confident the sales team is capable of handling this product?***

confidential *adjective* secret *or* not to be told or shown to other people; ***he sent a confidential report to the chairman; please mark the letter 'Private and Confidential'***

confidentiality *noun* being secret; **he broke confidentiality about the discussions** = he told someone about the secret discussions

confirm *verb* to say that something is definite *or* fixed; ***I am writing to confirm the printing prices which we gave you over the phone; we can confirm that the book will be published before the end of the year;*** **to confirm someone in a job** = to say that someone is now permanently in the job

confirmation *noun* **(a)** checking that something is definite; **confirmation of an order** = writing to say that an order is certain **(b)** something which confirms; ***he received confirmation from the bank that the cheque had been cleared***

confiscate *verb* to take something which belongs to someone, because it breaks the law; ***the Customs confiscated all the tapes***

conflate *verb* **(a)** to bring several pieces of text together to form one piece **(b)** *US* to bring together various parts of a book (text pages *or* colour illustrations *or* insert maps) before the book is bound; (NOTE: GB English is **collate**)

conflict *noun* **conflict of interest** = situation where a person may profit personally from decisions which he takes in his official capacity

conglomerate *noun* group of subsidiary companies which are linked together, but make very different types of products; ***the design studio is part of a large printing conglomerate***

conifer *noun* tree growing in temperate regions which grows fast and produces the softwood which is extensively used in papermaking

connect *verb* to link *or* to join; **connected dots** = block of halftone dots, which are joined together

connection *noun* **(a)** link *or* something which joins; ***there is no connection between us and the American company of the same name; both the authors are published by the same company, that is the only connection between them;*** **in connection with** = referring to; ***I want to speak to the managing director in connection with the sales forecasts*** **(b) connections** = people you know *or* customers *or* contacts; ***he has useful connections in the printing industry***

consider *verb* to think seriously about something; **to consider the terms of a contract** = to examine and discuss if the terms are acceptable

considerable *adjective* quite large; ***we sell considerable quantities of our books in Africa; they lost a considerable amount of money on the commodity market***

considerably *adverb* quite a lot; ***sales are considerably higher than they were last year***

consideration *noun* **(a)** serious thought; ***we are giving consideration to moving the head office to Scotland;*** **the project is under consideration** = we are still examining the project to decide whether to go ahead with it **(b)** something valuable exchanged as part of a contract; **for a small consideration** = for a small fee *or* payment

consign *verb* **to consign goods to someone** = to send goods to someone for him to use or to sell for you

consignation *noun* act of consigning

consignee *noun* person who receives goods from someone for his own use or to sell for the sender

consignment *noun* **(a)** sending goods to someone who will sell them for you; **consignment note** = note saying that goods have been sent; **books sent on consignment** = books sent overseas, where they will be kept by another company to be sold on the publisher's behalf for a commission (the consignee will send back sales reports and sales revenue, less commission, to the consignor at regular intervals) **(b)** group of goods sent for sale; ***a consignment of goods has arrived; we are expecting a consignment of children's books from Hong Kong***

consignor *noun* person who consigns goods to someone

COMMENT: on consignment deals are rarely favoured by accounting staff: it is difficult to establish whether a sale has been made, and the stock may have to be considered as if it were unsold warehouse stock. Ownership of the stock can prove difficult to establish in the case where the consignee goes into liquidation or is taken over (especially if, as usual, the consignee is in another country, operating under another legal system), and counting stock for valuation purposes is impossible

consistency *noun* **(a)** being always the same; ***a house style is designed to impose consistency on all the publisher's list*** **(b)** state of being liquid or solid, especially the percentage of fibre in paper pulp; ***the consistency of the pulp will depend on the amount of water added***

consolidate *verb* **(a)** to put the accounts of several subsidiary companies into the accounts of the main group **(b)** to group goods together for shipping

consolidated *adjective* **(a) consolidated accounts** = accounts of subsidiary companies grouped together into the accounts of the parent company **(b) consolidated shipment** = goods from different companies grouped together into a single shipment

consolidation *noun* grouping goods together for shipping

consortium *noun* group of companies which work together; ***a consortium of Canadian companies*** *or* ***a Canadian consortium; a consortium of French and British companies is hoping to win the contract for supply of printing equipment***

constat = CONTINUOUS STATIONERY

consult *verb* to ask an expert for advice; ***he consulted his accountant about his tax***

consultancy *noun* act of giving specialist advice; ***a consultancy firm; he offers a consultancy service***

consultant *noun* specialist who gives advice; ***a consultant on libel; management consultant; printing consultant***

consumable *noun* material (such as paper or ink) which is used up in a process; **consumable textbook** = school book with blank spaces in which the student writes notes or answers, and which cannot be reused by another student

contact 1 *noun* act of touching; **contact print** = print made where the paper touches the negative, and is therefore exactly the same size as the negative; **contact printing** =

photographic printing process in which the negative touches the light-sensitive paper; **contact screen** = type of screen used for making halftone blocks, where the screen touches the film **2** *verb* to touch; ***the print is made when the film contacts the paper***

contain *verb* to hold something inside; ***each crate contains two pallet loads of books; the book contains a lot of classified information; we have lost a file containing important documents; the disk contains the text of the first half of the book***

container *noun* **(a)** box *or* bottle *or* can, etc. which can hold goods; ***the gas is shipped in strong metal containers; the container burst during shipping;*** **container board** = strong cardboard used to make boxes **(b)** very large metal case of a standard size for loading and transporting goods on trucks, trains and ships; ***container ship; container berth; container port; container terminal; to ship goods in containers;*** **a container-load of dictionaries** = a shipment of dictionaries sent in a container

containerization *noun* putting into containers; shipping in containers

containerize *verb* to put goods into containers; to ship goods in containers

content *noun* the subject matter of a letter, book, etc.; **the content of the letter** = what the letter has to say

contents *noun* **(a)** things contained *or* what is inside something; ***the libel lawyers have examined the contents of the typescript; the customs officials inspected the contents of the crate;*** **the contents of the letter** = the words written in the letter **(b) table of contents** *or* **contents list** = list of the main chapters in a book, given usually at the beginning; **contents page** = page containing the contents list of a book *or* magazine

context *noun* words and phrases before and after a particular word in a sentence; **how a word is used in context** = how it goes together with other words and phrases to form a sentence; **quoted out of context** = without the surrounding text, so giving a misleading meaning

continue *verb* to go on doing something *or* to do something which you were doing earlier; ***the serial will be continued in our next issue; the article is continued on page 98; printing will continue all night;*** **'to be continued'** = words at the end of an article, showing that the serialization will be continued in the next issue

continual *adjective* which happens again and again; ***production was slow because of continual breakdowns in the paper feed***

continually *adverb* again and again; ***the photocopier is continually breaking down***

continuation *noun* act of continuing; **continuation page** = page *or* screen of text that follows on from a main page

continuity *noun US* **continuity book club** = book club where books are sent to members automatically, leaving the member free to return the book if he does not want to buy it; **continuity program** = sale by correspondence (especially of partworks); **continuity set** = series of volumes of a reference title (such as an encyclopaedia) which are updated and expanded by regular new publications

continuous *adjective* with no end *or* with no breaks; **continuous feed** = device which feeds continuous stationery into a computer printer; **continuous feeder** = device which feeds sheets of paper into a sheet-fed printing machine; **continuous sections** = arrangement of sections of a book, where each follows on from the next, as opposed to insetted sections; **continuous stationery** *or* **constat** = paper made as one long sheet, used in the computer printers; **continuous tone** *or* **contone** = image, such as a watercolour painting, where the tone shades between dark and light without being broken up into dots, as opposed to halftones (which use dots) and to line drawings (which use spaced lines for shading)

contone = CONTINUOUS TONE

contraband *noun* **contraband (goods)** = goods brought into a country illegally, without paying customs duty; ***the customs seized some contraband tapes***

contract 1 *noun* **(a)** legal agreement between two parties; ***to draw up a contract; to draft a contract; to sign a contract;*** **the contract is binding on both parties** = both parties signing the contract must do what is agreed; **under contract** = bound by the terms of a contract; ***the firm is under contract to deliver the goods by November;*** **to void a contract** = to make a contract invalid; **contract of employment** = contract between management and employee showing the conditions under which the employee works; **publishing contract** = agreement between a publisher and an author (or an agent, representing an author) by which the author grants the publisher the right to publish the work against payment of a fee, usually in the form of a royalty; **service contract** = contract between a company and a director showing all the director's conditions of work **(b)** agreement for supply of a service or goods; ***contract for the supply of spare parts; to enter into a contract to supply spare parts; to sign a contract for £10,000 worth of spare parts;*** **to put work out to contract** = to decide that work should be done by another company on a contract, rather than employing members of staff to do it; **to award a contract to a company** *or* **to place a contract with a company** = to decide that a company shall have the contract to do work for you; **to tender for a contract** = to put forward an estimate of cost for work under contract; ***conditions of contract*** *or* ***contract conditions;*** **breach of contract** = breaking the terms of a contract; **the company is in breach of contract** = the company has failed to do what was agreed in the contract; **contract proof** = colour, hardcopy representation of the intended printed image made from the films from which the final image carrier will be made; when signed off by the recipient, a contract is formed which states that if the final printed job is a close, visual match to the proof, the client will be satisfied; **contract work** = work done according to a written agreement **2** *verb* to agree to do some work by contract; ***to contract to supply 10,000 copies at 0.65p per copy;*** **to contract out of an agreement** = to withdraw from an agreement with the written permission of the other party

> COMMENT: in a publishing contract the publisher is granted the right to publish a work under certain conditions: the payment of a fee or royalty to the author; a definition of the markets in which the publisher can publish and sell the work; the defined right of the publisher to sublicense translations, book club editions, film adaptations, etc., on behalf of the author. For his part, the author guarantees that the book is original (i.e., that it is not copied from another book), is not libellous and that the author does in fact hold the rights to the book

contracting *adjective* **contracting party** = person or company which signs a contract

contractor *noun* person or company which does work according to a written agreement; **educational contractor** = bookseller who has a contract to supply schoolbooks to a local educational authority

contractual *adjective* according to a contract; **contractual liability** = legal responsibility for something as stated in a contract; **to fulfil your contractual obligations** = to do what you have agreed to do in a contract; **he is under no contractual obligation to buy** = he has signed no agreement to buy

contractually *adverb* according to a contract; ***the company is contractually bound to pay his expenses***

contrary *noun* **(a)** opposite; **failing instructions to the contrary** = unless different instructions are given; **on the contrary** = quite the opposite; ***the chairman was not annoyed with his assistant - on the contrary, he promoted him*** **(b)** material (such as pitch) found in paper, which should not be there

contrast *noun* difference between shades of colour *or* between bright and dark in an illustration; ***there is not enough contrast in***

these halftones; can you reduce the colour contrast on the cover?

contrasting *adjective* which show sharp differences; ***a cover design in contrasting colours***

contrasty *adjective* (photography) which has too much contrast

contribute *verb* to work with others on a book *or* newspaper *or* magazine; ***she contributed the articles on nineteenth century women's novels***

contribution *noun* article which is part of a newspaper *or* magazine; ***the editor rejected her second contribution because it was too long***

contributor *noun* person who contributes to a newspaper *or* anthology, etc.

control 1 *noun* **(a)** power *or* being able to direct something; ***the company is under the control of three shareholders; the family lost control of its business;*** **to gain control of a business** = to buy more than 50% of the shares so that you can direct the business; **to lose control of a business** = to find that you have less than 50% of the shares in a company, and so are not longer able to direct it **(b)** restricting *or* checking something *or* making sure that something is kept in check; **under control** = kept in check; ***expenses are kept under tight control; the company is trying to bring its overheads back under control;*** **out of control** = not kept in check; ***costs have got out of control;*** **budgetary control** = keeping check on spending; **credit control** = checking that customers pay on time and do not exceed their credit limits; **price controls** = legal measures to prevent prices rising too fast; **quality control** = making sure that the quality of a product is good; **stock control** = making sure that movements of stock are noted; **control group** = small group which is used to check a sample group; **control strip** = colour control bar which is printed on the edge of colour proofs; **control target** = image that contains specific elements designed to highlight variations in repro or printing **(c)** key on a computer which sends a signal instructing font, measure, page depth and other formatting commands; **control systems** = systems used to check that a computer system is working correctly **2** *verb* **(a) to control a business** = to direct a business; ***the business is controlled by a company based in Luxembourg; the company is controlled by the majority shareholder*** **(b)** to make sure that something is kept in check *or* is not allowed to develop; ***the company is trying to control editorial costs; it is impossible to control the rise in paper prices, because so much paper is imported;*** **controlled circulation magazine** = magazine which is not sold, but given free to a special list of readers

controller *noun* **(a)** person who controls (especially the finances of a company); **credit controller** = person in the accounts department who checks that invoices are paid on time; **production controller** = person in the production department of a publishing company who deals with printers and other suppliers; **stock controller** = person who notes movements of stock **(b)** *US* chief accountant in a company

convention *noun* international agreement; **the Berne Convention** = the international agreement on copyright, signed in Berne in 1886; **the Universal Copyright Convention (UCC)** = international agreement on copyright set up by the United Nations in Geneva in 1952

> COMMENT: both the Berne Convention and the UCC were drawn up to try to protect copyright from pirates; under the Berne convention, published material remains in copyright until 50 years after the death of the author and for 25 years after publication under the UCC. In both cases, a work which is copyrighted in one country is automatically covered by the copyright legislation of all countries signing the convention

conversion *noun* **(a)** change from one computer system to another **(b) conversion price** *or* **conversion rate** = rate at which a currency is changed into a foreign currency; **conversion table** = table for converting prices in a foreign currency to those of a local currency (used by some countries to regulate the retail price of imported books)

convert *verb* to change money of one country for money of another; ***we converted our pounds into Swiss francs***

converter *noun* device which converts from one computer system to another; *see also* BLACK BOX, PROTOCOL CONVERTER

convertibility *noun* ability of a currency to be exchanged easily for another

convertible *adjective* **convertible currency** = currency which can be exchanged for another easily

converting *noun* using paper or board to make stationery or packaging, with very little printing involved (envelopes, paper bags, gummed labels, etc.)

cookery book *US* **cookbook** *noun* book which gives recipes for preparing food; (NOTE: **cookbook** is always used in the US, and the term is becoming much more common in GB English)

co-operate *verb* to work together; ***the governments are co-operating in the fight against piracy; the two firms have co-operated on the computer project***

co-operation *noun* working together; ***without the co-operation of the workforce the project would never have been completed ahead of schedule***

co-operative 1 *adjective* willing to work together; ***the workforce has not been co-operative over the management's productivity plan;*** **co-operative advertising** = advertising where two companies share the costs (such as advertising by an agent and the publisher) **2** *noun* business run by a group of workers who are the owners and who share the profits; ***to set up a workers' co-operative***

coordinate *verb* to organize several things together; ***she is trying to coordinate the typesetting, printing and binding in various locations***

copier *noun* = PHOTOCOPIER **copier paper** = special paper used in photocopiers

copper *noun* red metal used for halftone blocks and in engravings

copperplate *noun* **(a)** plate of copper, used to make engravings; **copperplate printing** = printing method that uses a copper plate on which the image is etched, producing a very sharp image **(b)** type of handwriting *or* script with long ascenders and descenders sloping to the right, used in the 18th century in Britain, and taught as a model in schools

coproduction *noun* production of a large book *or* TV show where more than one company shares in the cost of production

coproperty *noun* ownership of property by two or more people together

coproprietor *noun* person who owns a property with another person or several other people

copublication *noun* action of copublishing a book; *see also* CO-EDITION

copublish *verb* to publish a book, together with one or more other companies who are involved in the origination of the book, and then sell it in different markets; ***we are copublishing the book with a Swedish publisher***

copublisher *noun* publisher who joins with another to publish a book

copy 1 *noun* **(a)** document which is made to look the same as another; **carbon copy** = copy made with carbon paper; **certified copy** = document which is certified as being the same as another; **file copy** = copy of a document which is filed in an office for reference; **top copy** = first or top sheet of a document which is typed with carbon copies; **copy machine** = photocopier, machine which makes photocopies; **copy paper** = special paper used in a photocopier **(b)** any document; **fair copy** *or* **final copy** = document which is written or typed with no changes or mistakes; **hard copy** = printout of a text which is on a computer *or* printed copy of something which is on microfilm; **rough copy** = draft of a document which, it is expected, will have changes made to it **(c)** text for typesetting *or* printing; any material which will be printed (including line drawings, etc.); ***she sent in the copy for the jacket blurb, with corrections made by the author; Tuesday is the last date for copy for the advertisement;*** **bad copy** = manuscript which is difficult to read *or* illegible; badly edited manuscript which the typesetter will not accept; **camera-ready copy** = bromide *or* artwork which is ready to be filmed for printing; **clean copy** = manuscript *or* text for typesetting which has no alterations and is easy to read; **publicity copy** = text of a proposed advertisement before it is printed; ***she writes copy for a travel firm;*** **knocking copy** = advertising material which criticizes competing products; **copy board** = part of a camera on which copy is fixed to be photographed; **copy block** = block of text which is dealt with as a single part of a design; **copy date** = date when copy for an article *or* advertisement has to be delivered to the newspaper or magazine publisher; **copy fitting** = deciding on the size of type, etc., which will be needed to fit a certain text into a certain fixed space; **copy-fitting table** = table showing the space taken by characters in a certain typeface and point size, used for casting off; **copy preparation** *or* **copy prep** = preparing MSS *or* typescripts to make them ready for the typesetter (by marking the typographical style to be used); **copy reader** = person who checks copy before printing **(d)** a book *or* a newspaper; ***we printed too many, and had to pulp 1500 copies; stock control say we have only 250 copies in the warehouse; for the reprint, the printer needs two clean copies to film from; have you kept yesterday's copy of the 'Times'? I read it in the office copy of 'Fortune'; where is my copy of the telephone directory?*** **2** *verb* **(a)** to make a second document which is like the first; ***he copied the company report at night and took it home*** **(b)** to make something which is similar to something else; ***the jacket designer simply copied the design from the other series; their commissioning editors have been told to copy good ideas from other publishers***

copy editing *noun* preparation work by an editor in a publishing company (correcting errors, changing the text to fit house style and marking up the typesetting style) to make a MS ready for typesetting

copy editor *noun* editor who prepares MSS *or* typescripts for typesetting, by correcting errors, making changes to conform to house style, and indicating typesetting style

copy holder *noun* **(a)** person who reads out the original text while a proof reader corrects the proofs **(b)** stand next to a computer, on which the keyboarder puts the copy to be keyboarded

copying *noun* making copies; ***limited copying from a book is allowed for private reference purposes; the company discovered cases of unauthorized copying of copyright material***

copying machine *noun* machine which makes copies of documents

copyright 1 *noun* an author's legal right to publish his or her own work and not to have it copied (lasting fifty years after the author's death under the Berne Convention); **Copyright Act** = an Act of Parliament (such as the Copyright Acts 1911, 1956, 1988, etc.) making copyright legal, and controlling the copying of copyright material; **copyright deposit** = depositing of a copy of a published work in a copyright library (usually the main national library) which is part of the formal copyrighting of published material; **copyright holder** *or* **copyright owner** = person *or* company who holds the copyright in a published work; **copyright law** = laws concerning copyright; **copyright line** = COPYRIGHT NOTICE **work which is out of copyright** = work by a writer who has been dead for fifty years; **work still in copyright** *or* **which is covered by copyright** = work by a living writer, or by a writer who has not been dead for fifty years; **infringement of copyright** *or* **copyright infringement** = act of illegally copying a work which is in copyright; **copyright notice** = note in a book showing who owns the copyright and the date of ownership, printed on the verso of the title page **2** *verb to confirm the copyright of a written work by inserting a copyright notice and publishing the work;* ***the book was copyrighted in the UK*** **3** *adjective* covered by the laws of copyright; ***it is illegal to photocopy a copyright work***

> COMMENT: copyright lasts for 50 years after the author's death according to the Berne Convention, and for 25 years according to the Universal Copyright Convention. In the USA, copyright is for 50 years after the death of an author for books published after January 1st, 1978. For books published before that date, the original copyright was for 28 years after the death of the author, and this can be extended for a further 28 year period up to a maximum of 75 years. In 1995, the European Union adopted a copyright term of 70 years after the death of the author. The copyright holder has the right to refuse or to grant permission to copy copyright material, though under the Paris agreement of 1971, the original publishers (representing the author or copyright holder) must, under certain circumstances, grant licences to reprint copyright material. The copyright notice has to include the symbol ©, the name of the copyright holder and the date of the copyright (which is usually the date of first publication). The notice must be printed in the book and usually appears on the reverse of the title page. A copyright notice is also printed on other forms of printed material such as posters. The change of the term of copyright in the European Union has created problems for publishers and copyright holders, in cases where the author died more than fifty years but less than seventy years ago; in effect, such authors have returned to copyright, and royalties, etc., are due to their estates until the seventy year term expires (this applies to well-known authors such as Beatrix Potter and James Joyce, as well as to composers, such as Elgar)

copy typing *noun* typing documents from handwritten originals, not from dictation; ***we sent his notes for copy typing***

copy typist *noun* person who types documents from handwritten originals, not from dictation

copywriter *noun* person who writes the text for advertisements

copywriting *noun* writing of copy for advertisements

CORA (= COMPUTER ORIENTATED REPRODUCER ASSEMBLY) the computer typesetting language used by Linotype

cords *noun* pieces of hemp string running across the back of a book, to which the signatures are sewn before the case is attached (in leather-bound books, the cords are either sunk into grooves in the back or may appear as raised ridges across the spine)

corner 1 *noun* **(a)** place where two sides join; ***the carton has to have specially strong corners; the corner of the crate was damaged*** **(b)** point where the sides of a page *or* cover of a book meet; ***in a half bound book, the spine and corners are covered in a different material from the sides, often leather;*** **rounded corners** = corners of pages which are not cut square, but are made round; **corner-rounding machine** = machine which rounds the corners of a sewn and gathered book, before it is bound; **corner marks** = marks on a piece of artwork *or* on colour separations, showing where the corners of the printed page fall, so as to help justification or colour register **2** *verb* to round the corners of a book block

corona *noun* electric discharge that is used to charge the toner within a laser printer; **corona wire** = thin wire that charges the powdered toner particles in a laser printer as they pass across it; ***if your printouts are smudged, you may have to clean the corona wire***

corporate *adjective* referring to a whole company; **corporate image** = idea which a company would like the public to have of it; **corporate plan** = plan for the future work of a whole company; **corporate planning** = planning the future work of a whole company; **corporate profits** = profits of a corporation

corporation *noun* **(a)** large company; **finance corporation** = company which provides money for hire purchase; **corporation tax** = tax on profits made by companies **(b)** *US* company which is incorporated in the United States

correct 1 *adjective* accurate *or* right; ***the references in the bibliographic section are not correct; is that the correct way to spell the author's name? the published accounts do not give a correct picture of the company's financial position*** **2** *verb* to remove mistakes from something; ***the proofreaders are still correcting the galleys; the galleys have been sent back to the typesetter for correcting; the accounts department have corrected the invoice; you will have to correct all these typing errors before you send the letter***

correction *noun* making something correct; change which makes something correct; ***he made some corrections to the text of the preface; corrections are charged to the author;*** **correction marks** *or* **correction signs** = signs used to indicate corrections (these are international signs, used by editors and typesetters) ⇨ APPENDIX; **correction overlay** = film on which corrections can be made to artwork; **author's corrections** = corrections made by the author (and usually charged to the author, if excessive); **colour corrections** = correction of colours by changes to colour separations; **printer's corrections** = corrections noted by the printer's reader on the top copy of the proofs before the proofs are sent to the publisher; **publisher's corrections** = corrections made by the publisher (either copying the author's corrections or making further editorial corrections)

COMMENT: corrections are usually indicated in different coloured inks, to show who is responsible for the alteration: author's and publisher's corrections are marked in blue; printer's errors are marked by the publisher in red; printer's corrections are marked by the printer in green

correspond *verb* **(a) to correspond with someone** = to write letters to someone **(b) to correspond with something** = to fit *or* to match something

correspondence *noun* letters which are exchanged; **business correspondence** = letters concerned with a business; **to be in correspondence with an author** = to write letters to an author and receive letters back; ***we are in correspondence with the printer about the latest invoice;*** **correspondence columns** = the letters page of a newspaper, where letters from readers to the editor are printed

correspondent *noun* **(a)** person who writes letters **(b)** journalist who writes articles for a newspaper on specialist subjects; ***a financial correspondent; the 'Times' business correspondent; he is the Paris correspondent of the 'Telegraph'***

corrigenda *noun* list of corrections printed in a book; **corrigenda slip** = list of corrections printed on a separate slip of paper and inserted in the bound book; *compare* ERRATUM (NOTE: the single noun (indication one correction only) is **corrigendum**)

corrugated *adjective* (paper *or* board) made with narrow folds on the surface; ***the books are packed in corrugated board***

COMMENT: corrugated paper is formed of several layers of paper which are folded concertina-fashion, in very small folds. If layers of corrugated paper are sandwiched between boards, the result is corrugated board

corrupt *adjective* (data *or* tape *or* disk) with incorrect *or* faulty information

cost 1 *noun* **(a)** amount of money which has to be paid for something; ***printing costs are 10% higher than last year; what is the cost of a four-colour jacket, as opposed to a two-colour job? computer costs are falling each year; we cannot afford the cost of two telephones;*** **to cover costs** = to produce enough money in sales to pay for the costs of production; ***the sales revenue barely covers the costs of advertising** or **the manufacturing costs;*** **to sell at cost** = to sell at a price which is the same as the cost of manufacture or the wholesale cost; **fixed costs** = business costs which do not rise with the quantity of the product made; **labour costs** = cost of hourly-paid workers employed to make a product; **manufacturing costs** *or* **production costs** = costs of making a product; **operating costs** *or* **running costs** = cost of the day-to-day organization of a company; **variable costs** = production costs which increase with the quantity of the product made (such as wages, raw materials); **cost analysis** = calculating in advance what a new product will cost; **cost centre** = group *or* machine whose costs can be itemized and to which fixed costs can be allocated; **cost, insurance and freight (c.i.f.)** = estimate of a price, which includes the cost of the goods, the insurance and the transport charges; **cost price** = selling price which is the same as the price which the seller paid for the item (i.e. either the manufacturing cost or the wholesale price); **cost of sales** = all the costs of a book sold, including manufacturing costs and the staff costs of the production department, together with the royalty due to the author; **cost sheet** = sheet used in a printing works *or* publisher's office which lists all the costs incurred in a piece of work **(b) costs** = expenses involved in a court case; **to pay costs** = to pay the expenses of a court case; ***the judge awarded costs to the defendant; costs of the libel case will be borne by the claimant*** **2** *verb* **(a)** to have a price; ***how much does the machine cost? this book costs £20 in hardback*** **(b) to cost a product** = to calculate how much money will be needed to make a product, and so work out its selling price

cost-cutting *adjective* reducing costs; ***we cancelled the order for a new telex as a cost-cutting exercise***

cost-effective *adjective* which gives value, especially when compared with something else; ***it is more cost-effective to have the artwork printed abroad; in the end it was more cost-effective to buy our own computer; we find advertising in the Sunday newspapers very cost-effective***

cost-effectiveness *noun* being cost-effective; ***can we calculate the cost-effectiveness of air freight compared with shipping by sea?***

costing *noun* calculation of the manufacturing costs, the marketing and distribution costs, and also the royalty, which allows the publisher to set the selling price of a book; ***the costings give us a retail price of $2.95; we cannot do the costing until we have details of all the manufacturing costs***

cost plus *noun* system of charging, where the selling price of a product is the same as the price paid by the seller, but with a percentage added; ***we are charging for the editorial work on a cost plus basis; we sell to our agents on a cost plus basis; the agreement gives a cost plus 25% selling price***

cotton *noun* thread and woven material from fibres from a tropical plant

> COMMENT: cotton rag was formerly an important source of raw material for papermaking, and rag paper is strong and white, and of very good quality. Because cotton rag is less easily available and in any case is not sufficient to meet increasing demand for good quality paper, most paper is now made from wood pulp

couch *verb* to move newly made wet paper from the wire mesh to a felt mat; **couching roll** = roll which squeezes wet paper as it leaves the mesh

coucher *noun* workman who takes the wet paper from the vatman and puts it onto the felt mat

count *verb* **(a)** to add figures together to make a total; to add the number of units to make a total; ***he counted up the sales for the six months to December; we will be counting the stock in the warehouse next week*** **(b)** to include; ***the book makes 325 pages, counting six pages of prelims and ten***

pages of appendix; the editorial department employs ten people, not counting part-timers; did you count my trip to New York as part of my sales expenses?

counting house *noun* department dealing with cash

counting keyboard *noun* keyboard which indicates how much space is left on a partly-completed line (the operator instructs the line lengths before keyboarding, and the program then either hyphenates the words at the ends of lines or allows the operator to hyphenate manually: the opposite is a 'non-counting keyboard')

counter *noun* **(a)** long flat surface in a shop for displaying and selling goods; **trade counter** = shop in a factory *or* warehouse where goods are sold to retailers; **counter pack** = box which displays books, designed to be placed on a bookshop counter; **counter staff** = sales staff who serve behind counters **(b)** space inside the curved part of a letter (the bowl), as in a 'b' or 'p' **(c)** device attached to a machine which counts the number of sheets used, books produced. etc.

counter- *prefix* against

counterfoil *noun* slip of paper kept after writing a cheque *or* an invoice *or* a receipt, as a record of the deal which has taken place

countersign *verb* to sign a document which has already been signed by someone else; ***all cheques have to be countersigned by the finance director; the sales director countersigns all my orders***

country *noun* land which is separate and governs itself; ***the contract covers distribution in the countries of the Common Market;*** **the managing director is out of the country** = he is on a business trip abroad; **country of origin** = country where a product is made

coupon *noun* **(a)** piece of paper used in place of money; **gift coupon** = coupon from a store which is given as a gift and which must be exchanged in that store **(b)** piece of paper which replaces an order form; **coupon ad** = advertisement with a form attached, which is to be cut out and returned to the advertiser with your name and address if you want further information about the product advertised; **reply coupon** = form attached to a coupon ad, which must be filled in and returned to the advertiser

courier 1 *noun* person who takes parcels and letters from one place to another **2** *verb* to send a package by courier

course *noun* series of lessons; ***she has finished her secretarial course; the company has paid for her to attend a course for trainee sales managers;*** **course book** = educational textbook

court *noun* place where a judge listens to a case and decides which of the parties in the argument is legally right; **court case** = legal action *or* trial; **to take someone to court** = to tell someone to appear in court to settle an argument; **a settlement was reached out of court** *or* **the two parties reached an out-of-court settlement** = the dispute was settled between the two parties privately without continuing the court case

courtesy discount *noun* special discount given by a supplier to a purchaser which is not a discount for resale (such as a special price at which a publisher sells books to other publishers or to authors)

courtesy line *noun* credit line, the note under a photograph showing the name of the photographer or the organization which provided the photograph for reproduction

cover 1 *noun* **(a)** thing put over a machine, etc. to keep it clean; ***put the cover over your micro when you leave the office; always keep a cover over the typewriter*** **(b)** (i) outside of a book (usually made of thicker paper or card); (ii) outside of a magazine (sometimes made of specially thick paper or art paper); ***the book has a leather cover; a magazine with a four-colour cover; we publish a cheap edition in paper covers;*** **cover copy** *or* **copy for the cover** = text which is to be printed on the cover; **cover design** = special design for a book *or* magazine cover; **cover designer** = designer who designs the cover of a book *or* magazine; **cover material** = (i) material out of which the cover is made; (ii) text which will be printed on a cover; **cover paper** *or* **cover stock** = board *or* thick paper used as the cover for magazines or pamphlets; **cover price** = retail price of a book (not always printed on the cover); **front cover** = cover at the front of a book *or* magazine (which normally has the title on it); **back cover** = cover at the back of a book *or* magazine (which can have publicity material *or* details about the author); **inside cover** = the inside of the cover; **cover story** = feature article which is illustrated by the picture on the front cover; ***the author's photograph appears on the back cover; the price is usually printed on bottom right hand corner of the inside front cover; we will start the blurb on the back and continue on the inside back cover*** **(c) insurance cover** = protection guaranteed by an insurance policy; ***do you have cover against libel?;*** **to operate without adequate cover** = without being protected by insurance **(d) to send something under separate cover** = in a separate envelope; **to send a magazine under plain cover** = in an ordinary envelope with no company name printed on it **2** *verb* **(a)** to put something over a machine, etc. to keep it clean; ***don't forget to cover your micro before you go home*** **(b)** to put a cover on a book *or* magazine; ***the book is covered in dark blue simili leather; the cheap edition will be paper covered;*** **covering material** = material used to make the cover for a book **(c) to cover a risk** = to be protected by insurance against a risk; **to be fully covered against libel** = to have insurance against all libel risks **(d)** to earn enough money to pay for costs, expenses etc.; ***we do not make enough sales to cover the expense of running a US office; breakeven point for this book is reached when sales cover all costs***

covering letter *or* **covering note** *noun* letter or note sent with documents to say why they are being sent

cpi *or* **CPI** = CHARACTERS PER INCH number of characters per inch of line, used as a guide to the total extent of a book

cpl *or* **CPL** = CHARACTERS PER LINE number of characters estimated in each line, used as a guide to the total extent of a book

cpp *or* **CPP** = CHARACTERS PER PAGE

cps *or* **CPS** = CHARACTERS PER SECOND number of characters printed *or* transmitted every second

CPU = CENTRAL PROCESSING UNIT

CR = CARRIAGE RETURN

craft books *noun* books dealing with work done by hand (such as knitting, sewing, making models, car repairs, etc.)

crash 1 *noun* **(a)** sudden failure of a computer system **(b)** *US* super, heavy gauze used to make the hinges for a binding; **crash finish** = coarse-grained paper or binding material **2** *verb (of a computer system)* to fail suddenly

crate 1 *noun* large wooden box **2** *verb* to put goods into crates

crawl *verb (of printing press)* to run at a low speed

crawling *noun* shrinking of ink on paper, because it has not penetrated the surface (also occurring when printing on plastic)

crc *or* **CRC** = CAMERA-READY COPY final text, illustrations, headings, folios, etc., pasted up ready to be filmed

cream *adjective* colour like yellowish-white; **cream laid paper** = white writing paper with faint lines running across it; **cream wove paper** = white paper which has been made on a woven wire mesh

crease 1 *noun* **(a)** fold in paper *or* board, made intentionally; ***the cover has a crease along the spine; the invoice should be torn off at the crease*** **(b)** wrong fold in flat paper; ***the publisher noted creases in the text paper; the creases in the cover were caused by damp*** **2** *verb* **(a)** to put a fold into paper *or* board usually by impressing a line, also called 'scoring'; ***the cover should be creased***

at the spine **(b)** to put a wrong fold into flat paper; ***the inside covers are creased and torn; creasing is a common fault in very lightweight papers***

credit 1 *noun* **(a)** time given to a customer before he has to pay an invoice; ***to give someone six months' credit; to sell on good credit terms;*** **extended credit** = credit on very long repayment terms; **interest-free credit** = arrangement to borrow money without paying interest on the loan; **long credit** = terms allowing the borrower a long time to pay; **short credit** = terms allowing the customer only a short time to pay; **credit agency** *or* *US* **credit bureau** = company which reports on the creditworthiness of customers to show whether they should be allowed credit; **credit control** = check that customers pay on time and do not owe more than their credit limit; **credit controller** = person in an accounts department who checks that customers pay invoices on time; **credit facilities** = arrangement with a bank or supplier to have credit so as to buy goods; **letter of credit** = letter from a bank, allowing someone credit and promising to repay at a later date; **irrevocable letter of credit** = letter of credit which cannot be cancelled; **credit limit** = fixed amount which is the most a customer can owe on credit; **he has exceeded his credit limit** = he has borrowed more money than he is allowed; **credit rating** = amount which a credit agency feels a customer should be allowed to borrow; **on credit** = without paying immediately; ***we buy everything on sixty days credit; the company exists on credit from its suppliers*** **(b)** money received by a person *or* company and recorded in the accounts; ***to enter £100 to someone's credit; to pay in £100 to the credit of Mr Smith;*** **account in credit** = account where the credits are higher than the debits; **debit and credit** = money which a company owes and which it receives; **credit balance** = balance in an account showing that more money has been received than is owed by the company; ***the account has a credit balance of £1,000;*** **credit column** = right-hand column in accounts showing money received; **credit entry** = entry on the credit side of an account; **credit note** = note showing that money is owed to a customer; ***the company sent the wrong order and so had to issue a credit note;*** **credit side** = right-hand side of accounts showing money received **(c)** **credits** = notes to acknowledge who is the owner of a copyright *or* who is the designer of a book *or* who is the photographer of a halftone illustration, etc. (these can be printed on the verso of the title page, or underneath an illustration); **credit line** = note under a photograph showing the name of the photographer or of the organization which provided the photograph, or under a quotation showing who was the author **2** *verb* to show who is the copyright owner *or* who is the designer *or* photographer, etc.; ***the cover design is credited to J. Smith***

credit card *noun* plastic card which allows you to borrow money and to buy goods without paying for them immediately

creditor *noun* person who is owed money; **creditors' meeting** = meeting of all persons to whom a bankrupt company owes money, to decide how to obtain the money owed

credit-worthy *adjective* able to buy goods on credit

creditworthiness *noun* ability of a customer to pay for goods bought on credit; ***printers will always want to check on the creditworthiness of a new publisher placing work with them***

creep *noun* movement of a cylinder blanket on the cylinder

crêpe paper *noun* crinkly paper, used as packaging material or as decoration

crime *noun* act which is against the law; **crime fiction** = stories about crimes, criminals and the police; **crime list** = series of books on crime or of crime fiction; ***he is a famous crime editor; they have a successful crime list***

critic *noun* person who writes reviews in a paper; ***the art critic of the 'Times'***

critical *adjective* **(a)** which criticizes; ***we had several critical reviews, and the author was extremely upset; the main review was***

critical of the errors in the index **(b)** very serious; ***the cash-flow position is critical; the pre-Christmas period is critical for supply to bookshops***

criticism *noun* words which criticize; ***his main criticism is of the cover design; we tried to answer the reviewer's criticisms***

criticize *verb* to say that something *or* someone is wrong *or* is working badly, etc.; ***the MD criticized the sales manager for not improving the volume of sales; the design of the new catalogue has been criticized; the book was criticized for sloppy proofreading***

crocking *noun* flaking of ink after it has dried

Cromalin *noun* trade name for pre-press proofing system using colour toners and a photo-sensitive substrate; cheaper than wet proofs if only one proof is needed

crop *verb* **(a)** to cut off parts of an illustration (such as a photograph); ***the photo has been cropped to remove most of the foreground; cropping the photograph makes it look as if the author was all alone in the room;*** **crop mark** = *(in DTP software)* printed mark that shows the edge of a page or image and allows it to be cut accurately **(b)** to cut off too much paper when binding; ***the book has been cropped so much that the outside margin has almost disappeared***

cropping *noun* removal of areas of artwork *or* of a photograph which are not needed; ***the photographs can be edited by cropping, sizing, touching up, etc.***

cross *verb* to write lines across something; **to cross a cheque** = to write two lines across a cheque to show that it has to be paid into a bank; **crossed cheque** = cheque which has to be paid into a bank

crossbar *noun* **(a)** short line crossing the main stem of a letter (such as the line across an 'f') **(b)** **crossbars** = metal cross-pieces which divide a chase into sections

cross-check **1** *noun* check made by referring to more than one source **2** *verb* to check by referring to more than one source; ***the sub-editor should cross-check the page references against the index; I checked the date in our reference library and cross-checked by ringing the author***

cross-direction *noun* direction across a web or sheet of paper, which is at right angles to the grain

cross folding *noun* folding paper against the grain

cross hatching *noun* series of lines in two directions to give shading to a line drawing

crosshead *or* **crossheading** *noun* heading of a paragraph *or* section which is centred over a column (crossheads are used in magazines to break up long columns of text)

cross index *verb* to provide with a cross-reference; ***'Hyde' is cross-indexed to 'Jekyll and Hyde'***

cross-line screen *noun* common screen for making halftones

cross marks *noun* register marks, the little crosses at the corners of sheets *or* overlays, which indicate where the different films are to be placed to achieve correct register

cross off *verb* to remove something from a list; ***he crossed my name off his list; you can cross him off our mailing list***

cross out *verb* to put a line through something which has been written; ***she crossed out £250 and put in £500; the paragraph had been crossed out by the author and reinstated by the editor***

cross-refer *verb* to make a cross-reference from one part of a book to another; ***this entry is cross-referred*** *or* ***cross-referenced to the appendix***

cross-reference **1** *noun* reference from one part of a book to another; ***the editors had not bothered to check the cross-references; you should add a cross-reference from 'Lincoln' to 'Gettysburg Address'*** **2** *verb* to make a reference to another part of the book;

the various paper sizes are cross-referenced to the appendix

cross-section *noun* view (in a drawing) as if something is cut through; ***the text is illustrated with a cross-section of the inside of the heart***

cross-shake *noun* shaking the paper pulp from side to side as it goes into the paper-making machine, thus setting the fibres into a certain direction

crown *noun* **(a) the Crown** = the King or Queen as representing the State; **Crown copyright** = copyright in British government publications, which belongs to the Stationery Office **(b)** size of book based on an old paper size of 15 x 20 inches (= 380 x 508mm) (the old paper was originally identified by a watermark of a crown); **crown octavo** = size of a book, formerly $7\frac{1}{2}$ x 5 inches, now 186 x 123mm; **crown quarto** = size of a book, formerly 10 x $7\frac{1}{2}$ inches, now 246 x 186mm

CRPU = CAMERA-READY PASTEUP

CRT = CATHODE RAY TUBE

crusher panel *noun* an area on a book cover blocked ready for title lettering to be blocked over it

crushing *noun* smashing *or* pressing of a sewn book, so as to remove air from between the pages, before it goes for binding

C/T = COLOUR TRANSPARENCY

CTN = CONFECTIONERS, TOBACCONISTS AND NEWSAGENTS small retail shops which carry some books, especially popular fiction, guide books and small reference books

CTP = COMPUTER TO PLATE

cumulative *adjective* which is added to automatically; **cumulative index** = index which grows as more references are added to it

curl 1 *verb* to roll into a curved shape; ***the paper has curled at the edges with damp*** **2** *noun* measurement of the amount by which paper curls in damp conditions

current *adjective* referring to the present time; **current list** *or* **list of current titles** = list of titles which are available at the present time; **current price** = today's price; **current rate of exchange** = today's rate of exchange

currently *adverb* at the present time; ***we are currently preparing the Spring Catalogue***

curriculum vitae (CV) *noun* summary of a person's life showing details of education and work experience; ***candidates should send a letter of application with a curriculum vitae to the personnel officer;*** (NOTE: the plural is **curriculums** *or* **curricula vitae.** Note also that the US English is **résumé)**

cursive *noun* typeface which is similar to handwriting, in that each letter flows on to the next, though without being completely joined

cursor *noun* marker on a VDU which shows where the next character will appear

> COMMENT: cursors can take several forms, such as a square of bright light, a bright underline or a flashing light

curve 1 *noun* **(a)** line which bends round; ***the graph shows an upward curve;*** **sales curve** = graph showing how sales increase or decrease **(b)** slang for digital expression of a colour separation specification (bending the curve means adjusting the colour balance or tonal range) **2** *verb* to make something bend; **curved electros** *or* **curved plates** = plates which are curved to fit on rotary printing presses

cushion *noun* soft pad on which a leather-bound book is placed for tooling

custom *noun* **(a)** use of a shop by regular shoppers; **to lose someone's custom** = to do something which makes a regular customer go to another shop; **custom-built** *or* **custom-made** = made specially for one customer; **custom-bound** = bound specially for a customer **(b) the customs** *or* **custom of the trade** = general way of working in a trade (in the 19th century, the customs of the trade between publishers and booksellers developed into the Net Book Agreement); ***according to the custom of the trade, overs are supplied up to 5% of the total order***

customer *noun* person *or* company which buys goods; ***the shop was full of customers; can you serve this customer first please? the company is one of our best customers;*** **customer appeal** = what attracts customers to a product; **customer file** = computer file which lists all a company's customers; **customer service department** = department which deals with customers and their complaints and orders

customize *verb* to change something to fit the special needs of a customer; ***we use customized computer terminals***

customs *noun* the government department which organizes the collection of taxes on imports; office of this department at a port *or* airport; **to go through customs** = to pass through the area of a port or airport where customs officials examine goods; **to take something through customs** = to carry something through the customs area (sometimes without declaring it); **customs broker** = person *or* company which takes goods through customs for a shipping company; **customs clearance** = document given by customs to a shipper to show that customs duty has been paid and the goods can be shipped; **customs declaration** = statement showing goods being imported on which duty will have to be paid; **customs duty** = tax paid on goods brought into or taken out of a country; **the crates had to go through a customs examination** = the crates had to be examined by customs officials; **customs formalities** = declaration of goods by the shipper and examination of them by customs; **customs officers** *or* **customs officials** = people working for customs; **customs tariff** = list of duties to be paid on imported goods

cut 1 *noun* **(a)** sudden lowering of a price *or* salary *or* numbers of jobs; ***price cuts*** *or* ***cuts in prices; salary cuts*** *or* ***cuts in salaries;*** **job cuts** = reductions in the number of jobs; **he took a cut in salary** = he accepted a lower salary **(b)** removing part of a text *or* photograph; ***the author objected to making any cuts in his text; we will have to make some drastic cuts if the text is to fit into 320 pages; the libel lawyers have asked for cuts to be made to chapter two*** **(c)** piece of metal used for printing an illustration; **line cut** = illustration on a metal block, using lines to show the picture; (NOTE: more used in the USA; the GB English for this is **block**) **2** *verb* **(a)** to lower suddenly *or* to reduce the number of something; ***we are cutting prices on all our models; the printrun was cut from 10,000 to 2,500; the company has cut back its sales force; we have taken out the telex to try to cut costs;*** **to cut (back) production** = to reduce the quantity of products made **(b)** to remove (part of a text *or* illustration, etc.); ***the editor has decided to cut the index to two pages; the author refuses to cut the preface; the libel lawyer suggested that several passages should be cut*** **(c)** to remove part of a sheet of paper; to separate a piece of paper using scissors *or* knife; ***the pages have been badly cut; the pages and cover should be cut flush;*** **cut edges** = the edges of a book which have been trimmed by a guillotine (i.e. the top, bottom and foredges); **cut flush** = book which has been trimmed so that the cover does not stick out further than the pages; **cut lines** = marks showing on a proof, which are left from the edges of film or paper patches on the original copy; *see also* CUTLINE *US* **cut marks** = marks on a sheet of paper, showing where it has to be guillotined; **cut sheet feeder** = mechanism that automatically feeds single sheets of paper into a printer

cut and paste *noun* **(a)** the normal way of doing a paste-up, where the various items are carefully cut out with a scalpel and positioned on a sheet **(b)** selecting section of text or data, copying it to the clipboard, then moving to another point or document and inserting it (often used in word-processors and DTP packages for easy page editing)

cutback *noun* reduction; ***cutbacks in government spending;*** **cutback binding** = ADHESIVE BINDING

cut down (on) *verb* to reduce suddenly the amount of something used; ***the office is trying to cut down on electricity***

consumption; we have installed a word-processor to cut down on paperwork

cut in *verb* to cut into a surface; **cut-in index** = index cut into the side of a page in steps, often used for address books; **cut-in notes** = printed notes set as a rectangular block of text in the outer edge of a paragraph of a page, with the main text shaped around them

cutline *noun US* caption to an illustration

cutoff *noun* **(a)** length of paper cut to make a sheet from a web press, equal to the plate cylinder circumference; **cutoff knife** = knife which cuts off the sheets on a rotary press; **cutoff rubber** = strip of rubber against which the cutoff knife cuts the sheets **(b)** paper which has been cut off

cut out *verb* **(a)** to remove something from a text by cutting; ***we have cut out all references to the Queen*** **(b)** to remove the background from an illustration, leaving the main part as a silhouette

cutout *noun* **(a)** piece of paper *or* card which is cut out from a large piece; **cutout book** = children's book, where the illustrations can be cut out to make models *or* figures, etc. **(b)** illustration where the background has been removed, leaving a silhouette

cutter *noun* machine which cuts

cutting *noun* **(a)** action of cutting paper; **cutting and creasing** = operation carried out on a letterpress cylinder machine, using dies to cut and crease paper or card into shapes; **cutting cylinder** = cylinder with knives which cut the printed section from the web; **cutting marks** = marks printed on the sheet showing where it has to be cut **(b) cost cutting** = reducing costs; ***we have made three secretaries redundant as part of our cost-cutting programme;*** **price cutting** = sudden lowering of prices; **price-cutting war** = competition between companies to get a larger market share by cutting prices **(c) press cutting agency** *or* **cutting service** = company which cuts out references to a client from newspapers and magazines and sends them on to him; **press cuttings** = references to a client *or* person *or* product cut out of newspapers or magazines; ***we have a file of press cuttings on our rivals' products***

CV *noun* = CURRICULUM VITAE ***please apply in writing, enclosing a current CV***

cyan *noun* a special blue, one of the three process colours

cyan-magenta-yellow-key (black)

see CMYK

cyberspace *noun* term used to describe the whole range of information resources available through computer networks

cyclohexylamine carbonate (CHC)

noun chemical used to remove the acid from paper

cylinder *noun* **(a)** long, round object, which is usually hollow; ***the posters are delivered in cardboard cylinders*** **(b) blanket cylinder** *or* **offset cylinder** *or* **transfer cylinder** = cylinder in an offset press which accepts the image onto the blanket; **plate cylinder** = part of a printing press, a heavy cylinder on which the plate is fixed; **cylinder press** *or* **flatbed cylinder press** = printing press where the paper is carried on a fixed cylinder which presses it onto the flat forme containing the inked type (as opposed to a rotary press, where the printing plate is on a cylinder); **cylinder brake** = device which stops the running of a printing press; **cylinder-dried paper** = paper which has been dried by running it over hot cylinders

Cyrillic *noun & adjective* the Russian alphabet, also used in some other Slavonic languages such as Ukrainian and Bulgarian

Dd

dagger *noun* typographical sign † used especially to indicate footnotes and references; **double dagger** = printing sign ‡ used to give a second reference level, used in cross-references

daily *adjective* published every day; **a daily newspaper** *or* **a daily** = newspaper which is produced every day; **popular dailies** = daily papers published for the mass market readership; **quality dailies** = daily papers aimed at the top end of the market

daisy-wheel *noun* wheel-shaped printing head, with characters on the end of spokes, used in a serial printer; **daisy-wheel printer** = serial character printer with characters arranged on interchangeable wheels, each wheel having characters of a different font or typeface (a daisy-wheel printer produces much better quality text than a dot-matrix, but is slower)

damp 1 *adjective* slightly wet **2** *noun* **the damp** = wet conditions; ***the books have been affected by damp***

dampen *verb* to make something damp; **dampening roller** *or* **damper** = roller which keeps the plate wet in lithographic printing

dancing roller = JOCKEY ROLLER

dandy roll *or* **dandy roller** *noun (in papermaking)* roller covered with wire mesh which presses the wet paper and can make watermarks on it if the mesh has a pattern on it; the dandy roller is the first of a series of rollers through which the wet paper passes

dark *adjective* not light; ***the cover is dark green, with gold lettering***

darken *verb* to make darker; to become darker; ***the picture needs darkening; the light cover paper will darken with age***

darkroom *noun* specially adapted room with no light, in which photographic film is processed

dash *noun* printing sign like a short line; **em dash** *or* **long dash** *or* **em rule** = dash which is the length of an em, used to separate words; **en dash** *or* **en rule** *or* **hyphen** = short dash, an en in length, used to link words

data *noun* information in the form of letters *or* figures which are available on computer; **data acquisition** = getting information; **bank of data** = databank; **data processing (DP)** = selecting and operating on data held in a computer to produce special information; **Data Protection Act** = Act which prevents confidential data about people being copied; **data storage** = ability to store date in the memory of a computer; (NOTE: **data** is usually singular: **the data is easily available**)

databank *noun* (i) large amount of data stored in a structured form; (ii) records stored in a computer

database *noun* store of information in a large computer in a structured form; ***we can extract the index from our database;*** **database publishing** = publishing information selected from a database, either on-line (where the user pays for it on a per-page inspection basis) or as a CD-ROM; **database setting** = typesetting of the information in a database directly from the codes written into the database

dataset *US* = MODEM

date *noun* **(a)** number of day, month and year; ***I have received your letter of yesterday's date;*** **date stamp** = rubber stamp for marking the date on letters received; **date of receipt** = date when something is received; **publication date** = (i) year when a book was published; (ii) day when a publisher says that a book is published (from that date, bookshops may sell the book); (iii) day when a newspaper or magazine is published **(b) up to date** = current *or* recent *or* modern; **to bring something up to date** = to add the latest information to something; **to keep something up to date** = to keep adding information to something so that it is always up to date; ***we spend a lot of time keeping our mailing list up to date*** **(c) out of date** = old-fashioned; ***their mailing list is years out of date; he is still using an out-of-date directory***

dateline *noun* line at the beginning of a newspaper report, giving the date and place from where the report was filed

day glow *noun* a range of fluorescent inks

d.c. = DOUBLE COLUMN

DCS format developed by Quark Inc that is an extension to the standard EPS format; DCS is used in process colour work and allows CMYK separations to be saved in a format that can be read by other applications

DD = DOUBLE DENSITY

deacidify *verb* to remove the acid from paper; *see* CHC

dead *adjective* **(a)** not alive; ***the author has been dead for sixty years, so his work is out of copyright*** **(b)** not working; **dead account** = account which is no longer used; **the line went dead** = the telephone line suddenly stopped working; **dead copy** = manuscript which has been keyboarded and typeset, and therefore is no longer needed; **dead keys** = keys on a keyboard that cause a function to occur rather than a character to print, such as the shift key; **dead letters** = letters still in the case, but which cannot be used because there is no more type left of one letter; **dead matter** = (i) manuscript text or phototypeset work which is not used; (ii) set metal type which is no longer any use and can be distributed; **dead metal** = parts of a metal printing plate which do not print **(c) dead white** = pure white, without the addition of blue or red which makes it more 'alive'

deadline *noun* date by which something has to be done; **to meet a deadline** = to finish something in time; ***we've missed our October 1st deadline; the deadline for advertising copy is next Tuesday***

deal 1 *noun* business agreement *or* affair *or* contract; ***to arrange a copublishing deal; the sales director set up a deal with a Russian import house; the deal will be signed tomorrow; they did a deal with an American agent;*** **to call off a deal** = to stop an agreement; ***when the chairman heard about the deal he called it off;*** **package deal** = agreement covering several different items at the same time; ***they agreed a package deal, covering the paperback rights, film rights and options on the author's next ten titles*** **2** *verb* **(a) to deal with** = to organize; ***leave it to the filing clerk - he'll deal with it;*** **to deal with an order** = to supply an order **(b)** to trade *or* to buy and sell; **to deal with someone** = to do business with someone

dealer *noun* person who buys and sells; **retail dealer** = person who sells to the general public; **wholesale dealer** = person who sells in bulk to retailers

dealing *noun* **fair dealing** = permission granted in the Copyright Acts, which allows photocopies of copyright works to be made for personal use and for private study, but not large numbers of copies for sale, or made by a teacher for the use of a class of students

debark *verb* to remove the bark from wood; **debarked wood** = wood which has had the bark stripped off, and is ready to be ground into pulp for papermaking

debit *noun* money which is owed; **debits and credits** = money which a company owes and money it receives; **debit balance** = balance in an account, showing that the company owes more money than it has received; **debit column** = left-hand column in accounts showing the money paid or owed to others; **debit entry** = entry on the debit side of an account; **debit side** = left-hand side of an account showing the money paid or owed to others; **debit note** = note showing that a customer owes money

debt *noun* money owed for goods or services; **to be in debt** = to owe money; **to pay off a debt** = to finish paying money owed; **to service a debt** = to pay interest on a debt; **bad debt** = money owed which will never be paid back; ***the company has written off £30,000 in bad debts;*** **debt collection** = collecting money which is owed; **debt collection agency** = company which collects debts for a commission; **debt collector** = person who collects debts; **debts due** = money owed which is due for repayment

debtor *noun* person *or* company which owes money; **debtor side** = debit side of an account; **aged debtor report** = computer report listing debtors, showing the length of time their payments are overdue

debug *verb* to test a program to locate and correct any errors; ***they spent weeks debugging the system***

decal *noun* sticker, a small piece of plastic which sticks to a surface, used often as an advertisement

decimal *noun* **decimal system** = system based on the number 10; **correct to three places of decimals** = correct to three figures after the decimal point (e.g. 3.485)

decimal classification *noun* classification of books in libraries, based on a series of units and subcategories

> COMMENT: the most common system is the Dewey Decimal Classification, based on ten subject areas, with numbers from 000 to 999 ⇨APPENDIX

decimal point *noun* dot which indicates the division between the whole unit and its smaller parts (such as 4.75); (NOTE: when it is printed above the base line it is known as a **raised point** or in US English **centered dot**)

> COMMENT: the dot should be raised above the line, though it is never printed in this way by computer printers. Note that the decimal point is used in English-speaking countries, and that in most other countries the decimal is indicated by a comma

decipher *verb* to read something which is badly written or printed; ***I find it difficult to decipher the author's handwriting***

deckle *noun* (i) raised edge of the wire tray in which handmade paper is made, which stops the pulp from running over the edge of the tray; (ii) the width of a machine which makes paper, hence the width of a piece of paper as it is made; **deckle edge** = (i) the uneven edge of a sheet of handmade paper; (ii) similar uneven edge given to machine-made paper (often used for expensive writing papers); **deckle edged paper** = paper with a deckle edge; **deckle frame** = wooden frame holding the wire on which handmade paper is made; **deckle strap** = flat piece of rubber along the edge of the wire mesh in a paper-making machine, which stops the pulp from running over the edge

> COMMENT: handmade paper always has a deckle edge, and this has to be cut off before printing, so that the lay of the paper is the same from sheet to sheet. An artificial deckle edge is given to machine-made writing paper to make it more attractive

decollate *verb* to separate continuous stationery into single sheets; to split two-part *or* three-part stationery into its separate parts (and remove the carbon paper)

decollator *noun* machine used to separate continuous stationery into single sheets *or* to split 2-part or 3-part stationery into separate parts

dedicate *verb* **(a)** *(of an author)* to print a special note in a book offering it to someone, usually a relative or friend, as a token of affection; ***he dedicated the book of poetry to his wife and daughters*** **(b)** to use for one purpose only; **dedicated communications link** = two or more sites linked with telecommunication lines which are for their sole use; no other users have access to the links; **dedicated word-processor** = small computer which has been configured to do only word-processing

dedication *noun* note, usually printed on a right-hand page after the title page, offering a book to someone as a token of affection or respect

deep *adjective* strong and dark (colour); ***the book has a deep blue cover with silver lettering***

deepen *verb* to make (a colour) deeper

deep-etch *verb* to etch the image very slightly below the surface of a printing plate, a process used in offset lithography to give a more intense print; **deep-etched halftone** = plate etched deeper than normal, often leaving white spaces (as opposed to a wipe-on or presensitized plate)

defamation *noun* **defamation (of character)** = statement in a book *or* newspaper which may damage the reputation of a person, and so is usually libellous

defamatory *adjective* which is damaging about a person or a person's character; ***he wrote a series of defamatory articles about the film star in a Sunday paper; the minister sued the paper for publishing defamatory articles about his private life***

default 1 *noun* **(a)** failure to carry out the terms of a contract, especially failure to pay back a debt; **in default of payment** = with no payment made; **the company is in default** = the company has failed to carry out the terms of the contract; **by default** = because no one else will act; **he was elected by default** = he was elected because all the other candidates withdrew **(b)** course of action taken automatically by a computer, unless the operator does something to change it **2** *verb* to fail to carry out the terms of a contract, especially to fail to pay back a debt; **to default on payments** = not to make payments which are due under the terms of a contract

defaulter *noun* person who defaults

defect *noun* something which is wrong *or* which stops a machine from working properly; ***a computer defect*** *or* ***a defect in the computer; there was a defect in the paper which made it tear easily***

defective *adjective* faulty *or* not working properly; ***the machine broke down because of a defective cooling system***

defer *verb* to put back to a later date *or* to postpone; ***to defer payment; the decision has been deferred until the next meeting***

deferment *noun* postponement *or* putting back to a later date; ***deferment of payment; deferment of a decision***

define *verb* to say what a word means; ***the word 'block' can be defined in several ways; the dictionary defines 'halftone illustration' as 'an illustration where shades of tone are indicated by dots'***

definition *noun* **(a)** meaning given to a word in a dictionary **(b)** ability of a reproduction *or* screen to display fine detail

definitive *adjective* which is final *or* which is the best and most complete work on a subject; ***this is the definitive biography of Jane Austen; they published the definitive work on sixteenth century printing; a definitive edition of Dickens***

degradation *noun* loss of picture *or* signal quality; ***line art can be reproduced on scanners or photocopied without much degradation;*** **image degradation** = loss of picture contrast and quality due to signal distortion *or* bad copying of a video signal

deink *verb* to remove the ink from printed paper as part of the recycling process

del. *abbreviation* instruction by a proofreader to a compositor to delete part of a text (either written 'del.' in the margin, or more usually indicated with a delete sign)

delete 1 *verb* to cut out words in a document *or* on a computer file; ***they want to delete all references to credit terms from the***

contract; the lawyers have deleted clause two; the sentence will be much clearer if you delete the first three words **2** *noun* **(a)** written sign used in proofreading, to show that a word should be deleted ⇨ APPENDIX **(b)** instruction given to a computer to remove a section of text; **delete character** = special code used to indicate data *or* text to be removed

deletion *noun* **(a)** action of deleting; ***the lawyers demanded the deletion of all references to their client*** **(b)** word *or* text which has been deleted; ***there were six deletions from the last page of the index; there were so many deletions that the text is now about two pages shorter***

> COMMENT: when you delete a computer file, you are not actually erasing it but you are making its space on disk available for another file

'Delibros' Spanish magazine dealing with books and publishers

deliver *verb* **(a)** to transport goods to a customer; ***when does the binder expect to deliver the bound copies?;*** **goods delivered free** *or* **free delivered goods** = goods transported to the customer's address at a price which includes transport costs; **delivered price** = price which includes packing and transport **(b)** to give a manuscript to a publisher; ***according to the contract, the author has to deliver the MS by the end of the year; the publisher cannot guarantee publication if the manuscript is not delivered on time; the author has still not delivered the last chapter***

delivery *noun* **(a)** handing of a manuscript to a publisher; ***the second part of the advance on royalties is payable on delivery of the manuscript*** **(b)** part of a printing machine where grippers move printed sheets from the machine and stack them; **delivery tapes** = broad ribbons which hold the printed sheets as they come out of the press **(c)** **delivery of goods** = transport of goods to a customer's address; ***we charge for delivery outside London; the delivery date for bound copies has been put back by three weeks; we guarantee delivery within 28 days; delivery is not allowed for*** *or* ***is not included in the price;*** **delivery instructions** = instructions to the printer or binder, saying where the sheets or bound copies of a book have to be sent; **delivery note** = list of goods being delivered, given to the customer with the goods; **delivery order** = instructions given by the customer to the person holding his goods, to tell him to deliver them; **delivery time** = number of days before something will be delivered; **delivery van** = goods van for delivering goods to retail customers; **to take delivery of goods** = to accept goods when they are delivered; ***we took delivery of the stock into our warehouse on the 25th*** **(d)** goods being delivered; ***we take in three deliveries a day; there were four pallets of books missing in the last delivery; the warehouse will close for Christmas and will not accept deliveries after December 20th***

de luxe edition *noun* special edition of a book, printed on very good quality paper and with an expensive binding, selling for a higher price than a standard edition

demand 1 *noun* **(a)** asking for payment; **payable on demand** = which must be paid when payment is asked for; **demand bill** = bill of exchange which must be paid when payment is asked for; **final demand** = last reminder from a supplier, after which he will sue for payment **(b)** need for goods at a certain price; ***there is a strong demand for TV tie-ins in the pre-Christmas period;*** **there is not much demand for this item** = not many people want to buy it; **this book is in great demand** *or* **there is a great demand for this book** = many people want to buy it; **on-demand publishing** = printing books as the demand arises (usually in very small quantities) as opposed to keeping larger quantities of books in stock; **supply and demand** = amount of a product which is available and the amount which is wanted by customers; **law of supply and demand** = general rule that the amount of a product which is available is related to the needs of potential customers **2** *verb* to ask for something and expect to get it; ***she demanded a refund; the suppliers are***

demanding immediate payment of their outstanding invoices

demy *noun* traditional British paper size; **demy octavo** = book format (formerly $8\frac{3}{4}$ x 5 inches, now 216 x 138mm); **demy quarto** = book format (formerly $1\frac{1}{4}$ x $8\frac{3}{4}$ inches, now 279 x 219mm)

densitometer *noun* (i) device for measuring the absorption of light (the percentage of light reflected and the light which passes through paper), used to calculate the thickness of ink required to print on a certain type of paper; (ii) device for measuring the size of dots in halftones

density *noun* **(a)** amount of light that a photographic negative blocks **(b)** darkness of a printed image, such as a photograph; **density dial** = knob that controls the density of a printed image; ***when fading occurs, turn the density dial on the printer to full black*** **(c)** dark appearance of a printed page, when the text is printed too close together **(d)** amount of data that can be packed into a space on a disk *or* tape; **double density** = system to double the storage capacity of a disk drive by doubling the number of bits which can be put on the disk surface; **double density disk (DD)** = disk that can store two bits of data per unit area compared to a standard disk; **single density disk (SD)** = standard magnetic disk able to store data

> COMMENT: scanner software produces various shades of grey by using different densities or arrangements of black and white dots and/or different sized dots

densometer *noun* device used for testing paper porosity by measuring the time taken for a certain volume of air to pass through a sample area of paper

dentelle *noun* gold decoration used on book covers, like a series of little teeth

department *noun* **(a)** specialized section of a large company; **accounts department** = section which deals with money paid or received; **editorial department** = department in a publishing company which deals with the in-house editing of books; **personnel department** = section of a company dealing with the staff; **head of department** *or* **department head** *or* **department manager** = person in charge of a department **(b)** section of a large store selling one type of product; **the reference department buyer** = person in a large bookshop who is responsible for buying reference books **(c)** section of the British government containing several ministries; ***the Department of Trade and Industry; the Department of Education and Science***

deposit 1 *noun* **(a)** money placed in a bank for safe keeping or to earn interest; **fixed deposit** = deposit which pays a fixed interest over a fixed period; **deposit account** = bank account which pays interest but on which notice has to be given to withdraw money; **deposit slip** = piece of paper stamped by the cashier to prove that you have paid money into your account **(b) legal deposit** = giving of a copy of a book to a deposit library as part of the process of publication; **deposit library** = national library to which a publisher has by law to give a copy of each book published **2** *verb* **(a)** to put money into a bank account; ***to deposit £100 in a current account*** **(b)** to give a copy of a book to a deposit library as part of the process of publishing the book

> COMMENT: in the British Isles, the deposit libraries are the British Library, the Bodleian Library at Oxford, Cambridge University Library, the National Library of Scotland and the Library of Trinity College Dublin; the Welsh National Library may also receive copies

depreciate *verb* **(a)** to reduce the value of assets in accounts; ***we depreciate our company cars over three years*** **(b)** to lose value; ***the pound has depreciated by 5% against the dollar***

depreciation *noun* reduction in value of an asset; **depreciation rate** = rate at which an asset is depreciated each year in the accounts

> COMMENT: publishers often write down the value of their stocks on the assumption that a book which is several years old is not likely to sell well, and

unsold stock is therefore less valuable. Depreciation has the effect of reducing profits in the year in which it is carried out, and increasing profits in subsequent years as the depreciated stock continues to sell. Depreciation does mean that stock can be remaindered without loss

dept = DEPARTMENT

depth *noun* **depth of field** = amount of a scene that will be in focus when photographed with a certain aperture setting; **depth of focus** = position of film behind a camera lens that will result in a sharp image; **depth of page** *or* **page depth** = measurement of the type area from the headline to the folio at the bottom of the page; **depth gauge** *or* **depth scale** = ruler used to measure the space between lines of type

descender *noun* part of a letter which falls below the base line ('j', 'y', 'p', 'g' and 'q' have descenders); **long descenders** = alternative characters in certain typefaces (such as Times Roman) that have longer descenders than the normal characters in the same face; **descender line** = line which marks the lowest level of the descenders in a particular face; *compare* ASCENDER

descending letters *noun* letters (like 'p', 'y', etc.) which have descenders

desensitize *verb* to wash an offset litho plate with chemicals to make sure the ink will not adhere to the non-printing areas

desiderata *noun* list of secondhand books that a dealer wants to buy

design 1 *noun* **(a)** planning *or* drawing of a product before it is manufactured; **book design** = design of a book, both the typography and the page layout; **jacket design** *or* **cover design** = planning of a book jacket; **design department** = department in a large company which designs the company's products or its advertising; **design studio** = independent firm which specializes in creating designs **(b)** a drawing which shows how a book *or* page *or* cover will look when finished; ***the designs for the cover were turned down by the author; the artist brought a portfolio of page designs to show the art director*** **2** *verb* to plan *or* to draw something before it is manufactured; ***he designed the covers for the whole series; she designs book jackets***

designer *noun* person who designs; **jacket designer** = person who designs book jackets

designation mark *noun* signature mark *or* letter or number, printed in very small type on the fold of the signature, so that the sequence of sections can be easily checked

desk *noun* **(a)** writing table in an office, usually with drawers for stationery; **desk diary** *or* **desk light** *or* **desk pad** = diary *or* light *or* pad of paper kept on a desk **(b)** **desk copy** = free copy of a book sent to someone who may read it to buy rights in it, or to order it in quantity for class use; **desk editor** = copy editor, an editor who works at a desk, preparing copy for the printer, checking proofs, collating corrections, etc. **(c)** section of a newspaper; **the city desk** = the section of a British newspaper which deals with business news

desktop *adjective* which sits on top of a desk; which can be done on a desk; **desktop computer** = small microcomputer system that can be placed on a desk; **desktop media** = combination of presentation graphics, desktop publishing and multimedia; this is a phrase that was originally used by Apple; **desktop PC** = normally refers to an IBM-compatible computer which can be placed on a user's desk: comprises a system unit (with main electronics, disk drive and controllers) and a separate monitor and keyboard.; **desktop publishing (DTP)** = design, layout and printing of documents, books and magazines using special software, a desktop computer and a high-resolution printer; the software normally provides a WYSIWYG preview to show what the printed page will look like

despatch = DISPATCH

destock *verb* to reduce the amount of stock in a shop *or* warehouse; ***bookstores have been destocking after the Christmas buying***

season and are returning thousands of copies of unsold paperbacks

detail 1 *noun* **(a)** small part of a drawing *or* photograph; ***the print is blurred, making it difficult to see the details; the detail of the drawing is very delicate;*** **detail paper** = thin transparent paper used for layouts and tracing **(b)** small part of a description; ***the catalogue gives all the details of the Autumn list; we are worried by some of the details in the contract*** **2** *verb* to list in detail; ***the catalogue details the payment arrangements for overseas buyers; the terms of the licence are detailed in the contract***

detailed *adjective* in detail; **detailed account** = account which lists every item; **detailed drawing** = drawing showing a lot of small details

detective *noun* policeman who tries to find who has committed a crime; **detective fiction** = crime fiction, with a detective as the main character

Deutsche Industrienorm (DIN) the German industrial standards organization

develop *verb* **(a)** to plan and produce; ***to develop a new papermaking technique*** **(b)** to apply a chemical process to exposed photographic film and paper to produce an image

developer *noun* chemical solution used to develop exposed film

device *noun* ornamental design used by a publisher *or* printer as part of his logo; **device independent** = programming technique that results in a program that is able to run with any peripheral hardware

Dewey decimal classification *noun* system of cataloguing library books, using a series of subject categories numbered from 000 to 999 ⇨ APPENDIX

diacritical marks *or* **diacritics** *or* **diacriticals** *noun* marks made above normal letters to show a change of pronunciation or stress

> COMMENT: the commonest diacritics are the accents in European languages and the dots indicating vowels in Arabic

diaeresis *US* **dieresis** *noun* printed sign, formed of two dots printed above a vowel

> COMMENT: in English the diaeresis is now uncommon, but was used in words such as 'naïve' and 'coördinate' to show that the two vowels were pronounced separately and not as a diphthong; it is still used in many European languages and indicates a change in pronunciation of a vowel. In German it is called the Umlaut

diagnostics *noun* tests that help a user find faults in hardware or software

diagram *noun* drawing which shows something as a plan *or* map; ***the book is illustrated with diagrams showing population densities; the diagram of organizational structures needs to be redrawn;*** **flow diagram** = diagram showing the arrangement of work processes in a series

diagrammatic *adjective* **in diagrammatic form** = in the form of a diagram; ***a chart showing the rainfall pattern in diagrammatic form***

diagrammatically *adverb* using a diagram; ***the chart shows the population growth diagrammatically***

dial *noun* a round display device, like the face of a clock, on which information is shown automatically by the movement of a hand or pointer; **dial micrometer** = machine for measuring paper thickness, where the reading is shown on a dial

dialogue *noun* conversation between characters in a film *or* play

diamond *noun* old size of type, equivalent to $4\frac{1}{2}$ point

diapositive *noun* positive transparency

diary *noun* book in which you can write notes or appointments for each day of the week; ***a diary publisher; a gardener's diary;*** **diary format** = format similar to that used for diaries, roughly 140 x 85mm

diazo paper *noun* specially treated paper used in the dyeline copying process; *see also* BLUEPRINT

dictate *verb* to speak words so that someone else can write them down; ***she spends two hours every morning dictating her novel to her secretary***

dictation *noun* action of dictating; **dictation speed** = number of words per minute which a secretary can write down from dictation

dictionary *noun* **(a)** book which lists words (usually in alphabetical order) and gives meanings for them; **monolingual dictionary** = dictionary where the meanings of the headwords are given in the same language; **bilingual dictionary** = dictionary which shows how words should be translated into another language; **multilingual dictionary** = dictionary where the headwords have translations into several different languages; ***a Russian-German bilingual dictionary; they publish a series of dictionaries for students*** *or* ***a series of student dictionaries; a multilingual dictionary of technical terms*** **(b)** part of a spelling checker program: the list of correctly spelled words against which the program checks a text

> COMMENT: the term 'dictionary' really applies to a book where the words are defined, but not necessarily explained; an 'encyclopaedia' is a book where the words are explained, but not always defined. A 'Dictionary of Gardening' is probably in fact an encyclopaedia, since it may give details of how to grow plants, rather than defining what each plant or process is. This present dictionary has many encyclopaedic sections, such as this one

didot *noun* **(a)** modern typeface with thick black vertical lines and hairline serifs, designed by Firmin Didot (1764-1836) **(b)** system of type sizes used in Europe, but not in the UK or the USA, introduced by F.-A. Didot (1730-1804); *compare* CICERO

> COMMENT: the basic Didot measurement is a point of 0.376mm, while the British and American point is 0.351mm. The cicero is the European equivalent to the British pica, but slightly larger (about 12.5 British points or 4.511mm)

die *noun* **(a)** matrix used for making a hot metal character; **die case** = case which holds the matrices for Monotype hot metal die casting; **die casting** = casting of metal type using hot metal and matrices **(b)** any metal stamp, used for cutting *or* stamping; **die cutting** = using sharp metal knives to cut out paper or cardboard in different shapes (as in making a cardboard box, or in making cutouts for pop-up books, usually on a letterpress cylinder machine); **die stamping** = stamping relief decorations *or* text on paper *or* card, as for example an address on stationery; **stamping die** = metal stamp for blocking the case of a book

differential spacing *noun* spacing where each character takes a space equivalent to its width ('m' taking more space than 'i')

digest *noun* book which summarizes a series of reports, especially one which collects summaries of court decisions, and is used as a reference tool by lawyers (a Law Digest); **digest-size** = book which is the same format as the 'Reader's Digest' (7 x 5 inches)

digester *noun* device which mixes ground wood, water and chemicals together and begins the process of papermaking

digipad *noun* digitizing pad, a device for inputting drawings into a computer system by digitizing them

digit *noun* **(a)** single number; ***a seven-digit phone number*** **(b)** printing sign ☞ used to point to something

digital *adjective* which represents data *or* physical quantities in numerical form (especially using a binary system in computer related devices); **digital computer** = computer which calculates on the basis of binary numbers; **digital data network** = network designed specifically for the transmission of digital data as distinct from networks such as the telephone system which are analog; **digital font** = font which has been digitized so that it can be stored in a computer; **digital image processing** = wide range of techniques used to generate, process and reproduce images by digital computers; **digital plotter** = machine which plots graphs based on information supplied on-line from a computer; **digital proofs** = proofs taken from digital files prior to film output at high or low resolution; **digital scanning** = reading of an image (such as a printed character) by a computer, and building it up as a series of dots in the computer memory

digitize *verb* to change analog movement *or* signals into a digital form which can be processed by computers, etc.; **digitized letterforms** = the shapes of characters which have been scanned and then stored as a series of dots in the computer memory; **digitized photograph** = image *or* photograph that has been scanned to produce an analog signal which is then converted to digital form and stored in a computer or displayed on a screen; **digitizing pad** *or* **digipad** = sensitive surface that translates the position of a pen into numerical form, so that drawings can be entered into a computer

digitization *noun* the action of converting shapes or signals into digital form

digitizer *noun* vector graphic input device which can be used to scan an existing image, capturing x, y co-ordinates at desired intervals

di litho = DIRECT LITHOGRAPHY

dime *noun US informal* ten cent coin; **dime novels** = cheap paperback novels

dimension *noun* measurement of something; **dimension marks** = marks on CRC showing a section that has to be enlarged or reduced; **vertical dimension** = the depth of a page from head to foot (that is, from top to bottom); (NOTE: when giving dimensions of a book in Britain the vertical dimension is always given first: this book is 198 x 129mm; if it were landscape format it would be 129 x 198mm. In many other countries, the width is given first. In the USA, dimensions are given in inches)

dimensional *adjective* referring to dimensions; **dimensional stability** = measurement of the ability of paper not to change its dimensions when subjected to heat, water, etc.

DIN = DEUTSCHE INDUSTRIENORM the German industrial standards organization

dingbats *noun US* ornaments and other symbols; (NOTE: UK English is **printer's flowers**)

dinky sheet *noun* narrow web of paper

diphthong *noun* two vowels which are pronounced together as one sound, sometimes printed together with a ligature (as in encyclopædia)

direct 1 *verb* to manage *or* to organize; ***he directs our South-East Asian operations; she was directing the development unit until last year*** **2** *adjective* straight *or* with no interference; **direct access** = the retrieval of stored data without having to read other data first; **direct colour separation** *see* DIRECT SCREENING **direct cost** = production *or* origination cost of a particular product; **direct-entry phototypesetting** = phototypesetting where the text is keyed directly onto a keyboard which allows it to be output as typesetting; **direct impression** = typesetting process where the image is created by something which hits the paper directly (as a typewriter); **direct input** = software which allows the keyboarder to input text directly into the computer typesetter using a direct-input keyboard; **direct lithography (di litho)** = lithographic process where the image is printed directly from the plate onto the paper (as opposed to offset lithography); **direct mail** = selling a product by sending publicity material to possible buyers through the post; ***these partworks are only sold by direct mail; the***

company runs a successful direct-mail operation; **direct-mail advertising** = advertising by sending leaflets to people through the post; **direct positive** = film produced by direct screening; **direct printing** = printing directly from a plate onto the paper (as opposed to offset); **direct processing** = method of photocopying which requires specially treated paper which captures the image from the original as it is exposed to light (as opposed to indirect process, used in plain-paper copiers); **direct screening** = method of originating colour separations, where the original is reproduced as screened separations using a halftone screen; **direct selling** = selling a product direct to the customer without going through a shop

direction *noun* **(a)** way in which something is moving; **direction of travel** = the direction in which the web of paper moves, either on a papermaking machine or through a printing press; **grain direction** *or* **machine direction** = way in which the grain of the paper lies in the same direction as the movement of the web along a papermaking machine; *compare* CROSS-DIRECTION **(b) directions for use** = instructions showing how to use something

directory *noun* list of people *or* businesses with information about their addresses and telephone numbers; ***a directory publisher; is there a directory for the publishing industry?;*** **classified directory** = list of businesses grouped under various headings, such as computer shops *or* newsagents; **commercial directory** *or* **trade directory** = book which lists all the businesses and business people in a town; **street directory** = list of people living in a street; map of a town which lists all the streets in alphabetical order in an index; **telephone directory** = book which lists all people and businesses in alphabetical order with their phone numbers; ***to look up a number in the telephone directory; his number is in the London directory***

dirty copy *noun* manuscript or typescript which has a large number of additions and changes, and is difficult to read (typesetting dirty copy is charged at a higher rate than clean copy); **dirty proof** = proof with many keyboarding errors or which has been heavily corrected

dis *informal* = DISTRIBUTE

disc *see* DISK

disclaimer *noun* legal refusal to accept responsibility

> COMMENT: publishers or authors may print disclaimers in their publications: 'the views expressed in the article are those of the author and do not represent the policy of the newspaper'; 'the characters in this novel are fictitious, and are not based on anyone living or dead'. Whether such disclaimers have any legal validity is open to question

discount 1 *noun* percentage reduction in the full price given by a seller to a buyer; ***to give a discount to trade customers; we give a special discount to schools;*** **to sell goods at a discount** *or* **at a discount price** = to sell goods below the normal price; **basic discount** = normal discount without extra percentages; ***we give 25% as a basic discount, but can add 5% for cash payment;*** *US* **long discount** = trade discount; **quantity discount** = discount given to people who buy large quantities; **10% discount for quantity purchases** = you pay 10% less if you buy a large quantity; **10% discount for cash** *or* **10% cash discount** = you pay 10% less if you pay in cash; **trade discount** = discount given by a manufacturer to a customer for goods for retail sale **2** *verb* to reduce prices to increase sales; **to discount bills of exchange** = to buy bills of exchange for less than the value written on them in order to cash them later

discounter *noun* person *or* company which sells goods at a discount

> COMMENT: discounts vary considerably from country to country. In the UK, the basic discounts given by publishers to booksellers, would be about 35%. Higher discounts will be given to wholesalers or large chains of bookshops, and also on mass-market

paperbacks. Lower discounts will apply to single copy orders (or a surcharge may be added), and especially to academic books. Educational books have a basic discount of 17.5%, because the bookseller is simply passing on orders for school purchases and is not buying the books speculatively for retail sale. Educational books are usually non-net, so that the bookseller can mark up the price if he wishes to hold them in stock and sell them from the shelf to the public

discretion *noun* being able to decide what should be done; **I leave it to your discretion** = I leave it for you to decide what to do; **at the discretion of someone** = if *or* as someone decides; ***the date of the next meeting will be fixed at the discretion of the committee***

discretionary *adjective* which can be done if someone wants; **the minister's discretionary powers** = powers which the minister could use if he thought he should do so; **discretionary hyphen** = hyphen, inserted by the keyboarder, which is different from the spelling used in the computer's H & J program

discrimination *noun* treating people in different ways because of class, religion, race, language, colour or sex; **sexual discrimination** *or* **sex discrimination** *or* **discrimination on grounds of sex** = treating men and women employees in different ways, usually to the disadvantage of the women

disk *noun* **(a)** round flat plate, coated with a substance that can be magnetized, used to store information in computers; ***the dictionary text is stored on disk; most typesetters will accept 3.25 inch disks;*** **floppy disk** = small disk for storing computerized information; **hard disk** = solid disk (used to store a large amount of computer information); **disk converter** = MULTI-DISK READER **disk drive** = part of a computer which makes a disk spin round, controlling the position of the read/write head in order to read it or store information on the disk; **disk operating system (DOS)** = section of the operating system in a computer that controls the disk and file management; **disk reader** = device which will read the contents of a disk into a main computer system **(b)** round flat plate with film matrices of different characters in a font, used in photomechanical typesetters **(c)** any round flat plate; **disk inking** = method of inking printing rollers, where the ink is spread from a turning plate; **disk ruling** = method of producing ruled paper, using disks to produce the rules

diskette *noun* very small floppy disk

COMMENT: computer disks may be single-sided or double-sided and can vary in diameter from 3 inch to 12 inches; $3\frac{1}{2}$ inch and $5\frac{1}{4}$ inch are common. The surface of a computer disk is divided into tracks which can be accessed individually. This gives a disk a considerable advantage over magnetic tape which does not allow random access

dispatch 1 *noun* **(a)** sending of goods to a customer; ***the strike held up dispatch for several weeks;*** **dispatch department** = department which deals with the packing and sending of goods to customers; **dispatch note** = note saying that goods have been sent **(b)** goods which have been sent; ***the weekly dispatch went off yesterday*** **2** *verb* to send goods to customers

dispatcher *noun* person who sends goods to customers

display 1 *noun* **(a)** showing of goods for sale; ***the bookshop has a window display of recent fiction; several new encyclopaedias are on display; an attractive display of gardening books;*** **display cabinet** *or* **display case** = piece of furniture with a glass top or glass doors for showing goods for sale (used particularly for antiquarian books); **display material** = posters, photographs, etc., to be used to attract attention to goods which are for sale; **display pack** *or* **display box** = special box for showing goods for sale; **display stand** *or* **display unit** = special stand for showing books for sale or at an exhibition **(b)** showing text on a computer screen; **display character** = graphical symbol which appears as a printed *or* displayed item, such as one of the letters of the alphabet *or* a number; **display colour** = colour of characters in a videotext display system; **display controller** = device that accepts character *or* graphics codes and instructions, and converts them into dot-matrix patterns that are displayed on a screen; **display format** = number of characters that can be displayed on a screen, given as lengths of rows and columns; **display highlights** = the emphasis of certain words *or* paragraphs by changing the colour of the display; **display line** = horizontal printing positions for characters in a line of text; **display mode** = way of referring to the character set to be used, usually graphics *or* alphanumerics; **display register** = register that contains character *or* control *or* graphical data that is to be displayed; **display resolution** = number of pixels per unit area that a display can show clearly; **display screen** = the physical part of a Visual Display Unit *or* terminal *or* monitor, which allows the user to see characters *or* graphics (usually a CRT, but sometimes LCD *or* LED displays are used); **display space** = memory *or* amount of screen available to show graphics *or* text; **display unit** = computer terminal *or* piece of equipment that is capable of showing data *or* information, usually by means of CRT; **gas discharge** *or* **plasma** *or* **electroluminescent display** = flat lightweight display screen that is made up of two flat pieces of glass covered with a grid of conductors, separated by a thin layer of gas which luminesces when a point of the grid is selected by two electrical signals; **visual display unit (VDU)** *or* **visual display terminal (VDT)** = screen attached to a computer which displays the information stored in the computer **(c)** special printing of headings, posters, etc.; **display advertisement** *or* **display ad** = advertisement which is well designed or placed in a box to attract attention; **display board** = coated coloured board, used as backing for exhibitions or displays; **display face** *or* **display type** = large typeface, used for posters, headings in bookwork, etc.; **display matter** = typeset material in a display face (such as a poster); **display paper** = thick paper used to print posters; **display size** = character size greater than 14 points, used in headlines rather than normal text (in hot metal setting, display sizes were not set on machine, but by hand); **display work** = printing posters, headings, etc. **2** *verb* **(a)** to show; ***the company was displaying its new range of children's books*** **(b)** to highlight part of a text, by setting it in a special face, putting it in a box, etc.; **displayed text** = text which is laid out by indenting or being placed in a box, so as to make it different from the rest of the text

Display PostScript ™ an extension of PostScript that allows PostScript commands to be interpreted and displayed on screen so that a user can see exactly what will appear on the printer

diss *informal* = DISTRIBUTE

dissect *verb* to remove the type which is to be printed in another colour (such as highlighted words in a children's dictionary)

distribute *verb* **(a)** to send out goods from a manufacturer's warehouse to retail shops; ***Smith Ltd distributes for several smaller companies; our books are represented and distributed by J. Smith & Co.*** **(b)** (i) to break up standing metal type and put each piece back into its case; (ii) in Monotype and Linotype machines, to melt down cast slugs after they have been used; ***the book was abandoned and the type was distributed*** **(c)** to spread ink evenly over the surface of a plate, using a distributing roller

distribution *noun* **(a)** act of sending goods from the manufacturer to the wholesaler and then to retailers; **distribution costs** = costs involved in distributing books from the warehouse to the customer, including picking, packing and transport; **channels of distribution** *or* **distribution channels** = ways of sending goods from the manufacturer to the retailer; **distribution network** = series of points *or* warehouses from which goods are sent all over a country **(b) distribution slip** = paper attached to a document *or* a magazine showing all the people in an office who should read it **(c)** breaking up standing metal type and putting it back into its case **(d)** spreading ink over the surface of a plate; **distribution rollers** =

rollers which distribute ink to the inking rollers

distributor *noun* **(a)** company which sells goods for another company which makes them; **sole distributor** = retailer who is the only one in an area who is allowed by the manufacturer to sell a certain product; **a network of distributors** = a series of distributors spread all over a country **(b)** **distributor rollers** = rollers which distribute the ink to the inking rollers or printing plates

distributorship *noun* position of being a distributor for a company

dither *verb* **(a)** to create a curve or line that looks smoother by adding shaded pixels beside the pixels that make up the image **(b)** to create the appearance of a new colour by a pattern of coloured pixels that appear, to the eye, to combine and form a new, composite colour (for example, a pattern of black and white dots will appear like grey); **dithered colour** = colour that is made up of a pattern of different coloured pixels

dittogram *noun* printing error caused by repeating the same letter twice

ditto marks *noun* two small lines (similar to double inverted commas set at the base line) used to show that the word above is repeated

divinity calf *noun* type of binding used for religious books, made of dark brown calf leather

division *noun* **(a)** main section of a large company; ***marketing division; production division; retail division; the ELT division of a major publishing group; he has been put in charge of one of the major publishing divisions of the company*** **(b)** way in which long words can be split at the end of lines; ***the rules of word division are quite different in French and English***

DIY = DO-IT-YOURSELF ***they publish a line of DIY handbooks***

DNS = DOMAIN NAME SERVICE

docket *noun* slip of paper on which a record can be kept; ***delivery docket; job docket; work docket***

doctor blade *noun* soft metal blade pulled across the surface of a gravure printing surface to remove excess ink

document *noun* paper with writing on it, especially an official piece of paper such as a legal document; **document paper** = special sized paper used for legal and other documents, which is suitable for writing on

document reader *noun* a mechanism for reading text into a computer

dog-eared *adjective* (book) with its corners bent, because it has been read often

dogsbody *noun informal* person who does all types of work in an office for very low wages; (NOTE: US English is **gofer**)

dogleg *noun US* leader line which bends to link the image to the text it refers to

do-it-yourself (DIY) *adjective* done by an ordinary person, not by a skilled worker; **do-it-yourself handbook** *or* **manual** = handbook showing you how to do repairs or construction work around the house; (NOTE: US English is **how-to book**) **do-it-yourself magazine** = magazine with articles on work which the average person can do repairs or construction work around the house; **do-it-yourself publishing** = publishing carried out by an ordinary individual from his or her own home; *compare* SAMIZDAT

dollar *noun* money used in the USA and other countries; **a five dollar bill** = a banknote for five dollars; (NOTE: usually written $ before a figure: **$250.** The currencies used in different countries can be shown by the initial letter of the country: **C$** (Canadian dollar) **A$** (Australian dollar), etc.)

dollar sign *noun* printed *or* written character ($) used in some computer languages to identify a variable as a string type

dolly *noun* device on wheels, such as a mobile microphone; **dolly truck** = truck which moves reels of paper from the paper store to the printing press

domain *noun* **(a)** area of responsibility; **public domain** = land *or* property *or* information which belongs to and is available to the public; **program which is in the public domain** = program which is not copyrighted; **public domain software** = software which is available for copying, without payment of a royalty **(b)** *(on the Internet)* part of the way of naming users on the Internet in which the domain name is the name of the service provider or company the user works for; in an electronic mail address, the domain name follows the '@' symbol; **domain name service (DNS)** = distributed database used on the Internet to convert a name to its IP address; for example, the domain name 'www.pcp.co.uk' is simple to remember and a DNS computer would convert this to its correct IP address such as 158.137.234.112

domestic *adjective* referring to the home market *or* the market of the country where the business is situated; **domestic market** = market in the country where a company is based; **domestic production** = production of goods for domestic consumption

door-to-door *adjective* going from one house to the next, asking the occupiers to buy something; ***door-to-door encyclopaedia selling; a door-to-door salesman***

DOS = DISK OPERATING SYSTEM section of the operating system in a computer that controls the disk and file management

dot *noun* **(a)** small round spot; ***the order form should be cut off along the line shown by the row of dots*** **(b)** small spot which forms part of a halftone photograph; **dot etching** = method of making a halftone darker or lighter, by reducing or increasing the size of the dots by etching them by hand; **dot-for-dot reproduction** = reproduction from a printed halftone, where each dot is matched and reproduced; **dot gain** = occurrence in halftone reproduction where the dots tend to enlarge slightly and may lead to dot spread; **dots per inch** *or* **d.p.i.** *or* **dpi** = standard method used to describe the resolution capabilities of a page printer *or* scanner; ***some laser printers offer high resolution printing at 400 dpi;*** **dot spread** = defect in halftone reproduction where the dots become too large

COMMENT: various shapes of dots are used for halftones, depending on the type of screen. Square dots give sharper edges to the image, while elliptical dots give a smooth gradation between tones

dotless 'i' *noun* the letter 'i' printed without a dot, used in some faces to give an IPA character, or in order to add a floating accent

dot-matrix printer *noun* printer in which the characters are made up by a series of closely spaced dots, it produces a page line by line; a dot-matrix printer can be used either for printing using a ribbon *or* for thermal *or* electrostatic printing

dotted line *noun* line made of a series of dots; ***please sign on the dotted line; do not write anything below the dotted line***

double 1 *adjective* twice *or* two times the size; **to be on double time** = to earn twice the usual wages for working on Sundays or other holidays; **double burn** = exposing two images on a film to give a special effect; **double case** = case which holds both upper case and lower case type; **double-coated paper** = paper which has been coated twice, giving a very hard gloss; **double column** = setting with two columns on the page; **double dagger** = typeset character used as a second reference mark; **double density** *see* DENSITY **double document** = error in photographing documents for microfilm, where the same image appears twice; **double elephant** = (i) large size of drawing paper (40 x 27 inches); (ii) *US* book size up to 50 inches high; **double exposure** = two images exposed on the same piece of photographic film, usually used for special effects; **double image** = two pictures formed when the plates are out of register; **double page spread (DPS)** *or* **double spread** = two facing pages, designed to be seen together, the illustrations or text forming one whole design; **double**

quotes *or* **double inverted commas** = punctuation marks (" ") indicating quotations; **double rule** = rule made of two lines; **double-sided disk** = computer disk which has been sensitized on both sides, and can store twice the amount of data; **double tone ink** = special ink for printing halftones, which spreads out from the centre of each dot as it dries and gives a stronger picture **2** *noun* traditional British paper size made when the short side of a sheet is doubled (if crown is 20 x 15 inches, double crown is 30 x 20: compare quad, where the long side is doubled)

doublures *noun* lining of the inside of the front and back boards, covering the edges of the leather which has been turned in (it may be plain or marbled paper, or even, in de luxe bindings, silk)

Dow etching *or* **Dow etch process** *noun* form of process engraving using magnesium alloy plates instead of zinc, giving very fine lines

downer *noun* break in the web, which makes the printing press stop

download *verb* (i) to load a program *or* section of data from a remote computer via a telephone line; (ii) to send printer font data stored on a disk to a printer (where it will be stored in temporary memory *or* RAM)

downloadable *adjective* which can be downloaded; **downloadable fonts** = fonts *or* typefaces stored on a disk, which can be downloaded *or* sent to a printer and stored in temporary memory *or* RAM

down stroke *noun* wide heavy section of a character (the main stroke when written with an ink pen)

down time *noun* time when a machine is not working

dp *or* **DP** = DATA PROCESSING selecting and operating on data held in a computer to produce special information

d.p.i. *or* **dpi** = DOTS PER INCH standard method used to describe the resolution capabilities of a page printer *or* scanner; ***a 300 d.p.i. black and white A4 monitor; a 300 dpi image scanner***

> COMMENT: 300 d.p.i. is the basic industry standard for a laser printer with 600 d.p.i the accepted standard for high-quality lase printers

DPS = DOUBLE PAGE SPREAD

draft 1 *noun* **(a)** first rough plan *or* document which has not been finished; ***the legal department drew up a draft contract; he drew up the draft agreement on the back of an envelope; the first draft of the contract was changed by the author's agent; the editor has seen the first draft of her new novel;*** **final draft** = last version of a text before it is typed *or* typeset; **rough draft** = plan of a document which may have changes made to it before it is complete; **draft printing** *or* **draft-quality printing** = low quality, high speed printing (as opposed to near-letter quality printing) **2** *verb* to make a first rough plan of a document; ***contract is still being drafted*** *or* ***is still in the drafting stage; she was asked to draft the blurb for the series;*** **drafting machine** = piece of equipment used in a drawing office, with rules, scales, set squares, a head for attaching a plotting pen, etc., all attached to an angled drawing board

draftsman *or* **draughtsman** *noun* person who draws plans, especially architectural plans

drag *verb* to move (a mouse) while holding the button down, so moving an image or icon on screen

dragon's blood *noun* red pigment used to cover etching plates to protect the parts which are not to be etched

drama *noun* plays (performed in the theatre *or* on radio *or* on TV); a single play; ***they are publishing a contemporary drama series;*** **drama critic** = reviewer for a newspaper who writes reviews of plays

dramatize *verb* to adapt for the theatre; ***the novel was dramatized by J. Smith***

dramatization *noun* act of adapting for the theatre

draughtsman *see* DRAFTSMAN

draw *verb* **(a)** to make a picture using a pencil *or* pen; ***she has drawn the designs for the new covers; the maps have all been drawn by hand*** **(b)** to pull; ***type which has not been secured may be drawn out of the forme by the printing rollers***

drawdown *noun* way of comparing two printing inks

> COMMENT: the inks are spread on paper with a spatula and their shades and opacity are compared when dry

drawer *noun* **(a)** person who draws **(b)** compartment in a piece of furniture which can be pulled out; ***the planchest has six drawers; the manuscripts are kept in the bottom drawer of the filing cabinet***

drawing *noun* picture which has been drawn by an artist; ***the book is illustrated with line drawings by the author;*** **drawing board** = large flat surface, on which an artist *or* designer can draw (sometimes with an adjustable sloping top); **drawing office** = office where plans are prepared; **drawing paper** = white cartridge paper, used by artists

drawing program software that allows the user to draw and design on screen; *see also* PAINT PROGRAM

drawing tools *plural noun* range of functions in a paint program that allows the user to draw; normally displayed as icons in a toolbar, the drawing tools might include a circle-draw, line-draw and freehand drawing tools

drawn-in *adjective* binding style, where the cords are pulled through holes in the cover boards and then glued down

drawn-on cover *noun* binding style where the cover is glued directly onto a book block made of one or more signatures sewn or glued together; **cover drawn on solid** = cover glued onto endpapers

draw up *verb* to write a document; ***to draw up a contract*** *or* ***an agreement; to draw up the acknowledgements list***

dressing *noun* **(a)** making ready printing cylinders by packing, to change the density of the impression **(b)** loading various fonts into a phototypesetter

drier *see* DRYER

drill *verb* to make holes in the margins of leaves for loose-leaf binding; **drilled and strung** = (book) which has been bound by making holes through each leaf (or signatures near the folds), and then attaching them together with a thread

drive 1 *noun* **(a)** energy *or* energetic way of working; **sales drive** = vigorous effort to increase sales **(b)** part of a machine which makes other parts work; **disk drive** = part of a computer which makes the disk spin round in order to store information on it **2** *verb* to make a machine work; to make a car *or* lorry, etc. go in a certain direction; **driven roller** = roller in a printing press which is driven by the motor, and which pulls the web through the press

drive out *verb* to expand the number of pages in a book by increasing the spaces between words or lines

drop 1 *noun* **(a)** fall; **drop guides** = bars at the side of a paper feed which place the sheets in the correct position **(b)** amount of space left when a text starts lower down the page than normal; ***there should be a 10mm drop at the beginning of the chapter*** *or* ***a 10mm chapter drop;*** **drop cap** *or* **drop initial** = large size initial letter at the beginning of a chapter, which runs down over several lines of text (typically a two-line drop initial, which takes up two lines of text); **drop folio** = page number printed at the foot of a page **(c) drop shipment** = delivery of a large order from the manufacturer direct to a customer's shop or warehouse without going through an agent or wholesaler; the invoice may be sent to the agent, though **2** *verb* **(a)** to fall; ***sales have dropped by 10%*** *or* ***have dropped 10%*** **(b)** to bring down the text, leaving a blank space; ***the chapter entry***

should be dropped six lines; **dropped (chapter) heads** = chapter heads (the first page of each chapter) which begin several lines down the page throughout a book **(c)** to unlock the forme after printing, so as to release the type which is then ready for distribution **(d)** to decide not to do something any more; ***we decided to drop the title from the Spring list; the education committee have dropped our Geography course from their list of adoptions*** **(e) drop ship** = to deliver a large order direct to a customer without going through an agent or distributor, though the invoice for the shipment may be sent to the agent

drop in *verb* to put a block of text or an illustration into a space left in a typeset page

drop-out *noun* **drop-out blue** = special blue pencil used to write on bromides or on other artwork, which does not reproduce when filmed; **drop-out halftone** = halftone which has no dots on the highlighted sections which are just white paper

drum *noun* large cylinder; **drum plotter** = computer output device that consists of a movable pen and a piece of paper around a drum that can be rotated, creating patterns and text when both are moved in various ways

dry 1 *adjective* **dry end** = the end of a fourdrinier papermaking machine where the wet web of paper is passed between hot rollers to dry it; **dry indicator test** = test of the resistance of paper to liquids; **dry ink** = powdered ink used in some photocopiers; **dry litho** = offset plate which does not need dampening to distribute the ink; **dry mounting** = way of mounting photographs so that they are flat, by using adhesives which stick when pressed; **dry offset** = letterpress process, using a letterpress plate on an offset litho press; **dry point** = method of etching with a needle directly onto a copper plate without using acid (used for retouching etched plates); **dry proofing** = method (such as Cromalin) of making colour proofs using dry inks **2** *verb* to remove wetness from something; **drying cylinder** = heated cylinder over which newly made sheets of paper pass to be dried; **drying time** = the time taken for ink to dry on a printed sheet

dryer *or* **drier** *noun* **(a)** machine which dries, especially one for drying ink **(b)** ingredient of ink which speeds up the drying process

dry-transfer lettering *or* **dry-transfer process** *noun* letters or other symbols which are on the back of a sheet of plastic and can be transferred to paper by rubbing (such as Letraset); **dry-transfer sheet** = sheet of letters used for the dry-transfer process

DTP = DESKTOP PUBLISHING the design, layout and printing of documents using special software, a desktop computer and a printer

dual pricing *noun* giving different prices to two books which are substantially the same (as one price for a book sold through retail outlets and a lower price for the same book, with possibly a different cover, sold by mail-order); *compare* PARTIAL REMAINDERING

duck-foot quotes *noun* brackets « and », used in Europe to indicate speech, when in English inverted commas would be used; *also called* GUILLEMETS

duct *noun* container for ink in a printing machine

duct roller *or* **ductor roller** *noun* roller which takes ink and supplies it to the distributing rollers which ink the forme

due *adjective* **(a)** owed; **to fall due** *or* **to become due** = to be ready for payment; **bill due on May 1st** = bill which has to be paid on May 1st; **balance due to us** = amount owed to us which should be paid **(b)** expected to arrive; ***the books are due to be delivered on Tuesday*** **(c) in due form** = written in the correct legal form; ***receipt in due form; contract drawn up in due form*** **(d)** caused by; ***the delay was due to a strike at the printing works; the company pays the wages of staff who are absent due to illness***

dues *noun* books for which orders have been taken, but which cannot be supplied until fresh stock arrives (either in the case of subscription orders recorded for a new title, or orders for a backlist title which is being reprinted)

duke *noun* old paper size (178 x 143), used for notepaper

dull *adjective* not shiny; **dull-coated paper** = coated paper which has a matt finish; (NOTE: **dull-coated paper** is preferred in US English; British English is **matt art paper**)

dummy *noun* imitation product to test the reaction of potential customers to its design, such as a book with a cover, but blank pages or with only a few specimen pages showing layouts; **dummy pack** = empty pack for display; **bulking dummy** = dummy book, made with the correct paper and binding, to test its weight, bulk and overall appearance

dump *verb* **to dump goods on a market** = to get rid of large quantities of excess goods cheaply in an overseas market

dump bin *noun* display container like a large box which is filled with goods for sale

dumping *noun* act of getting rid of excess goods cheaply in an overseas market; ***the government has passed anti-dumping legislation; dumping of cheap paperbacks on the European market***

duodecimo (12mo) *noun* book made from a sheet which is folded to give twelve leaves or twenty-four pages

duotone = DUPLEX HALFTONE

duplex *noun* **(a)** paper made of two sheets of different colour *or* finish, stuck together back to back; **duplex cut** = different widths of paper cut from the same reel; **duplex halftone** *or* **duotone** = two-colour halftone printed from a monochrome original, the screen angle of each negative being different (one giving dark shades, the other light) **(b)** communications channel permitting simultaneous transmission in both directions

duplicate 1 *noun & adjective* copy; ***he sent me the duplicate of the contract; we need a set of duplicate film for the Hong Kong reprint;*** **duplicate plates** = plates made from the original plates; **duplicate receipt** *or* **duplicate of a receipt** = copy of a receipt; **in duplicate** = with a copy; **receipt in duplicate** = two copies of a receipt; ***to print an invoice in duplicate*** **2** *verb* **to duplicate a film** *or* **a letter** = to make a copy of a film *or* letter

duplicating *noun* copying; **duplicating machine** = machine which makes copies of documents; **duplicating paper** = special paper to be used in a duplicating machine

duplication *noun* copying of documents

duplicator *noun* machine which makes copies of documents; **spirit duplicator** = machine which prints copies from a special stencil, the ink on the stencil being transferred to the copy paper by an alcohol solution; **duplicator paper** = absorbent paper used in a spirit duplicator

durable *adjective* which will last a long time; ***this cover material is not as durable as the previous batch***

dust cover *or* **dust jacket** *or* **dust wrapper** *noun* paper cover wrapped round a case-bound book; (NOTE: the term **dust wrapper** is used in the secondhand book trade, usually abbreviated in catalogues to **d.w.**)

dutiable *adjective* **dutiable goods** *or* **dutiable items** = goods on which a customs duty has to be paid

duty *noun* tax which has to be paid; **ad valorem duty** = duty calculated on the sales value of the goods; **customs duty** *or* **import duty** = tax on goods imported into a country; **stamp duty** = tax on legal documents (such as the conveyance of a property to a new owner)

Dvorak *noun* special computer keyboard which is adapted to the fingers

d.w. = DUST WRAPPER

dwell *noun* short time during which a hand-worked press is in contact with the paper, or when a blocking tool is in contact with cover material

dye 1 *noun* colouring substance, used to give a material a permanent colour; **dye transfer print** = full-colour print made from artwork direct onto coated paper, used for display material where only a few copies are required (the artwork is separated into three colours and gelatin matrices are made which absorb the dye and transfer it to the paper) **2** *verb* to give a material a permanent colour

dyeline *noun* **dyeline process** = cheap method of proofing where special coated paper is contacted to film and then developed (usually in blue or black); **dyeline paper** *or* **diazo paper** = specially treated paper used in the dyeline copying process; **dyeline print** = blueprint, a proof in the form of a print taken directly from film (same as an ozalid)

Ee

E13B font used in magnetic ink printing on cheques

e. & o.e. = ERRORS AND OMISSIONS EXCEPTED words written on an invoice or estimate to show that the company has no responsibility for mistakes in the invoice

EAN = EUROPEAN ARTICLE NUMBER form of bar code used in Europe

ear *noun* space at the side of the masthead on a newspaper, used for advertising

early selling *noun* selling of a book by a bookseller before the publication date set by the publisher

earmark *verb* to reserve for a special purpose; ***the board has earmarked funds for the encyclopaedia project; the grant is earmarked for technical course development***

earpiece *noun* small advertisement placed at the side of the masthead on a newspaper

earth station *noun* dish antenna and circuitry used for reception of data transmissions by satellite

easer *noun* substance added to ink to make it more fluid and less sticky

ECGD = EXPORT CREDIT GUARANTEE DEPARTMENT

edge *noun* **(a)** side of a flat thing; for a book, one of the three sides where the paper has been trimmed; ***the edges of the book are coloured; the printer has printed the figures right to the edge of the printout;*** **edge planing** = cutting the edge of a printing plate; **gilt edge** = foredge which has been covered with gold leaf; **sprinkled edge** = foredge which has been decorated with splashes of ink **(b)** advantage; ***having a local office gives us a competitive edge over Smith Ltd;*** **to have the edge on a rival company** = to be slightly more profitable *or* to have slightly larger share of the market than a rival

EDI = ELECTRONIC DATA INTERCHANGE system of sending commercial data over a network or telephone line using an electronic mail system

edit *verb* **(a)** to copy edit *or* to prepare a text for the printer *or* to make corrections to a text; ***she is editing the text on screen; the novel needed a lot of editing before it could be sent to the printer*** **(b)** to annotate *or* to add notes to an edition of a text; ***an edition of 'Macbeth' edited by Professor White*** **(c)** to be in charge of a newspaper *or* magazine *or* journal; ***he edits the 'Journal of Advanced Physics'*** **(d)** to make changes to a text; ***the review needs careful editing before we can quote it in our publicity material;*** **edit key** key which starts a function that makes an editor easier to use; **edit window** = area of the screen in which the user can display and edit text or graphics; **to edit down** = to reduce the extent of a text by cutting in the editorial department; ***they edited the autobiography down from 1,000 pages of single-spaced typescript to make a 250 page paperback;*** **to edit something out** = to delete something from the text; ***he asked the copy editing department to edit out all references to the Prime Minister***

editing *noun* action of preparing a manuscript for publication; ***the book is with the editing department; the editing of the text will take at least six months; can the editing be done directly on the screen?;*** **editing symbol** = character on microfilm to aid positioning, cutting and editing of the frames; **editing terminal** = computer terminal on which text is shown which can be edited

edition *noun* quantity of copies of a book printed and bound at the same time; ***the book has been published in an edition of 20,000; the African edition has to be ready for October; we are planning a paperback edition in eighteen months' time; the bibliography on the reverse of the title page shows six previous editions;*** **edition binding** = normal mass-produced binding style where the book is cased, with a plain cloth binding, usually covered with a jacket; **first edition** = first printing of a book, which may become rare and collectable; ***he has a collection of first editions;*** **limited edition** = edition of which only a certain number has been printed (usually for collectors); **numbered edition** = limited edition where each copy has a number written in it

editio princeps *noun* first edition

editor *noun* **(a)** person in charge of a newspaper *or* a section of a newspaper; ***the editor of the 'Times';*** **the City editor** = business *or* finance editor of a British newspaper **(b) copy editor** = person who prepares a manuscript for the printer; **desk editor** = specialist editor who only prepares manuscripts in a certain subject; ***we are looking for a desk editor in biological sciences*** **(c)** person in charge of a list in a publishing house; **acquisitions editor** *or* US **acquiring editor** = person who builds up a list by buying books *or* rights to books from packagers *or* other publishers; **commissioning editor** = person who asks authors to write books for the part of the publisher's list for which he or she is responsible; **children's editor** = person responsible for publishing books for children; **science editor** = editor responsible for a science list **(d)** person in charge of a learned journal; ***he is the editor of the 'Journal of New Science'*** **(e) text editor** = piece of software used to enter and correct text *or* modify programs under development

editorial 1 *adjective* referring to an editor; **editorial board** = group of editors (on a newspaper, etc.); **editorial duties** = the work of an editor or copy editor; **editorial staff** = (i) all staff working on the text of books (including commissioning editors and copy editors); (ii) all the staff working on the text of a newspaper or magazine (including the journalists and in-house editors) **2** *noun* **(a)** main article in a newspaper, written by the editor, expressing the newspaper's official point of view **(b)** text matter in a magazine which has been written by journalists (as opposed to advertising matter) **(c) editorial (department)** = copy editing department; ***the MS has been in editorial for six weeks***

editorship *noun* post of editor (especially on a newspaper)

EDP = ELECTRONIC DATA PROCESSING

educational *adjective* referring to education; **educational contractor** *or* **school contractor** = company which has a contract to supply a school with books, stationery and other items; **educational list** = group of books published by one publisher for the educational market; **educational publisher** = publisher who publishes books for use in schools *or* colleges; **educational representative** = publisher's representative who visits schools and colleges to show books to teachers; ***they have a strong educational salesforce; a small educational publisher is for sale***

effect 1 *noun* **(a)** result; **terms of a contract which take effect** *or* **come into effect from January 1st** = terms which start to operate on January 1st; **prices are increased by 10% with effect from January 1st** = new prices will apply from January 1st; **to remain in effect** = to continue to be applied; **we have made provision to this effect** = we have put into the contract terms which will produce this result **(b)** meaning; **clause to the effect that** = clause which means that; ***the editor made an announcement to the effect that the magazine would cease publication in two weeks' time*** **2** *verb* to carry out; **to effect a payment** = to make a payment; **to effect customs clearance** = to clear something through customs; **to effect a settlement between two parties** = to bring two parties together and make them agree to a settlement

effective *adjective* **(a) effective date** = date on which a rule *or* a contract starts to be applied; **clause effective as from January 1st** = clause which starts to be applied on January 1st **(b)** which works *or* which produces results; ***advertising in the Sunday papers is the most effective way of selling;*** *see* COST-EFFECTIVE

effectiveness *noun* working *or* producing results; ***I doubt the effectiveness of advertising learned journals on television;*** *see* COST-EFFECTIVENESS

effort *noun* using the mind or body to do something; ***the salesmen made great efforts to increase sales; thanks to the efforts of the finance department, overheads have been reduced; if we make one more effort, we should clear the backlog of orders***

EFL = ENGLISH AS A FOREIGN LANGUAGE

e.g. *abbreviation for the Latin phrase* 'exempli gratia', meaning for example *or* such as; ***the contract is valid in some countries (e.g. France and Belgium) but not in others***

EGA = ENHANCED GRAPHICS ADAPTER *(in an IBM PC)* popular standard for medium-resolution colour graphics display at a maximum resolution of 640x350 pixels

eggshell finish *noun* dull smooth finish to paper which has not been calendered; **eggshell antique** = bulky antique paper with an eggshell finish

Egyptian *noun* typeface with a slab serif

EIA = ELECTRONIC INDUSTRIES ASSOCIATION

eight to pica leads *noun* pieces of thin metal leading, eight of which form one pica

eighteenmo (18mo) *noun* old term for a sheet folded to make eighteen leaves (i.e. thirty-six pages)

electro *or* **electrotype** *noun* type of printing plate made from a mould and coated with copper or nickel

electronic *adjective* **electronic book** = term that describes a multimedia title; **electronic composition** = text manipulation by computer leading to automatic typesetting and page make-up; **electronic data interchange (EDI)** = system of sending commercial data over a network or telephone line using an electronic mail system; **electronic data processing (EDP)** = selecting and examining data stored in a computer to produce information; **electronic editing** = the electronic selecting and assembling of audio and visual material; there are no mechanical splices, lifts or reprints; **electronic keyboard** = keyboard that generates characters electronically in response to a key being pressed (rather than by mechanical means); **electronic editing** = electronic selecting and assembling of audio and visual material; there are no mechanical splices, lifts or reprints; **electronic mail** *or* **email** = sending and receiving messages over a telephone network, usually using a bulletin board; **electronic page composition (EPC)** = system comprising colour scanning, retouching and colour correction, proofing, page assembly and output of films by computer methods; **electronic point of sale (EPOS)** = system where sales are charged automatically to a customer's credit card and stock is controlled by the shop's computer; **electronic publishing** = use of desktop publishing packages and laser printers to produce printed matter *or* using computers to write and display information, such as viewdata; **electronic register control** = control of the register on web-fed presses, using electronic devices; **electronic rights** = right to publish and sell copyright material, using electronic devices such as CD-ROM, viewdata, teletext, etc.; **electronic scanner** = machine which produces colour separations by scanning colour artwork; **electronic typewriter** = typewriter using an electronic keyboard linked, via a buffer, to an electrically driven printing mechanism, also with the facility to send *or* receive character data from a computer

electronically *adverb* referring to operations using electronic methods; ***the text is electronically transmitted to an outside typesetter***

electronic publishing *noun* **(a)** (i) use of desktop publishing packages and laser printers to produce printed matter; (ii) using computers to write and display information, such as viewdata **(b)** publishing information selected from a database, either on-line (where the user pays for it on a per-page inspection basis) or as a CD-ROM

electronics *plural noun* applying the scientific study of electrons to produce manufactured products, such as computers, calculators or telephones

electrophotography *noun* general term for methods of recording optical images by means of light acting on a photoconducting insulator, static charge and an image created by a toner which is then fixed by heat or pressure

electrostatic printing *noun* copying process, where the surface of the paper is charged electrically and powdered ink is spread on it; the ink adheres to the charged surfaces and is then heated to fix it to the paper

electrotype *noun* type of printing plate made from a mould and coated with copper or nickel

element *noun* one part of a whole (such as a single piece of text or one illustration for a book)

elephant *noun* former book size, 23 x 14 inches; American book size, about 24 inches high; *see also* DOUBLE ELEPHANT

elhi *or* **El-Hi** *noun US* publishing for the elementary and high school markets; ***an elhi publisher; he has written a math course for the elhi market***

eliminate *verb* to remove; ***a spelling check program does not totally eliminate the need to proof read a text; using a computer should eliminate all possibility of error***

elision *noun* omitting a character which is not essential to understanding the meaning of a series of characters (as 1925 - 30, instead of 1925 - 1930)

elite *noun* typewriter typeface, giving twelve characters to the inch

ellipsis *noun* a series of three dots, used to show that part of a text is missing

Elmendorf tear test *noun* test carried out in paper mills to check the resistance of paper to tear (a slit is made in a sample of paper held in clamps and the force needed to completely tear the paper is measured)

ELT = ENGLISH LANGUAGE TEACHING

em *noun* **(a)** measure of width of type, equivalent to the point size used: one em in 8pt is 8pts wide **(b) pica em** = measure of width of type equivalent to 12 point or pica; **em dash** *or* **em rule** *or* **em score** = long dash (equivalent of 12pt); **em quad** = square piece of metal giving a space which is one em wide (also known as a mutton); **ems per hour** = rate of production of characters from a machine *or* operator; *see also* EMMAGE, EN

COMMENT: the em is taken as the width of a capital M which varies according to the point size of type. The pica em has been standardized at 4.23mm wide, which is equivalent to 12 points. It is also called mutton when referring to the width of the letter M

E-mail *or* **email** = ELECTRONIC MAIL system of sending messages to and receiving messages from other users on a network or over the Internet

embedded code *noun* sections *or* routines written in machine code, inserted into a high-level program to speed up *or* perform a special function; **embedded command** = printing command (such as indicating that text should be in italic) which is keyboarded into the text, and which appears on the screen but does not appear in the final printed document

emboldening *noun* making a word print in bold type

emboss *verb* to press a mould on the underside of something so that the surface stands out in relief; ***the address is embossed at the top of each piece of notepaper; the book has an embossed leather binding***

emerald *noun* former type size, equivalent to $6\frac{1}{2}$pt

emmage *noun* total area of the type, expressed in ems

emulsion *noun* light-sensitive coating on photographic film *or* paper; **emulsion side** = coated dull side of film which is placed in contact with the emulsion side of another film or plate, to give a clear image (for litho, printers normally require wrong reading positives, viewed from the emulsion side)

en *noun* measure of width of type which is half the size of an em; **en dash** *or* **en rule** *or* **en score** = short dash (like a hyphen), as long as an en, showing that two words *or* figures are joined together; **en quad** = space that is half the width of an em quad space, also called a nut; *see also* EM, ENNAGE

enamel paper *noun* paper which has been coated with a layer of clay and size to make it shiny and smooth; (NOTE: used especially in US English; GB English is **coated paper**)

encapsulate *verb* **(a)** to enclose perfume or chemicals in tiny capsules in paper **(b)** to enclose a printed sheet between two layers of clear plastic (used for maps, restaurant menus, book covers, etc.)

encapsulated *adjective* (something) contained within something else; **encapsulated PostScript (EPS)** = PostScript commands that describe an image *or* page contained within a file that can be placed within a graphics *or* DTP program; **encapsulated PostScript file (EPSF)** = file that contains encapsulated PostScript instructions together with a preview bitmap image

> COMMENT: an encapsulated PostScript file often contains a preview bitmap image of the page in TIFF or PICT format that can be easily displayed by a graphics application

enclose *verb* to put something inside an envelope with a letter; ***to enclose an invoice with a letter; I am enclosing a copy of the contract; letter enclosing a cheque; please find the cheque enclosed herewith***

enclosure *noun* document enclosed with a letter; ***letter with enclosures***

encrypt *verb* to convert plaintext to a secure coded form, using a cipher system; ***the encrypted text can be sent along ordinary telephone lines***

encryption *noun* conversion of plaintext to a secure coded form by means of a cipher system

encyclopaedia *noun* **(a)** reference book (sometimes in many volumes) containing articles on all subjects of human knowledge, usually presented in alphabetical order, with an index **(b)** reference book containing articles on a single subject, arranged usually in alphabetical order; ***a gardening encyclopaedia; the encyclopaedia of sport***

> COMMENT: an encyclopaedia is a book where the terms and concepts are explained, but not always defined, while a dictionary is a book where the words are defined, but not necessarily explained. The title 'dictionary' is often used in place of 'encyclopaedia': a 'Dictionary of Gardening' is probably an encyclopaedia, since it may give details of how to grow plants, rather than explaining what each plant or process is. This present dictionary has many encyclopaedic sections, such as this one

end 1 *noun* final point *or* last part; ***at the end of the contract period;*** **at the end of six months** = after six months have passed; **end of line** = LINE ENDING **end even** = making sure that the last line in a text being set is a full line; **end product** = manufactured product, made at the end of a production process; **end user** = person who will use a device *or* program *or* product; ***the company is creating a computer with the end user in mind*** **2** *verb* to finish; ***the distribution agreement ends in July; the chairman ended the discussion by getting up and walking out of the meeting***

end in *verb* to have as a result; ***the AGM ended in a fight between rival groups of shareholders; the libel case ended in an apology from the editor***

ending *noun* **(a)** action of coming to an end *or* of stopping something **(b)** end part of something; **line endings** = last words on each line of text, which may be need to be hyphenated, with the second part of the word carried over to the next line

end matter *noun* supplements *or* indexes *or* appendices, etc., which come at the back of the book, after the main text; (NOTE: US English is **back matter**)

endnotes *noun* notes which are printed at the end of a chapter (as opposed to footnotes which are printed at the bottom of the page)

endpapers *or* **endsheets** *noun* pages of thicker paper at the front and back of a book, glued to the first and last text pages and then glued to the cover; ***the limited edition has marbled endpapers***

engine-sized paper *noun* paper made from pulp to which size has been added (as opposed to tub-sized paper, where the size is added after the paper has been made)

English *noun* type size, no longer used, equivalent to the modern 14 point

English finish *noun US* type of smooth calendered paper finish, inferior in quality to coated paper; (NOTE: GB English is **imitation art paper**)

engrave *verb* to make an image on a metal plate by etching (burning away the surface with acid)

engraver *noun* person who engraves plates for printing; **engraver's proof** = proof of an engraving *or* line drawing

engraving *noun* **(a)** action of preparing a printing surface by etching the surface of a metal plate **(b)** illustration made by printing from an engraved plate

> COMMENT: the term 'engraving' does not mean the same in printing as it does in fine art. An artist engraves a plate by cutting fine lines on it with a burin (a type of sharp needle); the image is formed by putting ink into the cut lines, and wiping excess ink off the flat top surface. In printing, the opposite is the case, as photoengraving etches (with an acid) the non-printing surfaces, leaving the top surface to carry the ink. Photoengraving can be used either for reproducing line drawings (where tones are represented by lines of ink) or halftones (where the tones are conveyed by many little dots of different sizes)

enhance *verb* to make better *or* clearer; **enhanced dot matrix** = clearer character *or* graphics printout (using smaller dots and more dots per inch); **enhanced graphics adapter (EGA)** = popular standard for medium-resolution colour graphics display at a maximum

enlarge *verb* to make (a photograph) larger

enlargement *noun* (i) making larger; (ii) amount by which a photograph is made large; (iii) larger version of a photograph; ***an enlargement of the photograph was used to provide better detail***

enlarger *noun* device which makes photographic prints which are much larger than the negative

ennage *noun* total area of type, expressed in ens

entitle *verb* **(a)** to give a title to (a book); ***he is the author of a book entitled 'Decline and Fall'*** **(b)** to give the right to something; **he is**

entitled to a discount = he has the right to be given a discount

entitlement *noun* right; **holiday entitlement** = number of days' paid holiday which a worker has the right to take; ***she has not used up all her holiday entitlement***

entry *noun* **(a)** information put into a computer **(b)** item in a dictionary *or* encyclopaedia *or* catalogue; ***the dictionary has 25,000 entries; each entry has to be coded before typesetting can begin*** **(c)** written information put in an accounts ledger; **credit entry** *or* **debit entry** = entry on the credit *or* debit side of an account; **to make an entry in a ledger** = to write in details of a deal **(d)** act of going in; place where you can go in; **entry visa** = visa allowing someone to go into a country; **multiple entry visa** = entry visa which allows someone to enter a country as often as he likes

envelope *noun* folded flat paper cover for sending letters; **airmail envelope** = very light envelope for airmail letters; **aperture envelope** = envelope with a hole in it so that the address on the letter inside can be seen; **bankers envelope** = rectangular envelope with the flap along the top; **window envelope** = envelope with a hole covered with film so that the address on the letter inside can be seen; **sealed envelope** = envelope where the flap has been stuck down to close it; **unsealed envelope** = envelope where the flap has been pushed into the back of the envelope and not stuck down; **a stamped addressed envelope** = an envelope with your own address written on it and a stamp stuck on it to pay for return postage; ***please send a stamped addressed envelope for further details and our latest catalogue***

EPC = ELECTRONIC PAGE COMPOSITION

ephemera *noun* small printed item (such as a poster *or* card *or* ticket) which is intended to be thrown away, but which some people collect

epigraph *noun* quotation used at the beginning of a book, as part of the prelims

epos *or* **EPOS** = ELECTRONIC POINT OF SALE

EPS = ENCAPSULATED POSTSCRIPT digital file format used to save mono and colour images

EPSF = ENCAPSULATED POSTSCRIPT (FILE)

equal 1 *adjective* exactly the same; **equal opportunities programme** = programme to avoid discrimination in employment; (NOTE: the US equivalent is **affirmative action program**) **2** *verb* to be the same as; ***production this month has equalled our best month ever;*** **equals sign** *or* **equal sign** = printed sign (=) used to show that two things are equal

equally *adverb* to the same extent; ***costs will be shared equally between the two parties; they were both equally responsible for the disastrous launch***

equip *verb* to provide with machinery; ***to equip a printing works with new machinery; the office is fully equipped with word-processors***

equipment *noun* machinery and furniture required to make a factory or office work; ***office equipment*** *or* ***business equipment; office equipment supplier; office equipment catalogue;*** **capital equipment** = equipment which a factory *or* office uses to work; **heavy equipment** = large machines, such as for making cars or for printing

erase *verb* to delete something (a pencil mark, an entry on a computer); ***the whole text of the file has been erased; if a disk is reformatted, any data on the disk will be erased***

erratum *noun* mistake in a printed book; ***the reviewer pointed out several errata;*** **erratum slip** *or* **errata slip** = small piece of paper inserted into a book with corrections to important mistakes which have been noticed since the book was printed; (NOTE: plural of **erratum** is **errata**)

erroneous *adjective* wrong *or* not correct; ***an erroneous reading of the text***

error *noun* mistake; ***he made an error in calculating the total; the secretary must have made a typing error;*** **clerical error** = mistake made in an office; **computer error** = mistake made by a computer; **rejection error** = error by a scanner which is unable to read a character and leaves a blank; **scanning error** = error introduced while scanning an image; ***a wrinkled or torn page may be the cause of scanning errors;*** **substitution error** = error made by a scanner which mistakes one character *or* letter for another; **typographical error** = mistake in printing (i.e. using the wrong typeface *or* type size, etc.); **margin of error** = number of mistakes which can be accepted in a document *or* in a calculation; **errors and omissions excepted (e. & o.e.)** = words written on an estimate or invoice to show that the company has no responsibility for mistakes in the invoice; **error rate** = number of mistakes per thousand entries *or* per page; **in error** *or* **by error** = by mistake; ***the letter was sent to the London office in error***

escalator clause *noun* clause in a contract which allows for increased royalties as sales increase

> COMMENT: in such a clause, the royalty may only be 5% for the first printing of 2000 copies, but will increase to 7.5% for the next 2000 copies, then to 10% and finally 12.5% for sales beyond (say) 10,000 copies

escape *noun* getting away from a difficult situation; **escape clause** = clause in a contract which allows one of the parties to avoid carrying out the terms of the contract under certain conditions

esparto *noun* type of thick smooth paper made from a South American grass, which is very good for writing or printing, or as the body in coated papers, but is liable to tear and is now not often used

essay *noun* short piece of prose about a certain subject

essayist *or* **essay writer** *noun* person who writes essays

establish *verb* to set up *or* to make *or* to open; ***the company has established a branch in Australia; the business was established in Scotland in 1823; it is a young company - it has been established for only four years;*** **to establish oneself in business** = to become successful in a new business

establishment *noun* **(a)** commercial business; ***he runs an important printing establishment*** **(b) establishment charges** = cost of people and property in a company's accounts **(c)** number of people working in a company; **to be on the establishment** = to be a full-time employee; *see also* STAB **office with an establishment of fifteen** = office with a budgeted staff of fifteen

estate *noun* property left by a dead person; ***the royalties are payable to the author's estate***

estimate 1 *noun* **(a)** calculation of probable cost *or* size *or* time of something; **rough estimate** = very approximate calculation; **at a conservative estimate** = calculation which probably underestimates the final figure; ***their turnover has risen by at least 20% in the last year, and that is a conservative estimate;*** **these figures are only an estimate** = these are not the final accurate figures; ***can you give me an estimate of how much time was spent on the job?*** **(b)** calculation of how much something is likely to cost in the future, given to a client so as to get him to make an order; ***before we can give the order we must have an estimate of the total costs involved; to ask a typesetter for an estimate for typesetting 100,000 words of text;*** **to put in an estimate** = to give someone a written calculation of the probable costs of carrying out a job; ***three firms put in estimates for the printing job*** **2** *verb* **(a)** to calculate the probable cost *or* size *or* time of something; ***to estimate that it will cost £1m*** *or* ***to estimate costs at £1m; we estimate that this year's sales will be down 30% on last year's*** **(b) to estimate for a job** = to state in writing the future costs of carrying out a piece of work so that a client can make an order; ***three firms estimated for the fitting of the offices***

estimated *adjective* calculated approximately; ***estimated sales in the first year should cover all originating costs***

estimation *noun* approximate calculation

estimator *noun* person whose job is to calculate estimates for carrying out work

etc. and so on; ***the import duty is to be paid on luxury items including cars, watches, etc.;*** (NOTE: sometimes printed as **&c.**)

etch *verb* to use an acid to remove selected layers of metal from a metal printing plate leaving the printing surface untouched

etching *noun* illustration printed from a plate which has been etched

> COMMENT: etching consists of drawing the design on metal with etching ink, then exposing the metal to acid (the etching solution)

Ethernet standard defining the protocol and signalling method of a local area network

et seq. *abbreviation for the Latin phrase 'et sequens' meaning* and following

Europallet *noun* standardized pallet (120 x 100cm) used in Europe

European *adjective* referring to Europe; **European article number (EAN)** = form of bar code used in Europe; **European rights** = right to publish and sell a book in Europe

> COMMENT: the term 'Europe' has several meanings; geographically it refers to countries from Russia to the Atlantic. In publishing terms, it is often used to refer to countries from Germany and Austria to the Atlantic, and may not include the countries of Eastern Europe which have separate rights and copyright laws. Finally, in discussions between British and American publishers, the term 'Europe' is used to mean countries in Western Europe, but excluding the United Kingdom (and sometimes Ireland). This is particularly relevant where an American publisher licenses a British publisher to publish a book in British English, but retains the right to sell the original American version in Europe outside the UK: in this case, such a book may well legally be sold in the UK, in spite of the British publisher's exclusivity, because EU regulations encourage the free trade in goods within the Community

evaluate *verb* to calculate a value

evaluation *noun* calculation of value; **job evaluation** = examining different jobs within a company to see what skills and qualifications are needed to carry them out

even *adjective* (number) which can be divided by two (2, 4, 6, 8, etc.); **even pages** = pages with even numbers (even pages are always left-hand pages); **even small caps** *or* **even smalls** = small caps used for a whole word, without a full capital being used for the first letter; **even working** = number of printed pages printed in even sections without oddments; usually a number which can be divided by 16 or 32, but sometimes calculated in multiples of 24 or 48. 320 pages is an even working: 328 is an uneven working

ex- *preposition* **(a)** out of *or* from; **price ex warehouse** = price for a product which is to be collected from the manufacturer's or agent's warehouse and so does not include delivery; **price ex works** *or* **ex factory** = price not including transport from the maker's factory **(b) ex-directory** = telephone number which is not printed in the telephone book; ***he has an ex-directory number***

exceed *verb* to be more than; ***discount not exceeding 15%; last year costs exceeded 20% of income for the first time;*** **he has exceeded his credit limit** = he has borrowed more money than he is allowed

except *preposition & conjunction* not including; ***VAT is levied on all goods and services except books, newspapers and children's clothes; sales are rising in all markets except the Far East***

excepted *adverb* not including; **errors and omissions excepted** = note on an invoice to show that the company has no responsibility for mistakes in the invoice

exception *noun* item which is not included; **exception dictionary** = store of words which do not follow normal rules for hyphenation and have special word break requirements, used for word-processing and photocomposition; **exception listing** = listing of items which are not included in a computer program; **exception report** = report which only gives items which do not fit in the general rule *or* pattern

exceptional *adjective* not usual *or* different; **exceptional items** = items in a balance sheet which do not appear there each year

excerpt *noun* extract, a piece taken from a longer text; ***the paper has quoted excerpts from the review***

excise 1 *noun* **(a) excise duty** = tax on certain goods produced in a country (such as alcohol) **(b) Customs and Excise** *or* **Excise Department** = government department which deals with taxes on imports and with VAT **2** *verb* to cut out; ***please excise all references to the strike from the minutes***

exclamation mark *noun* printed sign (!) used to show surprise; (NOTE: in setting Spanish, two exclamation marks are required: one upside down at the beginning of the phrase, the other at the end of it)

exclude *verb* to keep out *or* not to include; ***certain territories are excluded from the market; damage by fire is excluded from the policy***

excluding *preposition* not including; ***all salesmen, excluding those living in London, can claim expenses for attending the sales conference***

exclusion *noun* act of not including; **exclusion clause** = clause in an insurance policy *or* warranty which says which items are not covered

exclusive *adjective* **(a) exclusive agent** = agent who is the only agent for the publisher's products in a certain territory; **exclusive agreement** = agreement making a person sole agent for a product in a market; **exclusive right to market a product** = right to be the only company to market the product in a certain area **(b) exclusive of** = not including; ***all payments are exclusive of tax; the invoice is exclusive of VAT***

exclusivity *noun* exclusive right to market a product in a certain area; ***the contract gives the British publisher exclusivity in the UK and Commonwealth***

execute *verb* to carry out (an order)

execution *noun* carrying out of an order; **stay of execution** = temporary stopping of a legal order; ***the court granted the company a two-week stay of execution***

executive 1 *adjective* which puts decisions into action; **executive committee** = committee which runs a society *or* a club; **executive director** = director who actually works full-time in the company; **executive powers** = right to put decisions into actions; ***he was made managing director with full executive powers over the European operation*** **2** *noun* person in a business who takes decisions *or* manager *or* director; ***sales executive; senior*** *or* ***junior executive;*** **account executive** = employee who is the link between his company and certain customers; **chief executive** = executive director in charge of a company; *US* **Chief Executive Officer (CEO)** = director of all a company's operations

exempt 1 *adjective* not covered by a law; not forced to obey a law; **exempt from tax** *or* **tax-exempt** = not required to pay tax; ***as a non-profit-making organization we are exempt from tax;*** **exempt from VAT** = (goods *or* services) to which VAT should not be applied **2** *verb* to free something from having tax paid on it or from having to pay tax; ***non-profit-making organizations are exempted from tax; food is exempted from sales tax; the government exempted trusts from tax***

exemption *noun* act of exempting something from a contract *or* from a tax; **exemption from tax** *or* **tax exemption** =

being free from having to pay tax; ***as a non-profit-making organization you can claim tax exemption***

> COMMENT: in the UK, books and newspapers are not exempt from VAT: they are zero-rated (in other words, VAT is levied on them at 0%). For the implications of this for the publishing trade, see the note at VAT

exercise 1 *noun* use of something; **exercise of an option** = using an option *or* putting an option into action **2** *verb* to use; **to exercise an option** = to put an option into action; ***he exercised his option to acquire sole marketing rights for the product; the chairwoman exercised her veto to block the motion***

ex gratia *adjective* **an ex gratia payment** = payment made as a gift, with no other obligations on the part of the person who pays

exhibit 1 *noun* **(a)** thing which is shown; ***the buyers admired the exhibits on our stand*** **(b)** single section of an exhibition; ***the British Trade Exhibit at the International Computer Fair*** **2** *verb* to show in an exhibition; ***they are exhibiting at the London Book Fair for the first time this year***

exhibition *noun* large show of goods intended to display what companies have to offer and to attract buyers; ***the government has sponsored an exhibition of English educational books in Saudi Arabia; we have a stand selling DIY books at the Ideal Home Exhibition;*** **exhibition room** *or* **hall** = place where goods are shown so that buyers can look at them and decide what to buy; **exhibition stand** = separate section of an exhibition where a company exhibits its products or services

exhibitor *noun* person *or* company which shows products at an exhibition

ex-libris *or* **bookplate** *noun* special piece of paper stuck into the inside of a book to show who owns it (sometimes designed and printed specially for a person, but otherwise bought from a stationer's)

exotic typefaces *noun* non-Latin typefaces, such as Russian, Arabic, Hebrew or Chinese

expand *verb* to increase *or* to get bigger *or* to make something bigger; ***the company is expanding fast; we have had to expand our sales force; the new edition has been considerably expanded;*** **expanded type** = computer-generated type which has been made wider than usual

expansion *noun* increase in size; ***the expansion of the domestic market; the company had difficulty in financing its current expansion programme;*** **expansion board** = printed circuit board which can be added to a system to increase its capacity or performance

expenditure *noun* amounts of money spent; **capital expenditure** = money spent on fixed assets (such as property or machinery); **the company's current expenditure programme** = the company's spending according to the current plan; **heavy expenditure on equipment** = spending large sums of money on equipment

expense *noun* **(a)** money spent; ***it is not worth the expense; the expense is too much for my bank balance;*** **at great expense** = having spent a lot of money; **he furnished the office regardless of expense** = without thinking how much it cost **(b) expense account** = money which a company allows a businessman to spend on travelling and entertaining clients in connection with his business; ***I'll put this lunch on my expense account; expense account lunches form a large part of our current expenditure***

expenses *noun* money paid to cover payments made by an individual while on company business; **all expenses paid** = with all costs paid by the company; ***the company sent him to San Francisco all expenses paid;*** **to cut down on expenses** = to try to reduce spending; **business expenses** = money spent on running a business, not on stock or assets; **entertainment expenses** = money spent on giving meals to business visitors; **fixed expenses** = money which is spent regularly (such as rent, electricity, telephone); **incidental expenses** = small amounts of money spent at various times, in addition to larger amounts; **legal expenses** = money spent on fees paid to lawyers; **overhead expenses** *or* **general expenses** *or* **running expenses** = money spent on the day-to-day cost of a business; **travelling expenses** = money spent on travelling and hotels for business purposes

expensive *adjective* which costs a lot of money; ***PVC binding is much more expensive than paper***

expiration *noun* coming to an end; ***expiration of a licence*** *or* ***of a copyright;*** **on expiration of the lease** = when the lease comes to an end; **expiration date** = (i) date at which a copyright comes to an end; (ii) last date at which photographic film *or* paper can be used with good results

expire *verb* to come to an end; ***the licence expires in 2001;*** **his passport has expired** = his passport is no longer valid

expiry *noun* coming to an end; **expiry date** = date when something will end

explode *verb* to make a picture of an object (such as a car engine) showing the parts inside, each part being shown separately but in the correct relationship to the rest

exploit *verb* to use something to make a profit; ***the company is exploiting its contacts in the Ministry of Trade; we hope to exploit the full marketing potential of the children's book range***

export 1 *noun* **(a) exports** = goods sent to a foreign country to be sold; ***exports to Africa have increased by 25%*** **(b)** action of sending goods to a foreign country to be sold; ***the export trade*** *or* ***the export market;*** **export department** = section of a company which deals in sales to foreign countries; **export duty** = tax paid on goods sent out of a country for sale; **export edition** = special edition printed for the export market; **export house** = company which specializes in the export of goods made by other manufacturers; **export licence** = government permit allowing something to be exported; ***the government has refused an export licence for computer parts;*** **export manager** = person in charge of an export department in a company; **Export Credit Guarantee Department (ECGD)** = British government department which insures exports sold on credit **2** *verb* to send goods to foreign countries for sale; ***50% of our production is exported; they have started exporting audio-visual aids to Arab countries***

exportation *noun* act of sending goods to foreign countries for sale

expose *verb* to allow light to fall on a photographic film for a certain amount of time; ***the film has all been exposed; I accidentally exposed the film as I was taking out of the camera;*** *see also* EXPOSURE

exposition *noun US* = EXHIBITION

exposure *noun* (i) allowing light-sensitive film to be exposed to light; (ii) the amount of time a photographic film is exposed to light; ***you need a very short exposure in bright light;*** **exposure meter** = instrument which calculates how much time a film should be exposed

express 1 *adjective* **(a)** rapid *or* very fast; ***express letter; express delivery*** **(b)** clearly shown in words; ***the contract has an express condition forbidding sale in Africa*** **2** *verb* **(a)** to put into words or diagrams; ***this chart shows home sales expressed as a percentage of total turnover;*** **expressed folio** = page number which is printed (as opposed to a blind folio) **(b)** to send very fast; ***we expressed the order to the customer's warehouse***

expressly *adverb* clearly in words; ***the contract expressly forbids alterations to the text without the approval of the author***

expurgated edition *noun* edition which has been cut to remove offensive material

expurgation *noun* cutting offensive material from a text

ext = EXTENSION

extend *verb* **(a)** to make longer; ***to extend a contract for two years; the copyright period has been extended for a further twenty years;*** **extended credit** = credit allowing the borrower a very long time to pay; ***we sell to Australia on extended credit;*** **extended delivery** = lengthening the time taken for a printing machine to deliver the printed sheet, so that ink will have time to dry before the next sheet is delivered **(b)** to make a typeface slightly wider than normal, so taking up more room on the line (as opposed to condensing, which takes up less room); ***the chapter heads are set in Extended Univers bold;*** *see also* EXPANDED

extended graphics array *see* XGA

extender *noun* **(a)** an ascender or descender **(b)** substance added to ink to make it less opaque

extension *noun* **(a)** allowing longer time; **to get an extension of credit** = to get more time to pay back money owed; **extension of a contract** = continuing the contract for a further period **(b)** *(in an office)* individual telephone linked to the main switchboard; ***can you get me extension 21? extension 21 is engaged; the sales manager is on extension 53***

extensive *adjective* very large *or* covering a wide area; ***an extensive network of sales outlets***

extent *noun* number of pages in a book; ***you need to put the extent and trimmed page size into the catalogue***

extra 1 *adjective* which is added *or* which is more than usual; ***there is no extra charge for corrections; they charge 10% extra for postage; he had £25 extra pay for working on Sunday; service is extra*** **2** *noun* **extras** = items which are not included in a price; ***packing and postage are extras***

extra bound book *noun* book which is specially bound and finished by hand

extract 1 *noun* **(a)** quotation which is part of another document; ***they have asked for permission the quote extracts from the play in their forthcoming anthology*** **(b)** printed document which is part of a larger document; ***he sent me an extract of the accounts*** **2** *verb* to remove required data *or* information from a database; ***we can extract the files required for typesetting***

> COMMENT: long extracts quoted in a text are often set indented, and in a smaller size than the text matter

Ff

f. & c. = FOLDED AND COLLATED

f. & g. = FOLDED AND GATHERED

face *noun* **(a)** part of a metal character which prints; ***the face stands above the beard*** **(b)** typeface, distinctively designed style of a character; ***Times and Helvetica are the two faces used for the text of this book;*** *see also* BOLDFACE **(c)** front cover of a book; **books displayed face out** = shown with the front cover displayed on a bookshop shelf (as opposed to spine out) **(d)** side of a film *or* printed page **2** *verb* to be opposite (another page); **facing page** = page opposite another page; **facing pages** = two pages which face each other; ***the text must be on the page facing the illustration; the legend refers to the map on the facing page;*** **facing editorial** = advertising space opposite editorial matter (charged at a higher rate than normal advertising space)

facility *noun* **(a)** being able to do something easily; ***we offer facilities for payment*** **(b)** total amount of credit which a lender will allow a borrower; **credit facilities** = arrangement with a bank *or* supplier to have credit so as to buy goods; **overdraft facility** = arrangement with a bank to have an overdraft **(c) facilities** = equipment *or* buildings which make it easy to do something; ***we have storage facilities for 60,000 books; transport facilities are provided by the Fair organizers; there are no facilities for unloading*** *or* ***there are no unloading facilities*** **(d)** *US* single large building; ***we have opened our new warehousing facility***

facsimile *noun* **facsimile character generator** = means of displaying characters on a computer screen by copying preprogrammed images from memory; **facsimile copy** = exact copy of a document; **facsimile edition** = reprint of an out-of-print book in exactly the same style as the original; **facsimile transmission (FAX)** = method of sending and receiving images in digital form over a telephone *or* radio link

factor 1 *noun* **(a)** thing which is important *or* which influences; ***the increase in the price of paper is an important factor in the company's lower profits;*** **cost factor** = problem of cost; **cyclical factors** = ways in which a trade cycle affects businesses; **deciding factor** = most important factor which influences a decision; **factors of production** = things needed to produce a product (land, labour and capital) **(b) by a factor of ten** = ten times **(c)** person or company responsible for collecting debts for companies, by buying debts at a discount on their face value **2** *verb* to buy debts from a company at a discount

factoring *noun* business of buying debts at a discount; **factoring charges** = cost of selling debts to a factor for a commission

factory *noun* building where products are manufactured; ***binding factory; paper factory;*** **factory hand** *or* **factory worker** = person who works in a factory; **factory inspector** *or* **inspector of factories** = government official who inspects factories to see if they are well run; **factory price** *or* **price ex factory** = price not including transport from the maker's factory; **factory unit** = single building on an industrial estate

factotum initial *noun* decorative square block, into which the initial letter of the paragraph is dropped

fade *verb* to lose colour; ***the cover material has faded; for a guidebook you need a cloth binding which will not fade;*** **non-fading material** = material which will not lose its colour

fade-out *noun* defect in printing, where the image becomes faint; **fade-out blue** = blue used to mark CRC (it does not show up on film); US **fade-out halftone** = halftone image which fades into the background at the edges; (NOTE: GB English is **vignette**)

fair 1 *adjective* **(a)** honest *or* correct; **fair comment** = criticism which is acceptable, and is not likely to be libellous; **fair deal** = arrangement where both parties are treated equally; **fair dealing** = permission granted in the Copyright Acts, which allows photocopies of copyright works to be made for personal use and for private study, but does not allow large numbers of copies to be made for sale, or by a teacher for the use of a class of students; **fair price** = good price for both buyer and seller; **fair trade** = (i) international business system under which countries agree not to charge import duties on certain items imported from their trading partners; (ii) US = RESALE PRICE MAINTENANCE **fair trading** *or* **fair dealing** = way of doing business which is reasonable and does not harm the consumer; GB **Office of Fair Trading** = government department which protects consumers against unfair or illegal business; **fair use** = use which can legally be made of a quotation from a copyright text without the permission of the copyright holder; **fair wear and tear** = acceptable damage caused by normal use; ***the insurance policy covers most damage, but not fair wear and tear to the machine*** **(b) fair copy** = document which is written or typed with no changes or mistakes **2** *noun* **trade fair** = large exhibition and meeting for advertising and selling a certain type of product; **book fair** = meeting where many publishers come together to show their books to buyers or to foreign publishers; **rights fair** = book fair (like the Frankfurt Book Fair, or the London Book Fair), where publishers sell rights in books to publishers from other countries, and also meet agents and representatives; **selling fair** = book fair (such as the Geneva Book Fair or the Paris Salon du Livre) where books can be sold to the public; ***the organizers of the Frankfurt Book Fair have sent out details of the new stand design; the London Book Fair is open from 9 a.m. to 5 p.m.; the computer fair runs from April 1st to 6th; there are two trade fairs running in Paris at the same time - the Salon du Livre and the computer dealers' fair***

fake 1 *noun* imitation *or* copy made for criminal purposes; ***a cover in fake leather; the shipment came with fake documentation; he was trying to sell a fake first edition;*** **fake process** = colour separation done by the designer who makes individual overlays by hand for each of the colours **2** *verb* to make an imitation for criminal purposes; ***a faked import licence***

faking *noun* putting in extra leading to make a page or column longer

fall 1 *noun* sudden drop *or* sudden decrease in value *or* loss of value; ***a fall in the exchange rate; a sudden fall in sales in the home market*** **2** *verb* **(a)** to drop suddenly to a lower price *or* lower figure; ***borrowing from libraries fell for the first time; his royalties have fallen from $10,000 a year to $200; the pound fell against other European currencies*** **(b)** to happen *or* to take place; ***the public holiday falls on a Tuesday;*** **payments which fall due** = payments which are now due to be made

fall away *verb* to become less; ***sales have fallen away since we increased our prices***

fall off *verb* to become lower *or* less; ***sales have fallen off since the tourist season ended***

fall out *verb* **the bottom has fallen out of the market** = sales have fallen below what previously seemed to be their lowest point

fall through *verb* not to happen *or* not to take place; ***the sale fell through at the last moment***

false *adjective* not true *or* not correct; ***to make a false entry in the balance sheet;*** **false bands** = strip of decorated leather *or* string glued to the top of the spine of the book block before the cover is put on

falsification *noun* action of making false entries in accounts

falsify *verb* to change something to make it wrong

family *noun* group of all the characters in the same typeface, including all the different fonts

fanfold *noun* method of folding continuous paper, one sheet in one direction, the next sheet in the opposite direction, allowing the paper to be fed into a printer continuously with no action on the part of the user

fancy *adjective* **fancy type** = strange *or* decorative typefaces, which are used for display *or* posters, but not usually for text

FAQ = FREQUENTLY ASKED QUESTIONS file that contains the answers to questions users most often ask about a particular topic

farm out *verb* **to farm out work** = to hand over work to another person *or* company to do for you; ***she farms out the editorial work to various freelancers***

fascicle *or* **fascicule** *noun* unbound section of a book which is published in separate parts, and will be collected by its purchaser with other sections and bound up into a volume; ***the tenth fascicle of the Latin dictionary will be published next year***

> COMMENT: the word fascicle is used of learned books, such as dictionaries *or* critical editions, etc. Popular books published in the same way are known as partworks

fashion boards *noun* boards with cartridge paper on one side and thin paper on the other, used for making artwork for blocks

fashion plate *noun* colour plate of a model wearing fashionable clothing

fast *adjective* **(a)** quick *or* quickly; ***the train is the fastest way of getting to our supplier's factory; home computers sell fast in the pre-Christmas period*** **(b)** (colour) which will not fade

fast-moving *or* **fast-selling** *adjective* **fast-selling items** = items which sell rapidly; ***dictionaries are not fast-moving stock; we place fast-moving bestsellers near the entrance***

fastness *noun* ability of a colour not to fade

fat *adjective* round *or* large; **fat face** *or* **fat type** = typeface with very thin serifs and very wide strokes, used in the 19th century for posters and other display work; **fat matter** = copy which is easy to set, such a copy with lots of white spaces; (the opposite is **lean matter**)

father *see* CHAPEL

fault *noun* **(a)** being to blame for something which is wrong; ***it is the stock controller's fault if the warehouse runs out of stock; the chairman said the lower sales figures were the fault of a badly motivated sales force*** **(b)** something wrong with a device or the way it operates; ***the binding line has developed a fault; printing was held up by a series of faults in the paper; the technicians are trying to correct a programming fault; we think there is a basic fault in the product design***

faulty *adjective* which does not work properly; ***faulty equipment was blamed for continual reel breaks; they installed faulty computer programs***

fax *or* **FAX** *noun & verb informal* = FACSIMILE TRANSMISSION ***we will send a fax of the design plan; I've faxed the documents to our New York office***

feasibility *noun* ability to be done; ***to report on the feasibility of a project;*** **feasibility report** = report saying if something can be done; **to carry out a feasibility study on a project** = to carry out an examination of costs and profits to see if the project should be started

feathering *noun* **(a)** blurred ink, caused by a fault in the paper (usually lack of sizing) **(b)** putting extra leading in phototypesetting, so as to make the type area of a page longer

featherweight *noun* very light weight; **featherweight antique paper** = light very thick paper, formerly used for children's books; (NOTE: US English is **high-bulk antique**)

feature **1** *noun* article in a paper *or* magazine, which is a report on a matter of interest, but not related to a particular news item; **features editor** = editor in charge of features **2** *verb* to promote something specially in a newspaper article

-fed *suffix* meaning 'which uses a certain type of paper'; **sheet-fed press** = press which prints on sheets of paper; **web-fed press** = press which prints on paper from a reel

fee *noun* **(a)** money paid for work carried out by a professional person (such as a proofreader *or* an accountant *or* a lawyer); ***we charge a small fee for our services; the libel lawyer charges a fee as a consultant; proofreaders' fees have gone up to #6 per hour*** **(b)** money paid for something; **copyright fee** *or* **permission fee** = money paid to a copyright holder for permission to reproduce something which is in copyright; **reading fee** = money paid to someone for reading a manuscript and commenting on it

feed **1** *noun* device which puts paper into a printer *or* into a photocopier; ***the paper feed has jammed;*** **continuous feed** = device which feeds continuous computer stationery into a printer; **sheet feed** = device which puts in one sheet at a time into a printer; **feed edge** = gripper edge, the edge of a sheet of paper which is held by the grippers and goes into the press first; **feed holes** = holes at the beginning of a paper tape which lead the tape into the reader; **feed roller** = roller which takes the web of paper into the printing machine **2** *verb* **(a)** to put paper into a machine; ***the paper is fed in at one end of the printing line;*** *see also* -FED **(b)** to put information into a computer

feedback *noun* **(a)** information about what people who sell or use products think of them; ***have you any feedback from the sales force about the bookshops' reaction to the new gardening series?*** **(b)** *(in computers)* output which returns to influence input

feeder *noun* device which feeds sheets of paper into a printing machine

feint (rules) *noun* very light lines running across writing paper and the paper in account books

felt **1** *noun* endless roll of soft material which carries the paper through the papermaking processes; **felt finish** = smooth finish on the top side of paper; **felt side** = smooth top side of paper (as opposed to the wire side, which may show the marks of the wire mesh) **2** *verb (of paper fibres)* to become interwoven like felt

> COMMENT: felt mats are used in making paper by hand: each damp sheet is placed on a mat, then another mat is placed on top of it, and another sheet of paper, making a pile of sheets and mats which is pressed to extract water

fenchel tester *noun* device for comparing the stability of two papers, when both are wet

festoon dryer *noun* method of drying paper by hanging it in loops over hot pipes

fibre *or US* **fiber** *noun* solid thread-like part of wood or rag, which is retained in the pulp and in the finished paper; **fibre optics** = thin strands of glass that transmit light and images, sometimes used in phototypesetters

> COMMENT: the fibres in wood or cotton rag are cellulose, and this is what gives paper its strength. Paper fibres lie in the direction of the movement of the web through the papermaking machine: this is known as the grain

fiction *noun* novels and stories which are invented by authors; ***the house specializes in new fiction; this is our new fiction catalogue; the fiction market*** *or* ***the market***

for fiction has been rising steadily; **children's fiction** = stories for children; **juvenile fiction** = stories for older children; **romantic fiction** = stories about love affairs; **science fiction** = stories dealing with imaginary events which may take place at some time in the future, based on existing scientific knowledge

fictitious *adjective* false *or* which do not exist; ***the author claims all the characters in her novel are fictitious***

field *noun* **(a) in the field** = outside the office *or* among the customers; ***we have sixteen reps in the field;*** **first in the field** = first company to bring out a product *or* to start a service; **field sales manager** = manager in charge of a group of salesmen; **field work** = examination of the situation among possible customers; ***he had to do a lot of field work to find the right market for the product*** **(b)** background of a picture; ***a red rose on a blue field***

figure *noun* **(a)** number *or* cost written in numbers; ***the figure quoted was for binding 2,000 copies; if you add all the costs together you arrive at a final figure of £25,000 for the cost of originating the books;*** **he put a very low figure on the value of the lease** = he calculated the value of the lease as very low **(b) figures** = written numbers, especially Arabic numbers; **sales figures** = total sales; **to work out the figures** = to calculate; **in round figures** = not totally accurate, but correct to the nearest 10 or 100; ***they have a workforce of 2,500 in round figures*** **(c) text figure** = illustration in a book (especially a line drawing) which is printed as part of the text (as opposed to a plate, which will be printed an special paper); ***see figure 10 for an illustration of the inside of the brain;*** **figure number** = number which refers to a text illustration; ***the figure numbers are printed in bold*** **(d)** grain which can be seen in a leather binding

file 1 *noun* **(a)** cardboard holder for documents, which can fit in the drawer of a filing cabinet; ***put these letters in the customer file; look in the file marked 'Scottish sales';*** **box file** = cardboard box for holding documents **(b)** documents kept for reference; **to place something on file** = to keep a record of something; **to keep someone's name on file** = to keep someone's name on a list for reference; **file copy** = copy of a document which is kept for reference in an office; copy of a published book, kept in the library of the publisher; **card-index file** = information kept on filing cards **(c)** section of data on a computer (such as a dictionary text, address list, customer accounts); ***how can we protect our computer files?;*** **file header** = information about the file stored at the beginning of the file; **file transfer protocol (FTP)** = TCP/IP standard for transferring files between computers; it is a file sharing protocol that operates at layers 5, 6 and 7 of an OSI model network **2** *verb* **(a) to file documents** = to put documents in order so that they can be found easily; ***the correspondence is filed under 'complaints'*** **(b)** to send in copy for a newspaper article; ***he filed a report yesterday on the revolution*** **(c)** to make an official request; **to file a petition in bankruptcy** = to ask officially to be made bankrupt *or* to ask officially for someone else to be made bankrupt **(d)** to register something officially; ***to file an application for a patent; to file a return to the tax office***

filing *noun* documents which have to be put in order; ***there is a lot of filing to do at the end of the week; the manager looked through the week's filing to see what letters had been sent;*** **filing basket** *or* **filing tray** = container kept on a desk for documents which have to be filed; **filing cabinet** = metal box with several drawers for keeping files; **filing card** = card with information written on it, used to classify information into the correct order; **filing clerk** = clerk who files documents; **filing system** = way of putting documents in order for reference

fill 1 *verb* **(a)** to make something full; ***we have filled our order book with orders for Africa; the production department has filled the warehouse with unsellable products*** **(b) to fill a gap** = to provide a product *or* service which is needed, but which no one has provided before; ***the new range of small***

handbooks fills a gap in the market **(c) to fill a post** *or* **a vacancy** = to find someone to do a job; ***your application arrived too late - the post has already been filled***

filler *noun* **(a)** something which fills a space, such as a small news item or a free advertisement in a newspaper; **stocking filler** = small item (such as a small format book) which can be used to put into a Christmas stocking; *see* SHELF FILLER **(b)** substance added to paper pulp to improve the opacity, also called 'loading'

fillet *noun* decoration on a binding *or* on a printed page (in the form of a decorative line)

fill in *noun* thin card used for filling in

filling in *noun* **(a)** printing fault where the ink runs and fills up the counters of round letters, such as 'g' or 'b', or where it fills in the spaces between halftone dots **(b)** sticking a thin layer of card onto boards after the leather has been put on in quarter or half binding, to make the surface level

fill out *verb* to write the required information in the blank spaces in a form; ***to get customs clearance you must fill out three forms***

film 1 *noun* **(a)** transparent strip of plastic, coated with a light-sensitive compound and used to produce photographs with the aid of a camera; **to develop a film** = to put exposed film into a solution of chemicals, so that the image becomes visible; **film advance** *or* **film feed** = movement forward of a roll of film in a phototypesetter as it leaves spaces between lines of setting and between pages; **film processing laboratory** = laboratory where exposed film is developed and fixed as negative; **film processor** = machine which processes film automatically; **negative film** = photographed film where the colours are reversed (black is white and white is black), from which normal prints can be made; **positive film** = film made from a negative, i.e. with the black showing as black, or with the same colours as the original; **right-reading film** = film which reads in the normal way, from left to right, when viewed from the emulsion side (as opposed to wrong-reading) **(b)** film which is made by photographing the camera-ready copy; ***the publisher has asked the printer to supply duplicate film of the text; the cover films have been lost in the post;*** **film assembly** = putting together all the film elements of a page, and mounting them on a foil; **final film** = film ready for platemaking; **film assembly** *or* **film make-up** = putting pieces of film in the correct places for making plates; **film mechanical** = camera-ready copy in the form of film **(c)** series of moving pictures shown on a cinema *or* TV screen; **film rights** = right to make a film based on a published book; **film script** = the text of a film, with the dialogue for the actors and the instructions for the director; ***the publisher keeps the film and TV rights; film rights were sold for $1 million*** **(d) film laminate** = very thin plastic film attached to the cover or jacket of a book in lamination; **film-wrapping** = wrapping a book in thin plastic sheet (same as shrink-wrapping) **2** *verb* to expose a photographic film to light by means of a camera, and so produce images; to photograph bromides to make a film for printing; ***the camera-ready copy has gone away for filming***

filmset *verb* to set text using a phototypesetter

filmsetting *noun* photocomposition *or* phototypesetting

filter *noun* sheet of coloured glass or plastic, which stops certain frequencies of light (used to make colour separations); **absorption filter** = filter that blocks certain colours

final *adjective* last *or* coming at the end of a period; ***to pay the final instalment; to make the final payment; to put the final details on a document;*** **final date for payment** = last date by which payment should be made; **final demand** = last reminder from a supplier, after which he will sue for payment; **final discharge** = last payment of what is left of a debt; **final draft** = corrected and edited copy sent for setting; **final edition of a newspaper** = last edition of a paper for a certain day; ***the story appeared in the final edition of the evening papers;*** **final film** = film used for platemaking; **final product** = manufactured product, made at the end of a production process; US **final proof** = last proof before passing for press

finalize *verb* to agree final details; ***we hope to finalize the agreement tomorrow; after six weeks of negotiations the loan was finalized yesterday***

finance 1 *noun* **(a)** money used by a company, provided by the shareholders or by loans; ***where will they get the necessary finance for the project?;*** **finance company** *or* **finance corporation** *or* **finance house** = company which provides money for hire-purchase; **finance market** = place where large sums of money can be lent or borrowed **(b) finances** = money *or* cash which is available; ***the bad state of the company's finances*** **2** *verb* to provide money to pay for something; ***the banks have agreed to finance the copublishing operation***

financial *adjective* concerning money; **financial adviser** = person *or* company which gives advice on financial matters for a fee; **financial assistance** = help in the form of money; **financial correspondent** = journalist who writes articles on money matters for a newspaper; **the financial press** = business newspapers and magazines; **financial resources** = money which is available for investment; **financial year** = the twelve months' period for a firm's accounts

financing *noun* providing money; ***the financing of the project was done by two international banks***

find *verb* **(a)** to get something which was not there before; ***to find backing for a project*** **(b)** to make a legal decision in court; ***the tribunal found that both parties were at fault;*** **the judge found for the defendant** = the judge decided that the defendant was right

findings *noun* **the findings of a commission of enquiry** = the recommendations of the commission

fine 1 *adjective* **(a)** very thin *or* small; ***the engraving has some very fine lines;*** **fine etching** = etching of dots on a halftone plate to make them sharper; **fine grain** = very small grain on a photograph (allowing delicate lines and sharp edges); **fine rule** = very thin printed line; **fine screen** = screen with very small dots (more than 120 lines per inch), making good quality halftones **(b)** very good; **fine papers** = good quality paper used for printing halftones or for writing **2** *adverb* very thin *or* very small; **we are cutting our margins very fine** = we are reducing our margins to the smallest possible **3** *noun* **fines** = defects in paper, where the fibres have become stuck together in lumps

finial *noun* decorative curved end to part of a letter which ends in a hook (such as a 'c')

finish 1 *noun* final appearance; especially the surface (rough or smooth) given to paper by rolling, coating or embossing; ***paper with a smooth finish; the cover has an attractive finish;*** **antique finish** = paper with a rough surface which looks as if it were handmade, or any bulky rough-finished paper, such as the paper used for watercolour painting; **eggshell finish** = dull smooth finish like the shell of an egg **2** *verb* **(a)** to do something *or* to make something completely; ***the order was finished in time; she finished the test before all the other candidates*** **(b)** to carry out the last part of the book production process; ***the book is finished in a dark red binding***

finished *adjective* which has been completed; **finished document** = document which is typed, and is ready to be printed; **finished goods** = manufactured goods which are ready to be sold; **finished rough** = presentation visual, artwork which is prepared for a presentation to show what the finished product will look like; *see also* MACHINE FINISHED

finishing *noun* (i) folding, gathering, stitching and binding the pages of a books after they have been printed; (ii) final part of the handbinding process, including lettering and tooling the covers

firewall *noun* computer connected to a local area network and the Internet that is used to protect an internal company network from hackers or unauthorised users gaining access via the Internet

firm 1 *noun* business *or* company *or* partnership; ***he is a partner in a law firm; a manufacturing firm; an important publishing firm*** **2** *adjective* **(a)** which cannot be changed; ***to make a firm offer for something; to place a firm offer for 10,000 copies; they are quoting a firm price of £1.22 per unit;*** **the books have been sold firm** = the seller will not take them back if they are unsold; **firm order** = order (for paper *or* books, etc.) which is at an agreed price and on agreed payment terms **(b)** not dropping in price, and possibly going to rise; ***paper prices are firmer than last year*** **3** *verb* to remain at a price and seem likely to go up; ***paper has firmed at $25 a tonne***

firm up *verb* to finalize, to agree final details; ***we expect to firm up the deal at the London Book Fair***

first *noun* person *or* thing which is there at the beginning *or* earlier than others; ***our company was one of the first to sell into the European market;*** **first colour** = the first of the colours to be printed (in four-colour printing); **first edition** = first printing of a book, which often has a higher value on the secondhand market; ***he collects modern first editions; this first edition of D.H. Lawrence is very rare;*** **first impression** *or* **first printing** = first printing of a book; **first option** = option giving the buyer first refusal on the rights for a book; **first proofs** = first proofs of a book from the printer (usually galley proofs); ***the book is in first proof stage; the first proofs have just come in from the printer;*** **first revise** = proof with corrections made to the first proofs; **first quarter** = three months' period from January to the end of March; **first half** *or* **first half-year** = six months' period from January to the end of June; **first in first out** = (i) redundancy policy, where the people who have been working longest are the first to be made redundant; (ii) accounting policy where stock is valued at the price of the oldest purchases

First Amendment *noun* the amendment to the US Constitution which guarantees freedom of speech, of the press, of religion, etc.

first-class *adjective & noun* **(a)** top quality *or* most expensive; ***he is a first-class jacket designer*** **(b)** most expensive and comfortable type of travel *or* of hotel; **first-class mail** = *GB* most expensive mail service, designed to be faster; *US* mail service for letters and postcards; ***a first-class letter should get to Scotland in a day***

fist *noun* index, a printing sign ☛ like a black hand, used to show a cross-reference

fit *noun* the space between typeset characters; the alignment of text and images on the page

fix *verb* **(a)** to arrange *or* to agree; ***we have to fix our promotion budget for the spring titles; can we fix a meeting for 3 p.m.? the publication date has still to be fixed*** **(b)** to arrange permanently; **fixed back** = cover which is glued to the back of the pages of the book; **fixed costs** = business costs which do not rise with the quantity of the product made; **fixed position** = position of an advertisement which is always in the same place in a newspaper or magazine; **fixed space** = space between characters or words which is always the same and cannot be changed when the line is justified **(c)** to mend; ***the technicians are coming to fix the telephone switchboard; can you fix the photocopier?*** **(d)** to treat a photograph with chemicals so that the image is kept permanently on film

fixative *noun* **(a)** chemical used to fix photographs **(b)** spray varnish put on drawings *or* paintings, so as to preserve the colours or prevent damage from dirt

fixing *noun* **(a)** arranging; ***fixing of charges; fixing of a mortgage rate*** **(b) price fixing** = illegal agreement between companies to charge the same price for competing products

flag 1 *noun* **(a)** mark which is attached to information in a computer so that the information can be found easily **(b)** tag attached to a sheet of paper to mark a special section of text *or* to a web of paper to mark where there is a fault or where a joint has been made **(c)** name of a newspaper *or* magazine, printed in a special style to identify the paper easily **2** *verb* to insert marks on information in a computer so that the information can be found easily

flagship (title) *noun* the most important *or* profitable publication published by a group

flap *noun* piece of paper which folds over; ***the flap of a book jacket; the blurb is continued on the back flap; gum down the flap of the envelope;*** **back flap** *or* **back jacket flap** = flap of a book jacket which is folded inside the back cover; **front flap** *or* **front jacket flap** = flap of a book jacket which is tucked into the front cover of a book, usually with a blurb on it

flash *noun* adding light in exposing a halftone, so as to make the dots on the picture stronger

flat 1 *adjective* **(a)** not folded or bent; **flat back** = spine of a book which is flat and not curved or 'rounded'; **flat sheets** = printed sheets of paper which are kept flat, and will be folded when it is necessary to bind them; **flat straw** = type of paper used for making cigarette papers **(b)** fixed *or* not changing; **flat rate** = charge which always stays the same; ***we pay a flat rate for electricity each quarter; he is paid a flat rate of £2 per thousand*** **(c)** *(of a photograph)* dull *or* with not enough contrast; ***the colours in the plates are flat*** **2** *noun* series of CRC pages stuck down ready for filming; imposed negatives positioned in holes on a sheet ready for platemaking

flatbed *noun* printing *or* scanning machine that holds the paper *or* image on a flat surface while printing or processing; ***scanners are either flatbed models or platen type, paper-fed models; paper cannot be rolled through flatbed scanners;*** **flatbed plotter** = movable pen that draws diagrams under the control of a computer on a flat piece of paper; **flatbed press** = mechanical printing machine where the printing plate lies flat on the bed of the machine, while the inking rollers and then the impression cylinder with the paper are rolled over it; **flatbed scanner** = scanner which scans a text or drawing which is lying flat; **flatbed transmitter** = device that keeps a document flat while it is being scanned before being transmitted by facsimile means

flat out *adverb* working hard *or* at full speed; ***the factory worked flat out to complete the order on time***

flat plan *noun* plan of sheets of a book *or* magazine, showing how colour sections, editorial matter and advertising pages are organized ➩APPENDIX

flat-planning *noun* organizing of flat plans

flat-stitching *noun* method of sewing sections of a book, where the thread is passed through the side of the section near the fold (as opposed to saddle-stitching, where the thread is sewn at the fold itself)

flat-wrapping *noun* wrapping a magazine flat in a plastic envelope for sending through the post

fleuron *noun* type of printed ornament ✻ shaped like a little flower; *see also* FLOWERS

flexiback binding *noun* binding where a special fabric or paper lining reinforces the spine

flexibility *noun* being easily changed; ***there is no flexibility in the company's pricing policy***

flexible *adjective* which can be bent *or* altered *or* changed; ***the guidebook is bound in a flexible PVC binding; the sales department has introduced a flexible pricing policy;*** **flexible binding** = binding where the cover adheres closely to the spine; this allows the spine to bend inwards (i.e. to become concave) so that the book will open flat; *compare* HOLLOW BACK, ROUNDED BACK, SQUARE BACK,

TIGHT BACK **flexible working hours** = system where workers can start or stop work at different hours of the morning or evening provided that they work a certain number of hours per day or week; ***we work flexible hours***

flexichrome *noun* photograph which has been coloured by hand

flexitime *noun* system where workers can start or stop work at different hours of the morning or evening, provided that they work a certain number of hours per day or week; ***we work flexitime; the company introduced flexitime working two years ago***

flexography *or* **flexographic printing** *noun* type of relief printing, using flexible rubber or plastic plates on a web press, popular in particular for printing packaging materials

flier *or* **flyer** *noun* **(a)** small advertising leaflet designed to encourage customers to ask for more information about the product for sale **(b) high flier** = (i) person who is very successful *or* who is likely to rise to a very important position; (ii) share whose market price is rising rapidly

flimsy *noun* very thin paper for making carbon copies or layouts

flip chart *noun* way of showing information to a group of people by writing on large sheets of paper which can then be turned over to show the next sheet

floating accent *noun (on a typewriter)* accent which is not fixed above any particular character, and can be typed above any character after backspacing (on a typewriter, an accented letter may need three keystrokes, one for the accent, then backspace, then key the letter)

flong *noun* papier mâché sheet used for making moulds for casting stereo plates

floor *noun* **(a) floor display** = rack for displaying books which stands on the floor and not on a counter; **floor space** = area of floor in an shop *or* office *or* warehouse; ***we have 3,500 square metres of floor space to let;*** **the factory floor** = main working area of a factory; **on the shop floor** = in the works *or* in the factory *or* among the ordinary workers; ***the feeling on the shop floor is that the manager does not know his job*** **(b)** lowest level of bids at an auction for rights in a book, established by the first bidders and rejected by the seller, but used as a basis for further bids

flop 1 *noun* failure *or* not being a success; ***the new novel was a flop*** **2** *verb* **(a)** to fail *or* not to be a success; ***the launch of the paperback series flopped badly*** **(b)** to turn a film to give a mirror image (i.e. the right is on the left), not the same as reverse

floppy 1 *adjective* **floppy disk** = small disk for storing information in a computer **2** *noun* small disk for storing computer information; ***the data is on 3.5-inch floppies***

floriation *noun* tooled decoration on leather binding, in the form of little flowers

flourish 1 *noun* decorative curling line, attached to a normal character; ***the foot of the upper case L ends in a flourish*** **2** *verb* to be prosperous *or* to do well in business; ***the company is flourishing; trade with Nigeria flourished***

flourishing *adjective* profitable; **flourishing trade** = trade which is expanding profitably; ***he runs a flourishing book remainder business***

flow 1 *noun* **(a)** movement; ***the flow of paper into the web press; the flow of ink over the rollers;*** **flow box** = headbox, a vat of liquid pulp from which the pulp passes onto the wire mesh to be made into paper **(b) cash flow** = cash which comes into a company from sales and goes out in purchases or overhead expenditure; **the company is suffering from cash flow problems** = cash income is not coming in fast enough to pay for the expenditure going out **(c) flow chart** *or* **flow diagram** = chart which shows the arrangement of work processes in a series **2** *verb* to move smoothly; ***production is now flowing normally after the strike***

flowers *noun* little standard ornaments, shaped like leaves or flowers, used by designers to create designs

fluff *noun* fibre dust which collects on the surface of paper, or inside line printers

fluffing *noun* formation of loose fibres of fluff on the surface of paper, especially found on soft paper

fluorescent *adjective* shining with a white glow (such as a substance added to paper stock to make very white paper)

flush *adjective & adverb* cut with the edge level with the cover; ***books with a flush edge*** *or* ***with a flush-cut edge*** *or* ***with flush boards; the books are cut flush; the covers are trimmed flush with the pages;*** **flush cover** *or* **flush binding** *or* **cut flush** = (book) which has been trimmed so that the edges of the cover do not stand out beyond the trimmed pages; **flush paragraph** = paragraph with no indentation *or* where the first line is not indented (a white line is added between paragraphs to divide them more clearly); *US* **flush and hang** = setting where the first line of a paragraph is flush with the left margin and the rest of the paragraph is indented; **flush left** *or* **flush right** = JUSTIFY, RANGE (NOTE: US English prefers **flush left** and **flush right** where GB English uses **range left** and **range right**)

flyer = FLIER

flying paster *noun* automatic reel change *or* device on a rotary printing press which changes the reel of paper automatically when it comes to an end

flyleaf *noun* extra blank page at the beginning or end of a book, one of the endpapers which is not glued to the cover but acts as a protection to the printed text pages (and is often used by book owners for writing notes)

FOB *or* **f.o.b.** = FREE ON BOARD

FOC = FATHER OF THE CHAPEL

focal length *noun* distance between the centre of an optical lens and the focusing plane, when the lens is focused at infinity

focus 1 *noun* image *or* beam that is clear and well defined; **the picture is out of focus** *or* **is not in focus** = the picture is not clear **2** *verb* to adjust the focal length of a lens so that the image is clear and well defined; ***the camera is focused on the foreground; they adjusted the lens position so that it focused correctly***

fog *noun* effect on photographic material which has been accidentally exposed to light, causing a loss of picture contrast

foil *noun* **(a)** very thin metal or plastic sheet on a backing, which is peeled off and used to block gold *or* silver letters on a book cover; **foil paper** = the paper backing to which the metal foil is attached; **gold foil** = gold-coloured foil (as opposed to real gold, which is called 'gold leaf') **(b)** clear stable film used as a carrying surface for film assembly **(c)** metallic paper used for decorative packaging

fold *verb* to bend a flat thing, so that part of it is on top of the rest; ***she folded the letter so that the address was clearly visible;*** **folded sheets** = sheets of a book which have been folded ready for gathering, sewing and binding; **folded and collated (f. & c.)** *or* **folded and gathered (f. & g.)** = sheets of a book which have been folded and put in order

folder *noun* **(a)** cardboard envelope for carrying papers; ***put all the documents in a folder for the chairman*** **(b)** machine which folds printed sheets **(c)** part of a web press where the paper is folded; **buckle folder** = device for folding paper where the sheet is made to buckle by pulling it through rollers against a metal plate; **knife folder** = device for folding paper at an angle to the web, by pushing a metal blade against the paper between two cylinders

folding *noun* action of folding sheets for gathering either in parallel folds, where each fold is parallel to the next, or in right-angle folds, where they are at right angles to each other; **folding blade** = strip of metal which pushes the sheet into the folding device; **folding cylinders** = cylinders between which the sheet is guided on a knife-folding machine; **folding jaws** = section of a folding machine which holds the paper pushed into it by the folding blade; **folding machine** = machine which automatically folds sheets; **folding stick** = bone strip used in hand folding; **folding strength** = strength of paper to resist tearing when folded several times

folding plate *noun* **(a)** large illustration which is tipped into a book, and which unfolds to make a double sized plate **(b)** plate on a buckle folding machine against which the sheet to be folded is pushed

fold-out *noun* pull-out, a sheet which is put folded into a magazine *or* book, and which can be unfolded to give a much wider page (used especially for plans and maps)

foliation *noun* numbering of pages of a manuscript (written on one side of the leaf only)

folio 1 *noun* **(a)** large book format, where the sheets of paper have been folded once, each sheet making two leaves or four pages; ***a folio edition of the book of drawings*** **(b)** number printed on a page; ***the folios are printed in 10 point Baskerville, centred;*** **blind folio** = page with no printed page number; **drop folio** = page number printed at the foot of the page; **expressed folio** = printed page number (as opposed to a blind folio) **(c)** page with a number, especially two facing pages in an account book which have the same number, or a page in a manuscript which has a number on one side only **2** *verb* to put a number on a page

follow *verb* **(a)** to come behind *or* to come afterwards; ***the samples will follow by surface mail; we will pay £10,000 down, with the balance to follow in six months' time*** **(b)** to do what someone says; to do the same as has been done before; **please follow copy** = please set exactly as the manuscript indicates; **follow style** = continue to set in the same style as the rest of the book (or as other books in the same series)

follow on *verb* to run on, to set printed text so that it continues directly from the previous text

font *or* **fount** *noun* set of characters all of the same size and face; **wrong font (wf)** = correction mark to a printer to show that a character is in the wrong font; **font change** = function on a computer to change the style of characters used on a display screen; **font disk** = (i) transparent disk that contains the master images of a particular font, used in a phototypesetting machine; (ii) magnetic disk that contains the data to drive a character generator to make up the various fonts on a computer display; **downloadable fonts** *or* **resident fonts** = fonts *or* typefaces which are stored on a disk and can be downloaded to a printer and stored in temporary memory; **font management system** = software which controls the font changes on a laser printer

COMMENT: each typeface will be available in many different fonts (Univers, for example, was designed in 21 different fonts) and these will include the different point sizes and weights, such as bold and italic. In metal setting, the font would contain different quantities of each character, according to the frequency of use of the characters. English fonts will contain capitals, small capitals, lower case, punctuation marks, numerals, ligatures and common symbols, making about 150 sorts in all. English fonts contain some accents and special characters, but many accents which are standard in, say German or Spanish fonts, are not included in English. British fonts contain the pound and the dollar signs, but American fonts are likely not to have the pound sign

foolscap *noun* large British size of paper; ***the letter was on six sheets of foolscap;*** **a foolscap envelope** = large envelope which takes foolscap paper

COMMENT: foolscap takes it name from a watermark of a clown's hat used in early papers; foolscap folio is $13\frac{1}{2}$ x $8\frac{1}{2}$ inches; foolscap quarto is $8\frac{1}{2}$ x $6\frac{3}{4}$ inches and foolscap octavo is $6\frac{3}{4}$ x $4\frac{1}{4}$ inches

foot 1 *noun* **(a)** bottom part of a page; ***he signed his name at the foot of the invoice; the cross-references are printed at the foot of the page*** **(b)** bottom of a metal type (i.e. the flat base divided into two feet, the opposite end to the face) **2** *verb* to be printed at the bottom of a page

footer *noun* text printed at the bottom of all the pages in a printed document (such as the page number); *compare* HEADER

footnote 1 *noun* note printed (usually in small type) at the bottom of a page; ***the footnotes are printed in 5pt Times; see the footnote on page 23*** **2** *verb* to put in footnotes

> COMMENT: footnotes are best printed at the bottom of a page, as the name suggests, if they are essential to the understanding of the text. They can also be printed at the end of a chapter or at the end of a book, especially if they are simply further references or supply bibliographic details. In learned journals it is common for them to be printed at the end of the chapter, which makes the typesetting of the main text much simpler. Reference numbers to footnotes are printed in small superscript numbers after the relevant word in the text, and in books the numbers usually run from the beginning of the text to the end of the book, consecutively. In journals formed of several different articles, each article has its own footnote numbering series

footprint *noun* **(a)** area covered by a transmitting device such as a satellite *or* antenna **(b)** area that a computer takes up on a desk

forbid *verb* to tell someone not to do something *or* to say that something must not be done; ***the contract forbids resale of the books to the USA; the staff are forbidden to use the front entrance; the government has forbidden the importation of more than 1,000 copies of any title;*** **forbidden books** = books which have been forbidden by a censor

fore and aft *noun* two-up, method of printing two copies of a book at the same time, with the pages joined head to head

foredge *or* **fore-edge** *noun* front edge of trimmed pages in a bound book (that is, the opposite edge to the spine); **foredge margin** = margin along the foredge of a book (as opposed to the gutter); **foredge painting** = painting along the foredge of a bound book, after the edge has been splayed out, so that the painting is only seen when the pages are splayed and not when the book is closed normally

> COMMENT: early bound books were displayed with this edge facing out on the shelf, hence the name; the title was written or printed on this edge of the pages

foreground *noun* **(a)** front part of an illustration (as opposed to the background); ***the foreground is in focus but the rest of the photograph is blurred;*** **foreground colour** = colour of characters and text displayed on a videotext screen **(b)** very important work done by a computer; **foreground processing** = region of a multitasking operating system in which high priority jobs *or* programs are executed; **foreground program** = high priority program in a multitasking system, whose results are usually visible to the user; *compare* BACKGROUND

foreign *adjective* not belonging to one's own country; **foreign language** = language spoken in another country *or* language which is not English; **foreign-language edition** = edition of an English-language text in translation; **foreign-language rights** = rights to translate an English-language text into a foreign language; **foreign rights** = rights to sell an English-language book in other countries (as licensed editions *or* translations *or* bilingual editions)

foreign exchange *noun* exchanging the money of one country for that of another; **foreign exchange transfer** = sending of money from one country to another

foreword *noun* text at the beginning of a book, sometimes by the author or more usually by another person, which introduces the book and its author

forfeit 1 *noun* taking something away as a punishment; **forfeit clause** = clause in a contract which says that goods *or* a deposit will be taken away if the contract is not fulfilled; **the goods were declared forfeit** = the court said that the goods had to be taken away from their owner **2** *verb* to have something taken away as a punishment; **to forfeit a patent** = to lose a patent because payments have not been made

forge *verb* to copy a signature illegally *or* to make a document which looks like a real one; ***he tried to enter the country with forged documents***

forger *noun* person who forges a document

forgery *noun* **(a)** making an illegal copy; ***he was sent to prison for forgery*** **(b)** illegal copy; ***the signature was proved to be a forgery***

fork-lift truck *noun* type of small tractor with two metal arms in front, used for lifting and moving pallets

form 1 *noun* **(a)** **form of words** = words correctly laid out for a legal document; **receipt in due form** = correctly written receipt **(b)** printed sheet with several pages of text printed on it **(c)** *US* = FORME complete set of metal type *or* blocks, assembled in a chase ready for printing **(d)** official printed paper with blank spaces which have to be filled in with information; ***you have to fill in form A20; customs declaration form; a pad of order forms;*** **application form** = form which has to be filled in to apply for something; **claim form** = form which has to be filled in when making an insurance claim **(e)** page of computer stationery; **form feed** = command to a printer to move to the next sheet of paper; **form handling equipment** = peripherals (such as decollator) which deal with output from a printer; **form letter** = standard letter into which personal details of each addressee are inserted, such as name, address and job; **form mode** = display method on a data entry terminal, the form is displayed on the screen and the operator enters relevant details; **form overlay** = heading *or* other matter held in store and printed out at the same time as the text; **form stop** = sensor on a printer which indicates when the paper has run out **2** *verb* to start *or* to organize; ***the brothers have formed a new company***

forma *see* PRO FORMA

format 1 *noun* **(a)** trim size of a book; ***the book is available in quarto and octavo formats; this is not a common format*** **(b)** layout of the design of a printed page; ***we are using a three column format for the dictionary*** **(c)** general style of a book, including illustrations, typeface used, binding style, etc.; ***we are reissuing the book in paperback format*** **2** *verb* **(a)** to put (a book) into a certain format **(b)** to prepare a blank disk to receive data by programming it to the system used by the computer **(c)** to layout a page of text held on computer; **formatting program** = program for automatically putting a computer text into a certain page format

formation *noun* way in which fibres in paper appear when the paper is held against the light

formatter *noun* hardware *or* software that arranges text *or* data according to certain rules; **print formatter** = software that converts embedded codes and print commands to printer control signals

forme *or US* **form** *noun* complete set of metal type *or* blocks, assembled in a chase ready for printing; **forme rollers** = rollers which apply ink to the forme

formula publishing *noun* publishing a series of books according to a certain principle (in identical format, for example, or written according to a set of instructions provided by the publisher)

forthcoming *adjective* which will be published shortly; ***'forthcoming titles for Autumn publication'; in his forthcoming biography of the Prime Minister, he writes about the collapse of the previous government***

forty-eightmo (48mo) *noun (old)* **(a)** printing 48 pages from a sheet of paper **(b)** book printed with 48 pages from a sheet

forward 1 *adjective* in advance *or* to be paid at a later date; **forward buying** *or* **buying forward** = buying currency *or* paper at today's price for delivery at a later date; **forward contract** = agreement to buy foreign currency *or* paper for delivery at a later date at a certain price; **forward (exchange) rate** = rate for purchase of foreign currency at a fixed price for delivery at a later date; **forward sales** = sales for delivery at a later date; **forward stock** = stock held in a section of a warehouse where it can be reached easily (this is the current stock, as opposed to the bulk stock which is held separately until needed) **2** *adverb* **(a) to date a cheque forward** = to put a later date than the present one on a cheque; **carriage forward** *or* **freight forward** = deal where the customer pays for transporting the goods; **charges forward** = charges which will be paid by the customer **(b) to buy forward** = to buy paper *or* foreign currency before you need it, in order to be certain of the exchange rate; **to sell forward** = to sell foreign currency for delivery at a later date **(c) balance brought forward** *or* **carried forward** = balance which is entered in an account at the end of a period and is then taken to be the starting point of the next period **3** *verb* **to forward something to someone** = to send something to someone; **please forward** *or* **to be forwarded** = words written on an envelope, asking the person receiving it to send it on to the person whose name is written on it

(freight) forwarder *noun* person *or* company which arranges shipping and customs documents for several shipments from different companies, putting them together to form one large shipment

forwarding *noun* **(a)** continuing the binding of a book after it has been sewn, by rounding, backing, casing-in, etc. **(b)** arranging shipping and customs documents; **air forwarding** = arranging for goods to be shipped by air; **forwarding agent** = FORWARDER **forwarding instructions** *or* **instructions for forwarding** = instructions showing how the goods are to be shipped and delivered **(c) forwarding address** = address to which a person's mail can be sent on

foul *adjective* **foul bill of lading** = bill of lading which says that the goods were in bad condition when received by the shipper; **foul copy** = badly written manuscript *or* typescript with many illegible changes; **foul proof** = proof with corrections instructed

founder *noun* **(a)** typefounder *or* person who casts type; **founder's type** = special type made by a typefounder, as opposed to the type cast in a typecasting machine **(b)** person who starts a company; **founder's shares** = special shares issued to the person who starts a company

foundry *noun* (i) factory which makes metal type; (ii) formerly, part of a letterpress printing house where matrices and stereos were made; **foundry chase** = chase which is used in making stereos; **foundry proof** *or* **press proof** = proof taken directly from a chase of metal type before a plate is made from it; **foundry type** = special display type which has to be bought from the foundry

fount *or* **font** *noun* set of characters, all of the same size and face; **wrong fount (wf)** = correction mark to a printer to show that a character is in the wrong fount

> COMMENT: the spelling 'fount' is mainly used in the UK, but is being superseded by 'font' which is used in the USA, and also in computer terminology. The two are both pronounced 'font'

fountain *noun* container for ink in a printing press; **fountain solution** = solution used in lithographic printing to prevent ink sticking to those parts of the plate which should not print

four-backed *adjective* printing of sheets with four colours on one side and one, two or four colours on the other (four-backed-one, four-backed-two, etc.)

four-colour *adjective* referring to printing using four colours (yellow, cyan, magenta, and black) to give full-colour printing;

four-colour press = printing press which prints four colours in one pass; **four-colour printing** *or* **four-colour process** = printing using the four process colours (yellow, cyan, magenta and black) to give a full range of colours at the same time; **four-colour reproduction** = reproducing a colour plate using four-colour printing

fourdrinier *noun* papermaking machine, where the paper is made by pulp draining through a continuous wire mesh; *see also* TWIN-WIRE

> COMMENT: the machine was patented by Henry Fourdrinier before 1810. In it, the white pulp enters from a vat at one end, and flows forward along the mesh becoming paper as the water drains away. It is then dried on heated cylinders. Fourdrinier machines produce webs of paper and can be adjusted to produce different thicknesses, weights and finishes

Fournier typeface designed by Pierre Simon Fournier (1712-1768), characterized by its very elegant italics

> COMMENT: Fournier was also the originator of the point system, which was revised and refined by Didot some years later

fourth cover *noun* back cover of a magazine

fourth estate *noun* newspapers and magazines, seen as the fourth power in the land (after the lords, the bishops and the ordinary people)

four-up *adverb* **to print four-up** = to print four copies of a page on the same sheet of paper (the books are cut apart after printing)

four-way entry *adjective* when referring to pallets indicates the pallet may be picked up by a fork-lift truck in any of the four directions

foxing *or* **fox marks** *noun* brown stain on paper, caused by damp which affects chemical impurities in the paper; also caused by the inks on other pages, especially from illustrations; **foxed page** = page with damp stains

fraction *noun* number shown as one figure above another; **piece fractions** = commonly-used fractions ($\frac{1}{2}$, $\frac{3}{4}$, etc.) which are available as a single piece of type; **split fraction** = fraction which has to be created by the typesetter, using superior and inferior figures separated by a dash

fraktur *noun* Gothic characters used in German typesetting

frame 1 *noun* **(a)** rule *or* border round an illustration **(b)** *(in DTP)* a movable, resizable box that holds text or an image; **frame window** = controls (including the minimise and maximise buttons, scroll bar and window title) and border that surround a window area **(c)** desk where a compositor works, with cases for type **2** *verb* to put a rule *or* border round an illustration

frame relay *noun* packet-switching protocol supporting data transmission rates of 1.5Mbps

franchise 1 *noun* licence to trade using a brand name and paying a royalty for it; ***he has bought a printing franchise*** **2** *verb* to sell licences for people to trade using a brand name and paying a royalty; ***his bookstall was so successful that he decided to franchise it***

franchisee *noun* person who runs a franchise

franchiser *noun* person who licenses a franchise

franchising *noun* act of selling a licence to trade as a franchise; ***he runs his chain of card shops as a franchising operation***

franchisor *noun* = FRANCHISER

franco *adverb* free

frank *verb* to stamp the date and postage on a letter; **franking machine** = machine which marks the date and postage on letters so that the sender does not need to use stamps

Frankfurt Book Fair the most important of the international book fairs, and one which has existed in one form or another since the later Middle Ages; the fair was superseded in the 18th and 19th centuries by the Leipzig Book Fair, but was reinstated as an international fair in 1949. Held each year in October, it is a meeting place for book publishers, printers, literary agents and booksellers

free 1 *adjective & adverb* **(a)** not costing any money; ***to be given a free ticket to the exhibition; the price includes free delivery; goods are delivered free; catalogue sent free on request;*** **carriage free** = the customer does not pay for the shipping; **free copy** = copy of a book sent out as a present; **free gift** = present given by a shop to a customer who buys a certain amount of goods; **free trial** = testing of a machine with no payment involved; ***to send a self-study course for two weeks' free trial;*** **free of charge** = with no payment to be made; **free on board (f. o. b.)** = (i) price including all the seller's costs until the goods are on the ship for transportation; (ii) *US* price includes all the seller's costs until the goods are delivered to a certain place; **free on rail** = price including all the seller's costs until the goods are delivered to the railway for shipment **(b)** with no restrictions; **free competition** = being free to compete without government interference; **free port** *or* **free trade zone** = port *or* area where there are no customs duties; **free of tax** *or* **tax-free** = with no tax having to be paid; **free of duty** *or* **duty-free** = with no duty to be paid; **free trade** = system where goods can go from one country to another without any restrictions; **free translation** = rough translation, which gives the meaning, without translating the text word for word **2** *noun* **frees** = free copies, books given away free (to representatives, agents, to the author, etc.); when estimating costs, the publisher will allow for a certain number of free copies

freedom *noun* being free to do something without restriction; **freedom of the press** = being able to write and publish in a newspaper what you wish without being afraid of prosecution, provided that you do not break the law; **freedom of speech** = being able to say what you want without being afraid of prosecution, provided that you do not break the law

freehand *adjective & adverb* (artwork) drawn by hand, without the use of rulers, stencils, or other guides

freelance 1 *adjective & noun* independent worker who works for several different companies but is not employed by any of them; ***we have about twenty freelances working for us*** *or* ***about twenty people working for us on a freelance basis; she is a freelance journalist*** **2** *adverb* selling one's work to various firms, but not being employed by any of them; ***he works freelance as a designer*** **3** *verb* **(a)** to do work for several firms but not be employed by any of them; ***she freelances for the local newspapers*** **(b)** to send work out to be done by a freelancer; ***we freelance work out to several specialists***

freelancer *noun* freelance worker

free sheet *noun* **(a)** newspaper given away free to each house in a district, its income coming solely from advertising **(b)** *US* woodfree paper (i.e., chemical or non-mechanical paper)

freeware *noun* software that is in the public domain and can be used by anyone without having to pay

freight 1 *noun* **(a)** cost of transporting goods by air, sea or land; ***at an auction, the buyer pays the freight;*** **freight charges** *or* **freight rates** = money charged for transporting goods; ***freight charges have gone up sharply this year;*** **freight costs** = money paid to transport goods; **freight forward** = deal where the customer pays for transporting the goods **(b) air freight** = shipping of goods in an aircraft; ***to send a shipment by air freight;*** **air freight charges** *or* **rates** = money charged for sending goods by air **(c)** goods which are transported; **to take on freight** = to load goods onto a ship, train or truck; **freight depot** = central point where goods are collected before being shipped **2** *verb* **to freight goods** = to send goods; ***we freight goods to all parts of the USA***

freightage *noun* cost of transporting goods

French fold *noun* sheet of paper which is printed on one side only and then folded twice, but not trimmed on the top edge, used to make greetings cards, etc.

French groove *or* **French joint** *noun* joint in binding, where space is left between the board and the spine, to allow the book to open flat

French sewing *noun* sewing signatures together without tapes, each signature being attached by sewing through the thread attaching the previous one

frequently asked questions *see* FAQ

fret *noun* design used for borders and on covers, made of an interlaced pattern

friar *noun* pale area, where there has not been enough ink; (NOTE: the opposite is **monk**)

friction feed *noun* printer mechanism where the paper is advanced by holding it between two rollers (as opposed to tractor feed which pulls on the sprocket holes)

friction glazing *noun* process of putting a high gloss on paper, by running the paper through rollers turning at different speeds

frisket *noun* small metal 'fingers' which hold the sheet to the tympan on a platen press

front *noun* **(a)** part of something which faces away from the back; ***the front of the book has a photograph of the author's house; the front page of the company report has a photograph of the managing director; our ad appeared on the front page of the newspaper; the design team has changed the front cover twice;*** **front board** = the board which forms the front of the book case; **front of book** = the first pages of a magazine, before the editorial matter; **front cover** = the cover on the front of a book or magazine, with the title and usually an attractive, eye-catching design; **front flap** *or* **front jacket flap** = flap of the jacket which is tucked into the front cover of a book, usually with a blurb printed on it; **front matter** = text of a book which appears before the main text (such as title page, preface, list of contents, etc.) **(b)** part of the metal type which faces the front, with a notch in it, so that the compositor can tell which way round the piece of type is **(c)** **money up front** = payment in advance; ***they are asking for £10,000 up front before they will consider the deal; he had to put money up front before he could clinch the deal***

front-end system *noun* typesetting system, where text is keyboarded on a terminal directly connected to the typesetting computer

frontlist *noun* new books just published or about to be published by a publisher (as opposed to the backlist)

> COMMENT: the frontlist contains all the new titles, and therefore is of particular interest to editors, production staff and sales staff. Promotion of the frontlist is heavy, and the frontlist carries most of a publisher's investment. On the other hand, a backlist which continues to sell is usually the most profitable part of a publisher's list, even though it may be disregarded by the editorial and even the sales staff, who find it more interesting to work on and sell the new titles

frontispiece *noun* illustration facing the title page (either printed on text paper or on art paper and then tipped in)

f.s.e. = FOLDED SEWN AND ENDPAPERED

FTP = FILE TRANSFER PROTOCOL

fudge 1 *noun* stop press, small section in a newspaper, reserved for very late items of news **2** *verb* to touch up a photograph by airbrushing or painting in

fugitive *adjective* (colour) which fades when exposed to light or chemicals; (NOTE: the opposite is **light-fast**)

fulfil *US* **fulfill** *verb* to complete something in a satisfactory way; ***the clause regarding payments has not been fulfilled;***

to fulfil an order = to supply the items which have been ordered; ***we are so understaffed that we cannot fulfil any more orders before Christmas***

fulfilment *noun* carrying something out in a satisfactory way; **order fulfilment** = supplying items which have been ordered

full *adjective* **(a)** with as much inside it as possible; ***is the container full yet?; when the disk is full, don't forget to make a backup copy*** **(b)** complete *or* including everything; **full binding** *or* **whole binding** = cased binding, where the case is completely covered with a piece of material (cloth, leather, etc., as opposed to half-binding); **full leather binding** = binding where the leather covers the whole book; **full bound book** = book with a full binding; **full colour** = colour work printed in four colours; ***a full colour illustration; the illustrations are printed in full colour;*** **full measure** = using the full width of the type area; **full out** = not indented, with the type area aligned to the left (or sometimes right) margin; **full page** = whole page; **a full-page photograph** = a photograph covering a whole page; **full price** = price with no discount; **full title** = complete title (as opposed to half-title)

full point = FULL STOP

full-scale *adjective* complete *or* very thorough; ***the MD ordered a full-scale review of credit terms***

full stop *noun* a punctuation mark, a dot showing that a sentence has come to an end; also used after some initials and abbreviations; (NOTE: US English often calls this a **period**)

full-time *adjective & adverb* working all the normal working time (i.e. about eight hours a day, five days a week); ***she is in full-time work*** *or* ***she works full-time*** *or* ***she is in full-time employment; he is one of our full-time staff***

full-timer *noun* person who works full-time

fully formed characters *noun* characters produced by a printer in a single action (as opposed to characters made up from dots, as in a dot-matrix printer); ***a daisy-wheel printer produces fully formed characters***

function 1 *noun* **(a)** duty *or* job; **management function** *or* **function of management** = the duties of being a manager **(b) function code** *or* **function key** = code or key which makes a part of a computer program work **2** *verb* to work; ***the advertising campaign is functioning smoothly; the new management structure does not seem to be functioning very well***

furnish *noun* final mixture of various substances from which paper is manufactured (formed of wood pulp, chemicals, and water)

furniture *noun* pieces of wood wedged round the edge of the metal type in a forme, to keep it tight and to make a margin; also similar pieces of wood used to make blank spaces in typeset text; *see also* REGLET

fuzzy *adjective* blurred (photograph); ***using art paper will eliminate fuzzy characters***

Gg

g = GRAM

galley *noun* **(a)** originally a long metal tray holding text in metal type; **galley press** = small press for taking galley proofs; **galley rack** = rack where galleys are stored **(b)** **galley** *or* **galley proof** *or* **slip proof** = long proof of text, printed as a continuous piece and not separated into pages; ***we have sent out the galley proofs to the author; the galleys have been sent back to the printer to be corrected; the book is at the galley stage, and should go into page next month;*** **page on galley** = long proof where the text is cut into page length pieces, but without headings and folios

> COMMENT: although originally used for proofs from a tray of metal type, the word 'galley' is now used for any proof on a long strip of paper

gang printing *noun* printing several jobs together on the same sheet (often used when printing several small advertising jobs)

gap *noun* empty space; **gap in the market** = opportunity to make a product which is needed but which no one has sold before

garbage *noun* data *or* information which is no longer required because it is out of date or incorrect; **garbage in garbage out (GIGO)** = expression meaning that the accuracy and quality of information that is outputted depends on the quality of the input

> COMMENT: GIGO is sometimes taken to mean 'garbage in gospel out', meaning that whatever wrong information is put into a computer people will always believe the output is true

gatefold *noun* page with two parallel folds towards the centre, so that it can be opened up like a double gate

gateway *noun* **(a)** (i) device that links two dissimilar networks; (ii) software protocol translation device that allows users working in one network to access another; ***we use a gateway to link the LAN to WAN*** **(b)** *(in electronic mail)* software that allows mail messages to be sent via a different route *or* to another network; **fax gateway** = computer or software that allows users to send an email or information as a fax transmission to a remote fax machine

gather *verb* **(a)** to collect together *or* to put together; ***he gathered his papers together before the meeting started; she has been gathering material for a book on the history of trade unions*** **(b)** to bring together printed signatures of a book for sewing and binding

gatherer *noun* = GATHERING MACHINE

gathering *noun* action of bringing printed sections together to be bound; **gathering machine** *or* **gatherer** = machine which gathers signatures for binding

gauge 1 *noun* device which measures thickness *or* width; **paper gauge** = device for measuring the thickness of paper; **type gauge** *or* *US* **line gauge** = special ruler used by printers and production staff, showing width in ems and points, used for calculating the width of a line or the depth of a page **2** *verb* to measure the thickness *or* width of something

gauze *noun* thin woven material, used to strengthen hinges in binding

gazetteer *noun* book which lists names of places and gives information about them

gear *noun* system of moving wheels, which connect together to give movement to a machine; **gear marks** = uneven printing caused by the rollers in a printing press moving at different speeds

gelatine *or* **gelatin** *noun* substance obtained from animal bones, used to make glue and size for coating paper

general *adjective* **(a)** ordinary *or* not special; **general expenses** = all kinds of minor expenses, money spent on the day-to-day costs of running a business; **general manager** = manager in charge of the administration of a company; **general office** = main administrative office of a company **(b)** referring to the ordinary public; **general books** = books which may interest the adult public (usually not including children's books, fiction or specialized books); **general books editor** *or* **trade editor** = editor who is in charge of a general list; **general list** = books published by a company for the general adult public; ***the general list has improved its sales this year, while the children's list has fallen back*** **(c)** dealing with everything *or* everybody; **general audit** = examining all the books and accounts of a company; **Annual General Meeting** = meeting of all the shareholders, when the company's financial situation is discussed with the directors; **Extraordinary General Meeting** = special meeting of shareholders to discuss an important matter

generate *verb* to use software *or* a computer device to produce codes, characters or programs automatically; ***the image is generated from digitally recorded data;*** **computer-generated** = produced using a computer; ***the book is illustrated with computer-generated graphics***

generation *noun* **(a)** action of producing characters *or* graphics using a computer; ***the computer is used in the generation of graphic images*** **(b)** reproduction of an image from an original

generic coding *noun* coding a document to specify headings, use of bold, roman and italic, etc.; ***ASPIC is a system of generic coding***

generic tags *noun* codes to identify headings and setting style for a manuscript

genre publishing *noun* publishing a fiction list, all of which is the same type of novel, such as science fiction, romantic fiction, westerns, etc.

gentleman's agreement *US* **gentlemen's agreement** *noun* verbal agreement between two parties who respect each other; ***they have a gentleman's agreement not to trade in each other's area***

get up *noun US* general format and style of a book

ghost 1 *noun* **ghost (writer)** = professional writer who writes a book for a famous person whose name then appears on the book as the author **2** *verb* to write a book for someone whose name then appears on the book as the author; **ghosted autobiography** = autobiography apparently written by a famous person, but in fact written by a ghost writer; ***his autobiography was ghosted by John Smith***

ghosting *noun* **(a)** effect when a text is printed out of register, so that a second text appears beside the first **(b)** faint image caused by a defect in the ink

GIF = GRAPHICS INTERFACE FORMAT graphics file format of a file containing a bit-mapped image; originally used on the CompuServe on-line system, now a standard for encoding colour bit-mapped images normally in either 16 or 256 colours with options for compression; **GIF file** = graphics file format of a file containing a bit-mapped image

gift *noun* thing given to someone; **gift book** = book which is given as a present, formerly often used for special anthologies which were given as presents; **gift coupon** *or* **gift token** *or* **gift voucher** = card, bought in a store, which is given as a present and which must be exchanged in that store for goods; **free gift** = present given by a shop to a customer who buys a certain amount of goods

gift-wrap *verb* to wrap a present in attractive paper; ***do you want this book gift-wrapped?***

gift-wrapping *noun* **(a)** service in a store for wrapping presents for customers **(b)** attractive paper for wrapping presents

gigabyte *noun* 10^9 bytes

GIGO = GARBAGE IN GARBAGE OUT

gilding *noun* putting gold leaf (on a binding *or* on the top edge or foredge of a book)

gilt *adjective* with gold leaf decoration; **book with a gilt edge** *or* **gilt top** = book where the foredge *or* top of the pages is decorated with gold leaf; **gilt in the round** = foredge which is gilded after the book has been rounded; **gilt in the square** = foredge which is gilded before the book has been rounded

gilt-edged *adjective* (book) with a gilt edge to the pages

GIP = GLAZED IMITATION PARCHMENT

glair *or* **glaire** *noun* glue made from egg white and vinegar, used to stick gold foil to the book cover when blocking

glassine *noun* thin transparent paper made from beaten pulp, used as wrapping paper or for the windows in window envelopes

glaze *noun* shiny coat given to art paper

glazed *adjective* shiny *or* glossy (paper); **glazed imitation parchment (GIP)** = shiny whitish paper, used for wrapping; **glazed morocco** = polished goatskin leather, used as a binding material; **glazed vellum** = shiny vellum, used for special documents, such as presentation scrolls

glitch *or* **glytch** *noun (informal)* anything causing the sudden failure of a computer

global *adjective* which covers everything; **global search and replace** = search and replace function which is applied to a whole computer file

gloss *noun* **(a)** shiny finish; **gloss paper** *or* **glossy coated paper** = paper with a shiny finish; **gloss art paper** = shiny art paper; *compare* MATT **(b)** explanation of a difficult word or comment on a difficult text, usually printed in the margin

glossary *noun* small book with a list of words referring to a particular subject, arranged in alphabetical order

glossy 1 *adjective* shiny (paper); ***the illustrations are printed on glossy art paper*** **2** *noun informal* photograph on glossy paper, the best quality for reproduction; **the glossies** = expensive magazines

> COMMENT: the glossiness of gloss paper is measured in terms of the ratio of reflected light from the paper surface to that from a polished black tile

glue 1 *noun* material which sticks items together; ***she put some glue on the back of the poster to fix it to the wall; the glue on the envelope does not stick very well*** **2** *verb* to stick things together with glue; ***the cover is glued to the endpapers; he glued the label to the box;*** **glueing machine** *or* **gluer** = machine which puts the glue onto book blocks before the cover is attached

> COMMENT: in hand binding, organic glues and pastes are used; these are flour paste or gelatine glue made from animal bones. In commercial binding, synthetic adhesives of the PVA type are used. These are often thermoplastic and set when cold; they remain flexible when set, while organic glues tend to set hard, and so may crack

glyphic *adjective* (typeface such as Perpetua) based on letters carved in stone

gm = GRAM **gm^2** *or* **gsm** = grams per square metre (the usual way of showing the weight of paper)

go *verb* **(a)** to be placed; ***the date goes at the top of the letter*** **(b)** *(of a newspaper)* **to go to bed** = to start printing; ***your story is too late for the first edition - the paper went to bed thirty minutes ago;*** *(of a book)* **to go to press** = to start printing; ***the author cannot make any more corrections - the book has gone to press***

go-ahead 1 *noun* **to give something the go-ahead** = to approve something *or* to say that something can be done; ***his project got a government go-ahead; the board refused to give the go-ahead to the dictionary project*** **2** *adjective* energetic *or* keen to do well; ***he is a very go-ahead type; she works for a go-ahead book packaging company***

goatskin *noun* leather from the skin of a goat, called morocco when used for binding

gofer *noun US* person who does all types of work in an office for low wages

going *adjective* **(a)** active *or* busy; **to sell a business as a going concern** = to sell a business as an actively trading company; **it is a going concern** = the company is working (and making a profit) **(b) the going price** = the usual *or* current price *or* the price which is being charged now; **the going rate** = the usual *or* current rate of payment; ***we pay the going rate for typists; the going rate for offices is £10 per square metre***

gold *noun* **gold blocking** = (i) the action of stamping decorations *or* letters in gold on the cover of a book; (ii) letters *or* decorations in gold leaf stamped onto the case of a book; **gold cushion** = soft pad on which gold leaf is kept ready for use; **gold foil** = gold-coloured metal foil, on a paper backing; **gold leaf** = very thin sheet of real gold, used to decorate tooling on a binding; **gold rubber** *or* **gold rug** = pad of soft leather used to wipe the cover of a book to remove bits of excess gold leaf; **gold tooling** = decorations in gold leaf stamped by hand on a binding

goldenrod *noun* orange paper used to mount films for platemaking

golden section *or* **golden rectangle** *noun* ideal elegant proportions of a page, based on the ratio of 34:21

> COMMENT: these proportions were first used in medieval manuscripts and were considered the ideal proportions for page design. In small formats they are also considered the ideal proportions for a type area. They were adopted by Penguin Books for their small paperback formats

golfball *noun* typewriter system, where the characters are on a metal ball which fits into the typewriter and rotates to allow the correct character to strike; **golfball typewriter** = typewriter that uses a golfball printhead

> COMMENT: a golfball contains all the characters of a single typeface; to change the face, the ball is taken out and replaced by another. The main defect of a golfball typewriter when used as a printer, is that it is slower than a dot-matrix printer

good *adjective* not bad; **good colour** = the ink is evenly spread over a whole printing job; *US* **good for press** = ready for printing; (NOTE: UK English is **passed for press**)

goodwill *noun* good reputation of a business; ***he paid £10,000 for the goodwill of the shop and £4,000 for the stock***

gothic *noun* **(a)** old typeface, similar to black letter, used in the first printed books; *see also* TEXTURA **(b)** *US* block letter, thick bold sans serif face

> COMMENT: the word 'gothic' was used in the 15th and 16th centuries by Italians (who preferred Roman and Italic type) to refer to the black letter faces used in Germany. By calling it gothic, they implied that it was barbaric. Gothic is still used to refer to the black letter faces used in Northern Europe

Goudy *noun* old face type, designed by the American typographer Frederic Goudy (1865-1947)

gouge *noun* tool used to impress decorative lines on a book cover

Government Printing Office *US* American government department which prints all government documents; (NOTE: the GB equivalent is **Her Majesty's Stationery Office (HMSO)**)

GPMU = GRAPHICAL, PAPER AND MEDIA UNION British trade union for the printing and paper industries formed by the amalgamation of NGA and SOGAT

gradation *noun* series of slight changes in colour *or* tone

grade *verb* **(a)** to sort something into different levels of quality **(b)** to make something rise in steps according to quantity; **graded advertising rates** = rates which become cheaper as you take more advertising space

graduate *noun* person who has a degree from a university or polytechnic; **graduate entry** = entry of graduates into employment with a company; ***the graduate entry into the civil service;*** **graduate training scheme** = training scheme for graduates; **graduate trainee** = person in a graduate training scheme

grain 1 *noun* **(a) grain direction** *or* **machine direction** = way in which the grain of the paper lies in the same direction as the movement of the web along a papermaking machine; **long grain** *or* **grain long** = sheet of paper where the grain runs with the long side of the sheet; **short grain** *or* **grain short** = sheet of paper where the grain runs across the sheet, parallel to the short side; **against the grain** = feeding paper into a printing press and printing on it across the grain of the paper **(b)** direction in which the fibres run in wood; ***wood engravings are cut across the grain*** **(c)** size of dots which form a photograph; **coarse grain** = larger dots (giving a rougher picture; **fine grain** = very small dots (giving a sharper picture) **(d)** spotted effect on fast photographic films due to the size of the light-sensitive silver halide crystals **2** *verb* to texture the surface of a lithographic plate to allow it to hold the ink

graining *noun* making a grainy effect on a picture

grainy *adjective* (photograph) with coarse grain; ***we will use grainy photographs to achieve an old-fashioned effect***

COMMENT: the grain on machine-made paper is formed as the wire mesh holding the pulp is shaken from side to side. The fibres in the pulp fall into line lengthwise with the web. In the case of handmade paper, the wire is also shaken, but in several directions, with the result that the fibres do not lie in one direction and the paper has no definite grain. In a reel of paper, the grain always runs in the direction of the web. Sheets can either have the grain along or across the sheet, depending on how the sheet is cut from the web. Books are normally printed with the grain (i.e. the grain runs down the page from top to bottom). Printing on paper against the grain (i.e. with the grain of the paper running from the foredge to the gutter) may avoid wrinkling of the pages in damp conditions, but it has other considerable disadvantages as it makes the book more difficult to keep flat when open and makes the pages curve. If paper is folded against the grain it will not lie flat. When printing in full colour it is desirable to print with the grain to avoid problems of register

gram *or* **gramme** *noun* measure of weight (one thousandth of a kilo); (NOTE: usually written **g** or **gm** with figures: **25g**)

grammage *noun* weight of paper, calculated as grams per square metre; (NOTE: usually shown as **gsm** : **80gsm paper**)

graph *noun* diagram which shows statistics in visual form, usually as a line or series of dots; ***to set out the results in a graph; to draw a graph showing the rise in profitability; the sales graph shows a steady rise;*** **graph paper** = special paper with many little squares, used for drawing graphs

graphic *adjective* **(a)** referring to drawings *or* illustrations; **graphic artist** *or* **graphic designer** = artist *or* designer who specializes in commercial design, involving text and illustrations **(b)** referring to illustrations produced by a computer; **graphic display (terminal)** = computer screen able to present graphical information; **graphic display resolution** = number of pixels that a computer is able to display on the screen; **graphic colour printer** = printer that can output colour graphics; **graphic object** = small graphic image imported from another drawing application and placed on a page; in most DTP, paint or drawing packages, the object can be moved, sized and positioned independently from the other elements on the page

graphical *adjective* referring to something represented by graphics

graphically *adverb* using pictures; ***the sales figures are graphically represented as a pie chart***

graphics *noun* pictures *or* illustrations *or* lines which are drawn on paper *or* on a screen to represent information; ***the computer will output graphics such as bar charts, pie charts, line drawings, etc.;*** **graphics accelerator** = video display board with its own graphics coprocessor and high-speed RAM that can carry out graphical drawing operations (such as fill) at high speed; often used to speed up software such as Windows or for graphics-intensive applications such as multimedia or DTP; **graphics art terminal** = typesetting terminal that is used with a phototypesetter; **graphics character** = preprogrammed shape that can be displayed on a non-graphical screen instead of a character, used extensively in videotext systems to display simple pictures; **graphics file** = (binary) file which contains data describing an image; ***there are many standards for graphics files including TIFF, IMG and EPS;*** **graphics file format** = method in which data describing an image is stored; *see also* GIF, PICT, TIFF **graphics mode** = videotext terminal whose displayed characters are taken from a range of graphics characters instead of text; **graphics pad** *or* **graphics tablet** = flat device that allows a user to input graphical information into a computer by drawing on its surface; **graphics printer** = printer capable of printing bit-mapped images; **graphics processor** *or* **graphics coprocessor** = secondary processor used to speed up the display of graphics: it calculates the position of pixels that form a line *or* shape and display graphic lines *or* shapes; **graphics terminal** *or* **graphics VDU** = special VDU which can display graphics

gratia *see* EX GRATIA

gratis *adverb* free, not costing anything; ***the author gets six gratis copies*** *or* ***six copies gratis***

grave accent *noun* small sign (è) placed over a vowel to show that it is pronounced in a special way *or* to distinguish it from others

> COMMENT: grave accents are used in French (à, è, ù) to indicate a pronunciation change or a spelling change; they are used in other languages to show stress

graver *noun* tool used in engraving

gravure *noun* photogravure, method of printing where the ink is in hollows etched into a copper surface, with the top surface being wiped clean so that when the paper is pressed onto the plate the ink from the hollows is transferred to it; *see also* PHOTOGRAVURE

gray goods *noun US* uncoloured cloth for binding

gray scale *see* GREY SCALE

greaseproof paper *noun* paper which is specially prepared to resist grease and oil, used to cover *or* wrap oily food

greasy ink *noun* ink used in lithography

> COMMENT: the image is drawn on the stone or plate with greasy ink; the surface is then wetted and printing ink is applied. The printing ink is repelled by the water but held by the greasy ink lines

greek *noun* meaningless mixed letters used to make typeset text used in layouts

Greek alphabet alphabet used in ancient and modern Greek; it contains 24 characters; some of these characters (such as π) have been adopted as international mathematical and scientific symbols

grey board *noun* pale grey cardboard used in binding

grey balance *noun* condition in a colour reproduction system where the values of the primary colours are balanced to give a visually neutral grey

grey scale *or* **gray scale** *noun* **(a)** shades of grey that are used to measure the correct exposure when filming **(b)** shades which are produced from displaying what should be colour information on a monochrome monitor

grid *noun* **(a)** system of numbered squares; **grid structure** = structure based on a grid **(b)** system of squares used to help when drawing; matrix of lines at right angles allowing points to be easily plotted *or* located; **grid gauge** = positioning tool for microfiche image display **(c)** details of specification which apply to several books in a series

> COMMENT: grids are used by designers and pasteup artists for laying out magazines and books, where the page size, type area and general layout remain the same for each page. The designer will prepare a master grid, showing the basic proportions of the page, with its trim size, type area, headlines, folio positions, margins, etc., and this is used when pasting up each page

grind *verb* to crush into tiny pieces; ***wood from softwood trees is ground up to make woodpulp***

grinder *noun* machine for crushing wood, as the first stage in papermaking

grip *see* GRIPPER EDGE

grippers *noun* little metal fingers which hold the paper in place and pull it through the printing press; **gripper edge** = feed edge, the edge of a sheet of paper which is held by the grippers and goes through the press first

groove *noun* low space between the cover board and the spine, where the covers hinge, and which, if it is large enough, will allow the book to lie flat when open; **American groove** *or* **French groove** = joint in binding where space is left between the board and the spine to allow the book to open flat

gross profit *noun* difference between revenue and direct costs

grot *or* **grotesque** *noun* any sans serif typeface

> COMMENT: sans faces are called 'grot' in British English and 'gothic' in US English. The first sans faces appeared in the first part of the 19th century and were called 'grotesque' because they seemed so strange

groundwood *noun US* mechanical wood pulp which has been ground by a machine; (NOTE: UK English uses only the term **mechanical pulp**)

gsm *or* **g/m²** = GRAMS PER SQUARE METRE (PER SHEET) way of showing the weight of paper used in printing

guard *noun* **(a)** something which protects, especially a card which protects an illustration or a strip of linen pasted onto the back fold of a signature **(b)** strip of paper sewn between sections of a book, to which tipped in illustrations can be glued; also used to increase the bulk at the spine, so as to allow space for folded maps or plates to be inserted (here also called a 'compensating guard')

guarding *noun* **(a)** joining a single sheet to a book *or* magazine **(b)** pasting a strip of paper *or* gauze to the fold of a signature to repair or strengthen it; heavy books often have the first and last signatures guarded

guide *noun* **(a)** book which shows how something should be used; ***a guide to the use of computers in typesetting*** **(b) travel guide** = book which tells you what is worth visiting in a place, and how to get there, which hotels to stay at, etc. **(c)** channel to allow paper to be fed into a machine; **drop guides** = bars at the sides of a paper feed which place the sheets in the correct position

guide bars *noun* special lines in a bar code that show the start and finish of the code; ***the standard guide bars are two thin lines that are a little longer than the coding lines***

guidebook *noun* book which describes a place for the benefit of visitors; ***a guidebook publisher; they publish a series of pocket guidebooks to European towns***

guideline *noun* **(a)** general instructions given to a compositor **(b)** unofficial suggestion from the management as to how something should be done; ***all editors should follow the guidelines for dealing with agents which have been laid down by the editorial director*** **(c)** line on artwork, showing the edge of the printing area

guild *noun* association of merchants *or* of shopkeepers; *see also* INDEPENDENT PUBLISHERS GUILD

guillemets *noun* small angled quotation marks (« ») used in some languages, but not in English; *see also* DUCK-FOOT QUOTES

guillotine 1 *noun* machine for cutting thick layers of paper or for trimming the edges of books **2** *verb* to cut paper with a guillotine

gum 1 *noun* type of glue which is made from plant resin; ***he stuck the label to the box with gum;*** **gum arabic** = gum made from resin from acacia trees, used as an adhesive on stamps, labels, etc. **2** *verb* to stick with glue; **gummed label** = label with dry glue on it, which has to be made wet to make it stick; **gummed paper** = paper with dry glue on it, which sticks if it is moistened; **gummed tape** = paper tape with glue on it, which sticks when moistened

gumming up *noun* covering a lithographic stone with a thin layer of gum arabic, to enhance the printed image

gusset *noun* folded paper which forms the expanding edge of a pocket

Gutenberg Johannes Gutenberg (1399?-1468), a German printer, and the inventor of printing as we know it. Gutenberg was the man who saw that separate pieces of metal type, one for each letter, could be duplicated by being cast from matrices; these separate pieces of type could then be put together in rows, clamped into chases, inked ;and multiple impressions taken from them by pressing the inked type onto sheets of paper. This method of typesetting did not materially change until the phototypesetting machines of the 1960s

gutter *noun* **(a)** (i) the two inside margins in a book *or* magazine; (ii) the space running between two facing pages near the spine (periodicals are often printed 'across the gutter' (i.e. with illustrations running across the centre fold) **(b)** *US* the space between columns of type **(c)** space between two imposed pages of type in a forme

gutter press *noun* newspapers which rely on sensational stories *or* murder reports *or* stories of the sex life of TV stars etc. to increase their circulation

Hh

H & J *or* **h & j** = HYPHENATION AND JUSTIFICATION

hache *noun* symbol to indicate space, or (especially in USA) to indicate the word 'number'; *see also* HASH

hack *noun* journalist who writes anything to order; **hack writer** = writer who will write anything to order; **hack work** = uninspired work written to order

haggle *verb* to discuss prices and terms and try to reduce them; ***to haggle about*** *or* ***over the details of a contract; after two days' haggling the contract was signed***

hair *noun* **hair space** = very thin space between characters (in letterpress, a half a point or one twelfth of an em wide)

hairline *noun* a very thin line; a thin stroke on a character, as opposed to the main stem; **hairline serif** = serif which is simply a thin straight line (as opposed to slab serifs, which are thick straight lines)

halation *noun* halo effect in the light parts of a photograph, caused by light reflecting back from the emulsion

half 1 *noun* one of two parts into which something is divided; ***the first half of the book is the text, and the rest is taken up with supplements;*** **the first half** *or* **the second half of the year** = the periods from January 1st to June 30th *or* from June 30th to December 31st; **the two sisters share the royalties half and half** = they share the royalties equally **2** *adjective* divided into two parts; **half measure** = setting type half the normal width (usually to leave space for an illustration); **a half-price sale** = sale of all books or other goods at half the normal price; **to sell books off at half price** = at 50% of the price for which they were sold before; **half space** = paper movement in a printer by half the amount of a normal character; **half stuff** = paper pulp ready for the beater; **half up** = illustration which is prepared at one and a half times the size it will be printed in the book

half binding *noun* binding of a hardcover book, where the spine and corners are covered with one type of material (such as leather) and the rest is left in ordinary cloth or paper

half bound *or* **half leather bound** *adjective* (book) with leather binding on the spine and part of the front and back, including the corners

half-calf *see* CALF

half line block *noun* line block where the lines appear greyer, made by using parallel cross-lines

half page *noun* half of a full page; ***the book has sixteen half page line drawings; we need to save a half page from the index***

half plate *noun* (i) illustration which takes half a page; (ii) common format for small photographs (6 x 4 inches)

half sheet work *noun* printing process, where both sides of a sheet are printed from the same forme, giving two identical copies; *see also* WORK AND TWIST

half-title *noun* first printed page of a book, with the title, sometimes laid out in decorative style, but smaller than on the title page and with no author's name or publisher's imprint (also called the bastard title)

halftone *or* **half-tone** *noun* **(a)** (i) continuous shading of a printed area; (ii) grey shade appearing to be half way between white and black; **halftone block** = illustration on a copper block where the image has been broken up by a screen so that it is made up of a series of dots of different sizes; **halftone process** *or* **halftoning** = making halftones from photographs; **halftone screen** = screen with cross lines used for preparing a halftone illustration **(b)** illustration made using the halftone process; ***the book is illustrated with twenty halftones; a book with 25 halftone illustrations; we need a full page halftone facing the beginning of the chapter***

> COMMENT: halftones are made by breaking up a continuous tone pattern into a series of dots of varying sizes. When printed, the dots appear to merge into a continuous tone, though if you look at them closely the dots are visible. The dots are created by scanning or by photographing the original through a screen, which is a mesh of criss-cross lines or a series of dots

half-year *noun* six months of an accounting period; **first half-year** *or* **second half-year** = first six months *or* second six months of a company's accounting year

half-yearly **1** *adjective* happening every six months; referring to a period of six months; ***a half-yearly magazine; half-yearly royalty statement*** **2** *adverb* every six months; ***we pay some royalties half-yearly***

halide *noun* silver compound that is used to provide a light-sensitive coating on photographic film and paper

halo *noun* **(a)** photographic effect seen as a dark region with a very bright line around it, caused by pointing the camera into the light **(b)** thicker ink at the edge of halftone dots, which makes the dots darker

hand *noun* **(a)** **to shake hands** = to hold someone's hand to show that an agreement has been reached; **to shake hands on a deal** = to shake hands to show that a deal has been agreed **(b)** **by hand** = using the hands, not a machine; ***the corrected pages will be made up by hand on the screen;*** **to send a letter by hand** = to ask someone to carry and deliver a letter personally, not sending it through the post; **hand lettering** = drawing letters by hand (used when designing publicity material); **hand mould** = small mould made of wood with a wire mesh at the bottom, used to make handmade paper; **hand sewing** = sewing the sections of a book together by hand **(c)** **in hand** = kept in reserve; **balance in hand** *or* **cash in hand** = cash held to pay small debts and running costs; **work in hand** = work which is in progress but not finished **(d)** **to change hands** = to be sold to a new owner; ***the bookshop changed hands for £100,000*** **(e)** printed sign ☞ indicating a reference or the beginning of a paragraph

handbill *noun* sheet of printed paper (printed on one side only) handed out to members of the public as an advertisement

handbinding *noun* binding where each book is bound separately by a trained operator

handbook *noun* book which gives instructions on how something is to be used; ***the handbook does not say how you open the photocopier; look in the operator's handbook to see how to set up the H & J program;*** **service handbook** = book which shows how to service a machine

handbound *adjective* (book) which has been bound separately by a trained operator; ***an illustrated edition of Shakespeare has been handbound in white leather***

hand-coloured *adjective* (line illustration) which has been coloured by hand; ***an early 19th century travel book with hand-coloured illustrations***

handle *verb* **(a)** to deal with something *or* to organize something; ***they can handle paper sizes up to 1200 x 1600mm; the accounts department handles all the cash; we can handle orders for up to 15,000 units; the agents handle all our overseas orders*** **(b)** to sell *or* to trade in (a sort of product); ***some bookshops will not handle stationery; they will not handle goods produced by other firms***

handling *noun* dealing with something; **handling charges** = money to be paid for packing and invoicing *or* for dealing with something in general *or* for moving goods from one place to another; ***the company adds on 5% handling charge for processing orders on our behalf;*** **handling stiffness** = amount of stiffness in paper which is handled a lot (such as newsprint); **materials handling** = moving materials from one part of a factory to another in an efficient way

handmade *adjective* made by hand, not by machine; **handmade paper** = paper which is made by hand, using a hand mould to take stock from a vat and then, after the water has been shaken out, dried on felt pads; ***he writes all his letters on handmade paper***

hand mould *noun* wooden frame with a wire mesh bottom, in which handmade paper is made

handout *noun* **publicity handout** = information sheet which is given to members of the public

hand press *noun* printing press (such as an Albion press) which is operated by hand, printing one sheet at a time; ***the book of poems was printed on his own hand press***

hand roller *noun* roller used to ink the type by hand on a hand press

hand set *verb* to set metal type by hand; **hand-set type** = type which has been set by hand; **hand-setting** = setting of a text in metal type by hand

handshake *or* **handshaking** *noun* standardized signals between two devices to make sure that the system is working correctly, equipment is compatible and data transfer is correct (signals would include ready to receive, ready to transmit, data OK)

handwriting *noun* writing done by hand; the particular way in which a person writes; ***can you read the handwriting on this copy? Spanish handwriting is not always easy to read;*** **send a letter of application in your own handwriting** = written by you with a pen, and not typed

handwritten *adjective* written by hand, not typed; ***we set twenty pages of handwritten author's corrections; it is more professional to send in a typed rather than a handwritten manuscript***

hang *verb* to attach something to a hook, nail, etc.; **hanging figures** = old-style figures, figures which have ascenders (6 and 8) and descenders (3, 4, 5, 7 and 9); **hanging indent** *or* **hanging indentation** *or* *US* **flush and hang** = type of indentation, where the first line is full out and the rest of the paragraph is indented; **hanging paragraph** = paragraph with the first line full width and rest indented

hard *adjective* **(a)** solid *or* not soft; **hard cash** = money in notes and coins which is ready at hand; **hard copy** = printout of a text which is on a computer *or* printed copy of a document which is on microfilm *or* artwork from which a digitized image is made; ***he made the presentation with diagrams and ten pages of hard copy;*** **hard disk** = computer disk which has a sealed case and can store large quantities of information; **hard hyphen** = hyphen which is part of the normal spelling of a word; **hard packing** = stiff paper used to wrap round a printing cylinder to give a sharp image when printing on hard paper **(b) hard bargain** = bargain with difficult terms; **to drive a hard bargain** = to make sure one gets good terms for oneself in negotiations; **to strike a hard bargain** = to agree a deal where the terms are favourable to you; **after weeks of hard bargaining** = after weeks of difficult discussions **(c) hard currency** = currency of a country which has a strong economy and which can be changed into other currencies easily; ***exports which can earn hard currency for the Soviet Union; these goods must be paid for in hard currency; a hard currency deal***

hardback *or* **hardcover edition** *noun* book bound in a stiff card *or* cased binding (as opposed to a paperback *or* soft cover edition); ***the book was published in hardback at £12.95 and simultaneously in paperback at £4.95; the hardcover edition is now out of print***

hardbound *adjective* (book) with a hard cased cover, as opposed to a paperback

hardcover *noun & adjective* version of a book with a cased binding (as opposed to paperback); ***we printed 4,000 copies of the hardcover edition, and 10,000 of the paperback***

hard sell *noun* **to give a product the hard sell** = to make great efforts to persuade people to buy it; **he tried to give me the hard sell** = he put a lot of effort into trying to make me buy

hard selling *noun* act of selling by using great efforts; ***a lot of hard selling went into that deal***

hard-sized paper *noun* paper containing a large quantity of size

hardware *noun* **computer hardware** = machines used in data processing, including the computers, keyboards, monitors and printers, but not the programs; *see also* SOFTWARE

hardwood *noun* wood from a tree which loses its leaves in winter (as opposed to conifers which give softwood); hardwood is used for wood engraving; **hardwood pulp** = paper pulp from hardwood trees, which gives a bulky opaque paper

Hart's Rules *'Rules for Compositors and Readers at the University Press'* book of instructions on spelling, hyphenation and punctuation, originally published for the benefit of staff at Oxford University Press, but used by most printers and publishers; (NOTE: the American equivalent is the **Manual of Style** published by the University of Chicago Press)

hash *noun US* printed sign (#) which indicates one of a series of numbers

hashmark *or* **hash mark** *noun* printed sign (#) used as a hard copy marker *or* as an indicator; (NOTE: in US usage # means number; **#32 = number 32** (apartment number in an address, paragraph number in a text, etc.). In computer usage, the pound sign £ is often used in the US instead of the hash to avoid confusion)

hatching *noun* series of lines drawn across an illustration to indicate tones

head 1 *noun* **(a)** most important person; **head of department** *or* **department head** = person in charge of a department; **head buyer** = most important buyer in a department store **(b)** top part *or* first part of a page; text on the top part of a page; **running heads** = text (such as the title of the book *or* a chapter) which appears as the first line at the top of a series of pages; **head margin** = margin between the text and the top of the page **(c)** top part of a book; ***we can trim 5mm off the head;*** **printed head-to-head** *or* **head-to-tail** = method of printing where two copies are printed from the same sheet, either with the heads of the two books together, or with the head of one connecting with the bottom edge of the other (this is used in paperback printing: the two books are cut apart when bound) **(d)** part of a printer that prints **(e) read/write head** = part of a disk drive that reads the information from a disk *or* writes the information on the disk; **head crash** = failure in a disk drive, where the read/write head touches the surface of the disk, causing damage and data loss **(f)** = HEADBOX **2** *verb* **(a)** to be the manager *or* to be the most important person; ***to head a department; he is heading a buying mission to China*** **(b)** to put a title to a chapter *or* page, etc.; ***see the paragraph headed 'Final Comments';*** **headed paper** = notepaper with the name of the company and its address printed on it

headband *noun* decorative strip (often in two colours) along the top of the back of the book, inside the spine

headbox *noun* vat of liquid pulp from which the pulp passes onto the wire mesh to be made into paper

headcap *noun* piece of leather binding on the spine, which folds over at the top and bottom and is tucked into the spine

header *noun* **(a)** information at the beginning of a list of data relating to the rest of the data; **header block** = block of data at the beginning of a file, which contains the file characteristics **(b)** words at the top of a page of a document (such as title, author's name, page number, etc.; *compare* FOOTER

heading *noun* **(a)** words at the top of a piece of text; ***the main headings are in 12pt Helvetica bold; the secondary headings are in 12pt Helvetica italic; items are listed under several headings; look at the figure under the heading 'Costs 95-96'*** **(b)** **letterheading** *or* **heading on notepaper** = name and address of a company printed at the top of a piece of notepaper

headline *noun* **(a)** line of type at the head of a book page (often called the 'running head'), usually consisting of the chapter title and a folio **(b)** display typesetting above a story in a newspaper or magazine

headliner *noun* typesetting machine which produces display setting

headpiece *noun* decorative design at the beginning of a chapter; *compare* TAILPIECE

head up *verb* to be in charge of; ***he has been appointed to head up our European organization***

headword *noun* main word in a dictionary *or* encyclopaedia, which begins an entry; ***a dictionary with 50,000 headwords***

heater *noun* device which heats; **heater box** = box in which a die is placed to be heated before tooling

heatsealed *adjective* (shrink-wrapping) which is sealed by heating

heat sealing *noun* sealing plastic shrink-wrapping by heating it

heat-set ink *noun* ink which dries when it is heated (used, for example, in a heat-set web offset machine)

heat transfer copier *noun* type of small copying machine which takes the print dye from printed paper and transfers it to another surface such as paper or cloth

heavy *adjective* thick *or* bold (type); ***book printed in heavy type;*** **heavy rule** = thick line

hectograph *noun* duplicating machine which uses gelatine plates as masters

height *noun* measurement of how tall *or* high something is; **character height** *or* **letter height** = measurement in millimetres from the bottom of the character to the top; **height to paper** = standard height of metal type (0.918 inches or 23.3mm in the UK and USA; the standard height varies in other countries); **x height** = height of the main central part of a printed character, such as the letter x, which does not have an ascender or descender

hell box *noun* box in which broken pieces of type or type which is in the wrong case can be put

hemp *noun* plant used for making rope and paper

> COMMENT: hemp waste or old ropes are used to make pulp: hemp paper is very thin, but strong and opaque. India paper and airmail paper can be made from hemp

hempel quoin *noun* quoin used to tighten a forme, by placing it in a corner of the forme and tightening it with a key

Hercules graphics adapter (HGA) *noun* standard for high-resolution mono graphics adapter developed by Hercules Corporation that can display text or graphics at a resolution of 720x348 pixels

Her Majesty's Stationery Office (HMSO) British government department which prints and publishes government documents; (NOTE: the US equivalent is the **Government Printing Office**)

Hewlett Packard LaserJet™ *or* **HP LaserJet** laser printer manufactured by Hewlett Packard that uses its PCL language to describe a page; **Hewlett Packard Printer Control Language (HP-PCL)** = standard set of commands developed by Hewlett Packard to allow a software application to control a laser printer's functions

HGA = HERCULES GRAPHICS ADAPTER

hickey *or* **hicky** *noun* dirty mark on the printed sheet made by dust or ink on a film *or* plate; **void hickey** = white spot on printed matter; (NOTE: plural of both spellings is **hickies**)

hide *noun* leather made from the skin of older animals than calf, used for binding large format books

hi-end *noun* pre-press system of larger capacity and range than a DTP system, found in specialized trade houses

high *adjective* **(a)** large *or* not low; **high gloss paper** = paper with a very shiny finish; **high sales** = large amount of revenue produced by sales; **high spaces** *or* **high quads** = spaces in letterpress which are the shoulder height of the type; **high volume (of sales)** = large number of items sold **(b) highest bidder** = person who offers the most money at an auction; ***the property was sold to the highest bidder;*** **a decision taken at the highest level** = decision taken by the most important person or group

high-bulk antique *noun US* light very thick paper, formerly used for children's books; (NOTE: UK English is **featherweight antique**)

high-grade *adjective* of very good quality; ***a high-grade art paper;*** **a high-grade trade delegation** = a delegation made up of very important people

high-level *adjective* **(a)** very important; **a high-level meeting** *or* **delegation** = meeting *or* delegation of the most important people (such as ministers, managing directors); **a high-level decision** = decision taken by the most important person or group **(b)** **high-level computer language** = programming language which uses normal words and figures

highlight *verb* (i) to add white parts to an illustration to make it appear more vivid; (ii) to mark a part of the text so that it stands out from the rest; ***the captions are highlighted with a double rule***

highlights *noun* (i) the main white or light-coloured parts of an illustration; (ii) characters *or* symbols treated to make them stand out from the rest of the text, often by using bold type; **highlight bump** = increasing the sharpness of the highlights in a halftone by exposing the film to the original a second time, after screening

high-resolution *or* **hi-res** *noun* ability to display *or* detect a very large number of pixels per unit area; ***high-resolution graphics; this high-resolution monitor can display 640 x 320 pixels; the new hi-res optical scanner can detect 300 dots per inch***

> COMMENT: currently, high-resolution graphics displays can show images at a resolution of 1024x1024 pixels, high-resolution printers can print at 600 or 800 dots per inch and a high-resolution scanner can scan at a resolution of 800 or 1200 dots per inch

highspeed skip *noun* rapid movement in a printer to miss the perforations in continuous stationery

hinge *noun* line along which the cover bends, where the front or back of a cover joins the spine, strengthened in cased books by a strip of gauze

hinged style *noun* type of cut flush paperback binding where the cover is creased in four places, head to foot, and glue is applied to the spine and about 3mm to first and last pages

hire 1 *noun* **(a)** paying money to rent a car *or* boat *or* piece of equipment for a time; **car hire firm** *or* **equipment hire firm** = company which owns cars *or* equipment and lends them to customers for a payment **(b)** *US* **for hire contract** = freelance contract; **to work for**

hire = to work freelance **2** *verb* **(a) to hire staff** = to engage new staff to work for you; **to hire and fire** = to employ new staff and dismiss existing staff; ***we have hired the best lawyers to represent us; they hired a small picture bureau to take the photographs*** **(b) to hire a car** *or* **a laser printer** = to pay money to use a car *or* a laser printer for a time

hi-res = HIGH RESOLUTION

histogram *noun* graph on which values are represented as vertical *or* horizontal bars

historic *or* **historical** *adjective* which goes back over a period of time; **historic(al) cost** = actual cost of something which was made some time ago; **historical figures** = figures which were current in the past; **historical novel** = type of fiction where the action is accurately placed in some definite time in the past

hit *noun* successful match *or* search of a database

HMSO = HER MAJESTY'S STATIONERY OFFICE

holding lines *noun* lines on a page design, showing where the artwork is to be placed

Holland cloth *noun* stiff cloth used to strengthen hinges

hollander beater *noun* machine for beating paper pulp

hollow 1 *adjective* empty *or* with nothing inside; **hollow back binding** = binding where the back is not glued to the spine of the book block, but is rounded to leave a space between it and the sewn signatures (as opposed to tight back binding); **Oxford hollow** = type of hollow back binding where a paper tube is placed between the back and the spine of the book block **2** *noun* **(a)** space between the back and the sewn signatures **(b)** paper tube glued to the spine of the book and to the covers, in order to strengthen the binding

hologram *noun* three-dimensional image, used on credit cards as a means of preventing forgery (also used sometimes on book covers)

holograph *noun* handwritten manuscript, as written by the author using a pen *or* pencil, but not typed; ***a holograph letter from T.S. Eliot***

home *noun* **home country** = country where a company is based; **home page** = *(on the Internet)* first page that is displayed when you visit a WWW site; ***if you visit the Peter Collin Publishing WWW site at 'http://www.pcp.co.uk' the home page is the first page that is displayed;*** **home sales** *or* **sales in the home market** = sales in the country where a company is based; **home-produced products** = products manufactured in the country where the company is based

honorarium *noun* money paid to a professional person, such as an accountant *or* a lawyer, when he does not ask for a fee; (NOTE: plural is **honoraria**)

hook down *noun* end of a line which runs over to the next line and is attached to the line below with a bracket

hooked plates *noun* plates which have a narrow folded edge which hooks round a printed section

hook up *noun* end of a line which runs over to the next line and is attached to the line above with a bracket

horizontal format *noun US* book format where the spine and foredge are shorter than the top and bottom edges; (NOTE: GB English is **landscape format**)

host computer *noun* **(a)** main controlling computer in a multi-user *or* distributed system **(b)** computer used to write and debug software for another computer, often using a cross compiler **(c)** computer in a network that provides special services *or* programming languages to all users

hot *adjective* **(a) hot-ground pulp** = paper pulp which has been ground with very little water, allowing the pulp to become hotter; **hot melt adhesive** = very hot adhesive used to stick covers to books (it sticks by absorption rather than by cooling); **hot press** = press used to block letters on a cover; **hot-pressed paper** = paper which is pressed between heated metal plates to make it smooth; **hot-pressing** = blocking letters on a cover with a hot stamp **(b) the news is hot off the press** *or* **it's a hot-press item** = the news is extremely recent

hotline *noun* special telephone number for rapid servicing of orders (used by publishers at particular times of year, such as Christmas or the beginning of a new academic buying season)

hot link *noun* command within a hypertext program that links a hotspot or hotword on one page with a second destination page which is displayed if the user selects the hotspot

hot metal composition *or* **hot type** *noun* form of typesetting (such as Linotype and Monotype) where characters *or* whole words *or* whole lines of type are set using molten metal, from instructions given to the setting machine on perforated tape produced by the compositor's keyboard; ***the book was set in hot metal; we used hot metal setting for his last book; how many typesetters still offer hot metal setting?***

> COMMENT: hot metal setting was used both for books and for newspapers for over 100 years. The 'Guardian' newspaper was still being set in hot metal in 1987. This type of setting is still occasionally used by jobbing printers

house *noun* company (especially a publishing company); ***one of the biggest software houses in the US; a French publishing house; the text was typed in house; we employ six in-house keyboarders; she works for a trade publishing house;*** **house ad** = advertisement in a magazine, advertising something offered for sale by the magazine itself (special subscription offer, binder for past issues, etc.), used to fill advertising space that has not been sold; *see also* FILLER **house copies** = copies of a magazine or book used in the publisher's offices; **house corrections** = corrections noted by the proofreaders employed by the printer *or* publisher (as opposed to author's corrections); **house editor** = editor employed by a publishing company; **house journal** *or* **house magazine** *or US* **house organ** = magazine produced for the workers or shareholders in a company to give them news about the company; **house reader** = proof reader employed by a printer *or* publishing house; **house telephone** = internal telephone for calling from one office to another

house-to-house *adjective* going from one house to the next, asking people to buy something; ***house-to-house encyclopaedia selling; the company sells its reference books house-to-house***

housekeeping *noun* tasks that have to be carried out regularly to maintain a computer system (such as checking that backup copies are kept, deleting old files, etc.)

house style *noun* style of spelling *or* layout *or* typography *or* general design, used by a company, especially one adopted by a publishing house in all its books; ***our house style is to spell 'organize' with a 'z' and not with an 's'***

> COMMENT: the aim of a house style is to give consistency to all the products of a publishing house, thus making them more recognizable to the reading public. In the case of magazines, contributors will be sent a style sheet which shows how they should lay out their contributions. A house style will cover many aspects of layout, such as headlines, position of folios, typefaces and sizes; it will also cover details of spelling and punctuation: the form for writing dates (1st January 1999 or January 1st, 1999 or 1st Jan. 1999 or 01.01.99, etc.); the use of full stops after abbreviation (Mr or Mr., P.O.Box or PO Box, etc.). Most publishing companies have their own style sheets which are given to editors and form part of the training programme for new editorial and production staff. Many printers as well as publishers have their own house style and many follow the style of one of the University Presses (Oxford and

Cambridge). See also HART'S RULES, MANUAL OF STYLE

how-to books *noun US* DIY books

HRG = HIGH RESOLUTION GRAPHICS

HSWO = HOT-SET WEB OFFSET

HTML = HYPERTEXT MARKUP LANGUAGE a series of special codes that define the typeface and style that should be used when displaying the text and also allow hypertext links to other parts of the document or to other documents; *see also* INTERNET, SGML, WWW

COMMENT: normally used to define screens used in the World Wide Web on the Internet, similar to SGML; for example, the '<p>' code means new paragraph, the '<b>' code means display in bold. A document coded in HTML can be displayed on any viewer software that understands HTML - such as any WWW browser, like Mosaic or Netscape Navigator

HTTP = HYPERTEXT TRANSFER PROTOCOL protocol used to identify the address of WWW pages stored on the Internet; the address of a WWW page is normally written as 'http://www.pcp.co.uk'

humidity *noun* amount of moisture in a substance (paper requires a constant humidity in order to avoid cockling and curling from damp, or shrinkage from dry conditions); **relative humidity** = the mass of moisture in a given volume of air expressed as a percentage of the moisture required to saturate the same volume of air at a certain temperature

Hunter Lab values *noun US* colour measurement scales used to measure colour values

hurt *verb* to harm *or* to damage; ***the bad publicity did not hurt our sales; the company has not been hurt by the cuts in educational expenditure; it won't hurt to let the author make a few changes;*** *US* **hurt books** = damaged *or* soiled books, which are then sold cheaply (they may have been damaged in the bookshop, in transit, or frequently they are simply returned stock)

hurts *noun* = HURT BOOKS

hybrid typeface *noun* computer-generated typeface which combines elements of several faces

hydrapulper *noun* tank in which dry pulp and other ingredients are added to water when making paper

hydration *noun* condition of paper pulp where water does not drain away from it through the mesh

hygrometer *noun* instrument which measures relative humidity

hype 1 *noun* excessive claims made in advertising; ***all the hype surrounding the launch of the new novel*** **2** *verb* to make excessive claims in advertising

hyperlink *noun* series of commands attached to a button or word in one page that link it to another page in a multimedia book, so that if a user clicks on the button or word, the hyperlink will move the user to another position in the book or display another page

hypertext *adjective* system of organising information; certain words in a document link to other documents and display the text when the word is selected; ***in this hypertext page, click once on the word 'computer' and it will tell you what a computer is;*** *see also* HTML, HTTP

hyphen *noun* printing sign (-), usually one en in length, which shows that two characters *or* words are joined together; ***do you spell 'coordinate' with a hyphen*** *or* ***does 'coordinate' take a hyphen? he omitted a hyphen in up-to-date;*** **hard hyphen** = hyphen which is part of the normal spelling of a word; **soft hyphen** = hyphen which is inserted when a word is split at the end of a line in word-processed text, but is not present when the word is written normally

hyphenate *verb* to put a hyphen between two characters; to separate a long word at the end of a line by inserting a hyphen; ***'coordinate' should be hyphenated; can you hyphenate 'bookshop' as 'books-hop'?***

hyphenated *adjective* written with a hyphen; ***the word 'high-level' is usually hyphenated***

hyphenation *noun* way of dividing a long word at the end of line by inserting a hyphen; **hyphenation exception dictionary** = list of words held in a computer memory, which either cannot be divided, or which are divided in an unusual way (this dictionary is stored in the H & J program of a typesetting computer); **hyphenation routine** = computer program which automatically divides words at the ends of line and inserts a hyphen; **hyphenation and justification (H & J) program** = computer program which automatically divides words correctly at the ends of lines at the same time as the lines are justified; ***an American hyphenation and justification program will not work with British English spellings***

hyphenless justification *noun* justification carried out without splitting words (this gives an easier read on wide lines, but in narrow columns can create large interword spaces)

hypo *abbreviation* photographic fixing solution, used to fix the image after the film has been developed

Ii

IBC = INSIDE BACK COVER

ibid *or* **ibidem** *abbreviation* meaning 'in the same place'; (NOTE: used especially in bibliographical references, where if several references are to the same book, the full title is not repeated, but is replaced by **ibid: 'ibid, page 324'**)

IBM compatible *adjective* able to accept the same peripherals as an IBM PC

icon *noun* small graphic symbol displayed on a screen, used in some DTP packages as an aid to the user

ICR = INTELLIGENT CHARACTER RECOGNITION

id. = IDEM

ideal *adjective* perfect *or* very good for something; ***this is the ideal size for a pocket dictionary;*** **ideal format** = standard large format for photographic negatives, used mainly in professional equipment

idem *or* **id** *noun* Latin word meaning 'the same', used to refer to a reference which has just been used

idiot copy *noun* keyboarded text without any formatting commands

idiot tape *noun* computer tape with plain text, without typesetting codes, which cannot be typeset until formatting data, such as hyphenation, justification, line width, and page size, has been added by a computer

idler *or* **idling roller** *noun* roller on a web press which turns freely

idle time *noun* time when a machine is not being used

IGT method *noun* method of testing paper absorbency (the paper is printed with a solution of Sudan Red in dibutylphthalate: the length of the printed area is inversely proportional to the absorbency of the paper); **IGT printability tester** = device for printing strips of paper under controlled conditions (used to measure oil absorbency and pick resistance)

ILL = INTER-LIBRARY LOAN

illegibility *noun* being illegible

illegible *adjective* which cannot be read; ***the keyboarders are complaining that the MS is illegible***

illicit *adjective* not legal *or* not permitted; ***the illicit sale of pornographic magazines***

illiteracy *noun* being unable to read; ***a campaign to stamp out adult illiteracy***

illiterate *adjective* (person) who cannot read; ***half our sports authors are illiterate;*** **he is computer illiterate** = he does not know how to use a computer

illuminate *verb* to draw pictures to illustrate a manuscript; ***some manuscripts of the Bible are beautifully illuminated***

illumination *noun* coloured drawing which illustrates an old manuscript

illustrate *verb* to put pictures in a book; to add pictures to a text; ***the book is illustrated with twenty-five full-colour plates; who illustrated the children's book series? the book is illustrated in colour; the manual is illustrated with charts and pictures of the car engine***

illustration *noun* **(a)** picture in a book (halftone or line drawing); ***there are several full-page illustrations of footballers*** **(b)** line drawing (as opposed to a halftone); **illustration board** = thick card used for artwork

illustrator *noun* person who illustrates a book; ***a children's book by a well-known illustrator***

image *noun* **(a)** picture *or* photograph *or* text, as it appears on a film or plate; **image area** = (i); *(in lithography)* part of the surface which takes ink and so prints the image (as opposed to the non-image area); (ii) part of a computer screen on which designs *or* characters can be displayed; **image master** = the master type from which characters used in phototypesetting are formed; **image scanner** = input device which converts documents *or* drawings *or* photographs into digitized machine-readable form; **image setter** = typesetting device that can process a PostScript page and produce a high-resolution output **(b)** general idea which the public has of a product *or* a company; ***they are spending a lot of advertising money to improve the company's image; the company has adopted a down-market image;*** **brand image** = picture which people have in their minds of a product associated with the brand name; **corporate image** = idea which a company would like the public to have of it; **to promote a corporate image** = to publicize a company so that its reputation is improved

imaging *noun* making and capturing images on a computer: the operator draws the design with an electronic pen

imitate *verb* to do what someone else does; ***they imitate all our sales gimmicks***

imitation *noun* thing which copies another; **beware of imitations** = be careful not to buy low quality goods which are made to look like other more expensive items; **imitation art paper** = smooth calendered paper which looks like art paper, but is not coated (the clay is added to the pulp before the paper is made); (NOTE: US English calls this **English finish**); **imitation cloth** = cover material which looks like cloth; **imitation leather binding** = binding in a plastic material which looks like leather; **imitation parchment** = tough paper which is slightly transparent because of having been beaten for some time

impact *noun* shock *or* strong effect; ***the impact of new technology on the printing industry; the new series cover design has made little impact on the buying public;*** **impact paper** = carbonless paper used to provide multiple copies without the use of carbon paper; **impact printer** = printer that prints text and symbols by striking an ink ribbon onto paper with a metal character (such as a daisy-wheel printer, as opposed to a non-impact printer like a laser printer); *see also* DAISY-WHEEL PRINTER, DOT-MATRIX PRINTER

imperfect *adjective* not perfect; ***sale of imperfect copies; to check a batch for imperfect products***

imperfection *noun* item which is not perfect (such as a book which has been badly printed or bound); ***to check a batch for imperfections; we have asked for a refund because of imperfections***

imperial *noun* traditional British large paper size (30 x 22 inches); **imperial octavo** = former book size (11 x $7\frac{1}{2}$ inches)

import 1 *noun* **(a) imports** = books *or* other goods brought into a country from abroad for sale; ***imports from Poland have risen to $1m a year;*** **invisible imports** = services (such as banking, tourism) which are paid for in foreign currency; **visible imports** = real goods which are imported **(b) import ban** = forbidding imports; ***the government has imposed an import ban on arms;*** **import duty** = tax on goods imported into a country; **import levy** = tax on imports, especially in the EU a tax on imports of farm produce from outside the EU; **import licence** *or* **import permit** = government licence *or* permit which allows goods to be imported; **import quota** = fixed quantity of a particular type of goods which the government allows to be imported;

the government has imposed an import quota on cars; **import surcharge** = extra duty charged on imported goods, to try to prevent them from being imported and to encourage local manufacture **2** *verb* to bring goods from abroad into a country for sale; ***the company imports cheap dictionaries from America; we use paper imported from Scandinavia***

importation *noun* act of importing; ***the importation of pornographic literature is forbidden***

importer *noun* person *or* company which imports goods; ***a paper importer; the company is a big importer of English paperbacks***

impose *verb* **(a)** to put a tax *or* a duty on goods; ***to impose a tax on imported paper; they tried to impose a ban on the sale of anti-government literature; the government imposed a special duty on newspapers*** **(b)** to arrange the film *or* type so that when the sheet is printed it will fold correctly into the right page order; **imposed page proofs** = last stage in page proofs, where the text is arranged in pages, in the correct position for making films and plates; **imposing stone** = heavy table on which metal type and blocks were formerly placed to be locked into the chase

imposition *noun* **(a)** putting a tax on goods or services **(b)** (i) arranging the pages of film *or* type so that when a sheet is printed, it will fold correctly into the right page order; (ii) putting together the metal type and blocks on the imposing stone, to be locked into a chase before printing; **imposition scheme** = plan showing how the pages of a book are imposed on the sheet

impression *noun* **(a)** the image printed on the paper by a printing press; **impression cylinder** = cylinder which prints the image onto the paper **(b)** printrun, all the copies of a book printed at one time; **the book is in its third impression** = the book has been reprinted twice

imprint *noun* name and address of the publisher or printer, which must appear on most printed matter; **joint imprint** = imprints of two publishers which appear on a book which has been published by the two companies jointly

> COMMENT: catalogues, advertisements and fliers do not need to have an imprint, but almost all other printed matter (books, newspapers, and even political leaflets) must carry two imprints: that of the publisher and of the printer. In a book, the imprints will normally appear on the reverse of the title page as part of the bibliographic information; in some countries it is usual to have the printer's imprint at the end of the book. In a magazine, imprints may be listed along with other details of the editors and other staff members

increment *noun* amount by which something is increased; **line increment** = minimum distance between two lines of type, which can be as small as one eighteenth of a point

incremental plotter *noun* plotter which receives positional data as increments to its current position rather than separate coordinates

incised *adjective* (typeface, such as Perpetua) based on letters cut in stone (also called 'glyphic')

inclusive type area *noun* type area which includes the headers and footers

incunabula *noun* early printed books (usually taken to be books printed before 1501); (NOTE: singular is **incunabulum**)

> COMMENT: the term incunabula (meaning 'baby linen' or 'cradle' in Latin) was first used to refer to the first stages or infancy of printing, and was subsequently used to refer to books printed before the beginning of the sixteenth century. The year 1500 is in fact meaningless in this connection, since printing and typographic developments continued from the 1440s to the 1530s, at which time both had developed to a stage which was not really superseded until the nineteenth century

indelible ink *noun* ink which cannot be removed

indent 1 *noun* **(a)** blank space at the beginning of a line of typesetting, which starts a little way in from the left-hand margin; ***each paragraph begins with a 2 em indent;*** **hanging indent** = type of indentation, where the first line is full out and the rest of the paragraph is indented **(b)** order placed by an importer for goods from overseas on credit; ***he put in an indent for a new stock of children's books*** **2** *verb* **(a)** to start a line of typesetting several spaces from the left-hand margin; ***indent the first line three spaces; each paragraph is indented 3 ems*** **(b) to indent for something** = to put in an order for something on credit; ***the department has indented for a new computer***

indentation *or* **indention** *noun* making an indent at the beginning of a line; **hanging indentation** = type of indentation, where the first line is full out and the rest of the paragraph is indented

independent *adjective* free *or* not controlled by anyone; **independent publisher** *or* **printer** = publishing *or* printing company which is not controlled by another company; **Independent Publishers Guild (IPG)** = British organization representing the interests of the many small (and some very large) publishers who are its members; **the independents** = shops *or* companies which are owned by private individuals and are not part of large groups

index 1 *noun* **(a)** list of items classified into groups or put in alphabetical order; **index board** = board used for printing index cards; **index card** = small card used for filing; **card index** = series of cards with information written on them, kept in a special order so that the information car be found easily; **index letter** *or* **number** = letter or number which identifies an item in an index **(b)** list printed, usually at the back of a book, giving references to items in the main part of the book; ***the catalogue contains an author and a title index; the atlas has an index of place-names;*** **general index** = index which covers all items in the book; **subject index** = index of subjects dealt with in a book or catalogue **(c)** regular statistical report which lists books published *or* rises and falls in prices, etc.; ***a cumulative book index; look it up on the microfiche index of books in print;*** **Index Translationum** = list of all translations published in the world, published each year by UNESCO; **cost-of-living index** = way of measuring the cost of living, shown as a percentage increase on the figure for the previous year; **retail price index** *or* *US* **consumer price index** = index showing how prices of consumer goods have risen over a period of time, used as a way of measuring inflation and the cost of living **(d)** fist, a printing sign ☛ like a black hand, used to show cross-references **(e) the Index (Index Librorum Prohibitorum)** = list of books banned by the Catholic Church (the last list was published in 1968); (NOTE: plural is **indexes** or **indices**, though **indices** is used more for statistical reports, and **indexes** for books) **2** *verb* **(a)** to write an index for a book; ***the book has been badly indexed; he earns his living from indexing journals*** **(b)** to put marks against items, so that they form an index

indexer *noun* person who compiles indexes for books

indexing *noun* **(a)** process of building and sorting a list of records; **indexing language** = language used in building library *or* book indexes **(b)** writing an index for a book; **computer indexing** = using a computer to compile an index for a book by selecting relevant words *or* items in the text

> COMMENT: an index is usually set in smaller type than the text and in two or more columns to the page. Normally an index will begin on a right-hand page, and will be folioed consecutively from the text pages. Bold and italic can be used to highlight important or less important items in an index (as, for example, the page references to illustrations). It is always useful to have a note at the beginning of an index to explain how it has been compiled and the meaning of the various typefaces or symbols used. Indexing was formerly done manually, with the indexer going

through the text and making filing cards for the items; there are now computer indexing programs, in which the words in the text are flagged and the computer then automatically lists them in alphabetical order, together with the numbers of the pages on which the words fall

India ink *or* **Indian ink** *noun* very black indelible ink, made from lampblack and glue

india paper *noun* extremely thin good quality opaque paper (about 30gsm), which is nevertheless quite strong, used for printing books with a large number of pages, such as Bibles, which would be very thick if ordinary paper were used

indicia *noun US* the mailing permit printed on a prepaid envelope or card

indirect *adjective* not direct; **indirect expenses** *or* **costs** = costs which are not directly attached to the making of a product (such as cleaning, rent, administration); **indirect labour costs** = costs of paying workers who are not directly involved in making a product (such as secretaries, cleaners); **indirect printing** = printing where the printing plate does not touch the paper (as in offset printing); **indirect process** = process of reproducing an image (as in a plain-paper copier), where an image of the original is transferred to the copy paper without the original touching the paper; **indirect screening** = colour origination method resulting in continuous tone separations

individual 1 *noun* one single person; ***savings plan made to suit the requirements of the private individual*** **2** *adjective* single *or* belonging to one person; ***each individual copy of the limited edition has been signed by the author and artist***

industry *noun* group of companies making the same type of product; ***the publishing industry; the printing industry; the newspaper industry***

inertia *noun* being lazy; **inertia selling** = method of selling items by sending them to people who have not ordered them and assuming that if they are not returned, the person who has received them is willing to buy them

inferior *adjective* **(a)** not as good as others; ***inferior products*** *or* ***products of inferior quality*** **(b) inferior figure** = small figure printed slightly lower than the base line of type; (NOTE: used in printing chemical formulae, such as: CO_2; inferior letters are also sometimes used, as in NO_x (nitrous oxides). The opposite is **superior**)

inform *verb* to tell someone officially; ***I regret to inform you that your manuscript is not acceptable for publication by this company; we are pleased to inform you that your book has been accepted for publication***

information *noun* **(a)** details which explain something; ***please send me information on*** *or* ***about your latest publications; I enclose this leaflet for your information; for further information, please write to the Sales Department*** **(b) information technology (IT)** = working with computer data; **information retrieval** = storing and then finding data in a computer **(c) information bureau** *or* **information office** = office which gives information to tourists *or* visitors; **information officer** = person whose job is to give information about a company *or* an organization *or* a government department to the public; person whose job is to give information to other departments in the same organization

infra red (IR) *noun* long invisible rays, below the visible red end of the colour spectrum; **infrared photography** = taking photographs using an infrared camera, which shows up heat sources; RADIATION DRYING

infringe *verb* to break a law *or* a right; **to infringe a copyright** = to copy a copyright text illegally

infringement *noun* breaking a law *or* a right; **infringement of copyright** *or* **copyright infringement** = act of illegally copying a work which is in copyright

ingrain paper *or* **ingrained paper** *noun* paper with a rough finish (similar to stone)

in-house *adverb & adjective* (working) inside a company's building; ***the in-house staff; we do all our data processing in-house; the colour artwork cannot be done in-house and has to be sent outside;*** **in-house training** = training given to staff at their place of work

initial 1 *adjective* first *or* starting; ***the initial response to the TV advertising has been very good;*** **initial capital** = capital which is used to start a business; ***he started the business with an initial expenditure or initial investment of £500;*** **initial printrun** = the first printrun of a new book; ***when the subscription orders began to come in, the initial printrun was increased from 10,000 copies to 25,000;*** **initial sales** = first sales of a new product **2** *noun* **(a)** first letter of a word *or* line; ***each paragraph should start with a 20 point initial;*** **initial caps** = instruction to make the first letter of each word a capital; **drop initial** = large size initial letter at the beginning of a chapter, which runs down over several lines of text (typically a two-drop initial, which takes up two lines of text); **stick-up initial** = initial letter set in a larger size than the text, but which is on the base line and rises above the ascenders of the rest of the text (the opposite of a drop initial); **swash initial** = ornamental swash letter used as the first letter of a chapter **(b) initials** = first letters of the words in a name; ***what do the initials IMF stand for? the chairman wrote his initials by each alteration in the contract*** **3** *verb* to write your initials on a document to show you have read it and approved it; ***to initial an amendment to a contract; please initial the agreement at the place marked with an X***

initiate *verb* to start; ***to initiate discussions;*** **initiating editor** = editor whose job is to start new projects, then pass them on to in-house copy editors for completion

initiative *noun* decision to start something; **to take the initiative** = to decide to do something; **to follow up an initiative** = to take action once someone else has decided to do something

injunction *noun* court order telling someone not to do something; ***he got an injunction preventing the company from publishing her memoirs; the company applied for an injunction to stop their rival from marketing a similar product***

ink 1 *noun* coloured liquid used for writing *or* printing; **book inks** = inks which are used for printing the text of books; **printing inks** = special types of ink only used in printing; **ink block** = block of hard black ink, used in Chinese and Japanese calligraphy (the calligrapher wets the block with water); **ink misting** = fault which can develop in very fast printing presses, where the ink becomes a fine mist and so prints a faint image; **ink rollers** = rollers for distributing ink on a printing press; **ink rub** = dirty marks on the printed paper, caused when it rubs against the ink on other pages during binding; **ink set-off** = defect in printing where the wet ink from one printed sheet marks another sheet; **ink slab** *or* **ink table** = flat surface across which the ink roller is rolled to make sure the ink is evenly distributed (as when printing on a hand press) **2** *verb* **(a)** to put ink on a plate *or* roller for printing; **inking pad** = small pad with ink on it, used for putting ink on a rubber stamp; *see also* OVERINK, OVERINKING **(b)** to draw lines on paper by pen *or* by the use of a plotter device

inker *noun* system of rollers and baths which put ink onto the printing surface

inking *noun* applying ink; **overinking** = applying too much ink; **inking rollers** = rollers that distribute the ink on a printing press

ink-jet printer *noun* computer printer that produces characters by sending a stream of tiny drops of electrically charged ink onto the paper (the movement of the ink drops is controlled by an electric field), the printer is a non-impact printer with few moving parts; ***colour ink-jet technology and thermal transfer technology compete with each other***

ink-jet printing *noun* printing process used in ink-jet printers

inland *adjective* inside a country; **inland postage** = postage for a letter to another part of the country; **inland freight charges** = charges for carrying goods from one part of the country to another

inline *noun* typeface where each character is formed of a black outline with the centre of the stroke left white

inner *adjective* inside *or* nearer the inside; **inner forme** = forme which carries the inside pages of a section, the outer forme carrying the outside pages, and prints on the other side of the paper; **inner margin** = margin on the side of a page nearest the binding; *compare* OUTER

innovate *verb* to bring in new ideas *or* new methods

innovation *noun* new idea *or* new method *or* new product

innovative *adjective* (person or thing) which is new and makes changes

innovator *noun* person who brings in new ideas and methods

in preparation *adverb (of book)* being prepared

in print *adjective* (book) which is currently available from the publisher; ***a list of current books in print; the book was first published in 1902 and is still in print;*** (NOTE: opposite is **out of print** *or* **O/P**)

input 1 *noun* **input of information** *or* **computer input** = data fed into a computer; **input device** = device such as a keyboard *or* bar code reader, which converts information into a form which a computer can understand and transfers the information to the processor; **input lead** = lead for connecting the electric current to the machine; **input tax** = VAT paid on goods or services which a company buys **2** *verb* **to input information** = to put data into a computer

in quires *noun* flat unbound printed sheets

inscribe *verb* to write, especially to write a note inside a book, when giving it to someone; ***the book is inscribed 'with best wishes to John, from the author'***

inscription *noun* note written in a book which is given to someone

insert 1 *noun* **(a)** sheet of paper which is put inside something; **an insert in a magazine mailing** *or* **a magazine insert** = advertising sheet put into a magazine when it is mailed; **loose insert** = insert which is not bound into the magazine **(b)** folded section of printed pages added between the pages of a signature or tucked into a pocket inside the book cover **(c)** material added to a text at proof stage; ***how can we possibly get this insert into the page without repaginating?*** **2** *verb* **(a)** to put something in; ***to insert a clause into a contract; to insert a publicity piece into a magazine mailing; to insert a section into a signature; the author wanted to insert two paragraphs on page one;*** **inserted book** = book with inserts added in the middle of signatures **(b)** to add new text inside a word *or* sentence

insertion *noun* **(a)** material inserted into a text; ***the author's insertions will cost a lot of money; the editors have made so many insertions that it will be simpler to reset the book*** **(b)** the act of putting an advertisement into a magazine *or* newspaper; ***some papers give three insertions for the price of two***

insert mode *noun* interactive computer mode used for editing and correcting documents

> COMMENT: this is a standard feature on most word-processing packages where the cursor is placed at the required point in the document and any characters typed will be added, with the existing text moving on as necessary; when the insert mode is off, new text will erase the existing text

inset 1 *noun* **(a)** section of printed pages inserted in the middle of a signature before it is sewn **(b)** small picture in a box inside a larger picture (as an enlarged detail of a piston might be shown in a box in the corner of a full-page illustration of an engine) **2** *verb* **(a)** to sew or glue a page or section in the middle of a signature; **insetted book** = book with insets added in the middle of signatures; **insetted imposition** = imposition in which sections are imposed to inset one inside another (also called 'quirewise') **(b)** to place a small drawing in a box in a larger drawing; ***there is a town-plan inset into the corner of the map***

insetter *noun* device which automatically inserts one signature inside another

inside *adjective & adverb* **(a) inside back cover** *or* **inside front cover** = advertising pages on the inside of the cover of a magazine; **inside edge** *or* **inside margin** = edge of text *or* margin which is near the binding **(b) inside worker** = worker who works in the office or factory (not in the open air, not a salesman); *see also* IN-HOUSE

inspect *verb* to examine in detail; ***to inspect a machine*** *or* ***an installation; to inspect the accounts;*** **to inspect printed sheets for defects** = to look at sheets in detail to see if they have any defects

inspection *noun* close examination of something; **inspection copy** = copy of an educational book, given to a teacher, who can look at it, decide to order it for the class and keep the free copy, or pay for the copy without buying any for the class, or return it to the publisher (also sometimes called 'desk copy')

inspector *noun* official who inspects; **inspector of factories** *or* **factory inspector** = government official who inspects factories to see if they are safely run

install *verb* to put (a machine) into an office *or* into a factory; ***to install a new perfector; to install a new data processing system***

installation *noun* putting new machines into an office *or* a factory; ***to supervise the installation of new equipment***

instalment *US* **installment** *noun* **(a)** part of a magazine *or* book which is published in parts; part of a radio *or* TV series; ***the novel has been serialized in ten instalments*** **(b)** part payment made regularly until the total amount has been paid; **the final instalment is now due** = the last of a series of payments should be paid now; **to miss an instalment** = not to pay an instalment at the right time

instant *adjective* immediately available; **instant publishing** = publishing of topical books immediately after the event (books on the World Cup, a Royal Wedding, etc.)

institutional *adjective* referring to an official organization; **institutional purchase** = buying of books by schools *or* local authorities *or* libraries

instruct *verb* to give an order to someone; **to instruct someone to do something** = to tell someone officially to do something; ***we instructed the typesetter to set in Times roman, and the whole text has been set in Helvetica italic***

instruction *noun* order which tells someone what should be done *or* how something is to be used; ***we gave clear instructions regarding the cover material; the designer is asking for instructions about the text of the title page;*** **to await instructions** = to wait for someone to tell you what to do; **to issue instructions** = to tell people what to do; **in accordance with** *or* **according to instructions** = as the instructions said or say; **failing instructions to the contrary** = unless someone tells you to do the opposite; **delivery instructions** *or* **shipping instructions** = details of how goods are to be shipped and delivered

insufficient *adjective* not enough; ***the schedule gives us insufficient time to read the proofs;*** **insufficient feed** = situation where the paper is not fed into the press quickly enough, increasing the tension on the paper actually in the press and so increasing the likelihood of a web break

intaglio process *noun* any printing process where the ink is in recesses cut into the plate, the flat surface of the plate being wiped clean before printing (gravure is an intaglio process)

integrate *verb* to link things together to form a united whole; **integrated book** = book with text and illustrations on the same page; **integrated digital network** = communications network that uses digital signals to transmit data; **integrated production system** = printing system where all the processes are linked automatically; **integrated publishing house** = publishing house which publishes in hardback and has its own paperback list; **integrated services digital network (ISDN)** = international digital communications network which can transmit sound, fax and data over the same channel

intellectual property *noun* ownership of something (such as a copyright *or* patent *or* design) which is in the mind of the inventor and cannot be seen or touched

intelligent character recognition (ICR) *noun* advanced form of OCR which can recognize a number of different typefaces

interactive *adjective* (system *or* piece of software) that allows the user to communicate with the computer; **interactive processing** = computer mode that allows the user to enter commands *or* programs *or* data and receive immediate responses; *compare* BATCH PROCESSING **interactive system** = computer system where the operator and the computer can communicate with each other (the computer responds to the operator by suggesting different courses of action); **interactive video** = system that uses a computer linked to a video disk player to provide processing power and images

COMMENT: this system is often used in teaching to ask the student questions, which, if he answers correctly, will produce a sequence of film from the video disk

intercalate *verb* to insert in between a series of items; ***blank pages are intercalated between each page of the book, so that the user can write notes***

intercharacter spacing *noun* word-processor feature that provides variable spacing between characters to create a justified line; *see also* INTERWORD SPACING

interface 1 *noun* link between two different computer systems, protocols, languages or pieces of hardware **2** *verb* to connect and act with; ***the office micros interface with the mainframe computer at head office***

interfere *verb* to get involved; to try to change something which is not your concern

interference *noun* the act of interfering; ***the editorial department complained of continual interference from the author's agent***

interlay *noun* paper *or* card placed under a letterpress printing plate to lift it to type height or to increase pressure on the dark image areas

interleaf *noun* (i) additional leaf of two blank pages added between the printed pages in a section of a book (used for example in a catalogue, to make additions or changes to the existing text); (ii) thin sheet of paper put between printed sheets to prevent set-off

interleave *verb* **(a)** to put blank sheets of paper *or* carbon paper between other sheets of paper; ***they interleaved the colour pages with thin paper to prevent set-off; an invoice pad with interleaved carbons*** **(b)** to bind blank sheets between each pair of pages, for writing notes

interleaving *noun* addition of blank paper between printed sheets to prevent set-off

inter-library loan (ILL) *noun* service to library users whereby a library obtains a book which is not in its own collection from another library

interlinear *adjective* between lines; *(on a phototypesetter)* **interlinear spacing** *or* **interline spacing** = leading, the insertion of spaces between lines of text (leaving a gap between lines of text is necessary to make the text more legible); **interlinear translation** = translation printed in small characters between the lines of a text

intermediates *noun* films used in intermediate stages of reproduction before producing the final films

internal *adjective* inside a company; **we decided to make an internal appointment** = we decided to appoint an existing member of staff to the post, and not bring someone in from outside the company; **internal audit** = audit carried out by a department within the company; **internal audit department** *or* **internal auditor** = department *or* member of staff who audits the accounts of the company he works for; **internal editorial department** = editorial department which works in a company; **internal sizing** = engine-sizing, adding size to the pulp before the paper is made; **internal telephone** = telephone which is linked to other phones in an office

internally *adverb* inside a company; ***the job was advertised internally***

international *adjective* working between countries; **international call** = telephone call to another country; **international dialling code** = number used to make a telephone call to another country; **international paper sizes** = ISO SIZES **international trade** = trade between different countries

International Standard Book Number (ISBN) number allocated to a book, which can be recognized internationally as referring only to that book

International Standard Serial Number (ISSN) number allocated to a journal *or* magazine, which can be recognized internationally as referring only to that issue of the magazine

International Standards Organization (ISO) organization which deals with setting up international standards of measurement

internegative *noun* colour negative

Internet *noun* international wide area network that provides file and data transfer, together with electronic mail functions for millions of users around the world; *see also* WWW

internet *noun* wide area network formed of many local area networks

internet protocol (IP) *noun* TCP/IP standard that defines how data is transferred across a network; **internet protocol address (IP Address)** = unique, 32-bit number which identifies each computer connected to a TCP/IP network

interpolation *noun* calculation of intermediate values between two points

> COMMENT: interpolation is often used in image manipulation software when resolution or size increases are required. It is the process by which pixel data is 'invented' to fill in the gaps between known points

interpret *verb* to translate what someone has said into another language; ***my assistant knows Greek, so he will interpret for us***

interpreter *noun* **(a)** person who translates what someone has said into another language; ***my secretary will act as interpreter*** **(b)** software used to translate high-level language into machine code

interrogation mark *see* QUESTION MARK

Intertype *noun* trade mark for a hot metal typesetting machine which casts slugs of type

interword spacing *noun* variable spacing between words in a text, used to justify lines; *see also* INTERCHARACTER SPACING

intranet *noun* one or more web sites accessible only by authorised users and kept behind a fire wall to prevent public access

in tray *noun* basket on a desk for letters *or* memos which have been received and are waiting to be dealt with

intro = INTRODUCTION first section of a text

introduce *verb* to make someone get to know a new person or thing; **to introduce a client** = to bring in a new client and make him known to someone; **to introduce a new**

product on the market = to produce a new product and launch it on the market

introduction *noun* **(a)** section at the beginning of a book where the author explains how the book is to be used *or* what were the reasons for writing it, etc. **(b)** letter making someone get to know another person; ***I'll give you an introduction or a letter of introduction to the MD - he is an old friend of mine*** **(c)** bringing into use; **the introduction of new technology** = putting new machines (usually computers) into a business or industry

introductory *adjective* which introduces; **introductory paragraphs** = paragraphs which introduce a subject *or* paragraphs at the beginning of a text; **introductory offer** = special price offered on a new product to attract customers

inventory 1 *noun US* stock *or* goods in a warehouse or shop; ***to carry a high inventory; to aim to reduce inventory;*** **inventory control** = system of checking that there is not too much stock in a warehouse, but just enough to meet requirements **2** *verb* to make a list of stock or contents

invert *verb* to turn upside down; ***the photograph on page two has been inverted***

inverted commas *noun* printed *or* written marks showing that a quotation starts or finishes (there are single inverted commas (' ') and double inverted commas (" "))

inversion *noun* turning upside down

investigate *verb* to examine something which may be wrong

investigative journalism *noun* type of journalism where reporters try to find out and publish the truth about corruption *or* government mismanagement, etc.

invisible *adjective* guide or object visible on a DTP page or graphics layout during the design phase, but is not printed

invoice 1 *noun* **(a)** note asking for payment for goods or services supplied; ***your invoice dated November 10th; they sent in their invoice six weeks late; to make out an invoice for £250; to settle or to pay an invoice;*** **the total is payable within thirty days of invoice** = the total sum has to be paid within thirty days of the date on the invoice; **VAT invoice** = invoice which includes VAT **(b) invoice price** = price as given on an invoice (including discount and VAT); **total invoice value** = total amount on an invoice, including transport, VAT, etc. **2** *verb* to send an invoice to someone; ***to invoice a customer;*** **we invoiced you on November 10th** = we sent you the invoice on November 10th

invoicing *noun* sending of an invoice; ***our invoicing is done by the computer;*** **invoicing department** = department in a company which deals with preparing and sending invoices; **invoicing in triplicate** = preparing three copies of invoices; **VAT invoicing** = sending of an invoice including VAT

inward *adjective* towards the home country; **inward mission** = visit to your home country by a group of foreign businessmen

ion deposition *noun* reproduction process, where toner adheres to an electrically charged area of paper

IP = INTERNET PROTOCOL TCP/IP standard that defines how data is transferred over a network; **IP address** = unique, 32-bit number which identifies computers that want to connect to a TCP/IP network

IPA = INTERNATIONAL PHONETIC ALPHABET characters adopted as an international system for representing the sounds used in speaking words ⇨APPENDIX

iph = IMPRESSIONS PER HOUR

IR = INFRA RED

irregular *adjective* **(a)** not regular *or* not straight; ***the spacing on page 25 is very irregular*** **(b)** not correct *or* not done in the correct way; ***irregular documentation; this procedure is highly irregular***

irregularity *noun* **(a)** not being regular *or* not being on time; ***the irregularity of the postal deliveries*** **(b) irregularities** = things which are not done in the correct way and which are possibly illegal; ***the auditors discovered serious irregularities in the company accounts; we are not aware of any irregularities in the way the contract was drawn up***

ISBN = INTERNATIONAL STANDARD BOOK NUMBER

> COMMENT: an international system for books, in which each book is given its own particular number. The ISBN is made up of ten digits; the first digit refers to the language (0 and 1 are the digits for English); the next group of digits (three, four or even six) refer to the publisher; the third group refer to the book; and the final digit is a check digit. ISBNs are used for cataloguing and ordering, and can be used for automatic stock movements if they are printed on the back of the book in the form of a bar code which can then be read with a light pen

ISDN = INTEGRATED SERVICES DIGITAL NETWORK standard method of transmitting digital data over a telephone network at high speeds - faster than a normal modem

ISO paper sizes *noun* international metric paper sizes (A, B and C paper sizes)

> COMMENT: the ISO sizes are based on a ratio of height to width of 1 to 1.414. The largest size is A0 (841 x 1189mm), and all other sizes are derived from this, with in each case the longer side being half the size of that of the previous size. ISO A papers are used for printing, B papers are for posters, and the C papers for envelopes

isotype *noun* symbol in the form of a little picture (developed by the Isotype Institute, in Vienna)

ISSN = INTERNATIONAL STANDARD SERIAL NUMBER

> COMMENT: an international system used on periodicals, magazines, learned journals, etc. The ISSN is formed of eight digits, which refer to the country in which the magazine is published, the date or issue number and the title of the publication

issue 1 *noun* all copies of a magazine published at the same time; ***the book was advertised in Friday's issue of magazine*** **2** *verb* to put out *or* to give out; to publish; ***the book has been issued in hardcover;*** *see also* REISSUE

IT = INFORMATION TECHNOLOGY

ital *abbreviation* ITALIC

italic *adjective & noun* style of typeface which slopes to right and is thinner than roman, used for display, to emphasize a piece of text, or to show a difference from roman; ***the headings can be printed in 9pt italic***

italicize *verb* to put a word into italics; ***the headings should be italicized***

italicization *noun* putting into italics

> COMMENT: as its name suggests, italic type was developed in Italy in the late fifteenth century, and was based on chancery script. It was originally used for complete texts, and only became used as a secondary face in the 18th century. True italic characters are designed to slope and match the roman characters for the same letters; they differ from them in design, however, notably the letters 'a' and 'g'. Computer-generated italics are not true italics, but are roman characters which are made to slope sideways. They are known as sloped roman. When marking a manuscript or proof, italic is instructed by underlining the word or character with a single line

itinerary *noun* list of places to be visited on one journey; ***a rep's itinerary***

ivory board *noun* fine white board made by laminating two layers of fine paper together

ivory paper *noun* thick creamy white writing paper

Jj

jacket 1 *noun* **book jacket** *or* **dust jacket** *or* **dust cover** *or* **dust wrapper** = decorated paper cover which is wrapped round a cased book; ***the book sells at £19.95, cased with a jacket; he designs jackets for several publishers; they gave me £1 off the price of the book because the jacket was torn*** **2** *verb* to put a jacket on a book; ***the book is available in paperback, or in boards jacketed; jacketing costs an extra 5p per copy; the books have been printed and bound, and are now in the jacketing department or are now being jacketed***

jam *verb* to stop working *or* to be blocked; ***the paper feed has jammed; the switchboard was jammed with calls***

Japanese paper *noun* thin white handmade paper, made from the bark of the mulberry tree, used for prints, drawings, etc.; **Japanese vellum** = thick Japanese paper

Java™ programming language developed by Sun Microsystems; it is used to develop applets for the Internet that can be downloaded automatically with a WWW page and run on the user's local computer

jaws *noun* set of teeth which hold something in a machine; **folding jaws** = section of a folding machine which holds the paper pushed into it by the folding blade

jerks *noun* sudden pulling of the paper as it passes through a web-fed printing machine

jet printing *noun* **laser jet printing** *or* **ink jet printing** = printing using a fine jet of ink; **ink jet printer** = computer printer that produces characters by sending a stream of tiny drops of electrically charged ink onto the paper (the movement of the ink drops is controlled by an electric field; the printer is a non-impact printer with few moving parts)

jiffy bag *noun* trademark for a type of envelope with soft padding, used to mail goods (such as books) which may be damaged in the post

job *noun* **(a)** piece of work; **to do odd jobs** = to do various pieces of (usually low-grade) work; **to be paid by the job** = to be paid for each piece of work done **(b)** printing order being worked on; ***we are working on six jobs at the moment; the bindery has a big job starting in August;*** **job bag** = bag used by a printer to contain all the documents and samples relating to a particular job; **job case** = case holding both capital and lower case letters of a particular font **(c)** regular paid work; ***he is looking for a job in publishing ; he lost his job when the factory closed; she got a job in a factory; to apply for a job in a publicity department;*** **job classification** = describing jobs listed under various classes; **job description** = official document from the management which says what a job involves; **job evaluation** = examining different jobs within an organization to see what skills and qualifications are needed to carry them out; **job satisfaction** = a worker's feeling of being happy in his or her place of work and pleased with the work being done; **job security** = feeling which a worker has of being able to stay in a job as long as he or she wants; **job specification** = very detailed description of what is involved in a job; **job title** = name given to a person in a certain job; **on-the-job training** = training given to workers at their place of work; **off-the-job training** = training given to workers away from their place of work (i.e. at a college) **(c) job lot** = group of miscellaneous items (such as remaindered books *or* used printing equipment) which are sold together, and where the buyer must buy the whole lot; ***he sold the contents of the paper warehouse as a job lot***

jobber *noun US* book wholesaler

jobbing *noun* doing small pieces of printing work; **jobbing chase** = JOB CASE **jobbing font** = display font used for advertisements and posters; **jobbing machines** = small printing machines (usually platens) used by jobbing printers; **vertical jobbing press** = small letterpress machine printing flat formes which move vertically and not horizontally; **jobbing printer** = person who does small general printing jobs, such as posters, letterheads, business cards, menus; **jobbing work** = small printing jobs, such as posters, letterheads, business cards, etc.

jockey roller *noun* first roller on a web-fed machine, which compensates for the uneven tension of the reel of paper

jogger *noun* device which knocks up sheets of paper to align them

joint *noun* point where the covers of a book are attached to the spine; **cloth joint** = strip of linen pasted along the fold of the endpaper to strengthen the joint

joint photographic expert group *see* JPEG

jordan refiner *noun* papermaking machine, where the pulp is torn and shredded

journal *noun* **(a) learned journal** = specialist periodical, usually edited by a university professor, which is published two or three times a year and deals with a specialized academic subject; **journals printing** = printing of specialized learned journals; ***he is the manager of our journals division; a printer who specializes in journal printing*** **(b)** specialist periodical; **house journal** = magazine produced for the workers in a company to give them news about the company; **trade journal** = magazine produced for people or companies in a certain trade

journalism *noun* work (especially as an editor or reporter) on newspapers *or* magazines

journalist *noun* person who works for a newspaper (especially a person employed by a newspaper to write articles for the paper)

journey *noun* long trip, especially a trip made by a salesman; ***he planned his journey to visit all his accounts in two days;*** **journey order** = order given by the shopkeeper to a salesman when he calls

journeyman *noun* qualified print worker who has completed his apprenticeship

JPEG = JOINT PHOTOGRAPHIC EXPERT GROUP ISO/CCITT standard for compressing images

> COMMENT: the compressed image is not as sharp as the original; JPEG can either work through hardware or software routines and works as follows: the image is divided into a matrix of tiny pixels, every other pixel is ignored and the grid is divided into blocks of 8x8 pixels, the algorithm then calculates the average of the blocks and so can delete one block - the decompression is the reverse of this process.

JPEG++ this is an extension to JPEG that allows parts of an image to be compressed differentially: for example, the background could be highly compressed (since it doesn't matter if this suffers a loss of quality)

judicature paper *noun* thick heavy paper on which legal documents are engrossed

jump *verb* to miss a page *or* a line *or* a space when printing; ***the typewriter jumped two lines; the paging system has jumped two folio numbers***

junk *noun* rubbish *or* useless items; **junk mail** = advertising material sent through the post

justification *noun* spacing the words and characters in a text, so that the right margin is straight; **hyphenation and justification (H & J) program** = computer program which allows the typesetting machine to justify lines automatically and to hyphenate correctly words which have to be split at the end of a line

justify *verb* **(a)** to change the spacing between words *or* characters in a document so that the left and right margins will be straight; ***the page is set in two columns, right justified; the newspaper is set in justified columns;*** **justify inhibit** = to prevent a word processor justifying a document; **hyphenate and justify** = to break long words correctly where they split at the ends of lines, so as to give a straight right margin; **left justify** = to print with a straight left-hand margin; **right justify** = to print with a straight right-hand margin; ***this book would look far neater if you right justified each line*** **(b)** to set lines of printed text as wide as possible in a certain page size

juvenile *noun & adjective* referring to children; book for children; **juvenile editor** = editor who specializes in books *or* magazines for children

juvenilia *noun* works written by an author as a child

Kk

K *abbreviation* one thousand; **'salary: £15K+ '** = salary more than £15,000 per annum

Kb *or* **Kbit** = KILOBIT measure of 1,024 bits

KB *or* **Kbyte** = KILOBYTE unit of measure for high capacity storage devices meaning 1,024 bytes; ***the new disk drive has a 100KB capacity***

K & N method *noun* test for measuring oil absorbency of paper

COMMENT: in the test (usually on smooth surfaced papers) K & N ink is applied to the paper with a spatula. Surplus ink is removed with an absorbent cloth after two minutes, and the colour density of the stain left on the paper is the measure of its absorbency. The darkness of the stain is measured with a spectrophotometer

kaolin *noun* china clay, or white clay used for loading or coating paper

kappa number *noun* number which expresses the ability of paper to be bleached (the paper pulp is tested with permanganate)

keep *verb* **(a)** to go on doing something; ***they keep making the same typographical errors; they kept working, even when the boss told them to stop; the other secretaries complain that she keeps singing when she is typing; you can't keep publishing the same sort of books year after year*** **(b)** to do what is necessary; **to keep an appointment** = to be there when you said you would be; **to keep the books of a company** *or* **to keep a company's books** = to note the accounts of a company accurately **(c)** to hold items for sale *or* for information; **we always keep this item in stock** = we always have this item in our warehouse *or* shop; **to keep someone's name on file** = to have someone's name on a list for reference **(d)** to hold things at a certain level; ***we must keep our mailing list up to date; to keep spending to a minimum; the backlist is selling strongly and keeps the company in profit; lack of demand for typewriters has kept prices down;*** **keep down** = do not use capitals if at all possible; **keep standing** = instruction to a typesetter to keep type (or possibly film) ready for reprinting; **keep up** = use capital letters throughout

kerfs *noun* shallow grooves in the back of a book section to house the threads used in sewing; (NOTE: also spelled **cerfs**)

kern 1 *noun* part of a piece of type which overlaps the next character (a common one is the lower case italic '*f*') **2** *verb* to make two characters overlap

kerning *noun* slight overlapping of certain printed character areas to prevent large spaces between them, giving a neater appearance

kettlestitch *noun* stitch at the top and bottom of each signature, which joins the signatures together

key 1 *noun* **(a)** part of a computer *or* typewriter *or* typesetting machine which is pressed with the fingers to make the machine work; ***there are sixty-four keys on the keyboard*** **(b)** *(names of keys)* **alphanumeric key** *or* **character key** = key which produces a character (letter *or* symbol *or* figure); **carriage return key** = key which marks the end of a line, when the machine goes to start a new line and the cursor *or* printhead moves to the beginning of the next line on screen *or* on a typewriter *or* in printing; **control key** = key on a computer which works part of a program; **function key** = key which has a specific task *or* gives a sequence of instructions; **shift key** = key which provides a second function for other keys, usually by making the typewriter *or* computer move to capital letters or which moves to another series of characters; **space key** *or* **space bar** = key which is pressed to make the machine leave a single space **(c)** list of words which refer to numbers on an illustration **(d)** small tool for holding the cords taut on a sewing frame while the book is being sewn **(e)** guiding; **key-drawing** = making an outline drawing which is used as a guide when separating colour film; **key plate** = initial printing plate used when printing colour images **2** *verb* to type information using a computer *or* typesetting machine; ***the entire text was keyed in Times italic; because of all the author's changes, we decided it would be quicker to key the whole text again;*** *see also* REKEY

keyboard 1 *noun* part of a typewriter, typesetting machine or computer with keys which are arranged in rows; **keyboard layout** = way in which various function and character keys are arranged; **azerty keyboard** = keyboard where the keys are arranged with the first line beginning A-Z-E-R-T-Y (used mainly in Europe); **qwerty keyboard** = English language keyboard, where the first letters are Q-W-E-R-T-Y; ***the computer has a normal qwerty keyboard;*** **keyboard operator** = person who types information on a keyboard **(f)** the colour black **2** *verb* to press the keys on a keyboard to type something; ***he is keyboarding our address list; the index has not been keyboarded yet***

keyboarder *noun* person who types information into a computer

keyboarding *or* **keying** *noun* act of entering data on a keyboard; ***keyboarding costs have risen sharply***

key in *verb* to key information so that it is captured by a computer; ***he is keying in the typesetting coordinates***

keyline *noun* rough sketch showing where finished artwork is to be placed

keypad *noun* small keyboard; **numeric keypad** = part of a computer keyboard which is a programmable set of numbered keys

keystroke *noun* action of pressing a key once; ***the text has two million keystrokes; we pay our keyboarders on a basis of £2 per thousand keystrokes;*** **keystroke count** = count of each keystroke made, often used to calculate keyboarding costs; **keystroke verification** = check made on each key pressed to make sure it is valid for a particular application

keyword *noun* (i) important *or* informative word in a title *or* document that describes its contents (and is used to retrieve information from a database *or* to access titles in a computerized library); (ii) word which is relevant *or* important to a text; **keyword and context (KWAC)** = library index system using important words from the text and title as index entries; **keyword in context (KWIC)** = library index system that uses keywords from the title *or* text of a book *or* document as an indexed entry, followed by the title *or* text it relates to; **keyword out of context (KWOC)** = library index system that indexes book *or* document titles under any relevant keywords

kg = KILOGRAM

kick copy *noun* copy of a newspaper *or* folded printed sheets, which is put out of line to show that a certain number of copies have been printed

kill *noun* to delete a whole story *or* article from a newspaper *or* magazine after it has been worked on; ***the editor told the production sub to kill the story about the minister;*** *compare* SPIKE

kilo *or* **kilogram** *noun* measure of weight (= one thousand grams); (NOTE: written **kg** after figures: **25kg**)

kilobit (Kb) *noun* measure of 1,024 bits of data

kilobyte *or* **KB** *or* **Kbyte** *noun* unit of measurement for high capacity storage devices meaning 1,024 bytes of data

kiosk *noun* small wooden shelter, for selling goods out of doors

kiss *noun* very light printing of an image

knib *noun* part of a setting rule which the compositor holds to pull it out of the composing stick

knife *noun* sharp instrument for cutting; **knife cheeks** = grippers which hold the paper which is being cut; **knife fold** = way of folding paper at an angle to the web, by pushing a metal blade against the paper between two cylinders

knocking copy *noun* advertising material which criticizes competing products

knock up *verb* to tap a pile of sheets of paper lightly on each side to straighten them

knotter *noun* device for removing hard knots in the wood which is to be pulped to make paper

kraft paper *noun* strong brown paper, used for wrapping parcels; **kraft liner** = strong paper made largely of sulphate, used to line corrugated containers; **kraft process** = SULPHATE PROCESS

Kurzweil *noun* trademark for an OCR reader, which can recognize typefaces and reads printed text into a computer, converting the printed signs to code

KWAC = KEYWORD AND CONTEXT

KWIK = KEYWORD IN CONTEXT

KWOK = KEYWORD OUT OF CONTEXT

Ll

L letter which causes problems in sans faces, where the lower case 'l' and the capital 'I' may look the same (as in the case of Univers); this confusion is one of the reasons why sans faces are less often used in the USA (because the abbreviation 'Ill.' for Illinois becomes impossible to read)

LA = LIBRARY ASSOCIATION

label 1 *noun* **(a)** piece of paper *or* card attached to something to show its price *or* an address *or* instructions for use; **gummed label** = label with dry glue on it, which is made wet to make it stick on the item; **self-sticking label** = sticky label, ready to stick on an item; **tie-on label** = label with a piece of string attached so that it can be tied on to an item; **label paper** = paper which is gummed on one side, used for printing labels **(b) address label** = label with an address on it; **price label** = label showing a price **(c)** wording on a diagram **2** *verb* to attach a label to something; **incorrectly labelled parcel** = parcel with the wrong information on the label

labelling *noun* putting a label on something; **labelling department** = section of a factory where labels are attached to the product

lace *verb* to thread a cord through holes; **lacing in** *or* **lacing on** = attaching the boards to a sewn book block by threading the cords through holes in the boards; **laced-on boards** = cased book where the book block is laced onto the boards

lacquer 1 *noun* varnish applied to paper to give it a gloss **2** *verb* to apply a varnish to paper

lading *see* BILL OF LADING

laid paper *noun* handmade paper which is made in a mould with thin wires across it and thicker wires (called chain lines) along it; *compare* WOVE **(antique) laid paper** = fine paper which imitates old handmade paper, with watermarks in the form of fine straight lines across the paper and thick lines along the grain

laminate 1 *noun* **(film) laminate** = plastic film used to cover the boards of a book cover or jacket; **liquid laminate** = liquid plastic coating, painted onto a cover to give it a glossy protective finish **2** *verb* **(a)** to cover (paper *or* card) with a thin layer of plastic, which is stuck to the paper by pressure and heat, giving the cover a glossy look; ***the book has a laminated jacket; laminated covers are easily wiped clean to remove dirt and grease*** **(b)** to paste thin boards together to produce some kinds of pasteboards

lamination *noun* **(a)** processing of laminating **(b)** the plastic film used to laminate

laminator *noun* machine which laminates

lampblack *noun* black pigment from burnt oil, used in the preparation of black ink

LAN *or* **lan** = LOCAL AREA NETWORK network where various terminals and equipment are all within a short distance of one another (at a maximum distance of about 500m, for example in the same building) and can be interconnected by cables; *compare with* WAN

landscape *noun* **landscape format** = book format where the top edge is longer than the foredge (as opposed to portrait format);

landscape photograph = photograph printed across the page, its width being greater than its height; (NOTE: US English is **horizontal**)

> COMMENT: landscape format is not a normal book format, in that a portrait format book is easier to hold in the hand. Landscape formats are used for art books where many illustrations may be horizontal. Landscape books, especially large art books, are heavy and tend to pull apart at the spine, thus distorting the pages. They also have the disadvantage of not being easy to put on bookshelves, and are especially awkward for bookshop shelves, where the need to show the spine and title makes the book stick out from the shelf much further than others

language *noun* words spoken or written by people in a certain country; ***the managing director conducted the negotiations in three languages;*** **foreign language** = language which is spoken by people of another country; **foreign language rights** = rights to translate a book into foreign languages; **programming language** = system of signs, letters and words used to instruct a computer

> COMMENT: there are three types of computer languages: machine code, assembler and high-level language. The higher the level the language is, the easier it is to program and understand, but the slower it is to execute. Common high-level languages are BASIC, C, COBOL, FORTRAN, PASCAL, PROLOG

lapse 1 *noun* stopping being valid; ***the lapse of copyright means that the book can be reprinted anywhere*** **2** *verb* to stop being valid *or* to stop being active; ***the copyright has lapsed;*** **to let an offer lapse** = to allow time to pass so that an offer is no longer valid

large *adjective* very big *or* important; ***the headings are in large capitals; the point size for the text should be at least two points larger than the footnotes; he is our largest customer; why has she got an office which is larger than mine?;*** **large crown octavo (8vo)** = book format (198 x 129mm); **large crown quarto (4o)** = book format (258 x 201mm); **large print books** *or* *US* **large type books** = books printed in a very large print size, intended for people who have difficulty in seeing (such books are normally bought by public libraries, and are not available in bookshops)

laser *noun* = LIGHT AMPLIFICATION BY STIMULATED EMISSION OF RADIATION device that produces coherent light of a single wavelength in a narrow beam, by exciting a material so that it emits photons of light; **laser beam recording** = production of characters on a light-sensitive film by a laser beam controlled directly from a computer; **laser disk** = plastic disk that contains information in the form of small etched dots that can be read by a laser, used to record images *or* sound in digital form; **laser printer** = high-resolution computer printer that uses a laser source to print high-quality dot matrix character patterns on paper (these have a much higher resolution than normal printers, usually 300 dpi)

last 1 *adjective & adverb* **(a)** coming at the end of a series; ***we passed the last proofs for press yesterday; this is our last board meeting before we move to our new offices; we finished the last items in the order just two days before the delivery date;*** **last colour** = the last of a series of colours printed in four-colour printing; **last quarter** = period of three months to the end of the financial year **(b)** most recent *or* most recently; ***where is the last batch of orders? the last ten orders were only for single copies*** **2** *verb* to go on *or* to continue; ***we have enough stock to last us for three months***

last in first out *noun* **(a)** redundancy policy, where the people who have been most recently appointed are the first to be made redundant **(b)** accounting method where stock is valued at the price of the latest purchases

late 1 *adjective* **(a)** after the time stated or agreed; **there is a penalty for late delivery** = if delivery is made after the agreed date, the supplier has to pay a fine **(b)** at the end of a period of time; **latest date for signature of the contract** = the last acceptable date for signing the contract **(c) latest** = most recent; ***here are the latest sales figures;*** **latest edition** = most recent printing of a newspaper **2** *adverb* after the time stated or agreed; ***the publisher was late in getting the corrected proofs back to the typesetter; the shipment was landed late***

lateral reversal *noun* reversing of an image to give an exact mirror image of the plate

latex *noun* rubber solution added to some papers to make them more durable

Latin alphabet *noun* **(a)** alphabet used in Roman times, with 21 letters (no j, u, w, y and z) **(b)** modern western alphabet, used in most European languages, except Greek and the Cyrillic languages (such as Russian and Bulgarian)

launch 1 *verb* to put a new product on the market (usually spending money on advertising it); ***they launched their new gardening series at the Chelsea Flower Show; the company is spending thousands of pounds to launch a new series of dictionaries*** **2** *noun* act of putting a new product on the market; ***the launch of the new fiction series has been put back three months; the company is geared up for the launch of the new series of school textbooks; the management has decided on a September launch date***

launching *noun* act of putting a new product on the market; **launching costs** = costs of publicity for a new product; **launching date** = date when a new product is officially shown to the public for the first time; **launching party** = party held to advertise the launching of a new product

law *noun* **(a) laws** = rules by which a country is governed and the activities of people and organizations controlled; **labour laws** = laws concerning the employment of workers **(b) law** = all the statutes of a country taken together; **civil law** = laws relating to people's rights and agreements between individuals; **commercial law** = laws regarding business; **company law** = laws which refer to the way companies work; **contract law** *or* **the law of contract** = laws relating to agreements; **copyright law** = laws concerning the protection of copyright; **law books** = books referring to the law (such as statutes, official publications, commentaries, etc.); **to break the law** = to do something which is not allowed by law; ***he is breaking the law by selling books on Sunday; you will be breaking the law if you try to take those books into the country without an import licence***

lawyer *noun* person who has studied law and can act for people on legal business; **commercial lawyer** *or* **company lawyer** = person who specializes in company law *or* who advises companies on legal problems; **copyright lawyer** = person who specializes in the law concerning copyright; **international lawyer** = person who specializes in international law

lay *noun* **(a)** way in which something is set out; **lay of the case** = way in which the different characters are placed in compartments in a case **(b)** one of two metal guides for paper in the printing press or folding machine; **lay boy** = device which collects the cut sheets after they have been printed and stacks them; **lay edge** = edge of the sheet of paper which touches one of the lays on the printing press (the front lay of the sheet is taken by the grippers, and the side lay is aligned against the side lay gauge); **lay gauge** = mechanism on the printing press which aligns with the lay edges of the paper, thus making sure that each sheet is printed in exactly the same place; **lay marks** = marks on the sheet showing which are the lay edges; **front lay** = lay at the front of the sheet of paper; **side lay** = edge of a sheet of paper, which is aligned by the side lay gauge

layer *noun* **(a)** thin film of a substance; ***in lamination, the card is covered with a thin layer of plastic and then heated*** **(b)** worker who feeds the sheets through the press

laying press *noun* lying press, a small press used to hold handbound books while they are being glued

lay out *verb* to design the way in which a page will be printed; ***the designer has laid out the text around the artist's colour drawings***

layout *noun* (i) arrangement of a page of a book *or* publicity leaflet, etc.; (ii) mock-up of a finished piece of printed work showing the positioning and sizes of text and graphics; ***the design team is working on the layouts for the new magazine; they altered the page layout to give more white space; the artist and author have approved the design layouts, so we can proceed to proofing specimen pages;*** **layout paper** *or* **detail paper** = thin transparent paper used for layouts and tracing; **layout sheet** = preprinted sheet with grids showing the basic design of a page, used by designers to prepare final layouts; **layout table** = light table used for laying out pages; **layout terminal** = keyboard and computer monitor on which page layouts can be prepared; *see also* COMPREHENSIVE

lc = LOWER CASE

LC = LIBRARY OF CONGRESS SYSTEM

L/C = LETTER OF CREDIT

LCD = LIQUID CRYSTAL DISPLAY liquid crystal that turns black when a voltage is applied, used in many small digital displays; **LCD shutter printer** = page printer that uses an LCD panel in front of a bright light to describe images onto the photosensitive drum; the LCD panel stops the light passing through, except at pixels that describe the image

lead[1] **1** *noun* **(a)** heavy soft metal (chemical symbol: Pb) used as the main part of the alloy in cast metal type (lead is too soft to use on its own, so it is strengthened with about 10% tin (to make it tough) and 20% antimony (to make it hard) **(b)** thin piece of metal used to separate lines of type; **thick lead** = lead of 3 pt; *see also* NONPAREIL **(c)** black material (graphite) used in pencils; ***a soft lead pencil*** **2** *verb* to make spaces between lines of typesetting, either with strips of metal *or* on the computer; ***the notes have not been leaded;*** *opposite is* UNLEADED

lead[2] **1** *noun* **(a)** main story in a newspaper *or* news programme on television **(b)** end of a web which is fed into the printing press **2** *verb* **(a)** to use as the first story; ***the paper led with the story about the refugees*** **(b)** to be the main person in a group; ***she will lead the trade mission to Nigeria; the tour of American factories will be led by the minister***

leader *noun* **(a)** person who manages *or* directs others; ***the leader of the print workers' union*** *or* ***the print workers' leader; she is the leader of the trade mission to Nigeria*** **(b)** product which sells best; **a market leader** = product which sells most in a market *or* company which has the largest share of a market; **loss-leader** = article which is sold very cheaply to attract customers **(c)** **leaders** *or* **leader lines** = series of short dashes or dots which run across a page (as between chapter titles and page numbers in a contents list) **(d)** blank tape at the beginning of a reel, which is fed into a machine **(e)** leading article, the main article in a newspaper, written by the editor, expressing the newspaper's official point of view

leading[1] *noun* space inserted between lines of typeset text, either as metal strips, or via the computer program; ***if we increase the leading from 1 to 2pt, the book will make twelve extra pages;*** **leading out** = action of spacing out the lines of typeset text

> COMMENT: the spaces between lines of text are called 'leading' because originally the lines were separated by thin strips of lead; the term is still used, even for computer setting, although here 'interlinear spacing' is more correct

leading[2] *adjective* **(a)** most important; ***they are the leading company in the reference field;*** **leading article** = main article in a newspaper, written by the editor, expressing the newspaper's official point of view **(b)** which goes into a machine first; **leading edge** = gripper edge *or* feed edge, the edge of a sheet of paper which is held by the grippers and goes through the press first

lead time *noun* time between deciding to place an order and receiving the product; ***the lead time on this item is more than six weeks***

leaf 1 *noun* **(a)** sheet of paper (which may be printed on both sides, making two pages) **(b)** thin sheet of real metal (as opposed to foil); ***the cover is leather tooled in gold leaf*** **2** *verb* **to leaf through a book** = to turn over the pages of a book rapidly, without reading it; (NOTE: plural is **leaves**)

leaflet *noun* small publicity sheet (usually folded in half); ***to mail leaflets*** *or* ***to hand out leaflets describing services; they made a leaflet mailing to 20,000 addresses***

lean matter *noun* copy to be set which poses problems (such as copy with mathematical symbols or copy which is closely typed); (NOTE: the opposite is **fat matter**)

learned journal *noun* academic journal published by a university *or* academic research body, usually edited by a university professor, which is published two or three times a year and deals with a specialized academic subject

leather *noun* material made from the skins of animals, used for binding expensive books; **full leather binding** = binding of a hardcover book where the whole book is covered with leather; **half leather binding** = binding of a hardcover book, where the spine and corners are covered with leather and the rest is left in ordinary cloth or paper; **quarter leather binding** = binding where the spine is covered with leather and the rest of the cover with paper; **leather cloth** = closely woven cloth, covered with a cellulose and oil mixture, which makes it look like leather; **simili leather** = material which looks like leather

leatherbound *adjective* **leatherbound book** = book which has been bound in leather

leatherette *noun* paper which has been embossed to look like leather

leave *verb* to let something stay as it is; ***leave the last page blank; leave three lines blank between the entries; the chapters should be left in their present order;*** **leave edge** = last edge of the sheet of paper as it goes into the press (as opposed to the leading edge)

leave out *verb* not to include; ***she left out the ISBN on the mailing piece; the contract leaves out any mention of a paperback edition***

LED = LIGHT-EMITTING DIODE **LED printer** = page printer (similar to a laser printer) that uses an LED light source instead of a laser; *see also* LASER PRINTER

ledger *noun* book in which accounts are written; **bought ledger** *or* **purchase ledger** = book in which expenditure is noted; **nominal ledger** = book which records a company's income and expenditure in general; **sales ledger** = book in which sales are noted; **ledger paper** = fine thick paper (formerly rag paper), tub-sized and coloured pale blue, grey or green, used for account books

left *adjective* opposite of right; ***the numbers run down the left side of the page; put the debits in the left column***

left-hand *adjective* belonging to the left side; **left-hand page** = left page of a double page spread (always with an even folio); ***begin each chapter on a left-hand page; left-hand pages should have even folio numbers; the debits are in the left-hand column in the accounts; he keeps the author contracts in the left-hand drawer of his desk***

left justification *noun* printing command that makes sure that the left hand margin of the text is even

leg *noun* column that is shorter than other columns

legal *adjective* **(a)** according to the law *or* allowed by the law; ***the company's action was completely legal*** **(b)** referring to the law; **to take legal action** = to sue someone *or* to take someone to court; **to take legal advice** = to ask a lawyer for advice about a legal problem; **legal adviser** = person who advises clients about the law; **legal claim** = statement that someone owns something legally; **legal costs** *or* **legal charges** *or* **legal expenses** = money spent on fees to lawyers; **legal department** *or* **legal section** = section of a company dealing with legal matters; **legal deposit** = giving of a copy of a book to a deposit library as part of the process of publication (in the British Isles, the deposit libraries are the British Library, the Bodleian Library at Oxford, Cambridge University Library, the National Library of Scotland and the Library of Trinity College Dublin; the Welsh National Library may also receive copies)

legend *noun* caption, a short text placed under an illustration

legibility *noun* being able to be read easily; ***the keyboarders complained about the legibility of the manuscript***

legible *adjective* which can be read easily; ***the manuscript is written in pencil and is hardly legible***

> COMMENT: legibility is one of the requirements of text matter. Text is more easily read in roman serif typefaces than in italic or in sans faces, and should have line spacing of about 2pts between the lines (i.e. there should be more spacing between the lines than between words). Sans faces and italic are less legible, and closely spaced lines, or lines which are irregularly spaced, are more difficult to read than lines of closely spaced words with extra spacing between the lines

legislation *noun* laws; **copyright legislation** = laws concerning copyright; **labour legislation** = laws concerning the employment of workers

lend *verb* to allow someone to use something for a period; ***the library lends several thousand books each week; the bank lent him £50,000 to start his business***

lender *noun* person who lends money

lending *noun* act of letting someone use something for a time; **lending library** = public library which lends books (as opposed to a reference library, where the books cannot be removed)

length *noun* **(a)** measurement of how long something is; **file length** = number of characters *or* bytes in a stored file; **line length** = number of characters which can fit into a set line of type **(b)** ability of ink to flow easily

lengthwise *adverb* along the length; ***the picture measures 29cm lengthwise***

Letraset *noun* trademark for a type of transfer lettering (lettering which can be transferred from a backing sheet to paper)

letter *noun* **(a)** piece of writing sent from one person *or* company to another to give information; **business letter** = letter which deals with business matters; **circular letter** = letter sent to many people; **covering letter** = letter sent with documents to say why they are being sent; **standard letter** = letter which is sent without change to various correspondents **(b) letter of acknowledgement** = letter which says that something has been received; **letter of appointment** = letter in which someone is appointed to a job; **letter of complaint** = letter in which someone complains; **letter of credit (L/C)** = letter from a bank allowing someone credit and promising to repay at a later date; **letters patent** = official document which gives someone the exclusive right to make and sell something which he has invented; **letter of reference** = letter in which an employer recommends someone for a new job **(c) air letter** = special piece of thin blue paper which when folded can be sent by air without an envelope; **registered letter** = letter which is noted by the post office before it is sent, so that compensation can be claimed if it is lost **(d)** written or printed sign (such as A, B, C, etc.); ***write your name and address in block letters*** *or* ***in capital letters;*** **letter fit** = the space between typeset characters

letterform *noun* shape of a letter; **digitized letterforms** = shapes of letters which are converted to digital codes and stored in a computer

letterhead *or* **letterheading** *noun* **(a)** name and address of a person or organization printed at the top of a piece of notepaper; ***business forms and letterheads can now be designed on a PC*** **(b)** sheet of paper with the name and address of a company printed at the top

lettering *noun* **(a)** calligraphy, the art of drawing letters by hand in a beautiful way **(b)** printing of letters; **spine lettering** = the printing of the title (and other details) on the spine of a book

letterpress *noun* **letterpress printing** = relief printing process, where metal type *or* blocks are covered with ink and the paper is pressed onto the block to make an image; **letterpress machine** = machine which prints letterpress

letter-quality (LQ) printing *noun* feature of some dot-matrix printers to provide characters of the same quality as a typewriter by using dots which are very close together; *see also* NLQ

letterset *noun* dry offset, the process of printing where ink is transferred from the plate to a blanket cylinder and then printed from the blanket onto paper

letter space *noun* the space between two typeset letters, especially a standard space

letter spacing *noun* extra spacing placed between letters for emphasis or to give a better visual effect

level *adjective* flat *or* not higher than the rest; **level small caps** = even small caps, printing in small capitals, without any large capitals at the beginning of words

levy 1 *noun* money which is demanded and collected by the government; **import levy** = tax on imports, especially in the EU a tax on imports of farm produce from outside the EU; **training levy** = tax to be paid by companies to fund the government's training schemes **2** *verb* to demand payment of a tax *or* an extra payment and to collect it; ***the government has decided to levy a tax on imported cars; to levy a duty on the import of luxury items***

lexicographical order *noun* order of items, where the words are listed in the order of the letters of the alphabet, as in a dictionary

lexicon *noun* a term for dictionary, now usually applied to a dictionary of Latin, Sanskrit, Hebrew or Greek

libel 1 *noun* untrue written statement which damages someone's reputation; **action for libel** *or* **libel action** = case in a law court where someone says that another person has written a libel **2** *verb* **to libel someone** = to damage someone's character in writing; *compare* SLANDER (NOTE: the GB spelling **libelling - libelled** but US spelling is **libeling - libeled**)

libellous *adjective* (written statement) which is untrue and damages someone's reputation

> COMMENT: libel only refers to writing and print; it can be used in connection with photographs and drawings, especially cartoons. Slander is the equivalent in spoken statements, including statements on radio and TV

librarian *noun* person who works in a library

librarianship *or* **library science** *noun* study of libraries and how they are organized and run

library *noun* **(a)** collection of books for lending *or* for reference; also a similar collection of records *or* tapes *or* films, etc.; ***the editors have checked all the references in the local library; a copy of each new book has to be deposited in the British Library; look up the bibliographical details in the library catalogue;*** **lending library** = library of books which are for lending to the public; **public library** = library owned by a town and open to the public to use either for reference or for borrowing books; **reference library** = section of a library which contains reference books (dictionaries *or* encyclopaedias) which can be read in the library but which cannot be taken away; **library binding** = specially solid binding used for books which are to be put in a library (especially full buckram binding for public libraries, and morocco quarter binding for private libraries); *GB* **library licence** = licence granted to a bookshop *or* to a local authority, allowing books to be bought at a discount for public libraries; **library purchase** = purchase of books by a library from a library supplier; **library supplier** = wholesaler who specializes in the supply of books to libraries; **library supply** = supplying books to libraries at a special discount

Library Association (LA) *noun* professional association representing British librarians

Library of Congress Catalog *noun* catalogue of the Library of Congress in the USA; **Library of Congress Catalog number (LOC)** = number of the reference in the Library of Congress Catalog, printed inside a book published in the USA; *compare* CIP **Library of Congress System (LC)** = cataloguing system used by the Library of Congress (it is different from the Dewey Decimal System) **(b)** **picture library** = collection of photographs and line drawings, which can be borrowed and reproduced for a fee

licence *US* **license** *noun* **(a)** official document which allows someone to do something; **import licence** *or* **export licence** = documents which allow goods to be exported or imported; *GB* **library licence** = licence granted to a bookshop *or* to a local authority, allowing books to be bought at a discount for public libraries **(b)** permission given by one manufacturer to another manufacturer to make copies of his products against payment of a fee; ***the software is manufactured in this country under licence;*** **goods manufactured under licence** = goods made with the permission of the owner of the copyright or patent

license 1 *noun US* = LICENCE **2** *verb* to give someone official permission to do something; ***the reprint has been licensed for sale in India***

licensee *noun* person who has a licence, especially a licence to manufacture something

licensing *noun* which refers to licences; ***a licensing agreement***

lift *verb* **(a)** to copy directly without any acknowledgement; ***the book contains whole chapters lifted from a book on the same subject published in the USA*** **(b)** to take away *or* to remove; ***the government has lifted the ban on imports from Japan; to lift trade barriers; the minister has lifted the embargo on the export of computers to East European countries***

ligature *noun* (i) two characters joined together on one stem to form a combined character; (ii) a short line connecting two characters

> COMMENT: the most common ligatures are between ff, fl and fi, though they also occur between vowels as in œ. Ligatures are less commonly used now, because it is difficult to keyboard them on personal computers, which are frequently used by authors to supply text to a publisher

light 1 *adjective* **(a)** not heavy *or* not thick; ***the book should be printed on light paper;*** **light face** = typeface (roman or italic) with thin lines, which appears light on the page (as opposed to bold face) **(b)** not dark **2** *noun* **light box** = viewer with a light inside and a matt transparent window, in which transparencies *or* films can be placed so that it is easy to see them; **light table** = table with a matt glass surface and a light underneath, on which film can be placed so that it is easy to see; **light-fast colours** = colours which do not fade when exposed to light; (NOTE: the opposite is **fugitive**) **light pen** = pen which contains a light-sensitive device that can detect pixels on a TV screen *or* the bars in a bar code and can send information back to a computer

light-emitting diode (LED) *noun* semiconductor diode that emits light when a current is applied

lighten *verb* to make less dark *or* less dense

light-sensitive *adjective* which is sensitive to light; ***the photograph is printed on light-sensitive paper***

lightweight *adjective* which is not heavy; ***the book is printed on thin, lightweight paper;*** **lightweight paper** = paper weighing less than 60gsm

limit 1 *noun* point at which something ends *or* point where you can go no further; **to set limits to imports** *or* **to impose import limits** = to allow only a certain amount of imports; **credit limit** = largest amount of money which a customer can borrow; **he has exceeded his credit limit** = he has borrowed more money than he is allowed; **time limit** = maximum time which can be taken to do something; ***to set a time limit for acceptance of the offer;*** **weight limit** = maximum weight **2** *verb* to stop something from going beyond a certain point; **each agent is limited to twenty-five units** = each agent is allowed only twenty-five units to sell

limitation *noun* act of allowing only a certain quantity of something; **limitation of liability** = making someone liable for only a part of the damage or loss; **time limitation** = amount of time available

limited *adjective* restricted *or* not open; **limited edition** = edition of which only a few copies are printed (usually no more than 1,000); ***the limited edition has been numbered and signed by the artist;*** **limited market** = market which can take only a certain quantity of goods; **limited liability company** = company where a shareholder is responsible for the company's debts only to the face value of his shares; **private limited company** = company with a small number of shareholders, whose shares are not traded on the Stock Exchange; **Public Limited Company (plc)** = company whose shares can be bought on the Stock Exchange

limp *adjective* which can bend *or* which is not stiff; **limp binding** = binding material which can bend easily (that is, paper and not stiff boards); *see also* CASE, YAPP **limp-bound edition** *or* **limp edition** = edition with a soft cover; ***the book is published in a limp edition and in a hardcover edition***

line *noun* **(a)** single long thin mark drawn by a pen *or* printed on a surface; ***the printer has difficulty in reproducing very fine lines; this paper has thin blue lines; I prefer notepaper without any lines; he drew a thick line across the bottom of the column to show which figure was the total;*** **line artwork** *or* **line copy** = black and white graphics, with no tones; **line block** *or* **line engraving** = block made from a line drawing for printing, usually made of zinc (it does not give tones, as a halftone does); (NOTE: US English is **cut**) **line colour** = coloured illustration made by printing line drawings in different colours; **line conversion** = process by which continuous tones are converted into lines; **line drawings** *or* **line illustrations** = illustrations for a book which are drawn with a pen, or have tints, but which do not need to be reproduced as halftones; ***the book is illustrated with twenty-five line drawings;*** **line and tone block** *or* **line/tone block** = block which combines both line artwork and halftones; (NOTE: the US English is **combination plate**) **(b)** row of characters (printed on a page *or* displayed on a computer screen *or* printer); ***each page has 52 lines of text; several lines of manuscript seem to have been missed by the compositor; can we insert an extra line of spacing between the paragraphs? the book has fifty lines per page; leave a line of white at the beginning of each paragraph; each paragraph should start a new line;*** **line casting machine** *or* **line caster** = machine (such as Linotype) which casts whole lines of type at a time; **line editor** = piece of software that allows the operator to modify one line of text from a file at a time; **line ending** = character which shows that a line has ended (instructed by pressing the carriage return key); **line feed (LF)** = (i) space between the base line of one line of text and the base line of the next; (ii) control on a printer *or* computer terminal that moves the cursor down by one line; **line folding** = move a section of a long line of text onto the next row; **line gauge** = instrument for measuring type, with picas, points, etc., marked on a type of ruler; **line increment** = minimum distance between two lines of type, which can be as small as one eighteenth of a point; **line length** = number of characters contained in a printed line *or* in a displayed line (on a computer screen this is normally 80 characters, on a printer often 132 characters); **line measure** = length of a line of typeset characters; **line space** = white space equivalent to one line of typesetting; **line spacing** = (i) leaving no white line between lines of type; (ii) distance between two rows of characters; **double line spacing** = leaving a white line between lines of text; **single line spacing** = leaving no white lines between lines of text; **lines per minute (LPM)** = number of lines printed by a line printer per minute; **bottom line** = last line in accounts, showing the net profit **(c)** **line of business** *or* **line of work** = type of business or work; **line of product** *or* **product line** = series of different products which form a group, all made by the same company; ***we do not stock that line; computers are not one of our best-selling lines; they produce an interesting line in garden books*** **(d)** **line chart** *or* **line graph** = chart or graph using lines to indicate values

lineage *noun* **(a)** measurement of how many lines a text will make **(b)** system for charging for advertisements by the number of column lines used

lined *adjective* **(a)** with lines; ***he prefers lined paper for writing notes*** **(b)** with a lining; ***the de luxe edition is in a slipcase lined with silk***

linen *noun* cloth made from the flax plant; **linen finish** = paper or board grained to look like linen; **linen paper** = strong paper used for banknotes; **linen tester** = magnifying glass used by printers

line printer *noun* device for printing draft quality information at high speeds, typical output is 200 to 3000 lines per minute

> COMMENT: line printers print a whole line at a time, running from right to left and left to right, and are usually dot matrix printers with not very high quality of print. Compare page printers, which print a whole page at a time

liner *noun* paper used to cover boards or other papers

lining *noun* **(a)** making a line of characters straight; **lining figures** *or* **lining numerals** = form of Arabic numerals which are aligned like capitals (as opposed to old face figures *or* non-lining figures, which have ascenders and descenders: Century is a face with lining figures) **(b)** (i) paper used to glue inside a board cover, to strengthen it and prevent warping; (ii) mull or kraft paper glued inside the spine of a book to strengthen it (mull is used as the first lining, and kraft paper as the second); **back lining** = piece of thin cloth or paper glued to the sewn spine of a book before the cover is attached; **lining papers** = endpapers, pages of thicker paper at the front and back of a book, glued to the first and last text pages and then glued to the cover **(c)** action of pasting paper inside the spine of a cased book to strengthen it

linocut *noun* (i) design made by cutting the surface of linoleum with a knife; (ii) print made from a linocut

> COMMENT: linocuts are broad and rather rough; they cannot give delicate lines, but can make striking designs

Linotron trademark for a phototypesetting machine developed by Linotype

Linotype trademark for a metal composing machine, which sets type in a metal strip as long as a line, as opposed to single characters

linotypist *noun* person who keyboards on a Linotype machine

> COMMENT: Linotype is easy to use and can be operated by a single keyboard operator; the main disadvantage as opposed to Monotype, is that, since each line is a single piece of metal (or 'slug'), even a small correction will involve resetting a whole line, and is therefore more expensive

Linson *noun* trademark for a strong binding paper which is patterned to resemble cloth

lint *noun* fluff, fibres which are detached from the surface of the paper as it is being printed

liquid crystal display (LCD) *noun* liquid crystal that turns black when a voltage is applied, used in many small digital displays; **LCD shutter printer** = page printer that uses an LCD panel in front of a bright light to describe images onto the photosensitive drum; the LCD panel stops the light passing through, except at pixels that describe the image

list 1 *noun* **(a)** several items written one after the other; ***list of products*** *or* ***product list; stock list; to add an item to a list; to cross an item off a list;*** **address list** *or* **mailing list** = list of names and addresses of people and companies; **black list** = list of goods *or* companies *or* countries which are banned for trade; **contents list** *or* **list of contents** = list of the main chapters in a book, given usually at the beginning; **picking list** = list of items in an order, but listed according to where they can be found in the warehouse **(b)** (i) catalogue of books which a publisher has for sale; (ii) special collection of books which a publisher has recently published and advertises in a special catalogue; ***three new biographies are mentioned in their Autumn List; he has built up an interesting military list;*** **list-building** = creation of a specialized series of titles; **list price** = price as given in a catalogue; *see also* BACKLIST, FRONTLIST **2** *verb* **(a)** to write a series of items one after the other; ***to list products by category; to list representatives by area; to list products in a catalogue; the catalogue lists twenty-three publications which have been delayed*** **(b)** to print *or* display certain items of information; **to list a program** = to display a program line by line in correct order

listing *noun* **(a)** **computer listing** = printout of a list of items taken from the data stored in a computer; **listing paper** = paper made as a long sheet, used in computer printers **(b)** **listings** = information items (such as what films are showing at which cinemas, etc.) listed in a newspaper

literacy *noun* being able to read and write; ***a campaign to increase adult literacy***

literal *noun* mistake made when keyboarding *or* printing when one character is replaced by another *or* when two characters are transposed; ***the reviewer found hundreds of literals in the index...who was the proofreader?;*** (NOTE: US English is **typo**)

literary *adjective* **literary agency** = office which represents authors in their negotiations with publishers, and finds publishers for new works by authors, for a commission (usually a percentage of the authors' royalties); **literary agent** = person who acts on behalf of an author, negotiates with publishers and takes a proportion of the author's income as a fee; **literary executor** = person appointed by an author in his will, to look after his unpublished works and papers after he dies; **literary property** = ownership of a copyright

'Literary Marketplace' American publication listing publishers, agents, translators, etc.; (NOTE: the British equivalent is the **Writers' and Artists' Yearbook**)

literate *adjective* (person) who can read; ***I think our editorial director's barely literate;*** **computer-literate** = able to understand expressions relating to computers and how to use a computer

lith film *noun* high quality and contrast photographic film used in lithographic printing

lithograph *noun* work of art printed from a stone or plate by lithography

lithographic *adjective* referring to lithography; **lithographic paper** = special fine paper for printing lithographs; **lithographic film** = LITH FILM

lithography *informal*

litho *noun* **(a)** printing process, where a design is applied to a smooth flat surface with greasy ink or a crayon (the surface is wetted and ink will adhere to the greasy parts, but not to the wet parts) **(b) offset lithography** = printing process used for printing books, where the ink sticks to image areas on the plate and is transferred to an offset cylinder from which it is printed on to the paper; *US* **litho prep** = make-up of film or repro

COMMENT: lithography was invented in 1798, by a German artist, Alois Senefelder. It was originally the art of drawing a design on stone in greasy ink, then printing from it. The surface now used is a metal plate, but the principle is the same: this is that a greasy surface attracts ink, while a wet surface repels ink. The design is drawn on the surface with greasy ink, the surface is then rolled with a damp roller to wet it, and then the inking roller passes over it, leaving ink on the parts which are greasy and not leaving ink on those parts which are wet

'Livres Hebdo' French weekly magazine dealing with books and publishing matters

LMP = LITERARY MARKETPLACE

load 1 *noun* **(a)** goods which are transported; **lorry-load** *or* **container-load** = amount of goods carried on a lorry or container; ***a container-load of books is missing*** **(b) workload** = amount of work which a person has to do; ***he has difficulty in coping with his heavy workload; my workload has doubled since the senior editor left*** **2** *verb* to put a program into a computer; ***load the word-processing program before you start keyboarding***

loading *noun* **(a)** substance (such as clay or gypsum) added to paper furnish during beating before the papermaking process, to make the paper more opaque and more solid; also china clay used for coating papers **(b)** the action of adding gypsum or clay to paper stock

loan *noun* **(a)** something (such as money *or* a book) which has been lent; **inter-library loan** = service to library users whereby a library obtains a book which is not in its own collection from another library **(b)** *(rare)* high quality rag paper, used for legal documents

LOC = LIBRARY OF CONGRESS NUMBER

local *adjective* referring to a particular area, especially one near where a publisher's office is based; **local author** = author who lives in the area served by a bookshop *or* local radio station, and who is given special promotion; **local authority** = elected body which runs a small area of the country; **local government** = elected administrative bodies which run areas of the country; **local interest titles** = books which are interesting to people living in a certain area, but not to anyone else; **local paper** = newspaper which sells in a certain area, and carries news about that area

local area network *or* **LAN** network where various terminals and equipment are all within a short distance of one another (at a maximum distance of about 500m, for example in the same building) and can be interconnected by cables; *compare with* WAN

locally *adverb* in the area near where an office or factory is based; ***we recruit all our staff locally***

loc. cit. *abbreviation for the Latin phrase 'loco citato' meaning* 'in the place quoted', used in a footnote to refer to another note

lock 1 *noun* (i) device for closing a door *or* box so that it can be opened only with a key; (ii) device to prevent a forme from moving **2** *verb* to close a door with a key, so that it cannot be opened; ***the manager forgot to lock the door of the computer room; the petty cash box was not locked***

lock up *verb* **to lock up type** = to screw the quoins tight in a chase so that the metal type cannot fall out

loft-dried paper *noun* paper which has been dried slowly in a special drying room

logo *noun* symbol *or* design *or* group of letters used by a company as a mark on its products and in advertising

logotype *noun* **(a)** single piece of metal type which prints a whole word, a trade mark, or the distinctive name of a newspaper, etc. **(b)** = LOGO

long *adjective* not short *or* which has a certain length; **long-bodied type** = bastard font, characters cast on a larger body (such as 8 point on 9), which means that leading is not needed; **long column** *or* **page** = page *or* column which is longer than the others, and has to be cut, or which is allowed to be longer than others to avoid an awkward widow; **long descenders** = alternative characters in a certain typeface (such as Times Roman) that have longer descenders than the normal characters in the same face; **long discount** = trade discount *or* discount from a manufacturer to a retailer; **long grain** = paper where the grain runs parallel to the longer side of the sheet; **long inks** = viscous inks, that is, inks which flow relatively easily; (NOTE: the opposite is **short inks**) **long run** = printrun which is longer than normal (say, 80,000 copies or more); **long s** = letter 's' in the form of an 'f', used in books printed before the end of the 18th century

longhand *noun* handwriting where the words are written out in full and not in shorthand; ***applications should be written in longhand and sent to the personnel officer***

looker out *noun* person who looks out books in a warehouse

look out *verb* to find books in a warehouse, according to the picking list

lookthrough *noun* how paper looks when it is held up to the light to examine it for finish or opacity

look-up table (LUT) *noun* collection of stored results that can be accessed very rapidly by a program without the need to calculate each result whenever needed

> COMMENT: for computer graphics a look-up table may be a table of pixel intensity or colour information which increases the range of values that can be displayed. Since the values are stored in a look-up table they do not have to be computed each time they are called up, and execution time is reduced

loop *noun* curved part of a letter, such as the top of an 'a'

loose-leaf book *noun* book with loose pages which can be taken out and fixed back again on metal rings in a special binder

lossless compression *noun* image compression techniques that can reduce the number of bits used for each pixel in an image without losing any information or sharpness (such as Huffman Encoding)

lossy compression *noun* image compression techniques that can reduce the number of bits used for each pixel in an image, but in doing so lose information (such as JPEG)

low *adjective* not high; type *or* blocks which are not as high as the forme, and have to be raised by interlaying; **low opacity paper** = transparent paper; **low sales** = small amount of money produced by sales; **low volume of sales** = small number of items sold

lower case (lc) *noun* small letters (a, b, c, d, etc.) as opposed to capitals (A, B, C, D, etc.); **upper and lower case** = printed with the first letter of each word in capitals, and the rest in small letters

low-level *adjective* **(a)** not very important; ***a low-level delegation visited the ministry; a low-level meeting decided to put off making a decision*** **(b) low-level computer language** = programming language similar to machine code

low-resolution graphics *or* **low-res graphics** *noun* ability to display character-sized graphic blocks *or* preset shapes on a screen rather than using individual pixels; *compare* HIGH-RESOLUTION

LPM = LINES PER MINUTE

LQ = LETTER QUALITY

Ludlow trademark for a type of composing machine which sets slugs of display type in large point sizes, used for headings

lump *noun* **lump sum** = money paid in one single amount, not in several small sums; ***he received a lump sum for the copyright, as opposed to an advance and a royalty***

lunch *noun* meal eaten in the middle of the day; **business lunch** = meeting between businessmen where they have lunch together to discuss business deals; **publishers' lunch** = extremely long lunch meeting common when publishers, agents, authors and other publishers meet

lunch hour *or* **lunchtime** *noun* time when people have lunch; ***the office is closed during the lunch hour** or **at lunchtimes***

LUT = LOOK-UP TABLE

luxe *see* DE LUXE, LUXURY

luxury *noun* expensive thing which is not necessary but which is good to have; **luxury edition** *or* **de luxe edition** = edition printed on fine paper with a superior binding

lwc = LIGHTWEIGHT COATED PAPER

lying press *noun* laying press, a small press used to hold handbound books while they are being glued

Mm

m = METRE

M *prefix* **(a)** = MEGA (i) one million; (ii) symbol for 1,048,576, used only in computer and electronic related applications; **MByte (MB)** = measurement of mass storage equal to 1,048,576 bytes **(b)** one thousand; *US* **M weight** = weight of one thousand sheets of paper

McCain sewing *see* SIDE SEWING

machine *noun* **(a) machine copy** = copy made by a copying machine; **copying machine** *or* **duplicating machine** = machine which makes copies of documents; **dictating machine** = machine which records what someone dictates, which a typist can then play back and type out; **machine shop** = place where working machines are **(b)** machine which makes paper; **machine-coated paper** = paper which is coated while being made in the papermaking machine, and is therefore cheaper than paper coated off the machine; **machine direction** = grain direction, the way in which the grain of the paper lies in the same direction as the movement of the web along a papermaking machine; **machine-finished paper (MF paper)** = calendered paper, paper which has been finished by passing through calenders on the papermaking machine; **machine-glazed paper (MG paper)** = paper which has been dried on a heated cylinder, giving a glossy finish to one side; **machine wire** = wire or plastic cloth in a fourdrinier papermaking machine, on which the paper is formed; **machine-made** *or* **machine-produced paper** = paper which has been manufactured by a machine, not handmade; ***the grain in machine-made paper runs along the web*** **(c)** machine which typesets *or* prints *or* binds; **machine binding** = binding by an automatic binding machine (as opposed to hand binding); **machine composition** = typesetting by the hot metal method, where the compositor keyboards and the machine sets the type in hot metal; **machine direction** = the direction in which the paper goes through a printing machine; **machine minder** = person in charge of a printing machine; **machine proof** = proof of sheets of a book, taken from the printing press; **machine revise** = final proof taken from the printing press before printing starts; **machine room** = section of a printing works where the printing takes place; **machine run** = PRINTRUN **(d)** a computer; **machine code** *or* **machine language** = instructions and information shown as a series of figures (0 and 1) which can be read by a computer; **machine-readable codes** = sets of signs or letters (such as bar codes, post codes) which a computer can read; **machine translation** = translation from one language into another carried out automatically by a computer

machinery *noun* machines; **idle machinery** *or* **machinery lying idle** = machines not being used; **machinery guards** = pieces of metal to prevent workers from getting hurt by the moving parts of a machine

machining *noun* printing on paper using a printing press

machinist *noun* person who works a machine

mackle *or* **mackled proof** *noun* blurred proof, which has been badly printed

macro *noun (computer)* block of instructions which is activated by a single keystroke

macron *noun* little line (¯) printed above a vowel to show that it pronounced long

made *adjective* produced *or* manufactured; **made endpapers** *or* **made ends** = specially thick endpapers which are made by glueing several sheets together; *see also* MAKE

mag *(informal)* = MAGAZINE

magazine *noun* **(a)** publication, usually with pictures, which is published regularly, every month or every week; **computer magazine** = magazine with articles on computers and programs; **do-it-yourself magazine** = magazine with articles on work which the average person can do to repair or paint the house; **house magazine** = magazine produced for the workers in a company to give them news of the company's affairs; **trade magazine** = magazine produced for people or companies in a certain trade; **travel magazine** = magazine with articles on holidays and travel; **women's magazine** = magazine aimed at the women's market; **magazine insert** = advertising sheet put into a magazine when it is mailed or sold; **to insert a leaflet in a specialist magazine** = to put an advertising leaflet into a magazine before it is mailed or sold; **magazine mailing** = sending of copies of a magazine by post to subscribers; **magazine publisher** = publishing house which publishes magazines; **magazine supplement** = supplement to a newspaper, in the form of a magazine format section, usually in colour, given free with the weekend edition of a newspaper **(b)** container on a Linotype machine which contains the matrices from which the slugs are cast; **magazine reel stand** = device which is near a web-fed press, with spare reels of paper

magenta *noun* red, one of the process colours (the others are cyan and yellow)

magnetic *adjective* **magnetic character reading (MCR)** *or* **magnetic ink character recognition (MICR)** = system that recognizes characters by sensing magnetic ink (used on cheques); **magnetic ink** = special ink with magnetic particles in it, used for printing cheques

magnetic tape *or* **mag tape** *noun* plastic tape for recording information on a large computer; **magnetic tape encoder** = device that directly writes data entered at a keyboard onto magnetic tape

> COMMENT: magnetic tape is available on spools of between 200 and 800 metres. The tape is magnetized by the read/write head. Tape is a storage medium which only allows serial access, that is, all the tape has to be read until the required location is found (as opposed to disk storage, which can be accessed randomly)

magnification *noun* amount by which something has been made to appear larger; process of magnifying a picture; ***the lens gives a magnification of 10***

magnify *verb* to make something appear larger; ***the photograph has been magnified 200 times***

mag tape *noun informal* = MAGNETIC TAPE

mail *noun* **(a)** system of sending letters and parcels from one place to another; **by mail** = using the postal services, not sending something by hand or by messenger; **to send a package by surface mail** = to send a package by land or sea, not by air; **by sea mail** = sent by post abroad, using a ship; **electronic mail** *or* **email** = system of sending messages from one computer to another, using the telephone lines **(b)** letters sent or received; **incoming mail** = mail which arrives; **outgoing mail** = mail which is sent out; **mail room** = room in an office where incoming letters are sorted and sent to each department, and where outgoing mail is collected for sending **(c) direct mail** = selling a product by sending publicity material to possible buyers through the post; ***the company runs a successful direct-mail operation; these calculators are sold only by direct mail;*** **direct-mail advertising** = advertising by sending leaflets to people by post; **mail shot** = leaflets sent by mail to possible customers

mail box *noun* (i) one of several boxes where incoming mail is put in a large building; box for putting letters, etc. which you want to post; (ii) storage in an electronic mail system, where messages are kept for subscribers to access through their computers

mailing *noun* sending something in the post; **direct mailing** = sending of publicity material by post to possible buyers; **mailing list** = list of names and addresses of people who might be interested in a product *or* list of names and addresses of members of a society; ***his name is on our mailing list; they are working to build up a mailing list of academics in Germany;*** **to buy a mailing list** = to pay a society, etc. money to buy the list of members so that it can be used to mail publicity material; **mailing piece** = leaflet suitable for sending by direct mail; **mailing shot** = leaflets sent by mail to possible customers

mail-merge *noun* word-processing program which allows a standard letter to be printed out to a series of different names and addresses

mail-order *noun* system of buying and selling from a catalogue, placing orders and sending goods by mail; **mail-order business** *or* **mail-order firm** *or* **mail-order house** = company which sells a product by mail; **mail-order catalogue** = catalogue from which a customer can order items to be sent by mail; **mail-order selling** *or* **mail-order sales** = sales made by mail-order

main *adjective* most important; **main entry** = catalogue entry containing the most important information about the document; **main index** = general index that directs the user gradually to more specific index areas; **main memory** *or* **main storage** = area of fast access time RAM whose locations can be directly and immediately addressed by the CPU

mainframe (computer) *noun* large-scale high-power computer system that can handle high-capacity memory and backing storage devices as well as servicing a number of operators simultaneously

maintenance *noun* keeping a machine in good working order; **maintenance contract** = contract with a company which will keep a piece of equipment in good working order

majuscule *noun* capital letter *or* upper case letter; (NOTE: the opposite is a **minuscule** or **lower case letter**)

make even *verb* to arrange type so that it runs the full width of the line; also, to arrange that the last line of a section being set is a full line

make good *verb* to repair *or* to compensate; ***the company will make good the damage; to make good a loss***

makegood *noun* advertisement which is run a second time because there was a mistake in the first run

maker *noun* person who makes something; **maker-up** = person who puts text into pages

make ready *verb* to get a printing machine ready for printing, by placing the plates in it, testing the paper and the impression, etc.; **make-ready time** = time taken by a printer to prepare the machines and plates for printing

make up *verb* **(a)** to compensate for something; **to make up a loss** *or* **to make up the difference** = to pay extra so that the loss or difference is covered **(b)** to split text into pages (with headlines, page numbers, etc.) and arrange typeset material into the correct page formats before printing

make-up *or* **makeup** *noun* **page make-up** = making printed text into the correct lengths for pages, fitting in illustrations and adding the headlines, page numbers, etc.; ***corrections made after page make-up are very expensive; we do our page make-ups directly on screen; computerized page make-up systems are available with any desktop publishing package***

making *noun* **(a)** production of an item; ***ten tonnes of paper were used in the making of the order*** **(b) making (order)** = order for paper to be specially made, when the printer *or* paper merchant does not have it in stock;

the printer says that the making of this paper will be at least five tonnes

making up *noun* bringing the printed sections of a book together before sewing

MAN = METROPOLITAN AREA NETWORK

management *noun* **(a)** directing *or* running a business; **line management** = way of organizing a business so that each manager is responsible for doing what his superior tells him to do; **product management** = directing the making and selling of a product as an independent item; **management accountant** = accountant who prepares specialized information for managers to help them make decisions; **management accounts** = financial information (on sales, costs, credit, profitability) prepared for a manager; **management consultant** = person who gives advice on how to manage a business; **management course** = training course for managers; **management by objectives** = way of managing a business by planning work for the managers and testing to see if it is completed correctly and on time; **management team** = a group of managers working together; **management techniques** = ways of managing a business; **management training** = training managers by making them study problems and work out ways of solving them; **management trainee** = young person being trained to be a manager **(b)** group of managers or directors; **top management** = the main directors of a company; **middle management** = the department managers of a company who carry out the policy set by the directors and organize the work of a group of workers

manager *noun* head of a department in a company; **accounts manager** = head of the accounts department; **area manager** = manager who is responsible for the company's work (usually sales) in a certain area; **general manager** = manager in charge of the administration in a large company

managerial *adjective* referring to managers; **to be appointed to a managerial position** = to be appointed a manager; **decisions taken at managerial level** = decisions taken by managers

managing *adjective* **managing director** = director who is in charge of a whole company; **chairman and managing director** = managing director who is also chairman of the board of directors

mandatory *adjective* **mandatory meeting** = meeting which all members have to attend

man-hour *noun* work done by one man in one hour; ***one million man-hours were lost through industrial action***

manifold paper *or* **manifold bank** *noun* very thin light paper *or* airmail paper

manilla *or* **manila** *noun* fibre from the leaves of a plant grown in the Philippines, used to make strong thick brown paper which is very difficult to tear; ***a manilla envelope;*** **manilla card** = board used in stationery

manipulate *verb* to move, edit and change text *or* data; ***an image processor that captures, displays and manipulates video images***

manipulation *noun* moving *or* editing *or* changing text *or* data; ***the high-speed database management program allows the manipulation of very large amounts of data***

manned *adjective* with someone working on it; ***the switchboard is manned twenty-four hours a day; the stand was manned by our sales staff***

manning *noun* people who are needed to do a work process; **manning levels** = number of people required in each department of a company to do the work efficiently; **manning agreement** *or* **agreement on manning** = agreement between the company and the workers about how many workers are needed for a certain job

manual 1 *adjective* (work) done by hand; (process) carried out by the operator without the help of a machine; **manual data processing** = sorting and processing information without the help of a computer;

manual entry *or* **manual input** = act of entering data into a computer, by an operator via a keyboard **2** *noun* book of instructions; **operating manual** = book showing how to operate a machine; **service manual** = book showing how to service a machine; **style manual** = book or notes prepared to show the details of the house style of a publisher or printer; **user's manual** = booklet showing how a device *or* system should be used

Manual of Style book of instructions on spelling, hyphenation and punctuation, published by the University of Chicago Press, and widely used by American editors, printers and publishers; (NOTE: the British equivalent is **Hart's Rules** published by Oxford University Press)

manually *adverb* done by hand, not by a machine; ***invoices have had to be made manually because the computer has broken down; the paper has to be fed into the printer manually***

manufacture 1 *verb* to make a product for sale, using machines; ***the company manufactures diskettes and magnetic tape*** **2** *noun* making a product for sale, using machines; **products of foreign manufacture** = products made in foreign countries

manufacturer *noun* person *or* company which produces machine-made products; **manufacturer's recommended price** = price at which the manufacturer suggests the product should be sold on the retail market, though often reduced by the retailer

manufacturing *noun* producing machine-made products for sale; **manufacturing capacity** = amount of a product which a factory is capable of making; **manufacturing costs** = costs of making a product; **manufacturing industries** = industries which take raw materials and make them into finished products; *US* **manufacturing clause** = clause in the American Copyright Act 1978, restricting the import into the USA of books written by Americans and published outside the USA (the aim was to force the reprinting of such books in the USA); the clause was abandoned in 1982

manuscript (MS) *noun* original draft copy of a book or article written *or* typed by the author, before it is sent for printing; ***this manuscript was written on a word-processor; the advance on royalties will be paid on acceptance of the completed manuscript for publication***

> COMMENT: manuscript means 'written by hand', but the word is now applied to typewritten works (also called typescripts), but (as yet) not to copy supplied on disk

map 1 *noun* drawing of a part of the world *or* town *or* country, etc., showing its main features in diagrammatic form; **physical map** = map which shows the physical features of an area (mountains, rivers, etc.); **geological map** = map which shows the types of rock and soil in an area; **four-colour map** = map printed in four colours; **sketch map** = rough map, not necessarily drawn exactly to scale; **map papers** = papers used for map work, with high opacity and good folding capacity **2** *verb* **mapping pen** = pen with a fine round point, used for drawing maps

> COMMENT: maps are now mainly computerized and are output on plotters. This allows the information on a map to be stored as a database, which can be used to produce maps on different scales, with different colour designs, etc.

marble *verb* to colour paper with a swirling pattern of colours, similar to patterns on marble; **marbled endpapers** = endpapers made with marbled paper

marbling *noun* coloured patterns used on endpapers

> COMMENT: marbling involves making an irregular pattern of lines of colour, as opposed to stippling, which is an irregular pattern of dots or spots of colour. In marbling, the paper is placed in a vat in which a gum solution made from Irish moss is covered with liquid

colours, which are moved into swirling patterns

marching display *noun* display device containing a buffer which allows the last few characters entered to be displayed

margin *noun* **(a)** blank space around the edge of the type area on a printed page; ***when typing the contract leave wide margins; the left margin and right margin are the two sections of blank paper on either side of the page;*** **to set the margin** = to define the size of a margin; **back margin** *or* **gutter margin** *or* **inside margin** = margin on the side of the page nearest to the spine; **bottom margin** *or* **foot margin** *or* **tail margin** = margin along the bottom of a page; **foredge margin** *or* **outside margin** = margin along the foredge of the page; **head margin** *or* **top margin** = margin at the top of the page **(b)** difference between the money received when selling a product and the money paid for it; **gross margin** = percentage difference between the unit manufacturing cost and the received price; **net margin** = percentage difference between received price and all costs, including overheads **(c)** extra space *or* time allowed; **margin of error** = number of mistakes which are accepted in a document *or* in a calculation; **safety margin** = time *or* space allowed for something to be safe; **margin of safety** = sales which are above the breakeven point

marginal *adjective* **(a)** in a margin; **marginal notes** = notes in small type printed in the outer margin of a page **(b) marginal cost** = cost of making a single extra unit above the number already planned; **marginal pricing** = making the selling price the same as the marginal cost; **marginal revenue** = income from selling a single extra unit above the number already sold

marginalia *plural noun* marginal notes

margination *noun* giving margins to a printed page

COMMENT: margins should be wide enough to allow the book to be trimmed not only when it is bound for the first time, but if it needs to be rebound in a library binding. The four margins are not usually the same width: the back margin is the narrowest and the foot margin the widest. The ratios between the four margins vary from book to book and from printer to printer, but common ratios are: (back : top : foredge : foot) 2 : 3 : 4 : 6 or 1.5 : 2 : 3 : 4. Note that the opposite is the case with magazines, where the top of the page is more important and has a wider margin than the foot

mark 1 *noun* **(a)** sign put on an item to show something; **proofreader's marks** *or* **correction marks** = special marks used to show changes to a proof **(b) reference mark** = special sign * which indicates that the reader is referred to a footnote **2** *verb* **(a)** to correct a proof, using the proofreader's marks; **marked proof** = proof which has been read by the printer's reader, with his corrections marked in green ink, sent to the publisher for his readers to read and instruct publisher's or author's corrections **(b)** to put a sign on something; ***to mark a product 'for export only'; article marked at £6.50; to mark the price on something***

mark down *verb* to make lower; **to mark down a price** = to lower the price of something; ***this range has been marked down to $24.99; we have marked all prices down by 30% for the sale***

mark-down *noun* **(a)** reduction of the price of something to less than its usual price **(b)** percentage amount by which a price has been lowered; ***we have used a 30% mark-down to fix the sale price***

marker *noun* **(a)** *(in binding)* bookmark, a piece of ribbon glued to the top of the spine, which hangs down between the pages of the book and is used to mark one's place; **marker pen** = felt pen which makes a wide coloured mark, used to indicate *or* highlight sections of text **(b)** code inserted in a file *or* text to indicate a special section; **block markers** = two markers inserted at the start and finish of a section of data to indicate a special block which can then be moved *or* deleted *or* copied as a single unit

market 1 *noun* **(a)** place where a product might be sold *or* group of people who might buy a product; **American market rights** = rights to sell in the USA; **British traditional market** = areas of the world representing the old British Empire, including Australia, New Zealand, Canada, India and much of Africa and the Caribbean (formerly included in publishing contracts to prevent the distribution of American editions of British titles in those areas; now largely abandoned); **home** *or* **domestic market** = market in the country where the selling company is based; ***sales in the home market rose by 22%*** **(b)** possible sales of a certain type of product *or* demand for a certain type of product; ***the market for computer books has fallen sharply; we have 20% of the educational market; there is no market for this type of book in Scandinavia;*** **a growth market** = market where sales are likely to rise rapidly; **to find a market niche** = to find a section of the market which is not catered for, and sell into it; **market analysis** = detailed examination and report on a market; **market leader** = company with the largest market share; **market opportunities** = possibility of finding new sales in a market; **market penetration** *or* **market share** = percentage of a total market which the sales of a company cover; **market research** = examining the possible sales of a product before it is put on the market; **market trends** = gradual changes taking place in a market **(c) closed market** = market where a supplier deals with only one agent or distributor and does not supply any others direct; **open market** = market where anyone can buy and sell **(d) up market** *or* **down market** = more expensive *or* less expensive; **to go up market** *or* **to go down market** = to make products which appeal to a wealthy section of the market *or* to a wider, less wealthy, section of the market **(e) market value** = value of a product *or* of a company if sold today; **to be in the market for a good bookshop** = to look for a bookshop to buy; **to come on to the market** = to become available for sale; ***this shop has just come on to the market;*** **to put something on the market** = to start to offer something for sale; ***I hear the company has been put on the market*** **2** *verb* to sell (products); ***this product is being marketed in all European countries***

marketable *adjective* which can be sold easily

marketing *noun* techniques used in selling a product (such as packaging, advertising, etc.); **marketing agreement** = contract by which one company will market another company's products; **marketing department** = department in a company which specializes in using marketing techniques to sell a product; **marketing manager** = person in charge of a marketing department; **marketing policy** *or* **marketing plans** = ideas of how the company's products are going to be marketed

mark up *verb* **(a)** to prepare copy for the compositor to set, by showing on the copy the typeface to be used, the line width, and other typesetting instructions; ***two manuscripts are in the editorial office for marking up; the sub-editor has marked up the copy and sent it to the printer for proofing; the text has been marked up for typefaces by the designer*** **(b)** to increase a price; **to mark prices up** = to increase prices; ***these prices have been marked up by 10%***

mark-up *noun* **(a)** action of instructing typographical details to the printer (the instructions regarding type size, font, line widths, etc., are written (or 'marked up') on the manuscript by a sub-editor or production editor **(b)** increase in price; ***we put into effect a 10% mark-up of all prices in June*** **(c)** amount added to the cost price to give the selling price; **we work to a 3.5 times mark-up** *or* **to a 350% mark-up** = we take the unit cost and multiply by 3.5 to give the selling price

mask 1 *noun* black overlay put over part of a film *or* illustration, so that it does not reproduce **2** *verb* to cover those parts of a photograph which are not to be reproduced; **masking paper** = paper used to mount films for platemaking; **masking tape** = adhesive tape used to cover parts of a film

mass *noun* **(a)** large group of people; **mass market** = very large market, covering a large proportion of a population; **mass market paperback** = paperback book aimed at the mass market; **mass marketing** = marketing which aims at reaching large numbers of people; **mass media** = means of communication which reach large numbers of people (such as radio, television, newspapers) **(b)** large number; ***they received a mass of orders*** *or* ***masses of orders after the TV commercials***

mass storage *noun* storage and retrieval of large amounts of data; **mass storage device** = computer backing store device that is able to store large amounts of data; ***disc drives and tape drives are common mass storage devices***

master *noun* **(a)** main text *or* original; **master file** *or* **master copy of a file** = main copy of a computer file, kept for security purposes; **master proof** *or* **master set of proofs** = (i) proofs kept in the editorial office, on which corrections from several proofreaders are collated; (ii) set of proofs from the printer, with his corrections marked, on which the publisher's and author's corrections are added and then returned to the printer; **master page** = standard layout for the pages of a book, prepared on screen in desktop publishing; **master tape** = main tape of a text held on computer, incorporating all the latest changes **(b)** text *or* plate which can be duplicated; ***a school textbook with ten pages of copy masters*** **(c)** experienced craftsman who trains others; **master printer** = printer who has passed qualifying examinations and trains others

masthead *noun* **(a)** name of a newspaper *or* magazine, which is usually set in a special design and printed at the top of the first page of each issue **(b)** *US* details of the ownership, issue number, and address of a newspaper or magazine, printed on the editorial page

mat *noun* = MATRIX (i) mould made from a page of standing metal type, used to make a stereo; (ii) mould used to cast a piece of metal type

match *verb* to make something the same as something else; to find something which is the same as something else; ***they tried to match the original colour in the reprint***

matchprint *noun* trade name for pre-press proofing system using colour toners and a photo-sensitive substrate; cheaper than wet proofs if only a proof is needed

material *noun* **(a)** substance which can be used to make a finished product; **synthetic materials** = substances made as products of a chemical process; **materials control** = system to check that a company has enough materials in stock to do its work; **materials handling** = moving materials from one part of a factory to another in an efficient way **(b)** **display material** = posters, photographs, etc., which can be used to attract attention to goods which are for sale; **point-of-sale material** *or* **POS material** = display material (posters, dump bins, spinners, etc.) advertising and displaying items to be sold at the place where they are being sold

mathematical *adjective* referring to mathematics; **mathematical setting** = specialized typesetting of mathematical texts; **mathematical symbols** = various signs and symbols in setting mathematical texts

> COMMENT: certain typesetters specialize in mathematical or scientific setting; such setting is normally more expensive than setting straight text

mathematics *noun* study of the relationship between numbers, their manipulation and organization to prove facts and theories logically

matrix *noun* **(a)** copper mould used to cast a piece of metal type **(b)** mould made from a page of standing metal type, used to make a stereo **(c)** pattern of the dots that make up a character in phototypesetting *or* on a computer screen; **matrix printer** *or* **dot-matrix printer** = printer in which the characters are made up by a series of dots printed close together, producing a page line by line; a dot-matrix printer can be used either for printing using a ribbon or for thermal *or* electrostatic printing; **character matrix** = pattern of dots that makes up a displayed character; (NOTE: plural is **matrices**)

matt *or* **matte** *adjective* not shiny *or* with a dull surface; **matt art paper** = coated paper, which is not glossy; (NOTE: US English is **dull-coated paper**) **matt finish paper** = art paper which is not shiny

matter *noun* **(a)** copy, text which has to be typeset and printed **(b)** main section of text on a page as opposed to titles *or* headlines **(c)** **printed matter** = printed books, newspapers, publicity sheets, etc.; **publicity matter** = sheets *or* posters *or* leaflets used for publicity; *see also* BACK MATTER, FRONT MATTER

mature *verb* to prepare paper for printing by exposing it to the temperature and humidity levels of the pressroom

maximum *noun* largest possible number *or* price *or* quantity *or* size; **maximum measure** = longest line which can be used

Mb = MEGABIT equal to 1,048,576 bits of storage, or equal to 131,072 bytes

Mbps = MEGABITS PER SECOND number of million bits transmitted every second

MB *or* **Mbyte** = MEGABYTE equal to 1,048,576 bytes of storage, or equal to 220 bytes; megabytes are used to measure the storage capacity of hard disk drives or main memory (RAM)

MBS = MIND BODY AND SPIRIT

MCGA = MULTICOLOUR GRAPHICS ADAPTER colour graphics adapter standard fitted in low-end IBM PS/2 computers

MCR = MAGNETIC CHARACTER READING

mean line *noun* height of lower case characters without ascenders

measure 1 *noun* **(a)** way of calculating size *or* quantity; **cubic measure** = volume in cubic feet or metres, calculated by multiplying height, width and length; **square measure** = area in square feet or metres, calculated by multiplying width and length **(b)** total length of a printed line of text (usually calculated in ems); **full measure** = setting to the widest possible width; **narrow measure** = setting an indented line **2** *verb* to find out the size *or* quantity of something; to be of a certain size *or* quantity; ***a package which measures 10cm by 25cm** or **a package measuring 10cm by 25cm; this book measures 198 x 129mm***

measurement *noun* **measurements** = size (in inches, centimetres, etc.); ***to write down the measurements of a package***

> COMMENT: in Britain, the measurements of paper sheets are normally given with the short side first (768 x 1008mm), while the physical measurements of a book are normally given with the height first and then the width. The format of this book is 198 x 129. Note that in many countries, the measurements are given with the width first and height second, leading to much confusion. The measurement of type is based on the point system (one point is 0.3515mm in Britain and the USA; 0.376mm in Europe)

mechanical 1 *adjective* **(a)** worked by a machine *or* produced by a machine; **mechanical composition** = typesetting by the hot metal method, where the compositor keyboards the text and the machine casts the type in hot metal; **mechanical overlay** = overlay which is cut out by a machine; **mechanical stipple** = stipple which is preprinted and can be applied to the design by the designer; **mechanical screen** *or* **mechanical tint** = shading in dots or lines, which is preprinted, and can be cut up and stuck down to give shading in artwork **(b)** (paper) made by machine from coarse chips of wood which have been crushed and ground with water to create the pulp; **mechanical paper** = paper made from untreated wood, used in printing newspapers and paperbacks; **mechanical pulp** = pulp made from ground untreated wood which still contains impurities; **mechanical pulp board** = card made from mechanical pulp **2** *noun* **mechanicals** = artwork, text and illustrations pasted down on board ready for filming

mechanical binding *noun* binding a book using a special device (such as spiral binding, comb binding, etc.)

COMMENT: the main types of mechanical binding are: plastic comb binding, where square holes are made in each leaf, into which the teeth of the comb fit; spiral binding, where the series of round holes are made in the leaves and a wire shaped like a spring is passed through them; ring binding, where only two or four holes are made in each leaf and heavy rings are fitted through them

mechanical reproduction *noun* reproduction by mechanical means (usually meaning, the reproduction of music on tape or record, and the reproduction of printed text by photocopying)

media *noun* **(a)** **the media** *or* **the mass media** = means of communicating information to the public (such as television, radio, newspapers); ***the product attracted a lot of interest in the media*** *or* ***a lot of media interest;*** **media analysis** *or* **media research** = examining different types of media (such as newspapers, television) to see which is best for promoting a certain type of product; **media coverage** = reports about something in the media; ***we got good media coverage for the launch of the new novel*** **(b)** form in which something is presented; **media converter** = multi-disk reader, device which can read data from various sizes and formats of disk

medical *noun* referring to the study or treatment of illness; **medical certificate** = certificate from a doctor to show that a worker has been ill; **medical publishing** = publishing of books on medical subjects; *see also* STM

medium 1 *adjective* middle *or* average; ***the company is of medium size;*** **medium face** = typeface which is halfway between bold and light; **medium screen** = halftone screen about 90-120 lines per inch **2** *noun* **(a)** one of the traditional non-metric paper sizes (broadside measuring 23 x 18 inches); **medium octavo** = traditional book format of 9 x $5\frac{3}{4}$ inches **(b)** way *or* means of doing something; **advertising medium** = type of advertisement (such as a TV commercial); ***the product was advertised through the medium of the trade press*** **(c)** material on which information is stored (such as a computer disk or mag tape) **(d)** substance in which printing ink is carried; (NOTE: plural is **media**)

mega- *prefix* meaning one million; **megabit (Mb)** = one million bits; **megabyte (MB)** = storage unit in computers, equal to 1,048,576 bytes, or to 10^{22} bytes

COMMENT: roughly speaking, a megabyte is equivalent to one million printed characters

melinex *noun* thick polyester base film

memo *noun* short message sent from one person to another in the same organization

memo pad *noun* pad of paper for writing short notes

memorandum *noun* short message; **memorandum (and articles) of association** = legal document setting up a limited company and giving details of its aims, directors, and registered office

memoirs *noun* autobiographical work, written in a less formal and more selective way than a full autobiography

memory *noun* facility for storing information in a computer

mending *noun* piece added to a printing plate

menu *noun* list of options *or* programs available to the user of a computer; **menu-driven software** = program where commands *or* options are selected from a menu by the operator; **menu selection** = choosing commands from a list of options presented to the operator; **main menu** = list of primary options available; **pull-down menu** = menu of options that can be displayed at any time, usually overwriting any other text

merchandise 1 *noun* goods which are for sale *or* which have been sold; ***the merchandise is shipped through two ports*** **2** *verb* **(a)** to sell goods by a wide variety of means, including display, advertising, sending samples, etc. **(b)** to derive products from other sources, such as books based on TV programmes or children's stationery based on books

merchandiser *noun* **(a)** person *or* company which organizes (i) the display and promotion of goods, or (ii) the production of products based on other sources **(b)** box or carton for the display of products such as books

merchandising *noun* organizing the display and promotion of goods for sale; ***merchandising of a product; merchandising department;*** **merchandising rights** = the right to produce products (books, mugs, T-shirts, balloons, etc.) based on a character in a TV programme or in a book

> COMMENT: merchandising can take many forms: it can include the production of children's plates and mugs based on a popular cartoon character; the sale of souvenirs linked to a famous tourist resort; special gifts tied into a special event such as the Olympic Games. Normally, if such products are based on characters in a book, the publisher will not be responsible for their manufacture, but will license a merchandiser to produce and sell them against payment of a royalty

merchant *noun* businessman who buys and sells goods (especially imported goods) in bulk for retail sale; **paper merchant** = company which buys paper wholesale from manufacturers and sells it retail to publishers and printers

merge *verb* **(a)** to combine two data files, but still retaining an overall order; ***the system automatically merges text and illustrations into the document;*** **merge sort** = software application in which the sorted files are merged into a new file; *see also* MAIL-MERGE **(b)** to join together; ***the two companies have merged; the firm merged with its main competitor; when we took the company over, its gardening list was merged with ours***

metal *noun* **(a) metal rule** = steel ruler, marked in centimetres, picas, etc., which allows a printed measure to be calculated **(b)** the alloy used to make the type in metal setting; **hot metal** = form of typesetting (such as Linotype and Monotype) where characters *or* whole words *or* whole lines of type are set using molten metal, from instructions given to the setting machine on perforated tape produced by the compositor's keyboard; ***the book was set in hot metal; we used hot metal setting for his last book; how many typesetters still offer hot metal setting?;*** **metal feeder** = device which lowers an ingot of metal slowly into the melting pot

metallic *adjective* made of metal; containing metal; **metallic ink** = ink with metal powder in it, normally gold, silver or copper, used to give a shiny effect

> COMMENT: the metal used in setting is an alloy of lead, tin and antimony, usually about 70% lead, 10% tin and 20% antimony. Lead is too soft to be used alone, and antimony is added to make it hard, while the tin makes the alloy tougher and also more fluid when liquid. Metal used in Linotype and Monotype machines has a higher proportion of lead

metamerism *noun* phenomenon whereby some colours change their hue in different lighting conditions

metre *US* **meter** *noun* measure of length (= 3.4 feet); (NOTE: usually written **m** after figures: **the case is 2m wide by 3m long**)

meterage *noun* length of a reel of paper in metres; ***all reels must be of standard meterage***

metric *adjective* **(a)** using the metre as a basic measurement; **metric ton** *or* **metric tonne** = 1000 kilograms; **the metric system** = system of measuring, using metres, litres and grams **(b)** system of book and paper measurement, calculated in millimetres

> COMMENT: the main metric stock paper sizes used in the UK are: metric quad crown (768 x 1008), metric large crown (816 x 1056), metric quad demy (888 x 1128), and metric quad royal (960 x 1272)

metropolitan area network (MAN) *noun* network extending over a limited area (normally a city); *compare with* LAN, WAN

mezzotint *noun* printing process using an etched copper plate

MF = MACHINE-FINISHED

MG = MACHINE-GLAZED **MG cylinder** = device attached to a papermaking machine to give a glaze to paper; **MG machine** = papermaking machine which has a MG cylinder; **MG paper** = paper which has been dried on a heated cylinder, giving a glossy finish to one side

mg = MILLIGRAM

MICR = MAGNETIC INK CHARACTER RECOGNITION system that identifies characters by sensing magnetic ink patterns (as used on bank cheques)

micro *noun* microcomputer; ***we put the sales statistics on to the office micro; our office micro interfaces with the mainframe computer in London***

micro- *prefix* very small

microcomputer *noun* small computer for general use in the home or office

microencapsulation *noun* use of tiny amounts of a substance surrounded by gelatine or plastic, for example to hold perfume in certain novelty inks

microfiche *noun* sheet of film with many microfilm photographs on it (especially used for catalogues, where fifty or more pages can be shown in one microfiche); ***we hold our records on microfiche;*** **microfiche reader** = machine used to read microfiches (the film is placed on a flat surface, and is then enlarged and has a light shone through it to appear full-size on a screen)

microfilm 1 *noun* roll of film on which a document is photographed in very small scale; ***we hold our records on microfilm*** **2** *verb* to make a very small scale photograph; ***send the 1990 correspondence to be microfilmed*** *or* ***for microfilming***

microfloppy *noun* small floppy disk (typically 3 or 3.5 inch in diameter)

micrographics *noun* images and graphics stored as microimages

microimage *noun* graphical image too small to be seen with the naked eye

micrometer *noun* device for measuring the thickness of materials, such as paper

micron *noun* metric measurement of the thickness of paper, one millionth of a metre; *compare* MIL

microphotograph *noun* very small scale photograph

microprocessor *noun* small computer processing unit

micropublishing *noun* publishing microfilms

Microsoft Network (MSN) a vast on-line service to provide information, weather reports, database links to the Internet and electronic mail especially for Windows 95 users

mid- *prefix* middle; **from mid-1997** = from the middle of 1997; **mid-space** *or* **middle space** = space which is one quarter the size of an em space

mil *noun* measurement of the thickness of paper mainly used in the USA (one thousand mils equal one inch); *compare* MICRON

milking machine *noun* portable machine which can accept data from other machines and then transfer it to a large computer

mill *noun* building where a certain type of material is processed or made; **paper mill** = factory where paper is made; **mill conditioned paper** = paper which has been conditioned for normal humidity; **mill edge** = the rough edge of paper as supplied from the mill; **mill finishing** = machine finishing, passing paper through calenders at the end of the papermaking process; **mill glazing** = machine glazing, drying paper on a heated cylinder, which gives a glossy surface to one side; **mill join** = joining of two webs done at the paper mill

millboard *noun* heavy board, made from waste paper, board or rope (but not straw), used for making book covers for quality bound books (such as those with leather bindings)

milligram *noun* one thousandth of a gram; (NOTE: usually written **mg** after figures)

millimetre *noun* one thousandth of a metre; (NOTE: usually written **mm** after figures)

mind body and spirit (MBS) *noun* category of books dealing with natural medicine, new faiths, oriental mysticism, etc.

mini- *prefix* very small

miniature *noun* small illustration in a medieval manuscript

minicomputer *noun* computer which is larger than a micro but smaller than a mainframe

minicontainer *noun* small container

minimum *noun* smallest possible (width *or* size *or* price, etc.)

miniweb *noun* web offset printing machine, using a narrow web of paper, typically printing 32 or 64 pages in black or eight A4 pages in colour

mint *noun* factory where coins are made; **in mint condition** = (secondhand book) which is in perfect condition; **mint stock** = stock of books in perfect condition

minus *or* **minus sign** *noun* printed *or* written sign (like a small dash) to indicate subtraction *or* to show a negative value; **minus colour** = colour which results if a colour is removed from white light (i.e. the opposite of the colour removed: if cyan is removed, the minus colour will be red); **minus setting** = tracking, reducing the spaces between letters, either to save space or to avoid awkward letter combinations (like L and T) which can leave gaps if spaced normally

minuscule *noun* lower case letter; (NOTE: the opposite is **majuscule** or **upper case letter**)

MIPS = MILLION INSTRUCTIONS PER SECOND measure of processor speed

misc = MISCELLANEOUS

miscellaneous *adjective* various *or* mixed *or* not all of the same sort; ***miscellaneous items; a box of miscellaneous pieces of equipment; miscellaneous expenditure***

miscellany *noun* book containing miscellaneous items, in verse and prose, and on several different subjects

misprint *noun* literal *or* mistake in setting; (NOTE: in US English **typo**)

misregister *noun* printing fault when the colour plates are out of register

mission *noun* group of people going on a journey for a special purpose; **trade mission** = visit by a group of businessmen to discuss trade; **inward mission** = visit to your home country by a group of foreign businessmen; **outward mission** = visit by a group of businessmen to a foreign country; **a fact-finding mission** = visit to an area to search for information about a problem

mitre *verb* to cut metal rules at the corners when making up a page of metal type

mixer *noun* vat containing strained pulp into which china clay or resin are added before the pulp passes through into the papermaking machine

mixing *noun* using different fonts and typefaces on the same line

mm = MILLIMETRE

mock-up *noun* (i) model of a new book or other product for testing or to show to possible buyers; (ii) draft layout or rough artwork

mode *noun* way of doing something; method of operating a computer; ***when you want to type in text, press this function key which will put the terminal in its alphanumeric mode;*** **insert mode** = interactive computer mode in which new text is entered within the previous text, which adjusts to accept it; **replace mode** = interactive computer mode in which new text entered replaces any previous text

modelling tint *noun* tint (usually blue or red) added to pure white to make it brighter

modem *or* **MODEM** *noun* = MODULATOR/DEMODULATOR device that allows data to be sent over telephone lines by converting binary signals from a computer into analog sound signals, which can be transmitted over a telephone line

modern *adjective* referring to the recent past or the present time; **modern face** = typeface with thin straight serifs, and where there is a marked difference between thick and thin strokes (developed by Didot and Bodoni in the early 19th century); **modern figures** *or* **numerals** = lining figures, Arabic numbers which are all of the same height, without descenders

modulator/demodulator *see* MODEM

moire (a) picture distortion which is caused by interference beats of similar frequencies **(b)** unwanted watery effect which is created by a set of closely spaced lines which are placed over another set (seen in film or prints); **moiré effect** = interference pattern (like watered silk) which occurs in colour printing when screens are set at wrong angles

moisture *noun* dampness *or* amount of water in the atmosphere or a material; **moisture content of paper** = amount of moisture in paper, shown as a percentage of the paper weight; **moisture-set ink** = ink which dries after the pigment and resin have been transferred to the paper and are separated from the vehicle by spraying with a fine moisture mist

mold *US* = MOULD

molly *US (informal)* = EM (NOTE: GB English is **mutton**)

monitor 1 *noun* screen (like a TV screen) on a computer; ***the page make-up has been done on monitor*** **2** *verb* to check *or* to examine how something is working; ***he is monitoring the progress of sales; how do you monitor the performance of the sales reps?;*** **monitored hyphenation** = hyphenation done by the keyboard operator (the word requiring hyphenation is highlighted on the monitor by the typesetting program)

monk *noun* printed area which has received too much ink and is very dark; (NOTE: the opposite is **friar**)

mono *adjective* black and white; ***the PC is supplied with a mono monitor***

monochrome *noun* (i) image in one colour, usually shades of grey and black and white; (ii) black and white photograph; **monochrome monitor** = computer monitor that displays text and graphics in black, white and shades of grey instead of colours

monogram *noun* device made of several initials linked together

monograph *noun* academic book, dealing with a single specialized subject

monoline *noun* typeface (such as Futura) where all the lines are the same thickness

Monophoto *noun* trade mark for a computerized phototypesetting system

monospacing *noun* system of typesetting where each character occupies the same amount of space, as on a typewriter (as opposed to proportional spacing)

Monotype *noun* trade mark for a composing machine, invented by Lanston in 1894, which casts separate pieces of type from hot metal using a special design of typefaces; **Monotype set system** = system where the basic em quad is a set size; **Monotype unit system** = system of computerizing typesetting, where each character is given a number of units (the base unit is one eighteenth of a point (about 0.0077 inch)

> COMMENT: in a Monotype machine, the compositor keyboards the text onto perforated paper tape, which is then passed through the casting machine, each character being cast separately, the metal type being arranged in order automatically with spacing to make up the justified lines. The Monotype system needs two processes (keyboarding and casting) which makes it slower than Linotype. However, because each character is separate, corrections are much easier and less costly on the Monotype system

montage *noun* illustration made from several photographs, drawings, etc., placed together and photographed

monthly *noun* magazine which appears once a month

moral right *noun* right of editors *or* illustrators etc., to have some say in the publication of a work to which they have contributed, even if they do not own the copyright

mordant *noun* fluid for etching a printing plate

morgue *noun (informal)* the reference library of a newspaper or magazine

morocco *noun* leather made from the skin of a goat, used in binding

mother set *noun* set of printing plates *or* of type, which is used only to make stereos and not for printing

> COMMENT: used particularly for reference books which reprint many times and where the stereos get worn out frequently

motion *noun* **(a)** moving about; **time and motion study** = study in an office *or* factory of the time taken to do certain jobs and the movements workers have to make to do them **(b) motion picture** = series of still pictures (each slightly different) which give the appearance of motion when projected on to a screen; **motion picture experts group (MPEG)** = full-motion video compression technique that is more efficient than the similar still-image compression scheme, JPEG; **motion picture rights** = film rights *or* movie rights, the right to make a filmscript from a book

mottled *adjective* area of solid colour which has a light and dark pattern, due to a defect in printing

mould *US* **mold** *noun* **(a)** plastic form taken from metal setting, used to make a stereo **(b)** tray with a wire mesh bottom in which handmade paper is made; **mould-made paper** = handmade paper

mount 1 *noun* **(a)** base in a forme on which a plate is placed to make it the same height as the standing type **(b)** backing or support to which something is fixed (such as a sheet of cardboard used as a backing for a photograph) **2** *verb* to fix a piece of artwork or film on a card backing or in a frame; **mounting board** = base on which printing plates are fixed; **mounted block** = letterpress block fixed on a mount to raise it to type height

mouse *noun* small hand-held input device moved on a flat surface to control the position of a cursor on the screen; **mouse-driven** = (software) which uses a mouse rather than a keyboard for input

moveable type *noun* type cast as individual metal units, as opposed to slugs (type cast as a whole line)

movie rights *US* = FILM RIGHTS

MPEG = MOTION PICTURE EXPERTS GROUP full-motion video compression technique that is more efficient than the similar still-image compression scheme, JPEG

MS = MANUSCRIPT (NOTE: the plural is MSS)

mull *noun* cloth glued to the back of a book block before the cased binding is attached; mull is thin cotton gauze which has been stiffened by being dipped in size

mullen *noun* bursting strength of paper; **mullen burst tester** = instrument for testing the burst strength of paper (a sample of paper is placed over a diaphragm which is inflated until the paper bursts)

multi- *prefix* referring to many things

multicolour *adjective* with several colours; *see* MCGA

multicolumn layout *noun* page layout with several columns (used especially in newspapers and magazines)

multi-disk reader *noun* device which can take in data from different sizes and formats of disk

multilingual *adjective* using several languages; **a multilingual dictionary** = dictionary giving translations in several languages for each main entry

Multilith *noun* trade name for a small offset printing press

multimedia *adjective* the combination of sound, graphics, animation, video and text within an application

multinational *noun* company which has branches *or* subsidiary companies in several countries; ***the company has been bought by one of the big multinationals***

multi-part stationery *noun* continuous stationery with two or more sheets together, either with carbons between or carbonless

multiplex *verb* to combine several messages in the same transmission medium

multiplexing *noun* combining several messages in the same transmission medium

multiplexor *noun* device that combines a certain number of inputs into a smaller number of outputs

multiplication *noun* mathematical operation that adds one number to itself a number of times; **multiplication sign** = printed *or* written sign (x) used to show that numbers are multiplied

multi-ring binder *noun* type of loose-leaf binding which uses a series of metal rings

multi-strike printer ribbon *noun* inked ribbon in a printer that can be used more than once

multivolume *adjective* (book) in several volumes

Murphy's law *noun* law, based on wide experience, which says that in commercial life if something can go wrong it will go wrong

mutton *noun* em *or* width of type equivalent to 12 points, taken as the width of a capital M; **mutton rule** = em rule; *see also* EM

Nn

nap *noun* surface of paper (usually referring to a rough surface); **nap roller** = ink roller used in lithography

national *adjective* referring to a whole country; **national advertising** = advertising which covers a whole country; **national press** = newspapers and magazines with a circulation covering the whole country (as opposed to the local press)

NB = NOTE

NBA = NET BOOK AGREEMENT

NCR paper = NO CARBON REQUIRED trade name for a carbonless paper which copies automatically onto a second sheet, without needing a piece of interleaved carbon paper

n.d. = NO DATE used in a bibliography to refer to a book *or* magazine whose publication date is not known

ND = NO DATE used in publishers' reports to indicate that it is not known when a book will be in stock; **RP/ND** = REPRINTING/NO DATE

NE = NEW EDITION used in publishers' reports to show that a new edition of a book will be published at some time in the future

near letter quality (NLQ) *noun* printing by a dot-matrix printer, giving high-quality type which is almost as good as a typewriter, by decreasing the spaces between the dots; ***switch the printer to NLQ for these circular letters***

neckline *noun* white line under a heading

needle *noun* tiny metal pin on a dot matrix printer which prints one of the dots

neg *(informal)* = NEGATIVE

negative 1 *adjective* **negative reading film** = film where the colours are reversed (black is white and white is black) **2** *noun* photographed film where the colours are reversed (black is white and white is black), from which normal prints can be made; **colour negative** = photographed colour film where the colours are replaced by their complements; **contact negative** = film which can be used to produce a print without any reduction *or* enlargement; **negative assembly** = assembling negatives ready to make a plate; *see also* POSITIVE

negotiate *verb* **to negotiate with someone** = to discuss a problem formally with someone, so as to reach an agreement; ***the management refused to negotiate with the union;*** **to negotiate terms and conditions** *or* **to negotiate a contract** = to discuss and agree terms of a contract; ***his agent negotiated an increased royalty rate***

negotiation *noun* discussion of terms and conditions to reach an agreement; **contract under negotiation** = contract which is being discussed; **a matter for negotiation** = something which must be discussed before a decision is reached; **to enter into negotiations** *or* **to start negotiations** = to start discussing a problem; **to resume negotiations** = to start discussing a problem again, after talks have stopped for a time; **to break off negotiations** = to refuse to go on discussing a problem; **to conduct negotiations** = to negotiate

NE/ND = NEW EDITION/NO DATE

NEP = NEW EDITION IN PREPARATION

net *adjective* **(a)** price *or* weight *or* pay, etc. after all deductions have been made; **net assets** *or* **net worth** = value of all the property of a company after taking away what the company owes; **net book** = book which is sold at a net price, which cannot be discounted; *see also* NON-NET **net cash flow** = difference between money coming in and money going out of a firm; **net income** *or* **net salary** = person's income which is left after taking away tax and other deductions; **net price** = price which cannot be reduced by a discount; **net profit** = result where income from sales is more than all expenditure plus overheads; **net receipts** = receipts after deducting commission *or* tax *or* discounts, etc.; **net sales** = sales less damaged or returned items; **net weight** = weight of goods after deducting the weight of packaging material and container; (NOTE: the spelling **nett** is sometimes used on containers) **net yield** = profit from investments after deduction of tax **(b)** **terms strictly net** = payment has to be the full price, with no discount allowed

Net Book Agreement (NBA) *noun* former legal agreement between publishers and bookshops in the UK, withdrawn in December 1995, which stipulated that a book must not be sold to the general public by a retail bookseller at less than the list price which was fixed by the publisher; fixed prices are still applied in several countries; *see also* RETAIL PRICE MAINTENANCE

NetScape™ *noun* very popular browser software used to view WWW pages on the Internet

network 1 *noun* system which links different points together; **a network of distributors** *or* **a distribution network** = series of points *or* warehouses from which goods are sent all over a country; **network architecture** = method in which a network is constructed, such as layers in an OSI system; **computer network** = shared use of a series of interconnected computers, peripherals and terminals; **local area network** *see* LAN **television network** = system of linked television stations covering the whole country; **wide area network** *see* WAN **2** *verb* to link together in a network; **to network a television programme** = to send out the same television programme through several TV stations; **networked system** = computer system in which several micros are linked together so that they all draw on the same database

new *adjective* recent *or* not old; **new edition** = edition of an old book which has been revised and corrected; **new technology** = electronic instruments which have recently been invented

news *noun* information about things which have happened; ***the business news is in the central pages of the paper; financial markets were shocked by the news of the devaluation;*** **news agency** = office which has reporters who write news reports which are then distributed to newspapers and television companies; **news bulletin** = report on TV or radio of the latest news; **news release** *or* **press release** = sheet giving information about an event which is sent to newspapers and TV and radio stations so that they can use it; ***the PR department is preparing a news release on our merger plans***

newsagent *US* **news dealer** *noun* person who runs a shop selling newspapers and magazines; *see also* CTN

newsboard *noun* grey cardboard made from waste newspapers

newsgroup *noun* collection of articles on the Usenet relating to one particular subject

newsletter *noun* printed sheet or small newspaper giving news about a company, a club or other organization

newspaper *noun* regular publication consisting of large sheets of paper printed with information and comment; **daily newspaper** *or* **weekly newspaper** = newspaper which appears each day of the week, except Sundays *or* newspaper which appears once a week; **Sunday newspaper** = newspaper which appears only on Sundays; (NOTE: **newspaper** is usually shortened to **paper**)

newsprint *noun* cheap paper, made mostly from mechanical pulp; it is used for printing newspapers, and cheap paperbacks, but it turns yellow quickly which means that it is not suitable for better quality books

newsstall *noun* kiosk, small outdoor shop selling newspapers and magazines

next to editorial *or* **next text** *noun* instructions from an advertiser to a magazine to place an advertisement next to editorial matter

NGA = NATIONAL GRAPHICAL ASSOCIATION British trade union with members working in the design and printing industries, merged with SOGAT to form the GPMU

niche *noun* special place in a market, occupied by one company or product

nick *noun* groove across the front of the stem of a piece of type, so that the compositor can easily tell which is the front of the piece; also a similar groove on a stamp used in tooling

nickel *noun* metal, used in electroplating; **nickel electro** = electro made of lead, and a coating of nickel and copper (they are used for long runs)

niger morocco *noun* good quality African leather, used for bindings

night *noun* period of time from evening to morning; **night shift** = shift which works at night; ***there are thirty men on the night shift; he works nights** or **he works the night shift***

nip 1 *noun* area where two rolls of paper are in contact **2** *verb* to hold a book tightly when binding, so as to press out any air from between the pages; **nip and tuck folder** = folding machine in which the sheet is pushed between gripping surfaces by a blade; **nip rolls** = two parallel rolls which take the paper and feed it into a folding machine

nipping *noun* pressing a sewn book so as to remove air from between the pages, before or after binding; (NOTE: US English is **smashing**)

NK NOT KNOWN report from a publisher, showing that a book which has been ordered was not published by them

nl = NEW LINE

NLQ = NEAR LETTER QUALITY

No. = NUMBER

No Carbon Required (NCR paper) *noun* trade name for a carbonless paper, a type of paper which copies automatically onto a second sheet, without needing an interleaved carbon paper

node *noun* interconnection point in a structure *or* network

noise *noun* random signal present in addition to any wanted signal, caused by static, temperature, power supply, magnetic or electric fields and also from the stars and the sun; ***the photographs were grainy, out of focus, and distorted by signal noise***

nominal weight *US* = BASIS WEIGHT

non- *prefix* not

non-book materials *noun* publications (such as videos, maps, cassettes, etc.) which are not books

non-bookshop outlets *noun* places which are not bookshops (such as food shops, garden centres, etc.) but which sell books

non-consumable textbook *noun* textbook which students should keep clean, without writing anything in it, so that it can be passed on to other students (the opposite is the consumable book, in which the student writes notes and answers to problems)

noncounting keyboard *noun* entry keyboard on a phototypesetter that produces a continuous output of characters on tape without hyphenation or justification instructions

non-delivery *noun* situation where something is not delivered

non-durables *plural noun* goods which are used up soon after they have been bought (such as food, newspapers)

nonfiction *noun* books which are not fiction, i.e. biography, travel, reference, instruction manuals, etc.

non-image area *noun* area on a lithographic plate which is not to be printed, and which does not take ink

non-impact printer *noun* printer (like an ink-jet printer) where the character form does not hit the paper

non-lining figures *noun* old-face figures, Arabic numerals with ascenders and descenders (as in Bembo), as opposed to lining figures

non-net *adjective* (book) which is not sold at a net price

> COMMENT: Formerly used to refer to educational books with low discounts, which amounted to a handling charge on orders from schools. If the bookseller wished to place educational books on his shelves to sell to the general public, he could mark up the price to give himself a higher margin

nonpareil *noun* old type size, equivalent to the modern 6 point

non-payment *noun* **non-payment of a debt** = not paying a debt due

non-printing codes *noun* codes that represent an action of the printer rather than a printed character

non profit-making organization *US* **non-profit corporation** *noun* organization (such as a charity, or some university presses) which is not allowed by law to make a profit; ***non-profit-making organizations are exempted from tax***

non-ranging figures = NON-LINING FIGURES

non-reflective ink *noun* ink used to print machine-readable codes and characters (as on cheques)

non-returnable *adjective* which cannot be returned; **non-returnable packing** = packing which is to be thrown away when it has been used and not returned to the sender

non-stock *adjective* **(a)** not held in stock; ***non-stock items have to be ordered specially and may take some time to reach the shop*** **(b)** not normal; ***the book is an odd format, and we had to use a non-stock size of paper***

non-union *adjective* **company using non-union labour** = company employing workers who do not belong to trade unions

non-woven *adjective* imitation cloth made from paper pulp, treated chemically to give it strength and embossed to imitate the woven surface of cloth

Nordsen glueing *noun* method of adding a strip of glue at the joints of a heavy book when casing in, to give more strength

not *noun* handmade paper pressed without metal plates, giving a very rough finish; *compare* HOT-PRESSED

notched binding *or* **notch binding** *noun* perfect binding process, where notches are cut into the spine of the folded untrimmed pages, helping the glue to penetrate and hold the sections together when the cover is glued in place

note 1 *noun* **(a)** short document *or* short piece of information; **advice note** = written notice to a customer giving details of goods ordered and shipped but not yet delivered; **covering note** = letter sent with documents to explain why you are sending them; **credit note** = note showing that money is owed to a customer; **debit note** = note showing that a customer owes money; **delivery note** = list of goods being delivered, given to the customer with the goods; **dispatch note** = note saying that goods have been sent **(b)** **bank note** *or* **currency note** = piece of printed paper money **2** *verb* to write down details of something and remember them; ***we note that the goods were delivered in bad condition; your order has been noted and will be dispatched as soon as we have stock; your complaint has been noted***

notebook *noun* book for writing notes in

notepad *noun* pad of paper for writing short notes

notepaper *noun* good quality paper for letters

notice *noun* **(a)** piece of written information; ***the company secretary pinned up a notice about the pension scheme;*** **copyright notice** = note in a book showing who owns the copyright and the date of ownership **(b)** official warning, such as that a contract is going to end *or* that prices are going to be changed; **until further notice** = until different instructions are given; ***you must pay £200 on the 30th of each month until further notice***

noticeboard *noun* (i) board fixed to a wall where notices can be put up; (ii) program for displaying information which can be accessed by users from home via modems

novel *noun* work of fiction at least 150 pages long; **crime novel** = novel concerning a crime, and the solving of it; **romantic novel** = novel, usually aimed at women readers, concerned with a love affair; (NOTE: as a group, novels are called **fiction: romantic fiction** is all romantic novels taken as a group)

novelist *noun* writer of novels

novella *noun* short novel, of less than 150 pages

np = NEW PARAGRAPH

NUJ = NATIONAL UNION OF JOURNALISTS British trade union with members working in newspaper and book publishing; also in radio and TV

number 1 *noun* written figure; **box number** = reference number used when asking for mail to be sent to a post office or when asking for replies to an advertisement to be sent to the newspaper's offices; ***please reply to Box No. 209;*** **index number** = (i) number of something in an index; (ii) number showing the percentage rise of something over a period; **page number** = folio, the number shown on a page of a book *or* magazine; (NOTE: the word **number** is often written **No.** with figures) **2** *verb* **(a)** to put a figure on a document; ***to number an order; I refer to your invoice numbered 1234*** **(b)** to put a number on a printed page; ***the pages are automatically numbered by the computer; the pages of the manuscript are numbered 1 to 395;*** **numbering machine** = (i) machine which numbers pages (such as the pages of a manuscript) automatically; (ii) printing machine which prints the numbers on tickets or invoices automatically

numeral *noun* number in typesetting *or* writing; **Arabic numeral** = number written 1, 2, 3, etc.; **Roman numeral** = number written I, II, III, etc.

numeric *or* **numerical** *adjective* referring to numbers; **in numerical order** = in the order of figures (such as 1 before 2, 33 before 34); ***file these invoices in numerical order;*** **numeric data** = data in the form of figures; **numeric keypad** = part of a computer keyboard which is a programmable set of numbered keys

nut *see* EN

NYO = NOT YET OUT (same as Not Yet Published)

NYP = NOT YET PUBLISHED publisher's report to a bookseller who has tried to order a book which has not been published

Oo

O & M = ORGANIZATION AND METHODS

OBC = OUTSIDE BACK COVER

obelisk *noun* printing sign like a small cross † used after the name of a person to show that he has died, and also used as a reference mark

obit *or* **obituary** *noun* article in a newspaper about the life and work of a person who has recently died

oblique *adjective* sloping; **oblique roman** = roman characters which slant to the right and look like italic; **oblique shading** = shading of the thick curved lines in old-face type, where the shading runs round the top and bottom of curved letters (such as 'p'), as opposed to the vertical shading used in modern faces; **oblique stroke** = solidus *or* slash, a line sloping to the right (/)

obliterate *verb* to erase *or* to remove or cover a piece of printing

obscene *adjective* offensive to a person's or to society's sense of what is decent and moral (especially in sexual matters); **obscene publication** = publication which is likely to deprave and corrupt people who read it or look at it

obscenity *noun* being obscene; **obscenity laws** = laws which define what constitutes obscenity (and setting out penalties for producing obscene material)

occasional publication *noun* magazine which does not appear on a regular basis

OCR **(a)** = OPTICAL CHARACTER READER device which scans printed *or* written characters, recognizes them, and converts them into machine-readable form for processing in a computer **(b)** = OPTICAL CHARACTER RECOGNITION process that allows printed *or* written characters to be recognized optically and converted into machine-readable code that can be input into a computer, using an optical character reader; **OCR font** = character design that can be easily read using an OCR reader

> COMMENT: there are two OCR fonts in common use: OCR-A, which is easy for scanners to read, and OCR-B, which is easier for people to read than the OCR-A font. OCR techniques are extremely useful in computerizing data which has been typeset but not computerized, allowing for example an old specialized dictionary to be converted to computer tape, or allowing direct input of typewritten pages from an author: they are read by a computer and are typeset without rekeying

octavo (8vo) *noun* page made when a sheet of paper is folded three times, giving eight leaves or a 16-page section; **crown octavo** = size of book ($7\frac{1}{2}$ x 5 inches) based on the crown paper size of 20 x 15 inches; **metric crown octavo** = size of book (186 x 123mm)

octodecimo = EIGHTEENMO

odd *adjective* **(a) odd numbers** = numbers (like 17 or 33) which cannot be divided by two; **odd pages** = pages with odd numbers (i.e. right-hand pages) **(b) odd sorts** = special characters which are not normally required (such as mathematical symbols, foreign accents, etc.)

oddment *noun* section of pages shorter than the normal signature (such as four pages) which has to be printed separately to make up the full extent of a book, because the book does not make an even working

odour-free ink *noun* ink (used to print on food packaging) which has no smell and which cannot harm the contents of the package

OFC = OUTSIDE FRONT COVER

offcut *noun* piece cut from a large sheet of paper when it is cut down to the correct size, which can be used for odd printing jobs (such as leaflets)

off-centre *adjective* not in the centre of a page *or* line; ***the map is slightly off-centre***

offer 1 *noun* **(a)** statement that you are willing to pay a certain amount of money to buy something; ***his agent is considering two offers from publishers*** **(b)** statement that you are willing to sell something; **offer for sale** = situation where a company advertises itself for sale **(c) he received six offers of jobs** *or* **six job offers** = six companies told him he could have a job with them **2** *verb* to say that you are willing to pay a certain amount of money for something; ***the American publisher offered $50,000 for the paperback rights***

off its feet *adjective* (type) which is not set straight on the base line

off-line *adverb* (i) (processor *or* printer *or* terminal) that is not connected to a network *or* central computer (usually temporarily); (ii) peripheral connected to a network, but not available for use; ***before changing the paper in the printer, switch it off-line;*** **off-line printing** = printout operation that is not supervised by a computer; **off-line processing** processing by devices not under the control of a central computer; (NOTE: opposite is **on-line**)

offprint *noun* extra printing of copies of a section of a journal (usually a single article), run on from the main printing and sold separately (or given to an academic author in lieu of payment); (NOTE: also called a **separate**)

offset 1 *noun* **(a) offset lithography** = printing process used for printing books, where the ink sticks to image areas on the plate and is transferred to an offset cylinder from which it is printed onto the paper; **offset blanket** = rubber sheet round a cylinder, to which the ink is transferred from the printing plate before being printed onto the paper; **offset cartridge** = paper with a rough basic texture (although it may be given a smooth surface), used in offset printing; **offset paper** = special paper for printing offset; **offset plate** = plate from which offset printing is carried out; **offset printing** = printing method that transfers the ink image to the paper via a second cylinder; *see also* PHOTO-OFFSET **(b)** = SETOFF **2** *verb* **(a)** to print an image by offset lithography; ***the image is offset onto the paper*** **(b)** to reproduce a book in a new edition by photographing a good copy of the previous edition **(c)** to balance one thing against another so that they cancel each other out; ***to offset losses against tax; foreign exchange losses more than offset profits in the domestic market***

off-the-job *adjective* **off-the-job training** = training given to workers away from their place of work (such as at a college or school)

oiled paper *noun* paper soaked in an oil, such as linseed oil, used for wrapping

OK Press = PASSED FOR PRESS

OKWC = OK WITH CORRECTIONS instruction from the editor to the typesetter to tell him to make corrections as indicated and then the text will be ready for press

Old English *noun* black letter typeface (as used in England)

old face *noun* one of the first roman typefaces (such as Bembo or Caslon), with oblique shading (not vertical) and which does not have much difference between fat and thin strokes; the serifs are bracketed and not hairline

old style *noun* **old style face** = typeface such as Caslon or Baskerville, with distinct serifs, derived from Classical Roman lettering; **old style figures** = Arabic figures in certain typefaces (such as Bembo or Caslon) where the 3, 4, 5, 7 and 9 go below the base line and the 6 and 8 go up to cap height; *compare* LINING FIGURES

> COMMENT: some old style faces are still widely used; Garamond, for example, is used especially for newspaper or magazine work

omit *verb* **(a)** to leave something out *or* not to put something in; ***the secretary omitted the date when typing the contract*** **(b)** not to do something; ***he omitted to tell the managing director that he had lost the documents***

omission *noun* thing which has been omitted; **errors and omissions excepted** = words written on an estimate or invoice to show that the company has no responsibility for mistakes in it

omnibus *noun* **omnibus agreement** = agreement which covers many different items; **omnibus edition** = edition of a series of books *or* short stories in one volume

OMR (a) = OPTICAL MARK READER device that can recognize marks, lines on a special forms (such as on an order form *or* a reply to a questionnaire) and that inputs them into a computer **(b)** = OPTICAL MARK RECOGNITION process that allows certain marks *or* lines on special forms (such as on an order form *or* a reply to a questionnaire) to be recognized by an optical mark reader, and input in a computer

oncosts *noun* fixed costs, amounts paid in producing a product which do not rise with the quantity of the product made

on-demand publishing *noun* printing books as the demand arises (usually in very small quantities) as opposed to keeping larger quantities of books in stock

one-man *adjective* **one-man** *or* **one-woman business** *or* **firm** *or* **company** *or* **operation** = business run by one person alone with no staff or partners

one-off *adjective* done or made only once; ***the new novel is a one-off item on their list***

one-shot binding *noun* adhesive binding using hot-melt glue only; *see* TWO-SHOT BINDING

one-shot periodical rights *noun* right to reprint part of a text in a single edition of a magazine *or* newspaper (as opposed to serialization)

one-sided *adjective* **(a)** which favours one side and not the other in a negotiation; ***one-sided agreement*** **(b)** printed on one side of a sheet only; **one-sided art paper** = paper which is coated on one side only, used for jackets

one-up *adverb* printed with one copy of the book at a time; *compare* TWO-UP

onion skin *noun* very thin paper made transparent by beating, used for airmail writing paper

on-line *or* **on line 1** *adverb* (terminal *or* device) connected to and under the control of a central processor; anything which is 'live', or actively connected to the line or system, etc.; ***the terminal is on-line to the mainframe equipment; the sales office is on line to the warehouse; we get our data on line from the stock control department; in the bindery, the wrappering is on line with the casing-in*** **2** *adjective* data or information that is available when a terminal is connected to a central computer via a modem; **on-line editing** = text editing by an editor *or* sub-editor on a terminal linked directly to the main computer; **on-line information retrieval** = system that allows an operator of an on-line terminal to access, search and display data held in a main computer; **on-line processing** = processing by devices connected to and under the control of the central computer (the user remains in contact with the central computer while the processing is being carried out); **on-line storage** = data storage equipment that is directly controlled by a computer; **on-line**

system = computer system that allows users who are on-line to transmit and receive information; **on-line transaction processing** = interactive processing in which a user enters commands and data on a terminal which is linked to a central computer, with results being displayed on-screen

on-the-fly *adverb* printing or outputting images as they are being processed

on-the-job *adjective* **on-the-job training** = training given to workers at their place of work

OO = ON ORDER publisher's report to a bookseller, informing him that a book he has ordered is on order by the publisher (either from a warehouse, or, in the case of a distributed book, from another publisher)

OP = OUT OF PRINT report from a publisher, showing that a book is not longer available; ***unless it is reprinted next month, the stock will run out and we shall let the book go OP; half the titles in the list were allowed to go OP***

opacity *noun* being opaque, not allowing light through

opaque 1 *adjective* which cannot be seen through *or* which does not allow light through **2** *verb* to remove spots, blemishes or other parts of a negative which are to be cut out from a plate, by painting over them with an opaque ink **3** *noun* ink used to cover up parts of a film

> COMMENT: mechanical pulp will produce opaque paper; if wood pulp is chemically treated or beaten to increase its strength, it will lose opacity, and if beaten long enough will become semi-transparent (like tracing paper). Printing opacity of paper is usually measured with an opacimeter. The measurement essentially involves finding the ratio of light reflected by one sheet of paper to that reflected by a thick pile of the same paper

op. cit. *abbreviation for 'opera citato' meaning* 'in the work quoted', used in notes and bibliographies to show that a reference is being made to a work which has already been referred to

open *adjective* **(a)** at work *or* not closed; ***some bookshops are open on Sundays*** **(b)** *(of book)* with the pages visible *or* not closed; **open flat** = book which lies flat when opened (if the binding is tight, or if the book is perfect bound, it will not open flat) **(c)** ready to accept something; **open to offers** = ready to accept a reasonable offer; **the company is open to offers for their fiction list** = the company is ready to discuss selling their fiction list **(d) open cheque** = cheque which is not crossed and can be cashed anywhere; **open credit** = bank credit given to good customers without security up to a certain maximum sum; **open market** = market where two publishers agree that both can sell the same book; **available on the open shelves** = (i) book which is available to any purchaser in a bookshop; (ii) available to any borrower in a library

open back binding *noun* hollow back binding, binding where the back is not glued to the spine of the book block, but has a hollow space between it and the sewn signatures, allowing it to be opened easily; (NOTE: the opposite is **tight-back**)

open-ended *US* **open-end** *adjective* (agreement *or* contract) with no fixed limit *or* with some items not specified

opening 1 *noun* **(a)** pages of a book which face each other **(b)** beginning part of a text **(c)** act of starting a business; **opening hours** = hours when a shop *or* business is open **(d) a market opening** = possibility of starting to do business in a new market **2** *adjective* at the beginning *or* first; **opening balance** = balance at the beginning of an accounting period; **opening stock** = stock at the beginning of the accounting period

open system *noun* system which is constructed in such a way that different operating systems can work together; **Open System Interconnection (OSI)** = standardized ISO network which is constructed in layer form, with each layer having a specific task, allowing different systems to communicate if they conform to the standard

open up *verb* **to open up new markets** = to work to start business in markets where such business has not been done before

operate *verb* **(a)** to work; ***the new terms of service will operate from January 1st; the rules operate on inland postal services*** **(b)** to **operate a machine** = to make a machine work; ***he is learning to operate the new word-processing package***

operating *noun* general running of a business *or* of a machine; **operating costs** *or* **operating expenses** = costs of the day-to-day organization of a company; **operating manual** = book which shows how to work a machine; **operating profit** *or* **operating loss** = profit or loss made by a company in its usual business; **operating system** = main program which operates a computer

operation *noun* business organization and work; **operations review** = examining the way in which a company or department works to see how it can be made more efficient and profitable; **a franchising operation** = selling licences to trade as a franchise

operative *noun* person who operates a machine which makes a product

operator *noun* person who works a machine; **keyboard operator** = person who operates a keyboard, either for computing purposes or to set type

opinion *noun* piece of expert advice; ***the lawyers gave their opinion on some chapters of the book; to ask an adviser for his opinion on a matter***

OPP oriented polypropylene, the film usually used for laminating book covers

opposite *noun* which is on the other side *or* facing; **opposite page** *or* **facing page** = the other page of a double-page spread

optical *adjective* (i) referring to *or* making use of light; (ii) referring to the eyes; ***an optical reader uses a light beam to scan characters or patterns or lines;*** **optical bar reader** *or* **bar code reader** *or* **optical wand** = optical device that reads data from a bar code; **optical brightener** = fluorescent dye added to paper pulp to make it white; **optical centre** = the centre of a page *or* design *or* line of type as it appears to the eye (not the actual centre, but slightly higher); **optical centering** = making a text look as though it is centred, when in fact it is not; **optical character reader (OCR)** = device which scans printed *or* written characters, recognizes them, and converts them into machine-readable codes for processing in a computer; **optical character recognition (OCR)** = process that allows printed *or* written characters to be recognized optically and converted into machine-readable code that can be input into a computer, using an optical character reader; **optical font** *or* **OCR font** = character design that can be easily read using an OCR reader; **optical mark reader (OMR)** = device that can recognize marks *or* lines on a special form (such as on an order form *or* a reply to a questionnaire) and that inputs them into a computer; **optical mark recognition (OMR)** = process that allows certain marks *or* lines on special forms (such as on an order form *or* a reply to a questionnaire) to be recognized by an optical mark reader, and input into a computer; **optical scanner** = equipment that converts an image into electrical signals which can be stored in and displayed on a computer; **optical letter spacing** *or* **optical spacing** = allowing variable spacing between different letters, so as to look as if the spacing is standard; **optical storage** = data storage using mediums such as microfiche, optical disk, etc.; **optical wand** = OPTICAL BAR READER

optically *adverb* by using an optical device; ***the text is scanned optically***

option *noun* **option to purchase** *or* **to sell** = giving someone the possibility to buy or sell something within a period of time; **first option** = allowing someone to be the first to have the possibility of deciding something; **to grant someone a six-month option on a book** = to allow someone six months to decide if he wants to be the agent *or* if he wants to manufacture the book in his territory; **to take up an option** *or* **to exercise an option** = to accept the option which has been offered and to put it into action; ***he exercised his option*** *or* ***he took up his option to acquire sole marketing rights to the product;*** **I want to leave my options open** = I want to be able to decide what to do when the time is right; **to take the soft option** = to decide to do something which involves the least risk, effort or problems; **option clause** = clause in an agreement between a publisher and an author which states that the author must offer the publisher his next work for publication

order 1 *noun* **(a)** arrangement of records (filing cards, invoices, etc.); **alphabetical order** = arrangement by the letters of the alphabet (A, B, C, etc.); **chronological order** = arrangement by the order of the dates; **numerical order** = arrangement by numbers **(b)** working arrangement; **machine in full working order** = machine which is ready and able to work properly; **the telephone is out of order** = the telephone is not working; **is all the documentation in order?** = are all the documents valid and correct? **(c)** official request to do something, for goods to be supplied; **printing order** = order from a publisher to a printer to print a certain number of copies of a book; **binding order** = request from a publisher to a binder to bind a certain number of copies of a book; **to fill** *or* **to fulfil an order** = to supply items which have been ordered; ***we are so understaffed we cannot fulfil any more orders before Christmas; to supply an order for twenty filing cabinets;*** **purchase order** = official paper which places an order for something; **order fulfilment** = supplying items which have been ordered; **terms: cash with order** = the goods will be supplied only if payment in cash is made at the same time as the order is placed; **items available to order only** = items which will be manufactured only if someone orders them; **on order** = ordered but not delivered; ***this item is out of stock, but is on order;*** **unfulfilled orders** *or* **back orders** *or* **outstanding orders** = orders received in the past and not yet supplied; **order book** = record of orders; **the company has a full order book** = it has enough orders to work at full capacity; **telephone orders** = orders received over the telephone; ***since we mailed the catalogue we have had a large number of telephone orders;*** *compare* TELEORDER **a pad of order forms** = a pad of blank forms for orders to be written on **(d)** item which has been ordered; ***the order is to be delivered to our warehouse;*** **order picking** = collecting various items in a warehouse to make up an order to be sent to a customer **(e)** instruction; **delivery order** = instructions given by the customer to the person holding his goods, telling him to deliver them **(f)** document which allows money to be paid to someone; ***he sent us an order on the Chartered Bank;*** **banker's order** *or* **standing order** = order written by a customer asking a bank to make a regular payment; ***he pays his subscription by banker's order;*** **money order** = document which can be bought for sending money through the post **2** *verb* **(a)** to ask for goods to be supplied; ***to order twenty filing cabinets to be delivered to the warehouse; they ordered a second reprint for delivery in June*** **(b)** to put in a certain way; ***the address list is ordered by country; that filing cabinet contains invoices ordered by date***

orientation *noun (in word-processing or DTP software)* direction of a page, either landscape (long edge horizontal) or portrait (long edge vertical)

origin *noun* where something comes from; **certificate of origin** = document showing where goods were made; **country of origin** = country where a product is manufactured

original 1 *adjective* which was used or made first; ***they sent a copy of the original invoice; he kept the original receipt for reference*** **2** *noun* **(a)** document (such as a letter, photograph or drawing) from which copies are made; ***we have lost the originals for the author's line drawings; please send the originals and not duplicate films*** **(b)** **paperback original** = book which is published first as a paperback (and which later may be issued in a hardcover edition)

originate *verb* to start *or* come from; ***the book was originated by a packager; the data originated from the new computer***

origination *noun* work involved in creating something, such as preparing a book from a manuscript right through to camera-ready copy *or* film; ***the origination of the artwork will take several weeks;*** **origination costs** = (i) costs of preparing a book to camera-ready copy *or* film; (ii) plant or fixed costs (as opposed to running costs)

ornament *noun* decoration, something added to make something look more attractive; **ornamented typeface** = typeface where the letters have extra decoration

orphan *noun* **orphan (line)** = first line of a paragraph which appears at the foot of a page or column and does not seem to be connected with the following text, normally avoided by taking it over to the next page; (NOTE: the opposite (where a short last line of a paragraph appears at the top of a page or column) is a widow)

orthochromatic film *noun* film which is sensitive to colours other than red (i.e. to yellow and blue)

orthography *noun* correct spelling

OS = OUT OF STOCK report from a publisher, showing a book which has been ordered is not in stock (and possibly is being reprinted)

oscillator rollers *noun* rollers which control the amount of ink being passed onto the impression cylinder

OSI = OPEN SYSTEM INTERCONNECTION

out 1 *adverb* **(a)** published; ***the book came out last week; we can't get the new cookery book out in time for Christmas*** **(b) to be out** = to be wrong in calculating something; ***the cast off was 60 pages out*** **(c) full out** = set to the left-hand edge, not indented **2** *noun* leaving part of the text out when composing

outdent *verb* to move part of a line of text into the margin; (NOTE: opposite is indent)

outer 1 *adjective* which is nearer the outside (as opposed to something inside); **outer forme** = forme which carries one side of the sheet, including the first and last pages (the inner forme prints the other side of the paper); **outer margin** = margin on the foredge of a page; *compare* INNER **2** *noun* imposed first and last pages of a book

out-house *adjective* working outside a company's buildings; ***the out-house staff; we do all our data processing out-house***

outlet *noun* place where something can be sold; **retail outlets** = shops which sell to the general public

outline 1 *noun* **(a)** edge round an illustration; **outline font** = printer or display font (collection of characters) stored as a set of outlines that mathematically describe the shape of each character (which are then used to draw each character rather than actual patterns of dots); outline fonts can be easily scaled, unlike bit-map fonts; *see also* BIT-MAPPED FONT **outline halftones** = halftones where the background has been removed, leaving the foreground as a kind of silhouette; **outline letters** = letters printed as lines round the edge of the letter shape, used for display purposes **(b)** general description, without giving many details; ***the agent submitted a two-page outline of the novel*** **2** *verb* **(a)** to put a line round the outer edge of an illustration **(b)** to make a general description; ***the chairman outlined the company's plans for the coming year***

out of court *adverb & adjective* **a settlement was reached out of court** = a dispute was settled between two parties privately without continuing a court case; ***they are hoping to reach an out-of-court settlement***

out of date *adjective & adverb* old-fashioned *or* no longer modern; ***their computer system is years out of date; they are still using out-of-date equipment***

out of focus *adjective* (photograph) where the image is blurred because the camera has not been focussed correctly

out of print (OP) *adjective* (book) of which the publisher has no copies left, and which is not going to be reprinted

out of register *adjective* with two printing plates incorrectly aligned, so giving a blurred image

out of square *adjective* (paper) not cut at right angles

out of stock (OS) *adjective & adverb* with no stock left; ***those gardening books are temporarily out of stock; several out-of-stock items have been on order for weeks; the publisher has reported the novel OS***

out of work *adjective & adverb* with no job; ***the recession has put millions out of work; the company was set up by three out-of-work engineers***

output 1 *noun* **(a)** amount which a company or a person or a machine produces; ***output has increased by 10%; 25% of our output is exported;*** **output per hour** = amount produced in one hour; **output bonus** = extra payment for increased production; **output resolution** = number of separate image points, spots, that a device is physically able to write **(b) outputs** = goods or services sold; **output tax** = VAT charged by a company on goods or services sold **(c)** information *or* data that is transferred from a main computer *or* the main memory to another device such as a monitor *or* printer *or* secondary storage device; **output device** = device such as a monitor *or* printer, which allows information in a computer to be displayed to the user; (NOTE opposite is **input**) **2** *verb* to transfer data from a computer to a monitor *or* printer; to produce (by a computer); ***finished documents can be output to phototypesetters; the printer will output colour graphs; that is the information outputted from the computer***

outright *adverb & adjective* completely; **to purchase something outright** *or* **to make an outright purchase** = to buy something completely, including all rights in it; **outright sale of a copyright** = sale of a copyright by an author to a publisher for a lump sum, with no royalty payable afterwards

outsert *noun* **(a)** wrapround, four-page section wrapped round a printed signature **(b)** leaflet or other promotional material sent outside a magazine which is mailed (as opposed to an insert)

outset = OUTSERT

outside *adjective & adverb* **(a)** near the edge of a page; **outside margin** = margin at the edge of a page, as opposed to the gutter **(b)** not in a company's office or building; **to send work to be done outside** = to send work to be done in other offices; **outside director** = director who is not employed by the company; **outside line** = line from an internal office telephone system to the main telephone exchange; **outside reader** = reader employed by a publisher on a fee basis to read manuscripts and comment on them; **outside worker** = worker who does not work in a company's offices **(c) outside sorts** = characters which are not frequently used (such as accents) and are kept in the outside compartments of a case **(d) outside front cover** *or* **outside back cover** = the two covers of a magazine

outstanding *adjective* not yet paid or completed; **outstanding debts** = debts which are waiting to be paid; **outstanding orders** = orders received but not yet supplied; **what is the amount outstanding?** = how much money is still owed?

out tray *noun* basket on a desk for letters or memos which have been dealt with and are ready to be dispatched

outturn sheets *or* **outturns** *noun* (i) sample sheets of paper taken from a shipment for approval by the purchaser; (ii) specimen printed sheets of a book sent to the publisher for confirmation

outward *adjective* going away from the home country; **outward mission** = visit by a group of businessmen to a foreign country

outwork *noun* **(a)** work which a company pays someone to do at home **(b)** specialist work which a printer subcontracts to another company (such as making up boxed sets, special typesetting, etc.)

outworker *noun* person who works at home for a company

over- *prefix* more than

overcapacity *noun* unused capacity for producing something

overcasting *noun* method of attaching leaves together to form a section which can be bound, used especially for the first and last sections (each signature is sewn in the usual way, and then all the signatures are sewn again from the front to the back, close to the fold); (NOTE: also called **oversewing, whipstitching**)

overcharge 1 *noun* charge which is higher than it should be; ***to pay back an overcharge*** **2** *verb* to ask too much money; ***they overcharged us for binding; we asked for a refund because we had been overcharged***

overdue *adjective* which has not been paid on time; **interest payments are three weeks overdue** = interest payments should have been made three weeks ago

overestimate *verb* to think something is larger or better than it really is; ***he overestimated the amount of time needed to fit out the factory; I think she is a very overestimated writer***

overexpose *verb* to expose film for too long a time, so that it is too pale

overexposure *noun* exposing a film for too long a time, so that the image is too pale

overfold *noun* paper which sticks out from the rest of the folded sheets, because the folding machine is off centre; (NOTE: the opposite (i.e. the paper which does not reach the edge of the other leaves) is **underfold)**

overhang cover = OVERLAPPING COVER

overink *verb* to use too much ink when printing; ***the pages have been badly overinked***

overinking *noun* using too much ink when printing; ***overinking makes the pages too dark***

overlap *verb (of cover material)* to stick out beyond the edge of the boards, so that it can be tucked in and glued; **overlapping cover** = paper cover which is not cut flush, but projects beyond the text pages

overlay 1 *noun* **(a)** transparent plastic sheet which is placed over a piece of artwork, on which the artist's instructions to the printer can be written **(b)** transparent sheet with colour separations, the colours being always shown as black **(c)** piece of paper placed round a printing cylinder, to adjust the impression **2** *verb* to change the height of type and blocks in letterpress printing, so as to alter the darkness of the printed text

overleaf *adverb* on the next page; ***see the chart overleaf***

overmanning *noun* having more workers than are needed to do a company's work; ***to aim to reduce overmanning***

overmatter *or* **overset** *noun* text which has been set into galley proofs, and which is too long for the space allowed and so is discarded (frequently found in newspapers and magazine work)

overprint *verb* to add further text on sheets which have already been printed; ***the catalogue is overprinted with the bookseller's address***

overrun 1 *noun* **(a)** taking text over to another line because of additions **(b)** remaking a line or lines of print, because of deletions or additions at proof stage **(c)** (i) making more paper than has been ordered; (ii) printing more sheets than specified; (NOTE: the opposite is **underrun) 2** *verb* **(a)** to be longer than anticipated; ***the text has overrun by two pages*** **(b)** to print more sheets than are required, in case any are faulty

overs *noun* extra items above the agreed total; extra sheets *or* bound copies supplied by a printer to allow for spoilage; ***the price includes 10% overs to compensate for damage***

overseas 1 *adjective* across the sea; to *or* in foreign countries; **an overseas call** = phone call to another country; **the overseas division** = section of a company dealing with trade with other countries; **overseas markets** = markets in foreign countries; **overseas trade** = trade with foreign countries **2** *noun* foreign countries; ***the profits from overseas are far higher than those of the home division***

overset = OVERMATTER

oversewing = OVERCASTING

oversize *adjective* too large; ***the block is oversize and will have to be trimmed; the paper merchant supplied oversize paper and will have to guillotine it***

overstock 1 *verb* to have more stock than is needed; **to be overstocked with certain titles** = to have too many copies of certain books in stock **2** *noun* **overstocks** = more stock than is needed to supply orders; ***we will have to sell off the overstocks to make room in the warehouse***

overstrike *verb* to print on top of an existing character to produce a new one (if a 'Y' is overprinted with an equals sign it will give a similar sign to that for 'yen')

overweight *adjective* **the package is sixty grams overweight** = the package weighs sixty grams too much

own brand books *noun* books specially packaged for a store with the store's name on them

own ends *noun* endpapers which are the blank first and last leaves of the text

Oxford hollow *noun* type of hollow back binding, where a paper tube is placed between the back and the spine of the book block

oxidation *noun* defect in lithographic printing plates, where the metal surface is corroded where it has not been correctly protected, and so creates little black spots on the printed paper

ozalid *noun* trade mark for a type of proof made from film by contacting it in a vacuum frame with special coated paper (similar to diazos or dyeline proofs) (NOTE: US English is **blue** or **Vandyke**)

COMMENT: ozalid proofs are normally made from the final films before plates are made, and so need to be checked particularly carefully

Pp

PA = PERSONAL ASSISTANT, PUBLISHERS ASSOCIATION

pack 1 *noun* **pack of items** = items put together in a container for selling; ***pack of twenty mini dictionaries;*** **binder's pack** = pack of books from a bindery; ***the books are delivered in binder's packs of forty copies;*** **blister pack** *or* **bubble pack** = type of packing where the item for sale is covered with a stiff plastic cover sealed to a card backing; **display pack** = specially attractive box for showing goods for sale; **dummy pack** = empty pack for display in a shop **2** *verb* to put things into a container for selling *or* sending; ***to pack books into cartons; the books are wrapped in paper, then packed in cartons and loaded onto pallets; the computer is packed in expanded polystyrene before being shipped***

package 1 *noun* **(a)** goods packed and wrapped for sending by mail; ***the Post Office does not accept bulky packages; the goods are to be sent in airtight packages;*** **package insert** = insert put into a package, not into a single publication **(b)** group of different items joined together in one deal; **package deal** = agreement where several different items are agreed at the same time; ***we are offering a package deal which includes warehousing, distribution, representation and credit control*** **(c)** set of computer programs designed for special purpose; **word-processing package** = computer programs for word-processing, including formatting and spelling checks; ***we bought a word-processing package for compiling our dictionaries*** **2** *verb* **(a) to package goods** = to wrap and pack goods in an attractive way **(b) to package books** = to produce books (commissioning authors, designers, typesetting, printing and binding) for sale as finished books to a publisher

packager *noun* company which creates a finished book for a publisher

> COMMENT: the packager usually conceives the product (that is, has the idea for the product), and commissions a sample of text from an author, and title page, cover and page layout from a designer. This is then made into a mock-up, which is presented to publishers to ask them to consider. In this case, the copyright will remain with the packager. Alternatively, a publisher may approach a packager with an idea for a book, and in this case the copyright may remain with the publisher. When a publisher decides to take the book, he will order a certain number of copies from the packager, at a certain price. This is a firm sale, and the books cannot be returned to the packager if the publisher is unable to sell them. The packager will usually retain rights in the book, either the copyright in the text and illustrations, or at least the right to sell adapted versions in other markets than those agreed with the first publisher. In the case of an illustrated book with a possible world-wide market, the packager may produce books in several languages at the same time, selling each one to a different publisher in each language market

packaging *noun* **(a)** the action of putting things into packages **(b)** production of finished books for a publisher **(c)** (i) material used to protect goods which are being packed; (ii) attractive material used to wrap goods for display; ***airtight packaging; lightweight packaging material for sending books by air mail***

packer *noun* person who packs goods

packet *noun* **(a)** small box of goods for selling; ***packet of envelopes** or **of filing cards;*** **postal packet** = small container of goods sent by post **(b)** group of bits of uniform size which can be transmitted as a group, using packet switched network; **packet switched data service** *or* **packet switched network (PSN)** = service which transmits data in packets of set length; **packet switching** = method of sending messages *or* data in uniform-sized packets

packing *noun* **(a)** action of putting goods into boxes and wrapping them for shipping; ***what is the cost of the packing? packing is included in the price;*** **packing case** = large wooden box for carrying easily broken items; **packing charges** = money charged for putting goods into boxes; **packing list** *or* **packing slip** = list of goods which have been packed, sent with the goods to show they have been checked; **packing paper** = strong paper used for packing books **(b)** material used to protect goods; ***packed in airtight packing;*** **non-returnable packing** = packing which is to be thrown away when it has been used and not returned to the sender **(c)** overlap on a cylinder to correct the pressure on the printing surface

pad 1 *noun* **(a)** pile of sheets of paper attached together along one side; **desk pad** = pad of paper kept on a desk for writing notes; **memo pad** *or* **note pad** = pad of paper for writing memos or notes; **phone pad** = pad of paper kept near a telephone for noting messages **(b)** soft material like a cushion; ***the machine is protected by rubber pads;*** **inking pad** = cushion with ink in it, used to put ink on a rubber stamp **2** *verb* **to pad out** = to add pages to make a book thicker; to add text to make an article *or* book longer

padded covers *or* **padded sides** *noun* covers of a de luxe book, where soft material is inserted between the cover and the boards of the binding case

padding *noun* adding text to make an article *or* book longer; text added in this way

page *noun* one side of a printed piece of paper forming a book *or* magazine *or* newspaper (as opposed to a leaf, which is a piece of paper printed on both sides, making two pages); ***the pages are numbered 1 to 78; the chapters all start on odd-numbered pages;*** **page break** = (i) point at which a page ends and a new page starts (in continuous text); (ii) marker used when word-processing to show where a new page should start; **page cord** = strong string used to tie type made up into page, before placing it in a chase; **page cutoff** = device which cuts off the ink from one page during printing; **page depth** = length of a page, measured from the headline down to the folio at the foot of the page; **page description language (PDL)** = software that controls a printer, and which makes the printer print out pages according to the user's instructions; *see also* POSTSCRIPT **page display** = showing a page of text on the screen as it will appear when printed out; **page gauge** = piece of metal with which the compositor can measure the depth of the page when making up type; **page layout** = arrangement of text and pictures within a page of a document; ***we do all our page layout using desktop publishing software;*** **page length** = length of a page (either in printing *or* in word-processing); **page make-up** = making printed text into the correct lengths for pages, fitting in illustrations and adding the headlines, page numbers, etc. (this may be done by hand or by computer using a VDU); **page numbering** = way in which pages in a book are numbered; **page on galley** = proof where the text is made up into pages, but printed on galley slips; *see also* SLIP PROOF **page preview** = graphical representation of how a page will look when printed, with different type styles, margins, and graphics correctly displayed; **page printer** = printer which composes one page of text within memory and then prints it in one pass (normally refers to laser printers); **page proofs** = proofs of a book which have been made up into pages, sometimes with headlines and folios; **page pull test** = test for the strength of the adhesive in perfect binding, where the book is lifted up by a single leaf to see if the glue will hold; **page reference** = cross-reference to text on a certain page; **page setup** = options within software that allow a user to set up how the page will look when printed - normally setting the margins, size of paper, and scaling of a page; **pages per minute (ppm)** = measurement of the speed of a printer as the number of pages of text printed every minute; **pages-to-view** = large sheet printed with imposed pages **2** *verb* **(a)** to put numbers on pages **(b)** to make up a text into pages

paginate *verb* to put numbers on the pages of a book

pagination *noun* numbering of pages in a book *or* magazine; putting a text into pages; arrangement of pages in a book

> COMMENT: page numbers usually start with a series of roman numerals (i, ii, iii, etc.) for the prelims, and then change to Arabic numerals for the main text pages. The main text is paginated from page 1 again, with the result that the last folio in a book is rarely the same number as the actual extent

paging *noun* (i) making up text into pages; (ii) putting the numbers on pages of a ledger, using a manual numbering machine

paint program *noun* software that allows a user to draw pictures on screen in different colours, with different styles of brush and special effects

> COMMENT: paint programs normally operate on bitmap images; drafting or design software normally works with vector-based images

palette *noun* range of colours which can be used (on a printer *or* computer display)

pallet *noun* **(a)** flat wooden base on which goods (sheets of paper, printed sheets, bound books, etc.) can be stacked for easy handling by a fork-lift truck; *see also* EUROPALLET, SKID, STILLAGE **(b)** *(in binding)* tool used for blind tooling on rounded leather backs

palletize *verb* to put goods on pallets; ***palletized cartons***

pamphlet *noun* small booklet of advertising material or of information, usually less than 32 pages and saddle-stitched

panchromatic film *noun* film which is sensitive to all colours

panel *noun* **(a)** flat surface standing upright; **display panel** = flat area for displaying goods in a shop window; **advertisement panel** = specially designed large advertising space in a newspaper **(b)** rectangular piece of paper on the spine of a book, giving the title and author; **panel back** = leather binding style, where decorated leather panels are put between the ribs on the spine **(c)** list of works by the same author printed on the page facing the title page **(d)** group of people; ***we have a panel of freelance editors whom we use from time to time;*** **panel of experts** = group of people who give advice on a problem; **consumer panel** = group of consumers who report on goods they have used so that the manufacturer can improve the goods, or use the consumers' reports in his advertising

pantograph *noun* device for copying or reducing or enlarging line work (a series of arms on pivots move a pen as the operator traces the lines on the original)

Pantone *noun* trademark for a system of colours, of which different shades are identified by numbers according to the Pantone Matching System (PMS)

> COMMENT: Pantone colours are identified by the letters PMS and a number. The colours can be made up according to the proportions of different inks shown. A typical instruction might be: 'blue is PMS 282 and red is Pantone warm red'

paper *noun* **(a)** thin material for writing on *or* for printing on *or* for wrapping; ***the book is printed on 80gsm paper; glossy paper is used for printing halftones; bad quality paper results in a bad printed image;*** **art paper** = shiny paper, coated on one or both sides with a mixture of china clay and water, used for illustrations, especially halftones;

bank paper = thin paper (less than 60gsm) used for flimsies, file copies of typed letters, etc.; **Bible paper** = extremely thin paper (about 30gsm), which is nevertheless quite strong; **bond paper** = good quality paper (60-100gsm) often used for correspondence; **brown paper** = thick paper for wrapping parcels; **carbon paper** = sheet of paper with dry black ink on one side used in a typewriter to make a copy; **cartridge paper** = good quality white paper for drawing *or* lithographic printing; **duplicating paper** = special paper to be used in a duplicating machine; **graph paper** = paper with small squares printed on it, used for drawing graphs; **headed paper** = notepaper with the name and address of the company printed on it; **lined paper** = paper with thin lines printed on it; **NCR paper** = coated paper for making copies without interleaved carbon paper; **onion skin paper** = very thin paper made transparent by beating, used for airmail paper; **typing paper** = thin paper for use in a typewriter; **wrapping paper** = paper for wrapping; *see also* ANTIQUE, LAID, MF, MG, WOVE **(b) paper bag** = bag made of paper; **paper cover** = wrapper for book which does not have a binding case; **paper cutter** = guillotine, a machine for cutting paper; **paper factory** = factory where paper is made; **paper feed** = device which puts paper into a printer or photocopier; **paper foils** = foils for blocking covers, with a paper backing; **paper merchant** = person *or* company which sells paper to printers or publishers; **paper mill** = factory which makes paper; **paper sizes** = various standard sizes of paper ⇨ APPENDIX; *US* **paper slew** = PAPER THROW **paper store** = storage area where stocks of paper are kept until needed; **paper surface efficiency (PSE)** = measurement of the suitability of the surface of paper for printing; **paper tape** = strip of paper into which holes are punched to record data, and which when fed into a computer can drive a typesetting machine, or can be used to drive a Monotype casting machine; **paper tape reader (PTR)** = machine which reads perforated paper tape; **paper throw** = rapid vertical movement of paper in a printer; **paper tray** = container used to hold paper to be fed into a printer **(c)** newspaper; **trade paper** = newspaper aimed at people working in a certain industry; **free paper** *or* **giveaway paper** = newspaper which is given away free, and which relies for its income on its advertising

> COMMENT: the first paper was made from old cloth, torn up, and mixed with water. Good quality paper is still made in this way, though most papers are now made from wood. The base material is wood which has been debarked, then shredded. If it is ground fine to make pulp it is called mechanical pulp; if it is mixed with various chemical substances to remove impurities and soften the tissues to form pulp, it is called chemical pulp. The pulp is laid on a wire mesh which retains the solid fibres and lets the water drain away. After most of the water has been removed, the paper is put through rollers which dry and calender it. Paper is made in many different qualities, each of which is suitable for a certain printing process, or for writing and drawing. Note that the paper usually constitutes the highest cost in book manufacture, especially where long printruns are concerned

paperback 1 *noun* book, usually printed on cheap paper, with a paper binding; ***we are publishing the book as a hardback and as a paperback;*** **mass-market paperback** = cheaply printed and bound book, which appeals to a very large public; **paperback house** = publisher of paperbacks; **paperback rights** = the right to publish a book in a paperback edition after it has been published in a cased edition **2** *verb* to publish a book in a paperback edition; ***the hardback is selling well, and the book will be paperbacked next spring***

paper-bound *or* **paper-covered** *adjective* (book) bound with a paper cover (as opposed to a hardbound or cased book)

paperclip *noun* piece of bent wire, used to hold pieces of paper together

paper-fed *adjective* (device) which is activated when paper is introduced into it, such as a paper-fed scanner

paperless *adjective* without using paper; **paperless office** = electronic office, an office which uses computers and other electronic devices for office tasks and is therefore supposed not to use much paper

paperweight *noun* heavy object, often of glass, used to place on loose papers to stop them blowing away

paper weight *noun* the weight of a certain quantity of paper; *see also* BASIS WEIGHT

> COMMENT: in Britain, the weight of paper is calculated in grams per square metre (gsm). In the USA, it is expressed as the weight of 500 sheets of paper (i.e. a ream) of a standard 25 x 38 inch size, measured in pounds

paperwork *noun* office work, especially writing memos and filling in forms; ***exporting to Russia involves a large amount of paperwork***

papeterie *noun* stiff paper used for cards

papier mâché *noun* mixture of paper pulp and water, used to make moulds (and called 'flong')

papyrus *noun* kind of reed growing in the Middle East, especially in Egypt, used from very early times to make a type of paper

paragraph *noun* group of several lines of writing which makes a separate section; ***the first paragraph of your letter*** *or* ***paragraph one of your letter; please refer to the paragraph in the contract on 'shipping instructions';*** **paragraph indentation** = moving the text in from the margin to indicate the beginning of a paragraph; **paragraph mark** *or* **paragraph opener** = printed sign used to show the beginning of a paragraph (it may be the traditional ¶, or a black dot, or a hand ☞, or any of several other symbols); **flush paragraph** = paragraph with no indentation *or* where the first line is not indented (a white line is added between paragraphs to divide them more clearly); **hanging paragraph** = paragraph with the first line full width and rest indented; **new paragraph** = editing mark to show the typesetter that the text should start a new paragraph; **plain paragraph** = paragraph with the first line indented and the rest full width

parallel *noun* sign || used as a reference mark for footnotes; **parallel folding** = method of folding paper (as in continuous stationery) where each fold is parallel to the next

parchment *noun* **(a)** leather from the split skin of a sheep or goat, soaked in lime and scraped to make it smooth, used in the Middle Ages as writing material for manuscripts **(b)** high-quality thick cream-coloured paper imitating old parchment

parchmentize *verb* to treat paper so that it becomes translucent and waterproof, like parchment

> COMMENT: before the invention of paper, parchment was the commonest writing material in the Western world. Skins of sheep were common in England; vellum is parchment made from skins of calves

parentheses *noun* punctuation sign ( ) used to show that part of the text is incidental to the rest (often incorrectly called 'brackets'); (NOTE: singular is **parenthesis**)

Parker board *noun* good quality wooden board for mounting metal plates

part *noun* one of a series; **two-part stationery** = stationery (invoices, receipts, etc.) with a top sheet and a copy sheet; **four-part invoices** = invoices with four sheets (a top sheet and three copies); *see also* MULTI-PART **part payment** = paying of part of a whole payment; **part delivery** *or* **part order** *or* **part shipment** = delivering *or* shipping only some of the items in an order

partial *adjective* not complete; **partial remaindering** = remaindering part of the excess stock of a book, while keeping some of the stock for sale at the original price

part-mechanical paper *noun* paper which is made from a mixture of half mechanical pulp and half chemical pulp

part-time *adjective & adverb* not working for the whole working day; **part-time work** *or* **part-time employment** = work for part of a working day

part-timer *noun* person who works part-time

part-title *noun* right-hand page with the title of a section of a book, similar to a half-title

partwork *noun* publication which comes out in sections, published usually once a month or every two weeks, which if collected and kept in a special binder, make a complete publication; *compare* FASCICLE

pass 1 *noun* **(a)** permit to allow someone to go into a building; ***you need a pass to enter the ministry offices; all members of staff must show a pass*** **(b)** complete run of a computer *or* printing machine *or* typesetting machine; ***the first pass from the computer will not include the typesetting codes*** **2** *verb* **(a)** to approve; ***the art director has to pass the covers before they are sent for proofing; the MS has been passed by our libel lawyer;*** **to pass for press** = to tell the printer that the proofs have been corrected and therefore that the book can be printed; **pass date** = date on which proofs have to be passed for press; **pass sheet** = specimen pull of a printed sheet at the beginning of the printrun, which is approved by the printer and which the publisher is required to accept; (NOTE: UK English is **'passed for press'** but US English is **'good for press'**) **(b)** to be successful; ***he passed his typing test; she has passed all her exams and now has a diploma in printing***

passage *noun* section of a text (which is quoted)

paste 1 *noun* light glue, used for sticking paper; **scissors and paste job** = (i) something put together from cut up sheets; (ii) book or article made almost entirely of passages from other works **2** *verb* **(a)** to stick something together with paste; ***the erratum slip is pasted into the back of the book*** **(b)** to attach webs together using an automatic paster **(c)** to insert text or graphics that has been copied or cut into a file; ***now that I have cut this paragraph from the end of the document, I can paste it in here;*** **cut-and-paste** = action of taking a section of text *or* data from one point and inserting it at another (often used in word-processors and DTP packages for easy page editing)

pasteboard *noun* thin board, made of several sheets of paper pasted together, used for mounting pictures, etc., but not for binding

paster *noun* **automatic paster** *or* **autopaster** *or* **flying paster** = device on a rotary printing press which changes the reel of paper automatically when one reel runs out; **paster tab** = gummed strip which attaches the end of one reel to the next when changing reels

paste up *verb* to stick together the various parts of a text and illustrations, to make finished camera-ready copy

paste-up *noun* (i) rough layout, made of galley proofs pasted down with rough illustrations and headings inserted; (ii) camera-ready copy made by pasting the various sections of finished text and illustrations on a piece of board ready to be photographed

patch *noun* **(a)** (i) correction which is inserted into a bromide or film by stripping in; (ii) process of making small additions to a PostScript file without altering the original code underneath **(b)** one of a series of test colour prints in a control strip on a colour proof

patch up *verb* **(a)** to add pieces of packing paper to raise the type if it is too low **(b)** to paste positives in the correct places, ready for filming **(c)** to make temporary repairs to a machine

pattern *noun* **(a)** series of regular lines *or* shapes which are repeated again and again; **pattern book** = book showing examples of design **(b)** general way in which something usually happens; **pattern of trade** *or* **trading pattern** = general way in which trade is carried on

patterned *adjective* decorated with a pattern

PC = PERSONAL COMPUTER

PDF = PORTABLE DOCUMENT FORMAT provides a data file generated from PostScript that is platform independent, application independent and font independent; ***Acrobat™ is Adobe's suite of software used to generate, edit and view PDF files***

PDL = PAGE DESCRIPTION LANGUAGE

PE = PRINTER'S ERROR note made by a publisher's reader on proofs to show that the mistake was made by the typesetter

pearl *noun* old type size, similar to 5 point

peculiar *adjective* unusual character, such as an accent or phonetic character

pel = PICTURE ELEMENT smallest area on a screen that can be individually controlled; (NOTE: this is not necessarily the same as a pixel, since a pel could be made up of several pixels)

pen *noun* **felt pen** = pen with a point made of hard cloth; **light pen** = type of pen which contains a light-sensitive device that, when passed over a bar code can read it and send information back to a computer; **mapping pen** = special pen with a fine round tip, used for making maps; **marker pen** = pen which makes a wide coloured mark, used to highlight sections of text; **technical pen** = special pen with a fine tip, used for making technical drawings; **pen and ink drawing** = drawing done with pen and ink (as opposed to pencil, etc.); **pen ruling** = printing rules on paper using grooved pens on a flatbed letterpress machine; *compare* DISK RULING

pen name *noun* name taken by an author which is not his or her real name

penalty *noun* punishment (such as a fine) which is imposed if something is not done; **penalty clause** = clause which lists the penalties which will be imposed if the contract is not obeyed; ***the contract contains a penalty clause which fines the company $10,000 for every week the completion date is late;*** *US* **penalty copy** = manuscript which is difficult to set, and for which typesetting is charged at a higher rate than usual

penalize *verb* to punish *or* to fine; ***to penalize a supplier for late deliveries; they were penalized for bad service***

pencil *noun* writing instrument, consisting of a central core of graphite or coloured material in a thin cylinder of wood (usually made of cedar); **pencil case** = binding imperfection, where an endpaper is not stuck correctly at the fold, making a small tube of paper; **pencil drawing** = drawing done with a pencil, as opposed to pen and ink, etc.; **hard pencil** = pencil with a hard lead making precise grey lines; **soft pencil** = pencil with a soft lead making dense black lines; **indelible pencil** = pencil which makes marks that cannot be erased

> COMMENT: pencils are classified according to the hardness of the lead; 4B is very soft and 4H is very hard; HB is medium

perfect 1 *adjective* completely correct *or* with no mistakes; ***we check each batch to make sure it is perfect; she did a perfect typing test;*** **perfect copy** = (i) book block ready for binding; (ii) MS which has no errors or changes; (iii) very good quality antiquarian or secondhand book **2** *verb* **(a)** to develop something until it is as good as it can be; ***he perfected the process for printing from stone; the system was first used in 1935, but was not perfected until the 1960s*** **(b)** to print on the other side of a sheet which has already been printed on one side **(c)** to print using a perfector (i.e., printing both sides of the sheet at the same time)

perfect binding *noun* binding system used mainly for paperbacks, where the folds of paper at the back of the book block are cut off, and the cut ends of the pages are stuck into the binding case with special glue

perfect bound *adjective* (book) which has a perfect binding

COMMENT: perfect binding requires glue which does not dry out completely. The first perfect bound books tended to crack when opened, because the glue was too dry. Modern perfect binding allows even very large books to be bound in paper bindings; even some dictionaries are now perfect bound. A stronger form of perfect binding is notched binding, where notches are cut into the back of the folded sections instead of trimming off, so allowing the glue to penetrate the folds

perfector *US* **perfecting press** *noun* printing machine which prints the two sides of the sheet of paper at the same time

perforate *verb* to make holes in something; **perforated tape** = paper tape, a long strip of tape on which data can be recorded in the form of punched holes; **perforating machine** = machine which makes perforations in paper

perforations *noun* (i) row of tiny holes in a sheet of paper, allowing it to be torn easily; (ii) tiny holes made on press or on a folding machine to help with the folding of thick pages (a letterpress printing press can be adapted to make perforations in sheets of paper)

perforator *noun* (i) machine that punches holes; (ii) keyboard which produces a perforated tape

perform *verb* (i) to act in a play *or* film; (ii) to put on a play; to play a piece of music in public; **performing rights** = right to perform a copyright work

performance *noun* putting on a play *or* film *or* playing a piece of music; **performance rights** *or* **performance fees** = fees paid for the right to read poetry *or* prose *or* to put on a production of a play, etc., to a paying audience

period *noun* **(a)** length of time; **accounting period** = period of time at the end of which the firm's accounts are made up **(b)** *US* full stop, a printing sign used at the end of a piece of text

periodic *or* **periodical 1** *adjective* from time to time; ***a periodic review of the company's performance*** **2** *noun* **periodical** = magazine which is published at regular intervals

peripherals *noun* items of hardware (such as terminals, printers, monitors, etc.) which are attached to a main computer system

permanence *noun* ability of paper not to yellow or to become brittle with age

permanent *adjective* which will last for a very long time *or* for ever; **permanent ink** = ink which will not fade; **permanent paper** = acid-free paper

permission *noun* being allowed to do something; **written permission** = document which allows someone to do something; **verbal permission** = telling someone that he or she is allowed to do something; **to give someone permission to do something** = to allow someone to do something; ***they asked for permission to reproduce the photograph on the cover of the new book;*** **rights and permissions department** = department in a publishing company which deals with requests to reproduce material which is in the company's copyright or the copyright of its authors, where the authors have licensed the company to act on their behalf

permit 1 *noun* official document which allows someone to do something; **export permit** *or* **import permit** = official document which allows goods to be exported *or* imported; **work permit** = official document which allows someone who is not a citizen to work in a country **2** *verb* to allow someone to do something; ***the author will not permit his work to be performed in certain countries; we were not permitted to photograph the interior of the President's palace***

per pro = PER PROCURATIONEM with the authority of; ***the secretary signed per pro the manager***

petal printer = DAISY-WHEEL PRINTER

pH measure of the concentration of hydrogen ions in a solution, which shows how acid or alkaline it is; **pH meter** = meter which measures the pH value of a solution

> COMMENT: the pH value is shown as a number. A value of 7 is neutral; lower values indicate increasing acidity and higher values increasing alkalinity. The maximum reading is pH10, which is completely alkaline. Paper should be less acid (i.e. should have a pH value of 7 or more) if it is to be used for books which are likely to have a long life. Acid-free paper (with a very high pH value) is used in libraries to wrap and protect valuable books and manuscripts. Newsprint has a low pH value (5 or less) and so ages rapidly. The glues used in binding should also be alkaline, with a pH value of 6 or more

phoneme *noun* single item of sound used in speech; ***the phoneme 'oo' is present in the words 'too' and 'zoo'***

phonetic *adjective* referring to phonetics; ***the pronunciation is indicated in phonetic script***

phonetics *noun* written symbols that are used to represent the correct pronunciation of a word; *see also* IPA

photo **1** *prefix* referring to light **2** *abbreviation of* PHOTOGRAPH

photocompose *verb* to set text using a phototypesetting machine; **photocomposing machine** = machine which carries out photocomposition

photocomposer *noun* machine which carries out photocomposition

photocomposition *noun* method of typesetting on film or paper from film matrices or a digital font, as opposed to hot metal or strike-on methods

photocopier *noun* machine which makes a copy of a document by photographing and printing it

photocopy **1** *noun* copy of a document made by reproducing and printing it on a photocopier; ***make six photocopies of the contract*** **2** *verb* to make a copy of a document by reproducing and printing it with a photocopier; ***she photocopied the contract***

photocopying *noun* making photocopies; ***photocopying costs are rising each year;*** **photocopying bureau** = office which photocopies documents for companies which do not possess their own photocopiers; **there is a mass of photocopying to be done** = there are many documents waiting to be photocopied

photoengrave *verb* to make a photoengraving

photoengraver *noun* person who makes photoengravings

photoengraving *noun* **(a)** process of preparing letterpress plates from illustrations **(b)** halftone produced by photoengraving; ***the book is illustrated with ten photoengravings***

> COMMENT: the term 'engraving' does not mean the same in printing as it does in fine art. In printing, photoengraving etches (with an acid) the non-printing surfaces, leaving the top surface to carry the ink. Photoengraving can be used either for reproducing line drawings (where tones are represented by lines of ink) or halftones (where the tones are conveyed by many little dots of different sizes). On the other hand, an artist engraves a plate by cutting fine lines on it with a burin (a type of sharp needle); the image is formed by putting ink into the cut lines, wiping excess ink off the top surface.

photograph **1** *noun* image formed by light striking a light-sensitive surface; ***it's a photograph of the author's mother; he took six photographs of the house to use in his book; we will be using a colour photograph of the author on the back of the jacket;***

colour photograph = photograph which reproduces the subject in colour; **black and white photograph** = photograph which uses tones of black to show the image; **sepia photograph** = photograph using tones of sepia brown; **photograph library** = library of photographs which can be borrowed and reproduced for a fee **2** *verb* to take pictures on sensitive film, using a camera

photographer *noun* person who takes photographs

photographic *adjective* referring to photography *or* photographs; ***the copier makes a photographic reproduction of the printed page;*** **photographic composition** *or* **typesetting** = PHOTOTYPESETTING **photographic paper** = paper used to printing photographs; **photographic print** = photograph printed onto paper; **photographic studio** = place where photographs are made or where films are developed and printed

photographically *adverb* using photography; ***the text film can be reproduced photographically***

photography *noun* method of creating images by exposing light-sensitive film to light, using a camera

photogravure *noun* gravure, an intaglio printing process in which the paper is pressed directly onto the printing cylinder; the ink is held in a mass of tiny cells etched on the surface; used especially for printing long runs of colour works

photolithography *or* **photo-litho** *noun* printing using a lithographic printing plate prepared by photographic methods and not by hand

photomechanical composition = PHOTOCOMPOSITION

photomechanical transfer (PMT) *noun* (i) system for transferring line drawings and text photographically onto film before printing; (ii) photographic print made by this process; (NOTE: US English is **velox**)

photomontage *noun* montage made of several photographs

photo-offset = OFFSET LITHOGRAPHY

photopolymer plate *noun* printing plate which has a layer of photosensitive plastic bonded to a flexible metal plate; **photopolymer resin** = photosensitive plastic material which coats a plate

photoprint *noun* photograph used as an illustration

photosensitive *adjective* (paper *or* film) which is sensitive to light

photosetting = PHOTOCOMPOSITION

photostat 1 *noun* trade mark for a type of photocopy **2** *verb* to make a photostat of a document

phototext *noun* characters and text that have been produced by a phototypesetter

phototypesetter *noun* **(a)** company which specializes in phototypesetting **(b)** device that can produce very high-resolution text on photo-sensitive paper or film

> COMMENT: the phototypesetter, rather like a large laser printer, normally uses the PostScript page description language and can generate type at 2,540 dpi; if the device is capable of outputting text and half-tone images, it is normally called an image setter

phototypesetting *noun* method of typesetting that creates characters using a computer and exposing a sensitive film in front of a mask containing the required character shape

> COMMENT: this is the method by which most new publications are typeset, superseding metal type, since it produces a good quality result in a shorter time

photounit *noun* part of a phototypesetting machine in which the image of the character is created

pi *US* = PIE

pic = PICTURE (plural is **pix**)

pica *or* **pica em** *noun* **(a)** measurement used in composition, being equivalent to 12 points or 0.166 inch, used especially to give a line width measurement **(b)** width of characters in a typewriter, usually twelve characters per inch

pi characters = SPECIAL SORTS extra items not carried in the normal type font (such as odd fractions or accents); **pi font** = font of pi characters

pick *noun* fibres pulled from the surface of paper by tacky ink on the printing plate

picking *noun* **(a)** pulling fibres from the surface of paper as it is being printed, caused by poor paper surface or tacky ink on the plates; **picking resistance** = ability of paper to withstand picking **(b) order picking** = collecting various items in a warehouse to make up an order to be sent to a customer; **picking list** = list of items in an order, listed according to where they can be found in the warehouse

pick up *verb US* to use the text or illustrations from one book in another

PICS file format used to import a sequence of PICT files on a Macintosh

PICT = PICTURE *(Apple Macintosh)* graphics file format that stores images in the QuickDraw vector format

pictogram *or* **pictograph** *noun* little picture used to represent something

> COMMENT: used often in guide books. A bath shows if the hotel bedrooms have baths; a knife and fork shows the quality of a restaurant; a fish shows that fishing is allowed, etc.

pictorial *adjective* expressed in pictures; ***a pictorial record of the Queen's visit to Canada***

picture 1 *noun* printed *or* drawn image of an object or scene; ***this picture shows the new design;*** **picture agency** = office which has a picture library and lends illustrations to publishers for a fee; **picture book** = book with a large number of illustrations; **picture department** = department in a publisher's office which looks for pictures to be used in books; **picture element** *or* **pixel** = smallest single unit *or* point on a display whose colour *or* brightness can be controlled; *see also* PEL, PIXEL **picture library** = library of pictures (usually photographs, but also including old lithographs, etc.) which a publisher can borrow and reproduce for a fee; **picture pages** = pages of a book *or* magazine which have illustrations; **picture processing** = analysis of information contained in an image, usually by computer, providing analysis *or* recognition of objects in the image; **picture research** = looking for pictures which can be used in a book *or* magazine *or* TV documentary, etc.; **picture researcher** = person who looks for pictures to be used in a book *or* magazine *or* TV documentary, etc.; **picture transmission** = transmission of images over a telephone line; *see also* FACSIMILE TRANSMISSION **2** *verb* to visualize an object *or* scene; ***try to picture the layout before starting to draw it in***

picturization book rights *noun* the right to publish a book containing pictures or cartoons which have been published separately in newspapers

pie 1 *noun* **printer's pie** = type which has become mixed up and is meaningless **2** *verb* to mix up loose type by accident; ***the line was dropped and pied, so had to be reset;*** (NOTE: US English is spelt **pi**)

piece *noun* **(a)** small part of something; ***to sell something by the piece; the price is 25p the piece;*** **mailing piece** = leaflet suitable for sending by direct mail **(b) piece accent** = floating accent; **piece fraction** = fraction made up of two small figures (one superior, the other inferior), separated by a hyphen

piece rate *noun* rate of pay calculated per unit produced *or* for a piece of work done and not paid for at an hourly rate

piecework *noun* work that is paid for at a set rate per unit produced and not at an hourly rate

pie chart *noun* diagram where information is shown as a circle cut up into sections of different sizes

pierced block *noun* letterpress block with a hole cut through it, leaving a large area of white

pigment *noun* colouring substance in ink; **pigment foils** = foils for blocking covers, which give a colour to the letters or design

pin 1 *noun* **(a)** sharp piece of metal for attaching papers together, etc.; **drawing pin** = pin with a flat head for attaching a sheet of paper to something hard; ***she used drawing pins to pin the poster to the door*** **(b)** sharp projecting piece of metal; **pin feed** = device for feeding paper tape or computer stationery into a printer, which has pins which fit into the holes in the paper; **pin mark** = small depression on a piece of type, made by the pin which pushes the type out of the mould; **pin register** = method of aligning film, by using pins set in holes in the corners of each piece of film **2** *verb* to attach with a pin; ***she pinned the papers together; pin your cheque to the application form***

pin holes *noun* defect in paper, in the form of tiny holes

pipe roller *noun* idler *or* idling roller, the roller on a web press which turns freely

piping *noun* small ridges which occur in paper

PIRA = PRINTING INDUSTRIES RESEARCH ASSOCIATION British organization which does research into printing techniques and offers advice to member companies and training to their staff; **PIRA SOAT** = PIRA SURFACE OIL ABSORBENCY TESTER

> COMMENT: the PIRA SOAT method for measuring surface oil absorption time requires a brass roll carrying a drop of liquid paraffin to roll across the paper, transferring some of the liquid to it. The time taken for the paper to absorb 75% of the liquid is the surface oil absorption time

piracy *noun* copying of patented inventions *or* copyright works

pirate 1 *noun* person who copies a patented invention or a copyright work and sells it; ***a pirate copy of a book*** **2** *verb* to copy a copyright work; ***a pirated book*** *or* ***a pirated edition*** *or* ***a pirated design; the designs for the new system were pirated in the Far East; he used a cheap pirated disk and found the program had bugs in it***

> COMMENT: the items most frequently pirated are books which can easily be printed from photocopied originals, music from cassettes or records, or computer programs on magnetic disks and tapes which are relatively simple to copy

pitch *noun* **(a)** number of characters which will fit into one inch of line, when the characters are typed in monospacing (used on line printers, the normal pitches available being 10, 12 and 17 characters per inch); **pitch edge** = the edge of the paper as it is fed into a printing machine **(b) pitch marks** = lines drawn on cover material to allow it to be placed quickly and correctly once the glue has been applied **(c)** sticky substance in softwood, which is present in mechanical pulp and can damage the papermaking machinery

pix *plural noun informal* pictures (used in advertising or design)

pixel *or* **picture element** *noun* smallest single unit *or* point of a display whose colour *or* brightness can be controlled

> COMMENT: in high resolution display systems the colour or brightness of a single pixel can be controlled; in low resolution systems a group of pixels are controlled at the same time

place 1 *noun* position in a text; ***she marked her place in the text with a red pen; I have***

lost my place and cannot remember where I have reached in my keyboarding **2** *verb* to put; **to place a contract** = to decide that a certain company shall have the contract to do work; **to place a manuscript** = to find a publisher willing to publish a book; **to place something on file** = to file something; **to place an order** = to order something; ***he placed an order for 250 cartons of paper***

plagiarism *noun* copying another person's writings, and passing them off as one's own

plagiarist *noun* person who copies another person's work

plagiarize *verb* to copy another person's work and pass it off as one's own

plain *adjective* simple; ***the design of the cover is in plain blue and white squares; we want the school edition to have a plain design;*** **plain paragraph** = paragraph with the first line indented and the rest of the text full width

plain cover *noun* **to send something under plain cover** = to send something in an ordinary envelope with no company name printed on it

plain-paper copier *noun* photocopier which can use ordinary paper (such as headed stationery), and does not need special sensitized paper

plan 1 *noun* **(a)** organized way of doing something; ***the firm has announced its publishing plans for the next year*** **(b)** drawing which shows how something is arranged *or* how something will be built; ***the designers showed us the first plans for the new offices;*** **flat plan** = plan of sheets of a book *or* magazine, showing how colour sections, editorial matter and advertising pages are organized; **street plan** *or* **town plan** = map of a town showing streets and buildings **2** *verb* to organize carefully how something should be done; ***they are planning to launch a new paperback fiction list next autumn; the printers have planned to increase their capacity by 25%***

planchest *noun* piece of furniture with wide flat drawers, in which large plans *or* artwork can be kept

plane *verb* to smooth a surface; to reduce a surface by removing a thin layer from it

planer *noun* wooden block used to tap the metal type to fit it in place

planner *noun* **desk planner** *or* **wall planner** = book *or* chart which shows days *or* weeks *or* months so that the work of an office can be shown by diagrams

planning *noun* **(a)** putting film onto a grid **(b)** organizing the imposition of a book or magazine; **flat-planning** = organizing flat plans **(c)** assembly of type and illustrations into final film ready for platemaking

planographic printing *noun* printing from a flat printing plate (as in lithography) where the lines which produce the image are not raised above the surface (as in letterpress) or sunk below the surface of the plate (as in gravure printing), but are greasy, so that the ink stays on the image and is repelled by the rest of the wet ;surface of the plate

plant *noun* **(a)** machinery; **plant costs** = (i) the costs of installing and maintaining equipment; (ii) the fixed costs of producing a book, as opposed to the running costs **(b)** originated material (blocks, film, etc.) which belong to the publisher

Plantin popular typeface designed by Christopher Plantin (1514 - 1589)

plastic *noun* **plastic comb binding** = mechanical binding process where separate sheets have holes punched in them into which the teeth of a plastic comb fit; **plastic proofing** *see* DRY PROOFING **plastic wrapping** = thin transparent plastic sheets, used to wrap magazines for distribution

plate *noun* **(a)** illustration in a book, usually printed separately and on better quality paper than the text and then tipped into a book **(b)** printing surface with an image on it, that conveys the ink to the paper; **litho plate** = the printing surface in lithography; **plate cylinder** = cylinder in a printing machine to which a printing plate is fixed; **plate proof** = pull, a proof taken directly from the printing plate; **plate slap** = noise made by a plate which does not fit tightly around the cylinder **(c)** photographic image using a sheet of glass as the backing material; **plate camera** = camera which takes pictures on glass plates

plate-making *noun* making of plates for printing

> COMMENT: printing plates are usually made from metal (sometimes plastic or paper), and can be flat or curved to fit round the cylinder. Photographic plates are now used mainly in high quality, large-format professional cameras while the most popular backing material is still acetate film

platen *noun* **(a)** roller which supports the paper in a printer *or* typewriter **(b) platen press** = letterpress printing machine where the paper is placed on the type and a flat plate (the platen) presses down on it **(c)** device that keeps film in a camera in the correct position

plating *noun* action of fitting the plates to the plate cylinder; **plating sequence** = order in which the plates are fixed to the cylinder

plot *verb* to draw an image (especially a graph) based on information supplied as a series of coordinates; **plotting mode** = ability of some word-processors to produce graphs by printing a number of closely spaced characters rather than individual pixels (this results in a broad low-resolution line)

plotter *noun* computer peripheral that draws straight lines between two coordinates; **plotter driver** = dedicated software that converts simple instructions issued by a user into complex control instructions to direct the plotter; **plotter pen** = instrument used in a plotter to mark the paper with ink as it moves over it; **digital plotter** = plotter which receives the coordinates in digital form which it plots; **drum plotter** = computer output device that consists of a movable pen and a piece of paper wrapped round a drum that rotates, creating patterns and text; **incremental plotter** = plotter which receives positional data as increments to its current position rather than separate coordinates; **x-y plotter** *or* **graph plotter** = plotter which plots to supplied coordinates, by moving the pen in two planes while the paper remains stationary

> COMMENT: plotters are used for graph and diagram plotting and can plot curved lines as a number of short straight lines

plough *noun* hand cutter for cutting the edges of cased books

PLR = PUBLIC LENDING RIGHT

plucking = PICKING

plug 1 *noun* **(a)** device at the end of a wire used to connect a machine to the electricity supply; **adapter plug** = plug which allows devices with different plugs (two-pin, three-pin, etc.) to be fitted into the same socket; **plug-compatible** = computer or peripheral which can be used with another system simply by plugging it in with a special plug **(b) to give a plug to a new product** = to publicize a new product **2** *verb* **(a) to plug in** = to attach a machine to the electricity supply **(b)** to publicize *or* to advertise; ***they ran six commercials plugging holidays in Spain; she used her appearance on the chat show to plug her new novel***

plus *preposition* added to; **cost plus** = basis for calculating a price, based on the unit cost with an additional percentage (for example, cost plus 90%)

plus *or* **plus sign** *noun* printed *or* written sign (+) showing that figures are added *or* showing a positive value

-ply *suffix* indicating the number of layers of paper or board which are glued together to give greater strength

PMA = POST MORTEM AUCTORIS

PMS = PANTONE MATCHING SYSTEM

PMT = PHOTOMECHANICAL TRANSFER

pocket *noun* **(a)** paper folded like an envelope and glued inside the cover of a book to hold a map or other insert **(b)** type of envelope with a triangular flap

pocket book *noun* **(a)** small notepad which can be kept in the pocket **(b)** *US* small paperback

point 1 *noun* **(a)** measurement system used in typesetting (one point is equal to 0.351mm); ***the text of the book is set in 9 point Times; if we increase the point size to 10, will the page extent increase?;*** **point size** = height of a type; (NOTE: usually written **pt** after figures: **10pt Times Bold**)

> COMMENT: in the UK and the USA, point sizes are based on the pica system; one point equals 0.3515mm (or 0.01384 inch); 12 points being one sixth of an inch, or 4.21mm or one pica em. In Europe, point size is based on the Didot point: one point equals 0.3759mm (or 0.0148 inch), and 12 points are one cicero

(b) *US* measurement of the thickness of card (equal to one thousandth of an inch) **(c)** place *or* position; **breakeven point** = position at which sales cover costs but do not show a profit; **customs entry point** = place at a border between two countries where goods are declared to customs **(d)** round dot; **full point** *or* **full stop** = round printed dot in a text marking the end of most sentences; (NOTE: US English uses **period**) **decimal point** = dot which indicates the division between a whole unit and its smaller parts (such as 4.25); (NOTE: that in many countries the decimal is indicated by a comma, not a full point) **2** *verb* **to point out** = to show; ***the report points out the mistakes made by the company over the last year; he pointed out that the results were better than in previous years***

pointer *noun* graphical symbol used to indicate the position of a cursor on a computer display; ***desktop publishing on a PC is greatly helped by the use of a pointer and mouse***

point of presence (POP) *noun* a telephone access number for a service provider that can be used to connect to the Internet via a modem

point-of-sale (POS) *noun* the place where goods in a shop are paid for; **point-of-sale material** = display material (such as posters, dump bins) to advertise a product where it is being sold; **point-of-sale terminal** *or* **POS terminal** = computer terminal at a point-of-sale, used to provide detailed product information and connected to a central computer to give immediate stock control information; **electronic point-of-sale (EPOS)** = system that uses a computer terminal at a point-of-sale site for electronic funds transfer, as well as for product identification and stock control; **point to point protocol** *see* PPP

polished foil *noun* foil for blocking book covers, giving a shiny finish in many different colour shades

polystyrene *noun* **expanded polystyrene** = light solid plastic used for packing; ***the books were delivered packed in expanded polystyrene chips***

polythene *noun* thin plastic film used for wrapping

polyurethane binding (PUR) *noun* strong adhesive binding used for heavy reference books offering good open-flat qualities

polyvinyl acetate (PVA) *noun* synthetic cold-melt glue used in binding

polyvinyl chloride *noun see* PVC

POP = POINT OF PRESENCE

popular *adjective* liked by many people; **popular edition** = cheap edition; **popular prices** = prices which are low and therefore liked

pop-up book *noun* book with illustrations which are cut out in paper in such a way that when the book is opened the illustrations stand up in three-dimensional form

> COMMENT: used mainly for children's books, but also for some adult or more serious educational material

pornographic *adjective* obscene, aiming to arouse sexual excitement

pornography *noun* books, films, etc. with obscene subject matter

porosity *noun* ability to allow fluids to pass through

porous *adjective* which allows fluids to pass through

port *noun* socket, a physical connection allowing data transfer between a computer's internal communications channel and another external device

portable 1 *adjective* which can be carried; **portable colour duct** = device which can be attached to a printer to change the colour of the printing ink; **Portable Document Format** *see* PDF **2** *noun* **a portable** = a computer *or* typewriter which can be carried

portfolio *noun* large folder containing samples of a designer's work

portrait *noun* **(a)** picture of a person's face; ***there is a portrait of the author facing the title page*** **(b)** written description of a person; ***a book of portraits of famous politicians*** **(c) portrait format** = vertical format (with the height greater than the width, as opposed to landscape format)

POS *or* **p.o.s.** = POINT OF SALE

position 1 *noun* **(a)** place where something is; ***we will have to change the position of the text to take in the second illustration*** **(b)** situation *or* state of affairs; **what is the cash position?** = what is the state of the company's current account?; **bargaining position** = statement of intentions by one group during negotiations **2** *verb* to place something; ***position this photograph at the top right-hand corner of the page***

positive 1 *adjective* (film) made from a negative, i.e. with the black showing as black, or with the same colours as the original; **positive reading** *or* **right reading** = (film) which is positive **2** *noun* film which shows the colours as in the original (i.e. black is black); *compare* NEGATIVE

post- *prefix* later; **post-editing** = editing and modifying text after it has been compiled *or* translated by a machine; **post-formatted** = (text) arranged into pages at the printing stage rather than on screen

postage *noun* payment for sending a letter or parcel by post; **postage paid** = words printed on an envelope to show that the sender has paid the postage even though there is no stamp on it; **postage stamp** = small piece of paper attached to a letter or parcel to show that you have paid for it to be sent through the post

postal 1 *adjective* referring to the post; **postal charges** *or* **postal rates** = money to be paid for sending letters or parcels by post; ***postal charges are going up by 10% in September;*** **postal order** = document bought at a post office, as a method of paying small amounts of money by post **2** *noun* size of board which is not an ISO size (572 x 725mm)

post-binding *noun* type of loose-leaf binding using metal posts which pass through the holes in the leaves (as opposed to ring binding)

postcard *noun* piece of cardboard for sending a message by post (often with a picture on one side), usually $3\frac{1}{2}$ x $5\frac{1}{2}$ inches in size

poster *noun* large notice *or* advertisement to be stuck up on a wall; **poster paper** = paper which is glossy on one side and rough on the other; **poster stick** = large composing stick which can hold the large type needed for printing posters; **poster type** = very large type faces used for posters (often made of wooden blocks)

> COMMENT: the standard format for a single sheet poster is double crown (30 x 20 inches)

posthumously *adverb* after a person's death; ***his last novel was published posthumously***

post mortem auctoris (PMA) *Latin phrase meaning* 'after the death of the author' (used in copyright law)

post office *noun* (i) building where the postal services are based; (ii) shop where you can buy stamps, send parcels, etc.; **the Post Office** = national organization which deals with sending letters and parcels; **Post Office box number** = reference number given for delivering mail to a post office, so as not to give the actual address of the person who will receive it

postpone *verb* to arrange for something to take place later than planned; **they postponed publication until the spring** = they arranged for publication to take place later than planned, in the spring

postponement *noun* arranging for something to take place later than planned; ***I had to change my appointments because of the postponement of the meeting with the printers***

postscript *or* **post scriptum** *or* **PS** *noun* addition to a letter, added after the signature

PostScript™ standard page description language developed by Adobe Systems; PostScript offers flexible font sizing and positioning; it is most often used in DTP systems, high-quality laser printers and phototypesetters; ***if you do a lot of DTP work, you will benefit from a PostScript printer;*** **Display PostScript** = graphics language system that allows a user to see on the screen exactly what would appear on the printer; *see also* COMPUTER TO PLATE

> COMMENT: an Encapsulated PostScript file contains PostScript commands that describe an image or page, the commands are stored in a file and this can be placed on a page; an encapsulated PostScript file often contains a preview image in TIFF or PICT format

pot *noun* container for molten metal on a typecasting machine

potboiler *noun* work written to earn money (and with no literary merit)

pound *noun* **(a)** measure of weight (= 0.45 kilos) (in the USA, paper weight is calculated in pounds per 500 sheets); (NOTE: usually written **lb** after a figure: **25lb**) **(b)** money used in the UK and many other countries; **pound sterling** = official term for the British currency; (NOTE: usually written **£** before a figure: **£25.** Note also that the pound sign is used in the USA in place of the hash mark to avoid confusion in cases where the hash mark means 'number'. See note at HASH)

powderless etching *noun* method of etching blocks without needing to use dragon's blood (using magnesium alloy plates instead of zinc, giving very fine lines); (NOTE: also called **Dow etching**)

pp = PAGES

p.p. *verb* = PER PROCURATIONEM **to p.p. a letter** = to sign a letter on behalf of someone; ***the secretary p.p.'d the letter while the manager was at lunch***

PPA = PERIODICAL PUBLISHERS ASSOCIATION

ppi = PAGES PER INCH *see also* BULK

PPP = POINT TO POINT PROTOCOL protocol that allows a computer to use the TCP/IP protocol over a telephone connection

PR = PUBLIC RELATIONS ***a PR firm is handling all our publicity; he is working in PR; the PR people gave away 100,000 balloons***

predesigned *adjective* (graphic material) provided to the customer already designed; ***there is a wide selection of predesigned layouts to help you automatically format typical business and technical documents***

pre-edit *verb* to change text before it is run through a machine to make sure it is compatible

preface 1 *noun* text at the beginning of a book, after the title page and bibliographical page, which introduces the book and thanks people for helping in making it; *compare* FOREWORD, INTRODUCTION **2** *verb* to write or say something before the main part of a text; ***he prefaced his article with a quotation from Dickens***

> COMMENT: a preface is usually written by the author, and explains briefly why the book has been written and who the readers are expected to be. A foreword, on the other hand, can be written by the author, but is more usually by another person, often a famous person whose name might be expected to increase the sales of the book

prefatory note *noun* note addressed to the reader, printed at the beginning of a book

preferred position *noun* position of an advertisement in a magazine, which is particularly asked for by the advertiser

prefix *noun* **(a)** code *or* instruction *or* character at the beginning of a message *or* instruction **(b)** word attached to the beginning of another word to give it a special meaning; ***'kilo-' is the prefix meaning 'one thousand', so a kilogram is a thousand grams***

prejudice 1 *noun* harm done to someone; **without prejudice** = without harming any interests (words written on a letter to indicate that the writer is not legally bound to do what he offers to do in the letter); **to act to the prejudice of a claim** = to do something which may harm a claim **2** *verb* to harm (someone's claim)

prekey *verb* to keyboard a text before sending it for typesetting

preliminary *adjective* early *or* happening before anything else; **preliminary discussion** *or* **a preliminary meeting** = discussion *or* meeting which takes place before the main discussion *or* meeting starts; **preliminary matter** = PRELIMS

prelims *or* **preliminary pages** *noun* pages at the beginning of a book, before the actual text; (NOTE: US English is **front matter**)

> COMMENT: the prelims occupy several pages. They will normally include a half-title, the title page, the title page verso with bibliographical details, a contents page, and list of illustrations, preface, introduction and acknowledgements. They may also include a list of books by the same author (on the blank page facing the title page or half-title), a frontispiece (illustration facing the title page), etc. The prelims are usually numbered in roman figures (i, ii, iii, etc.) and these numbers do not count towards the page numbers of the text. A catalogue might note that a book has 24pp prelims and 222pp text. In British and American books the printer's imprint appears on the bibliographical page following the title page

pre-make-ready work *noun* (i) routine in a composing room to prepare a forme before making ready on a letterpress machine; (ii) preparing an offset machine for printing, including platemaking

premium book *noun* book offered as a gift to subscribers to another book or series of books, or offered at a very cheap price as a come-on to members of a book club

prep = PREPARATION

prepack *or* **prepackage** *verb* to pack something before putting it on sale; ***the guides are prepacked*** *or* ***prepackaged in a plastic display stand***

prepaid *adjective* paid in advance; **carriage prepaid** = indication that the transport costs have been paid in advance; **prepaid reply card** = stamped addressed card which is sent to someone so that he can reply without paying the postage

prepay *verb* to pay in advance

prepayment *noun* payment in advance; **to ask for prepayment of a fee** = to ask for the fee to be paid before the work is done

preparation *noun* getting something ready; **copy preparation** = sub-editing, marking up the copy for the printer; **data**

preparation = conversion of data into a machine-readable form (usually by keyboarding) before data entry

pre-press *adjective* before going to press; **pre-press costs** = origination costs, the costs of preparing a book or magazine up to the camera-ready copy stage or film; **pre-press proof** = proof made from the film, before printing starts; **pre-press work** = preparing an offset machine for printing, including platemaking and making ready;. (NOTE: also called **pre-make-ready work**)

preprint 1 *noun* **(a)** section of a book printed before the rest and sent out in advance as publicity matter **(b)** printed material which is then overprinted (such as colour sections without text) **2** *verb* to print something before the rest of the job; **preprinted cover** = cover which is printed in advance of the main binding (as, for example, covers to be used for display purposes, or for reps to use when subscribing the title); **preprinted form** = paper used for printing databases *or* applications programs that already contain some information printed on it; **preprinted stationery** = computer stationery (such as invoices) which has already been printed with the company's logo and address as well as the blank columns, etc.

pre-publication *adjective* before publication; **pre-publication advertising** = advertising carried out before the publication of a book; **pre-publication sales** = sales which are recorded before the publication of a book; **pre-publication selling** = advance selling, the selling of a book by a retail bookseller before the publication date set by the publisher

prescribed text *noun* educational book which has been listed as required for a course of study *or* for an exam

presensitized *adjective* (offset litho plate) which has a sensitive coating ready for processing

presentation *noun* **(a)** **presentation copy** = special copy of a book (either in special binding *or* with a special inscription) which is given to someone at an official ceremony **(b)** demonstration *or* exhibition of a proposed plan; ***the distribution company made a presentation of the services they could offer; we have asked two PR firms to make presentations of proposed publicity campaigns;*** **presentation visuals** = artwork which is used in a presentation, to show what the finished work will look like

preset *verb* to set something in advance; ***the printer was preset with new page parameters***

pre-shrunk packaging *US* = SHRINK-WRAPPING

press 1 *noun* **(a)** **printing press** = machine for printing; **the book has been passed for press** = the proofs have been accepted by the publisher and the printer has been told to go ahead and print; **the book is on the press** = the book is being printed; **the book is going to press on Monday** = the printing of the book will start on Monday; **press costs** = printing costs, including making plates, paper, machining, binding, etc.; **press date** = date on which a book *or* magazine is printed; **press proofs** = final proofs which are run off just before the printing run starts **(b)** name often given to (i) a company which prints books *or* magazines *or* newspapers; (ii) a publishing company, especially one which is attached to a university *or* learned society **(c)** **the press** = newspapers and magazines; **the local press** = newspapers which are sold in a small area of the country; **the national press** = newspapers which sell in all parts of the country; ***the new car has been advertised in the national press; we plan to give the product a lot of press publicity; there was no mention of the new product in the press;*** **press agency** = company which sells news items and features to newspapers and journalists; **press agent** = person who looks after the publicity for an author, entertainer or other famous person; *US* **press clipping agency** = PRESS CUTTING AGENCY **press conference** = meeting at which reporters from newspapers are invited to hear news of an important event or person and ask questions; **press copies** = copies of a new book which are sent to newspapers; **press coverage** = reports about something in the press; ***we were very disappointed by the press coverage of the new encyclopaedia;*** **press cutting** = piece cut out of a newspaper *or* magazine, which refers to an item which a certain customer may find interesting; ***we have kept a file of press cuttings about our authors;*** **press cutting agency** = company which makes press cuttings for other companies; **press release** = sheet giving news about something which is sent to newspapers and TV and radio stations so that they can use the information; ***the company sent out a press release about the launch of the new series of ecology titles*** **(d)** action of pushing down on something; **press rolls** = heavy rollers which crush the paper as it is going through the papermaking process **2** *verb* to push down on paper to finish it; **hot-pressed paper** = paper which is pressed between metal plates to make it smooth; *see also* NOT

pressing *noun* action of flattening printed signatures; **pressing boards** = stiff cardboard plates between which the printed pages are pressed to flatten them before going for binding

presspahn hollow *noun* type of hollow used in the spine of cased books

pressroom *noun* part of a printing works where the printing is actually carried out

pressrun *noun* US number of books printed at one time; (NOTE: GB English is **printrun**)

presswork *noun* the work of carrying out a printing job, whether it is printing leaflets or posters, or a multivolume reference work in full colour (in book printing, also called machining)

preview *verb* to display text *or* graphics on a screen as it will appear when it is printed out; **preview screen** = screen on which text or graphics can be previewed

previewer *noun* feature that allows a user to see on screen what a page will look like when printed; ***the built-in previewer allows the user to check for mistakes***

price 1 *noun* money which has to be paid to buy something; **agreed price** = price which has been accepted by both the buyer and seller; **all-in price** = price which covers all items in a purchase (goods, insurance, delivery, etc.); **bargain price** = very cheap price; **book club price** = special price to members of a book club (usually 75% or less of the normal retail price in the publisher's edition); **catalogue price** *or* **list price** = price as marked in a catalogue or list; **cost price** = selling price which is the same as the price which the seller paid for the item (either the manufacturing price or the wholesale price); **export price** = special price put on a book for the export market, which does not bear any relation to the catalogue price in the publisher's home market; **fair price** = good price for both buyer and seller; **firm price** = price which will not change; **to sell books off at half price** = to sell books at half the price at which they were being sold before; **net price** = price which cannot be reduced by a discount when sold retail; **published price** = price at which a book is published (usually the price which is marked in the publisher's catalogue, or printed on the book, or at any rate, the price listed in the national list of books in print); **retail price** *or* **selling price** = price at which the retailer sells to the final customer; **retail price index** = index which shows how prices of consumer goods have increased or decreased over a period of time; **price control** = legal measures to stop prices rising too fast; **price cutting** = sudden lowering of prices; **price differential** = difference in price between products in a range; **price fixing** = illegal agreement between companies to charge the same price for competing products; **price label** *or* **price sticker** *or* **price tag** = label which shows a price; **price list** = sheet giving prices of goods for sale; **price range** = series of prices for similar products from different suppliers; **price war** *or* **price-cutting war** = competition between companies to get a larger market share by cutting prices; **to increase in price** = to become more expensive; ***books have increased in price in line with the increase in the cost-of-living;*** **to increase prices** *or* **to raise prices** = to make items more expensive; ***several***

publishers increase backlist prices on January 1st; **we will try to meet your price** = we will try to offer a price which is acceptable to you; **to cut prices** = to reduce prices suddenly **2** *verb* to give a price to a product; **competitively priced** = sold at a low price which competes with that of similar products from other companies

pricing *noun* giving a price to a product; **pricing policy** = a company's policy in giving prices to its products; ***our pricing policy aims at producing a 35% gross margin;*** **common pricing** = illegal fixing of prices by several businesses so that they all charge the same price; **competitive pricing** = putting a low price on a product so that it competes with similar products from other companies; **marginal pricing** = making the selling price the same as the cost of a single extra unit above the number already planned

primary *adjective* first *or* basic *or* most important; **primary colours** *or* **colour primaries** = the three primary colours (red, green and blue) which make white light, or the three process colours (cyan, magenta and yellow) used, with black, in four-colour process work; **primary publishing** = publishing of school books for use in primary schools (schools teaching children up to about the age of 11); **primary school textbook** = textbook used in schools teaching children up to about eleven years old; *compare* SECONDARY, TERTIARY

primer *noun* manual, a simple instruction book with instructions and examples to show how a new program *or* system operates

print 1 *noun* **(a) in print** = published and available for sale; ***she has twenty-four novels in print;*** **the book is out of print (OP)** = the book is no longer available from the publisher; **to put a book out of print** = to decide not to reprint a book; **250,000 copies in print** = 250,000 copies of the book have been printed, though possibly in several editions and over several years **(b)** words made (on paper) with a machine; ***you get clearer print from a daisy-wheel printer than from a line printer;*** **to read the small print** *or* **the fine print on a contract** = to read the conditions of a contract which are often printed very small so that people will not be able to read them easily; **print control character** = special character which directs a printer to perform an action *or* function (such as change font), rather than print a character; **print hammer** = (i) moving arm in a typewriter that presses the metal character form onto the inked ribbon, leaving a mark on the paper; (ii) moving part in an impact printer, which presses the character onto the printer ribbon; **print life** = number of characters a component can print before needing to be replaced; ***the printhead has a print life of over 400 million characters;*** **print modifiers** = codes in a document that cause a printer to change mode, i.e. from bold to italic; **print pause** = temporarily stopping a printer while printing (to change paper, etc.); **print spooling** = automatic printing of a number of different documents in a queue at the normal speed of the printer, while the computer is doing some other task; **print style** = typeface used on a certain printer *or* for a certain document **(c)** printed copy of a etching, etc., made from a film *or* plate; ***he collects 18th century prints; the office is decorated with Japanese prints*** **(d)** positive photographic image in which black is black and white is white; *compare with* NEGATIVE **print contrast ratio** = difference between the brightest and darkest areas of an image **2** *verb* **(a)** to make copies of a book *or* newspaper, by running paper through a printing press; ***the book was printed last month and already a reprint has been ordered; the magazine is printed in Italy;*** **to print to paper** = to print as many copies as there is paper available, rather than asking for a precise number of copies which might be uneconomical; **print order** = order from a customer asking a printer to print (specifying quantity, paper, binding, etc.); **print number** = printrun, the number of copies of a book which are printed at one time **(b)** to make letters on paper with a machine; ***printed agreement; printed regulations; the printer prints at 60 characters per second;*** **printed matter** = papers such as leaflets, brochures, newspapers, books, which have been printed (subject to special postage rates) **(c)** to write in capital letters; ***please print your name and address on the top of the form***

printable *adjective* (paper) which can be printed on

printer *noun* **(a)** company which prints books *or* newspapers, etc.; ***the book will be sent to the printer next week; we are using Japanese printers for some of our magazines;*** **printer's imprint** = special mention of the name and address of the printer on the inside of a book *or* periodical **(b)** person who typesets and prints; **printer's devil** = apprentice or young helper in a printing workshop; **printer's error (PE)** = mistake made by the printer (usually an error in typesetting); **printer's flowers** = ornaments available in metal type or transfer lettering; **printer's pie** = type which has become mixed up and is meaningless **(c)** machine which prints; **computer printer** *or* **line printer** = machine which prints information from a computer, printing one line at a time; **bidirectional printer** = printer which is able to print characters from left to right and from right to left as the head moves backwards and forwards; **chain printer** = printer whose characters are located on a continuous belt; **daisy-wheel printer** = printer with characters arranged on interchangeable wheels; **dot-matrix printer** = printer which forms characters from a series of tiny dots printed close together; **impact printer** = printer that prints text and symbols by striking an inked ribbon onto paper with a metal character; **ink-jet printer** = printer that produces characters by sending a stream of tiny drops of electrically charged ink onto the paper (the movement of the ink drops is controlled by an electric field); **laser printer** = high-resolution printer that uses a laser source to print high quality dot-matrix characters; **line printer** = printer which prints draft-quality information at high speed (typical output is 200 - 3000 lines per minute); **page printer** = printer which composes one page of text, then prints it rapidly; **thermal printer** = printer where the character is formed on thermal paper with a printhead containing a heating element; **printer buffer** = temporary store for character data waiting to be printed (used to free the computer before the printing is completed making the operation faster); **printer control characters** = command characters in a text which transmit printing commands to a printer; **printer driver** = dedicated software that converts and formats the user's commands ready for a printer; **printer-plotter** = high resolution printer that is able to operate as a low resolution plotter; **printer quality** = standard of printed text from a particular printer (high resolution dot-matrix printers produce near letter quality, daisy-wheel printers produce letter quality); **printer ribbon** = roll of inked material which passes between a printhead and the paper

printhead *noun* (i) row of needles in a dot matrix printer that produce characters as a series of dots; (ii) metal form of a character that is pressed onto an inked ribbon to print the character on paper

printing *noun* **(a)** art of printing books *or* magazines, including typesetting, etc.; ***she is studying printing at college;*** **printing cylinder** = cylinder on a press which carries the printing plate; **printing head** = PRINTHEAD **printing history** = details of the printing of a book (the date of the original printing, and the dates of reprints) usually listed on the bibliographic page after the title page; **printing house** = company which prints; **printing ink** = ink, made from carbon mixed with oil, used in printing; **printing papers** *or* **printings** = types of paper which can be used for printing (as opposed to wrappings and writings); **printing processes** = methods of printing, such as letterpress, litho, gravure, screenprinting and flexography; **printing sequence** = the order in which the four colours are printed in four-colour work; **the printing trade** = all printers and allied companies; **printing works** = factory where books *or* newspapers are printed **(b)** quantity of copies of a book printed at the same time; ***the second printing has sold out and a third has been ordered***

printing down *noun* preparation of a printing plate by exposing it to a prepared film in a printing-down frame, and subjecting it to light; **printing-down frame** = vacuum frame used for printing down when making a plate from a film

Printing Industries Research Association *see* PIRA

printing press *noun* **(a)** company *or* factory which prints books *or* magazines, etc. **(b)** machine which prints books *or* newspapers

printmaking *noun* printing art prints (lithographs, etchings, linocuts, etc.)

print out *verb* to print information from a computer through a printer

printout *noun* **computer printout** = printed copy of information from a computer; ***the sales director asked for a printout of the agents' commissions***

printrun *noun* print number, the number of copies of a book printed at one time; (NOTE: US English is **pressrun**)

printshop *noun* shop where jobbing printing takes place

printwheel *noun* daisy-wheel, a wheel made up of a number of arms, with a character at the end of each arm, used in a daisy-wheel printer

privacy *noun* the right of an individual to limit the extent of, and control access to, the data that is stored about him; **privacy of data** = rule that data is secret and must not be accessed by users who have not been authorized; **privacy of information** = rule that unauthorized users cannot obtain data about private individuals from databases *or* that each individual has the right to know what information is being held about him on database

private *adjective* belonging to a single person, not a company *or* the state; **letter marked 'private and confidential'** = letter which must not be opened by anyone other than the person it is addressed to; **private press** = printing press which prints limited numbers of handset books, and sells them to collectors

privately *adverb* **privately printed book** = book printed by a private press; **privately published book** = book which has been printed at the author's expense

pro 1 *preposition* for; **pro tem** = for the time being *or* temporarily; **per pro** = with the authority of; ***the secretary signed per pro the manager;*** **pro forma** = invoice sent to a buyer before the goods are sent, so that payment can be made in advance **2** *verb slang* original artwork and transparencies ready for scanning

process *noun* **process camera** = camera designed for the stages required in preparing illustrations for printing, such as tone and colour separation; **process colours** = the three basic primary colours (cyan, magenta, yellow), which with black are used in combinations to produce all other colours; **process colour printing** = printing of colour plates, using four-colour plates (one for each process colour); **process engraving** = (i) method of making line or halftone letterpress blocks, where the originals are photographed and then etched; (ii) a block made for letterpress printing; **process plates** = colour plates used in four-colour printing; **process white** = special white paint used to cover unwanted block lines on artwork (it does not show when photographed); **process work** = printing in four colours

processing *noun* **(a)** developing and printing a film **(b)** sorting of information; **batch processing** = computer system, where information is collected into batches before being loaded into the computer; **data processing** *or* **information processing** = selecting and examining data in a computer to produce information in a special form; **word processing** *or* **text processing** = working with words, using a computer to produce, check and change texts, reports, letters, etc.

processor *noun* **word processor** = small computer which is used for working with words, to produce texts, reports, letters, etc.

product *noun* manufactured item for sale; **product advertising** = advertising a particular named product, not the company which makes it; **product analysis** = examining each separate product in a company's range to see why it sells *or* who buys it, etc.; **product design** = design of consumer products; **product development** = improving an existing product line to meet the needs of the market; **product engineer** = engineer in charge of the equipment for making a product; **product line** *or* **product range** = series of different products made by the same company which form a group (such as cars in different models, pens in different colours, etc.); **product management** = directing the making and selling of a product as an independent item; **product mix** = the particular combination of products made by the same company

production *noun* making *or* manufacturing of goods for sale; **domestic production** = production of goods in the home market; **rate of production** *or* **production rate** = speed at which items are made; **production control** = control of the manufacturing of a product (using computers); **production controller** = person in the production department of a publishing company who deals with printers and other suppliers; **production cost** = cost of making a product; **production department** = section of a company which deals with the making of the company's products, in a publishing company the department dealing with typesetting, proofing, paper buying, printing, and binding; **production ledger** = accounts ledger where a publisher keeps note of all production costs incurred in making a book, from origination to bound books; **production manager** = person in charge of the production department; **production and progress record** = record kept giving details of the production of a book; **production schedule** = timetable for the production of a book; **production unit** = separate small group of workers producing a certain product

profession *noun* (i) type of work which needs special skills learnt over a period of time; (ii) group of specialized workers; **the legal profession** = all lawyers; **the medical profession** = all doctors

professional *adjective* **(a)** referring to one of the professions; ***the accountant sent in his bill for professional services; we had to ask our lawyer for professional advice on the contract;*** **professional books** *or* **a professional list** = books on professional subjects, such as accountancy, law, medicine, etc.; **professional and reference publishing** = publishing of special books for the professions and also reference titles; **a professional man** = man who works in one of the professions (such as a lawyer, doctor, accountant); **professional qualifications** = documents showing that someone has successfully finished a course of study which allows him to work in one of the professions **(b)** expert *or* skilled; ***his work is very professional; they did a very professional job in designing the new logo***

profile *noun* brief description (of an author, of a company); ***he asked for a company profile of the possible partners in the joint venture; the customer profile shows our average buyer to be male, aged 25-30, and employed in the service industries***

pro forma *noun* **pro forma (invoice)** = invoice sent to a buyer before the goods are sent, so that payment can be made in advance

program 1 *noun* **computer program** = instructions to a computer telling it to do a particular piece of work; ***to buy a word-processing program; the accounts department is running a new payroll program*** **2** *verb* to write a program for a computer; **to program a computer** = to install a program in a computer; ***the computer is programmed to print labels***

programme *US* **program** *noun* plan of future action; ***development programme; research programme; training programme; to draw up a programme of future publications*** *or* ***a publishing programme***

programmable *adjective* which can be programmed

programmed learning *noun* use of educational software to give a learner a course of instruction

programmer *noun* **computer programmer** = person who writes computer programs

programming *noun* **computer programming** = writing programs for computers; **programming engineer** = engineer in charge of programming a computer system; **programming language** = software that allows a user to write a series of instructions to define a particular task, which will then be translated to a form that is understood by the computer

> COMMENT: programming languages are grouped into different levels: the high-level languages such as BASIC and PASCAL are easy to understand and use, but offer slow execution time since each instruction is made up of a number of machine code instructions; low-level languages such as ASSEMBLER are more complex to read and program in but offer faster execution time

progress *noun* movement of work forward; ***to report on the progress of the work*** *or* ***of the negotiations;*** **to make a progress report** = to report how work is going; **in progress** = which is being done but is not finished; **work in progress** = value of goods being manufactured which are not complete at the end of an accounting period

progress card *noun* progress sheet card or sheet on which details of a job's progress can be kept

progress chaser *noun* person whose job is to check that work is being carried out on schedule *or* that orders are being fulfilled on time, etc.

progressive *adjective* which moves forward in stages; **progressive proofs** *or* **progressives** *or* **progs** = set of colour proofs from process colour printing, showing first one colour, then with the second added, etc., until the whole colour illustration is shown, presented in this way so that the publisher and printer can check each colour; **bastard progressives** = progressive colour proofs showing different combinations of colours, not necessarily in the order of printing

progs = PROGRESSIVES

project *noun* **(a)** plan; ***he has drawn up a project for developing new markets in Europe*** **(b)** particular job of work which follows a plan; ***we are about to start work on a large reference book project; the company will start work on the project next month;*** **project analysis** = examining all costs *or* problems of a project before work on it is started; **project manager** = manager in charge of a project

projected *adjective* planned *or* expected; **projected sales** = forecast of sales; ***projected sales in Europe next year should be over £1m***

projection *noun* **(a)** act of showing an illustration on a screen, using a projector **(b)** forecast of something which will happen in the future; ***projection of profits for the next three years; the sales manager was asked to draw up sales projections for the next three years***

promote *verb* **(a)** to give someone a more important job; ***he was promoted from salesman to sales manager*** **(b)** to advertise; **to promote a new product** = to try to increase the sales of a new product by a sales campaign *or* TV commercials *or* free gifts

promotion *noun* **(a)** moving up to a more important job; **to earn promotion** = to work hard and efficiently and so be promoted **(b)** **promotion of a product** = selling a new product by publicity *or* sales campaign *or* TV commercials *or* free gifts; **author promotion tour** = tour made by an author to promote his book (appearing on local TV programmes, at signing sessions in bookshops, etc.); **promotion copies** = free copies of an unpublished book given to salesmen and the publicity department to use in pre-selling the book

promotional *adjective* **(a)** used in an advertising campaign; ***the admen are using balloons as promotional material;*** **promotional budget** = forecast cost of promoting a new product; **promotional material** = posters, carrier bags, etc., which are used to publicize a book **(b)** *US* **promotional book** = cheap, highly illustrated book, similar to a coffee table book, but sold at a bargain price

prompt *noun* message which appears on a computer screen, reminding the operator to do something

proof 1 *noun* sheet with text *or* pictures printed on it, for the publisher *or* author *or* designer to examine and make corrections; **proof copy** = page proofs of a book, bound in a paper cover, used for publicity purposes; **proof corrections** = changes made to the text, layout or illustrations on proofs; **proof correction marks** = special marks used to indicate changes (deletions, addition, more space, etc.) ⇨APPENDIX; **proof room** = place in a print works where proofs are made; **author's proof** = proof sent to the author to read and make corrections (which are charged to the author if they exceed a certain amount); **block proof** = proof contacted from a letterpress block; **foundry proof** = proof taken directly from a chase of metal type before a plate is made from it; **galley proofs** = proofs in the form of long pieces of text, not divided into pages, printed on long pieces of paper; **machine proof** = proof of imposed pages taken from the printing press; **master proof** *or* **master set of proofs** = (i) proofs kept in the editorial office, on which corrections from several proofreaders are collated; (ii) set of proofs from the printer, marked with his corrections, which are returned after the publisher's and author's corrections have been added; **ozalid proof** = proof made from film, on photographic paper; *see also* BLUE, DIAZO, VANDYKE **page proof** = proof of the pages of a book, sometimes with headlines and page numbers; **page on galley proofs** = proofs printed on long sheets of paper, but showing the text divided into pages; **press proof** = MACHINE PROOF **repro proof** = proof taken on high-quality paper which can be photographed and used for reproduction; **revised proof** = proof of text with the corrections made to it; **slip proofs** = proofs of pages, each printed on a separate sheet of paper **2** *verb* to make proofs of a text; ***the corrected text has gone for proofing***

-proof *suffix* which prevents something getting in *or* getting out *or* harming; ***dustproof cover; inflation-proof pension; soundproof studio***

proofer *noun* machine which produces proofs, as opposed to finished printed pages; ***output devices such as laser proofers and typesetters***

proofing *noun* producing proofs of a book, which then have to be read and corrected; **proofing press** *or* **proof press** = special press used only to produce proofs

proof read *verb* to read proofs and note corrections to them

proofreader *noun* person whose job it is to read and correct proofs; **proofreader's marks** = special marks used by proofreaders to show changes which have to be made to the proof by the typesetter ⇨APPENDIX

proofreading *noun* stage in the production process, where readers and the author read the proofs and mark corrections

> COMMENT: the stages of proofing are galley proofs, page on galley (where the pages are indicated, but the proofs are still printed on long pieces of paper), and page proofs. It is usual to miss out some of these stages, and many books are proofed in pages from the start. Proofs from film are in the form of ozalids, blues, diazos, etc.

property *noun* **intellectual property** *or* **literary property** = ownership of something (such as the words forming the text of a book *or* a copyright *or* patent *or* design *or* the image on a photograph) which cannot be seen or touched

proportional *adjective* directly related; ***the increase in profit is proportional to the reduction in overheads***

proportional spacing *noun* system used in typesetting, which makes a space proportional to the character width ('i' taking less space than 'm'); *compare* MONOSPACING

pro rata *Latin phrase meaning* 'for the rate': at a rate which varies according to the size or importance of something

prose *noun* text which is not verse (as, for example, in a novel)

prospectus *noun* printed leaflet giving details of a forthcoming publication (often with a specimen page) to attract buyers

protect *verb* to defend something against harm; ***the information is protected by copyright; the computer is protected by a plastic cover; the cover is supposed to protect the machine from dust;*** **copy protect** = switch used to prevent copies of a disk being made; ***all the disks are copy protected;*** **write protect tab** = tab on a disk which will prevent writing information to the disk *or* erasing information already on the disk

protection *noun* thing which protects; **consumer protection** = protecting consumers against unfair *or* illegal traders; **copy protection** = preventing copies being made; ***a hard disk may crash because of faulty copy protection; the new product will come without copy protection;*** **data protection** = making sure that data is not copied by an unauthorized user; **Data Protection Act** = act which prevents confidential data about people being copied

protective *adjective* which protects; **protective tariff** = tariff which tries to ban imports to stop them competing with local products; **protective cover** = cover which protects a machine

protest *noun* statement *or* action to show that you do not approve of something; ***to make a protest against high prices;*** **sit-down protest** = action by members of the staff who occupy their place of work and refuse to leave; **protest literature** = literature written and published to protest against something, usually a political situation; *see also* SAMIZDAT

protocol *noun* pre-agreed signals, codes and rules to be used for data exchange between systems; **protocol converter** = device used for converting protocols from one computer system to another, such as for converting data from a micro to a phototypesetter; **protocol standards** = standards laid down to allow data exchange between any computer system conforming to the standard

proud *adjective* (text) which projects a little into the margin; also used to describe a piece of type which stands higher than the normal type height

prove *verb* to pull a proof from a printing plate

provincial press *noun* newspapers published for areas of the country away from the capital city

P.S. *noun* = POST SCRIPTUM additional note at the end of a letter

PSE = PAPER SURFACE EFFICIENCY

PSTN = PUBLIC SWITCHED TELEPHONE NETWORK

pseudonym *noun* false name used by a writer

pseudonymous *adjective* (book) written by a writer under a pseudonym

PTR = PAPER TAPE READER

pubdate = PUBLICATION DATE

public 1 *adjective* referring to all the people in general; **public domain** = document *or* text that has no copyright and can be copied by anyone; **Public Lending Right (PLR)** = right of an author to receive a payment from a library, when a book has been borrowed by a member of the public; **public library** = library which is open to the general public, and for which citizens of the town can have borrowers' tickets; **public library system** = system of public libraries covering the whole country; **public prints** = newspapers **2** *noun* **the public** *or* **the general public** = the people

public relations (PR) *noun* keeping good relations between a company *or* a group and the public so that people know what the company is doing and can approve of it; ***a public relations man; he works in public relations; a public relations firm handles all our publicity;*** **a public relations exercise** = a campaign to improve public relations

public switched telephone network (PSTN) *noun* national telephone system, with country and world-wide exchanges, lines and telephone sets that are all interconnected and can be used by the public

publication *noun* **(a)** making something public; ***the publication of the latest trade figures*** **(b)** printed document which is to be sold *or* given to the public; ***he asked the library for a list of government publications; government publications can be bought at special shops; the company specializes in publications for the business reader;*** **official publication** = document published by an official organization, such as a government department; **the company has six business publications** = the company publishes six magazines or newspapers dealing with business matters

publication date *or* **date of publication** *noun* (i) year when a book was published; (ii) day when a publisher says that a book is published (from that day, bookshops may sell the book); (iii) day when a newspaper or magazine is published

publicity *noun* attracting the attention of the public to products or services by mentioning them in the media; **publicity agency** *or* **publicity bureau** = office which organizes publicity for companies who do not have publicity departments; **publicity budget** = money allowed for expenditure on publicity; **publicity campaign** = period when planned publicity takes place; **publicity copy** = text of an advertisement before it is printed; **publicity department** = section of a company which organizes the company's publicity; **publicity expenditure** = money spent on publicity; **publicity manager** = person in charge of a publicity department; **publicity matter** = sheets *or* posters *or* leaflets used for publicity

publicize *verb* to attract people's attention to a product for sale *or* a service *or* an entertainment; ***the campaign is intended to publicize the services of the tourist board; we are trying to publicize our products by advertisements on buses***

publish *verb* to have a document (such as a catalogue *or* book *or* magazine *or* newspaper) written and printed and then sell *or* distribute it to the public; ***the society publishes its list of members annually; the government has not published the figures on which its proposals are based; the company publishes six magazines for the business market; the book was published last week;*** **published price** = price at which a book is published (usually the price which is marked in the publisher's catalogue, or printed on the book, or at any rate, the price listed in the national list of books in print)

publishable *adjective* which can be published; ***the libel lawyers has advised that the book is not publishable in its present form***

publisher *noun* **(a)** company which arranges for books *or* software to be made and sells them to the public, usually through a retail bookseller; **publisher's agreement** = contract between a publisher and the copyright holder *or* author *or* agent *or* another publisher, which lays down the terms under which the publisher will publish the book for the copyright holder; **Publishers Association (PA)** = organization which represents the interests of publishers in Great Britain; **publisher's binding** = edition binding, a binding style where the book is cased, with a plain cloth binding; **publisher's cloth** = cloth used to cover books in publisher's binding; **publisher's reader** = person who reads manuscripts for a publisher and suggests ones which might be worth publishing; **publisher's list** *or* **catalogue** = list of books which a publisher has for sale, both new titles and backlist; **publisher's list price** = price of a book as stated in a publisher's catalogue; **publisher's**

representative = salesman who visits bookshops on behalf of a publisher and persuades the bookshop buyer that a book should be ordered **(b)** *(in a large publishing company)* person in charge of a specialized list **(c) newspaper publisher** = owner of a newspaper

'Publishers Weekly' American weekly magazine, dealing with publishing matters

publishing *noun* the business of printing books *or* newspapers and selling *or* distributing them to the public; **publishing company** *or* **publishing house** = company which publishes books or magazines; **publishing date** = publication date, the date on which a book will be published; **desktop publishing (DTP)** = design, layout and printing of documents using special software, a small computer and a printer; **electronic publishing** = (i) use of desktop publishing packages and laser printers to produce printed matter; (ii) using computers to write and display information (such as viewdata); **professional publishing** = publishing books on law, accountancy, and other professions

'Publishing News' British weekly magazine dealing with publishing matters

pull 1 *noun* **(a)** proof from letterpress **(b) repro pull** = perfect proof ready to be reproduced **2** *verb* **(a)** to make a proof **(b)** not to publish a story in the newspaper, after it has been written *or* typeset

pull away *noun* part of a signature consisting of blank pages which is removed from a book when binding

pull-down menu *noun* menu which can be displayed on the screen at any time by pressing the correct key

pullout *noun* folded insert in a book *or* paper, which is tipped in, and which when opened out makes a large sheet (used for maps, etc.)

pulp 1 *noun* **(a)** material produced from rags or ground wood, mixed with water, used for making paper; **pulp board** *or* **pulp card** = thin board made from paper pulp, used for the cover boards of a book; **woodpulp** = fibrous material made from crushed wood, mixed with water, used to make paper; *see also* CHEMICAL, MECHANICAL **(b) pulp fiction** = cheap fiction which is considered by critics to have no literary value; (NOTE: US English is **dime novels**) **2** *verb* **(a)** to take torn rags *or* ground wood and mix this with water and chemicals to produce smooth pulp for making paper **(b)** to take printed paper *or* waste paper and produce pulp from it for making paper again; ***the unsold copies in the warehouse were sent away to be pulped***

pulping *noun* sending unsold or erroneous printed copies to be pulped

pulpwood *noun* softwood used for making paper

punch 1 *noun* **(a)** device for making the matrix from which type is cast (the punch is a steel stamp with the letter cut into it in relief; this is then pressed into a metal alloy, which becomes the matrix); **punch cutting** = making a punch by cutting the design on it **(b)** device for making holes in punched cards **2** *verb* to make a hole; **punched card** = card with holes in it which a computer can read and store as information; **punched card reader** = device that transforms data on a punched card to a form that can be recognized by a computer; **punched tape** = strip of paper tape that contains holes to represent data, formerly used in phototypesetting, but now replaced by magnetic tapes and disks

punctuate *verb* to add punctuation marks to a text

punctuation *noun* putting special symbols in a written text, to help the reader understand it; **punctuation mark** = printed or written symbol, which cannot be spoken, but which divides up the text and helps to make its meaning clearer

> COMMENT: the main punctuation marks are the question mark and exclamation mark; inverted commas (which show the type of text being written); the comma, full stop, colon and semicolon (which show how the words

are broken up into sequences); the apostrophe (which shows that a letter or word is missing); the dash and hyphen and brackets (which separate or link words)

PUR = POLYURETHANE

pure paper *noun* paper made from woodfree or chemical pulp

put to bed *verb* to make (especially a newspaper) ready for printing

PVA = POLYVINYL ACETATE

PVC = POLYVINYL CHLORIDE plastic material often used for covers of reference books because it can stand a great deal of handling

COMMENT: printing on PVC is not as simple as printing on paper, since PVC is not absorbent. Designs have to be bold, with few details, and thin lines cannot be printed easily. Printing on PVC is usually done by screen printing

Qq

QA = QUERY AUTHOR

qty = QUANTITY

quad 1 *noun* **(a) quad (sheet)** = traditional measurement of a sheet of paper four times as large as a basic sheet, i.e. it is twice as wide and twice as long; **quad royal** = sheet of paper measuring 50 x 40 inches **(b)** (i) piece of metal type which has no character on it, used to give a space between words or characters; (ii) space between characters in computer setting; **em quad** = space printed that is equal in size to an em (the same width as the point size of the type used); **en quad** = space that is half the width of an em quad space **2** *verb* to insert spaces to fill out a line (especially to complete a short line which is left justified, such as a heading); **quad left** = set lines flush to the left margin; **quad right** = set lines flush to the right margin

quadding *noun* insertion of spaces into text to fill out a line

> COMMENT: metric quad paper sizes are (in millimetres): quad crown (768 x 1008), quad large crown (816 x 1056), quad demy (888 x 1128), quad royal (960 x 1272)

quadrant balance *or* **scale** *noun* device used to measure grammage of paper

> COMMENT: a sample of paper 100 x 100mm is taken and placed on the scale; the grammage values are printed on a semicircular scale, the pointer runs across the scale when the piece of paper is spiked on a pin. The readings on the scale give the gsm (i.e. the weight of the piece of paper multiplied by one hundred)

quadrat *noun* quad, a piece of metal type which has no character on it, used to give a space between characters

quadrille *noun* paper ruled in small squares, like graph paper

quadruplicate *noun* **in quadruplicate** = with the original and three copies; ***the invoices are printed in quadruplicate***

quaint characters *noun* old-fashioned ligatures that are no longer used

quality *noun* **(a)** what something is like *or* how good or bad something is; ***there is a market for good quality secondhand computers;*** **high quality** *or* **top quality** = very best quality; ***the firm specializes in high quality four-colour printing;*** **the quality dailies** *or* **weeklies** *or* **Sundays** *or* **the quality press** = newspapers and magazines aiming at a high level of readership **(b) quality control** = checking that the quality of a product is good; **quality controller** = person who checks the quality of a product

quantity *noun* amount *or* number of items; **quantity discount** = discount given to a customer who buys large quantities of goods

QuarkXPress™ page composition software with typographic functions; ***with the addition of extensions QuarkXPress can be built up into a customised production system***

quarter *noun* **(a)** one of four equal parts; **quarter binding** = binding of a cased book, where the spine is covered with one material (such as leather *or* cloth) and the rest of the cover is covered with another material, such as paper; **quarter-bound book** = book with a quarter binding; **quarter leather** = binding where the spine is covered with leather and the rest of the cover with another material; **quarter page folder** = device which folds a sheet of folded paper twice **(b)** period of three months; **first quarter** = period of three months from January to the end of March; **second quarter** = period of three months from April to the end of June; **third quarter** = period of three months from July to the end of September; **fourth quarter** *or* **last quarter** = period of three months from October to the end of the year; **quarter day** = day at the end of a quarter, when rents *or* fees, etc. should be paid

quarterly 1 *adjective & adverb* happening every three months *or* happening four times a year; ***there is a quarterly charge for consultancy; we agreed to pay the royalty quarterly*** *or* ***on a quarterly basis*** **2** *noun* magazine that is published four times a year

quarto *or* **4o** *noun* size of book made by folding a standard sheet of paper twice, to make four leaves or an eight page signature

query 1 *noun* **(a)** question, especially a note asking the author or editor to check the text; **query author (qy** *or* **QA)** = note asking the author to check the text **(b)** question mark **2** *verb* to ask a question about something *or* to suggest that something may be wrong; ***the sub-editor has queried the date given in the index***

question mark *noun* printing and written sign (?) which shows that a question is being asked; (NOTE: in Spanish, two question marks are printed, one upside down at the beginning of the phrase, the second at the end of it)

questionnaire *noun* printed list of questions, especially used in market research; ***to send out a questionnaire to test the opinions of users of the system; to answer*** *or* ***to fill in a questionnaire about holidays abroad***

quick-setting ink *noun* ink which is specially made to set rapidly

QuickTime™ *(in an Apple Macintosh)* graphics routines built into the Macintosh's operating system that allow windows, boxes and graphic objects to be displayed

'Quill and Quire' Canadian magazine dealing with publishing matters

quire *noun* **(a)** 24 or 25 sheets of paper (twenty quires make one ream) **(b)** section of gathered pages

quirewise *adverb* folded sheets which are automatically folded and placed inside each other; **quirewise imposition** = imposition in which sections are imposed to inset one inside the other (also called 'insetted imposition')

> COMMENT: for ordinary writing paper and handmade paper, a ream is 480 sheets, or 20 quires of 24 sheets each. For office paper or printing paper a ream is 500 sheets, or 20 quires of 25 sheets

quit *verb (in computing)* to leave a system *or* a program; ***do not forget to save your text before you quit the system***

quoin 1 *noun* metal wedge which fits into the space between the type and the edge of a chase, and is tightened to fix the metal type in place; **quoin key** = key used to tighten or loosen a quoin **2** *verb* to lock up type; (NOTE: quoin is pronounced 'coin')

quota *noun* fixed amount of something which is allowed; **import quota** = fixed quantity of a particular type of goods which the government allows to be imported; **quota system** = system where imports *or* supplies are regulated by fixing maximum amounts; **to arrange distribution through a quota system** = to arrange distribution by allowing each distributor only a certain number of items

quotation *noun* **(a)** part of a text which is mentioned in another text; **quotation marks** = inverted commas *or* signs printed at the beginning and end of text to show that it has been quoted from another source, or to show the title of something; **single quotation marks** *or* **double quotation marks** = printed signs (' ') and (" "), used to show that a piece of text has been quoted **(b)** estimate of how much something will cost; ***we asked for quotations for supplying 2 tonnes of 80gsm paper; their quotation was much lower than all the others*** **(c) quotations** = special long hollow metal strips, used to fill in blanks in the typeset text

> COMMENT: when setting quotations, it is essential to show clearly where the quotation begins and ends, so as to distinguish it from the text proper. Normally, a quotation consisting of a few words will be put in double quotes; a longer quotation (a paragraph or more) should either be indented or set in a smaller size, or both. A quotation from a poem can be set smaller, or even can be set in italic, provided it is not too long

quote 1 *verb* **(a)** to repeat words used by someone else; to repeat a reference number; ***the author has quoted a whole paragraph from the speech without any acknowledgement; in reply, please quote this number; when querying the invoice, please quote the reference number printed at the top of the statement; he replied, quoting the number of the account;*** **quoted matter** = printed text which is quoted from another text, usually indicated by quotation marks **(b)** to estimate *or* to say what costs may be; ***to quote a price for supplying stationery; their prices are always quoted in dollars; he quoted me a price of £1,026; can you quote for supplying 20,000 envelopes?*** **2** *noun informal* **(a) quotes** = quotation marks; **single quotes** = single inverted commas; **double quotes** = double inverted commas (" "); ***the name of the company should be put in double quotes*** **(b)** quotation from another text; ***have you checked the quotes from the film scenario against the original text?*** **(c)** estimate of how much something will cost; ***to give someone a quote for supplying two tonnes of paper; we have asked for quotes for printing and binding 10,000 copies; their quote was the lowest of three and we always accept the lowest quote***

q.v. *abbreviation for the Latin phrase* quod vide, meaning 'which see', used to indicate a cross-reference

qwerty *or* **QWERTY** *noun* **qwerty keyboard** = English language keyboard for a typewriter *or* computer, where the first letters are Q-W-E-R-T-Y; ***the computer has a normal qwerty keyboard;*** *see also* AZERTY

qy = QUERY

Rr

RA sizes sizes of stock sheets of printing paper which are slightly larger than the comparable A sizes

COMMENT: there are three RA sizes: RA0 (860 x 1220mm), RA1 (610 x 860mm) and RA2 (430 x 610mm); see also SRA sizes, which are larger still

rack *noun* frame to hold items for display; ***card rack; display rack; magazine rack;*** **rack jobber** = wholesaler who sells goods by putting them on racks in retail shops; **rack jobbing** = selling books from racks in supermarkets and newsagents

radiation drying *noun* drying ink by ultra-violet and infra-red radiation; **radiation drying unit** = drying unit fitted to a printing press to dry ink or varnish using UV or IR radiation

radio *noun* medium used for the transmission of speech, sound and data over long distances by radio frequency electromagnetic waves; **radio and TV rights** = rights for the adaptation of a text for broadcasting on radio and TV

rag paper *noun* good-quality paper made from cotton or linen rags; **rag content** = amount of rag in paper (some papers are part woodpulp and part rag); **rag pulp** = pulp from torn rags, which is boiled before being used to make paper

COMMENT: rag paper is less widely made now because it is expensive, and cotton and linen rags are not easy to find; man-made fibres, which are often used in clothing, are not suitable for papermaking

ragged *adjective* not straight *or* with an uneven edge; **ragged left** = printed text with a flush right-hand margin and uneven left-hand margin; **ragged right** = printed text with a flush left-hand margin and uneven right- hand margin; **ragged text** = unjustified text *or* text with a ragged right margin

COMMENT: ragged right setting is quite often used, and in narrow measures makes the setting more even, with no wide gaps between characters or words. It is often used in newspapers and magazines which are set in narrow columns. Ragged left setting is not common

raise *verb* **(a)** to make something higher; **raised bands** = raised strips on the spine of a leather-bound book covering the cords; **raised initial** = stick-up initial, an initial letter set in a larger size than the rest of the text, the letter being on the base line and rising above the ascender line (the opposite of a 'drop initial'); **raised printing** = thermography, printing process which uses heat to produce raised characters (very thick ink is used; this is dusted with powder, then heated to weld it to the paper. The process is often used for letterheads) **(b)** to increase *or* to make higher; ***we are raising all prices by 10% in our new catalogue*** **(c) to raise an invoice** = to write or print out an invoice

RAM = RANDOM ACCESS MEMORY memory that allows access to any location in any order, usually in the form of integrated circuits; **RAM chip** = chip which stores information. allowing random access; **RAM disk** = section of RAM that is made to look like and behave like a high-speed disk drive; (NOTE: there is no plural for RAM, and it often has no article: **512K of RAM; the file is stored in RAM)**

random 1 *adjective* done without making any special choice; **random access** = ability to access immediately memory locations in any order; ***disk drives are random access; magnetic tape is not, it is sequential access memory;*** **random access memory (RAM)** = memory that allows access to any location in any order, usually in the form of integrated circuits; **random access storage** = memory that allows access to any location in any order; **random check** = check on items taken from anywhere within a group without any special choice being made; **random error** = computer error which has no special reason; **random sample** = sample for testing taken without any choice being made; **random sampling** = choosing samples for testing without any special selection **2** *noun* sloping top part of a composing frame

range *verb* to give an even edge to lines of type; **ranged** *or* **ranging numerals** = lining numerals, Arabic figures which are all of even height; **range left** = to align the type with a straight left-hand edge; **range right** = align the text with a straight right-hand edge; *compare* ALIGN (NOTE: US English is **flush left, flush right)**

rare *adjective* not common; ***experienced salesmen are rare these days; it is rare to find a small business with good cash flow;*** **rare books** = relatively modern books which are not in print and are not easy to find

raster *noun* **raster scanning** = system of scanning the whole of a screen with a picture beam which moves down the screen one line or one pixel at a time; **raster graphics** = graphics where the image is built up in lines running across the screen or page; **raster image processor (RIP)** = raster which translates software instructions into an image *or* complete page which is then printed by a printer *or* typesetter

rata *see* PRO RATA

rate *noun* **(a)** money charged for time worked *or* work completed; **all-in rate** = price which covers all items in a purchase (such as delivery, tax and insurance, as well as the goods themselves); **fixed rate** = charge which cannot be changed; **flat rate** = fixed charge, a payment which is the same for everyone; ***a flat-rate increase of 10% on all typesetting costs; we pay a flat rate for typesetting of £10 per page; the keyboarders are paid a flat rate of £2 per thousand;*** **the going rate** = the usual *or* the current rate of payment; **the market rate** = normal price in the market; ***we pay the going rate or the market rate for typists; the going rate for offices is £10 per square foot*** **(b) exchange rate** *or* **rate of exchange** = rate at which one currency is exchanged for another; **to calculate costs on a fixed exchange rate** = to calculate costs on an exchange rate which does not change; **forward rate** = rate for purchase of foreign currency at a fixed price for delivery at a later date; **freight rates** = charges for transporting goods; **letter rate** *or* **parcel rate** = postage (calculated by weight) for sending a letter *or* a parcel **(c)** amount *or* number *or* speed compared with something else; **call rate** = number of calls (per day *or* per week) which a salesman makes on customers; **depreciation rate** = rate at which an asset is depreciated each year in the company accounts; **error rate** = number of mistakes per thousand entries *or* per page; **rate of sales** = speed at which units are sold

rate card *noun* list of charges for advertisements in a newspaper or magazine, or for commercials on TV or radio ⇨APPENDIX

rattle *noun* noise made by paper when it is handled, giving an indication of its stiffness

raw *adjective* in the original state *or* not processed; **raw data** = (i) pieces of information that have not yet been input into a computer system; (ii) data in a database which has to be processed to provide information to the user; **raw materials** = substances which have not been manufactured (such as wool, wood, sand); **raw stock** = paper which is to be coated; **raw tape** = tape without formatting commands

RC paper = RESIN-COATED PAPER

read *verb* to look at printed words and understand them; ***the terms and conditions are printed in very small letters so that they are difficult to read; has the managing director read your report on sales in India? can the OCR read typeset characters?;*** **can the computer read this information?** = can the computer take in this information and understand it or analyse it?; **read only memory (ROM)** = memory device that has data written into it at the time of manufacture, so that its contents can only be read and not changed

readability *noun* being easy *or* pleasant to read; ***the readability of a novel; the readability of a typeface***

readable *adjective* which can be read easily with pleasure; ***the new novel is very readable;*** **machine-readable codes** = sets of signs or letters (such as bar codes, post codes) which can be read and understood by a computer; **the data has to be presented in computer-readable form** = in a form which a computer can read

reader *noun* **(a)** proofreader, person who reads proofs and marks corrections; **reader's marks** = proof correction marks, special marks used to indicate changes (deletions, additions, more space, etc.) ⇨APPENDIX; **reader's proof** = proof sent to a proofreader and marked with his corrections **(b)** person who reads manuscripts for a publisher and advises whether they should be published **(c)** any person who reads books *or* newspapers; ***the new list is aimed at the general reader*** **(d)** educational book with text for students to practise reading **(e)** machine which can read tape *or* machine-readable codes; **reader-printer** = device which reads a microfilm, and then puts out a copy

readership *noun* all the readers of a book *or* newspaper

reading *noun* **(a)** action of reading proofs *or* a manuscript and making comments; **reading copy** = copy of a finished book *or* proof copy of the pages of a book, sent to librarians *or* other publishers who might be interested in buying it **(b)** action of reading books *or* newspapers; **reading list** = list given to a student of books which he or she ought to read; **the reading public** = the members of the public who actually read books **(c)** action of reading printed text; **right-reading film** = film which reads in the normal way, from left to right, when viewed from the emulsion side (as opposed to wrong-reading)

read/write head *noun* device in a disk drive that can read data on a disk or add data to a disk

readvertise *verb* to advertise again; **to readvertise a post** = to put in a second advertisement for a vacant post; ***all the candidates failed the test, so we will just have to readvertise***

readvertisement *noun* second advertisement for a vacant post

ready *adjective* fit to be used *or* to be sold; ***the order will be ready for delivery next week; the driver had to wait because the shipment was not ready;*** **make-ready time** = time to get a machine ready to start production

real time *noun* actions *or* processing time that is of the same order of magnitude as the problem to be solved; **real-time system** = computer system where data is inputted directly into the computer which automatically processes it to produce information which can be used immediately

ream *noun* number of sheets of paper

> COMMENT: for ordinary writing paper and handmade paper, a ream is 480 sheets, or 20 quires of 24 sheets each. For office paper or printing paper a ream is 500 sheets, or 20 quires of 25 sheets

ream-wrapped *adjective* sheets wrapped in parcels of 500

reback *verb* to take the leather back off the spine of an old book and replace it

rebind 1 *noun* action of binding sheets of a book which were not bound when the book was first printed; ***the book is out of stock at the moment, but the rebind should come in***

next week **2** *verb* **(a)** to remove an old binding from a book and replace it with another one; ***the stock of paperback copies have been rebound in PVC*** **(b)** to bind up sheets left over from a previous print and bind order

> COMMENT: rebinding means that the old covers have to be stripped off, new covers attached and the pages trimmed again. At least one or two millimetres will be lost at each of the three trimmed edges

recast *verb* to write (a text) again; ***the author was asked to recast the first chapter in the light of the reader's comments***

recd = RECEIVED

receipt *noun* **(a)** paper showing that money has been paid *or* that something has been received; **receipt book** *or* **book of receipts** = book of blank receipts to be filled in when purchases are made **(b)** act of receiving something; **to acknowledge receipt of a letter** = to write to say that you have received a letter; ***we acknowledge receipt of your letter of the 15th; the publisher never even acknowledged receipt of my manuscript***

record 1 *noun* **(a)** report of something which has happened; ***the chairman signed the minutes as a true record of the last meeting;*** **for the record** *or* **to keep the record straight** = to note something which has been done; **on record** = correctly reported *or* recorded; **off the record** = unofficially *or* in private; ***he made some remarks off the record about the disastrous home sales figures*** **(b) records** = documents which give information; ***the names and addresses of authors are kept in the company's records; we find from our records that our invoice number 1234 has not been paid*** **(c)** description of what has happened in the past; **track record** = success or failure of a company *or* salesman in the past; ***he has a good track record as a salesman; the company has no track record in the computer market*** **(d)** success which is better than anything before; **record sales** *or* **record losses** *or* **record profits** = sales *or* losses *or* profits which are higher than ever before; ***1997 was a record year for the company; sales for 1997 equalled the record of 1990; our top salesman has set a new record for sales per call;*** **we broke our record for June** = we sold more than we have ever sold before in June **2** *verb* **(a)** to make a recording of music *or* speech, etc., on tape or disk; **recording rights** = rights to make a record of a piece of music *or* poetry, etc. **(b)** to note *or* to report; ***the company has recorded another year of increased sales; your complaint has been recorded and will be investigated;*** **recorded delivery** = mail service where the letters are signed for by the person receiving them

record-breaking *adjective* which is better than anything which has happened before; ***we are proud of our record-breaking profits in 1996***

recover *verb* to put a new cover on a book; ***we asked the binder for an estimate for stripping off the old covers and recovering in the new design***

rectification *noun* correction

rectify *verb* to correct something *or* to make something right; ***we will rectify the entry in the next edition of the bibliography***

recto *noun* right hand page of a book (usually given an odd number); **start the text recto** = start the text on a right-hand page; *compare* VERSO

recycle *verb* to take waste material and process it so that it can be used again; **recycled paper** = paper made from waste paper

redraft *verb* to draft again; ***the whole contract had to be redrafted to take in the chairman's amendments***

redraw *verb* to draw again; ***the artwork will have to be redrawn; can the computer redraw the graphics showing the product from the top view***

reduce *verb* **(a)** to make (a photograph *or* a type size) smaller; ***the text will have to be reduced by 10% to fit the format*** **(b)** to make smaller *or* lower; ***we are reducing prices on***

some of our backlist titles to try to clear the stock

reducer *noun* additive which reduces the tacking of ink or varnish

reduction *noun* **(a)** act of reducing; proportion by which something, such as a photograph, is made smaller; ***we need a 25% reduction to fit the halftone in the space;*** **reduction print** = print of a photograph which is smaller than the original **(b)** lowering (of prices, etc.); ***reduction in demand has led to a fall in keyboarding prices; the reduction in printing prices has meant that more printing is being done in the Far East***

redundant *adjective* (data) that can be removed without losing any information

redundant matter *noun* text which is not needed *or* which is too long

reel *noun* large heavy roll of paper used in a web-fed printing press; **reel bogie** *or* **reel truck** = truck which moves reels of paper from the paper store to the printing press; **reel-fed press** = web-fed press, a printing press which takes paper from reels (as opposed to sheet-fed); **reel-stand** = stand for holding a reel of paper at the feed end of a web press; **reel-up** = spool which reels paper in a papermaking machine; **reel width** = the width of the paper on a reel

ref = REFERENCE **cross-ref** = CROSS-REFERENCE

refer *verb* **(a)** to mention *or* to deal with *or* to write about something; ***we refer to your estimate of May 26th; he referred to an article which he had seen in the 'Times'; referring to your letter of June 4th*** **(b)** to direct the reader's attention to another part of the text or to another text; ***the author refers the reader to the index; the bold entries in the index refer to titles mentioned in the text*** **(c)** to pass a problem on to someone else to decide; ***we have referred your complaint to our supplier***

referee *noun* person who can give a report on someone's character *or* ability *or* speed of work, etc.; ***she gave the name of her boss as a referee; when applying please give the names of three referees***

reference *noun* **(a)** action of referring to another text; **references** = list of books or articles, etc., which are referred to in notes; **reference mark** = printing sign * which indicates that the reader should look up the word in a footnote; **reference numbers** = numbers *or* letters which identify a document and make it easier to find when it has been filed; ***our reference: PC/MS 1234; thank you for your letter (reference 1234); please quote this reference in all correspondence; when replying please quote reference 1234*** **(b)** **reference book** = book of information, usually a book such as a dictionary or encyclopaedia in which information is set out in a certain order or classification; **reference library** = library of reference books; **reference publishing** = publishing reference books; **reference publisher** = company which publishes reference books; **the reference section of a bookshop** *or* **library** = part of a bookshop *or* library where reference books are kept (the books in the reference section of a public library cannot be borrowed); **work of reference** = important and well-known reference book; ***it is the standard work of reference on tropical diseases*** **(c)** written report on someone's character *or* ability, etc.; **to ask a company for trade references** *or* **for bank references** = to ask for reports from traders *or* a bank on the company's financial status and reputation; **letter of reference** = letter in which an employer *or* former employer recommends someone for a job; ***he enclosed letters of reference from his two previous employers*** **(d)** person who reports on someone's character *or* ability, etc.; ***to give someone's name as reference; please use me as a reference if you wish***

refiner *noun* machine which takes woodpulp and passes it through rapidly turning rollers to give it certain texture

reflection copy *noun* artwork or photograph which is photographed using reflected light (as opposed to back-lit copy, which is a transparency)

reformat *verb* **(a)** to change the format of a text *or* book; ***the book was reformatted as a B format paperback*** **(b)** to change the page layout of a page on a computer **(c)** to format a disk again (if the disk contains data, the data will be erased)

refresh *verb* **(a)** to update regularly the contents of dynamic RAM by reading and rewriting stored data to ensure data is retained **(b) refresh rate** = number of times every second that the image on a CRT screen is redrawn; **screen refresh** = to update regularly the images on a CRT screen by scanning each pixel with a picture beam to make sure the image is still visible

refusal *noun* **(a)** saying no; **right of first refusal on a text** = right of a publisher to see and offer to publish the next text by an author **(b)** situation where one ink will not print on top of other ink

refuse *verb* to say that you will not do something *or* will not accept something; ***the publisher refused to pay until the printer had replaced the defective copies***

register 1 *noun* **(a)** official list; ***to enter something in a register; to keep a register up to date;*** **companies' register** *or* **register of companies** = list of companies, showing their directors and registered addresses **(b)** large book for recording details (as in a hotel, where guests sign in, or in a registry where deaths are recorded) **(c)** location of data in a computer storage system **(d)** superimposing two or more images correctly; **the text is in register with the colour sections** = the text is correctly aligned with the colour sections; **the type on the back of the sheet is exactly in register with the type on the front** = the two type areas are exactly in line with each other; **the two colours are out of register** = the colours are not correctly positioned one on top of the other; **register marks** = marks (usually crossed lines) at the corners of a film *or* overlay *or* artwork, used to help in lining up the images; **register pins** = pins which go through holes made by a register punch in artwork to help line up the images correctly; **register punch** = punch which makes holes for register pins; **register sheet** = proof which is pulled to see if the register is correct **(d)** *(bookbinding)* thin ribbon attached to the spine of a book, used as a bookmark **2** *verb* **(a)** to write something in an official list; ***to register a trademark*** **(b)** to make sure that different plates printing on the same sheet are correctly aligned (such as the different colours used in colour work)

reglet *noun* thin piece of wood used to make spaces between lines of type

regular *adjective* ordinary *or* standard; **regular edition** = ordinary edition (as opposed to a de luxe edition, cheap edition, book club edition, etc.); **regular size** = ordinary size (smaller than economy size, family size, etc.)

rehyphenation *noun* changing the hyphenation of words in a text after it has been put into a new page format *or* line width

reimpose *verb* to impose pages again

reimposition *noun* changing the imposition of pages, because of different paper size, a different folding machine or the addition of extra pages

> COMMENT: a cased book may need to be reimposed when being made into a perfect bound paperback, since the paperback needs wider gutters to allow for trim

reimpression = REPRINT

reinforced binding *noun* binding which is strengthened at the joints for heavy wear (as in a library) or for a particularly heavy book

reinstate *verb* to put back text which was deleted; ***the frontispiece has been reinstated at the author's insistence***

reissue 1 *noun* publication of a book, which has been out of print for some time, in a new format, sometimes with a new title, treated as a new book **2** *verb* to publish a book, which has been out of print, in a new format, with a newly designed cover, possibly with a new title; ***the three***

biographies were all reissued in the paperback series

reject *verb* to refuse to accept *or* to say that something is not satisfactory; ***the manuscript was rejected by several major publishers, and the author decided to publish it himself;*** **the company rejected the takeover bid** = the directors recommended that the shareholders should not accept the bid

rejection *noun* **(a)** refusal to accept; **rejection slip** = note from a publisher rejecting a manuscript; ***his novel collected twenty-two rejection slips before being published by a small publisher in Wales; the rejection letter contained a lot of useful advice from the publisher's reader*** **(b)** book which is rejected because of an imperfection or defect

rekey *verb* to key text again; ***the entire text had to be rekeyed in Times italic; because of all the author's changes, we decided it would be quicker to rekey the whole text***

relative humidity *noun* the mass of moisture in a given volume of air expressed as a percentage of the moisture required to saturate the same volume of air at a certain temperature

release 1 *noun* **(a)** setting free; **release paper** = special paper (used as backing for sticky labels) which can easily be peeled off when the label is to be used **(b) day release** = arrangement where a company allows a worker to go to college to study for one day each week; ***the junior sales manager is attending a day release course*** **(c) press release** = sheet giving news about something which is sent to newspapers and TV and radio stations so that they can use the information in it; ***the company sent out*** *or* ***issued a press release about the launch of the new TV series*** **(d) new releases** = new records put on the market **2** *verb* **to release dues** = to send off orders which had been piling up while a product was out of stock

relief *noun* **relief block** = printing block where the characters *or* image are higher than the surface, and carry the ink; **relief map** = map which shows how high or low land is by using different colours to indicate height; **relief printing** = printing process in which the ink is held on a raised image such as the metal character in letterpress printing or on a woodcut block

religious *adjective* referring to religion; **religious publishing** = publishing of books about a certain religion, or which are used in religious services; **a religious press** = a publishing company which specializes in religious books; **the religious press** = religious newspapers and magazines

remainder 1 *noun* **(a)** things left behind; ***the remainder of the stock will be sold off at half price*** **(b) remainders** = quite new books which are sold off cheaply because they have not been successful; **remainder house** *or* **remainder merchant** = book dealer who buys unsold new books from publishers at a very low price for resale; **remainder binding** = cheap binding for surplus folded sheets which are sold off through the remainder trade **2** *verb* **to remainder books** = to sell new books off cheaply; ***the shop was full of piles of remaindered books***

remake *verb* to change the layout of a page or pages

remove 1 *verb* to take something away; ***we can remove his name from the mailing list; the author has removed the name of his secretary from the acknowledgements*** **2** *noun* quotation which is printed in smaller type than the rest of the text

renew *verb* to pay to continue a subscription to a magazine or journal

renewal *noun* payment to continue a subscription

renumber *verb* to give new numbers to pages *or* to index cards

reorder 1 *noun* further order for something which has been ordered before; ***the book has only been published ten days and we are already getting reorders;*** **reorder level** = minimum amount of stock of an item (when stock falls to this amount, the item must be reordered) **2** *verb* to place a new order for something; ***we must reorder these paperbacks because the stock level is getting low***

rep 1 *noun* = REPRESENTATIVE ***to hold a reps' meeting; our reps make on average six calls a day;*** **commission rep** = representative who is not paid a salary but receives a commission on sales **2** *verb informal* = REPRESENT ***he reps for two firms on commission***

repack *verb* to pack again; ***the books with the wrong covers had to be repacked and sent back to the binder***

repaginate *verb* to change the numbers of pages; ***because the author added three pages to the first chapter, the whole book had to be repaginated***

repeat 1 *noun* **(a)** second or later printing of an advertisement; second or later broadcasting of a radio or TV programme **(b)** = REPEAT ORDER **2** *verb* **to repeat an order** = to order something again

repeat order *noun* new order for something which has been ordered before; ***the book has been published only ten days and we are already flooded with repeat orders***

repetitive letter *noun* form letter *or* standard letter into which the details of each addressee (such as name and address) are inserted

replace *verb* to put someone *or* something in the place of something else; ***the cost of replacing damaged stock is very high; the photocopier needs replacing; the company will replace any defective copy free of charge; the third paragraph should be deleted and replaced by the new text as shown***

report 1 *noun* **(a)** statement describing what has happened *or* describing a state of affairs; ***the sales manager reads all the reports from the sales team;*** **progress report** = document which describes what progress has been made **(b)** computer printout showing a situation; **aged debtor report** = computer report listing debtors, showing the length of time their payments are overdue; **dues report** = listing of titles and the number of dues which have been logged; **sales report** = computer printout showing the sales over a certain period; **stock report** = computer printout showing the number of copies *or* items in stock **(c) a report in a newspaper** *or* **a newspaper report** = article *or* news item; ***can you confirm the report that the company is planning to buy a chain of bookshops?*** **2** *verb* **(a)** to make a statement describing something; ***the salesmen reported an increased demand for the gardening titles*** **(b)** to produce a computer printout showing a state of affairs; ***the book has been reported out of print; the publisher reports the book as reprinting no date*** **(c) to report to someone** = to be responsible to *or* to be under someone; ***he reports direct to the managing director; the salesmen report to the sales director*** **(d)** to go to a place *or* to attend; ***to report for an interview; please report to our London office for training***

reposition *verb* to put something back in a new position; ***using spray adhesive allows a designer to reposition artwork***

rep finished paper *or* **repped paper** *noun US* paper with a ribbed finish

represent *verb* **(a)** to work for a company, showing goods or services to possible buyers; ***he represents a children's publisher in Scotland; our French distributor represents several other competing firms*** **(b)** to act as a symbol for something; ***the hash sign is used to represent a number in a series***

representation *noun* act of selling goods for a company; ***we offered them exclusive representation in Europe; they have no representation in the USA***

representative 1 *adjective* which is an example of what all others are like; ***we displayed a representative selection of our product range; the sample chosen was not representative of the printrun as a whole*** **2** *noun* **(a) sales representative** *or* **sales rep** = person who works for a company, showing goods or services for sale; ***we have six***

representatives in Europe; they have vacancies for representatives to call on accounts in the north of the country **(b)** company which works for another company, selling their goods; ***we have appointed Smith & Co our exclusive representatives in Europe***

reprint 1 *noun* **(a)** printing of copies of a book after the first printing; ***the mistake on the title page in the first printing will be corrected in the reprint; we ordered a 10,000 copy reprint;*** **reprint house** = publishing company which specializes in reprinting out-of-print titles; **reprint rights** = right of another publisher to reprint a book published and possibly still in print (as in another country *or* in a cheap edition *or* in a book club edition, etc.) **(b)** reprinting of an out-of-print book, or of a very old book, now out of copyright **2** *verb* to print more copies of a document *or* book; ***the book is being reprinted; the book reprinted twice in its first year***

repro = REPRODUCTION **(a)** finished artwork *or* camera-ready copy, ready for filming and printing **(b)** process of achieving this by camerawork or scanning; **repro paper** = coated paper used to produce final high quality proofs for photographic reproduction; **repro proof** *or* **repro pull** = perfect proof ready to be reproduced

reproduce *verb* **(a)** to originate by photography or scanning, from artwork or illustrations, and produce films from which printing plates can be made **(b)** to copy; ***permission to reproduce part of the illustration in our new book***

reproduction *noun* action of copying; **reproduction rights** = right to allow a picture or text to be reproduced in a printed work; **reproduction fee** = fee paid to the copyright owner for permission to reproduce a copyright text or picture; **reproduction proof** *or* **reproduction pull** *or* **repro pull** = (i) perfect proof of text ready for photographic reproduction; (ii) proof taken on fine paper from letterpress or engraving

reprography *noun* producing copies from an original (as photocopies, carbon copies, etc.)

republication *noun* publishing again; ***we are looking at our out-of-print backlist to see if any of the titles are suitable for republication***

republish *verb* to publish again; ***the book has been out of print for some years, but has now been republished in an edition of modern classics***

reputable *adjective* with a good reputation; ***we only use reputable carriers; his father founded a very reputable firm of law publishers***

reputation *noun* opinion of someone *or* something held by other people; ***a printing company with a reputation for quality; he has a reputation for being difficult to negotiate with***

request 1 *noun* asking for something; **on request** = if asked for; ***'catalogues available on request'*** **2** *verb* to ask for; ***I am sending a catalogue as requested***

require *verb* **(a)** to ask for *or* to demand something; ***to require a full explanation of expenditure; the law requires you to submit all documentation to the tax authorities*** **(b)** to need; ***the document requires careful study; to write the program requires a computer specialist***

required hyphen *or* **hard hyphen** *noun* hyphen which is always in a word, even if the word is not split (as in 'all-in price'); *see also* SOFT HYPHEN

requisition *noun* order placed by an institution, such as a college to the college bookstore, asking for books to be ordered for students taking a certain course

resale *noun* selling goods which have been bought; ***the contract forbids resale of the book in the USA***

resale price maintenance (RPM) *noun* system (as in the former Net Book Agreement) where the price for an item is fixed by the manufacturer and the retailer is not allowed to sell it for a lower price

rescreen *verb* to reproduce a screened photograph again, using a new screen angle which does not conflict with the original screen (avoiding a moiré effect)

research 1 *noun* trying to find out facts *or* information; **research assistant** = person who helps a writer by doing research for him or her; **market research** = examining the possible sales of a product and the possible customers for it before it is put on the market; **picture research** = looking for suitable illustrations for a book **2** *verb* to study *or* to try to find out information about something; ***to research the history of the Second World War***

researcher *noun* person who carries out research; **picture researcher** = person who looks for suitable illustrations to be used in a book *or* magazine *or* TV documentary, etc.

reserve *verb* to keep for a time until needed; ***the library will reserve a book for a borrower for ten days;*** **all rights reserved** = note placed on the imprint page of a book, showing that the publisher holds all rights in the book

reset *verb* **(a)** to typeset again; ***there are so many literals the whole index will have to be reset; the book has been completely reset in a bolder typeface*** **(b)** to set a register *or* counter to its initial state; ***when it reaches 999 this counter resets to zero***

resetting *noun* typesetting again

resident font *noun* font data which is always present in a printer *or* device and which does not have to be downloaded

residual rights *or* **residuals** *noun* **(a)** rights which are held by an author, which have not been sold to a publisher **(b)** rights held in recorded material by the actors or musicians who performed it (giving payments when the material is reused, as in the case of a repeat of a TV programme)

resin *noun* sticky oil which comes from some types of conifer, used both in papermaking and in ink production; **resin-coated paper** *or* **RC paper** = paper coated with resin, used for photographic and reproduction use

resist *noun* coating on a printing plate which protects part of the plate from acid

resolution *noun* (i) clearness of a photograph or other graphic image; (ii) number of pixels that a screen *or* printer can display per unit area (measured in dots per inch (dpi)); ***the resolution of most personal computer screens is not much more than 70 dpi (dots per inch);*** **graphic display resolution** = number of pixels that a computer is able to display on the screen; **high resolution (hi-res)** = ability to display *or* detect a very large number of pixels per unit area; **low resolution (low-res)** = ability to display preset shapes on the screen rather than individual pixels

resticker *verb* to print new stickers and attach them to stock (usually to change the price)

restock *verb* to order more stock; ***to restock after the Christmas selling period***

restocking *noun* ordering more stock

restraint *noun* control; **restraint of trade** = (i) situation where a worker is not allowed to use his knowledge in another company if he changes jobs; (ii) attempt by companies to fix prices *or* create monopolies *or* reduce competition, which could affect free trade

restrict *verb* to limit *or* to impose controls on; ***the contract restricts our market to the UK only;*** **to sell into a restricted market** = to sell goods into a market where the supplier has agreed to limit sales to avoid competition

restrictive *adjective* which limits; **restrictive trade practices** = arrangement between companies to fix prices *or* to share the market, etc.

resume *verb* to start again; ***the magazine has resumed publication***

résumé *noun* **(a)** summary of a text; ***a résumé of the planned biography is attached to this proposal*** **(b)** *US* summary of a person's life story with details of education and work experience; (NOTE: GB English is **curriculum vitae**)

resumption *noun* starting again; **we expect an early resumption of negotiations** = we expect negotiations will start again soon

retail 1 *noun* sale of small quantities of goods to ordinary customers; **retail bookshop** = bookshop which sells to the general public; **retail bookseller** = bookseller who buys books at a discount from publishers and sells them at the full price to the public; **retail price** = full price paid by a customer in a shop; **retail price index** = index showing how prices of retail goods have risen over a period of time; **retail price maintenance** = legal agreement (such as the former Net Book Agreement) between producers and retailers, that the retailer cannot sell an item at a lower price than the price fixed by the producer; **retail shop** *or* **retail outlet** = shop which sells goods to the general public; **the retail trade** = all people *or* businesses selling goods retail; **stock with a retail value of £500,000** = stock which would sell for £500,000 if sold in a bookshop **2** *verb* **(a) to retail goods** = to sell goods direct to the public **(b)** to sell for a price; **these books retail at** *or* **for £9.25p** = the retail price of these books is £9.25p

retailer *noun* person who runs a retail business, selling goods direct to the public

retailing *noun* selling of full price goods to the public

retain *verb* **(a)** to keep; ***the author has retained film rights in the book*** **(b) to retain a lawyer to act for a company** = to agree with a lawyer that he will act for you (and pay him a fee in advance)

retainer *noun* money paid in advance to someone so that he will work for you, and not for someone else; ***we pay him a retainer of £1,000***

reticulation *noun* effect caused by wet ink drying on a previously inked surface, where the second inking does not dry properly but gives a spotted result

retouch *verb* to paint over marks on a film, photograph or illustration by hand or by electronic means, to make it clearer or to change the detail; ***I retouched the scratch mark on the last print; the artwork for the line drawings needs retouching in places; the picture needs some retouching to take out part of the crowd***

retoucher *noun* person who retouches

retouching *noun* action of changing an illustration or film by hand to make it clearer or to change the detail in some way

retransfer *noun* image taken from a lithographic plate to make a duplicate plate; *see also* TRANSFER

retree *noun* damaged sheets of paper sold off cheaply

retrieval *noun* getting back; **data retrieval** *or* **information retrieval** = getting information from the data stored in a computer; **retrieval system** = system which allows information to be retrieved

retrieve *verb* to get back (information) which is stored in a computer; ***all of the information was accidentally wiped off the computer so we cannot retrieve our sales figures for the last month***

return 1 *noun* **(a)** sending back; **return address** = address to send something back to; **these goods are all on sale or return** = if the retailer does not sell them, he sends them back to the supplier, and pays only for the items sold **(b) returns** = books *or* magazines *or* newspapers which have not been sold and which are sent back to the supplier; ***paperback returns are running at over 20% in the first part of the year, as booksellers are destocking;*** **returns level** *or* **level of returns** = the number of books returned to the publisher by booksellers, shown as a percentage of the quantity originally sold; **returns policy** = policy adopted by a publisher on allowing booksellers to send back unsold stock for credit; **returns provision** = provision in a publishing agreement showing how returns are to be treated when calculating author's royalties **(c)** profit *or* income from money invested; **return on investment (ROI)** *or* **on capital** = profit shown as a percentage of money invested **(d) official return** = official report; **to make a return to the tax office** *or* **to make an income tax return** = to send a statement of income to the tax office; **to fill in a VAT return** = to complete the form showing VAT receipts and expenditure; **stock return** = details which a printer supplies to a publisher showing the stocks he holds of books or printed sheets; **nil return** = report showing no sales *or* income *or* tax etc.; **daily** *or* **weekly** *or* **quarterly sales return** = report of sales made each day *or* week *or* quarter **(e)** key on a keyboard used to indicate that all the required data has been entered; ***you type in your name and code number then press return*** **2** *verb* **(a)** to send back; ***to return unsold stock to the wholesaler; to return a letter to sender*** **(b)** to make a statement; ***to return income of £15,000 to the tax authorities***

> COMMENT: publishers would like to discourage returns, but in most cases, they have to accept that a certain proportion of books will not sell, and therefore will be returned by the booksellers. The main concern of the publisher is to limit the returns to a manageable proportion of the original printing. A publisher knows that if he refuses to accept returns, the bookseller may refuse to subscribe copies of further new books published by him. In contracts, returns may be provided for in two ways: in a publishing agreement, the publisher may hold back royalties due to cover the possibility of books being returned unsold by the bookseller, after having been sold to the bookseller by the publisher (this is called the 'returns provision'); in an agency agreement, there is normally a clause dealing with what happens to the stock held by the agent at the end of the agreement (usually, the agent will have to pay for the carriage back to the publisher if the agent terminates the agreement, but the publisher will pay if he terminates the agreement)

retype *verb* to type again; ***the manuscript had to be retyped, as the corrections were illegible***

reversal *noun* **(a)** (i) turning in the opposite direction; (ii) reproduction, changing right to left, positive to negative or black to white; **reversal film** = photographic film with a positive image; (NOTE: often called **slide** *or* **transparency film**) **(b)** change from being profitable to unprofitable; ***the company suffered a reversal in the Far East***

reverse 1 *adjective* opposite *or* in the opposite direction; **reverse characters** = characters which are displayed in the opposite way to other characters for emphasis (as black on white *or* white on black, when other characters are the opposite); **reverse indent** = hanging indent, a type of indentation, where the first line is full out and the rest of the paragraph is indented; **listed in reverse order** = listed in order starting at the last (or smallest, or last in the alphabet); *(of a film)* **reverse reading** = reading from right to left when viewed from the emulsion side (so that when printed it will be the right way round) **2** *noun* opposite side of a piece of paper, also called the verso; ***bibliographic details are usually printed on the reverse of the title page*** **3** *verb* to change something so that it is the other way round (one can reverse black to white, left to right or positive to negative); **reverse left to right** *or* **reverse L to R** = change the picture so that the right side becomes the left (i.e. as a mirror image); **to reverse out** = to make a black image appear as white out of black or out of a colour; the white area may then be filled in with another colour; ***the title is reversed out of the photograph of the house***

reversible *adjective* which can go backwards; **reversible printing unit** = printing unit which can print with the web running in either direction

reversion *noun* return of property to an original owner; **reversion of copyright** =

return of rights to the author if the publisher fails to keep the book in print; **reversion clause** = clause in a publishing agreement which allows for the reversion of copyright after a period of time, or if the publisher allows the book to go out of print

reversionary *adjective* (property, such as a copyright) which passes to another owner on the death of the present one

revert *verb (of property)* to go back to its original owner; ***the rights revert to the illustrator after ten years***

review 1 *noun* **(a)** written comments on a book which are published in a newspaper *or* magazine; ***the book has had some very good reviews;*** **book reviews page** = special page of a newspaper where new books are reviewed; **review copy** = copy of a book sent to a newspaper asking them to review it; **review list** = list of people *or* newspapers to whom copies of books are sent for review; **review slip** = note sent with a review copy, giving information about the book (author, price, publisher, etc.) and a mention of the publication date (when reviews are supposed to appear) **(b)** magazine *or* monthly or weekly journal **2** *verb* **(a)** to read a book and write comments about it in a magazine *or* newspaper; ***the book has been extremely well reviewed*** **(b)** to examine something generally; ***the price list will be reviewed at the end of the year; the company has decided to review freelance payments in the light of the rising cost of living;*** **to review discounts** = to look at discounts offered to decide whether to change them; **to review salaries** = to look at all salaries in a company to decide on increases

reviewer *noun* person who reviews books

revise 1 *noun* proof after corrections have been made; ***the publisher sent back the revises with yet another mass of author's corrections*** **2** *verb* to change something which has been written *or* calculated *or* planned; ***the revised version has no mistakes; sales forecasts are revised annually;*** **new and revised edition** = new edition of a text which has been corrected; **revised proofs** = proofs to which corrections have been made

reviser *noun* person who revises a text

revision *noun* act of revising; ***the book has had a thorough revision to bring it up to date***

rewrite 1 *verb* to write a text again, making changes; ***the text has been rewritten twice; the libel lawyer said the book would need complete rewriting to make it publishable*** **2** *noun* act of writing something again; ***the chapter is in its second rewrite***

RGB = RED, GREEN, BLUE **(a)** colour separation using the primary colours **(b)** the three colour picture beams used in a colour CRT; *compare* CMYK

RGB display *or* **monitor** *noun* high-definition monitor system that uses three separate input signals controlling red, green and blue colour picture beams

RI = REISSUE

ribbon *noun* long thin flat piece of material; ***printer ribbons*** *or* ***typewriter ribbons***

rider *noun* **(a)** additional clause; ***to add a rider to a contract*** **(b) rider rollers** = additional rollers used to maintain pressure on the paper as it is being wound onto a reel

right 1 *adjective* not left; ***the credits are on the right side of the page;*** **right justify** = to align the right margin so that the text is straight; **right justification** = aligning the text and spacing characters so that the right margin is straight **2** *noun* legal title to something; ***right of renewal of a contract; she has a right to the property; he has no right to the patent; the staff have a right to know how the company is doing***

right-angled *adjective* which is at right angles to something; **right-angled fold** *or* **right-angle fold** = fold of paper which is at right angles to the one before (as opposed to parallel folds)

rightful *adjective* legally correct; **rightful owner** = legal owner

right-hand *adjective* belonging to the right side; ***the credit side is the right-hand column in the accounts; he keeps the address list in the right-hand drawer of his desk;*** **right-hand page** = recto, the right page of a double page spread, always with an odd folio; ***begin each chapter on a right-hand page; right-hand pages should have odd folio numbers***

right-reading *adjective* film *or* text which reads from left to right, when viewed from the emulsion side (as opposed to wrong-reading)

rights *noun* legal right to publish a book, extracts from a text, pictures, maps, etc.; **book club rights** = right to publish a book in a book club edition; **foreign rights** = legal right to sell a book in a foreign country or in a translation; **hardback rights** = right to publish a hardback edition of a book which was originally published as a paperback; **paperback rights** = right to publish a paperback edition of a book which was previously published as a hardback; **serial rights** = right to reproduce a book chapter by chapter in a magazine or newspaper over a period of time; **subsidiary rights** = right to adapt the book (for film *or* TV *or* into a foreign language), or to serialize it in a magazine; **volume rights** = right to publish a text as a book during its term of copyright (either in the original edition or in cheap paperback versions, or by licensing the right to publish it to another publisher); **all rights reserved** = note placed on the imprint page of a book, showing that the publisher holds all rights in the book; **rights and permissions department** = department in a publishing company which deals with rights to reproduce sections of copyright material, and with other copyright matters; **rights manager** = person in charge of a rights department

Rinco process *noun* process of making gravure positives by photographing a proof of white letters on a black background

ring binder *noun* binder made of two hard covers with a ring attachment into which papers can be put, with holes punched in each sheet of paper to slip over the metal rings

ring binding *noun* the binding of loose sheets in a ring binder

RIP (a) = REST IN PROPORTION printing instruction to indicate that all the material is to be reduced *or* enlarged in the same proportion **(b)** = RASTER IMAGE PROCESSOR raster which translates software instructions into an image *or* complete page which is then printed by a printer *or* imagesetter

rise 1 *noun* increase *or* becoming higher; ***the rise in the price of paper has increased manufacturing costs by 10%*** **2** *verb* to move upwards *or* to become higher; ***prices are rising faster than inflation; interest rates have risen to 15%;*** **rising space** *or* **rising type** = defect in locking the forme, which makes the type or spaces rise above the normal height

river *noun* long white space running down a printed page, caused when wide spacing occurs between words on every line

ROB = RUN OF BOOK

roe chlorination number *noun* measurement of how much chlorine a sample of paper pulp will absorb, thus showing how easily it can be bleached

ROI = RETURN ON INVESTMENT

roll *noun* **(a)** something which has been turned over and over to wrap round itself; ***the desk calculator uses a roll of paper;*** **roll-wrapped** = magazine which is rolled up before being wrapped for mailing **(b)** heavy brass roller used to press a continuous design on the flat cover of a book

roller *noun* round metal bar, used in a printing press to guide the paper through the machine

rolling headers *noun* titles *or* headers of (teletext) pages displayed as they are received

rolling plan *noun* plan which runs for a period of time and is updated regularly for the same period

ROM = READ ONLY MEMORY **CD-ROM** = (compact disc-ROM) small plastic disc that is used as a high capacity ROM device; data is stored in binary form etched on the surface which is then read by a laser; **ROM cartridge** = software stored in a ROM mounted in a cartridge that can be easily plugged into a computer; (NOTE: there is no plural for ROM, and it is often used without the article: **the file is stored in ROM**)

rom = ROMAN

roman[1] *noun* ordinary upright typeface, neither italic nor bold; ***the text is set in Times Roman;*** **sloped roman** = form of italic found in dot-matrix printers, where the characters are roman and have been made to slope to the side by the computer (as opposed to true italic which is a specially designed face of a certain font); (NOTE: the word **roman** is also sometimes used to mean **sans-serif type**)

> COMMENT: roman characters were developed in Italy in the late 15th century, and have become the most widely used of the type styles. It is generally believed that roman characters are easier to read than either italic or bold, possibly because people are more accustomed to roman than to other faces. In the sixteenth century, italic was just as common as roman for continuous text, and for several centuries black letter type was widely used for all printing, especially in Germany

roman[2] *noun* French word meaning 'novel'; **roman à clef** = novel with characters drawn from real life (where the reader and critics usually try to find out who the characters are based on)

Roman *adjective* referring to ancient Italy, and especially to the Latin script; **the Roman alphabet** *or* **Latin alphabet** = (i) alphabet used for Latin, with 21 characters (no j, u, w, y or z); (ii) modern European alphabet with 26 letters, used in most European languages

Romanization *noun* transliterating a non-Western script into Roman characters

Romanize *verb* to transliterate a non-Western script into Roman characters; ***a romanized version of Chinese***

roman numerals *or* **roman figures** *noun* figures written I, II, III, IV, or i, ii, iii, iv, etc. (as opposed to Arabic numerals such as 1, 2, 3, 4)

ROP = RUN OF PAPER

rotary *adjective* which turns round; **rotary machine** *or* **rotary press** = printing press whose printing plate is curved and attached to a cylinder; **rotary printing** = printing process using a curved plate attached to a cylinder, which prints onto the paper as it lies flat; **rotary strainer** = large round cylinder with holes in it, which turns round in the vat of stock, removing large particles from it

rotogravure *noun* web-fed gravure printing on a rotary press, used particularly for colour printing of long runs, such as catalogues or magazines

rough 1 *adjective* **(a)** approximate *or* not very accurate; **rough calculation** *or* **rough estimate** = approximate answer **(b)** not finished; **rough copy** = draft of a document which will have changes made to it before it is complete; **rough draft** *or* **rough sketch** = sketch showing how the finished layout will look; **rough proof** = proof which shows in general how the layout looks, used to indicate changes to the layout; **rough trimmed** = art book whose pages are not all trimmed to the same measure (i.e., where the excessively long or wide pages only are trimmed) **2** *noun* rough sketch of artwork; ***the designer showed some roughs for the main double-page spread***

rough out *verb* to make a draft *or* a general design; ***he roughed out some sketches for the covers***

round 1 *adjective* circular; **round brackets** = parentheses, printing signs used to show that part of the text is separated from the rest **2** *verb* to make the spine of a book round;

round and back *or* **rounding and backing** = process in binding where the book is given a rounded spine and a concave foredge, also giving the book a hinge; **book with a rounded back** = book with a convex spine

rout *verb* to cut away the blank parts of a plate so that there is no chance of their printing by accident

routing *noun* cutting away redundant blank parts from a plate

row *noun* (i) line of printed *or* displayed characters; (ii) horizontal line on a punched card; ***the figures are presented in rows, not in columns; each entry is separated by a row of dots;*** **row of dots** = series of dots printed one after the other, used to indicate that something is missing or to lead the eye across the page

ROW = RUN OF WEEK

royal *adjective* traditional size of book and paper (broadside is 25 x 20 inches)

> COMMENT: the metric royal paper sizes are: royal octavo (234 x 156mm), royal quarto (312 x 237mm); the quad royal sheet is (1272 x 960mm)

royalty *noun* money paid to a writer for the right to use his property (usually a certain percentage of sales, or a certain amount per sale); **royalty cheque** = cheque covering royalties for a certain period; **royalty clerk** = clerk in a publisher's office who calculates the royalties due to authors; **royalty statement** = printed statement from a publisher showing how much royalty is due to an author; **sliding royalty** = royalty where the percentage increases with the number of copies sold

> COMMENT: royalties can vary considerably. An established author may receive 10% of the list price on hardback sales and 15% for paperback sales. Royalties can be based on the list price (i.e., the price of the book before it is discounted to the bookshop), or on the receipts, which are the money received by the publisher from the bookshop. It is common to pay a royalty on receipts in the case of sales overseas, since they are usually at very high discounts. Royalty statements will normally show the numbers of copies sold in various markets, together with the list price and the discounted receipts. In Scandinavia (but not in the UK) it is normal for the author to insist on being told the quantity of copies printed, as this will indicate the numbers given away for review or as specimen copies. In Russia, royalties are not based on sales, but on the size of the book: a royalty would be X roubles per 1000 characters or per 10 pages 'signature'. In the UK, sliding royalties are common on paperbacks, where the author gets an increased royalty as the quantity sold increases. In Russia, the opposite is the case, where the author gets a smaller percentage royalty from reprints

RP = REPRINTING report made by a publisher to a bookseller who has ordered a book which is currently being reprinted; **RP/ND** = REPRINTING/NO DATE report from a publisher showing that a book will be reprinted, but no date can be given for copies being available (usually this indicates that the book is out of stock, but the publisher is considering a reprint and waiting for sufficient dues to build up before deciding on the reprint quantity); **RPUC** = REPRINT UNDER CONSIDERATION report used by publishers to encourage bookshops to order out-of-print titles, and so record dues; when enough dues are recorded the reprint may go ahead

RPM = RESALE PRICE MAINTENANCE

RRP = RECOMMENDED RETAIL PRICE

RS-232C EIA approved standard used in serial data transmission, covering voltage and control signals

RTF = RICH TEXT FORMAT text file format that includes text commands that describe the page, type, font and formatting; ***the RTF format allows formatted pages to be exchanged between different word processing software***

rub *verb* to damage by repeated movement of one surface on another; **to rub out** = to erase, to remove pencil notes with a rubber; **rub resistance** = ability of a printed surface not to be damaged by rubbing (an important factor in printing packaging material)

rubber *noun* **(a)** elastic material from the juice of a tree; **rubber blanket** = rubber sheet which goes round the cylinder in an offset press and takes the image from the cylinder to be printed on the paper **(b)** eraser, material used to remove pencil marks

rubilith *noun* red masking film used for photographic masking

rubric *noun* heading of a book chapter *or* section, printed in red

ruby *noun* old printing size, similar to 5 point; (NOTE: US English is **agate**)

rule 1 *noun* (i) long thin continuous line in printing; (ii) strip of metal of type height used in letterpress for printing lines; ***the border round the illustration is a thin rule;*** **em rule** = dash as long as an em, used to show that words are separated; **en rule** = dash as long as an en, used to show that words are joined **2** *verb* to make a thin line; **ruled paper** = paper with lines printed on it

ruler *noun* tool with a straight edge, used for measuring or drawing straight lines; designers and typographers use steel rulers with measurements in millimetres, inches and picas

ruling *noun* making lines on paper, by pen ruling or disk ruling

run 1 *noun* **(a)** making a machine work; **a cheque run** = series of cheques processed through a computer; **a computer run** = period of work of a computer; **test run** = trial made on a machine; **run of book (ROB)** *or* **run of paper (ROP)** = advertiser's order to the advertising department of a publication in which he buys space at the basic rate without specifying the position in which the advertisement should appear (the customer leaves the layout department to position the advertisement where it fits best); **run of week (ROW)** = advertiser's order to the advertising department of a publication in which he buys space at the basic rate and does not specify in which issue the advertisement will appear **(b)** material produced by a machine (such as a batch of paper produced by a papermaking machine, a series of printed sheets from a printing press, or a series of bound books from a bindery); **printrun** *or* *US* **pressrun** = number of copies of a book printed at one time **2** *verb* **(a)** to print **(b)** to work a machine; ***do not run the photocopier for more than four hours at a time; the computer was running invoices all night***

run around *or* **run round 1** *noun* type which is not set to the full width but goes round an illustration **2** *verb* to change the layout of text so that it goes round an illustration; ***run the blurb text round the photograph of the author***

run back *verb US* to move text from the beginning of one line back to the end of the previous line *or* from the top of one page back to the bottom of the previous page; (NOTE: GB English is **take back**)

run down *verb US* to move text from the end of one line to the beginning of the next line *or* from the bottom of one page to the top of the next page; (NOTE: GB English is **take over**)

run in *verb US* = RUN ON

runnability *noun* ability of paper to run easily through a printing press

runner *noun* small line number printed in the margin of a text

running *noun* **(a)** **running foot** = line of print which appears at the foot of each page; **running headline** *or* **running head** = headline which runs from page to page throughout a book, usually the title or a chapter title, but in dictionaries, directories and encyclopaedias it is usually the first and last headwords on each page (running heads help the reader to find his place in the text); **running on** = printing sheets after the machine has been made ready; **running**

sheet = printed sheet taken from the machine at the beginning of a print run so as to check if it is printing correctly; **running text** = main text of a book which continues over the pages, in which notes, illustrations etc., have only a set limited position; **running total** = total carried from one column of figures to the next **(b) running costs** *or* **running expenses** *or* **costs of running a business** = money spent on the day-to-day cost of keeping a business going

> COMMENT: In book production, running or variable costs are all the costs which vary with the printrun (paper, printing and binding costs); fixed or plant costs include typesetting, reproduction, editorial costs

run off *verb* to print rapidly; ***they run off six hundred leaflets before lunch***

run on *verb* **(a)** to print more sheets after the first number have been printed; **run-on price** = price for the extra sheets run on after the main quantity has been printed; ***can you quote for 5,000 print run and 1,000 run on? we decided to run on 3,000 copies to the first printing*** **(b)** to make the text continue without a break, or without a line break; ***the quotation should run on from the line above;*** **run on chapter** = chapter which does not start a new page; (NOTE: in this sense, US English is **run in**)

run-out *noun* bromide produced by a phototypesetter

run out of *verb* to have nothing left *or* to use up all the stock; ***we have run out of headed notepaper; the laser printer has run out of paper***

runover *noun US* block of text which has been reset

run over *verb* to allow text to go onto the next line *or* page; ***the last two lines of the quotation can run over onto the following page***

run round *verb see* RUN AROUND

run through *adjective* (rule) which goes right across the sheet of paper

rush 1 *noun* **(a)** doing something fast; **rush job** = job which has to be done fast; **rush order** = order which has to be supplied fast **(b) rushes** = positive cinema or video film which is printed from the negatives, and which has not been edited **2** *verb* to make something go fast; ***to rush an order through the factory; to rush a shipment to Africa;***

Ss

saddle *noun* device on which an unbound booklet is placed to be stitched

saddle-stitched *adjective* bound with saddle-stitching

saddle-stitcher *noun* machine for saddle-stitching

saddle-stitching *noun* binding where the signature is stitched through the middle of the fold, usually with wire, usually for small books up to 96 pages maximum; **saddle-wire stitching** = saddle-stitching using metal wire, like staples

safe *adjective* out of danger; **keep the documents in a safe place** = in a place where they cannot be stolen or destroyed; **see-safe** = agreement where the publisher who has sold books to a bookseller will give credit for unsold books at the end of a period under certain conditions (such as against an order for more stock of other titles); ***we bought the stock see-safe***

sale *noun* **(a)** act of selling *or* of giving an item in exchange for money; **cash sale** = selling something for cash; **credit card sale** = selling something for credit, using a credit card; **sale or return** = system where the retailer sends stock back if it is not sold, and receives credit from the supplier for unsold items; ***we have taken 400 copies on sale or return;*** **conditions of sale** = agreed ways in which a sale takes place (such as discounts and credit terms) **(b) sales campaign** = planned work to achieve higher sales; **sales conference** *or* **sales meeting** = meeting of sales managers, representatives, publicity staff, etc., to discuss results and future sales plans; **cost of sales** = all the costs of a product sold, including manufacturing costs and the staff costs of the production department; **sales department** = section of a company which deals with selling the company's products; **domestic sales** *or* **home sales** = sales in the home market; **sales drive** = vigorous work to increase sales; **sales executive** = person in a company in charge of sales to certain clients; **sales figures** = total sales, or sales broken down by category; **sales force** = group of salesmen; **sales forecast** = calculation of future sales; **sales literature** = printed information (such as leaflets, prospectuses) which helps sales; **sales manager** = person in charge of a sales department; **sales plan** = plan for marketing a book; **sales promotion** = sales techniques aimed at increasing sales, such as free gifts and competitions; **sales representative** = person who visits customers on behalf of a company and tries to persuade them to buy goods

salesman *noun* **(a)** man who sells goods (such as encyclopaedias) to members of the public; **door-to-door salesman** = man who goes from one house to the next, asking people to buy something **(b)** person who represents a company, selling its products or services to retail shops; ***we have six salesmen calling on accounts in central London***

Salon du Livre book fair in a French-speaking country (such as the Paris Salon du Livre)

same size (s/s) *noun* instruction on artwork, showing that it has to be kept the same size and not reduced or enlarged

samizdat *noun* publishing carried on by private individuals or groups in a country where the state has a monopoly of publishing and where publishing is strictly censored

COMMENT: originally applied to Russia ('samizdat' is an abbreviated form of the Russian for 'do-it-yourself-publishing'); the term is now used for any country. See also UNDERGROUND

sample *noun* specimen, a small part of an item which is used to show what the whole item is like; ***ask the paper merchant to send us a sample of the paper*** *or* ***a paper sample;*** **sample book** *or* **book of samples** = book showing samples of different types of cloth *or* paper, etc.; **sample cover** = proof of a cover of a book, used as sales material; **sample pages** = proof of pages of a book, showing the layout and part of the text, used as sales material

sand trap *noun* set of bars in a trough which trap heavy particles of grit which may have got into the pulp before it goes into the papermaking process

sans *or* **sans-serif** *or* **sanserif** *noun* typeface without serifs (the decorative strokes at the ends of the characters); commonly used sans faces are Univers, Helvetica and Futura; (NOTE: often simply called **sans: the headwords are set in a 9pt sans face**)

COMMENT: sans faces are less easy to read than seriffed faces (see comment at SERIF) and they are rarely used for continuous text, although some magazines use them for text matter. Nevertheless, legibility is not always what the typographer is aiming for; immediate recognizability of a word is possibly easier with sans faces, and this is why they are commonly used for road signs and other public notices. Sans faces are not as common in the USA as in Europe

save *verb* **(a)** not to waste *or* to use less; **to save a line** = to take back text so as to reduce the lines by one **(b)** to store data on a computer disk; ***do not forget to save your files when you have finished keyboarding them***

saveall *noun* device in a paper mill to save useful fibres from the white water drained out of pulp

sawing *noun* cutting notches in the sewn signatures for cords to lie in when hand binding

SBN *see* ISBN

sc (a) = SMALL CAPS instruction to the compositor to set text in small capitals, indicated by the copy editor on the MS with two lines under the text **(b)** = SINGLE COLUMN

s/c = SUPERCALENDERED

scale 1 *noun* **(a)** relationship between the dimensions of an object and the dimensions of a drawing or model or map which represents it; **map drawn to scale of 1cm to the kilometre** = map on which a distance of 1 centimetre equals 1 kilometre on the ground; **the illustrations are drawn to scale** = the various parts of the thing illustrated have the same relationship to each other as they do in reality; **scale drawing** = drawing which is done to scale; **type scale** = special ruler used by printers and production staff, showing width in ems and points, used for calculating the width of a line or the depth of a page; (NOTE: US English is **line gauge**) **(b)** system which is graded into various levels; **scale of charges** *or* **scale of prices** = list showing various prices; **sliding scale of royalties** = system, where the percentage royalty changes according to the number of copies sold **2** *verb* **(a)** (i) to indicate on artwork how it should be reduced or enlarged; (ii) to calculate how much an illustration should be enlarged or reduced to fit **(b) to scale down** *or* **to scale up** = to make smaller *or* bigger in proportion

scale out *verb* to show how many copies each store in a chain will take, according to a system based on the size of the shop

scale-out *noun* system of ordering different numbers of copies for different stores in a chain

scalpel *noun* very sharp knife, used by designers when cutting artwork or film

scan 1 *noun* examination of an image *or* object to obtain data; **scan plate** = engraved printing plate made by electronic photoengraving **2** *verb* to produce data from the shape *or* state of an object *or* drawing, by examining the image and capturing it as computer data; ***he scanned the map for Teddington; the facsimile machine scans the picture and converts this to digital form before transmission; the machine scans at up to 300 dpi resolution;*** **scan area** = section of an image read by a scanner

scanner *noun* electronic device that scans, especially a device that scans original material and converts it to computer data; **flat-bed scanner** = device with a flat sheet of glass on which the image *or* photograph *or* document is placed; the scan head moves below the glass and converts the image into data which can be manipulated by a computer; **image scanner** = input device that converts documents *or* drawings *or* photographs into digitized machine-readable form; **optical scanner** = equipment that converts an image into electrical signals which can be stored in and displayed on a computer

> COMMENT: a scanner can be a device using photoelectric cells as in an image digitizer, or a device that samples data from a process. One type of scanner reads the bar code on the product label using a laser beam and photodiode; another can read text and by recognizing characters, stores them as data on a computer; yet another type will scan colour originals and carry out colour separations

scanning *noun* **(a)** action of examining and producing data from the shape of an object *or* drawing; **scanning device** = device that allows micrographic images to be selected rapidly from a reel of film; **scanning error** = error introduced while scanning an image; **scanning rate** = time taken to scan one line *or* image; **scanning resolution** = ability of a scanner to register small pixels (the usual resolution is 300 dpi); **scanning speed** = the speed with which a line *or* image is scanned; ***throughput is 1.3 inches per second scanning speed; its scanning speed is 9.9 seconds for an 8.5 x 11 inch document*** **(b)** carrying out colour separations electronically

scatter proof *noun* proof showing several illustrations, printed together on the same sheet, and not as they will appear in the final page layout

scenario *noun* (i) screenplay, the text of the dialogue for a film; (ii) summary of the plot of a play or film

schedule *noun* **(a)** timetable, a plan of time drawn up in advance; **editorial schedule** = list of dates for all the editorial processes of a book (copy editing, design, author's queries, libel checking, etc.); **production schedule** = list of dates for all the production processes of a book (copy to typesetter, layouts, proofing, cover work, etc.); **publication schedule** = list of dates of publication of a series of books over a period of time; **to be ahead of schedule** = to be early; **to be on schedule** = to be on time; **to be behind schedule** = to be late **(b)** list (especially additional documents attached to a contract); ***please find enclosed our schedule of charges; schedule of territories to which a contract applies; see the attached schedule*** *or* ***as per the attached schedule***

scheduling *noun* drawing up a plan *or* a timetable

scholarly books *or* **scholarly publishing** *noun* academic books, publishing books on university subjects; **scholarly press** = publishing company which publishes scholarly books

school *noun* **school books** = educational books, books published for use in schools; **school book supply** = method of supplying books to schools; **school edition** = edition of a book specially made for sale to schools; **school rep** *or* **educational rep** = representative who calls on schools to show books to teachers who may then order them for the students

science *noun* study *or* knowledge based on observing and testing; **science fiction** *or* **sci-fi (SF)** = fiction which deals with what may happen in the future, based on existing scientific facts and extending them into a future time

scientific *adjective* referring to science; **scientific technical and medical (STM) publishing** = publishing specialized books in science, technology and medicine

sci-fi = SCIENCE FICTION

scissors and paste job *noun* **(a)** preparing a design paste-up or camera-ready copy for reproduction, by taking various piece of artwork or film and pasting them in position **(b)** book or article made almost entirely of passages from other works

sci-tech *noun US* scientific and technical publishing

scoop *noun* (i) exciting news story which a reporter is the first to find, which no other newspaper has reported; (ii) signing a sought-after author, etc., to write for one's newspaper or publishing company

score *verb* to draw lines with a sharp edge *or* rule across paper *or* card, so that it can fold more easily

scoring *noun* making lines on paper or board so that it will fold more easily (used on the covers of paper-bound books, so that the covers bend easily)

Scotchprint™ trade mark for a coated repro film, used for making litho originals from letterpress blocks

scout *noun* person who looks out for something; **literary scout** = person who looks for suitable books for a publisher to publish in another country (either as translations or adaptations)

scrap 1 *noun* waste material *or* pieces of paper; **scrap paper** = pieces of waste paper which can be recycled **2** *verb* to throw (something) away as useless; ***they had to scrap 10,000 covers and reprint them with the correct title***

scraperboard *noun* board used by artists, either a white board with a black coating, or a black board with a white coating; when the coating is scratched away with a knife, the result looks rather like an engraving

scratch *verb* to draw a little line through a character to show that it is wrong

screamer *noun (informal)* **(a)** exclamation mark **(b)** *US* very large headline in a newspaper

screen 1 *noun* **(a)** grid of dots or lines placed between the camera and the artwork, which has the effect of dividing the picture up into small dots, creating an image which can be used for printing; **halftone screen** = screen with cross lines or a grid of dots used for preparing a halftone illustration; **mechanical screen** = shading in dots or lines, which is preprinted, and can be cut up and stuck down to give shading in artwork; **silk-screen printing** = SCREEN PROCESS PRINTING **screen angle** = angle at which a screen is set before the photograph is taken (different angles are used for the four process colours so as to avoid a moiré effect); the normal angles are black: 45°; magenta: 75°; yellow: 90°; cyan: 105°; **screen print** = print taken from a film which has been screened; **screen printing** *or* **screen process printing** = printing process where a design is inked through a fine screen (formerly silk, now usually nylon) parts of which are covered by a stencil to prevent the ink passing through; **screen ruling** = number of lines per inch on a screen or the number of dots per inch on a halftone; **screen tint** = mechanical screen, shading in dots or lines, which is preprinted, and can be cut up and stuck down to give shading in artwork **(b)** glass surface on which computer information *or* TV pictures, etc., can be shown; ***he brought up the information on the screen;*** **screen editor** *or* **text editor** = software that allows the user to edit text on-screen, with one complete page of information being displayed at a time; **screen format** = way in which a screen is laid out; **on-screen** = with information being displayed on a screen; ***the text is edited on-screen*** **2** *verb* to photograph artwork using a halftone screen; **screened print** = print made using a screen

screenful *noun* complete frame of information displayed on a screen

screenplay *noun* scenario, text of the dialogue of a film

screenwriter *noun* person who writes scenarios for films

> COMMENT: photographic screens have varied degrees of fineness. according to the subject matter and type of paper used. The dots vary between 40 and 200 lines per inch. Typical screens are 50 to 60 for newsprint, 80 to 100 for MF and SC papers, 120 to 133 for imitation art papers and 150 or more for high-grade art papers

script 1 *noun* **(a)** manuscript *or* text of a book; ***we have three scripts to copy edit in a week*** **(b)** text of a play *or* film *or* TV documentary, etc. **(c)** typeface which looks like sloping handwriting **2** *verb* to write the script for a play *or* film *or* TV documentary, etc.; ***the show was scripted by Joe Smith***

scriptwriter *noun* person who writes a film *or* TV *or* radio script

scroll *verb* to move displayed text vertically up *or* down the screen, one line *or* pixel at a time; **scroll mode** = terminal mode that transmits every key press and displays what is received; **smooth scroll** = text that is moved up a screen pixel by pixel rather than line by line, which gives a smoother movement

scrub *verb* to wipe information off a disk; to remove data from store; ***scrub all files referring to 1994 taxes***

scuffing *noun* roughening of the paper surface due to rubbing

scumming *noun* situation where the non-image areas of a lithographic print take in ink, giving black marks in the white areas; (NOTE: also called **catch up**)

search 1 *noun* process of identifying a character *or* word *or* section of data in a document *or* file; **search and replace** = feature on some word processors that allows the user to find certain words *or* phrases, then replace them with another word *or* phrase; **global search and replace** = word-processor search and replace function covering a complete file *or* document; **search engine** = software that performs the search on a database or title; **search key** = (i) word *or* phrase that is to be found in a text; (ii) field and other data used to select various records in a database; **search routine** = software which allows the user to search for an item in a database **2** *verb* to look for an item of data

second *adjective* **second colour** = the colour which is printed second in two-colour work; **second cover** = the inside front cover of a magazine

secondary *adjective* **(a)** second in importance; **secondary colours** = colours formed by mixing primary colours **(b)** more advanced than primary; **secondary education** = education after primary schools (from about 11 years to 18 years old); ***they specialize in the publishing of secondary school books;*** **secondary publishing** = publishing books for use in secondary schools; *see also* PRIMARY, TERTIARY

second-class *adjective & adverb* less expensive *or* less comfortable; ***to travel second-class; the price of a second-class ticket is half that of a first class; I find second-class hotels are just as comfortable as the best ones;*** **second-class mail** = (i) *GB* less expensive, slower, mail service; (ii) *US* mail service for sending newspapers and magazines; ***a second-class letter is slower than a first-class; send it second-class if it is not urgent***

second half *noun* period of six months from 1st July to end of December; ***the figures for the second half are up on those for the first part of the year***

secondhand *adjective & adverb* used *or* not new *or* which has been owned by someone before; ***a secondhand bookshop; the shop has both new books and a small secondhand stock***

section *noun* **(a)** (i) signature, part of a book made from one sheet of paper; (ii) supplement to a newspaper *or* magazine; ***the book is printed in 32-page sections; the paper has a special travel section on Saturdays;*** **section mark** = SIGNATURE MARK **(b)** printed sign showing a paragraph division or that a footnote is being referred to **(c)** department in a company; **legal section** = department in a company dealing with legal matters

sector *noun* smallest area on a disk that can be accessed by a computer

> COMMENT: a disk is divided into many tracks, each of which is then divided into a number of sectors which in turn hold a certain number of bits

secure system *noun* system that cannot be accessed without authorization

security *noun* being protected *or* being secret; **security in this office is nil** = nothing can be kept secret in this office; **security paper** = paper with a special watermark to prevent it being imitated; **security printer** = printer who prints paper money, company reports, secret government documents, etc.

see copy *verb* instruction to the typesetter to look at the original manuscript to see how the text setting is instructed; **see overleaf** *or* **see the following page** = instruction to the reader to look at a reference on the next page

see-safe *noun* agreement where the publisher who has sold books to a bookseller will give credit for unsold books at the end of a period under certain conditions (such as against an order for more stock of other titles); ***we bought the stock see-safe***

see-through *noun* situation where text on the verso of a page can be seen through the paper

seize *verb* to take hold of something *or* to take possession of something; ***the customs seized the shipment of books; the court ordered the company's funds to be seized***

seizure *noun* taking possession of something; ***the court ordered the seizure of the books***

select *verb* to choose; ***the novel has been selected as a book club choice***

selection *noun* choice; thing which has been chosen; **book club selection** = book which is specially chosen as a lead title for a book club; **main selection** = book which is the first choice offered to the club members (and is heavily promoted); **alternate selection** = book which is the second choice offered to the club members

self- *prefix* referring to the thing itself

self-adhesive *or* **self-seal envelope** *noun* envelope which sticks without needing to be wetted

self-copy paper *see* NCR

self-cover *noun* cover which is printed on the same paper as the text of the book (used for brochures and small books)

self-endpapers *or* **self-ends** *noun* endpapers which are part of the printed book, and not added specially

self-mailer *noun* mailing piece which does not need an envelope

self-sealing *adjective* (envelope) which sticks itself, without needing to be wetted

self-wrapper *noun* self-cover, cover made from the same paper as the rest of the book

seller *noun* thing which sells; ***this book is a steady seller;*** **bestseller** = item (especially a book) which sells very well

selling 1 *noun* **direct selling** = selling a product direct to the customer without going through a shop; **mail-order selling** = selling by taking orders and supplying a product by post; **selling costs** = amount of money to be paid for advertising, reps' commissions, etc., involved in selling something **2** *suffix* **fast-selling items** = items which sell quickly;

best-selling novel = novel which sells better than other novels

semi- *prefix* half

semi-bold *noun* typeface which is between light and bold

semichemical pulp *noun* pulp which is prepared partly by mechanical means and partly by chemical

semicolon *noun* printing sign (;) which indicates a separation between parts of a sentence *or* marks the end of a program line in computing

semi-display advertisement *noun* advertisement inside a box in the classified advertisements section of a newspaper

semi-finished *adjective* **semi-finished products** = products which are partly finished

sensitive *adjective* **(a)** (device *or* film) which can sense even small changes; ***the computer is sensitive even to very slight changes in current; light-sensitive film changes when exposed to light*** **(b)** likely to cause offence *or* likely to cause legal problems; ***the book contains some sensitive information about the armed forces*** **(c)** able to feel something sharply; ***the market is very sensitive to the result of the elections;*** **price-sensitive product** = product which will sell less if the price is increased

sensitivity *noun* being sensitive; **sensitivity guide** = strip of film which can be used to show what exposure to use

sensitize *verb* to make something sensitive; **sensitized paper** = paper which has had chemicals added to it or has been coated with a substance, to make it sensitive to light

sentence *noun* series of words which form a separate section of a text, usually starting with a capital letter and ending with a full stop; ***the copy editor has been instructed to try to reduce the number of sentences without verbs; one of Joyce's sentences runs to ten pages without any punctuation***

separate 1 *adjective* not together; **to send something under separate cover** = to send something in a different envelope **2** *noun* offprint, single article from a journal which is reprinted separately **3** *verb* **(a)** to divide the colours needed in a four-colour printing; **separated artwork** = artwork which has been separated into the printing colours, each of which has a different film **(b)** to divide; ***the personnel are separated into part-timers and full-time staff;*** **separated graphics** = displayed characters that do not take up the whole of a character matrix, resulting in spaces between them

separation *noun* **(a) colour separation** = separating the various colours from a design into the process colours (magenta, cyan, yellow and black) to make a series of four films for printing; **separation filter** = one of the three filters used to make colour separations **(b) colour separations** = overlays prepared by an artist for the various colours needed in a design

> COMMENT: the colours are separated either by scanning or by photographing the original using filters to isolate each colour in turn. Each colour is then produced as a separate proof for checking purposes

sepia *noun* brown ink, often used to give an old-fashioned look to photographs

sequence *noun* **(a)** order in which something is set out; ***the designer has indicated the sequence of photographs*** **(b)** series of books which follow one after the other; ***the 'Dance to the Music of Time' sequence*** **(c)** series of scenes of a play *or* shots of a film *or* sections of a book, etc.

sequential access *noun* method of retrieving data from a storage device by starting at the beginning of the medium (such as tape) and reading each record until the required data is found; **sequential access storage** = storage medium whose data is accessed sequentially

serial *noun* **(a)** publication which comes out in several separate parts over a period of time; **serial publication** = publishing a book in parts in several issues of a magazine *or* newspaper; **serial rights** = right to reprint a whole book in parts (as in several issues of a magazine); **first serial rights** = right to publish sections of a book in a magazine *or* newspaper before the book itself is published; **second serial rights** = right to publish sections of a book in a magazine *or* newspaper after the book has been published **(b)** radio *or* TV programme which appears regularly, with the same characters; ***the book is a spinoff from the children's TV serial*** **(c)** classification in a series; **serial number** = number in a series

serialization *noun* publishing a book in parts in a magazine *or* newspaper

serialize *verb* to publish a book in parts in a magazine *or* newspaper

series *noun* **(a)** group of books dealing with similar subjects, published as a group, all in the same format; **series title** = title given to a series of books, each one of which has its own separate title; ***'At Lady Molly's' is the seventh title in the 'Dance to the Music of Time' series*** **(b)** all the different point sizes available in a typeface

serif *noun* little stroke added to the top or bottom end of the main stroke of characters in certain typefaces; **bracketed serif** = serif which is joined to the main part of a letter with a curved line; **slab serif** = serif which is a thick straight line; **sans serif** = typeface without serifs; ***Times and Baskerville are faces with serifs*** *or* ***are serif faces;*** *see also* SANS

seriffed *adjective* with serifs; ***Times Roman is a seriffed typeface; seriffed type is more legible than sans serif***

> COMMENT: serifs can be straight, or sloping, or curved. They derive from Roman letters cut in stone. The purpose of adding serifs to letters is first to keep the letters apart, while at the same time making it possible to link one letter to the next, and secondly, to make the letters distinct, in particular the top parts which the reader recognizes when reading. To test this, cover the bottom half of a line of seriffed face text and do the same for a line of sans face text: then compare the legibility of the top parts of the letters. In the USA, seriffed faces are preferred because some sans faces do not distinguish between the capital 'I' and the lower case 'l', making it impossible to write the word 'Illinois', or particularly its abbreviation 'Ill'

serigraphy *noun* silk screen printing, where the ink is forced through a fine cloth onto the paper behind

server *noun* dedicated computer *or* peripheral that provides a function to a network

set 1 *noun* **(a)** group of items which go together *or* which are used together; group of books which are sold together; ***we keep a set of duplicate films in the office;*** **boxed set** = set of books sold together in a box **(b)** width of a printed character in a certain typeface; **set size** = measurement of horizontal dimensions in sets (one set equals one point); **set width** = width of the body of a printed character (some faces are wider than others: Baskerville, for example, is particularly wide) **2** *adjective* **(a)** fixed *or* which cannot be changed; **set format** = format which is used for all titles in a series and cannot be changed **(b)** which has been typeset; **the text is set solid** = typeset without any leading between the lines **3** *verb* **(a)** to compose *or* to typeset *or* to put a text into printed characters; ***the manuscript has been marked up and sent to the typesetters for setting; the page is set in 12 point Times Roman;*** *(instructions to compositors)* **'set flush'** = set with no indents; **'set solid'** = set without any leading between the lines; *see also* TYPESET **(b)** *(of ink)* to dry

set off *verb* to transfer ink from one sheet to another

set-off *or* **setting-off** *noun* printing defect where a sheet is marked with wet ink from another newly printed sheet; **set-off spray** *or* **anti-set-off spray** = fine powder used on a press to prevent set-off between printed sheets

setting *noun* **(a)** action of composing text into typeset characters; ***the MS has been sent to the typesetter for setting; setting charges have increased since last year;*** **computer setting** = typesetting using a computerized typesetting machine; **setting costs** = cost of typesetting a text; **setting rule** = part of a composing stick which has measurements on it, so that the compositor can measure the width of the text; **setting stick** = composing stick, sort of narrow box in which the compositor places the pieces of type as he sets each line **(b)** arranging the final form of the spine of a book

setting up costs *or* **setup costs**

noun costs of getting a machine *or* a factory ready to make a new product after finishing work on another one; **setting-up time** *or* **setup time** = time taken to get a machine ready for printing

set up *verb* to begin (something); **to set up a machine** = to get a machine ready for printing; **set-up time** = time taken to load programs and attach the input devices to a typesetting machine

sew *verb* to attach using a needle and thread; **sewn binding** = binding where the signatures are attached with thread; **wire-sewn** = wire-stitched, method of binding where the signatures are attached with wire staples (as opposed to sewn binding)

sewer = SEWING MACHINE

sewing *noun* part of the binding process, when gathered pages are sewn together in signatures, and then attached to form the book block; **sewing machine** = machine for sewing signatures; **sewing thread** = thread used in a sewing machine; **flexible sewing** = sewing sections round cords or tapes, leaving a hollow in the spine to allow the book to open easily; **French sewing** = sewing signatures together without tapes, each signature being attached by sewing through the thread attaching the previous one

SF = SCIENCE FICTION

SGML = STANDARD GENERALIZED MARKUP LANGUAGE hardware-independent standard which defines how documents should be marked up to indicate bolds, italics, margins and so on; *see also* HTML

> COMMENT: generally used to code data for database entry or to mark up a book before it is typeset

shade 1 *noun* (i) variation in a printed colour due to added black; (ii) quantity of black added to a colour to make it darker; ***the cover is in three shades of green*** **2** *verb* to give a shade to an area of illustration; **shaded areas** = darker parts of an illustration; **shaded letters** = display letters which give a shadow effect

shading *noun* showing darker sections of a line drawing by adding dark colour *or* by drawing criss-cross lines

shadow *noun* dark part of a photograph *or* halftone; **shadow mark** = paper defect where marks left by the rollers can be seen

shank *noun* stem, the main part of a piece of metal type

shareware *noun* software which is available free to sample, but if kept the user is expected to pay a fee to the writer (often confused with public domain software which is completely free)

sharp *adjective* very clear (image); ***the reproduction is not sharp enough - the edges are fuzzy***

sharpen *verb* to make sharper

sharpness *noun* clearness of a printed image; ***the cover lacks sharpness***

shaving *noun* trimming pages so much that part of the text is cut off; **shavings** = thin strips of paper cut off at the paper mill or during binding

sheepskin *noun* white binding material made from the skin of sheep; *compare* PARCHMENT

sheet *noun* **(a)** **sheet of paper** = flat piece of paper, especially a large piece of paper for printing, which has not been folded; **sheet cutter** = machine that cuts reeled paper into sheets; **sheet feed** = device which puts one sheet at a time into a printer *or* photocopier; **sheet feed attachment** = device which can be attached to a printer to allow single sheets of paper to be fed in automatically; **sheet-fed press** = printing press which takes single sheets of paper, as opposed to a web press which takes reels of paper; **sheet sizes** = standard sizes of paper available in sheets; **sheet wander** = defect caused when the web of paper moves from side to side while passing through the press **(b)** large piece of paper, printed with the text of a book, which is to be folded, sewn and bound; ***we have 10,000 copies of the book in cased binding, and 25,000 in sheets waiting for the cases to be made;*** **sheet stock** = stock of printed sheets of a book, which are not yet bound; **flat sheet stock** = stock of printed sheets, stored flat; **sheet work** = printing on both sides of a sheet of paper to produce one copy; *compare* HALF SHEET WORK, WORK-AND-TURN **(c)** **sales sheet** = paper which gives details of a product and explains why it is good; **time sheet** = paper showing when a worker starts work and when he leaves work in the evening

sheeter *noun* machine for cutting a web of paper into sheets

sheetwise *adverb* printed on one side of a sheet of paper at a time

shelf *noun* flat surface attached to a wall *or* in a cupboard on which items for sale are displayed; ***the shelves in the bookshop were full of items before the Christmas rush;*** **shelf filler** = person whose job it is to make sure that the shelves in a shop are kept full of items for sale; **shelf space** = amount of space on shelves in a shop; **shelf talker** = card which advertises a book, placed on a shelf next to the stock of the book itself

shelfback *noun* spine of a book

shelve *verb* to postpone *or* to put back to another date; ***when costs rose to £100,000 the company decided to shelve the project; the publication of the new reference series has been shelved***

shelving *noun* **(a)** rows of shelves *or* space on shelves; ***we installed new metal shelving in the paperback department*** **(b)** postponing; ***the shelving of the project has resulted in six redundancies***

shift **1** *noun* group of workers who work for a period, and then are replaced by another group; period of time worked by a group of workers; **day shift** = shift worked during the daylight hours (from early morning to late afternoon); **night shift** = shift worked during the night; ***there are 150 men on the day shift; he works the day shift or night shift; we work an 8-hour shift; the management is introducing a shift system or shift working*** **2** *verb* to move *or* to sell; ***we shifted 20,000 items in one week***

shift key *noun* key on a typewriter *or* computer which provides a second function for other keys (usually by making the typewriter *or* computer move to capital letters or which moves to another series of characters)

shift work *noun* system of work in a factory with shifts

shilling stroke *or* **shilling mark** *noun* solidus *or* oblique stroke

shiner *noun* light spot in paper

shining *noun* holding printed sheets up to the light to see that the printed areas on the two sides are in register

ship *verb* to send (goods), but not always on a ship; ***to ship goods to the USA; we ship all our stock by rail; the consignment of paperbacks was shipped abroad last week;*** **to drop ship** = to deliver a large order direct to a customer's shop or warehouse, without going through an agent, though the invoice may be sent to the agent

shipment *noun* goods sent; ***two shipments were lost in the fire; a shipment of school books was damaged; we make two shipments a week to France;*** **bulk shipment**

= shipments of large quantities of goods; **consolidated shipment** = goods from different companies grouped together into a single shipment; **drop shipment** = delivery of a large order from a manufacturer direct to a customer's shop or warehouse, without going through an agent, though the invoice may be sent to the agent

shipper *noun* person who sends goods *or* who organizes the sending of goods for other customers

shipping *noun* sending of goods; **shipping agent** = company which specializes in the sending of goods; **shipping clerk** = clerk who deals with shipping documents; **shipping costs** = costs of sending goods; **shipping instructions** = details of how goods are to be shipped and delivered; **shipping note** = note which gives details of goods being shipped

shives *noun* small pieces of wood fibre still visible in finished paper

shoo flies *noun* devices which move the leading edge of the printed sheet up so that it goes out of the press easily

shoot *verb* to take a photograph or film; ***the illustrations were shot in the author's own kitchen***

shooting stick *noun* short stick used to lock up or unlock formes

shop *noun* **(a)** place where goods are stored and sold, such as a bookshop; **retail shop** = shop where goods are sold only to the public; **shop assistant** = person who serves customers in a shop; **shop front** = part of a shop which faces the street, including the entrance and windows; **shop window** = window in a shop where goods are displayed so that customers can see them *or* place where goods or services can be exhibited; (NOTE: US English usually uses **store** so **bookstore, paperback store,** etc.) **(b)** place where goods are made *or* workshop; **binding shop** = section of a printing factory where the books are bound; **machine shop** = place where working machines are kept; **repair shop** = small factory where machines are repaired; **on the shop floor** = in the factory *or* in the works *or* among the ordinary workers; ***the feeling on the shop floor is that the manager does not know his job*** **(c) closed shop** = system where a company agrees to employ only union members in certain jobs; ***the union is asking the management to agree to a closed shop***

shoplifter *noun* person who steals goods from shops

shoplifting *noun* stealing goods from shops

shop-soiled *adjective* dirty because of having been on display in a shop

short *adjective* **(a)** not tall *or* not long; **short and** = printing sign (&) which means 'and'; **short column** = column which has been printed with fewer lines than the other columns in the same book; **short descenders** = descenders in certain typefaces which are shorter than in other typefaces (faces such as Goudy or Plantin are noted for their short descenders); **short discount** = discount which is less than the normal trade discount (such as the discount on educational books); **short grain paper** = paper where the grain is parallel to the shorter side of the sheet; **short inks** = inks which do not flow easily; (NOTE: the opposite is **long inks**) **short page** = page which has been printed with fewer lines than the other pages (either as a mistake, or to avoid a design problem); **short story** = piece of fiction between three and ten pages long **(b)** for a small period of time; **short credit** = terms which allow the customer only a little time to pay; **in the short term** = in the near future *or* quite soon **(c)** not as much as should be; ***the printing was 2,000 copies short;*** **short of** = with less than needed *or* with not enough of; ***we are short of staff*** *or* ***short of money; the editorial department is short of new ideas***

shortage *noun* **(a)** lack *or* not having enough; ***a chronic shortage of skilled staff; we employ part-timers to make up for staff shortages; the import controls have resulted in the shortage of spare parts;*** **manpower shortage** *or* **shortage of manpower** = lack of workers; **there is no shortage of advice on what the company should publish** = there are plenty of people who want to give the company advice on publishing **(b)** the number of copies of a book *or* magazine which have not been printed

shorten *verb* to make shorter; ***the blurb needs to be shortened to fit the jacket flap***

shorthand *noun* rapid way of writing using a system of signs; **shorthand secretary** = secretary who takes dictation in shorthand; **shorthand typist** = typist who can take dictation in shorthand and then type it; **to take shorthand** = to write using shorthand

shortlist 1 *noun* list of some of the better people who have applied for a job, who can be asked to come for a test or an interview; list of books selected for a prize **2** *verb* to make a shortlist; ***shortlisted candidates will be asked for an interview***

short-range *adjective* **short-range forecast** = forecast which covers a period of a few months

short run *noun* printrun of relatively few copies, usually taken to be less than 1,000 copies; ***he operates a profitable short-run printing company; they specialize in short-run reprints for academic publishers; the laser printer is good for short-run leaflets***

shorts *noun* books which have not been printed in sufficient quantity; (NOTE: opposite is **overs**)

shot *noun* **(a)** photograph; ***the illustration facing the title page is a shot of the Prime Minister on a horse*** **(b) mail shot** *or* **mailing shot** = leaflets sent by post to possible customers

shoulder *noun* **(a)** edge of the spine of a book, which sticks out slightly; **shoulder heads** = heads printed in a line on their own; **shoulder notes** = notes printed in the margin at the level of the first line of type **(b)** sloping surface between the bevel of the metal type and the edge of the stem

shout *noun* short slogan advertising a book, which is printed in large letters, in advertisements or on the book jacket

showcard *noun* piece of cardboard with advertising text, put near an item for sale, sometimes on the counter

showcase *noun* cupboard with a glass front or top to display items

showroom *noun* room where goods are displayed for sale; **educational showroom** = room where educational books and equipment are on show, so that teachers can look at them and decide what to buy

show side *noun* side of a binding material which is visible

show-through *noun* (i) paper defect, where the paper is not opaque enough; (ii) defect in printing, where the printed text on the back of a page can be seen through the page from the other side; *compare* STRIKE-THROUGH

> COMMENT: when the printing on one side of the paper can be seen from the other side, this is due either to show-through or to strike-through. Show-through is caused by inadequate opacity of the paper, while strike-through results from the vehicle (the liquid component) of an oil-based ink penetrating right through the sheet

shred *verb* to tear paper into very small pieces (usually meaning to destroy confidential documents in a special machine)

shredder *noun* machine for destroying documents, by tearing them into very small pieces

shrink *verb* to get smaller; ***the drawing was shrunk to fit the space; the educational market has shrunk by 20%; the company is having difficulty selling into a shrinking market***

shrinkage *noun* **(a)** amount by which something gets smaller; ***to allow for shrinkage*** **(b)** *(informal)* losses of stock through theft (especially by members of the staff of a shop)

shrink-packed *or* **shrink-wrapped** *adjective* covered in tight plastic protective cover

shrink-packaging *or* **shrink-wrapping** *noun* act of covering a book, cassette, record etc., in a tight plastic cover which is heated to seal it; (NOTE: US English is also **pre-shrunk packaging**)

shrink-wrap *noun* the plastic film used in shrink-wrapping

side *noun* **(a)** one of the surfaces of a flat object; ***please write on one side of the paper only;*** **side-sewing** *or* **side-stitching** = sewing a book through the sides of the folded sheets, and not at the fold; **side wire binding** *or* **side wire stitching** = binding by stapling through the sides of the folded sheets **(b)** part of something near the edge; **side heading** *or* **side head** = heading which is ranged to the left with text run on; **side lay** = edge of a sheet placed flush with the guide lines on the press; **side notes** = notes printed in the margin; **side sorts** = pi characters *or* special sorts; **side stick** = piece of wood placed along the side of the page inside a forme

siding *noun* finishing a quarter- or half-binding by glueing paper or cloth over the boards, covering the edges of the leather

sig *(informal)* = SIGNATURE ***there are plates wrapped round sigs 2 and 5***

sign 1 *noun* **(a)** printed *or* written character; ***a pound sign (£) is used in some American computer programs in place of the hash mark*** **(b)** advertising board *or* notice which advertises something; ***they have asked for planning permission to put up a large red shop sign; advertising signs cover most of the buildings in the centre of the town*** **2** *verb* **(a)** to write your name in a special way on a document to show that you have written it or approved it; ***to sign a letter*** *or* ***a contract*** *or* ***a document*** *or* ***a cheque; the contract is signed by the managing director*** **(b)** *(of an author or illustrator)* to write one's signature on a copy of a book or illustration; **signing session** = ceremony where an author visits a bookshop and signs copies of the book which members of the public have bought; **copies signed by the author** *or* **signed by the illustrator** = copies of a book with the signature of the author *or* illustrator in them; **signed limited edition** = small number of copies of a book, specially bound and numbered, with the author's or illustrator's signature in them

signatory *noun* person (or company) who signs a contract, etc.; ***you have to get the permission of all the signatories to the agreement if you want to change the terms; the United States was not a signatory to the Berne Convention***

signature *noun* **(a)** name written in a special way by someone; ***a pile of letters waiting for the managing director's signature; the book is worth more if it has the signatures of both the author and illustrator in it*** **(b)** section, a printed sheet, folded into 16, 32 or 64 pages; **signature (mark)** = letter or number printed at the foot of the first page of a section, showing the order in which the signatures have to be gathered for binding

> COMMENT: note that the folded set of printed pages is technically speaking a 'section' while the 'signature' is the identifying number or letter on it; 'signature' is however commonly used to mean the set of pages themselves

silhouette *noun* illustration where the foreground is solid colour and the background is white

silk-screen printing *noun* screen process printing, printing process where a design is inked through a fine screen such as silk or nylon, parts of which are covered by a stencil to prevent the ink passing through

Silurian *noun* type of paper where coloured fibre is added to the stock, giving a spotted appearance

simple mail transfer protocol (SMTP) standard protocol which allows electronic mail messages to be transferred from one system to another

simultaneous *adjective* happening at the same time; ***simultaneous publication in London and New York***

simultaneously *adverb* happening at the same time; ***the book was published simultaneously in England and Australia***

singer sewing *noun* thread sewing through the spine of an insetted book

single *adjective* one alone; **single copy** = one copy of a book; **single-copy orders** = orders for one copy of a book (which may be uneconomical for a large warehouse, and which may have a surcharge applied by the supplier); **single leaf** = cancel page of one sheet of paper; **single line display** = small screen which displays a single line of characters at a time; **single quotes** *or* **single quotation marks** = printed signs (' '), used to show that a piece of text has been quoted; **single revolution printing** = letterpress process where the cylinder rotates and prints one impression with every turn; **single sheet feed** = device attached to a printer to allow single sheets of paper to be used instead of continuous stationery; **single sided disk** = computer disk which can only be used to store data on one side

sink *noun* hollow in the surface of a printing plate

sinkage *noun* amount of drop in a chapter heading or other heading

sisal *noun* plant fibre, used to make rope and also kraft paper

sixteen *number* 16; ***the magazine is printed in sixteen-page sections***

sixteenmo (16mo) *noun* (i) size of page where the sheet of paper is folded four times to give 32 pages; (ii) book which is printed in 32-page sections; (iii) American book size about 6 or 7 inches high

sixtyfourmo (64mo) *noun* (i) size of page where the sheet of paper is folded six times to give 128 pages; (ii) book which is printed in 128-page sections; (iii) American book size about 3 inches high

size 1 *noun* **(a)** measurements of something *or* how big something is *or* how many there are of something; **page size** = physical dimensions of a printed page; ***our page sizes vary from 220 x 110 to 360 x 220;*** **ISO paper sizes** = international metric paper sizes (A, B and C paper sizes) (The largest size is A0 (841 x 1189mm), and all other sizes are derived from this, with in each case the longer side being half that of the previous size) ⇨APPENDIX; **type size** *or* **size of type** = size of type, calculated in 'points' which refer to the height of the printed character, not its width **(b)** sort of glue added to paper pulp to make the paper stiffer, or used to paint onto paper or card to seal the surface **2** *verb* to add size to paper pulp; **sized paper** = paper with size added; **tub-sized paper** = paper which has been dipped into size; it is stiff and smooth, and is used for writing papers and legal documents

sizing *noun* **(a)** reducing *or* enlarging a picture to fit; ***photographs can be edited by cropping, sizing, etc*** **(b)** (i) coating with size; (ii) the material used for coating paper; **tub sizing** = sizing of paper by dipping it in a vat containing size or gelatine

> COMMENT: size is a mixture of resin and aluminium sulphate, added to paper pulp to make the paper stiff and less absorbent. Surface sizing is now standard practice on most paper and board. It increases surface strength, water resistance, stability of the dimensions of the paper, and gives a smooth surface for printing

sketch 1 *noun* rough drawing to show how a finished illustration *or* design should look; ***the designer brought in some sketches for the new logo*** **2** *verb* **(a)** to make a rough drawing to show how something should look when finished; ***the design director had to choose between several sketches which the designers had submitted*** **(b)** to write a rough description of something; ***the author sketched out the plan of a series of cookery books***

skid *noun US* flat wooden base on which goods (sheets of paper, printed sheets, bound books, etc.) can be stacked for easy handling by a fork-lift truck; (NOTE: UK English is **pallet**)

skip *verb* to move from one stage to the next-but-one, missing out the stage in between; ***the printer skipped the next three lines of text;*** **skip capability** = feature of certain word-processors to allow the user to jump backwards *or* forwards by a quantity of text in a document; **high-speed skip** = rapid movement of paper in a printer, ignoring the normal line advance

skiver *noun* leather made by splitting a sheepskin, used as a cover material for de luxe books

slab *verb* to finish the preparation of an electrotype, by making the printing surface even

slab serif *noun* Egyptian, typeface where the serifs are thick straight lines

slack *adjective* not tense *or* not taut; **slack sheet** = situation where the paper in a web press is not tight enough

slander 1 *noun* untrue spoken statement which damages someone's character; **action for slander** *or* **slander action** = case in a law court where someone says that another person had slandered him **2** *verb* **to slander someone** = to damage someone's character by saying untrue things about him; *compare* LIBEL

slant = SOLIDUS

slash 1 *noun* solidus, the printing sign (/) **2** *verb* to cut *or* to reduce sharply; ***to slash prices*** *or* ***credit terms; prices have been slashed in all departments; the bank has been forced to slash interest rates***

slashed zero *noun* a printed *or* written sign like an 0 with a line through it, used in computers

sleeper *noun* book which does not sell well on publication, but which suddenly starts to sell some time later

slew *noun US* rapid vertical movement of paper in a printer

slice *noun* adjustable meter to control the flow of the pulp onto the wet end of the paper machine

slide *noun* **(a)** positive transparent photograph in a card mount; *see also* TRANSPARENCY **(b) slide rule** = device, like a ruler with a sliding central part, which allows rapid mathematical calculations

sliding *adjective* which rises in steps; **a sliding scale of royalties** = royalty where the percentage increases with the number of copies sold

slip *noun* **(a)** small piece of paper; **slip pages** = page on galley proofs, proofs where the text is made up into pages but without headlines or folios; **slip proofs** = galley proofs printed on long lengths of paper, not divided into pages; **slip sheets** = pieces of paper placed between printed sheets to prevent set-off; **compliments slip** = piece of paper with the name of the company printed on it, sent with documents, gifts, etc., instead of a letter; **distribution slip** = paper attached to a document *or* to a magazine, showing all the people in an office who should read it; **rejection slip** = note from a publisher to an author telling him his manuscript has not been accepted for publication **(b)** end of a cord *or* tape used in binding by being glued to the cover boards **(c)** mistake; ***he made a couple of slips in laying out the tables***

slipcase *noun* card box for an expensive book, which is open at one side so that the spine of the book is visible

slip-up *noun* mistake; ***there have been some serious slip-ups in the dispatch department***

slit *verb* to cut through a sheet of paper *or* along a web of paper; **to slit on press** = to cut a web lengthwise as it is going through the press before the paper is folded

slitter *noun* set of knives which cut a printed sheet *or* a web of paper; **slitter marks** = marks in the centre of a sheet of paper, showing where it has to be cut

slogan *noun* **publicity slogan** = group of words which can be easily remembered, and which is used in publicity for a product; ***we are using the slogan 'Smiths can sell it' on all our publicity***

sloped roman *noun* form of italic found in dot-matrix printers, where the characters are roman and have been made to slope to the side by the computer (as opposed to true italic which is a specially designed face of a certain font)

slot *noun* square hole punched in leaves in some types of ring binding

slotted binding = NOTCHED BINDING

slug *noun* line of metal type cast in a casting machine in hot metal setting (made in a Linotype or Intertype machine)

slur *noun* printing defect in letterpress, where the image is blurred, caused by movement of the paper or forme

slush pile *noun* unsolicited manuscripts which are sent to publishers or agents (and which may never be read)

slush pulp *noun* liquid pulp which is pumped straight into the papermaking process

small *adjective* not large; **small ads** = short private advertisements in a newspaper (selling small items, asking for jobs, etc.); **small capitals** *or* **small caps** *or* **smalls** = capital letters which are smaller than normal, only rising to the x-height of the lower case letters (instructed by underlining the text twice or writing 'sc'); **small pica** = old type size, similar to the modern 11 point

small orders *noun* orders for small quantities of books; **small order surcharge** = extra charge added by some publishers to an order under a certain quantity or value

smalls = SMALL CAPS

smash *verb* **(a)** to break (a record) *or* to do better than (a record); ***to smash all production records; sales have smashed all records for the first half of the year*** **(b)** to press a folded signature before binding, so that it takes less room

smashing *noun US* crushing *or* pressing of a sewn book, so as to remove air from between the pages, either before or after binding; (NOTE: GB English is **nipping**)

smudge 1 *noun* unwanted dark mark made by rubbing ink **2** *verb* to make a mark by rubbing ink which has been printed

smudge-proof ink *noun* ink which cannot smudge

SOAT = SURFACE OIL ABSORBENCY TESTER **PIRA SOAT** = test for the absorbency of paper, where a brass roll carrying a drop of liquid paraffin transfers some of the liquid to the paper; the time taken for 75% of the liquid to be absorbed is measured

soda pulp *noun* paper pulp made from wood chips cooked in caustic soda

soft *adjective* **(a)** not hard; **soft binding** = paper covered (i.e., not cased); **soft cover** = paper cover; **soft currency** = currency of a country with a weak economy, which is cheap to buy and difficult to exchange for other currencies; **soft-focus lens** = lens which deliberately does not focus correctly; **soft-focus shot** = photographic picture where the focus is deliberately not correct, so as to give a blurred effect; **soft font** = fonts *or* typefaces stored on a disk, which can be downloaded *or* sent to a printer and stored in temporary memory *or* RAM; **soft loan** = loan (from a company to an employee or from a government to another government) at very low or nil interest; **to take the soft option** = to decide to do something which involves least risk, effort or problems; **soft sell** = persuading people to buy by encouraging them, but not forcing them to do so **(b) soft copy** = text displayed on screen (as opposed to hard copy on paper); **soft dot** = halftone dot which is less dense round the edge than in the centre; **soft hyphen** = hyphen which only appears on the computer screen, and does not print out in hard copy

software *noun* computer programs (as opposed to machines, which are 'hardware'); **software development** = processes required to produce working programs from an initial idea; **software documentation** = information, notes and diagrams that describe the function, use and operation of a piece of software; **software house** = company which develops and sells computer programs; **software licence** = agreement between a user and a software house, giving details of the rights of the user to use *or* copy the software; **software package** = complete set of programs (and the manual) that allow a certain task to be performed; **software piracy** = illegal copying of software for sale; **software specification** = detailed information about a piece of software's abilities, functions and methods; **software system** = all the programs required for one or more tasks

softwood *noun* wood from conifers used in papermaking

SOGAT 82 = SOCIETY OF GRAPHICAL AND ALLIED TRADES UK union whose members work in the printing industry, merged with NGA to form the GPMU

soiled copies *noun* copies of a book that have been made dirty in a shop or warehouse

sole *adjective* only; **sole agency** = agreement to be the only person to represent a company *or* to sell a product in a certain area; **sole agent** = person who has the sole agency for a product in an area; **sole distributor** = retailer who is the only one in an area who is allowed to sell a certain product; **sole owner** = person who owns a business on his own, with no partners; **sole trader** = person who runs a business by himself but has not registered it as a company

solid *adjective & adverb* (i) (printed text) set with no spaces between the lines; (ii) (printed colour) which is 100% colour, without any tints; **solid font printer** = printer which uses a whole character shape to print in one movement, such as a daisy-wheel printer; **solid matter** *or* **solid type** = text without any leading between the lines; ***the index is set in 7pt solid***

solidus *noun* slash, printing sign (/)

solus (advertisement) *noun* advertisement which does not appear near other advertisements for similar products

sort 1 *noun* **sorts** = different pieces of metal type (in a font, each sort is supplied in different quantities, according to the frequency of use of the particular letter); **outside sorts** = characters which are not frequently used (such as accents or ligatures) and are kept in the outside compartments of a case **2** *verb* to put (cards *or* addresses) in order; ***she is sorting index cards into alphabetical order;*** *see also* ALPHASORT

SORT = SURFACE OIL RESISTANCE TIME

source *noun* place where something comes from; ***the source of the quotations is not referred to in the acknowledgements***

space 1 *noun* **(a)** empty place between characters in setting; white line between lines of type in setting; **em space** = space which is one em wide; **en space** = space which is one en wide; **line space** = white space equivalent to one line of typesetting; **word space** = white space left between two words in continuous text; **space bands** = metal wedges which are inserted between words in the Linotype slug and expand to fill out the correct line width; **space dots** = row of dots showing that a space is left blank (used in tabular work, price lists or catalogues); **space mark** = proofreader's mark showing that a space is needed **(b)** piece of metal type, which is not as tall as a character, used to make a space between characters or words **(c)** empty place *or* empty area; **advertising space** = space in a newspaper set aside for advertisements; **to take advertising space in a newspaper** = to book space for an advertisement in a newspaper **2** *verb* to set spaces between characters; ***the line of characters was evenly spaced across the page***

space bar *or* **space key** *noun* long bar at the bottom of a keyboard on a typewriter *or* computer which makes a single space into the text when pressed

space out *verb* to leave large spaces between characters; ***the company name is written in spaced-out letters;*** **spaced-out line** = line with wide spaces to make it justify without the need for hyphenation

spacer *noun* **intelligent spacer** = facility on a word processing system used to prevent words from being hyphenated *or* separated at the wrong point

spacing *noun* putting spaces between characters *or* between lines of type; **spacing material** = pieces of metal used for spacing between letters, words or lines; *see also* DIFFERENTIAL, LEAD, QUAD **word spacing** = spaces between words (which are made wider or narrower to fit the characters into a fully justified line); **double spacing** = typed with a white line between each line of text; **line spacing** = (i) leaving no white line between lines of type; (ii) distance between two rows of characters; **double line spacing** = leaving a white line between lines of text; **single line spacing** = leaving no white lines between lines of text

spec = SPECIFICATION

special *adjective* different *or* not normal *or* referring to one particular thing; **special character** = character which is not a normal one in a certain font (such as a certain accent *or* a symbol); **special colour** = printing colour other than one of the four process colours (cyan, magenta, yellow, black); **special order** = order which is different or more important than other orders; ***we have had a special order from Canada for 5,000 copies of the new title, but the Canadian publisher insists on having his own title page;*** **special sales** = sales of books by a publisher as a one-off deal (not going through the normal agents); **special sorts** = extra items not carried in the normal type font (such as odd fractions or accents); (NOTE: **also called pi characters**)

specialist *noun* person *or* company which deals with one particular type of product or one subject; **specialist bookshop** = bookshop that specializes in one type of book

specifications *noun* detailed information about what is needed *or* about a product to be supplied; **job specification** = very detailed description of what is involved in a job; **to work to standard specifications** = to work to specifications which are acceptable anywhere in the industry; **the work is not up to specification** *or* **does not meet our specifications** = the product is not made in the way which was detailed; **type specification** *or* **type spec** = details of the typeface, point size, leading, etc., which are to be used in a book

> COMMENT: a book specification is either the details of book (unit price, royalty terms, quantity printed, etc.) which a publisher uses to work out the selling price, or the instructions which a publisher gives to a printer on typeface, paper quality, format, etc.

specify *verb* to state clearly what is needed; ***a paper buyer must specify in detail the type of paper required; do not include VAT on the invoice unless specified***

specimen *noun* thing which is given as a sample; **specimen page** = typeset page which a printer prepares specially for a publisher; the publisher uses it either to decide on the final style of the book or to show to potential copublishing partners

spectrophotometer *noun* instrument used to measure colour; it can measure the colour of a printed surface giving a wavelength-by-wavelength analysis of the light reflected from the surface

spectrum *noun* range of colours

speed *noun* **(a)** rate at which something moves; **dictation speed** = number of words per minute which a secretary can write down in shorthand; **typing speed** = number of words per minute which a typist can type **(b)** measure of the sensitivity of a photographic material (film *or* paper) to light; ***high speed film is very sensitive to light***

speed up *verb* to make something go faster; ***we are aiming to speed up our delivery times***

spell *verb* to indicate the letters which make up a word; **spell in full** = write out an abbreviation in full

spellcheck *verb* to check the spelling in a text by comparing it with a dictionary held in the computer

spellchecker *or* **spelling checker** *noun* (i) program which looks at the words of a text in a computer, checks them against a dictionary of correctly spelled words, and indicates the words which are incorrect; (ii) dictionary of correctly spelled words, held in a computer, and used to check the spelling of a text; ***the program will be upgraded with a word-processor and a spelling checker***

spelling *noun* way in which words are spelled; ***the book is printed in American spelling***

spex *US* = SPECIFICATIONS

spike *verb* to refuse to print a news story; *compare* KILL

spine *noun* back edge of a bound book, usually with the title and publisher's imprint or logo on it; back fold of a sheet or signature; ***the book is bound in calf, with gold lettering on the spine; the author's name and the title are usually shown on the spine as well as on the front cover;*** **spine brass** = stamp with the words to be used on a spine; **spine lettering** = words (such as the title and author's name) as they appear on the spine of a book, usually written from top to bottom; they should be correctly placed for reading when the book is lying flat with the front cover upwards, but there is unfortunately no standardization about this; **to show a book spine out** = to put a book on the bookshop shelf with the spine outwards (less eye-catching than face out, where the whole of the front cover is seen)

spinner *noun* display rack for books, which turns round

spin off *verb* to develop other products from an existing product; ***they are planning to spin off a series of information booklets from their encyclopaedia database***

spinoff *noun* useful product developed as a secondary item from a main product; ***the books are spinoffs from a successful children's TV series***

spiral *noun* thing which twists round and round getting higher all the time; **spiral binding** = type of mechanical binding, where a coil of wire is passed through holes made in the back margins of the sheets; **spiral bound book** = book in a spiral binding; **spiral roller** = inking roller with a spiral groove running round it, allowing ink to be spread evenly over the plate

spirit duplicator *noun* short-run printing machine using alcohol to transfer ink from a stencil to the paper

splice *verb* to join up a web of paper which has broken, or to join a web to another web

split 1 *noun* dividing up; **royalty split** = way in which a royalty is divided between several authors or author and illustrator **2** *verb* to divide into parts; **split boards** = binding boards which are split to take the edge of a waste sheet and tapes in hardbound books; **split duct** *or* **split fountain** = division of the ink duct to allow two colours to be printed on different parts of the sheet at the same time; **split fraction** = fraction printed as one figure above another, the two figures being set as superior and inferior figures separated by a dash; **split run** = (i) printrun which is so large that it has to be done at two different printers; (ii) printrun of which only a small part is completed as a test; (iii) printrun of a newspaper *or* magazine which is stopped from time to time to insert a new plate (as for local news, change of advertisements); **split screen** = system where more than one text can appear on the screen at the same time (such as the text being worked on and a second text which can be called up for reference)

spoil *verb* to ruin *or* to make something bad; ***half the shipment was spoiled by water; the***

company's results were spoiled by a disastrous last quarter

spoilage *noun* **(a)** paper *or* binding material wasted as a book is being printed; (NOTE: US English is **makeover**) **(b)** wasting of material during printing **(c)** allowance of extra material to allow for wastage on the machine; ***we have allowed an extra 10% of paper for spoilage***

spoils *noun* sheets which are badly printed (at the beginning of a run) and are waste

sponsor 1 *noun* **(a)** person *or* company which pays money to help publish a book; company which pays to help a sporting event, in return for advertising rights **(b)** company which advertises on TV **(c)** director in a publishing company who is responsible for a particular book (the director has to approve the books published by his editors) **2** *verb* **(a)** to pay money to help publish a book; to pay to help someone study; ***several trainees on the course are sponsored by their firms;*** **sponsored book** = book which has been published with money from a sponsor **(b)** **sponsoring editor** = editor who is responsible for building a list by acquiring titles from packagers *or* from other publishers (also called an 'acquisitions editor')

sponsorship *noun* act of sponsoring; ***government sponsorship of overseas selling missions***

spot *noun* **(a)** round mark; **spot colour** = the use of small areas of colour on a page (as for headings or small diagrams) **(b)** **TV spot** = short period on TV which is used for commercials; ***we are running a series of TV spots over the next three weeks***

spotting *noun* retouching *or* covering up marks on artwork *or* film before printing

spray *noun* liquid in the form of small drops, such as the substance put onto newly-printed sheets to avoid setoff; **spray adhesive** = glue which is applied in a spray, especially glue which allows repositioning of artwork; *see also* ANTI-SET-OFF SPRAY

spread 1 *noun* **(a)** two facing pages in a book *or* magazine, which are treated as a single item and designed together; **double page spread** *or* **double spread** = two facing pages designed to be seen together, the illustrations *or* text forming one whole design **(b)** tendency of ink to creep outwards by absorption into the paper **2** *verb* to thicken the lines of an image to make them reproduce better

spreadsheet *noun* (i) computer program which allows tabulations spreading over many columns; (ii) computer printout showing a series of columns of figures

spring back *noun* **(a)** tendency for a flat sheet to go back to its original flat shape after being folded **(b)** binding for account books and other bound stationery which allows the pages to lie flat when open

sprinkled edge *noun* edge of a book which has been sprayed with splashes of ink for decoration

sprocket *or* **sprocket wheel** *noun* wheel with teeth round it which fit into holes in continuous stationery *or* punched tape

sprocket feed *noun* paper feed, where the printer pulls the paper by turning sprocket wheels which fit into a series of holes along each edge of the sheet; *see also* TRACTOR FEED

sprocket holes *noun* series of small holes on each edge of continuous stationery, which allow the sheet to be pulled through the printer

spur *noun* little line running sideways from the rounded bowl of a letter 'g' or up from the loop of an 'f'

square 1 *noun* **(a)** shape with four equal sides and four right angles; ***graph paper is drawn with a series of small squares;*** **square back** *or* **square spine** = style of binding where the back of the book is flat and not rounded; **square brackets** = printing sign [], used to separate text, often used in technical literature, to show a comment from the editor of a newspaper, to enclose phonetics; **square**

serif = face where the serifs are straight and thicker than other strokes **(b)** way of measuring area, by multiplying the length by the width; ***paper weight is measured in grammes per square metre*** **(c) squares** = projection of the boards of a cased book beyond the size of the trimmed page (usually the overhang is about 3mm) **2** *verb* **squared paper** = graph paper, paper printed with a series of small squares; **to square corrections** = to add in text in order to balance deleted text, thus avoiding remake-up of pages; **to square up illustrations** = to adjust illustrations by cropping or airbrushing to make them level and rectangular; *see also* OUT OF SQUARE

squash *noun* spread of ink beyond the correct image area

squeegee *noun* rubber sponge for spreading ink through the screen in screen process printing

SRA sizes sizes of stock sheets of printing paper for printing bled work; they are larger than the comparable A sizes

> COMMENT: there are three SRA sizes: SRA0 (900 x 1280mm), SRA1 (640 x 900mm) and SRA2 (450 x 640mm); see also RA sizes, which are slightly smaller

s/s = SAME SIZE instruction to a layout designer that a photograph or illustration is to be printed the same size as the original

stab = ESTABLISHMENT number of people working in a company

stabbing *or* **stab-stitching** *noun* side-stitching, sewing a very thick book with wire through the sides of the folded sheets, and not at the fold

stack 1 *noun* **(a)** pile *or* heap of things on top of each other; ***stack of paper in a warehouse; there is a stack of replies to our advertisement*** **(b)** *(in a library)* section where books are kept which are not on open access **(c)** *(in papermaking)* set of calenders in a calendering machine **2** *verb* to pile things on top of each other; ***the binder's boxes are stacked in the warehouse***

stacking *noun* **(a)** action of piling items up one on top of the other **(b)** metal *or* wooden shelves for storing large quantities of books *or* paper in a warehouse

staff *noun* permanent employees; **staff writer** *or* *US* **staffer** = reporter employed full-time on a newspaper

stage *noun* period, one of several points of development; ***the different stages of the production process; the text is ready for the printing stage;*** **the contract is still in the drafting stage** = the contract is still being drafted

stain 1 *noun* permanent colour mark; ***the MS was covered with round stains from coffee cups*** **2** *verb* to give the edges of pages a permanent colour; ***the tops of the pages are stained blue***

stamp 1 *noun* **(a)** device for printing designs on a cover **(b)** device for making marks on documents; mark made in this way; ***the invoice has the stamp 'Received with thanks' on it; the manuscript was stamped with the office stamp to show when it was received;*** **date stamp** = stamp with rubber figures which can be moved, used for marking the date on documents; **rubber stamp** = stamp made of hard rubber cut to form words; **stamp pad** = soft pad of cloth with ink on which a stamp is pressed, before marking the paper **(c) stamp duty** = tax on legal documents (such as the conveyance of a property to a new owner) **2** *verb* **(a)** to block, to press a design on the cover of a book, using gold leaf, foil or ink **(b)** to mark a document with a stamp; ***to stamp an invoice 'Paid'; the documents were stamped by the customs officials*** **(c)** to put a postage stamp on (an envelope, etc.); **stamped addressed envelope** = envelope with your own address written on it and a stamp stuck on it to pay for the return postage; ***send a stamped addressed envelope for further details and catalogue***

stamping *noun* blocking, making a design on the cover of a book, using gold leaf or ink; **stamping die** = metal plate for blocking the case of a book; **blind stamping** = stamping a design on the cover material without using any ink or gold leaf; **die stamping** = stamping relief decorations *or* text on paper *or* card, as for example an address on stationery

stand *noun* arrangement of shelves *or* tables, etc. at an exhibition for showing a company's products; **display stand** = special stand for displaying goods for sale; **exhibition stand** = separate section of an exhibition where a company exhibits its products or services; (NOTE: US English is booth) **news stand** = small wooden shop on a pavement, for selling newspapers

standard 1 *noun* normal quality *or* normal conditions which other things are judged against; **standard of living** *or* **living standards** = quality of personal home life (such as amount of food or clothes bought, size of family car, etc.); **production standards** = quality of production; **up to standard** = of acceptable quality; ***this printing is not up to standard*** *or* ***does not meet our standards*** **2** *adjective* normal *or* usual; **standard document** *or* **standard form** *or* **standard paragraph** *or* **standard text** = normal printed document *or* form *or* paragraph which is used many times; **standard agreement** *or* **standard contract** = normal printed contract form; **standard letter** = letter which is sent without any change of text to various correspondents; **standard page** = largest page size which can be printed on a press; **standard paper sizes** *see* ISO SIZES

standardization *noun* making sure that everything fits a standard *or* is produced in the same way; ***standardization of cover design in a series***

standardize *verb* to make sure that everything fits a standard *or* is produced in the same way

standing *adjective* **standing order** = order to a publisher to send the same quantity of books at regular intervals (such as a standing order for 20 copies of all new titles in a series); **standing type** = pages of a book in metal type which are kept by the printer in case a reprint is needed, and for which the publisher pays rent; **keep standing** = instruction to a printer not to distribute the metal type, (or possibly film) but to keep it ready for further printings

staple 1 *noun* small piece of bent metal for attaching papers together; ***he used a pair of scissors to take the staples out of the documents*** **2** *verb* **to staple papers together** = to attach papers with staples; ***he could not take away separate pages, because the documents were stapled together***

stapler *noun* small device used to attach papers together with staples

star *noun* printing reference mark, an asterisk (*)

starred *adjective* with a star printed *or* written on it; ***the starred paragraphs are to be indented;*** **star signature** *or* **starred signature** = signature with a signature mark followed by a star, showing that it has to be bound as an insert inside another section

stat *US* = PHOTOSTAT

state publishing *noun* publishing which is organized by a government

statement *noun* **(a)** saying something clearly; **statement of expenses** = detailed list of money spent; **royalty statement** = detailed account from a publisher to an author, concerning the number of copies of a book sold, the revenue and the royalty earned by the author **(b) statement of account** = list of invoices and credits and debits sent by a supplier to a customer at the end of each month

state-of-the-art *adjective* very modern *or* as technically advanced as possible

station *noun* one of the points on a collating machine

stationery *noun* office supplies for writing, such as paper, carbons, pens, etc.; **stationery binding** = binding style which is used for books which are to be written in, and therefore must lie flat when open (also called 'account-book binding'); **computer stationery** = paper specially made for use in a computer printer; **continuous stationery** = paper made as a long sheet used in computer printers; **preprinted stationery** = computer stationery (such as invoices) which is preprinted with the company heading and a form onto which the details will be printed by the computer; **Her Majesty's Stationery Office (HMSO)** = British government agency which prints and publishes all government documents

statute *noun* law made by parliament; **statute book** = list of laws passed by parliament

statutory *adjective* fixed by law; **statutory deposit copy** = copy of a book or other publication which has to be deposited with a National Library according to law

steel *noun* **steel engraving** = engraved plate, used for printing delicate designs such as banknotes

stem *noun* **(a)** vertical main part of a printed letter **(b)** body, the main part of a piece of metal type

stencil *noun* **(a)** sheet of special paper which can be written or typed on, and used in a duplicating machine **(b)** piece of material with shapes and symbols already cut out, allowing designers to draw components and other symbols rapidly; ***the stencil has all the electronic components on it; the plan looks much neater if you use a stencil*** **(c)** prepared piece of silk or other material used in screen process printing

stencilled *adjective* copies made with a stencil

step 1 *noun* **(a) step index** *or* **cut-in index** = index where the outside margin of the book is cut away in a series of steps down the page, each step being marked with a tag and a letter of the alphabet, often used for address books **(b) stepmark** *see* BLACK STEP **2** *verb* to cut in steps

step and repeat *noun* method of taking a single image and repeating it many times on a sheet of paper (used when printing stamps, for example)

stereo *or* **stereotype** *noun* duplicate printing plate, cast in metal or plastic from a mould taken from metal type

stet 1 *Latin word meaning* 'let it stand'; instruction to a printer to leave something without making any corrections which have been instructed **2** *verb* not to change something; ***he phoned the printer to tell him to stet the correction on the last page of proofs***

> COMMENT: when instructing the compositor not to change a typeset text, the part to be left without changes is underlined with a dotted line and the word 'stet' is written in the margin (nowadays, a tick is used)

stick 1 *noun* **composing stick** = sort of narrow box in which the compositor places the pieces of type as he sets each line **2** *verb* to attach with glue; ***to stick a stamp on a letter; they stuck a poster on the door***

sticker 1 *noun* small piece of gummed paper or plastic to be stuck on something as an advertisement *or* to indicate a price; **airmail sticker** = blue sticker with the words 'By air mail' which can be stuck on an envelope or parcel to show that it is being sent by air **2** *verb* to put a price sticker on an article for sale; ***we had to sticker all the stock;*** *see also* RESTICKER

stick-up initial *or* **raised initial** *noun* initial letter set in a larger size than the rest of the text, the letter being on the base line and rising above the ascender line (the opposite of a drop initial)

stiff *adjective* hard *or* which does not bend easily; **stiff cover** = cased cover, cover in thick boards, as opposed to a limp cover; **stiff leaf** = piece of paper which has been strengthened by having another leaf pasted onto it

stiffener *noun* strip of thin card glued to the inside of a cloth spine to make it stiff

still *noun* photograph of one frame from a motion film

stillage *noun* pallet, flat wooden base on which goods (sheets of paper, printed sheets, bound books, etc.) can be stacked for easy handling by a fork-lift truck

stipple 1 *noun* pattern of irregular dots to produce a tone; **mechanical stipple** = stipple which is preprinted and can be applied to the design by the designer **2** *verb* to put a pattern of coloured dots on paper; **stippled endpapers** = endpapers decorated with a pattern of colours

> COMMENT: stippling involves making irregular patterns of dots or patches of colour, as opposed to marbling which involves irregular swirling patterns of lines of colour

stipulate *verb* to demand that a condition be put into a contract; ***to stipulate that the contract should run for five years; to pay the stipulated charges; the company failed to pay on the date stipulated in the contract; the contract stipulates that the author is liable for libel costs***

stipulation *noun* condition in a contract

stitch *verb* to sew the folded pages of a signature together; to sew the sewn signatures of a book together; *see also* SADDLE STITCH, SIDE-STITCH, WIRE-STITCH

stitcher *noun* machine for stitching pages together

stitching *noun* action of attaching pages together with wire or thread; **metal stitching** = attaching the sections of a book together with metal staples

STM = SCIENTIFIC, TECHNICAL AND MEDICAL

stock 1 *noun* **(a)** quantity of materials for use in manufacture; **paper stocks** = quantities of paper kept in stock (either by a publisher *or* by a printer) for use at some later date **(b)** quantity of goods (such as books) for sale; **opening stock** = details of stock at the beginning of an accounting period; **closing stock** = details of stock at the end of an accounting period; **stock code** = number and letters which indicate an item of stock; **stock control** = making sure that enough stock is kept and that quantities and movements of stock are noted; **stock depreciation** = reduction in value of stock which is held in a warehouse for some time; **stock figures** = details of how many goods are in the warehouse *or* store, etc., on a certain date; **stock level** = quantity of goods kept in stock; ***we try to keep stock levels low during the summer;*** **stock return** = details which a printer supplies to a publisher showing the stocks he holds of books or printed sheets; **stock turn** *or* **stock turnround** *or* **stock turnover** = total value of stock sold in a year divided by the average value of goods in stock; **stock valuation** = estimating the value of stock at the end of an accounting period; **to buy a shop with stock at valuation** = to pay for the stock the same amount as its value as estimated by the valuer; **stock in hand** = stock held in a shop *or* warehouse; **to purchase stock at valuation** = to pay for stock the price it is valued at; (NOTE: US English uses **inventory** instead of **stock**) **(c) in stock** *or* **out of stock** = available *or* not available in the warehouse *or* store; ***we hold 2,000 titles in stock; the title went out of stock just before Christmas but came back into stock in the first week of January; we are out of stock of this series;*** **to take stock** = to count the items in a warehouse **(d)** normal *or* usually kept in stock; ***we use the printer's stock 80gsm paper;*** **stock paper** = paper which a printer always carries in stock, usually in a range of qualities and in sizes which fit his printing machinery; **stock size** = normal size; ***the book is in an odd format and needs a non-stock paper which had to be ordered in*** **(e)** furnish, the mixture of various substances from which paper is manufactured (formed of wood pulp, chemicals, and water); **stock chest** = container in which stock is kept before it is drawn off into the papermaking machine **(f)** paper used for a certain purpose **2** *verb* to hold goods for sale in a warehouse *or* store *or* shop; ***the wholesaler stocks 2000 titles***

stock controller *noun* person who notes movements of stock; ***the stock controller monitors the current stock of each title***

stock-in-trade *noun* goods held by a business for sale

stockist *noun* person *or* shop which stocks a certain item

stocklist *noun* list of items carried in stock

stockroom *noun* room where stores are kept

stocktaking *noun* counting of goods in stock at the end of an accounting period; ***the warehouse is closed for the annual stocktaking;*** **stocktaking sale** = sale of goods cheaply to clear a warehouse before stocktaking

stock up *verb* to buy supplies of something which you will need in the future; ***they stocked up with computer paper***

COMMENT: stock depreciation is calculated by the publisher according to a system agreed with the company's auditors. Stock is generally depreciated according to its saleability: a reference book or popular classic which might continue to have a steady sale over a period of years may not be depreciated at all. On the other hand, a topical book (such as one on the current Olympic Games) may be written off completely, since it will not sell at all once the event it commemorates has passed. The effect of depreciation is to lower the profit in the current year, and (if the book continues to sell) to increase the profit in the following year. Depreciated stock can be sold to remainder merchants

stone *noun* **(a)** flat surface, usually metal, on which the pages of metal type are made up into formes; **stone hand** *or* **stoneman** = person who imposes pages; *US* **stone proofs** = press proofs, final proofs which are run off just before the printing run starts **(b)** hard mineral surface, formerly used in lithography; **stone engraving** = engraving of a lithographic stone

stop 1 *noun* **(a)** end of an action, such as not supplying an account; **account on stop** = account which is not supplied because it has not paid its latest invoices; **to put an account on stop** = to stop supplying a customer (usually because he has not paid); **to put a stop on a cheque** = to tell the bank not to pay a cheque which you have written; **stop cylinder** = letterpress cylinder which rotates once to print a sheet, then prints the next sheet after the bed has returned to its place **(b)** point where a line ends where it meets another line at right angles (as in a stopped heading) **2** *verb* **(a)** to make (something) not to move any more; **stopped heading** = heading which runs across the top of columns in an account book, the vertical rules end where they meet the heading **(b) to stop an account** = not to supply an account any more on credit because bills have not been paid; **to stop a cheque** = to ask a bank not to pay a cheque you have written; **to stop payments** = not to make any further payments

stop out *verb* to paint out parts of a negative to make sure they will be etched when blocks are being made

stop press *noun* fudge, small section in a newspaper, reserved for very late items of news

storage *noun* **(a)** keeping in store *or* in a warehouse; **storage capacity** = space available for storage; **storage facilities** = equipment and buildings suitable for storage **(b)** cost of keeping goods in store; ***storage was 10% of value, so we scrapped the stock*** **(c)** facility for storing data in a computer; ***disk with a storage capacity of 10Mb;*** **storage unit** = device attached to a computer for storing information on disk or tape

store 1 *noun* **(a)** (i) place where goods are kept; (ii) quantity of items *or* materials kept because they will be needed **(b)** large shop; **chain store** = one store in a number of stores; **department store** = large store with sections for different types of goods; *see also* BOOKSTORE **2** *verb* **(a)** to keep in a warehouse; ***to store goods for six months*** **(b)** to keep for future use; ***we store our pay records on computer;*** **store and forward** = communications system that stores a number of messages before retransmitting them

storekeeper *or* **storeman** *noun* person in charge of a storeroom

storeroom *noun* room where stock can be kept *or* small warehouse attached to a factory

storyboard *noun* board with details of the pictures to be taken for a TV commercial

storyline *noun* rough description of the story of a sequence of photographs or other illustrations

straight *adjective* **(a)** (line) with no curves; **straight edge** = paper edge which is cut straight (as opposed to a deckle edge) **(b)** **straight matter** *or* **straight text** = text which is continuous, with no changes of layout; ***the MS is 105 pages of straight text;*** **straight run** = printing on a press with no changes of plate

strain *verb* to remove impurities *or* solid matter from a liquid by passing it through a mesh

strainer *noun* metal container through which paper pulp is passed to remove impurities

strawboard *noun* board used for cheap cased bindings, made from straw

stream *noun* mass of things (such as people *or* traffic), all going in the same direction; **to come on stream** = to start production; **stream feeder** = device for moving sheets of paper into the press, each sheet slightly overlapping the next

streamer *noun* **(a)** device for attaching a tape storage unit to a computer **(b)** large headline running across a page of a newspaper **(c)** long strip of paper *or* ribbon, used for publicity purposes or as a decoration

streaming *noun* reading data from a storage device in one continuous operation, without processor intervention

streets = RIVERS

stress marks *noun* small marks which indicate where the stress falls on a word (used in phonetics)

strike *verb* **(a)** to hit; ***the printing head strikes the ribbon and the paper at the same time*** **(b)** to make a matrix for casting type, by hitting the blank metal with a punch

strike-on *noun* method of typing text for printing, where the type hits a carbon ribbon and leaves an impression on paper (as in a typewriter); *see also* COLD COMPOSITION, TYPEWRITER COMPOSITION

strike out *verb* to cross out (a word *or* text)

strike-through *noun* ink which seeps through paper and is visible on the other side of the page; *compare* SHOW-THROUGH

COMMENT: when the printing on one side of the paper can be seen from the other side, this is due either to show-through or to strike-through. Show-through is caused by inadequate opacity of the paper, while strike-through results from the vehicle (the liquid component) of an oil-based ink penetrating right through the sheet. The more a paper is oil-absorbent, the greater the possibility of strike-through

stringer *noun* journalist who works freelance for a newspaper (he is paid by the article), covering events in a particular town or country

strip 1 *noun* narrow piece of paper *or* film **2** *verb* to remove; ***they stripped the covers off the book and replaced them with new covers***

strip cartoon *noun* series of humorous drawings telling a story

strip in *verb* to insert a small patch of paper or film in a hole cut in the main sheet of paper or film; ***the corrections to the text have been stripped in on the film***

stripping *noun* imposition for offset printing, by making film up into imposed pages, sticking the pieces of negative or positive film onto backing, ready for filming; **stripping-in** = making a correction to a film or bromide by cutting a hole in the original to remove incorrect text and insert correct text; **stripping-film** very thin film used for making corrections

stroke *noun* **(a)** basic curved *or* straight line that makes up a character; **up stroke** *or* **down stroke** = line made by moving the pen up *or* down the piece of paper **(b) (oblique) stroke** = solidus, the printed character (/)

stub *noun* small section of paper left after folding; **cheque stub** = small piece of paper left in the cheque book after a cheque has been removed; **stub binding** = binding process where the folded sections are sewn to stubs of paper which are then glued to form the spine

studio *noun* place where designers, film producers, artists, etc., work; **design studio** = independent firm which specializes in creating designs for companies; **film studio** *or* **photographer's studio** = place where films are shot *or* where a photographer takes photographs

study aids *noun* materials (books, cassettes, computer programs) for sale to students who want to learn by self-study at home

stuff *verb* to put papers, etc., into envelopes; ***we pay casual workers £2 an hour for stuffing envelopes*** *or* ***for envelope stuffing***

stuffer *noun* **(a)** advertising paper to be put in an envelope for mailing **(b)** ingredients for making paper

style *noun* way of doing *or* making something; **house style** *or* **style of the house** = editorial style (spellings, punctuation, etc.) which is adopted in a publishing company; ***the house style adopts the -ize ending for verbs;*** **style sheet** = printed sheet, listing all the rules of house style for a publishing company *or* for contributors to a magazine, which has to be followed by authors and editors

COMMENT: the aim of a house style is to give consistency to all the products of a publishing house, thus making them more recognizable to the reading public. In the case of magazines, contributors will be sent a style sheet which shows how they should lay out their contributions. A house style will cover many aspects of layout, such as headlines, position of folios, typefaces and sizes; it will also cover details of spelling and punctuation: the form for writing dates (1st January 1999 *or* January 1st,1999 *or* 1st Jan. 1999 *or* 01.01.99 etc.); the use of full stops after abbreviations (Mr *or* Mr., P.O.Box *or* PO Box, etc.). Most publishing companies have their own style sheets which are given to editors and form part of the training programme for new editorial and production staff. Many printers as well as publishers have their own house style; many printers and publishers follow the style of one of the University Presses (Oxford and Cambridge). See also HART'S RULES, MANUAL OF STYLE

stylus *noun* **(a)** instrument with a sharp point for engraving on metals **(b)** special pen used for graphics

sub 1 *noun* **(a)** wages paid in advance **(b)** = SUB-EDITOR, SUBSCRIPTION **2** *verb* to sub-edit (a text); **subbing** *or* **sub-editing** = editing of a manuscript before it is sent for typesetting

sub- *prefix* under *or* less important

sub-agency *noun* small agency which is part of a large agency

sub-agent *noun* person who is in charge of a sub-agency

subdivision *noun* section of a text within a division

sub-edit *verb* to read, mark and correct a manuscript text, so that it fits house style as regards spellings, syntax, etc.; also making sure that the facts in it are correct, that the illustrations are obtained and are correctly referred to in the text, that the index and page numbers are correct, etc.; ***the sub-editing of the MS will take about four weeks***

sub-editor *noun* **(a)** member of staff of a publishing house who sub-edits a manuscript; (NOTE: the department dealing with the sub-editing of manuscripts is called the **editorial department**) **(b)** member of staff of a newspaper or magazine who edits text by journalists

sub-heading *or* **sub-head** *noun* heading used to divide up a chapter into separate sections

subject *noun* the matter which a book is written about; **subject catalogue** *or* **subject index** = catalogue which lists books according to their subjects (such as cookery, gardening, etc.); **subject entry** = entry in a subject index *or* catalogue

subject to *adjective* depending on; **the contract is subject to government approval** = the contract will be valid only if it is approved by the government; **agreement** *or* **sale subject to contract** = agreement *or* sale which is not legal until a proper contract has been signed; **offer subject to availability** = the offer is valid only if the goods are available

sub judice *adverb* being considered by a court (and so not to be mentioned in the media); ***the papers cannot report the case because it is still sub judice***

sublicense *verb* to license the use of something which you have been licensed to use

COMMENT: for example, a publisher who has been licensed to publish a translation of a text, may (with the agreement of the original copyright holder) sublicense another publisher to reprint the translated text locally

submission *noun* act of submitting

submit *verb* **(a)** to put (something) forward to be examined; ***to submit a proposal to the committee; he submitted a claim to the insurers; the reps are asked to submit their expenses claims once a month*** **(b)** to send a manuscript to a publisher, asking for it to be considered for publication; ***he submitted the MS to six publishers before getting a positive response***

subscribe *verb* **(a) to subscribe to a magazine** = to pay in advance for a series of issues of a magazine **(b)** *(of a bookseller)* to place orders for a book in advance of publication **(c)** *(of a publisher's rep)* to visit bookshops to ask buyers to order copies of a book before publication; ***the book will be subscribed during the summer for publication in October***

subscriber *noun* **(a) subscriber to a magazine** *or* **magazine subscriber** = person who has paid in advance for a series of issues of a magazine; ***the extra issue is sent free to subscribers*** **(b) telephone subscriber** = person who has a telephone

subscript *noun* figure printed in smaller size and lower down than a normal figure (i.e. below the base line); *see also* SUPERSCRIPT (NOTE: used in chemical formulae: CO_2)

subscription *noun* **(a)** money paid in advance for a series of issues of a magazine *or* for membership of a society; ***did you remember to pay the subscription to the computer magazine? he forgot to renew his club subscription;*** **to take out a subscription to a magazine** = to start paying for a series of issues of a magazine; **to cancel a subscription to a magazine** = to stop paying for a magazine; **subscription library** = library run on a commercial basis, where the members pay to borrow books; **subscription price** = special price (lower than individual issue price) for a magazine; **subscription rates** = amount of money to be paid for a series of issues of a magazine **(b)** orders for a new book placed by bookshops before publication; ***the subscription has reached 2,500*** *or* ***we have 2,500 subscriptions for the book***

subsidiary 1 *adjective* (thing) which is less important; ***they agreed to most of the conditions in the contract but queried one or two subsidiary items;*** **subsidiary company** = company which is owned by a parent company; **subsidiary rights** = rights other than the right to publish a book in its first form, such as paperback rights, rights to adapt the book (for film *or* TV *or* into a foreign language), rights to serialize it in a magazine, etc. **2** *noun* company which is owned by a parent company; ***most of the group profit***

was contributed by the subsidiaries in the Far East

subsidize *verb* to help by giving money; ***the government has refused to subsidize the car industry;*** **subsidized publication** = publication which is partly paid for by a subsidy from an official body *or* from a sponsor

subsidy *noun* money given to help something which is not profitable; ***the country's publishing industry exists on government subsidies***

substance *noun* weight of paper, as shown by the grammage (number of grams per square metre) or in the USA, as pounds per 500 sheets

substitute 1 *noun* person *or* thing which takes the place of someone *or* something else **2** *verb* to put something to take the place of something else; ***in the section on earthquakes, substitute 1997 for 1995***

substrate *noun* (i) paper, the surface on which text *or* illustration is printed; (ii) card or board, used for making boxes

subtitle 1 *noun* title printed under a main title **2** *verb* to give a subtitle to a book; ***the book is subtitled 'A study in African politics'***

subtractive *noun* (colour) which is the complement of another (i.e. it filters out that colour from white light); **subtractive primaries** = the process primaries, cyan, magenta and yellow, which, when combined, make black; **subtractive process** = origination using the three subtractive primaries

suction *noun* action of sucking air *or* liquid out; **suction box** = device which removes water from paper as it is formed, by sucking the liquid out under a vacuum as the paper passes over the box; **suction feeder** = machine which lifts a sheet of paper with suction caps before feeding it into a printing press; **suction roll** *or* **rotary suction box** = metal cylinder with perforations, which has a suction box inside it

sue *verb* to take someone to court *or* to start legal proceedings against someone to get money as compensation; ***he is suing the publisher and the author for libel***

suffix *noun* syllable or letters attached to the end of a word which alter the meaning of the word; *compare* PREFIX

sulphate process *US* **sulfate process** *noun* alkaline process for digesting wood pulp, where groundwood is heated with caustic soda and sodium sulphide, giving a strong pulp used to make kraft paper

sulphite process *US* **sulfite process** *noun* acid process for digesting wood pulp, where groundwood is heated with lime and sulphur dioxide to produce the pulp from which chemical paper is made. The paper is of better quality than that made by the sulphate process, and if beaten becomes translucent; **sulphite pulp** = pulp which has been treated by the sulphite process

summarize *verb* to give a short description of something; ***the document summarizes the advantages of the new distribution system***

summary *noun* text which is a shortened version of a longer text; ***the author has sent in a summary of the novel***

sunk cord sewing *noun* binding process where the cords lie in notches cut in the backs of the signatures

super *noun* thick gauze used to make the hinge between the boards and the book block

supercalender *noun* machine through which damp paper is passed after it has left the papermaking machine, used to make smooth, hard and glossy paper

supercalendered paper *noun* paper with a smooth shiny surface made by passing it through a supercalender

supercalendering *noun* giving a very smooth finish to paper by passing it through a supercalender

superimpose *verb* to print one thing on top of another; ***to superimpose one colour on another***

superimposition *noun* enhancing an image by blocking part of a negative and exposing it again

superior *adjective* **superior figures** *or* **superior letters** = superscripts, figures *or* letters which are set in smaller size and printed higher up above the x-height; NOTE: used in scientific setting: 10^{-12}

supermarket *noun* large store, usually selling food, where customers serve themselves and pay at a checkout desk; ***sales in supermarkets*** *or* ***supermarket sales are more and more important to mass market publishers***

superscript *noun* small character printed higher than the normal line of characters; *compare with* SUBSCRIPT NOTE: used often in scientific setting: 10^{5}

supershift *noun* level of shift on a typesetting keyboard which makes another font available

super VGA *see* SVGA

supplement 1 *noun* **(a)** material printed at the back of a book; ***a useful supplement gives details of hotels and their room rates*** **(b)** extra volume *or* section in a reference book, containing new material which is not in the main text **(c)** special extra section of a newspaper, usually on a special subject; ***the travel supplement comes with the weekend issue of the paper*** **2** *verb* to add to; ***we will supplement the warehouse staff with six part-timers during the Christmas rush***

supplier *noun* person *or* company which supplies *or* sells goods or services; **educational supplier** *or* **school book supplier** = wholesaler who specializes in supplying educational equipment or books to schools

supply 1 *noun* **(a)** providing something which is needed; ***problems concerning the supply of books to schools;*** **supply and demand** = amount of a product which is available and the amount which is wanted by customers; **the law of supply and demand** = general rule that the amount of a product which is available is related to the needs of the possible customers **(b)** stock of something which is needed; **office supplies** = goods needed to run an office (such as paper, pens, typewriters) **2** *verb* to provide something which is needed; ***the wholesalers will supply almost any title at 24 hours notice***

suppress *verb* to prevent something being published; ***the biography was suppressed by his family, after several months of legal battles***

suppression *noun* preventing something being published

surcharge *noun* extra charge; **import surcharge** = extra duty charged on imported goods, to try to stop them from being imported and to encourage local manufacture; **small order surcharge** = extra amount charged by a publisher for a bookshop order which does not reach a minimum quantity or a minimum value

surface *noun* outside layer of something; **surface paper** = coated paper with a shiny smooth surface, which has been coated with a mixture of china clay and size; **surface plate** = normal litho plate (not deep-etched); **surface-sizing** = TUB-SIZING **surface strength** = ability of the surface of paper not to stick to a sticky substance; **surface oil absorbency tester (SOAT)** = method for measuring the surface oil absorption time; **surface oil absorption time (SOAT)** *or* **surface oil resistance time (SORT)** = time taken for oil to be absorbed by paper

> COMMENT: the PIRA SOAT method for measuring surface oil absorption time requires a brass roll carrying a drop of liquid paraffin to roll across the paper, transferring some of the liquid to it. The time taken for the paper to absorb 75% of the liquid is the surface oil absorption time

suspend *verb* to stop (something) for a time; ***we have suspended payments while we***

are waiting for news from our agent; mailings have been suspended until the autumn; deliveries have been suspended during the mail strike

suspension *noun* stopping something for a time; **suspension points** = series of dots (usually three dots), printed close together, to show a hesitation

SVGA = SUPER VGA enhancement to the standard VGA graphics display system which allows resolutions of up to 800x600 pixels with 16 million colours

swap up *verb (of a representative)* to exchange one of a company's books for that of another publisher (in a bookshop)

swash letters *noun* ornamental italic letters with elegant curves at the ends of the strokes; **swash initial** = swash letter used as the initial letter of a paragraph

swatch *noun* small sample; **colour swatch** = small sample of colour which the finished product must have

swell *noun* particularly thick part of sewn sections, caused by the thread

swelled rule *noun* ornamental rules which are fatter in the centre than at the ends

switch *verb* to change from one thing to another; **we have switched printers** = we have stopped using one printer and are now using another

switch over to *verb* to change to something quite different; ***we have switched over to a French supplier; the factory has switched over to web-fed machines***

swop = SWAP

swung dash *noun* printing symbol (~) used in dictionaries to show that a headword is being repeated; sign used in some computer programs to indicate a carriage return

symbol *noun* sign *or* picture *or* object which represents something; ***this dictionary uses the symbol ⇨ to indicate cross-references; they use a series of symbols to show different classes of hotels***

syndicate *verb* to produce an article, drawing, etc., which is published in several newspapers or magazines at the same time

syndicated *adjective* published in several newspapers or magazines; ***he writes a syndicated column on personal finance***

synonym *noun* word which means the same thing as another word

synonymous *adjective* meaning the same; ***the words 'error' and 'mistake' are synonymous***

synopsis *noun* short text, giving the basic details of a book; ***he sent in a synopsis of his new novel***

synthetic paper *noun* paper made using man-made fibres (it does not contain any cellulose)

syQuest *noun* disk for storing digital data, available in 44, 88 or 200 Mb

system *noun* **computer system** = set of programs, commands, etc., which run a computer; **systems analysis** = using a computer to suggest how a company should work by analyzing the way in which it works at present; **systems analyst** = person who specializes in systems analysis

Tt

tab *noun* **(a)** = TABULATOR, TABULATION **tab rack** *or* **ruler line** = graduated scale, displayed on the screen, showing the position of tabulation columns; **tab stops** *or* **tabulation stops** = preset points along a line, where the printing head *or* cursor will stop for each tabulation command **(b)** small piece of paper, attached to a sheet *or* card to draw attention to something; **tab card** = card with a small tab, used as an index card in a card-index; **tab index** = index to a book, where little tabs with the letters of the alphabet are stuck to the edges of the pages

tabbing *noun* movement of the cursor in a word-processing program from one column to the next; ***tabbing can be done from inside the program;*** **decimal tabbing** = adjusting a column of numbers so that the decimal points are aligned vertically

table *noun* list of figures *or* facts set out in columns (sometimes with rules separating the columns); **table matter** = text in columns with rules between them; **table of contents** = list of contents in a book or magazine, usually printed at the beginning (in some countries it is printed at the back of a book); **table rolls** = rollers which hold up the wire mesh in a small paper mill

tablet *noun* **graphics tablet** = graphics pad, a flat device that allows a user to input graphical information into a computer by drawing on its surface

tabloid *noun* **(a)** trimmed page size for newspapers, 400 x 300mm (about half the normal newspaper format) **(b)** small format newspaper, usually aimed at a down-market readership

tabular *adjective* **in tabular form** = arranged in a table; **tabular material** *or* **tabular matter** = figures *or* text set out in columns; **tabular setting** = setting in columns

tabulate *verb* to set out text in columns, with the cursor moving to each new column automatically as the text is keyboarded

tabulation *noun* (i) arrangement of a table of figures; (ii) moving a printing head *or* cursor to a preset distance along a line; **tabulation markers** = symbols displayed to indicate the position of tabulation stops; **tabulation stops** = preset points along a line at which a printing head *or* cursor will stop at for each tabulation command

tabulator *noun* part of a typewriter *or* computer which sets words or figures automatically in columns

tack *noun (of ink, coating or glue)* stickiness; **tack value** = measurement of how sticky a substance is

tag *noun* **(a)** tie-on label **(b)** one section of a computer instruction **(c)** identifying characters attached to a file *or* item (of data); ***each file has a three-letter tag for rapid identification***

tag image file format *see* TIFF

tail *noun* **(a)** (i) downstroke of a letter; (ii) curved end stroke of a letter (such as the capitals R or K) **(b)** bottom edge of a book *or* page; **tail cap** = piece of leather binding on the spine, which folds over at the bottom and is tucked into the inside of the spine; **tail margin** = margin between the text and the bottom of the page

tailband *noun* decorative strip (often in two colours) along the bottom of the back of the book, inside the spine; ***a quarto with blue headbands and tailbands, and gilt edges***

tailpiece *noun* decoration printed towards the bottom of a page at the end of a piece of text, either at the end of a chapter, or at the end of a whole book; *compare* HEADPIECE

take 1 *noun* part of a large job given to a compositor to set **2** *verb* **(a)** to receive *or* to get; **the shop takes £20,000 a week** = the shop receives £20,000 a week in cash sales **(b)** to do a certain action; **to take stock** = to count the items in a warehouse

take back *verb* to move text from the beginning of one line back to the end of the previous line *or* from the top of one page back to the bottom of the previous page; *see also* TAKE OVER (NOTE: US English is **run back**)

take in *verb* to put more text into the material already typeset; ***take in three lines from the next galley***

take out *verb* to remove; ***the lawyers asked the publisher to take out all references to the Prime Minister in the text***

take over *verb* to move text from the end of one line to the beginning of the next line *or* from the bottom of one page to the top of the next page; *see also* TAKE BACK (NOTE: US English is **run down**)

talking book *noun* text of a book, read and recorded on a cassette

tape *noun* **(a)** long, flat, narrow piece of sensitized plastic; **magnetic tape** = narrow length of thin plastic coated with a magnetic material used for recording information; **computer tape** = magnetic tape used in computers; **tape merging** = taking two tapes with data and combining them (usually a master tape is combined with corrections or additions on a second tape) **(b)** long flat narrow strip of paper; **punched tape** = strip of paper on which information can be recorded in the form of punched holes; **tape punch** = machine that punches holes into paper tape; **tape reader** = machine that reads punched holes in paper tape *or* signals on magnetic tape **(c)** long flat narrow strip of woven material, glued to the back of the sewn signatures to strengthen the back of the book **(d)** strip of material or leather which carries paper from one part of a printing machine to another

target 1 *noun* thing to aim for; **production targets** = amount of units a factory is expected to produce; **sales targets** = amount of sales a representative is expected to achieve; **target market** = market in which a company is planning to sell its goods **2** *verb* **to target a market** = to plan to sell goods in a certain market

TCP = TRANSMISSION CONTROL PROTOCOL standard data transmission protocol that provides full duplex transmission, the protocol bundles data into packets and checks for errors

TCP/IP = TRANSMISSION CONTROL PROTOCOL/INTERFACE PROGRAM data transfer protocol used in networks and communications systems (often used in Unix-based networks)

teacher's book *or* **teacher's manual** *noun* book published to go with a set of student's books, giving the teacher answers to questions, suggestions for teaching, etc.

tear *verb* to split by being pulled apart; **to tear off** = to remove a sheet from a pad of paper, by tearing (usually along perforations); **tear factor** = ratio of the paper weight to the tear strength of a piece of paper across the grain; **tear strength** = measurement of the resistance of paper to tearing; **tear test** = test to see how strong paper is or to show in which direction the grain lies

tearsheet *noun* page removed from a book *or* periodical, and sent to an advertiser as proof that his advertisement has been placed

technical *adjective* referring to particular machine *or* process; ***the document gives all the technical details on the new computer typesetting machine;*** **technical books** =

books which deal with technical subjects; **technical editor** = editor on the staff of a specialist magazine, who is responsible for testing, writing about and reviewing equipment; **the technical press** = specialist periodicals dealing with technical subjects; **technical translator** = translator who specializes in translating technical books; **technical writer** = author of specialized books on technical subjects

technical profile *noun* describes the values of the printing variables that must be: (i) considered by anyone who is producing repro for a particular publication; and (ii) also followed by companies making colour proofs of the material for that publication

> COMMENT: the technical profile should include: substrate type, inks used, tone transfer characteristic - solid density and dot gain

technological *adjective* referring to technology; **the technological revolution** = changing of industry by introducing new technology

technology *noun* applying scientific knowledge to industrial processes; **information technology** = technology involved in acquiring, storing, processing, and distributing information by electronic means (including radio, TV, telephone and computers); **the introduction of new technology** = putting new electronic equipment into a business or industry

tel = TELEPHONE

telecommunications *noun* technology of passing and receiving messages over a distance (as in telephone, cable, radio, etc.)

teleorder *noun* order placed through the teleordering system

teleordering *noun* book ordering system, in which the bookseller's orders are entered into a computer which then puts the order through to the central computer at the end of the day, the orders being sent on to the publisher's distribution service the following day

telephone 1 *noun* machine used for speaking to someone over a long distance; **house telephone** *or* **internal telephone** = telephone for calling from one room to another in an office or hotel; **telephone book** *or* **telephone directory** = book which lists all people and businesses in alphabetical order with their telephone numbers; **telephone orders** = orders received by telephone; ***since we mailed the catalogue we have received a large number of telephone orders*** **2** *verb* **to telephone a place** *or* **a person** = to call a place *or* someone by telephone; **he telephoned the order through to the warehouse** = he telephoned the warehouse to place an order

teleprocessing (TP) *noun* processing of data at a distance (as on a central computer from outside terminals)

telesales *plural noun* sales made by telephone

teletypesetter *noun* setting machine operated from paper tape

teletypesetting (TTS) *noun* typesetting operated by a punched paper tape, often over a telegraphic system, formerly much used by newspapers

teletypewriter *noun* keyboard and printer attached to a computer system which can input data either direct *or* by making punched paper tape

teletext *noun* method of transmitting text and information with a normal TV signal, usually as a serial bit stream that can be displayed using a decoder and an ordinary TV set

> COMMENT: teletext constantly transmits pages of information which are repeated one after the other; the user can stop one to read it. This is different from viewdata, where the user calls up a page of text using a telephone line

television (TV) *noun* (i) system for broadcasting pictures and sound using high-frequency radio waves, captured by a receiver and shown on a screen; (ii) device that can receive broadcast signals with an aerial and display images on a CRT screen with sound; **television receive only** *see* TVRO **television rights** *or* **TV rights** = right to adapt a work for the television

temp *noun* **(a)** = TEMPORARILY **TEMP/OS** = TEMPORARILY OUT OF STOCK report from a publisher to a bookseller, showing that a book is out of stock at present, but should be in stock soon **(b)** temporary secretary; ***we have had two temps working in the office this week to clear the backlog of letters;*** **temp agency** = office which deals with finding temporary secretaries for offices

template *noun* (i) plastic *or* metal sheet with cut-out symbols to help the drawing of flowcharts and circuit diagrams; (ii) *(in text processing)* standard text (such as a standard letter *or* invoice) into which specific details (company address *or* prices *or* quantities) can be added; **template command** = command that allows functions *or* other commands to be easily set; ***a template paragraph command enables the user to specify the number of spaces each paragraph should be indented***

tensile strength *noun* strength of paper to withstand pulling; **tensile strength tester** = instrument to test the tensile strength of paper

tension *noun* tightness (of a web of paper as it passes through a printing press)

term *noun* **(a)** period of time when something is legally valid; ***the term of a contract; the term of the loan is fifteen years; the term of copyright is fifty years from the death of the author;*** **short-term** = for a period of months; **long-term** = for a long period of time; **medium-term** = for a period of one or two years **(b) terms** = conditions *or* duties which have to be carried out as part of a contract; arrangements which have to be agreed before a contract is valid (such as conditions agreed between a publisher and an author, between a publisher and a printer, or between a publisher and a bookshop); ***he refused to agree to some of the terms of the contract; by*** *or* ***under the terms of the contract, the company is responsible for all damage to the property; to negotiate for better terms;*** **terms of payment** *or* **payment terms** = conditions for paying something; **terms of sale** = conditions attached to a sale; **cash terms** = lower terms which apply if the customer pays cash; **'terms: cash with order'** = terms of sale showing that payment has to be made in cash when the order is placed; **export terms** = special terms offered to booksellers who are buying for export, or to booksellers in other countries (usually a longer credit period, and also a higher discount); **net terms** = terms offered by a publisher to an agent or bookseller on the basis of an agreed net price (without further discount); **trade terms** = special discount for people in the same trade; **wholesale terms** = special terms offered by a publisher to a wholesaler (usually at least 50% discount) **(c) terms of employment** = conditions set out in a contract of employment

terminal *noun* **(a)** end part, or tail, of a letter **(b) computer terminal** = keyboard and screen, by which information can be put into a computer or can be called up from a database; ***computer system consisting of a microprocessor and six terminals***

terminable *adjective* which can be terminated

terminate *verb* to end (something) *or* to bring (something) to an end; ***to terminate an agreement; his employment was terminated; the option terminates on July 31st***

termination *noun* **(a)** bringing to an end; **termination clause** = clause which explains how and when a contract can be terminated **(b)** *US* leaving a job (resigning, retiring, or being fired or made redundant)

territory *noun* area covered by a representation agreement *or* visited by a salesman; ***the territories covered by the agreement are South-East Asia and Hong Kong; we are expanding the rep force and reducing the reps' territories; his territory covers all the north of the country***

tertiary *adjective* **tertiary level publishing** = publishing for the educational market after secondary school level (i.e. for adult education, polytechnics and universities); *see also* PRIMARY, SECONDARY

test **1** *noun* **(a)** examination to see if something works well; **market test** = examination to see if a sample of a product will sell in a market **(b)** **test case** = legal action where the decision will fix a principle which other cases can follow; **test print** = printing a small run experimentally before a big run; ***we did a test print of the new magazine before going to press with 1.5 million copies*** **2** *verb* to examine something to see if it is working well; **to test the market for a product** *or* **to test market a product** = to show samples of a product in a market to see if it will sell well; ***we are test marketing the language course in the Netherlands***

text *noun* **(a)** written part of something; ***he wrote notes at the side of the text of the agreement;*** **continuous text** = written matter which continues without any break for illustrations, charts, etc.; **text-editing facilities** = word-processing system that allows the user to add, delete, move, insert and correct sections of text; **text-editing function** = option in a program that provides text-editing facilities; ***the program includes a built-in text-editing function;*** **text editor** = piece of software that provides the user with text-editing facilities; **text file** = stored file on a computer that contains text rather than digits *or* data; **text formatter** = program that arranges a text file according to preset rules, such as line width and page size; **text management** = facilities that allow text to be written, stored, retrieved, edited and printed; **text manipulation** = facilities that allow text editing, changing, inserting and deleting; **text processing** = word-processing, using a computer to keyboard, edit and output text, in the forms of letters, labels, etc.; **text retrieval** = information retrieval system that allows the user to examine complete documents rather than simply a reference to a single document **(b)** printed matter which forms the main part of a book *or* article; **text area** = part of the printed page which is covered by printed text (as opposed to the margins); **text illustrations** = illustrations printed on the text pages, and not on separate paper; **text pages** = printed pages with the text of a book, not including the prelims, specially printed plates, maps, etc.; **text paper** = (i) any paper suitable for printing text matter, but not halftones; (ii) the paper used for printing the text of a book (as opposed to art paper for the plates) or for printing the inside pages of a magazine (as opposed to the cover); **text type** = typeface used for the text of a book, as opposed to the chapter headings, etc. **(c)** **Text** = TEXTURA

textbook *noun* schoolbook *or* academic book, used in course of study; **textbook publisher** = educational publisher

textual *adjective* referring to text; ***the editors made several textual changes before the proofs were sent back for correction***

Textura *or* **Text** *noun* technical name for black letter or gothic type

TF = TO FOLLOW report from a publisher to a bookseller, showing that a book will be sent soon

thermal *adjective* referring to heat; **thermal copier** = copying machine which copies text using heat to take an image from the carbon in the original and transferring the image to heat-sensitive paper; **thermal paper** = special paper whose coating turns black when heated, allowing characters to be printed by using a matrix of small heating elements; **thermal printer** = type of printer where the character is formed on thermal paper with a printhead containing a matrix of small heating elements (this type of printer is very quiet in operation since the printing head does not strike the paper)

thermal transfer *noun* method of printing where the ink is attached to the paper by heating; ***a thermal transfer printer; colour ink-jet technology and thermal transfer technology compete with each other***

thermographic copier *noun* thermal copier, copying machine which copies text using heat to take an image from the carbon in the original and transferring the image to heat-sensitive paper

thermographic printing *or* **thermography** *noun* printing process which uses heat to produce raised characters (very thick ink is used; this is dusted with powder, then heated to weld it to the paper. The process is often used for letterheads)

thermoplastic *adjective* (substance, such as glue) which becomes soft when heated; **thermoplastic binding** *or* **adhesive binding** = binding for perfect bound books, where plastic glue is heated to attach the cover to the trimmed pages; **thermoplastic plates** = printing plates made of thermoplastic material, which can be bent to fit round the cylinder

thermo-mechanical pulp *noun* pulp made from wood chips which have been heated

thermoprinting *noun* printing on plastic wrapping material, using heat

thermosetting *adjective* material which can be moulded when hot, but which does not become plastic; **thermosetting plates** = printing plates made in thermosetting material, which are moulded into a curved shape to fit round a cylinder

thesaurus *noun* **(a)** book which gives words, not in alphabetical order like a dictionary *or* encyclopaedia, but listed under certain headings **(b)** book of writings on a certain subject; (NOTE: plural is **thesauri** or **thesauruses**)

thick leading *or* **thick space** *noun* normal space between words, which is one third of an em

thickness dummy *noun* book made from the correct paper and binding materials, but without any printed text, used to check the weight and bulk of the finished product

thin leading *or* **thin space** *noun* space which is one fifth of an em; **thin typeface** = typeface with very slender lines

third cover *noun* inside back cover of a magazine (used for advertisements)

thirtytwomo (32mo) *noun* (i) page size where the paper is folded to give 32 leaves (or 64 pages); (ii) book printed in this format; (iii) American book format about 4 or 5 inches high

thousand characters *or* **thousand keystrokes** *noun* number of characters or keystrokes used to calculate keyboarding costs; ***the keyboarding charge is £3.00 per thousand keystrokes***

thread *noun* strong thin cord used for sewing books; **thread sealing** = binding system where plastic staples are inserted and sealed to sew the sections, then the sewn sections are glued with a gauze backing; **thread sewing** *or* **thread stitching** = attaching collated sections of a book together with thread; **thread sewn book** = book where each signature is sewn and then collated with other signatures and sewn together before binding

three-colour *adjective* using three colours; ***the series will have three-colour covers;*** **three-colour process** = colour printing process in which the three colours (yellow, magenta and cyan) are printed one after the other, followed if necessary by black for the text; **three-colour processing** = making blocks for three-colour printing

three-decker *noun* large Victorian novel, published in three volumes

three-knife trimmer *noun* guillotine with three knives which trim books and magazines along three edges

three-quarter binding *noun* binding where the leather covering the spine and the corners also covers most of the front and back boards

three-up *adverb* printing three copies of a text at the same time; **book which is printed three-up** = book which is printed and bound three copies at a time; *see also* TWO-UP

throwaway *noun* (i) cheap little advertising flyer; (ii) free sheet

throw out *verb* **(a)** to design a section of a book or periodical so that it can be unfolded to make a page larger than double page size **(b)** to reject *or* to refuse to accept; ***the proposal was thrown out by the editorial committee; the board threw out the draft contract submitted by the union*** **(c)** to get rid of (something which is not wanted); ***we threw out the old telephones and installed a computerized system; the sales director threw out the old reporting system***

throw-out *noun* fold-out, a section of a book or periodical which can be unfolded to larger than page size

thumb hole *noun* rounded hole cut in the foredge of a book as part of a thumb index

thumb index *noun* method of indexing, where rounded holes are cut into the foredge of a book, with a piece of stiff card stuck on the relevant page, allowing a thumb to be placed in the hole and the book to be opened at the correct page quickly

thumb-index *verb* to provide a book with a thumb index; ***the dictionary is thumb-indexed***

tick *noun* sign ✓ written in the margin to show that the typeset text is correct (now used in place of 'stet'); (NOTE: US English is **check**)

tied letters *noun* ligatures

tie-in *noun* book which is derived from or published together with a TV *or* radio programme

TIFF = TAG IMAGE FILE FORMAT standard file format used to store graphic images

COMMENT: TIFF is probably the most common image interchange format used by DTP software. Developed by Aldus and Microsoft, TIFF can handle monochrome, grey-scale, 8-bit or 24-bit colour images. There have been many different versions of TIFF that include several different compression algorithms

tight *adjective* **(a)** which does not allow any movement; ***producing two hundred pages of setting in a day is a very tight schedule, and I don't think we can do it; getting three hundred pages of MS into 160 pages of printed text is going to be tight; production expenses are kept under tight control;*** **tight back** *or* **tight spine** = binding where the cover is glued to the back of a book without any hollow; **tight-edged** = reel of paper which has dried at the edges, so that the edges are tight and the centre of the reel is slack **(b)** (text) which is closely set with very little spacing

-tight *suffix* which prevents something getting in; ***the computer is packed in a watertight case; send the films in an airtight container***

tilde *noun* printed accent used over the letter 'ñ' in Spanish, or over 'ã' and 'õ' in Portuguese

tiling *noun* process by which an image, too large for the device handling it to be output on a single piece of film or paper, is broken into a number of smaller pieces, which, when brought together later, can be reassembled as a single picture

tiling fill *or* **tiled fill** *noun* means by which a repeating pattern (like wallpaper) can be produced from a single, patterned element (tile) and used to decorate an area confined by a complete boundary

tilt and swivel *adjective* (monitor) which is mounted on a pivot so that it can be moved to point in the most convenient direction for the operator

time *noun* **(a)** period when something takes place (such as one hour, two days, fifty minutes, etc.); **computer time** = time when a computer is being used (paid for at an hourly rate); **real time** = time when a computer is working on the processing of data while the problem to which the data refers is actually taking place **(b)** hours worked; **he is paid time and a half on Sundays** = he is paid the normal rate plus 50% extra when he works on Sundays; **full-time** = working for the whole normal working day; **overtime** = hours worked more than the normal working time; **part-time** = not working for a whole working day **(c)** period before something happens; **delivery time** = number of days before something will be delivered; **lead time** = time between placing an order and receiving the goods; **time limit** = period during which something should be done; **to keep within the time limits** *or* **within the time schedule** = to complete work by the time stated

time and motion study *noun* study in an office *or* factory of the movements of workers as they perform tasks, with the aim of improving efficiency of production

time rate *noun* rate for work which is calculated as money per hour *or* per week, and not money for work completed

time scale *noun* time which will be taken to complete work; ***our time scale is that all work should be completed by the end of August; he is working to a strict time scale***

time-sharing *noun* sharing a computer system, with different users using different terminals

time work *noun* work which is paid for at a rate per hour *or* per day, not per piece of work completed

Times New Roman typeface designed by Stanley Morison (1899-1967) for the 'Times' newspaper in 1932, now one of most widely used text faces

tin *noun* metal used as part of the alloy in metal type and in hot metal setting (it makes the lead tougher and also more fluid when heated)

tint 1 *noun* **(a)** pale background colour formed of dots of a colour (the smaller the dots, the paler the tint) **(b) mechanical tint** *or* **mechanical screen** *or* **mechanical stipple** = shading, dots, hatching or stippling which is preprinted on film or dry-transfer lettering sheets and can be applied to the design by the designer; **tint-laying** = creation of a tint by stripping in film **2** *verb* to colour with a tint; **a tinted paper** = paper which is coloured

tinting *noun* mechanical tint *or* stipple which is preprinted and can be applied to the design by the designer

tip in *verb* to stick an extra leaf (usually with a colour plate *or* folding map, etc.) into the pages of a bound book; ***a book with six tipped-in plates***

tip-in *noun* extra leaf tipped into a bound book

tissue paper *noun* very thin paper made from chemical pulp, used to wrap fragile objects, and in binding, placed in front of engraved plates, so as to prevent the ink setting off onto the facing pages

titanium oxide *noun* chemical added to paper stock to make the paper whiter and more opaque

title *noun* **(a)** name given to a book *or* play *or* poem, etc.; ***the books are catalogued under title and author;*** **title index** = index of books (in a library *or* publisher's catalogue) listed under their titles; **title piece** = display lettering on a title page; **title signature** = first signature of a book, the signature which contains the title page **(b)** book in a publisher's catalogue; ***we are publishing a series of six titles on popular medicine; a catalogue of spring titles*** **(c)** name given to a person in a certain job; ***he has the title 'Chief Executive'*** **(d)** = TITLE PAGE **title verso** *or* **reverse of title** = TITLE PAGE VERSO *see also* HALF-TITLE

title page *noun* page at the beginning of a book which gives the title (usually in display typography), the name of the author, and the imprint of the publisher; **title page verso** *or* **title verso** = page on the back of the title page, where the bibliographical details and the copyright notice are printed

> COMMENT: The title page is always a right-hand page. From the designer's point of view, a title page is designed both to attract the reader and at the same time give some idea of the contents of the book: this must be done using typography alone, although some

title pages have illustrations or vignettes. The jacket or cover is designed in order to attract the purchaser to the book in the shop; the title page is designed to make the reader want to read it when he or she opens it

titling (font) *noun* typeface font which only exists in capital letters and is used in book titles and other headings (for example Othello); in hot metal, a titling font uses the full width and depth of the body

token *noun* **(a)** thing which acts as a sign *or* symbol; **token charge** = small charge which does not cover the real costs; **token damages** = damages awarded by a court which are very small (such as one penny), to show that the harm done was more technical than real; **token payment** = small payment to show that a payment is being made **(b) book token** = card bought in a bookshop which is given as a present and which must be exchanged in a bookshop for books; ***we gave her a book token for her birthday***

tolerance *noun* deviation from the specifications allowed in dimensions; ***we agreed with the binder on a tolerance of 5%***

tombstone *noun* large advertisement placed in a newspaper or periodical for a legal reason (such as to announce a will, or to give the terms of a government loan)

ton *noun* measure of weight; *GB* **long ton** = measure of weight (= 1016 kilos); *US* **short ton** = measure of weight (= 907 kilos); **metric ton** = tonne *or* 1,000 kilos

tone *noun* shade of colour; ***the graphics package can give several tones of blue;*** **tone value** = degree of tone of a colour; **tone work** = halftone work (using screening to produce tones in a printed work, as distinct from line work, which has no tones)

toner *noun* powder put into a photocopier *or* photographic device to develop the image; **toner cartridge** = sealed cartridge containing toner, which can be easily replaced in a photocopier; ***change toner and toner cartridge according to the manual; the toner cartridge and the imaging drum can be replaced as one unit when the toner runs out***

tonnage *noun* **(a)** space for cargo in a ship, measured in tons **(b)** weight of paper, in tonnes

tonne *or* **metric tonne** *noun* 1,000 kilos

COMMENT: the metric tonne is used in the UK for calculating paper requirements

tool 1 *noun* **(a)** *(in binding)* metal instrument which is used to press designs onto the case of a book **(b) tools** = set of utility programs (backup, format, etc.) in a computer system **2** *verb* to make a design on the case of a book (either cloth or leather) by pressing on the case with a tool which has been heated; ***book in tooled morocco binding***

tooling *noun* pressing designs by hand onto the cover of a book, using a punch; **blind tooling** = pressing designs with a cold tool; **gold tooling** = pressing designs with a heated tool and gold leaf

TOP = TEMPORARILY OUT OF PRINT

top 1 *adjective & noun* **(a)** upper edge of a bound book *or* upper part of the page; **book with the top edge coloured** *or* **stained** = book where the tops of the pages are coloured; **top edge gilt** = book with gilding on the top edge; **top margin** = margin at the top of a printed page; **top space** = number of blank lines left at the top of a printed text **(b)** first; **top copy** = first sheet of a document which is typed with several carbon copies or photocopies **2** *verb* to go higher than *or* to make a higher offer; ***the New York agent bid $500,000 which topped all other bids;*** **topping bid** = bid which is higher than all others

top-selling *adjective* which sells better than all other products; ***top-selling author of detective stories***

top side *noun* **(a)** *(of paper)* the side which is being printed on **(b)** felt side, the smooth top side of paper (as opposed to the wire side, which may show the marks of the wire mesh)

top-weighting *noun* designing a page so that the emphasis is to the top part (used in magazine design, rather than in books; the pages may have heavy headings and wide margins at the top); *see the note at* MARGIN

TOS = TEMPORARILY OUT OF STOCK

trace *verb* to copy a design by placing a sheet of transparent paper over it and drawing a copy of the design seen through the paper; **tracing paper** = special transparent paper, used to trace designs

track *noun* one of a series of concentric rings on a disk or lines on magnetic tape, which the read/write head accesses and on which data is stored in sectors

tracking *noun* **(a)** minus setting, reducing the spaces between letters, either to save space or to avoid awkward letter combinations (like L and T) which can leave gaps if spaced normally **(b) tracking lines** = imaginary lines running from the front edge of a printing plate to the back (ink density and colour density are constant along the tracking lines) **(c)** lines on magnetic tapes or disks along which information is carried

tractor feed *noun* method of feeding paper into a printer, where sprocket wheels on the printer connect with the sprocket holes on either edge of the paper to pull the paper through

trade *noun* **(a)** business of buying and selling; **export trade** *or* **import trade** = the business of selling to other countries *or* buying from other countries; **foreign trade** *or* **overseas trade** *or* **external trade** = trade with other countries; **home trade** = trade in the country where a company is based; **trade cycle** = period during which trade expands, then slows down, then expands again **(b) fair trade** = international business system where countries agree not to charge import duties on certain items imported from their trading partners; **trade agreement** = international agreement between countries over general terms of trade; **trade bureau** = office which specializes in commercial enquiries; **trade description** = description of a product to attract customers; *GB* **Trade Descriptions Act** = act which limits the way in which products can be described so as to protect customers from wrong descriptions made by manufacturers; **trade directory** = book which lists all the businesses and business people in a town; **trade mission** = visit to a country by a group of foreign businessmen to discuss trade; **to ask a company to supply trade references** = to ask a company to give names of traders who can report on the company's financial situation and reputation **(c)** people *or* companies dealing in the same type of product; ***he is in the secondhand book trade; she is very well known in the printing trade;*** **trade association** = group which links together companies in the same trade; **trade discount** *or* **trade terms** = reduction in price given to a customer in the same trade (as by a publisher to another publisher, or to a bookseller); **trade fair** = large exhibition and meeting for advertising and selling a certain type of product; **trade journal** *or* **trade magazine** *or* **trade paper** *or* **trade publication** = magazine or newspaper produced for people and companies in a certain trade; **trade press** = all magazines produced for people working in a certain trade; **trade price** = special wholesale price paid by a retailer to the manufacturer or wholesaler **(d)** *(specifically)* **the book trade** *or* **the publishing trade** = commercial activities involved in making and selling books; **trade binding** *or* **edition binding** = binding style of a book for sale through retail bookshops (i.e. not the same as an educational book *or* a library book *or* a mail-order book); **trade book** = book which is published for sale to the retail bookshops; **trade catalogue** *or* **trade list** = publisher's catalogue listing books for sale through retail bookshops; **trade counter** = shop in a publisher's office *or* section of a warehouse where small quantities of books are sold to booksellers in person; **trade customs** *or* **customs of the trade** = particular customs relating to the printing and publishing trades; **trade edition** = edition of a book for sale through retail book shops (as opposed to an edition for sale through book clubs *or* to the educational market, etc.); **trade paperback** = paperback book with a higher price and lower discount than a mass-market paperback, for sale through ordinary retail bookshops (usually well-made on good quality paper, with good illustrations, being the same as a trade book, but with a paper binding); **trade publisher** = publisher specializing in books for sale through retail bookshops **(e)** *(specifically)* **the printing trade** = commercial activities involved in printing books, newspapers, ephemera, etc.; **trade binding** = binding of sheets of a book by a binder for another printer which has printed them; **trade house** = specialist printing or binding company which does work mainly for other printers or binders (such as typesetting, laminating, or making jackets)

trade mark *or* **trade name** *noun* particular name, design, etc., which has been registered by the manufacturer and which cannot be used by other manufacturers

trader *noun* **sole trader** = person who runs a business, usually by himself, but has not registered it as a company

trailing blade coater *noun* device for scraping off excess coating from paper

train *verb* to teach (someone) to do something; to learn how to do something; ***he trained as an accountant; the company has appointed a trained printer as its managing director***

trainee *noun* person who is learning how to do something; ***we employ a trainee sub-editor to help in the office at peak periods; graduate trainees come to work in the pressroom when they have finished their courses at university;*** **management trainee** = young member of staff being trained to be a manager

traineeship *noun* post of trainee

training *noun* being taught how to do something; ***there is a ten-week training period for new staff; the shop is closed for staff training;*** **industrial training** = training of new workers to work in an industry; **management training** = training staff to be managers, by making them study problems and work out solutions to them; **on-the-job training** = training given to workers at their place of work; **off-the-job training** = training given to workers away from their place of work (such as at a college or school); **training levy** = tax to be paid by companies to fund the government's training schemes; **training officer** = person in a company who deals with the training of staff

transceiver *noun* transmitter and receiver, a device which can both transmit and receive signals (such as a terminal *or* modem)

transcribe *verb* (i) to copy something by hand; (ii) to transfer data from one system to another *or* from one medium to another

transcription *noun* action of transcribing data *or* of copying a text

transfer *noun* **(a)** image on a special sheet which can be printed onto a piece of paper by pressing; **transfer diffusion copier** = type of photocopying device for producing PMTs, transforming negatives into positives for use in litho origination; **transfer letters** *or* **transfer lettering** *or* **transfer type** = system of letters which can be transferred to a sheet of paper by pressing, available in many different fonts and point sizes (such as Letraset) **(b)** image taken from a letterpress plate and used to make a litho plate

translate *verb* **(a)** to put something which is said *or* written in one language into another language; ***he asked his secretary to translate the letter from the German agent; we have had the contract translated from French into Japanese*** **(b)** *(graphics)* to move an image on screen without rotating it

translation *noun* the act of translating; book or other text which has been translated; ***she passed the translation of the letter to the accounts department;*** **translation bureau** = office which translates documents for companies; **translation rights** = rights to translate a book into another language; ***he paid $10,000 for the English translation rights***

translator *noun* person who translates

transliterate *verb* to write words of one language in the characters of another; ***'pinyin' is Chinese transliterated into Western characters***

transliteration *noun* writing words of one language using the characters of another (such as Arabic into English); *see also* ROMANIZATION

translucent *adjective* through which light can pass, but which cannot be seen through

transmission control protocol *see* TCP

transparency *noun* transparent positive film, which can be projected onto a screen *or* to make film for printing

transparent *adjective* through which light can pass and through which one can see; **transparent copy** = transparencies used for printing; **transparent ink** = ink which when printed over other inks allows the first ink to show through (these are used in four-colour printing to create many different colours and shades)

transponder *noun* communications device that receives and retransmits signals

transpose *verb* to put two things (such as letters in words *or* illustrations *or* lines of text) in place of each other; ***the captions to the two illustrations were transposed in pasteup;*** (NOTE: as an instruction to a printer, the text or letters to be moved are indicated with a curled line and an arrow in the margin)

transposition *noun* changing the order of a series of characters (as 'comupter' for 'computer' or '1899' for '1998'

travel *verb* to go from one place to another, especially to show a company's goods to buyers and take orders from them; ***he travels in the north of the country for a paperback house;*** **travel book** = book which describes a journey undertaken by the author, or the author's impressions of a foreign country (but not giving factual details of hotels, museums, etc. which will be found in a guide book); **travel list** = series of travel books published by a publisher

traveller *US* **traveler** *noun* **commercial traveller** = salesman who travel round an area visiting customers on behalf of his company; **travellers' meeting** = meeting of all the salesmen of a company, when new books are shown to them by the editorial staff

treatment *noun* synopsis of a proposed book, which shows how the author will write it, the point of view the author will put forward, etc.

trial *noun* **(a)** court case to judge a person accused of a crime; ***he is on trial*** *or* ***is standing trial for piracy*** **(b)** test to see if something is good; **trial sample** = small piece of a product used for testing; **free trial** = testing of a product (such as a language course) with no payment involved

trichromatic *adjective* using three colours; **trichromatic ink** = one of the three process colours (magenta, cyan and yellow)

trim 1 *noun* action of cutting the edges of the folded pages of a book as it is being bound; ***the trim may be as much as 4mm*** **2** *verb* **(a)** to cut the edge of a photograph *or* other sheet of paper to make a certain size, or to remove unwanted material; ***you will need to trim three millimetres from the top part of the photograph to make it fit*** **(b)** to cut away the edges of the folded pages of a book as it is being bound; ***the printed pages are trimmed to 198 x 129mm; if we strip off the cover and recover with the new design, the books will have to be trimmed again;*** **trim marks** = marks printed on a sheet which indicate where the sheet has to be trimmed; (NOTE: US English is **cut marks**) **trim to bleed** = instruction to trim the printed sheets until the edge of the page cuts into the printed area; **trim size** *or* **trimmed size** = measurements of a page of a book after it has been cut *or* of a sheet of paper after it has been cut to size **(c)** to cut a price; ***we have trimmed our prices to meet the competition***

trimmer *noun* machine which cuts the edges of the pages of a book as it is being bound; *see also* THREE-KNIFE TRIMMER

trimmings *noun* pieces of paper cut off the edges of pages

tri-metal plate *noun* plate used for long print runs made of three layers of metal

trindles *noun* flat pieces of metal which hold a book flat while the foredge is being trimmed

triple lining *noun* very strong binding using linings on the spine

triplex paper *noun* paper made of three layers

triplicate *noun* **in triplicate** = with an original and two copies; **invoicing in triplicate** = preparing three copies of invoices

trs = TRANSPOSE instruction to a typesetter to change the place of letters *or* pieces of text

true *adjective* correct *or* accurate; **true copy** = exact copy; ***I certify that this is a true copy; certified as a true copy;*** **true italic** = designed italic face in a font (as opposed to the italic in dot matrix printers, which is sloped Roman)

TS = TYPESCRIPT

TTS = TELETYPESETTING

tub sizing *noun* sizing of paper by dipping it in a vat containing gelatine (as opposed to engine-sizing, where the size is added to the pulp before the paper is made)

> COMMENT: tub-sized paper is stiff and smooth, and is used for writing papers and legal documents

tucker *noun* folding blade, a strip of metal which pushes the sheet into the folding device

tumbler work *see* WORK AND TUMBLE

turkey *noun US (informal)* book which doesn't sell

turn 1 *noun* **(a) stock turn** = total value of stocks sold in a year divided by the average value of goods in stock; ***the company has a stock turn of 6.7*** **(b)** metal character which has been put in upside down, because the correct character was not available; **taking out turns** = replacing turns by correct characters **2** *verb* **(a)** to change direction *or* to put something in a different way; ***the illustration has been turned to appear landscape*** **(b) to turn a letter** = to set a letter upside down because the correct letter is not available

turnaround time *noun* **(a)** time taken for a product to be made and delivered after an order has been received **(b)** time taken to activate a computer program and produce the result which the user has asked for

turner bars *noun* metal rods on a rotary press which turn the web of paper so that it is running in a different direction

turn in *verb* to bend cover material over the edge of the binding board and glue it there

turn over *verb* **(a)** to have a certain amount of sales; ***we turn over £20,000 a week*** **(b)** = TURN IN

turnover *noun* **(a)** part of a hyphenated word which has been taken over to the next line **(b)** *GB* amount of sales; ***the company's turnover has increased by 235%; we based our calculations on the forecast turnover;*** **stock turnover** = total value of stock sold in a year divided by the average value of goods held in stock **(c)** *US* number of times something is used *or* sold in a period (usually one year), expressed as a percentage of a total

turnround *noun* value of goods sold during a year divided by the average value of goods held in stock

TV *see* = TELEVISION

TVRO = TELEVISION RECEIVE ONLY equipment for reception and display without transmission

twelvemo (12mo) *noun* (i) duodecimo, a book made from a sheet which is folded to give twelve leaves or twenty-four pages; (ii) book with this format; (iii) American book size, 7-8 inches high

twentyfourmo (24mo) *noun* (i) format produced when the printed sheet is folded to give 24 leaves, or 48 pages; (ii) book with this format; (iii) American book size, 5-6 inches high

twice-up *or* **two-up** *adjective* (illustration) drawn twice the size it will be when printed

twin-wire fourdrinier *noun* papermaking machine with two wire meshes, making two layers of paper which are joined together back to back while still wet, so the finished paper is smooth on both sides; **twin-wire paper** = smooth paper made on a twin-wire machine

two-colour press *noun* printing press which can print two colours at the same time; **two-colour process** = separating artwork for printing in two colours

two-line drop capital *noun* initial capital letter which occupies two lines, sometimes used decoratively at the beginning of a chapter (the opposite of a stick-up initial)

two-part *noun* paper (for computers *or* typewriters) with a top sheet for the original and a second sheet for a copy

two revolution printing *noun* letterpress process where the cylinder rotates twice for each impression

two set *noun* putting two sets of plates on a printing cylinder, so that two impressions are made at the same time

two-shot binding *noun* adhesive binding using both hotmelt and cold PVA glues

two-up *adverb* **(a)** printing two copies of a book at the same time with the pages joined head to head (used for paperback binding); **book which is printed two-up** = book which is printed and bound two copies at a time; *see also* ONE-UP, THREE-UP, FOUR-UP **(b)** *(in hand binding)* sewing two sections together **(c)** = TWICE-UP

tympan *noun* bed on which the paper is placed in a hand-operated press; bed of sheets used to raise the printing paper to the correct height

> COMMENT: type area and type depth can be described as inclusive or exclusive; inclusive includes the running heads and any footlines (which may involve the folio), and exclusive counts only the area of text without running heads or footlines

type 1 *noun* **(a)** (i) a single metal letter *or* character; (ii) metal slugs with raised characters used for printing; **the book has been set in type** = the text has been typeset and is ready for printing **(b)** characters used in printing *or* characters which appear in printed form; ***they switched to italic type for the heading;*** **type area** = the space on a page which is occupied by the printed text, including headings; **type family** = various forms of the same typeface (roman, bold, italic, condensed, etc.); **type gauge** *or* **type scale** *or* **type rule** = special ruler used by printers and production staff, showing width in ems and points, used for calculating the width of a line or the depth of a page; (NOTE: US English is **line gauge**) **type height** = standard height of the main section of a metal character (all characters are the same height, 23.32mm, so that the pressure on the paper remains the same); **type holder** = tool holding the type of words to be blocked onto a cover; **type metal** = the metal (a mixture of lead, tin and antimony) used in metal setting; **type page** = type area, the area of a page which is covered with printing, surrounded by the margins; **type series** = all the different point sizes available in a typeface; **type size** = size of type, calculated in 'points' which refer to the height of the printed character, but not its width; **type spec** = details of the typeface, point size, measure, leading, etc., which are to be used in a book; **type specimen** = printed specimen showing samples of various typefaces or of the typeface to be used for a particular job; **type style** = general style of type (roman, bold, italic, etc.) in which a job will be set **2** *verb* to write with a typewriter; ***the MS should be typed on one side of the paper only, using***

double spacing; all his reports are typed on his portable typewriter

typecasting *noun* the process of casting type in hot metal (individual letters in Monotype and slugs in Linotype)

typecutter *noun* person who cuts the punches to make the matrices to cast type

typeface *noun* **(a)** cut surface of a piece of type, which prints on the paper **(b)** type style *or* font *or* set of characters designed in a certain style and given a special name; ***typefaces such as Baskerville and Times Roman are very often used for bookwork***

typefounder *noun* person who casts metal type

typefoundry *noun* workshop where metal type is cast

type-high *adjective* (bearer *or* block) which is as high as type (i.e. 23.32mm)

typematter *noun* text which has been typeset (as opposed to illustrations)

typescript *noun* manuscript of a book, typed by the author *or* a typist on a typewriter

typeset *verb* to set text in type for printing; ***in desktop publishing, the finished work should look almost as if it had been typeset***

typesetter *noun* person *or* company *or* machine which typesets; ***the text is ready to be sent to the typesetter***

typesetting *noun* action of setting text in type; ***typesetting costs can be reduced by supplying the typesetter with prekeyed disks;*** **typesetting machine** = composing machine, a machine which sets type automatically in hot metal, from instructions given on a paper tape, punched by the compositor using a keyboard similar to a typewriter keyboard; **computer typesetting** = typesetting which is done automatically by a computer, using instructions keyed on disk or tape; *see also* PHOTOTYPESETTING

typewriter *noun* machine which prints letters *or* figures on a piece of paper when a key is pressed, by striking an inked ribbon onto the paper with a character type; ***she wrote the letter on her portable typewriter; he makes fewer mistakes now he is using an electronic typewriter;*** **typewriter composition** = method of typing text for filming and printing, where the text is written on a typewriter; **typewriter faces** = size and font of characters available on a typewriter

typewritten *adjective* written on a typewriter; ***his manuscripts are never typewritten and cause the editorial staff a lot of problems***

typing *noun* writing documents with a typewriter; **typing error** = mistake made when using a typewriter; **typing pool** = group of typists, working together in a company, offering a secretarial service to several departments; **copy typing** = typing documents from handwritten originals, not from dictation

typist *noun* person whose job is to write letters using a typewriter; **copy typist** = person who types documents from handwritten originals not from dictation; **shorthand typist** = typist who takes dictation in shorthand and then types it

typo *noun* US *(informal)* typographical error which is made while typesetting; (NOTE: GB English is also **literal**)

typographer *noun* **(a)** person who designs the printed pages of a book; person who designs typefaces **(b)** person who sets a book in type; (NOTE: more usually called a **compositor**)

typographic(al) *adjective* referring to typography *or* to typesetting; a typographical error made while typesetting is called a 'literal; **typographical error** = misprint *or* literal (mistake made while typesetting); **typographic quality** = text set by a laser printer which is the same quality as if it had been phototypeset

typography *noun* (i) laying out of text in a pleasing way or in a way which best conveys meaning on the typeset page; (ii) design of typefaces

Uu

u & lc *or* **u/lc** = UPPER AND LOWER CASE instruction to a typesetter to set the first letter of a word in capitals and the rest in lower case

uc = UPPER CASE

UCC = UNIVERSAL COPYRIGHT CONVENTION

UCR = UNDERCOLOUR REMOVAL

ultraviolet (light) (UV) *noun* electromagnetic radiation with a wavelength just greater than the visible spectrum, from 200 to 4000 angstrom; **ultraviolet drying** = drying ink or varnish by radiation of UV light

> COMMENT: UV light is used to dry inks and cover varnishes. UV varnishing is cheaper than lamination, but does not have as glossy a finish

umlaut *noun* accent consisting of two dots over a German a, o or u

unabridged *adjective* which has not been abridged; ***the book is available in an unabridged edition in hardback***

unacceptable *adjective* which cannot be accepted; ***the terms of the contract are quite unacceptable***

unauthorized *adjective* not permitted; **unauthorized edition** *or* **unauthorized reprint** = pirate edition of a book which has not been authorized by the publisher; **unauthorized returns** = unsold books returned from a bookshop without authorization from the publisher or his representative

unavailability *noun* not being available

unavailable *adjective* not available; ***the following items on your order are temporarily unavailable***

unbacked *adjective* a sheet of paper printed on one side only

unbleached kraft (paper) *noun* strong matt brown paper used for making paper bags, wrapping paper, etc. (bleaching makes paper white, but also weakens it)

unbound *adjective* (sheets) which have not been bound

uncensored *adjective* which has not been changed by the censor

unchecked *adjective* which has not been checked; ***a set of unchecked proofs***

uncoated paper *noun* paper which is not coated (not suitable for halftones)

uncorrected *adjective* not corrected; ***to send a set of uncorrected proofs to the proofreader***

uncut pages *noun* pages of a book which have been bound but not trimmed, so that some pages are still attached by folds at the foredge and head

underblanket *noun* packing sheet under the blanket on a blanket cylinder in offset printing

undercolour removal (UCR) *noun* removing unwanted colour in litho separations as part of the achromatic colour origination system

undercut *noun* (in process engraving) the cutting action of acid which eats under the edges of the image areas

underexposed *adjective* (photograph) which has not been exposed for long enough and so is dark

underexposure *noun* not exposing a photograph long enough, with the result that it is dark

underfold *noun* paper which does not reach the edge of the other leaves because the folding machine is off centre; (NOTE: the opposite (i.e. the paper which sticks out from the rest of the folded sheets) is **overfold**)

underground press *noun* illegal newspapers published in a country where publications are censored; **underground literature** = literature published by the underground press; *compare* SAMIZDAT

underlay 1 *verb* to raise the height of a printing plate by putting something such as a piece of card under it **2** *noun* card used to raise the height of a block or plate

underline 1 *noun* **(a)** line drawn *or* printed under a piece of text; ***the chapter headings are given a double underline and the paragraphs a single underline*** **(b)** *US* caption printed under an illustration **2** *verb* to print *or* write a line under a piece of text; **underlining** = word-processing command which underlines text

> COMMENT: underlining is used by editors and designers to indicate different type styles: single underline is an instruction to set in italic; double underline, in small caps; three lines indicate caps. (These are all straight lines). A wavy underline is used to instruct setting in bold

undermentioned *adjective* mentioned lower down in a document

underrun *noun* (i) printing fewer sheets than were ordered; (ii) delivering or making less paper than was ordered

underscore = UNDERLINE

unearned advance *noun* money received as an advance on royalties, which has not been covered by the royalties from the sales so far

> COMMENT: a publishing contract often allows an author an advance payment against future royalties; the author will not receive any further royalties until the amount paid in advance has been earned by sales of the book. Most advances on royalties are considered to be non-returnable (i.e., the publisher cannot ask for his money back if the book does not sell). Some publishers may have reason to ask for an advance back, especially if the author produces a MS which is not of publishable quality

unedited *adjective* which has not been edited; ***the unedited text is with the publisher for editing***

uneven *adjective* **(a)** not even *or* not uniform; **uneven inking** = inking where some parts of the sheet are darker than others **(b) uneven working** = page extent which does not fit the printer's imposition scheme (usually in multiples of 8 or 16); ***the book is likely to make 358 pages, but the printer says this is an uneven working and we must reduce the text to 352 pages***

unexpurgated *adjective* (text) which contains pornographic *or* explicit material which is cut out of other editions; *compare* BOWDLERIZE

unfair *adjective* **unfair competition** = trying to do better than another company by using techniques such as importing foreign goods at very low prices or by wrongly criticizing a competitor's products

unfinished *adjective* **(a)** (book) which has not been finished; ***at his death he left the unfinished manuscript of his tenth novel*** **(b)** (paper) which has not been through the final stages of papermaking

unfulfilled *adjective* (order) which has not yet been supplied

ungathered *adjective* sheets which have been printed and folded, but not gathered

uniform *adjective* (design) which is exactly the same; ***the letters are not of***

uniform height; the colour is a uniform pale yellow; **uniform edition** = series of different books all with the same design

uniform resource locator (URL) (Internet) system used to standardize the way in which WWW addresses are written; ***the URL of the Peter Collin Publishing home page is 'http://www.pcp.co.uk'***

union *noun* **(a) union kraft** *or* **union paper** = waterproof paper made of two layers of kraft paper with a tar coating between them **(b) union catalogue** = catalogue listing books in several libraries

unit *noun* **(a)** single product for sale; **unit cost** = the cost of one book (i.e total product costs divided by the number of units produced); **unit price** = the price of one item **(b)** separate piece of equipment or furniture; **unit type press** = press with several printing units; **desk top unit** = computer *or* machine that will fit onto a desk; **display unit** = special stand for showing goods for sale **(c)** width of a letter (typically one em equals eighteen units and one en nine units, although these may vary with different typefaces); **Monotype unit system** = system of computerizing typesetting, where each character is given a number of units (the base unit is one eighteenth of a point (about 0.0077 inch)

Univers sans face designed by Adrian Frutiger (1957) and now very widely used

Universal Copyright Convention (UCC) *noun* international agreement on copyright set up by the United Nations in Geneva in 1952

> COMMENT: both the Berne Convention of 1886 and the UCC were drawn up to try to protect copyright from pirates; under the Berne Convention, published material remains in copyright until 50 years after the death of the author and for 25 years after publication under the UCC. In both cases, a work which is copyrighted in one country is automatically covered by the copyright legislation of all countries signing the convention

university press *noun* **(a)** printing press belonging to a university, which prints university documents (such as examinations, the university statutes, etc.) **(b)** publishing company belonging to a university

unjustified *adjective* not justified (i.e. with an uneven edge to the text matter)

> COMMENT: the text can be ranged left or right, leaving the other margin unjustified. In American English, this is called 'ragged left' or 'ragged right'

unlawful *adjective* against the law *or* not legal; **unlawful copying** *or* **unlawful reproduction** = copying a text *or* illustration without the permission of the copyright holder

unleaded *adjective* with no leading between lines; *see also* LEAD[1]

unlined *adjective* **unlined paper** = paper with no lines printed on it

unpublishable *adjective* (manuscript) which no publisher will publish

unpublished *adjective* (manuscript) which has not been published

unsealed envelope *noun* envelope where the flap has been pushed into the back of the envelope, and is not stuck down

unseen *adjective* which has not been seen; **they ordered 250 copies sight unseen** = they bought them without having seen them

unseriffed *adjective* (typeface) without serifs

unsewn *adjective* (binding) where the pages are not sewn together, but are cut and glued to the cover; *see also* PERFECT BINDING

unsharp masking (USM) function available on a scanner to give increased definition to an un-sharp original

unshift *verb* to move to lower case characters on a keyboard (i.e. to cancel a shift key operation)

unsold *adjective* not sold; ***unsold copies will be returned for credit***

unsolicited *adjective* which has not been asked for; **unsolicited manuscript** = manuscript which is sent to a publisher by the author, without the publisher having asked to see it; **unsolicited testimonial** = letter praising someone *or* a product without the writer having been asked to write it

untitled *adjective* without a title

untranslated *adjective* which has not been translated

untrimmed *adjective* (sheet of paper) which has not been trimmed; (book) where the pages have not been trimmed; **untrimmed size** = size of a piece of paper *or* printed page which has not been trimmed

unwinding stand *noun* stand which holds a web of paper which is to be passed through another process, such as supercalendering

unwritten *adjective* **unwritten agreement** = agreement which has been reached in speaking (such as in a telephone conversation) but has not been written down

-up *suffix* meaning the number of plates printed at one time on one side of a sheet; **book printed two-up** = book printed two copies at a time from the same web of paper (the two copies are separated after the books are bound)

UPC = UNIVERSAL PRODUCT CODE American bar coding system used on packaging and book covers

update 1 *noun* (i) information added to something to make it up to date; (ii) printed information which is an up-to-date revision of earlier information **2** *verb* to revise a text so that it is up to date; ***the guidebook is updated annually***

up front *adverb* in advance; **money up front** = payment in advance; ***they are asking for £100,000 up front before they will consider the deal; he had to put money up front before he could talk about paperback rights***

upper case *noun* capital letters and other symbols on a typewriter *or* keyboard, which are accessed by pressing the shift key; ***the headline is printed in upper and lower case (u & lc);*** *see also* LOWER

COMMENT: to instruct upper case, the editor underlines the text with three lines. The term 'upper case' comes from the case in which metal type was kept in front of the compositor. The case was divided into many little compartments, the top half being for capitals and the bottom part for small letters

URL = UNIFORM RESOURCE LOCATOR

usage *noun* how something, such as a language, is used; ***the sub-editor should have a good knowledge of modern English usage***

Usenet *noun* section of the Internet that provides forums (called newsgroups) in which any user can add a message or comment on other messages

user *noun* person who uses something; **end user** = person who actually uses a product; **user's guide** *or* **handbook** = book showing someone how to use something

user-friendly *adjective* which a user finds easy to work; ***these programs are really user-friendly***

USM = UNSHARP MASKING

UV (light) = ULTRAVIOLET (LIGHT) **ultraviolet drying** = drying ink or varnish by radiation of UV light; **UV varnish** = coating applied to book covers to make them shiny and more durable; this type of varnish can be dried on machine under UV light. UV varnishing is cheaper than lamination, but does not have as glossy a finish

Vv

vacuum *noun* state with no air; **vacuum forming** = plastic moulding used in packaging (as in making boxes for kits or display); **vacuum frame** = frame from which the air can be extracted to make a vacuum, so that the film and the plate are tight together, without any buckling of the film; **vacuum pads** = suction caps which are used to lift a sheet of paper

valuation *noun* estimate of how much something is worth; ***to ask for a valuation of the stock before making an offer for a company;*** **stock valuation** = estimating the value of stock at the end of an accounting period; **to buy a bookshop with stock at valuation** = to pay for the stock the same amount as its value as estimated by a valuer

value 1 *noun* **(a)** amount of money which something is worth; ***the valuer put the value of the stock at £25,000;*** **asset value** = value of a company calculated by adding together all its assets; **book value** = value as recorded in the company's accounts; **'sample only - of no commercial value'** = not worth anything if sold **(b)** *US* **value publishing** = publishing high quality bargain books **(c)** strength of a colour (i.e. its darkness or lightness) **2** *verb* to estimate how much money something is worth; ***he valued the stock at £25,000***

Value Added Tax (VAT) *noun* tax imposed as a percentage of the invoice value of goods and services

valuer *noun* person who estimates how much money something is worth

vandyke *or* **Van Dyke** *noun US* trade mark for a type of photographic proof made from film printed onto special paper; *see also* BLUE, DIAZO, OZALID

vanity publisher *noun* publisher who publishes books which are paid for by their authors; **vanity publishing** = publishing books which are paid for by their authors

variable *adjective* which changes; **variable costs** = money paid to produce a product which increases with the quantity made (such as wages, raw materials), as opposed to fixed costs or plant costs; **variable spacing** = spacing between words which can change, used in justifying lines

varnish 1 *noun* shiny coating applied to book covers or jackets, to make them more durable (similar in appearance to lamination, but cheaper); **UV varnish** = coating applied to book covers to make them shiny and more durable; this type of varnish can be dried on machine under UV light **2** *verb* to coat a book cover with varnish; **varnishing machine** = machine which applies varnish to book covers; **UV varnishing** = coating a cover with UV varnish

vat *noun* large container for liquid; **vat machine** = cylinder machine, a type of machine used in the paper industry for making board (a gauze-covered cylinder revolves in a drum of paper pulp); **vat paper** = paper made in a vat machine

VAT = VALUE ADDED TAX ***the invoice includes VAT at 15%; the government is proposing to increase VAT to 17.5%; some items (such as books) are zero-rated for VAT; he does not charge VAT because he asks for payment in cash;*** **VAT declaration** = statement declaring VAT income to the VAT office; **VAT invoicing** = sending of an invoice including VAT; **VAT invoice** = invoice which shows VAT separately; **VAT inspector** = government official who examines VAT returns and checks that VAT is being paid; **VAT office** = government office dealing with the collection of VAT in an area

vatman *noun* **(a)** worker who makes handmade paper **(b)** = VATman

VATman *noun* VAT inspector

> COMMENT: in the UK books and newspapers are not exempt from VAT; VAT is levied on them at 0%, that is, they are 'zero-rated'. This is important for publishers, since it keeps the price to the customer low, and encourages the buying of books. It has another advantage in that a publisher (like any other trader) can claim back from the Customs and Excise Department any VAT which he has spent which is more than the VAT he has charged on his sales. Since books have 0% VAT charged on them, a publisher can claim back all VAT which he spends on purchasing stationery, equipment, typesetting, etc. Finished books are charged at 0% VAT by the printer; if typesetting is done by the printer, it is included on the invoice at 0% VAT, since it is part of the finished book; if typesetting is done separately, then VAT is charged on it by the typesetter at the normal rate (and can eventually be claimed back by the publisher)

VCR = VIDEO CASSETTE RECORDER

VDU *or* **VDT** = VISUAL DISPLAY UNIT *or* VISUAL DISPLAY TERMINAL

vector *noun* coordinate that consists of a magnitude and direction; **vector graphics** *or* **vector image** *or* **vector scan** = computer drawing system that uses line length and direction from an origin to plot lines and so build up an image rather than a description of each pixel, as in a bitmap; ***a vector image can be easily and accurately re-sized with no loss of detail;*** *compare with* BIT MAP

vector font *noun* shape of characters within a font that are drawn using vector graphics, allowing the characters to be scaled to almost any size without changing the quality; *compare with* BIT-MAPPED FONT

vehicle *noun* the liquid part of printing ink, which carries the pigment

vellum *noun* **(a)** parchment, made from the underside of calf-skin or goatskin, which has been scraped and soaked in lime; vellum was formerly used in the Middle Ages for manuscripts, and also for binding books; today it is used for binding some de luxe editions **(b)** thick cream-coloured writing paper

velox *US* = PHOTOMECHANICAL TRANSFER

venture *noun* business *or* commercial deal which involves a risk; **joint venture** = very large business project where two or more companies, often from different countries, join together to share development costs and eventual profits; **venture capital** = capital for investment which may easily be lost in risky projects, but can also provide high returns

verification *noun* (i) checking if something is correct; (ii) checking that data has been keyboarded correctly *or* that data transferred from one medium to another has been transferred correctly

verify *verb* to check to see if something is correct

version *noun* a copy *or* statement which is slightly different from others; ***the latest version of the software includes a graphics routine***

verso *noun* back of a leaf of a book (i.e. the left-hand page, usually with an even number, a right-hand page being the recto); **title page verso** = the page after the title page, normally reserved for bibliographic details; *see also* RECTO, REVERSE

> COMMENT: the title page verso normally carries the imprints (the names and addresses of both publisher and printer), the copyright line, the ISBN and possibly other copyright details (such as the CIP information), and, if translated or adapted, details of its original publication

vertical *adjective* upright *or* straight up or down; **vertical alignment** = spacing of matter so that the items are correctly placed above each other on the page; **vertical communication** = communication between senior managers via the middle management to the workers; **vertical integration** = joining two businesses together which deal with different stages in the production or sale of a product (as when a publisher buys a bookseller, or a printer buys a typesetter); **vertical jobbing press** = small letterpress machine printing flat formes which move vertically and not horizontally; **vertical justification** = adjustment of the spacing between lines of text to fit a section of text *or* column into a page; **vertical scrolling** = displayed text that moves up or down the computer screen one line at a time; **vertical tab** = number of lines that should be skipped before printing starts again

vertically *adverb* from top to bottom *or* going up and down at right angles to the horizontal; ***the page has been justified vertically***

VGA = VIDEO GRAPHICS ARRAY *(in an IBM PC)* standard of video adapter developed by IBM that can support a display with a resolution up to 640x480 pixels in up to 256 colours, superseded by SVGA

vide *Latin word meaning* 'see', used in cross-references; **vide infra** = see below; **vide supra** = see above

video *noun* referring to images viewed on a television screen; **video cassette** = cassette with video tape in it (either blank for recording, or with a prerecorded film); **video cassette recorder (VCR)** = device attached to a TV set, which can be programmed to record TV programmes on videotape and play them back at another time; **video disk** = read-only optical disk able to store TV pictures and sound in binary form, also capable of storing large amounts of computer data; **video display** = device which can display text *or* graphical information, such as a CRT; **video graphics array** *see* VGA **video monitor** = device able to display, without sound, signals from a TV camera (that are then recorded onto video tape); **video player** = device that can play back video recordings but cannot record; **video recorder** = device for recording TV images and sound onto video tape; **videotape** = magnetic tape used in a video recorder, for storing TV pictures and sound information; **video terminal** = keyboard with a monitor

videotext *or* **videotex** *noun* system for transmitting text and displaying it on a screen

> COMMENT: this covers information transmitted either by TV signals (teletext) *or* by signals sent down telephone lines (viewdata)

view *noun* **to print 8 pages to view** = to print 8 pages at a time on each side of the sheet of paper

viewdata *noun* interactive system for transmitting text *or* graphics from a database to a user's terminal by telephone lines

> COMMENT: the user calls up the page of information required, using the telephone and a modem, as opposed to teletext, where the pages of information are repeated one after the other automatically

viewer *noun* light box with an eyepiece through which a person can look at film *or* transparencies

vignette *noun* **(a)** very small illustration, often used to decorate a title page, a bibliographical page, the last page of a book etc. **(b)** halftone illustration which fades into the background at the edges; (NOTE: US English is also **fade-out halftone**)

vinyl foils *noun* foils for blocking plastic covers

virgin *adjective* blank *or* unused; **virgin tape** = (tape) that has not been recorded on before

virgule *noun* oblique stroke *or* solidus (the printing sign:; /)

viscosity *noun* degree of fluidity of ink, glue or varnish

viscous *adjective* liquid, but which does not run freely

visual 1 *adjective* which can be seen; **visual display unit (VDU)** *or* **visual display terminal (VDT)** = screen attached to a computer which shows the information stored in the computer; **visual space** = leading between lines of text **2** *noun* (i) rough sketch; (ii) finished artwork *or* graphics *or* photographs *or* illustrations, used as part of a printed output; ***the designer has sent in some visuals for the covers;*** (NOTE: US English is **comprehensive)**

viz *abbreviation* for the Latin word 'videlicet' meaning 'namely', used to give an example

vocabulary *noun* (i) book containing a list of words, usually a small book with a list of words on a specialized subject, or classified in some way; (ii) list of words with translations given at the back of a foreign language text

void 1 *adjective* **(a)** not legally valid; **the contract was declared null and void** = the contract was said to be no longer valid **(b) void hickey** = hickey in the form of a white spot on print **2** *verb* **to void a contract** = to make a contract invalid

volatile memory *or* **volatile store** *or* **volatile storage** *noun* memory *or* storage medium which loses data stored in it when the power supply is switched off

volume *noun* **(a)** one book, usually part of a series of books, such as one of a reference series; ***volume three of the complete works of Dickens is temporarily out of stock; the series was planned to be completed in twenty volumes, but it was scrapped after volume four because of lack of sales;*** **multi-volume** = with many volumes; ***a multi-volume encyclopaedia;*** **volume rights** = right to publish a text as a book during its term of copyright (either in the original edition or in cheap paperback versions, or by licensing the right to publish it to another publisher) **(b)** set of issues of a newspaper *or* magazine, usually the issues published in a calendar year **(c)** bulk *or* thickness of paper; ***we need to use a thicker paper to give the book more volume;*** **volume factor** *or* **volume number** = thickness of paper shown as the millimetre thickness of 100 sheets of 100gsm paper; in the USA, bulk is usually shown as ppi (pages per inch), the number of pages which make up one inch of bulk **(d)** quantity of items; **volume discount** = discount given to customer who buys a large quantity of goods; **volume of output** = number of items produced; **volume of sales** *or* **sales volume** = number of items sold; **low** *or* **high volume of sales** = small *or* large number of items sold

voucher copy *noun* free copy of a periodical given to an advertiser; free copy of a book given to a person who has worked on it (such as an editor or author's agent)

voucher proof *noun* proof sent by the printer for information only, not for correction

Ww

waive *verb* to give up (a right); **to waive a payment** = to give up the right to receive a payment

waiver *noun* giving up (a right) *or* removing the conditions (of a rule); **waiver clause** = clause in a contract giving the conditions under which the rights in the contract can be given up

wall chart *or* **wall map** *noun* chart *or* map which is made to hang up or to be pinned up on a wall

WAN = WIDE AREA NETWORK network where the various terminals are far apart and linked by radio, satellite and cable; *compare with* LAN

want *noun* thing which is needed; **want ads** = advertisements listed in a newspaper under special headings (such as 'property for sale', or 'jobs wanted'); **to draw up a wants list** = to make a list of things (such as out-of-print books) which you need

warehouse 1 *noun* large building where goods are stored; **warehouse capacity** = space available in a warehouse; **price ex warehouse** = price for a product which is to be collected from the manufacturer's or agent's warehouse and so does not include delivery **2** *verb* to store (goods) in a warehouse

warehouseman *noun* person who works in a warehouse

warehousing *noun* act of storing goods; ***warehousing costs are rising rapidly***

warp *verb (of boards)* to bend or curve because of damp conditions

warpage *or* **warping** *noun* becoming bent or curved

warranty *noun* **(a)** promise in a contract (as a promise in a contract between an author and a publisher that the work is the author's own work and has not been plagiarized from another author); **breach of warranty** = failing to do something which is a part of a contract **(b)** statement made by an insured person which declares that the facts stated by him are true

wash-up *noun* cleaning of a printing press after use

wastage *noun* amount lost by being wasted; ***allow 10% extra material for wastage***

waste 1 *noun* rubbish, things which are not used **2** *adjective* not used; **waste paper** = paper which is not used, and which can be collected for recycling; cardboard is made from recycled waste paper; **waste paper basket** = container near an office desk into which pieces of rubbish can be put; **waste sheet** = sheet of paper in the endpapers, which is kept to protect the other sheets during binding and is then cut out

water-immersion test *noun* test to show how effective size is on paper

waterleaf *noun* freshly-made paper which has not been sized

watermark 1 *noun* design which is made in paper, by impressing the wet pulp with a design on the dandy roll in machine-made papers or by using a wire design in the wet pulp mould for handmade papers; ***the paper has a watermark showing it was made in***

Ireland in 1911 **2** *verb* to put a watermark in paper

> COMMENT: watermarks are most often used in banknote paper, but they also appear in handmade paper and other fine papers. They are a useful way of dating old documents or antiquarian books

waterproof *adjective* which will not let water through; ***the books are sent packed in waterproof paper***

water-soluble ink *noun* ink which can dissolve in water

wavy line *noun* line which goes up and down regularly; ***to instruct bold face, underline the word or words with a wavy line;*** **wavy paper** = paper which crinkles at the edges, because of irregular damping

wax engraving *noun* method of electrotyping for maps and charts; engraved wax is used as a mould for the electro

wax paper *or* **waxed paper** *noun* paper made from chemical pulp, coated with a layer of wax to make it more or less waterproof and used as wrapping paper

waygoose *or* **wayzgoose** *noun* annual celebration of a printing company

wear and tear *noun* **fair wear and tear** = acceptable damage caused by normal use; ***the insurance policy covers most damage but not fair wear and tear to the machine***

web *noun* **(a)** large roll of paper, which is fed into a printing machine (as opposed to separate sheets); **web break detector** = device which senses if the web of paper breaks and stops the machine running; **web offset printing** = offset printing, using paper from a large roll; **web paper** = paper supplied in large rolls; **web perfector** = web machine which prints both sides of the web at the same time; **web press** *or* **web machine** = printing machine which uses rolls of paper (as opposed to a sheet-fed press); **miniweb** = web offset printing machine, using a narrow web of paper, typically printing 32 or 64 pages in black or eight A4 pages in colour; **web wander** *see* SHEET WANDER **(b)** continuous wire mesh on which paper is made on a fourdrinier machine

web-fed *adjective* (printing press) which takes paper from rolls; *compare* SHEET-FED

wedge serif *noun* serif with a straight slope (as opposed to bracketed serifs which are curved)

weekly *adjective* done every week; **a weekly magazine** *or* **a weekly** = magazine which is published each week

weigh *verb* **(a)** to measure how heavy something is; ***he weighed the packet at the post office*** **(b)** to have a certain weight; ***the paper weighs 70gsm***

weight *noun* **(a)** measurement of how heavy something is; **gross weight** = weight of both the container and its contents; **net weight** = weight of goods after deducting the packing material and container **(b)** thickness of the strokes in a printed character (bold characters have more weight than roman) **(c)** **paper weight** = weight of paper, calculated as grammes per square metre (written gsm)

> COMMENT: paper weight is usually calculated in gsm, and varies from about 30gsm (Bible paper) to about 150gsm (heavy cartridge). Board for paper covers is also calculated in gsm: a common cover weight is 240gsm. In the USA, paper weight is calculated in pounds per 500 sheets. Note that a heavy paper is not necessarily bulkier (thicker) than a lightweight paper

wet *adjective* **wet beaten stuff** = beaten pulp at the wet end of a papermaking machine; **wet carbon process** = colour correction process used in gravure, involving three-colour carbon tissues; **wet end** = part of a paper-making machine where the wet pulp passes onto the wire mesh; **wet expansion** = measurement of the increase in length of a piece of paper when it is put in water; **wet felt** = felt which has absorbed water, used as the base on which the paper moves through the papermaking machine; **wet flong** = flong made of alternate layers of tissue paper and blotting paper pasted together and used wet; **wet plate** = photographic negative or positive made by a collodion method; **wet proofing** = taking proofs off plates, as opposed to plastic or dry proofs such as Cromalin; **wet stock** = paper pulp before it is processed to make paper; **wet strength** = strength of paper when wet; **wet strength paper** = paper which remains strong even when wet, because of the addition of resin to the pulp

wet-on-wet printing *noun* method of printing where one colour is printed on top of another before the first colour is dry

wf = WRONG FONT proofreader's note, showing that a character is not printed in the correct font

> COMMENT: marked by the reader in the margin, while the incorrect character is circled (now it is more usual to put a cross in a circle in the margin)

WF = WOODFREE PAPER

What You See Is What You Get (WYSIWYG) *noun* program where the output on the screen is exactly the same as the output on printout; including graphics and special fonts

whipstitching *noun* method of attaching leaves together to form a section which can be bound, used especially for the first and last sections (each signature is sewn in the usual way, and then all the signatures are sewn again from the front to the back, close to the fold); (NOTE: also called **overcasting, oversewing**)

whirler *noun* machine for evenly sensitizing printing plates

white line *noun* line space between two lines of printed text

white out *verb* **(a)** to reverse out, to print a text as white lettering out of a black or coloured background; ***the cover will use white-out lettering on a dark blue background*** **(b)** to space out type matter **(c)** to paint out part of the copy on artwork so that it does not reproduce

white sale *noun US* sale of selected academic and very specialized books

white space *noun* part of a printed page with no printing on it

white water *noun* water which has drained out the paper pulp and which is strained to retrieve fibrous matter

whole binding *noun* cased binding, where the case is completely covered with a piece of material (cloth, leather, etc., as opposed to half-binding)

whole bound book *noun* fullbound book, a book which has been completely covered in a binding material (such as leather)

wholesale *noun & adverb* buying goods from manufacturers and selling in large quantities to traders who then sell in smaller quantities to the general public; **wholesale bookseller** *or* **wholesaler** = bookseller who buys and sells books in large quantities to institutions or government purchasing organizations or retail bookshops, etc., and does not sell to the public; (NOTE: the US English is **book jobber**) **the wholesale trade** = the business of buying large quantities of merchandise from a manufacturer and selling it on to retail dealers

wholesaler *noun* bookseller who buys books from publishers in bulk and sells them on to retail bookshops or government purchasing organizations, etc., and does not sell to the public

Wickersham quoin *noun* steel quoin which can be extended with a key

wide area network (WAN) *noun* network where the various terminals are far apart and linked by radio, satellite and cable; *compare with* LAN

> COMMENT: WANs use modems, radio and other long distance transmission methods; LANs use cables *or* optical fibre links

wideband *noun* transmission with a bandwidth greater than that of a voice channel

widow *noun* short line which ends a paragraph and appears at the top of a page *or* column, normally avoided by taking it back to the bottom of the previous page; (NOTE: the opposite (where the first line or heading of a new paragraph appears at the bottom of a page) is an **orphan** or **club line**)

width *noun* **page width** *or* **line width** = number of characters across the type area of a page *or* in a line; **width of a character** = distance across a printed character (which is not related to its weight, or the thickness of the strokes)

WIMP = WINDOW, ICON, MOUSE, POINTER description of an integrated software system that is entirely operated using windows, icons, and a pointer controlled by a mouse

window *noun* **(a)** **shop window** = large window in a shop front, where customers can see goods displayed; **window display** = display of goods in a shop window; **window dresser** = person who arranges a window display; **window envelope** = envelope with a hole in it covered with plastic like a window, so that the address on the letter inside can be seen **(b)** *(in word-processing and designing on computer)* (i) reserved section of screen used to display special information, that can be selected and looked at at any time and which writes over information already on the screen; (ii) part of a document currently displayed on a screen; ***you can connect several remote stations to the network and each will have its own window onto the hard disk; the operating system will allow other programs to be displayed at the same time in different windows;*** **edit window** = area of the screen in which the user can display and edit text *or* graphics; **text window** = window in a graphics system, where the text is held in a small space on the screen before being allocated to a final area **(c)** black square placed on the repro where a halftone is to be inserted (this will appear as a clear space when the negative is made, ready for the halftone negative to be stripped in) **(d)** hole cut in the card backing into which a piece of film is inserted

windowing *noun* (i) action of setting up a window to show information on the screen; (ii) displaying *or* accessing information via a window

wipe *noun* printing defect where the ink blurs and forms lines at the edge of the type area

wipe-on plate *noun* printing plate which is not presensitized but needs to have a light-sensitive coating wiped on by hand

wire *noun* **(a)** thin thread of metal; **wire side** = the side of a piece of paper which lies on the wire mesh when it is being made, and sometimes has the marks of the mesh on it (the opposite side is called the felt side, and is smooth) **(b)** small metal staple, used for binding; **wire binding** = binding the pages of a book with a wire which runs through holes in the margins of the pages; **wire bound** *or* **wire stitched** = book where the pages are attached with wire, as opposed to sewn binding using thread; **wire-o binding** = trade mark for a method of binding using a spiral wire running through holes in the margin of the pages of a loose-leaf book; **wire stabbing** = method of binding very thick books, where metal staples are passed through the edge of folded sheets from front to back; **wire stitching** = attaching the sections of a book by metal staples

withdraw *verb* to take a book out of sale; ***after complaints from the widow of the subject, the book was withdrawn***

wood *noun* **wood block** = block of hard wood, cut to make an illustration (either a woodcut or a wood engraving); **wood furniture** = pieces of wood used to fill spaces in a forme; **wood letters** *or* **wood type** = very large letters, cut in hard wood, used for posters

woodcut *noun* illustration made by printing from a block of hard wood, where the design is cut into the wood along the grain

(making a less delicate design than a wood engraving)

wood engraving *noun* illustration made by printing from a block of wood, where the design is cut into the end grain of the wood, against the grain, making the design sharper and more durable than a woodcut

woodfree paper *noun* paper which is made from chemical pulp, and not from mechanical woodpulp (note that in spite of its name, it is still made from wood); (NOTE: US English is **free sheet**)

woodpulp *noun* material made from crushed wood, mixed with water, used to make paper

> COMMENT: woodpulp is either crushed from small pieces of wood by machine (mechanical pulp) or dissolved using chemicals (chemical pulp)

word *noun* separate item of language, which is used with others to form speech *or* writing which can be understood; **words per minute (wpm)** = method of measuring the speed of a printer *or* shorthand typist; **word break** = point where a long word can be divided by a hyphen at the end of a line; **word count** = counting the number of words in a text; ***the word-processing program has a word count facility;*** **word division** = way of splitting words at the ends of lines, inserting a hyphen; *see also* HYPHENATION **word space** = white space left between two words in continuous text; **word spacing** = spaces between words (which are made wider or narrower to fit the characters into a fully justified line); **word wrap** *or* **wraparound** = system in word processing where the operator does not have to indicate the line endings, but can keyboard continuously, leaving the program to continue the text on the next line

wordage *noun* number of words in a text, used often as a method of payment for work such as keyboarding or translation

wording *noun* series of words; ***did you read the wording on the contract?***

word-process *verb* to edit, store and manipulate text using a computer

word-processing (WP) *noun* working with words, using a computer to produce, check and change texts, reports, letters, etc.; ***load the word-processing program before you start keyboarding;*** **word-processing bureau** = office which specializes in word-processing for other companies

word-processor *noun* **(a)** small computer *or* typewriter with a computer in it, used for working with words to produce and store texts, reports, letters, etc. **(b)** word-processing package, a program for a computer which allows the editing and manipulation and output of text, such as letters, labels, address lists, etc.

work 1 *noun* **(a)** book *or* play, etc., which has been written and published; ***the complete works of Shakespeare;*** **work which is out of copyright** = book which is no longer in copyright **(b)** things done using the hands *or* brain; **casual work** = work where the workers are hired for a short period; **clerical work** = work done in an office; **work in progress** = value of goods being manufactured which are not complete at the end of an accounting period **(c)** job *or* something done to earn money; ***he goes to work by bus; she never gets home from work before 8 p.m.; his work involves a lot of travelling; he is still looking for work; she has been out of work for six months;*** **work permit** = official document which allows someone who is not a citizen to work in a country **2** *verb* to do things with the hands *or* brain, for money; ***the factory is working hard to complete the order; she works better now that she has been promoted;*** **to work a machine** = to make a machine function

work and tumble *adverb* printing imposition, where one side of the sheet of paper is printed, then the paper is turned upside down to print the other side from the same forme, changing the edge which is fed to the grippers

work and turn *adverb* printing imposition, where one side of the sheet of paper is printed, then the paper is turned over (without changing the gripper edge) to print the other side; the material for both sides of the sheet is set in one plate; the paper is printed first on one side, then turned and printed on the other side, ;giving two sets of printed pages

work and twist *adverb* printing imposition, where one side of the sheet of paper is printed, then the paper is turned over, twisted through 90° and printed on the other side, changing the edge which is fed to the grippers

workbook *noun* book with blank spaces for a student to write answers in

working *noun* a single pass through a printing machine which will complete the printing of a sheet (three-colour printing will require three workings on a single-colour machine); **even working** = number of printed pages printed in even sections without oddments; usually a number which can be divided by 16 or 32, but sometimes calculated in multiples of 24 or 48. 320 pages is an even working: 328 is an uneven working

workspace *noun* memory, the space available on a computer for temporary work

workstation *noun* desk with a computer terminal, printer, telephone, etc., where a word-processing operator works

workup *noun* black mark on a printed sheet caused by a piece of lead which has moved and caught the ink

world rights *noun* the right to sell copies of a book anywhere in the world

World Wide Web *see* WWW

WORM = WRITE ONCE READ MANY times memory optical disc storage system that allows the user to write data to the disc once, but the user can then read the data from the disc many times

wove *noun* paper with an antique finish, which does not show laid lines but shows the marks of the mesh on the dandy roll

WP = WORD PROCESSING

wpm = WORDS PER MINUTE

wrap 1 *noun* four-page section wrapped round a signature before binding and bound up with it **2** *verb* **(a) to wrap (up)** = to cover something all over (in paper); ***he wrapped (up) the parcel in green paper*** **(b) to wrap round** = to put a four page section round a signature before the book is bound; ***there are sixteen pages of plates wrapped round sigs 2, 4, 5 and 6***

wraparound *or* **word wrap** *noun* **(a)** system in word processing where the operator does not have to indicate the line endings, but can keyboard continuously, leaving the program to continue the text on the next line; **horizontal wraparound** = movement of a cursor on a computer display from the end of one line to the beginning of the next **(b) wraparound plates** = flexible plates wrapped round the steel cylinders on rotary letterpress or flexography **(c)** *US* = WRAPROUND

wrapper *noun* **(a)** drawn-on cover, the cover of a paperback **(b)** dust jacket, a paper cover which is put round a cased book to protect the binding

wrappering *noun* putting paper covers on paperbacks

wrapping *noun* **(a)** putting periodicals into plastic or paper envelopes for mailing; **wrapping paper** = special coloured paper for wrapping presents; **gift-wrapping** = (i) service in a store for wrapping presents for customers; (ii) coloured paper for wrapping presents **(b) wrappings** = term for papers used for wrapping (as opposed to printings and writings)

wrapround *noun* (i) outset, a four-page section of printed pages such as a set of plates, which is wrapped round a signature; (ii) cover which is wrapped round a book

wrinkle *noun* small crease in paper caused by damp conditions which make the paper stretch

write *verb* to put words *or* figures on to paper *or* into a computer; ***she wrote a best-selling novel; he wrote a letter of complaint to the editor; the telephone number is written at the bottom of the notepaper***

write in *verb* to add matter to a text

write out *verb* to write in full; ***she wrote out the minutes of the meeting from her notes;*** **to write out a cheque** = to write the words and figures on a cheque and then sign it

write protect *verb* to make it impossible to write to a floppy disk *or* tape by moving a special tab; **write-protect tab** = tab on a floppy disk which if moved, prevents any writing to *or* erasing from the disk

writer *noun* person who writes, especially one who makes a living by writing books, or articles for newspapers

writing *noun* **(a)** something which has been written; ***to put the agreement in writing; he has difficulty in reading my writing;*** **writing paper** = good quality paper used for writing letters **(b) writings** = special paper for writing (as opposed to printings and wrappings)

wrong font (wf) *noun* note from a proofreader showing that a character is in the wrong typeface

wrong-reading film *noun* film which reads in the wrong way, from right to left, when viewed from the emulsion side (as opposed to right-reading)

WWW = WORLD WIDE WEB *(within the Internet)* thousands of pages of formatted text and graphics (stored in HTML) that allow a user to have a graphical user interface to the Internet rather than a less user-friendly command-line interface

WYSIWYG = WHAT YOU SEE IS WHAT YOU GET

Xx Yy Zz

X.25 CCITT standard that defines the connection between a terminal and a packet-switching network

x height *noun* height of the main central part of a printed character such as the letter x, which does not have an ascender or descender; **x line** = line marking the top of the main part of a printed character such as the letter x (the bottom is the base line)

xerographic *adjective* referring to xerography; **xerographic copier** = plain paper copier, where the image of the original is transferred to the copy paper by electrostatic means; **xerographic printer** = printer (such as a photocopier) where copies are made by electrostatic means (ink is attracted to charged areas of a picture)

xerography *noun* copying method that relies on powdered ink being attracted to charged area of an image

Xerox 1 *noun* **(a)** trade mark for a type of photocopier; ***to make a xerox copy of a letter; we must order some more xerox paper for the copier; we are having a new xerox machine installed tomorrow*** **(b)** photocopy made with a xerox machine; ***to send the other party a xerox of the contract; we have sent xeroxes to each of the agents*** **2** *verb* to make a photocopy with a xerox machine; ***to xerox a document; she xeroxed all the file***

XGA = EXTENDED GRAPHICS ARRAY standard for colour video graphics adapter for PCs, developed by IBM, which has a resolution of 1,024x768 pixels with 256 colours on an interlaced display; **XGA-2** = provides a resolution of 1,024x768 pixels with 64,000 colours

X-Y *noun* coordinates for drawing a graph, where X is the vertical and Y the horizontal value; **X-Y plotter** = device for drawing lines on paper between given coordinates

yankee machine *noun* MG machine, a papermaking machine which has a machine glazing cylinder

yapp binding *noun* binding with a soft binding material, whose edges project over the trimmed pages (used often for Bibles)

year *noun* period of twelve months; **calendar year** = year from January 1st to December 31st; **financial year** = the twelve month period for a firm's accounts; **fiscal year** = twelve month period on which taxes are calculated (in the UK it is April 6th to April 5th of the following year); **year end** = the end of the financial year, when a company's accounts are prepared

yearbook *noun* reference book which is published each year with updated or new information

yellow 1 *adjective & noun* one of the three process colours (the others are cyan and magenta) **2** *verb* to turn yellow; **yellowing** = tendency of some paper to turn yellow when exposed to the light

yellow pages *noun* section of a telephone directory (printed on yellow paper) which lists businesses under various headings (such as computer shops or newsagents, etc.)

yellow press *noun* the gutter press, newspapers which rely on sensational news to attract readers

yellow-magenta-cyan-black *see* YMCK

YMCK = YELLOW-MAGENTA-CYAN-BLACK colour definition based on these four colours used in graphics and DTP software when creating separate colour film to use for printing; (NOTE: normally written as CMYK)

zap *verb* to wipe off all data currently in the workspace; ***he pressed CONTROL Z and zapped all the text***

zero *noun* nought *or* number 0

zero-rated *adjective* (item) which has a VAT rate of 0%

zero-rating *noun* rating of an item at 0% VAT

zinc *noun* **zinc etching** = line engraving, a block used to print illustrations with no tones, such as line drawings

zinco *or* **zincograph** *noun* letterpress line block made of zinc

zip-a-tone *noun* mechanical tint on self-adhesive film, used when preparing artwork

zone *noun* region *or* part of a screen defined for specialized printing; **hot zone** = text area to the left of the right margin in a word-processed document, if a word does not fit completely into the line, a hyphen is automatically inserted

SUPPLEMENT

International Book Fairs

The following are the most important international book fairs, with their regular venue and date

Title	*Town, Country*	*Month*
Cairo International Book Fair	Cairo, Egypt	January
Tokyo International Book Fair	Tokyo, Japan	January
Calcutta Book Fair	Calcutta, India	January
Feria Internacional del Libro	Mexico	March
Jerusalem International Book Fair	Jerusalem, Israel	March
London International Book Fair	London, UK	March/April
Fiera del Libro per Ragazzi	Bologna, Italy	April
Feria Internacional del Libro	Bogota, Colombia	April/May
Salon International du Livre et de la Presse	Geneva, Switzerland	April/May
Feria Internacional del Libro	Buenos Aires, Argentina	April/May
Warsaw International Book Fair	Warsaw, Poland	May
Salon du Livre	Paris, France	May
BookExpo America	Chicago, USA	June
Liber	Various cities, Spain	June
Malaysian Book Fair	Kuala Lumpur, Malaysia	August
Singapore International Book Fair	Singapore	August/Sept
Philippine Book Fair	Manila, Philippines	September
Beijing Book Fair	Beijing, China	September
Moscow International Book fair	Moscow, Russia	September
Frankfurt Book Fair	Frankfurt, Germany	October
Salon du Livre	Montreal, Canada	November

Book Prizes & Awards

Some of the more important literary prizes and awards.

Arthur C. Clarke Award Given for the best British science fiction novel.

Aurora Award Highest Canadian award for science fiction and fantasy books

Australian Children's Book Awards Awards for children's literature made by the Children's Book Council of Australia

Bargate (Verity) Award An annual UK award for a new and unperformed play

Benjamin Franklin Award Award which recognizes excellence in independent publishing, sponsored by the Publishers Marketing Association of America

Besterman Medal Awarded annually by the Library Association for an outstanding bibliography or guide to the literature first published in the United Kingdom during the preceding year

Booker Prize for Fiction An annual prize of £20,000 for a novel written in English by a citizen of Great Britain, The Irish Republic or South Africa. Sponsored by Booker McConnell plc

Caldecott Book Awards Presented by the American Library Association (ALA), these awards are the most prestigious in children's literature

The Canada Council for the Arts: Governor General's Literary Awards Annual literary awards made by the Canada Council

Carnegie Medal An award made by the British Library Association to the writer of an outstanding book for children. The book must be written in English and have been published in the United Kingdom during the year preceding the presentation of the award.

Children's Book Award An award founded in 1980 and given to authors of fiction for children under the age of 14 by the Federation of Children's Book Groups

Cholmondeley Awards Annual award made by the Society of Authors (q.v.) for th encouragement of poets

Commonwealth Writers' Prizes Annua awards sponsored by the Commonwealt Foundation, for works of fiction in a numbe of categories

Cookson (Catherine) Fiction Prize Annua award for an unpublished novel of at leas 70,000 words

Cooper (Duff) Memorial Prize An annua UK award for a literary work of biograph history, politics, or poetry in English o French

Crime Writers' Association (CWA) A U organisation responsible for several annua literary awards: *Cartier Diamond Dagge Award* (outstanding title), *John Crease Memorial Dagger* (best crime novel by a unpublished author), *Gold and Silver Dagge Awards for Fiction* (best crime novel published in the UK)

Dillons First Fiction Award An annua prize for the best first-time novelist i English

Earthworm Children's Book Award A annual UK award of Friends of the Ear Trust to promote environmental awareness i children's literature

Edgar Allan Poe Awards Presented by Th Mystery Writers of America for the best i mystery, fiction, and non-fiction

Elgin (Mary) Award An annual UK awar made by Hodder & Stoughton Ltd t encourage new writers of fiction

Emil Award An award organised by th Book Trust and given annually for th children's book 'in which text an illustration are both excellent and perfect harmonious'; now combined with th Maschler (Kurt) Award (q.v.)

Book Prizes & Awards

Ewart-Biggs (Christopher) Memorial Prize A biennial prize for a work in English or French that contributes to peace and understanding in Ireland, or to co-operation between members of the European community

Faber (Geoffrey) Memorial Prize An award in alternate years for a volume of verse, and a volume of prose fiction of the best literary merit by young Commonwealth or UK authors

Farmer (Prudence) Poetry Prize An annual UK award made for the best poem published in the *New Statesman* magazine

Fawcett Society Book Prize An annual award (alternate years for fiction and non-fiction) for a book that has contributed to the understanding of women's position in society. All submitted work is placed in the Fawcett Library

Fletcher (Sir Banister) Award An annual UK prize of the Authors Club for the best book on architecture of the arts

Florio (John) Prize A biennial prize for the best translation into English

Greenaway (Kate) Medal An award, made by the British Library Association annually with the intention of recognising the importance of illustrations in children's books, to the artist who in the opinion of the Library Association has produced the most distinguished work in the illustration of children's books during the year preceding the award. The work must have been originally published in the United Kingdom. A list of books awarded the medal is published in the Library Association Year Book

Gregynog Prize Biennial awards to Welsh publishers for high standards in book production, for adult books, and for children's books

Guardian Children's Fiction Prize An annual prize instituted in 1967 by the *Guardian* Newspaper for an outstanding work of fiction for children written by a British or Commonwealth author

Guardian Fiction Prize An annual award made by the *Guardian* Newspaper for a work of fiction published by a British or Commonwealth writer

Hawthornden Prize An annual award by the Hawthornden Trust for a work of imaginative literature by a young British author

Higham (David) Prize for Fiction Administered by the Book Trust, and awarded for a first novel or book of short stories by a UK or Commonwealth author

Holtby (Winifred) Memorial Prize An annual award of the Royal Society of Literature for the best regional work of fiction or non-fiction by a UK, Irish or Commonwealth author

Jones (Mary Vaughan) Award Awards by the Welsh National Centre for Children's Literature for various categories of Welsh and English children's literature

Kent (Sir Peter) Conservation Book Prize An annual award administered by the Book Trust for a book on environmental issues published in the UK

King (Coretta Scott) Awards Annual awards, established 1970, given for the most outstanding text, and most imaginative illustrations by a black author and illustrator for children's books. Presented by the American Library Association

King (Martin Luther) Memorial Prize An annual UK award for a literary work reflecting the ideals of Dr King, published in the UK

McColvin Medal Awarded annually by the Library Association for an outstanding reference book first published in the United Kingdom during the preceding year

Book Prizes & Awards

McLeod (Enid) Prize An annual award of the Franco-British Society for a book contributing to Franco-British understanding

Macmillan Silver Pen Award An annual award for an outstanding UK novel; sponsored by Macmillan, and administered by the English Centre of PEN International

McVitie's Prize An annual award for a literary work in any form by a Scottish resident; submission in English, Scots or Gaelic.

Maschler (Kurt)/Emil Award Annual UK award for 'a work of imagination in the children's field in which text and illustration are of excellence and so presented that each enhances yet balances the other'

Mind Book of the Year/Allen Lane Award An annual award administered by the UK charity MIND for a book which furthers public understanding of mental illness

Mother Goose Award An award given to the most exciting newcomer to British Children's book illustration

National Medal for Literature An award made annually to a living American author for the whole corpus of his or her work

NCR Book Award An award of £30,000 sponsored by the computer manufacturers NCR for a new work of non-fiction. First awarded 1988

New Writers' Award An annual award for the best unpublished romantic novel, given by the Romantic Novelists Association (UK)

Noma Award A prize awarded by the Japanese publishing firm Kodansha to African writers whose work is published in Africa, to encourage the African publishing industry.

Poetry Society of America Awards Several awards and medals awarded annually by the Poetry Society of America, including the Frost Medal, the Shelley Memorial Award, and William Carlos Williams Award

RITA Awards Awarded by the Romance Writers of America for excellence in the romantic genre

Runciman Award An annual prize offered by the Anglo-Hellenic League and administered by the Book Trust, for a literary work about Greece

Scott Moncrieff Prize An annual UK award of the Translator's Association for the best translation published of a French twentieth century work

Smarties Book Prize An award organised by the Book Trust, and given for children's books in three age categories

Smith (W.H.) Annual Literary Award A cash award which has been offered by W.H. Smith & Son Ltd annually since 1959. The Award is made to the Commonwealth author whose book (originally written in English and published in the United Kingdom within the previous 24 months ending on 31 December) makes, in the opinion of the judges, the most outstanding contribution to literature

Stanford (Winifred Mary) Prize A biennial award offered by Hodder & Stoughton for a UK-published book inspired by the Christian faith

Thomas (Dylan) Award Offered by the Poetry Society (UK) in alternate years for poetry and short stories

Times Educational Supplement Book Awards Two annual awards for authors of the best information books for children published in the UK or Commonwealth. One award is for a book for children up to the age of nine, the other for a book for children aged 10 - 16

Trask (Betty) Awards Annual awards administered by the Society of Authors for young Commonwealth authors of romantic fiction

3ook Prizes & Awards

Vhitbread Literary Awards Annual prizes warded to authors living in the UK or Eire ɔr books published in those countries; five ategories - novel, first novel, biography, ildren's novel, poetry - are selected, of 'hich one is further declared *Whitbread ook of the Year.* Administered by the ooksellers Association of Great Britain and 'eland.

Whitfield Prize An annual award made by the Royal Historical Society for the best UK-published work on English or Welsh history by a young author

Proof correction marks

Mark in Text	Meaning	Mark in Margin
/	delete	
	delete and close up	
- - - - -	do not change	
	insert	
/	substitute	new word
	wrong fount	
word	italic	
word	bold	
word	caps	
word	small caps	
	replace caps by lower case	
	replace italic by light	
	insert full stop	
	insert semi-colon	;
	insert comma	,
	start new paragraph	
	run on (i.e. no paragraph)	
	indent	
	full out	
	take over to next line	
	take back to preceding line	
↑	raise	
↓	lower	
	close up	
	insert space	
	reduce space	

A HISTORY OF PRINTING

The development of typesetting and printing came about in Europe in the later Middle ages. As a newly literate middle class arose, so the previous methods of dis-emination of literature proved quite incapable of satis-fying the demand for large amounts of reading material Hitherto, manuscripts had been copied in monasteries for wealthy patrons, and even if a dictating pool system was adopted, where ONE person read the text and several others coppied it down, production was slow and expensive, and output very small.

Wood blocks were also used, first for making small pic tures that could be reproduced cheaply, then for making whole pages of text. This system had the dis-advantage of inflexibility, and required skilled wood carvers. It was only when Gutenbreg saw that thousands

of identical pieces of metal type could be cast from a single matrix (each piece representing a letter of alpha-bet), and that pieces of type slotted together to form words could be fitted into pages and used for printing large numbers of identical copies of the same text, that modern typesetting and printing was born. From his invention the enormous expansion of the printed word proceeded.

Alphabets

Baskerville

ABCDEFGHIJKLMNOPQRSTUVWXYZ
abcdefghijklmnopqrstuvwxyz 1234567890 ,.;:!?

ABCDEFGHIJKLMNOPQRSTUVWXYZ
abcdefghijklmnopqrstuvwxyz 1234567890 ,.;:!?

ABCDEFGHIJKLMNOPQRSTUVWXYZ
abcdefghijklmnopqrstuvwxyz 1234567890 ,.;:!?

Helvetica

ABCDEFGHIJKLMNOPQRSTUVWXYZ
abcdefghijklmnopqrstuvwxyz 1234567890 ,.;:!?

ABCDEFGHIJKLMNOPQRSTUVWXYZ
abcdefghijklmnopqrstuvwxyz 1234567890 ,.;:!?

ABCDEFGHIJKLMNOPQRSTUVWXYZ
abcdefghijklmnopqrstuvwxyz 1234567890 ,.;:!?

Rockwell

ABCDEFGHIJKLMNOPQRSTUVWXYZ
abcdefghijklmnopqrstuvwxyz 1234567890 ,.;:!?

ABCDEFGHIJKLMNOPQRSTUVWXYZ
abcdefghijklmnopqrstuvwxyz 1234567890 ,.;:!?

ABCDEFGHIJKLMNOPQRSTUVWXYZ
abcdefghijklmnopqrstuvwxyz 1234567890 ,.;:!?

Times

ABCDEFGHIJKLMNOPQRSTUVWXYZ
abcdefghijklmnopqrstuvwxyz 1234567890 ,.;:!?

ABCDEFGHIJKLMNOPQRSTUVWXYZ
abcdefghijklmnopqrstuvwxyz 1234567890 ,.;:!?

ABCDEFGHIJKLMNOPQRSTUVWXYZ
abcdefghijklmnopqrstuvwxyz 1234567890 ,.;:!?

Accents and non-Roman alphabets

Accents

à á ä â ã å
è é ë ê
í ï î
ò ó ö ô õ
ù ú ü û
č ç
ñ

International Phonetic Alphabet

æ	e	ɪə	g	r
ɑː	eə	uː	h	s
ɒ	eɪ	ʊ	j	ʃ
aɪ	ə	ʌ	k	t
aʊ	əʊ	b	l	tʃ
aɪə	əʊə	d	m	θ
aʊə	ɜː	ð	n	v
ɔː	iː	dʒ	ŋ	w
ɔɪ	ɪ	f	p	z
				ʒ

Greek Alphabet

Α α	Ν ν
Β β	Ξ ξ
Γ γ	Ο ο
Δ δ	Π π
Ε ε	Ρ ρ
Ζ ζ	Σ σ *or* ς
Η η	Τ τ
Θ θ	Υ υ
Ι ι	Φ φ
Κ κ	Χ χ
Λ λ	Ψ ψ
Μ μ	Ω ω

Russian Alphabet

А а	Р р
Б б	С с
В в	Т т
Г г	У у
Д д	Ф ф
Е е	Х х
Ж ж	Ц ц
З з	Ч ч
И и	Ш ш
Й й	Щ щ
К к	Ь ь
Л л	Ъ ъ
М м	Ы ы
Н н	Э э
О о	Ю ю
П п	Я я

Dewey Decimal System

LIBRARY CLASSIFICATION

The main classifications:

000–099	general works covering all branches of knowledge, such as encyclopaedias and other general reference books, including books about library classification
100–199	philosophy, psychology, ethics
200–299	religion, mythology
300–399	social sciences, sociology, economics
400–499	languages, including books about language
500–599	science
600–699	applied science and technology
700–799	fine arts, crafts; sport
800–899	literature, including books about literature
900–999	history, geography, biography, travel

ASCII IN DECIMAL, HEXADECIMAL

dec.	HEX	CHAR	dec.	HEX	CHAR	dec.	HEX	CHAR	dec.	HEX	CHAR
0	00	NUL	32	20	SP	64	40	@	96	60	
1	01	SOH	33	21	!	65	41	A	97	61	a
2	02	STX	34	22	"	66	42	B	98	62	b
3	03	ETX	35	23	#	67	43	C	99	63	c
4	04	EOT	36	24	$	68	44	D	100	64	d
5	05	ENQ	37	25	%	69	45	E	101	65	e
6	06	ACK	38	26	&	70	46	F	102	66	f
7	07	BEL	39	27	'	71	47	G	103	67	g
8	08	BS	40	28	(	72	48	H	104	68	h
9	09	HT	41	29	)	73	49	I	105	69	i
10	0A	LF	42	2A	*	74	4A	J	106	6A	j
11	0B	VT	43	2B	+	75	4B	K	107	6B	k
12	0C	FF	44	2C	,	76	4C	L	108	6C	l
13	0D	CR	45	2D	-	77	4D	M	109	6D	m
14	0E	SO	46	2E	.	78	4E	N	110	6E	n
15	0F	SI	47	2F	/	79	4F	O	111	6F	o
16	10	DLE	48	30	0	80	50	P	112	70	p
17	11	DC1	49	31	1	81	51	Q	113	71	q
18	12	DC2	50	32	2	82	52	R	114	72	r
19	13	DC3	51	33	3	83	53	S	115	73	s
20	14	DC4	52	34	4	84	54	T	116	74	t
21	15	NAK	53	35	5	85	55	U	117	75	u
22	16	SYN	54	36	3	86	56	V	118	76	v
23	17	ETB	55	37	7	87	57	W	119	77	w
24	18	CAN	56	38	8	88	58	X	120	78	x
25	19	EM	57	39	9	89	59	Y	121	79	y
26	1A	SUB	58	3A	:	90	5A	Z	122	7A	z
27	1B	ESC	59	3B	;	91	5B	[	123	7B	{
28	1C	FS	60	3C	<	92	5C	\	124	7C	¦
29	1D	GS	61	3D	=	93	5D	]	125	7D	}
30	1E	RS	62	3E	>	94	5E	↑	126	7E	~
31	1F	US	63	3F	?	95	5F	_	127	7F	DEL

THE ASCII SYMBOLS

NUL	*Null*
SOH	*Start of Heading*
STX	*Start of Text*
ETX	*End of Text*
EOT	*End of Transmission*
ENQ	*Enquiry*
ACK	*Acknowledge*
BEL	*Bell*
BS	*Backspace*
HT	*Horizontal Tabulation*
LF	*Line Feed*
VT	*Vertical Tabulation*
FF	*Form Feed*
CR	*Carriage Return*
SO	*Shift Out*
SI	*Shift In*
DLE	*Data Link Escape*
DC	*Device Control*
NAK	*Negative Acknowledge*
SYN	*Synchronous Idle*
ETB	*End of Transmission Block*
CAN	*Cancel*
EM	*End of Medium*
SUB	*Substitute*
ESC	*Escape*
FS	*File Separator*
GS	*Group Separator*
RS	*Record Separator*
US	*Unit Separator*
SP	*Space (Blank)*
DEL	*Delete*

Publisher's Request for a Quotation

Quotation Enquiry No: ....

Date: ....

Quotation required by: ....

Printing specification

Title: .... Quantity: ....

Paper cover: .... Text: .... Size: ....

Print Colours Cover: .... Text: ....

Finish – Cover: .... Finish – Text: .... Binding: ....

Origination: ....

....

Schedule: ....

....

Delivery to: ....

....

....

Other specifications: ....

....

....

Signed: ....

Printer's Quotation

A. Publishing Co. Ltd
20 Common Road
London WC1

Estimate: Number: 1234
Date:

Title: PRINTING MADE EASY

Trimmed Page Size: 198 x 129mm

Description:

EXTENT:	256 pages
TEXT:	printed black from positive films supplied
CASE:	Printed four colour from disk/artwork supplied laminate 220gsm boards
PAPER:	80gsm High Opaque
DELIVERY:	to one UK address in shrink-wrapped parcels
	4000 £3840.00 5000 £4440.00

Prices estimated are firm for labour content until April 1998 All prices are subject to sight of artwork supplied It is assumed that disks supplied are fully formatted, ready to output Material prices may be subject to any trade increase

TERMS: 30 days net from date of invoice

W.P. Smith
Estimator

Publisher's House Estimate

Series title______________ Date ______________
Title ______________ Paper ______________
Page size ______________ Cased/Limp ______________

Extent______ Publication month/year______ Illustrations: Line______ Halftone______

Quantity					
Author fee					
Text picture permissions					
Typesetting					
Corrections					
Make-up					
Artwork/illustrations					
Colour origination					
Jacket	Artist				
	origination				
Total fixed costs					
Text printing	machining				
	paper				
Jacket printing	machining				
	paper				
Total					
Total sheet cost					
Total binding cost					
Unit sheet cost					
Unit binding cost					
Unit production cost					
Unit royalty					
Unit marketing cost					
Unit cost					
Booksellers' discount					
Profit margin					
% Margin price obtained					
Published price					

Paper Order

Order no: ....

Date: ....

To: ....

Title: ....

Paper type: ....

Quantity: ....

Size: ....

Volume: ....

Substancc: (gsm) ....

(........grams per 1000 sheets/metres)

Grain: short/long

Printing: 1/2/4 colour printing

Print process: litho/letterpress

sheet fed/web

Price: £ .... per tonne

(£ .... per 1000 sheets/metres)

Delivery date: ....

Delivery address: ....

Packing: guillotine trimmed/ precision trimmed

reels/sheets/ream wrapped/bulk packed on pallets

Marks: ....

Signed: ....

Print Order

Order no: ....

Date: ....

To: ....

Title: ....

ISBN: ....

Your estimate: ....

Text:

Page size: ....

Extent: ....

Colours: ....

HTs included? ....

Paper: you supply/we supply by .... (date)

size/quantity

We supply CRC/films

Imposition: ....

Cover/Jacket:

Size: ....

Colours: ....

Quantity: ....

Paper: ....

Finish: ....

We supply: ....

Delivery date: ....

Delivery address: ....

Other details: ....

Signed: ....

Binding order

Order no: ....

Date: ....

To: ....

Title: ....

ISBN: .... Your estimate ....

Page size: .... Extent: ....

Sheets size .... supplied to you from ....

Imposition ...... Sewn/unsewn/insetted two wires

Sections of 16/24/32 pages Ends printed/plain/no ends/self-ends

<u>Limp</u>:

Lined Cut flush 3 edges

Covers drawn on to spine/Covers scored 4 times, drawn on hinged style

<u>Cased</u>:

Lined Rounded and backed/square backed Jacketted?

Boards: ....microns Hollows: ....microns

Cover material (you supply/we supply): ....

Blocking (spine/front) in (colour) .... from brasses supplied by you/us

Headbands/tailbands/ribbon marker Other requirements: ....

Packing: Binder's parcels .... copies per parcel

Cartons:: .... copies per carton

Bulk-packed and shrink wrapped on pallets (size ....)

Delivery date: ......

Delivery address: ....

Signed:

Printer's job sheet

CUSTOMER. . . . .
. . . .
ADDRESS. . . . .
. . . .
. . . .

JOB NUMBER

CUSTOMER'S O/No. DATE
LAST DOCKET No. EST. No.
LAST INV. No.

DESCRIPTION OF JOB

FINISHED SIZE

DATE REQUIRED:

QUANTITY

PROOFS SENT:

RETURNED:

COMPOSING ROOM

TYPEFACE LINE LENGTH
IMPOSITION POINT SIZE
Proofs: Rough/Colour/Machine
Date proofs wanted by: Read by Corrections checked by
Quantity of proofs required: **Galley Nos.** . . . .

SUPPLIER: Order No

DESIGN

ART WORK
PASTE-UP
LETRASET
CALLIGRAPHY

SUPPLIER: Order No

CAMERA WORK/COLOUR SEPARATION

SIZE
NEGATIVE
POSITIVE
PMT/BROMIDE

CROMALIN PROOF
PRESS PROOF
PROGRESSIVE PROOF
QUANTITY RESERVED
AMOUNT ISSUED

SUPPLIER: Order No

BINDERY

SUPPLIER: Order No

DESPATCH INSTRUCTIONS

Use Gwynne/Plain labels

Six file copies to be kept with each job

DELIVERIES

DATE	QUANTITY	METHOD	Advice Note No

Book formats and Paper sizes

British Book formats: trimmed (vertical measurement first; in millimetres)

Crown octavo	186 × 123
Crown quarto	246 × 189
Large Crown octavo	198 × 129
Large Crown quarto	258 × 201
Demy octavo	216 × 138
Demy quarto	276 × 219
Royal octavo	236 × 156
Royal quarto	312 × 237

ISO Paper sizes (vertical measurement first)

A0	841 × 1189	B0	1000 × 1414
A1	594 × 841	B1	707 × 1000
A2	420 × 594	B2	500 × 707
A3	297 × 420	B3	353 × 500
A4	210 × 297	B4	250 × 353
A5	148 × 210	B5	176 × 250
A6	105 × 148	B6	125 × 176
A7	74 × 105	B7	88 × 125
A8	52 × 74	B8	62 × 88
A9	37 × 52	B9	44 × 62
A10	26 × 37	B10	31 × 44
RA0	860 × 1220	SRA0	900 × 1280
RA1	610 × 860	SRA1	640 × 900
RA2	430 × 610	SRA2	450 × 640

Envelope sizes

C3	460 × 324
C4	324 × 229
C5	229 × 162
C6	162 × 114

Note that in many countries the smaller measurement is automatically given first, even if the book or sheet is seen as portrait format. Note also that, in the USA, most sizes are given in inches.

Imposition schemes

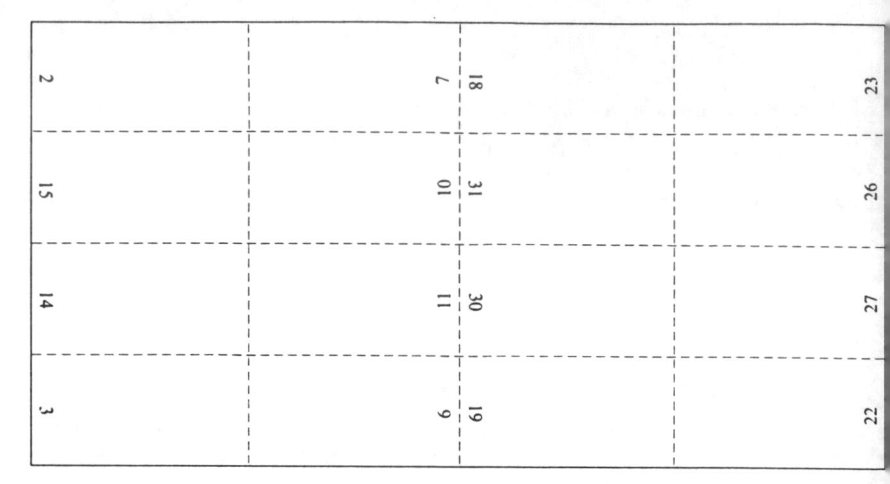

32-page section
(16 to view)

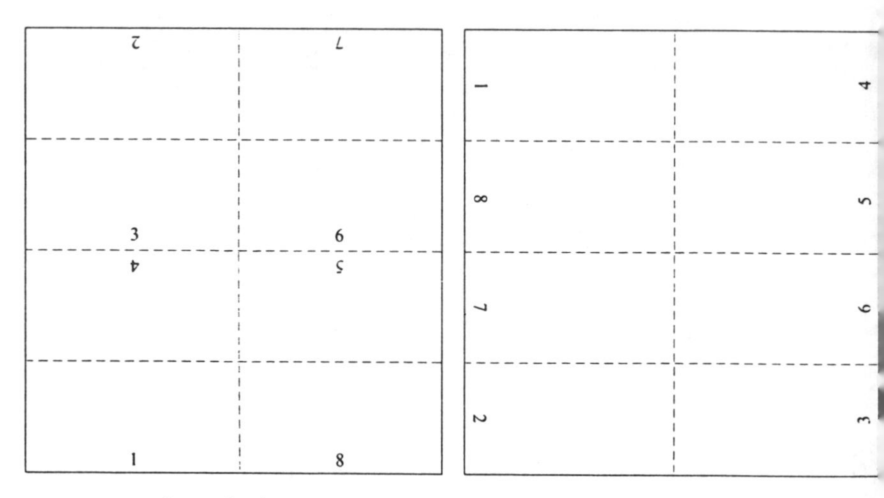

8-page landscape

8-page portrait

Flatplan

1	2 3	4 5	6 7	8 9	10 11	12 13	14 15	16	Section	Date	Note
17	18 19	20 21	22 23	24 25	26 27	28 29	30 31	32	Section	Date	Note
33	34 35	36 37	38 39	40 41	42 43	44 45	46 47	48	Section	Date	Note
49	50 51	52 53	54 55	56 57	58 59	60 61	62 63	64	Section	Date	Note
65	66 67	68 69	70 71	72 73	74 75	76 77	78 79	80	Section	Date	Note
81	82 83	84 85	86 87	88 89	90 91	92 93	94 95	96	Section	Date	Note
97	98 99	100 101	102 103	104 105	106 107	108 109	110 111	112	Section	Date	Note
113	114 115	116 117	118 119	120 121	122 123	124 125	126 127	128	Section	Date	Note

Technical Information for a Periodical

MECHANICAL DATA

Frequency:	Monthly
Publication day:	First Thursday in month
Printing process:	Offset litho
Binding:	Wire-stitched
Trim size:	285 x 210mm
Screen:	Black & White 120/48 line per cm Colour 150/60 lines per cm
Bleeds:	bleed trim on all trimmed edges is 3mm
Materials required:	
Colour:	screened positives, emulsion side down, right-reading, with progressives
Black & White:	screened positives, emulsion-side down, right-reading
Copy for setting:	double space typed

Advertising Rates for a Periodical

RATE CARD

ADVERTISEMENT RATES: DISPLAY

Size	*Number of Insertions*		
	1	**3**	**6**
Black and White			
Full page	£1000	£950	£900
Half page	600	575	550
Third page	450	425	400
Quarter page	350	325	300
Four colour			
Full page	£1600	£1500	£1350
Half page	1100	1000	850
Two colour			
Full page	£1250	£1100	£1000
Half page	800	700	600
Inside covers full colour	£1900	£1500	£1250

Facing editorial: basic card rate plus 10%

Full page bleed: basic card rate plus 10%

Inserts

Preprinted inserts can be accepted folded

Rates:		
	one issue:	£1000
	three issues:	£2500
	six issues:	£4500

ADVERTISEMENT RATES: CLASSIFIED

Recruitment:	
Full page	£750
Half page	£400
Single column centimetre	£10.00
Double column centimetre	£19.00
Three column centimetre	£25.00

Classified under headings:

For Sale	Wanted	Property
Freelance offered	Technical Services	Marketing
Business Supplies	Personal	Educational

Single Column Centimetre	£9.00
Double Column Centimetre	£15.00

All advertisements must be pre-paid
Box numbers £5.00 per insertion
Copy required by 5p.m. four working days before publication

For further details, please tick the titles of interest and return this form to:

Peter Collin Publishing, 1 Cambridge Road, Teddington, TW11 8DT, UK
fax: +44 181 943 1673 tel: +44 181 943 3386 email: info@pcp.co.uk

Title	*ISBN*	*Send Details*
English Dictionaries		
Accounting	0-948549-27-0	❑
Agriculture, 2nd ed	0-948549-78-5	❑
American Business	0-948549-11-4	❑
Automobile Engineering	0-948549-66-1	❑
Banking & Finance	0-948549-12-2	❑
Business, 2nd ed	0-948549-51-3	❑
Computing, 2nd ed	0-948549-44-0	❑
Ecology & Environment, 3ed	0-948549-74-2	❑
Government & Politics, 2ed	0-948549-89-0	❑
Hotel, Tourism, Catering Mg	0-948549-40-8	❑
Human Resource & Personnel, 2ed	0-948549-79-3	❑
Information Technology, 2nd ed	0-948549-88-2	❑
Law, 2nd ed	0-948549-33-5	❑
Library & Information Management	0-948549-68-8	❑
Marketing, 2nd ed	0-948549-73-4	❑
Medicine, 2nd ed	0-948549-36-X	❑
Printing & Publishing, 2nd ed	0-948549-99-8	❑
Science & Technology	0-948549-67-X	❑
Vocabulary Workbooks		
Banking & Finance	0-948549-96-3	❑
Business	0-948549-72-6	❑
Computing	0-948549-58-0	❑
Colloquial English	0-948549-97-1	❑
Hotels, Tourism, Catering	0-948549-75-0	❑
Law	0-948549-62-9	❑
Medicine	0-948549-59-9	❑
Professional/General		
Astronomy	0-948549-43-2	❑
Economics	0-948549-91-2	❑
Multimedia, 2nd ed	1-901659-01-1	❑
PC & the Internet	0-948549-93-9	❑
Bradford Crossword Solver	0-948549-39-4	❑
Bilingual Dictionaries		
French-English/English-French Dictionaries		❑
German-English/English-German Dictionaries		❑
Spanish-English/English-Spanish Dictionaries		❑
Swedish-English/English-Swedish Dictionaries		❑

- -

Name: ....

Address:...

....

....Postcode:.........................